# MATHEMATICAL ELEMENTS FOR COMPUTER GRAPHICS

## Second Edition

### David F. Rogers
*Professor of Aerospace Engineering*
*United States Naval Academy, Annapolis, Md.*

### J. Alan Adams
*Professor of Mechanical Engineering*
*United States Naval Academy, Annapolis, Md.*

Boston, Massachusetts   Burr Ridge, Illinois
Dubuque, Iowa   Madison, Wisconsin   New York, New York
San Francisco, California   St. Louis, Missouri

This book was computer typeset by Nancy A. Rogers using TEX.
The font is Computer Modern Roman. Phototypesetting was done at the AMS.
The editor was B. J. Clark;
the production supervisor was Louise Karam.
The cover was designed by Caliber Design Planning, Inc. and David F. Rogers.

## McGraw-Hill

A Division of The McGraw·Hill Companies

**MATHEMATICAL ELEMENTS FOR COMPUTER GRAPHICS**

11 12 HAM/HAM 0 9 8 7 6 5 4 3 2

ISBN  0-07-053529-9  {hard cover}

ISBN  0-07-053530-2  {soft cover}

Cover/dust jacket illustration credits:

Front cover/dust jacket: A sphere and its defining rational B-spline polygon net. (David F. Rogers)

Back cover/dust jacket: The America's Cup yacht Stars & Stripes defined as a B-spline surface. (George Hazen).

Library of Congress Cataloging in Publication Data

Rogers, David F., (date).
    Mathematical elements for computer graphics/David F. Rogers
    and J. Alan Adams — 2nd ed.
        p.    cm.
    Bibliography: p.
    Includes index.
    ISBN 0-07-053529-9   ISBN 0-07-053530-2 (soft)
    1. Computer graphics.  I.      Adams, J. Alan (James Alan), (date).
II. Title.
T385.R6    1990
006.6 — dc19
                                                  89-2308

# MATHEMATICAL ELEMENTS FOR COMPUTER GRAPHICS

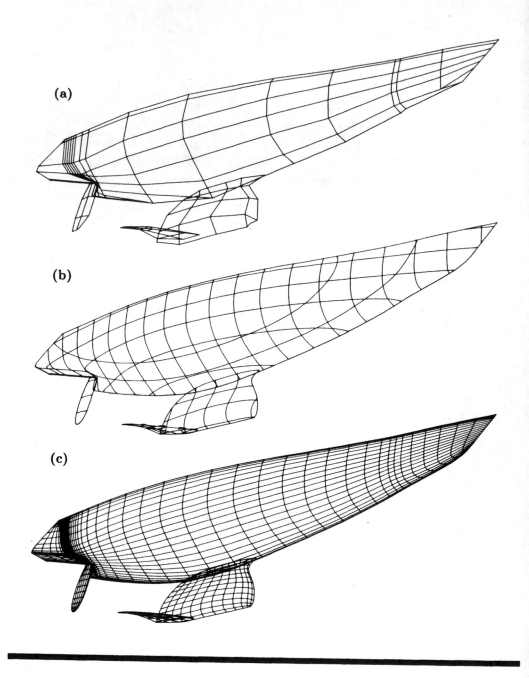

(a)

(b)

(c)

The America's Cup yacht Stars & Stripes defined as a B-spline surface.
(a) Defining polygon net; (b) body, buttock and waterlines;
(c) parametric net. (Courtesy of George Hazen.)

*To our wives*
*Nancy A. Rogers and Virginia F. Adams*
*and our families*
*Stephen, Karen and Ransom Rogers*
*and*
*Lynne, David and Alan Adams*

# CONTENTS

# FOREWORD

Since its inception more than a decade ago, the field of computer graphics has captured the imagination and technical interest of rapidly increasing numbers of individuals from many disciplines. A high percentage of the growing ranks of computer graphics professionals has given primary attention to computer-oriented problems in programming, system design, hardware, etc. This was pointed out by Dr. Ivan Sutherland in his introduction to Mr. Prince's book, *Interactive Graphics for Computer-aided Design* in 1971 and it is still true today. I believe that an inadequate balance of attention has been given to application-oriented problems. There has been a dearth of production of useful information that bears directly on the development and implementation of truly productive applications. Understanding the practical aspects of computer graphics with regard to both the nature and use of applications represents an essential and ultimate requirement in the development of practical computer graphics systems. Mathematical techniques, especially principles of geometry and transformations, are indigenous to most computer graphic applications. Yet, large numbers of graphic programmers and analysts struggle over or gloss over the basic as well as the complex problems of the mathematical elements. Furthermore, the full operational potential of computer graphics is often unrealized whenever the mathematical relationships, constraints, and options are inadequately exploited. By their authorship of this text, Drs. Rogers and Adams have recognized the valuable relevance of their background to these practical considerations. Their text is concise, is comprehensive and is written in a style unusually conducive to ease of reading, understanding and use. It exemplifies the rare type of work that most practitioners should wish to place in a prominent location within their library since it should prove to be an invaluable ready reference for most disciplines. It is also well suited as the basis for a course in computer science education curriculum.

I congratulate the authors in producing an excellent and needed text, *Mathematical Elements for Computer Graphics*.

S. H. "Chas" Chasen
Lockheed Georgia Company, Inc.

# PREFACE

In the fourteen years since the first edition of this book was published, computer graphics has both changed and come of age. Computer graphics is now an important discipline for computer scientists, engineers, scientists, mathemamaticians, physicians and artists, to name only a few. Old concepts have matured and new concepts have developed. However, much of the underlying mathematics remains virtually unchanged. As then, mastery of the fundamental mathematical concepts is still central to understanding and to continued development of computer graphics. This book provides the material necessary to master these concepts.

This second edition is not just a revision; it is almost a total rewrite. A large number of new illustrations and more detailed examples are included. Suggested problems and programming projects are provided. Algorithms which implement the mathematical theory are now presented in pseudocode. The book is typeset.

Chapter 1 includes new coverage of raster refresh and flat panel displays, laser printers, ink jet and thermal plotters, and color film cameras, as well as expanded coverage of previous topics related to computer hardware.

Chapter 2 provides expanded coverage of two dimensional transformations, including new topics in solid body transformations, reflections and geometric interpretation of homogeneous coordinates.

Chapter 3 has been greatly expanded. New topics or discussions of multiple transformations, rotation about arbitrary axes, reflections through an arbitrary plane, oblique projections, including the details of cabinet and cavalier projections, vanishing points, photographic transformations, an expanded discussion of stereo and a comparison of object fixed and center of projection fixed techniques for generating perspective projections are included.

Chapter 4 now provides an expanded discussion of conics. A detailed discussion of techniques for the use of conic sections appears in this edition.

Chapter 5 has been rewritten for increased clarity and understanding. More complete discussions of parabolic blending, Bézier and B-spline curves are included. A discussion of generalized parabolic blending is given. A discussion of periodic uniform B-spline curves is now included, as are discussions of B-spline curve fitting and subdivision. Extensive discussion of rational uniform and nonuniform B-spline curves (NURBS) has been added.

Chapter 6 has also been almost totally rewritten. The discussions of Coons surfaces, both linear and bicubic, and of ruled and developable surfaces have been expanded. New discussions of surfaces of revolution, sweep, quadric, Bézier and B-spline surfaces, B-spline surface fitting, surface subdivision and Gaussian curvature and mathematical surface fairness are included. Both nonrational and rational uniform and nonuniform B-spline surfaces (NURBS) are thoroughly discussed.

Extensive appendices on computer graphics software, matrix methods, a pseudocode definition, a B-spline surface file format, problems, programming projects and pseudocoded algorithms are included.

The new topics have been carefully arranged and presented to insure that the text is still suitable for undergraduate as well as graduate students. The material in the book can be used for a semester-long formal course in computer graphics at either the senior undergraduate or graduate level. A second semester course based on its companion volume *Procedural Elements for Computer Graphics* naturally follows. This is the way it is used by the authors. If broader material coverage in a single semester course is desired, then the two volumes can be used together. Suggested topical coverage is: Chapter 1 of both volumes, followed by Chapters 2 and 3 with selected topics from Chapter 4 (e.g., 4–1 to 4–8) of the present volume; then selected topics from Chapter 2 (e.g., 2–1 to 2–5, 2–7, 2–15 to 2–19, 2–22, 2–23 and 2–28), Chapter 3 (e.g., 3–1, 3–2, 3–4 to 3–6, 3–9, 3–11, 3–15 and 3–16), Chapter 4 (e.g., 4–1, part of 4–2 for backplane culling, 4–3, 4–4, 4–7, 4–9, 4–11 and 4–13) and Chapter 5 (e.g., 5–1 to 5–3, 5–5, 5–6 and 5–14) of *Procedural Elements for Computer Graphics*. The first author has successfully used this arrangement both for formal and for short courses. The book is also designed to be useful to professional programmers, engineers and scientists. Further, the detailed algorithms, worked examples and numerous illustrations make it particularly suitable for self-study at any level. Sufficient background is provided by college-level mathematics through calculus and a knowledge of a higher-level programming language.

A word about the production of the book may be of interest. The book was computer typeset using TEX by Nancy A. Rogers. The Computer Modern Roman family of fonts was used. Macros necessary to conform to McGraw-Hill Publishing Co. specifications were written by David F. Rogers. Two computers were used: an IBM AT and a Zenith 386. The manuscript was coded directly from handwritten copy. After screen previewing, galleys and page proofs were produced on a 300 dpi laser printer for editing and page makeup. The final madeup pages, ready for art insertion, in the form of TEX .dvi files were phototypeset by the American Mathematical Society.

No book is ever written without the assistance of many individuals. Thanks are due the first author's students at the Johns Hopkins University Applied Physics Laboratory Center who reviewed an early version of the first five chapters of the book. Their many suggestions and comments were especially helpful.

Special thanks are due John Dill and Fred Munchmeyer, two valued and much appreciated long time colleagues, who read the entire manuscript, red pen in hand. Their many suggestions and comments served to make this a better book. Special thanks are due our colleague Linda Adlum who not only read the entire manuscript but also checked *all* the examples. Thanks are extended to Stephen D. Rogers who read the manuscript and checked the examples in the first five chapters. Mike Gigante's comments on the first five chapters are also greatly appreciated. Bill Gordon's review of the work on Bézier and B-spline curves and surfaces was most useful.

Virginia Adams' efforts in proofreading the final copy are also appreciated. Thanks are due Barbara Beeton for her unfailing patience in answering questions about the details of TEX. A special note of appreciation to Joost Zalmstra, whose timely development of TEX page makeup macros made that task immensely easier. The usually fine McGraw-Hill editing was supervised by Jim Bradley. The very extensive illustration program was expertly supervised by Mel Haber. A very special thanks are due B. J. Clark who has been our editor at McGraw-Hill for nearly two decades. He has always been receptive to our sometimes rather unorthodox ideas.

David F. Rogers
J. Alan Adams
Annapolis
February 1989

# PREFACE

A new and rapidly expanding field called "computer graphics" is emerging. This field combines both the old and the new: the age-old art of graphical communication and the new technology of computers. Almost everyone can expect to be affected by this rapidly expanding technology. A new era in the use of computer graphics, not just by the large companies and agencies who made many of the initial advances in software and hardware, but by the general user, is beginning. Low-cost graphics terminals, time sharing, plus advances in mini- and microcomputers have made this possible. Today, computer graphics is practical, reliable, cost effective and readily available.

The purpose of this book is to present an introduction to the mathematical theory underlying computer graphics techniques in a *unified* manner. Although new ways of presenting material are given, no actual 'new' mathematical material is presented. All the material in this book exists scattered throughout the technical literature. This book attempts to bring it all together in *one* place in *one* notation.

In selecting material, we chose techniques which were fundamentally mathematical in nature rather than those which were more procedural in nature. For this reason the reader will find more extensive discussions of rotation, translation, perspective and curve and surface description than of clipping or hidden line and surface removal. First-year college mathematics is a sufficient prerequisite for the major part of the text.

After a discussion of current computer graphics technology in Chapter 1, the manipulation of graphical elements represented in matrix form using homogeneous coordinates is described. A discussion of existing techniques for representing points, lines, curves and surfaces within a digital computer, as well as computer software procedures for manipulating and displaying computer output in graphical form, is then presented in the following chapters.

Mathematical techniques for producing axonometric and perspective views are given, along with generalized techniques for rotation, translation and scaling of geometric figures. Curve definition procedures for both explicit and parametric representations are presented for both two-dimensional and three-dimensional curves. Curve definition techniques include the use of conic sections, circular arc interpolation, cubic splines, parabolic blending, Bézier curves and curves based on B-splines. An introduction to the mathematics of surface description is included.

Computer algorithms for most of the fundamental elements in an interactive graphics package are given in an appendix as BASIC† language subprograms. However, these algorithms deliberately stop short of the coding necessary to actually display the results. Unfortunately there are no standard language commands or subroutines available for graphic display. Although some preliminary discussion of graphic primitives and graphic elements is given in Appendix A, each user will, in general, find it necessary to work within the confines of the computer system and graphics devices available to him or her.

The fundamental ideas in this book have been used as the foundation for an introductory course in computer graphics given to students majoring in technical or scientific fields at the the undergraduate level. It is suitable for use in this manner at both universities and schools of technology. It is also suitable as a supplementary text in more advanced computer programming courses or as a supplementary text in some advanced mathematics courses. Further, it can be profitably used by individuals engaged in professional programming. Finally, the documented computer programs should be of use to computer users interested in developing computer graphics capability.

## Acknowledgments

The authors gratefully acknowledge the encouragement and support of the United States Naval Academy. The academic environment provided by the administration, the faculty, and especially the midshipmen was conducive to the development of the material in this book.

No book is ever written without the assistance of a great many people. Here we would like to acknowledge a few of them. First, Steve Coons who reviewed the entire manuscript and made many valuable suggestions, Rich Reisenfeld who reviewed the material on B-spline curves and surfaces, Professor Pierre Bézier who reviewed the material on Bézier curves and surfaces and Ivan Sutherland who provided the impetus for the three-dimensional reconstruction techniques discussed in Chapter 3. Special acknowledgement is due past and present members of the CAD Group at Cambridge University. Specifically, work done with Robin Forrest, Charles Lang, and Tony Nutbourne provided greater insight into the subject of computer graphics. Finally, to Louie Knapp who provided an original Fortran program for B-spline curves.

The authors would also like to acknowledge the assistance of many individuals at the Evans and Sutherland Computer Corporation. Specifically, Jim

---

†BASIC is a registered trade mark of Dartmouth College

Callan who authored the document from which many of the ideas on representing, preparing, presenting and interacting with pictures is based. Special thanks are also due Lee Billow who prepared all of the line drawings.

Much of the art work for Chapter 1 has been provided through the good offices of various computer graphics equipment manufacturers. Specific acknowledgment is made as follows:

| | |
|---|---|
| Fig. 1–3 | Evans and Sutherland Computer Corporation. |
| Fig. 1–5 | Adage Inc. |
| Fig. 1–7 | Adage Inc. |
| Fig. 1–8 | Vector General, Inc. |
| Fig. 1–11 | Xynetics, Inc. |
| Fig. 1–12 | CALCOMP, California Computer Products, Inc. |
| Fig. 1–15 | Gould, Inc. |
| Fig. 1–16 | Tektronix, Inc. |
| Fig. 1–17 | Evans and Sutherland Computer Corporation. |
| Fig. 1–18 | CALCOMP, California Computer Products, Inc. |

David F. Rogers

J. Alan Adams

# INTRODUCTION TO COMPUTER GRAPHICS

Computer graphics is now a mature technology. However, a number of terms and definitions are still rather loosely used in this field. In particular, computer aided design (CAD), interactive graphics (IG), computer graphics (CG) and computer aided manufacturing (CAM) are frequently used interchangeably or in such a manner that considerable confusion exists as to the precise meaning. Of these terms CAD is the most general. CAD may be defined as *any* use of the computer to aid in the design of an individual part, a subsystem or a total system. The use does not have to involve graphics. The design process may be at the system concept level or at the detail part design level. It may also involve an interface with CAM.

Computer aided manufacturing is the use of a computer to aid in the manufacture or production of a part exclusive of the design process. CAM requires the use of geometric description and motion control part programming languages, such as APT (Automatic Programmed Tools), to generate the necessary commands to control a machine tool. The machine tool controller is generally a micro- or minicomputer. The CAD system may generate the required machine control commands directly. Alternately, a standard data format, e.g., the Initial Graphics Exchange Standard (IGES), may be generated. A separate program is subsequently used to convert this data to the required format for the machine controller. Figure 1-1 shows a typical numerically controlled machining center and its controller.

Computer graphics is the use of a computer to define, store, manipulate, interrogate and present pictorial output. This is essentially a passive operation. The computer prepares and presents stored information to an observer in the form of pictures. The observer has no direct control over the picture being presented. The application may be as simple as the presentation of the graph of a single function or as complex as the simulation of the automatic reentry and landing of a space vehicle or an aircraft.

Dynamic interactive computer graphics (hereafter called interactive graphics

1

for short) also uses the computer to prepare and present pictorial material. However, in interactive graphics the observer can influence the picture as it is being presented; i.e., the observer interacts with the picture in real time. To see the importance of the real time restriction, consider the problem of rotating a reasonably complex three-dimensional picture composed of 1000 lines at a reasonable rate, say, 15°/second. As we shall see subsequently, the 1000 lines of the picture are most conveniently represented by a 1000 × 4 matrix of homogeneous coordinates of the end points of the lines, and the rotation is most conveniently accomplished by multiplying this 1000 × 4 matrix by a 4 × 4 transformation matrix. Accomplishing the required matrix multiplication requires 16,000 multiplications, 12,000 additions and 1000 divisions. If this matrix multiplication is accomplished in software, the time may be significant. To see this, consider a single user general purpose computer with a hardware floating-point accelerator that requires 3.6 microseconds to multiply two numbers, 2.6 microseconds to add two numbers, and 5.2 microseconds to divide two numbers. Thus, the matrix multiplication requires approximately 0.1 seconds.

Since computer displays that allow dynamic motion require that the picture be redrawn (refreshed) at least 30 times each second in order to avoid flicker,

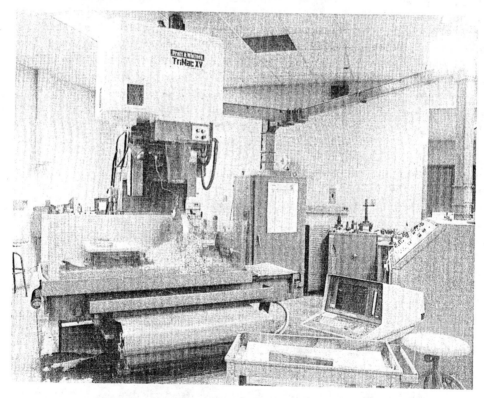

**Figure 1-1**  Numerically controlled machining center.

it is obvious that the picture cannot change smoothly.  Even if it is assumed that the picture is recalculated (updated) only 15 times each second, i.e., every degree, it is still not possible to accomplish a smooth rotation in software. Thus, this is no longer real time dynamic interactive graphics. To regain the ability to interactively present the picture several things can be done. A faster computer, at additional expense, can be used. Clever programming can reduce the time to accomplish the required matrix multiplication. However, a point will be reached where this is no longer possible. The complexity of the picture can be reduced. In this case, the resulting picture may not be acceptable. However, the matrix multiplication required to manipulate the above example picture and indeed for more complex pictures can be accomplished by using microcoded or special-purpose digital hardware matrix multipliers. Historically, and currently, this is the most performance and cost effective approach.

 With this terminology in mind the remainder of the chapter gives an overview of computer graphics and discusses the various types of graphic devices available.

## 1–1    OVERVIEW OF COMPUTER GRAPHICS

Computer graphics is a complex and diversified technology. To begin to understand the technology it is necessary to subdivide it into manageable parts. This can be accomplished by considering that the end product of computer graphics is a picture. The picture may, of course, be used for a large variety of purposes; e.g., it may be an engineering drawing, an exploded parts illustration for a service manual, a business graph, an architectural rendering for a proposed construction or design project, an advertising illustration, or a single frame from an animated movie. The picture is the fundamental cohesive concept in computer graphics. We must therefore consider how:

> Pictures are represented in computer graphics.
> Pictures are prepared for presentation.
> Previously prepared pictures are presented.
> Interaction with the picture is accomplished.

Here 'picture' is used in its broadest sense to mean any collection of lines, points, text, etc. displayed on a graphics device.

## 1–2    REPRESENTING PICTURES

 Although many algorithms accept picture data as polygons or edges, each polygon or edge can in turn be represented by points. Points, then, are the fundamental building blocks of picture representation. Of equal fundamental importance is the algorithm which explains how to organize these points. To illustrate this, consider a unit square in the first quadrant. The unit square can be represented by its four corner points (see Fig. 1–2):

$$P_1(0,0) \qquad P_2(1,0) \qquad P_3(1,1) \qquad P_4(0,1)$$

An associated algorithmic description might be

$$\text{Connect } P_1P_2P_3P_4P_1 \text{ in sequence}$$

The unit square can also be described by its four edges:

$$E_1 \equiv P_1P_2 \quad E_2 \equiv P_2P_3 \quad E_3 \equiv P_3P_4 \quad E_4 \equiv P_4P_1$$

Here, the algorithmic description is

$$\text{Display } E_1E_2E_3E_4 \text{ in sequence}$$

Finally, either the points or edges can be used to describe the unit square as a single polygon, e.g.,

$$S_1 = P_1P_2P_3P_4P_1 \qquad \text{or} \qquad P_1P_4P_3P_2P_1 \qquad \text{or} \qquad S_1 = E_1E_2E_3E_4$$

The fundamental building blocks, i.e., points, can be represented as either pairs or triplets of numbers depending on whether the data are two- or three-dimensional. Thus, $(x_1, y_1)$ or $(x_1, y_1, z_1)$ would represent a point in either two- or three-dimensional space. Two points would represent a line or edge, and a collection of three or more points a polygon. The representation of curved lines is usually accomplished by approximating them by short straight line segments.

The representation of textual material is quite complex, involving in many cases curved lines or dot matrices. However, fundamentally textual material is again represented by collections of lines and points and an organizing algorithm. Unless the user is concerned with pattern recognition, the design of special character fonts or the design of graphic hardware, he or she need not be concerned with these details, since almost all graphic devices have built-in hardware or software character generators.

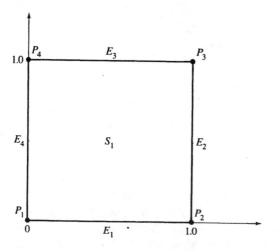

**Figure 1–2**   Picture data descriptions.

## 1–3 PREPARING PICTURES FOR PRESENTATION

Pictures ultimately consist of points and a drawing algorithm to display them. This information is generally stored in a file prior to being used to present the picture. This file is called a data base. Very complex pictures require very complex data bases, which require a complex algorithm to access them. These complex data bases contain data organized in various ways, e.g., ring structures, B-tree structures, quadtree structures, etc., generally referred to as a data structure. The data base itself may contain pointers, substructures and other nongraphic data. The design of these data bases and the algorithms which access them is an ongoing topic of research, a topic which is clearly beyond the scope of this text. However, many computer graphics applications involve much simpler pictures for which the user can readily invent simple data structures which can be easily accessed. The simplest is, of course, a lineal list. Surprisingly, this simplest of data structures is quite adequate for many reasonably complex pictures.

Since points are the basic building blocks of a graphic data base, the fundamental operations for manipulating these points are of interest. There are three fundamental operations when treating a point as a (geometric) graphic entity: move the beam, pen, cursor, plotting head (hereafter called the cursor) invisibly to the point; draw a visible line to a point from an initial point; or display a dot at that point. Fundamentally there are two ways to specify the position of a point: absolute or relative (incremental) coordinates. In relative or incremental coordinates the position of a point is defined by giving the displacement of the point with respect to the previous point. All computer graphics software is based on these fundamental operations. Section 1–22 and Appendix A more fully discuss computer graphics software fundamentals.

When specifying the position of a point, either real (floating point) numbers or integers may be used. If integers are used, difficulties arise because of the limited word length of most graphics support computers. For integer coordinate specification, a full computer word is generally used. The largest positive integer, assuming equal positive and negative ranges, that can be specified by a full computer word is $2^{n-1} - 1$, where $n$ is the number of bits in the word. For a 16-bit word this number is 32767. For many applications this is acceptable. However, difficulties are encountered when larger integer numbers than can be specified are required. At first, we might expect to overcome this difficulty by using relative coordinates to specify a number such as $60,000$, i.e., using an absolute coordinate specification to position the cursor to $(30000, 30000)$ and then a relative coordinate specification of $(30000, 30000)$ to position the cursor to the final desired point of $(60000, 60000)$. However, this does not work, since an attempt to accumulate relative position specifications beyond the maximum representable integer value results in integer overflow. On most machines integer overflow results in the generation of a number of opposite sign and erroneous magnitude.

The way out of this dilemma is to use homogeneous coordinates to represent the data. The use of homogeneous coordinates introduces some additional complexity, some loss in speed and some loss in resolution. However, these disadvantages are far outweighed by the advantage of being able to represent large integer numbers with a computer of limited word size. For this reason, as well as others presented later, homogeneous coordinate representations are generally used in this book.

In homogeneous coordinates an $n$-dimensional space is represented by $n + 1$ dimensions; i.e., three-dimensional data, where the position of a point is given by the triplet $(x, y, z)$, is represented by four coordinates $(hx, hy, hz, h)$, where $h$, the homogeneous coordinate, is an arbitrary number.

If each of the coordinate positions represented in a 16-bit computer were less than 32767, then $h$ would be made equal to 1 and the coordinate positions represented directly. If, however, one of the coordinates is larger than 32767, say, $x = 60000$, then the power of homogeneous coordinates becomes apparent. In this case we let $h = 1/2$; and the coordinates of the point are then defined as $(30000, y/2, z/2, 1/2)$, all acceptable numbers for a 16-bit computer. However, some resolution is lost since $x = 60000$ and $x = 60001$ are both represented by the same homogeneous coordinate. In fact, resolution is lost in all the coordinates even if only one of them exceeds the maximum expressible integer number of a particular computer.

## 1-4  PRESENTING PREVIOUSLY PREPARED PICTURES

The data used to prepare the picture for presentation is rarely the same as that used to present the picture. The data used to present the picture is frequently called a display file. The display file represents some portion, view or scene of the picture represented by the total data base. The displayed picture is usually formed by rotating, translating, scaling and performing various projections on the data. These basic orientation or viewing preparations are generally performed using a $4 \times 4$ transformation matrix operating on the data represented in homogeneous coordinates (see Chapters 2 and 3). When a sequence of transformations is required, each individual transformation matrix can be sequentially applied to the points to achieve the desired result. If, however, the number of points is substantial, this is inefficient. An alternate, and more desirable, method is to multiply the individual matrices for each transformation together. The result is a single combined (or concatenated) transformation matrix. This matrix operation is called concatenation. The points are then multiplied by the single combined $4 \times 4$ transformation matrix to yield the transformed points. This technique results in significant time savings when performing compound matrix operations on sets of data points.

Hidden line or hidden surface removal, shading, transparency, texture or color effects may be added before final presentation of the picture. If the picture represented by the entire data base is not to be presented, the appropriate portion must be selected. This is a process called clipping. Clipping may be two- or three-dimensional, as appropriate. In some cases, the clipping window or volume may have holes in it or may be irregularly shaped. Clipping to standard two- and three-dimensional regions is frequently implemented in hardware. A complete discussion of these effects is beyond the scope of the present text. They are thoroughly discussed by Rogers in Ref. 1–1.

Two important concepts associated with presenting a picture are windows and viewports. Windowing is the process of extracting a portion of a data base by clipping the data base to the boundaries of the window. Performance of the windowing or the clipping operation in software generally is sufficiently time con-suming that real-time interactive graphics is not possible. Again, sophisticated graphics devices perform this function in special-purpose hardware or microcode. Clipping involves determining which lines or portions of lines in the picture lie outside the window. Those lines or portions of lines are then discarded and not displayed; i.e., they are not passed on to the display device.

In two dimensions a window is specified by values for the left, right, bottom and top edges of a rectangle. The window edge values are specified in user or world coordinates, i.e., the coordinates in which the data base is specified. Floating point numbers are usually used.

Clipping is easiest if the edges of the rectangle are parallel to the coordinate axes. Such a window is called a regular clipping window. Irregular windows are also of interest for many applications (see Ref. 1–1). Two-dimensional clipping is represented in Fig. 1–3. Lines are retained, deleted or partially deleted, depend-ing on whether they are completely within or without the window or partially within or without the window. In three dimensions a regular window or clipping volume consists of a rectangular parallelepiped (a box) or for perspective views

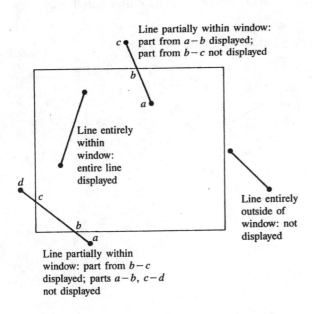

**Figure 1–3**    Two-dimensional windowing (clipping).

a frustum of vision. A typical frustum of vision is shown in Fig. 1–4. In Fig. 1–4 the near (hither) boundary is at $N$, the far (yon) boundary at $F$ and the sides at $SL$, $SR$, $ST$ and $SB$.

A viewport is an area of the display device on which the window data are presented. A two-dimensional regular viewport is specified by giving the left, right, bottom and top edges of a rectangle. Viewport values may be given in actual physical device coordinates. When specified in actual physical device coordinates they are frequently given using integers. Viewport coordinates may be normalized to some arbitrary range, e.g., $0 \le x \le 1.0$, $0 \le y \le 1.0$, and specified by floating point numbers. The contents of a single window may be displayed in multiple viewports on a single display device as shown in Fig. 1–5. Keeping the proportions of the window and viewport(s) the same prevents distortion. The mapping of windowed (clipped) data into a viewport involves translation and scaling (see Appendix A).

An additional requirement for most pictures is the presentation of alphanumeric or character data. There are in general two methods of generating characters — software and hardware. If characters are generated in software using lines, they are treated in the same manner as any other picture element. In fact, this is necessary if they are to be clipped and then transformed along with other picture elements. However, many graphics devices have hardware character generators. When hardware character generators are used, the actual characters are generated just prior to being drawn. Up until this point they are treated as character codes. Hardware character generation yields significant efficiencies. However, it is less flexible than software character generation, since it does not allow for clipping or general transformation; e.g., usually only limited rotations and sizes are possible.

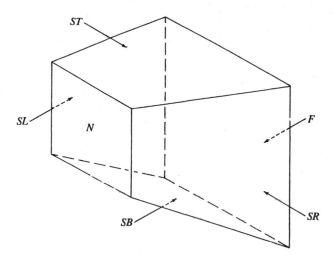

**Figure 1–4**   Three-dimensional frustum of vision.

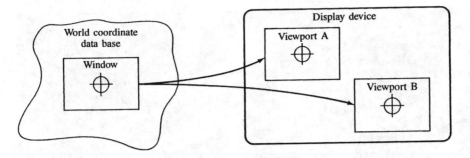

**Figure 1–5**   Multiple viewports displaying a single window.

When a hardware character generator is used, the program which drives the graphics device must first specify size, orientation and the position where the character or text string is to begin. The character codes specifying these characteristics are then added to the display file. Upon being processed the character generator interprets the text string, looks up in hardware the necessary information to draw each character, and draws the characters on the display device.

## 1–5   INTERACTING WITH THE PICTURE

Once the picture has been presented, interaction with, or modification of, the picture is required. To meet this requirement a number of interactive devices have been developed. Among these devices are tablets, light pens, joysticks, mice, control dials, function switches or buttons and of course the common alphanumeric keyboard. Before discussing these physical devices it is appropriate to discuss the functional capabilities of interactive graphics devices. The functional capabilities are generally considered to be of four or five logical types (see Refs. 1–2 to 1–4). The logical interaction devices, as opposed to the physical devices discussed below, are a locator, a valuator, a pick and a button. A fifth functional capability called keyboard is frequently included because of the general availability of the alphanumeric keyboard. In fact, a keyboard can conceptually and functionally be considered as a collection of buttons.

The locator function provides coordinate information in either two or three dimensions. Generally the coordinate numbers returned are in normalized coordinates and may be either relative or absolute. The valuator function provides a single value. Generally this value is a real number between zero and some real maximum. The button function is used to select and activate events or procedures which control the interactive flow. It generally provides only binary (on or off) digital information. The pick function identifies or selects objects or subpictures within the displayed picture. The logical keyboard processes textual information. A typical physical keyboard is shown in Fig. 1–6.

**Figure 1–6** An alphanumeric keyboard. (Courtesy of Evans & Sutherland Computer Corp.)

The tablet is the most common locator device. A typical tablet is shown in Fig. 1–7. Tablets may be used either in conjunction with a CRT graphics display or stand alone. In the latter case they are frequently referred to as digitizers. The tablet itself consists of a flat surface and a penlike stylus (or puck) which is used to indicate a location on the tablet surface. Usually the proximity of the stylus to the tablet surface is also sensed. When used in conjunction with a CRT display, feedback from the CRT face is provided by means of a small tracking symbol called a cursor, which follows the movement of the stylus on the tablet surface. When used as a stand-alone digitizer, feedback is provided by digital readouts.

Tablets provide either two- or three-dimensional coordinate information. A three-dimensional tablet is shown in Fig. 1–8. The values returned are in tablet coordinates. Software converts the tablet coordinates to user or world coordinates. Typical resolution and accuracy is 0.01 to 0.001 inch.

A number of different principles have been used to implement tablets. The original RAND tablet (see Ref. 1–5) used an orthogonal matrix of individual wires beneath the tablet surface. Each wire was individually coded such that the stylus acting as a receiver picked up a unique digital code at each intersection. Decoding yielded the $x,y$ coordinates of the stylus. The obvious limitations on the resolution of such a matrix-encoded tablet were the density of the wires and the receiver's ability to resolve a unique code. The accuracy was limited by the

**Figure 1–7**    A typical tablet. (Courtesy of Adage, Inc.)

linearity of the individual wires as well as the parallelism of the wires in the two orthogonal directions.

Another interesting implementation for a tablet used sound waves. A stylus was used to create a spark which generated a sound wave. The sound wave moved outward from the stylus on the surface of the tablet in a circular wave

**Figure 1–8**    A three-dimensional sonic tablet. (Courtesy of Science Accessories Corp.)

front. Two sensitive ribbon microphones were mounted on adjacent sides of the tablet. Thus, they were at right angles. By accurately measuring the time that it took the sound wave to travel from the stylus to the microphones, the coordinate distances were determined. This technique could be extended to three dimensions (see Fig. 1–8).

The most popular tablet implementation is based on a magnetic principle. In this tablet implementation strain wave pulses travel through a grid of wires beneath the tablet surface. Appropriate counters and a stylus containing a pick-up are used to determine the time it takes for alternate pulses parallel to the $x$ and $y$ coordinate axes to travel from the edge of the tablet to the stylus. These times are readily converted into $x,y$ coordinates.

A locator device similar to a tablet is the touch panel. In a typical touch panel, light emitters are mounted on two adjacent edges with companion light detectors mounted in the opposite edges. Anything, e.g., a finger, interrupting the two orthogonal light beams yields an $x,y$ coordinate pair. Because of its poor resolution, the touch panel is most useful for gross pointing operations. In this capacity it is frequently mounted in front of a CRT screen.

Locator devices such as the joystick, track ball and mouse are frequently implemented using sensitive variable resistors or potentiometers as part of a voltage divider. Control dials which are valuators are similarly implemented. The accuracy is dependent on the quality of the potentiometer, typically 0.1 to 10 percent of full throw. Although resolution of the potentiometer is basically infinite, use in a digital system requires analog-to-digital (A/D) conversion. Typically the resolution of the A/D converter ranges from 8 to 14 bits, i.e., from 1 part in $2^8$ (256) to 1 part in $2^{14}$ (16384). Valuators are also implemented with digital shaft encoders which, of course, provide a direct digital output for each incremental rotation of the shaft. Typical resolutions are 1 part in $2^8$ (256) to 1 part in $2^{10}$ (1024) for each incremental rotation of the shaft.

A typical locator is the joystick. A joystick is shown in Fig. 1–9. A movable joystick is generally implemented with two valuators, either potentiometers or digital shaft encoders, mounted in the base. The valuators provide results proportional to the movement of the shaft. A third dimension can readily be incorporated into a joystick, e.g., by using a third valuator to sense rotation of the shaft. A tracking symbol is normally used for feedback.

The track ball shown in Fig. 1–10 is similar to the joystick. It is most often seen in radar installations, e.g., in air traffic control. Here, a spherical ball is mounted in a base with only a portion projecting above the surface. The ball is free to rotate in any direction. Two valuators, either potentiometers or shaft encoders, mounted in the base sense the rotation of the ball and provide results proportional to its relative position. In addition to feedback from the normal tracking symbol, users obtain tactile feedback from the rotation rate or angular momentum of the ball.

The joystick has a fixed location with a fixed origin. The mouse and track ball, on the other hand, have only a relative origin. A typical mouse consists of an upside-down track ball mounted in a small, lightweight box. As the mouse is moved across a surface, the ball rotates and drives the shafts of two valuators,

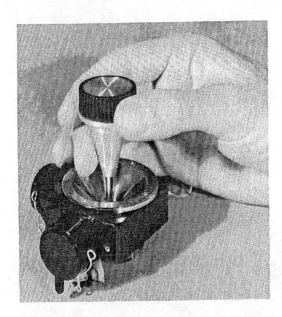

**Figure 1–9**    Joystick. (Courtesy of Measurement Systems, Inc.)

either potentiometers or digital shaft encoders. The cumulative movement of the shafts provides $x,y$ coordinates. A typical mouse is shown in Fig. 1–11. The mouse can be picked up, moved and set back down in a different orientation. In this case the coordinate system in which data is generated, i.e., the mouse, is changed, but not the data coordinate system itself. Under these circumstances

**Figure 1–10**    Track ball. (Courtesy of Measurement Systems, Inc.)

**Figure 1–11**   Mouse. (Courtesy of Apple Computer, Inc.)

the tracking symbol used for feedback does not move when the mouse is not in contact with the surface. The mouse suffers from inaccuracies due to slippage. Recently mice that work on both optical and magnetic principles have become available, eliminating the inaccuracies due to slippage.

Perhaps the simplest of the valuators is the control dial. Control dials, shown in Fig. 1–12, are essentially sensitive rotating potentiometers or accurate digital shaft encoders. They generally are used in groups and are particularly useful for activating rotation, translation, scaling or zoom functions.

Buttons or function switches, shown in Fig. 1–13, are either toggle or push-button switches. They may be either continuously closed/continuously open or momentary-contact switches. The most convenient type of function switch incorporates both capabilities. Software-controlled lights indicating which switches or buttons are active are usually provided. Buttons and switches are frequently incorporated into other devices. For example, the stylus of a tablet usually has a switch in the tip activated by pushing down on the stylus. A mouse also incorporates one or more buttons.

The light pen is the only true pick device. The pen, shown schematically in Fig. 1–14, contains a sensitive photoelectric cell and associated circuitry. Since the basic information provided by the light pen is timing, it depends on the picture being repeatedly produced in a predictable manner. This precludes its use with a storage tube CRT display. (See Sec. 1–7.) The use of a light pen is limited to refresh displays, either line drawing or raster scan.

Figure 1–12    Control dials. (Courtesy of Evans & Sutherland Computer Corp.)

On a line drawing refresh display (see Sec. 1–8), if the light pen is activated and placed over an area of the CRT which is subsequently written on, the change in intensity sends a signal to the display controller. This signal allows the particular instruction in the display buffer being executed at that time, and hence, e.g., the particular line segment, object or subpicture that was picked, to be determined. A light pen can also be used as a locator on a line drawing refresh device by using a tracking symbol.

Figure 1–13    Function switches. (Courtesy of Adage, Inc.)

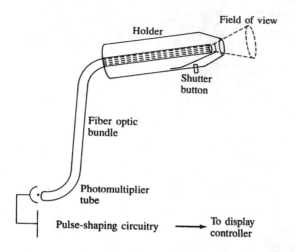

**Figure 1–14** Schematic of a light pen.

Since in a raster scan display the picture is generated in a fixed sequence, the light pen is used to determine the horizontal scan line ($y$ coordinate) and the position on the scan line ($x$ coordinate). Again, this allows the particular line segment, object or subpicture to be determined. The actual process is somewhat complicated by the interlace scheme (see Sec. 1–12). The above description also indicates that, on a raster scan device, a light pen can be used as a locator rather than as a pick device.

Although physical devices are available to implement all the logical interactive devices, an individual graphics device may not have the appropriate physical devices available. Thus, simulation of the logical interactive devices is required. An example is shown in Fig. 1–15, where a light pen is being used to simulate a logical button function by picking light buttons from a menu.

The tablet is one of the most versatile of the physical devices. It can be used as a digitizer to provide $x,y$ coordinate information. In addition, it can readily be used to simulate all the logical interactive functions. This is shown in Fig. 1–16. The tablet itself is a locator (a in Fig. 1–16). The button function can be implemented by using a tracking symbol. The tracking symbol is positioned at or near menu buttons using the tablet stylus. The tablet coordinates are compared with the known $(x, y)$ coordinates of the menu buttons. If a match is obtained, then that button is activated (b in Fig. 1–16). A keyboard can be implemented in a similar manner (c in Fig. 1–16).

A single valuator is usually implemented in combination with a button. The particular function for evaluation is selected by a button, usually in a menu. The valuator is then simulated by a 'number line' or 'sliderbar' (d in Fig. 1–16). Moving the tracking symbol along the line generates $x$ and $y$ coordinates, one of which is interpreted as a percentage of the valuator's range.

**Figure 1–15**   A light pen used to simulate a logical button function via menu picking. (Courtesy of Adage, Inc.)

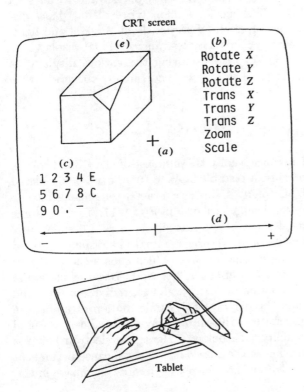

**Figure 1–16**   A tablet used to simulate all the logical interactive functions. (a) Locator; (b) button; (c) keyboard; (d) valuator; (e) pick.

The pick function can be implemented using a locator by defining the relative $x$ and $y$ coordinates of a small 'hit window.' The hit window is then made the tracking symbol, and the stylus is used to position it. The $x,y$ coordinates of each of the line segments, objects or subpictures of interest are then compared with those of the current location of the hit window. If a match is obtained then that entity is picked. Implemented in software, this can be slow for complex pictures. Implemented in hardware, there is no noticeable delay. Although a light pen or a mouse cannot be used as a digitizer, like the tablet they can also be used to simulate all the logical interactive functions.

## 1–6  DESCRIPTION OF SOME GRAPHICS DEVICES

The display medium for computer graphics-generated pictures has become widely diversified. Typical examples are cathode ray tube (CRT) displays, flat panel displays, pen-and-ink plotters, dot matrix, electrostatic or laser printer plotters and film. In addition to display devices, image capture devices are becoming of increasing importance.

The three most common types of CRT display technologies are direct-view storage tube (line drawing), calligraphic (line drawing) refresh and raster scan (point plotting) refresh displays. The most common types of flat panel displays include plasma-gas discharge, electroluminescent, liquid crystal and light-emitting diode technologies. With recent advances, an individual display may incorporate more than one technology. In discussing the various displays we take a user's, or conceptual, point of view; i.e., we are generally concerned with functional capabilities.

## 1–7  STORAGE TUBE GRAPHICS DISPLAYS

The direct-view storage tube[†] is conceptually the simplest of the CRT displays. The storage tube display, also called a bistable storage tube, can be considered a CRT with a long-persistence phosphor. A line or character remains visible (up to an hour) until erased. A typical display is shown in Fig. 1–17. To draw a line or character on the display the electron beam intensity is increased sufficiently to cause the phosphor to assume its bright 'storage state'. The display is erased by flooding the entire tube with a specific voltage, which causes the phosphor to assume its dark state. Erasure takes about 1/2 second. Because the entire tube is flooded, all lines and characters are erased. Thus, individual lines and characters cannot be erased, and the display of dynamic motion or animation is not possible. An intermediate state (write-through mode) is sometimes used to provide limited refresh capability (see below). Here, the electron beam is intensified to a point that is just below the threshold that will cause permanent storage but is still sufficient to brighten the phosphor. Because the image in this

---

[†]Storage tube graphics displays are no longer manufactured. However, there are still literally thousands of them in use, hence the discussion.

**Figure 1–17**   Storage tube graphics display. (Courtesy of Tektronix Inc.)

mode does not store, it must be redrawn or repainted continuously in order for it to be visible.

A storage tube display is flicker-free (see below) and capable of displaying an 'unlimited' number of vectors. Resolution is 1024 × 1024 addressable points (10 bits) on an 8 × 8 inch square (11-inch-diagonal) CRT or 4096 × 4096 points (12 bits) on either a 14 × 14 inch square (19-inch-diagonal) CRT or an 18 × 18 inch square (25-inch-diagonal) CRT. Typically only 78 percent of the addressable area is viewable in the vertical direction.

A storage tube display is a line drawing or random scan display. This means that a line (vector) can be drawn directly from any addressable point to any other addressable point. Hard copy is relatively easy, fast and inexpensive to obtain. Conceptually, a storage tube display is somewhat easier to program than a calligraphic or raster scan refresh display. Storage tube CRT displays can be combined with microcomputers into stand-alone computer graphics systems or incorporated into graphics terminals. When incorporated into terminals, alphanumeric and graphic information are passed to the terminal by a host computer over an interface. Although parallel interfaces are available, typically a serial interface which passes information 1 bit at a time is used. Because of the typically low interface speed and the erasure characteristics, the level of interactivity with a storage tube display is lower than with either a refresh or raster scan display.

## 1–8   CALLIGRAPHIC REFRESH GRAPHICS DISPLAYS

In contrast to the storage tube display, a calligraphic (line drawing or vector) refresh CRT display uses a very short persistence phosphor. These displays are frequently called random scan displays. Because of the short persistence of the phosphor, the picture painted on the CRT must be repainted or refreshed many times each second. The minimum refresh rate is at least 30 times each second, with a recommended rate of 40 to 50 times each second. Refresh rates much lower than 30 times each second result in a flickering image. The effect is similar to that observed when a movie film is run too slowly. The resulting picture is difficult to use and disagreeable to look at.

The basic calligraphic refresh display requires two elements in addition to the CRT. These are the display buffer and the display controller. The display buffer is contiguous computer memory containing all the information required to draw the picture on the CRT. The display controller's function is to repeatedly cycle through this information at the refresh rate. Two factors which limit the complexity (number of vectors displayed) of the picture are the size of the display buffer and the speed of the display controller. A further limitation is the speed at which picture information can be processed, i.e., transformed and clipped, and textual information generated.

Figure 1–18 shows block diagrams of two high-performance calligraphic refresh displays. In both cases it is assumed that picture transformation such as rotation, translation, scaling, perspective and clipping are implemented in hardware in the picture processor. In the first case (Fig. 1–18a) the picture processor is slower than the refresh rate for useful pictures (4000 to 5000 vectors). Thus, the picture data sent by the host central processing unit (CPU) to the graphics display is processed before being stored in the display buffer. Here the display buffer contains only those precise instructions which are required by the vector/character generator to draw the picture. Vectors are generally held in screen coordinates. The display controller reads information from the display buffer and sends it to the vector/character generator. When the display controller reaches the end of the display buffer, it returns to the beginning and cycles through the buffer again.

This first configuration also gives rise to the concepts of double buffering and separate update and refresh rates. Since in this configuration the picture processor is too slow to generate a complex new or updated picture within one refresh cycle, the display buffer is divided into two parts. While an updated picture is being processed and written into one-half of the buffer, the display controller is refreshing the CRT from the other half of the buffer. When the updated picture

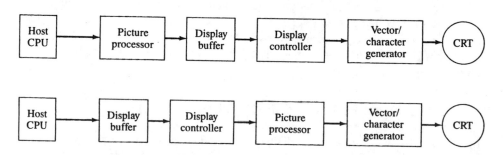

**Figure 1–18**   Conceptual block diagrams of calligraphic refresh displays.

is complete, the buffers are swapped and the process is repeated. Thus, a new or updated picture may be generated every second, third, fourth, etc. refresh cycle. Double buffering prevents part of the old picture being displayed along with part of the new updated picture during one or more refresh cycles.

In the second configuration (see Fig. 1–18b) the picture processor is faster than the refresh rate for complex pictures. Here, the original picture data sent from the host CPU is held directly in the display buffer. Vectors are generally held in user (world) coordinates as floating point numbers. The display controller reads information from the display buffer, passes it through the picture processor and sends it to the vector generator in one refresh cycle. This implies that picture transformations are performed 'on the fly' within one refresh cycle.

In either configuration, each vector, character and picture drawing instruction exists in the display buffer. Hence, any individual element may be changed independent of any other element. This feature, in combination with the short persistence of the CRT phosphor, allows the display of dynamic motion. Figure 1–19 illustrates this concept. Figure 1–19 shows the picture displayed during four successive refresh cycles. The visible solid line is the displayed line for the current refresh cycle, and the invisible dotted line is for the previous refresh cycle. Between refresh cycles the location of the end of the line $B$ is changed. The line appears to rotate about the point $A$.

In many pictures only portions of the picture are dynamic. In fact, in many applications the majority of the picture is static. This leads to the concept of segmentation of the display buffer. Figure 1–20 illustrates this idea. Here, the baseline, the cross-hatching and the letter $A$ used to show the support for the line $AB$ are static; i.e., they do not change from refresh cycle to refresh cycle. In contrast, the location of the end of the line $AB$ and the letter $B$ change from refresh cycle to refresh cycle to show dynamic motion. These separate portions of the picture are placed in separate segments of the display buffer. Since the static segment of the display buffer does not change, it can be ignored by the picture processor for the configuration shown in Fig. 1–18. This significantly

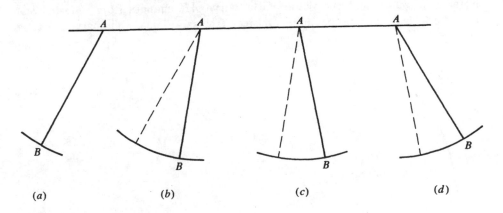

(a)          (b)          (c)          (d)

**Figure 1–19**   Dynamic motion.

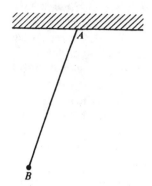

**Figure 1–20**   Display buffer segmentation.

reduces the work load on the picture processor when updating a picture. In this case, only the picture in the dynamic segment need be updated. Further, it reduces the amount of data that needs to be transmitted from the host CPU to the picture processor during each picture update.

For the configuration shown in Fig. 1–18b a different type of segmentation is possible. Recall that for this configuration the picture data is stored in the display buffer in world (user) coordinates and picture processing occurs on the fly once each refresh cycle. For the picture in Fig. 1–20 two segments are created in the display buffer, a static and a dynamic segment. Update of the information in the dynamic segment is accomplished using functions available in the picture processor. Thus, picture update occurs locally within the graphics device, and communication with the host CPU is unnecessary. For the particular case shown in Fig. 1–20 the only picture processor function required for local dynamic update is rotation about the point $A$.

Figure 1–21 illustrates a picture for which dynamic update requires communication with the host CPU, i.e., intelligent update of the picture. Again two segments are created, a static segment comprised of the baseline, cross-hatching and the letter $A$, and a dynamic segment comprised of the curve $AB$ and the letter $B$. Assume that the shape of the curve $AB$ changes from refresh cycle to refresh cycle depending upon physical factors. Thus, the shape must be

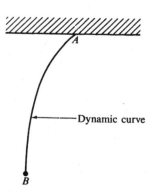

Dynamic curve

**Figure 1–21**   Intelligent display buffer segmentation.

computed by an application program running in the host CPU. In order to update the dynamic picture segment, new data, e.g., curve shape, must be sent to and stored in the display buffer.

Although the concept of picture segmentation has been introduced through dynamic motion examples, it is not limited to dynamic motion or animation. Any picture can be segmented. Picture segmentation is particularly useful for interactive graphics programs. The concept is similar to modular programming. The choice of modular picture segments, their size and their complexity depends on the particular application. Individual picture elements can be as simple as single points or as complex as complete object descriptions. A typical calligraphic refresh display is shown in Fig. 1–22.

To illustrate the importance of the communication speed, or bandwidth, between the host CPU and the graphics device, consider the requirements for intelligently updating a curved line with 250 segments or points describing it. Each point is described by three coordinates. If we assume that a floating point representation with six significant figures (characters) is used, and that a single 8-bit byte is used to represent a character, then for a refresh rate of 30 frames/second and an update every refresh cycle the required communication bandwidth is

30[(no. points)(no. coor./point) (no. of sig. figs./point)(no. bits/char.)]

or                30(250)(3)(6)(8) = 1,080,000 bits/second

Thus, the required bandwidth can easily exceed 1 megabit/second. For complicated three-dimensional sculptured surfaces, the required bandwidth can easily

**Figure 1–22**    Calligraphic refresh display. (Courtesy of Evans & Sutherland Computer Corp.)

exceed 10 times this, i.e., 10 megabits/second. In most cases this dictates a parallel or direct memory access (DMA) interface between the host CPU and the graphics device to support real-time intelligent dynamic graphics.

## 1–9  RASTER REFRESH GRAPHICS DISPLAYS

Both the storage tube CRT display and the calligraphic (random scan) refresh display are line drawing devices. That is, a straight line can be drawn directly from any addressable point to any other addressable point. In contrast, the raster CRT graphics display is a point plotting device. A raster graphics device can be considered a matrix of discrete cells, each of which can be made bright. It is not possible, except in special cases, to directly draw a straight line from one addressable point, or pixel,† in the matrix to another addressable point or pixel. The line can only be approximated by a series of dots (pixels) close to the path of the line. Figure 1–23a illustrates the basic concept. Only in the special cases of completely horizontal, vertical or, for square pixels, 45° lines does a straight line of dots or pixels result. This is shown in Fig. 1–23b. All other lines appear as a series of stair steps. This is called aliasing or the 'jaggies'. Antialiasing techniques are discussed in Ref. 1–1.

The most common method of implementing a raster CRT graphics device uses a frame buffer. A frame buffer is a large, contiguous piece of computer memory. As a minimum there is one memory bit for each pixel (picture element) in the raster. This amount of memory is called a bit plane. A $512 \times 512$ element square raster requires $2^{18}$ ($2^9 = 512$; $2^{18} = 512 \times 512$) or 262,144 memory bits in a single bit plane. The picture is built up in the frame buffer 1 bit at a time. Since a memory bit has only two states (binary 0 or 1), a single bit plane yields a black-and-white (monochrome) display. Since the frame buffer is a digital device, while the raster CRT is an analog device, conversion from a digital representation to an analog signal must take place when information is read from the frame buffer and displayed on the raster CRT graphics device. This is accomplished by a digital-to-analog converter (DAC). Each pixel in the frame buffer must be accessed and converted before it is visible on the raster CRT. A schematic diagram of a single-bit-plane, black-and-white frame buffer, raster CRT graphics device is shown in Fig. 1–24.

Color or gray levels are incorporated into a frame buffer raster graphics device by using additional bit planes. Figure 1–25 schematically shows an $N$-bit-plane gray level frame buffer. The intensity of each pixel on the CRT is controlled by a corresponding pixel location in each of the $N$ bit planes. The binary value (0 or 1) from each of the $N$ bit planes is loaded into corresponding positions in a register. The resulting binary number is interpreted as an intensity level between 0 (dark) and $2^N - 1$ (full intensity). This is converted into an analog

---

†A pixel is addressed or identified by its lower left corner. It occupies a finite area to the right and above this point. Addressing starts at 0,0. This means that the pixels in an $n \times n$ raster are addressed in the range 0 to $n-1$. Thus, e.g., the top and right-most lines in Fig. 1–23 do not represent addressable *pixel* locations.

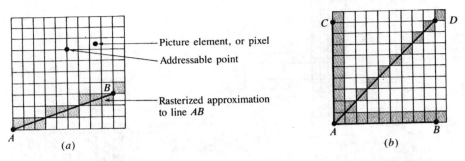

**Figure 1–23**    Rasterization. (a) General line; (b) special cases.

voltage between 0 and the maximum voltage of the electron gun by the DAC. A total of $2^N$ intensity levels are possible. Figure 1–25 illustrates a system with 3 bit planes for a total of $8\,(2^3)$ intensity levels. Each bit plane requires the full complement of memory for a given raster resolution; e.g., a 3-bit-plane frame buffer for a $512 \times 512$ raster requires 786,432 $(3 \times 512 \times 512)$ memory bits.

An increase in the number of available intensity levels is achieved for a modest increase in required memory by using a lookup table. This is shown schematically in Fig. 1–26. Upon reading the bit planes in the frame buffer, the resulting number is used as an index into the lookup table. The lookup table must contain $2^N$ entries. Each entry in the lookup table is $W$ bits wide. $W$ may be greater than $N$. When this occurs, $2^W$ intensities are available; but only $2^N$ different intensities are available at one time. To get additional intensities the lookup table must be changed (reloaded).

Since there are three primary colors, a simple color frame buffer is implemented with three bit planes, one for each primary color. Each bit plane drives

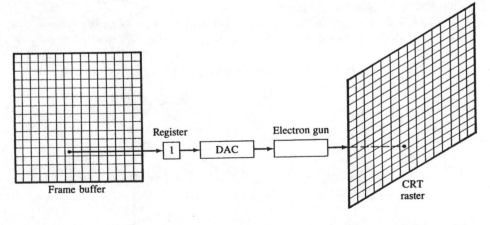

**Figure 1–24**    A single-bit-plane black-and-white frame buffer raster CRT graphics device.

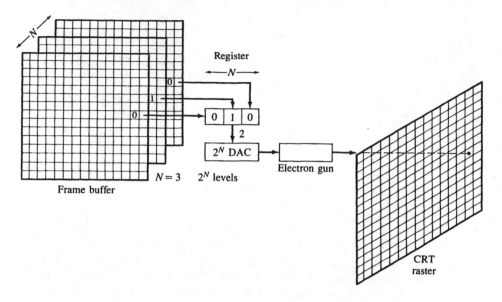

**Figure 1–25**    An $N$-bit-plane gray level frame buffer.

an individual color gun for each of the three primary colors used in color video. These three primaries (red, green and blue) are combined at the CRT to yield eight colors as shown in Table 1–1. A simple color raster frame buffer is shown schematically in Fig. 1–27.

Additional bit planes can be used for each of the three color guns. A schematic of a multiple-bit-plane color frame buffer with 8 bit planes per color, i.e., a 24-bit-plane frame buffer, is shown in Fig. 1–28. Each group of bit planes drives an 8-bit DAC. Each group generates 256 $(2^8)$ shades or intensities of red, green or blue. These are combined into 16,777,216 $[(2^8)^3 = 2^{24}]$ possible colors. This is a 'full' color frame buffer.

The full color frame buffer can be further expanded by using the groups of bit planes as indices to color lookup tables. This is shown schematically in Fig. 1–29.

**Table 1–1 Simple 3-bit plane frame buffer color combinations**

|           | Red | Green | Blue |
| --------- | --- | ----- | ---- |
| Black     | 0   | 0     | 0    |
| Red       | 1   | 0     | 0    |
| Green     | 0   | 1     | 0    |
| Blue      | 0   | 0     | 1    |
| Yellow    | 1   | 1     | 0    |
| Cyan      | 0   | 1     | 1    |
| Magenta   | 1   | 0     | 1    |
| White     | 1   | 1     | 1    |

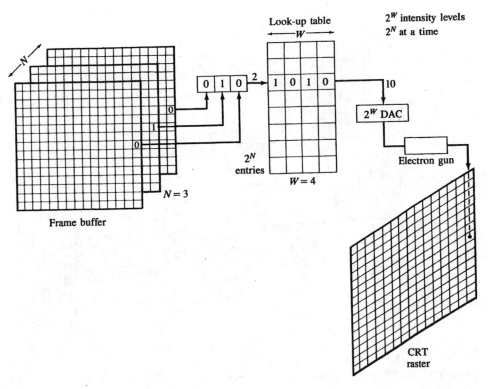

**Figure 1-26**   An $N$-bit-plane gray level frame buffer with a $W$-bit-wide lookup table.

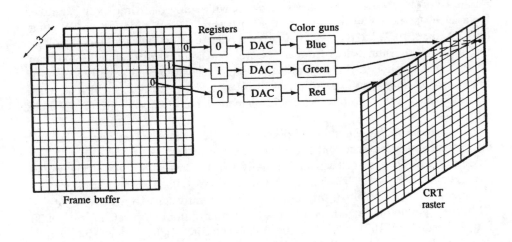

**Figure 1-27**   Simple color frame buffer.

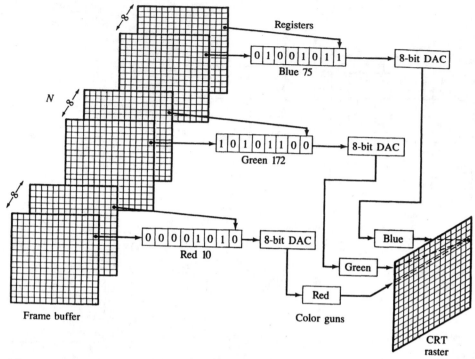

**Figure 1-28**    A 24-bit-plane color frame buffer.

For $N$ bit planes/color with $W$-bit-wide color lookup tables, $(2^3)^N$ colors from a palette of $(2^3)^W$ possible colors can be shown at any one time. For example, for a 24-bit-plane ($N = 8$) frame buffer with three 10-bit-wide ($W = 10$) color lookup tables, 16,777,216 ($2^{24}$) colors from a palette of 1,073,741,824 ($2^{30}$) colors, i.e., about 17 million colors from a palette of a little more than 1 billion, can be obtained. Although three separate lookup tables are schematically shown in Fig. 1-29, for small numbers of physical bit planes (up to about 12) it is more advantageous if the lookup tables are implemented contiguously with $(2^3)^N$ table entries.

Because of the large number of pixels in a raster scan graphics device, achieving real-time performance and acceptable refresh or frame rates is difficult. For example, if pixels are accessed individually with an average access time of 200 nanoseconds ($200 \times 10^{-9}$ second), then it requires 0.0524 second to access all the pixels in a $512 \times 512$ frame buffer. This is equivalent to a refresh rate of 19 frames (pictures)/second, well below the required minimum refresh rate of 30 frames/second. A $1024 \times 1024$ frame buffer contains slightly more than 1 million bits (1 megabit) and, at 200 nanoseconds average access time, requires 0.21 second to access all the pixels. This is 5 frames/second. A $4096 \times 4096$ frame buffer contains 16.78 million bits per memory plane! At a 200-nanosecond access time per pixel it requires 3 seconds to access all the pixels. To achieve a refresh

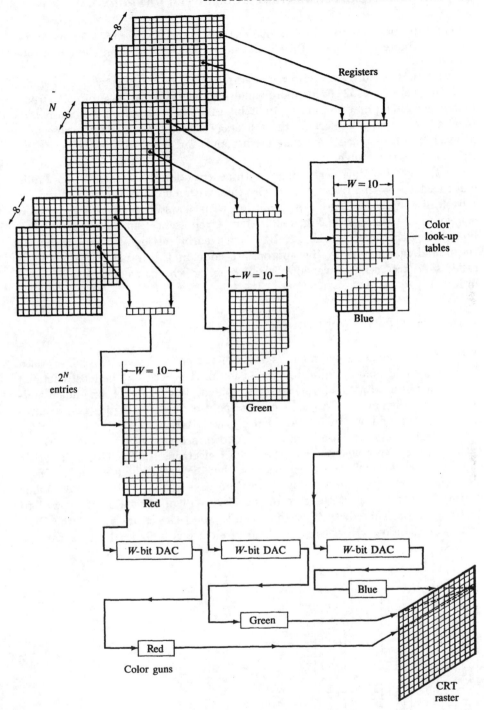

**Figure 1–29**    A 24-bit-plane color frame buffer with 10-bit-wide lookup tables.

rate of 30 frames/second a $4096 \times 4096$ raster requires an average effective access rate of 2 nanoseconds/pixel. Recall that light travels two *feet* in this small time period.

Real-time performance with raster scan devices is achieved by accessing pixels in groups of 16, 32, 64 or more simultaneously. In the case of color frame buffers each pixel may contain up to 32 bits; i.e., all bit planes for an individual pixel are accessed together. With an average access time of 1600 nanoseconds for each group of pixels, real-time performance for $512 \times 512$ and $1024 \times 1024$ frame buffers is possible.

Although real-time performance with acceptable refresh rates is more difficult to achieve with a raster CRT device than with a calligraphic or line drawing refresh display, solid figure representation with a raster device is conceptually simple. This is shown in Fig. 1–30. Here a representation of the solid figure bounded by the lines L1, L2, L3, L4 is achieved by setting all the pixels within the bounding polygon to the appropriate code in the frame buffer. This is called solid area scan conversion. Algorithms for scan conversion are discussed in Ref. 1–1.

## 1–10   CATHODE RAY TUBE BASICS

A frame buffer as described above is not itself a display device. It is simply used to assemble and hold a digital representation of the picture. The most common display device used with a frame buffer is a video (TV) monitor. An understanding of raster displays, and to some extent line drawing refresh displays, requires a basic understanding of CRTs and video display techniques.

The CRT used in video monitors is shown schematically in Fig. 1–31. A cathode (negatively charged) is heated until electrons 'boil' off in a diverging cloud (electrons repel each other because they have the same charge). These electrons are attracted to a highly charged positive anode. This is the phosphor coating on the inside of the face of the large end of the CRT. If allowed to continue uninterrupted, the electrons simply flood the entire face of the CRT with a bright glow. However, the cloud of electrons is focused into a narrow,

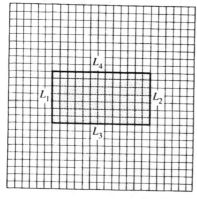

**Figure 1–30**   Solid figures with a raster graphics device.

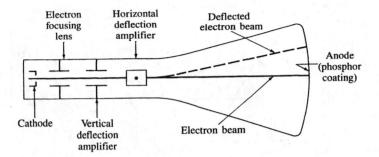

**Figure 1–31** Cathode ray tube.

precisely collimated beam with an electron lens. At this point the focused electron beam produces a single bright spot at the center of the CRT. The electron beam is deflected or positioned to the left or right of the center and/or above or below the center by means of horizontal and vertical deflection amplifiers.

It is at this point that line drawing displays, both storage and refresh, and raster scan displays differ. In a line drawing display the electron beam may be deflected directly from any arbitrary position to any other arbitrary position on the face of the CRT (anode). A perfectly straight line results. In contrast, in a raster scan display the beam is deflected in a set, rigidly controlled pattern. This pattern comprises the video picture.

## 1–11   COLOR CRT RASTER SCAN BASICS

A color raster scan CRT is similar to the standard black-and-white CRT described in the previous section. In the color raster scan CRT there are three electron guns, one for each of the three primary colors, red, green and blue. The electron guns are frequently arranged in a triangular pattern corresponding to a similar triangular pattern of red, green and blue phosphor dots on the face of the CRT (see Fig. 1–32). To ensure that the individual electron guns excite the correct phosphor dots (e.g., the red gun excites only the red phosphor dot), a perforated metal grid is placed between the electron guns and the face of the CRT. This is the shadow mask of the standard shadow mask color CRT. The perforations in the shadow mask are arranged in the same triangular pattern as the phosphor dots. The distance between perforations is called the pitch. The color guns are arranged so that the individual beams converge and intersect at the shadow mask (see Fig. 1–33). Upon passing through the hole in the shadow mask the red beam, for example, is prevented or masked from intersecting either the green or blue phosphor dot. It can only intersect the red phosphor dot. By varying the strength of the electron beam for each individual primary color, different shades (intensities) are obtained. These primary color shades can be combined into a large number of colors for each pixel. For a high-resolution display there are usually two to three color triads for each pixel.

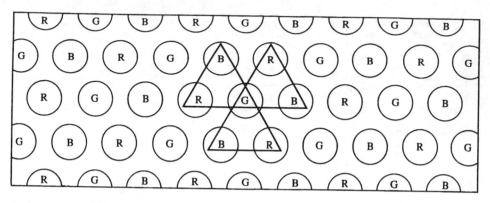

**Figure 1–32**  Phosphor dot pattern for a shadow mask CRT.

## 1–12    VIDEO BASICS

The process of converting the rasterized picture stored in a frame buffer to the rigid display pattern of video is called scan conversion. The scanning pattern and the frequency of repetition are based on both visual perception and electronic principles. The human visual perception system requires a finite amount of time to resolve the elements of a picture. If individual images are presented at a rate greater than the time required for the visual system to resolve individual images, one image persists while the next is being presented. This persistence of vision is used to achieve flicker-fusion. The result is perceived as a continuous presentation. A number of factors affect flicker, including image brightness and the particular CRT screen phosphor used. Experience indicates that a practical minimum picture presentation or update rate is 25 frames/second, provided the minimum refresh or repetition rate is twice this, i.e., 50 frames/second. This is actually what is done with movie film. With movie film 24 frames/second are presented, but the presentation of each frame is interrupted so that it is

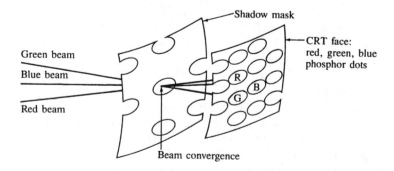

**Figure 1–33**    Color CRT electron gun and shadow mask arrangement.

presented twice for an effective repetition rate of 48 frames/second. Thus, for film the update rate is 24 and the refresh rate is 48. The same effect is achieved in video using a technique called interlacing.

Video is a raster scan technique. The American standard video system uses a total of 525 horizontal lines with a frame or viewing aspect ratio of 4:3; i.e., the viewing area is three-quarters as high as it is wide. The repetition or frame rate is 30 frames/second. However, each frame is divided into two fields, each containing one-half of the picture. The two fields are interlaced or interwoven. The fields are presented alternately every other 1/60 second. One field contains all the odd-numbered scan lines (1, 3, 5,... ), and the other the even-numbered scan lines (2, 4, 6,... ). The scanning pattern begins at the upper left corner of the screen with the odd field. Each line in the field is scanned or presented from the left to the right. As the electron beam moves across the screen from left to right, it also moves vertically downward but at a much slower rate. Thus, the 'horizontal' scan line is in fact slightly slanted. When the beam reaches the right edge of the screen, it is made invisible and rapidly returned to the left edge. This is the horizontal retrace which usually requires approximately 17 percent of the time allowed for one scan line. The process is then repeated with the next odd scan line. Since half of 525 is 262 1/2 lines, the beam is at the bottom center of the screen when the odd scan line field is complete (see Figs. 1–34 and 1–35). The beam is then quickly returned to the top center of the screen. This is the odd field vertical retrace. The time required for the vertical retrace is equivalent to that for 21 lines. The even scan line field is then presented. The even scan line field ends in the lower right hand corner. The even field vertical retrace returns the beam to the upper left hand corner, and the entire sequence is repeated. Thus, two fields are presented for each frame, i.e., 60 fields per second. Since the eye perceives the field repetition rate, this technique significantly reduces flicker.

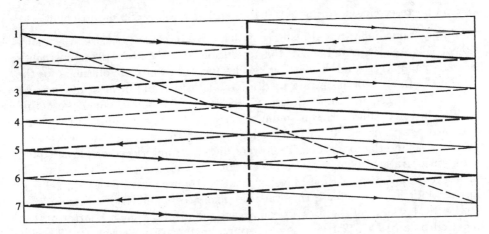

**Figure 1–34**  Schematic of a 7-line interlaced scan line pattern. The odd field begins with line 1. The horizontal retrace is shown dashed. The odd field vertical retrace starts at the bottom center. The even field vertical retrace starts at the bottom right.

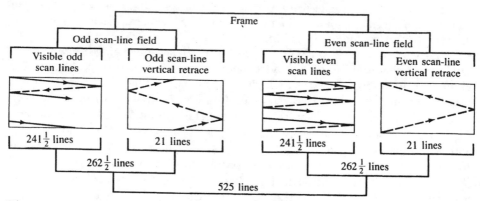

**Figure 1–35**　A 525-line standard frame schematic.

Although the American standard video system calls for 525 lines, only 483 lines are actually visible because a time equivalent to 21 lines is required to accomplish the vertical retrace for each field.[†] During this time the electron beam is invisible or blanked. The time available for each scan line is calculated for a frame repetition rate of 30 as

$$1/30 \text{ second/frame} \times 1/525 \text{ frame/scan lines} = 63\tfrac{1}{2} \text{ microseconds/scan line}$$

Since approximately $10\tfrac{1}{2}$ microseconds is required for horizontal retrace, the visible portion of each scan line must be completed in 53 microseconds. With a normal video aspect ratio of 4:3, there are 644 pixels on each scan line. The time available to access and display a pixel is thus

$$53 \text{ microseconds/scan line} \times 1/644 \text{ scan line/pixels} = 82 \text{ nanoseconds}$$

Many frame buffer-based raster scan displays sample the picture at a resolution of 512 pixels per scan line. At this resolution approximately 103 nanoseconds is available to access and display a pixel. Equivalent results are obtained for the 625-line 25-frame repetition rate used in Great Britain and in most of Europe.

The interlaced technique described above is not required when presenting a video picture. However, this noninterlaced picture is not compatible with a standard television set. In fact, most high quality raster scan graphics devices present a noninterlaced picture. To prevent flicker, noninterlaced displays require a repetition rate of 60 frames/second. This, of course, reduces the available pixel access and display time by a factor of 2. Higher scan line and pixel-per-line resolutions also decrease the available pixel access and display time, e.g., a $1024 \times 1024$ resolution requires a pixel access and display time a quarter of that required by a $512 \times 512$ resolution — approximately 25 nanoseconds. Thus, a very fast frame buffer memory, a very fast frame buffer controller, an equally fast DAC and a very high bandwidth monitor are required.

---

[†] Many raster scan graphics devices use this time for processing other information.

## 1–13    FLAT PANEL DISPLAYS

Although today the CRT is unrivaled as the computer graphics display of choice, it is bulky, heavy, fragile, and currently limited in size to about 30 inches diagonally. For these as well as other reasons, flat panel displays are becoming of increasing importance. All flat panel displays are raster refresh displays.

Flat panel displays are broadly divided into those based on active (light-emitting) and passive (light-modulating) technologies. Among the active technologies are flat CRTs, plasma-gas discharge, electroluminescent (EL) and vacuum fluorescent displays. Liquid crystal (LC) and light-emitting diodes (LED) are representative of the passive technologies.

Of the active flat panel display technologies, plasma-gas discharge and electroluminescent based displays are currently most suitable for the relatively large sizes and high resolutions required by computer graphics applications. Except for applications with special requirements, e.g., avionics where light emitting diode-based displays have certain advantages, liquid crystal based displays are the most suitable of the passive technologies.

As shown in Fig. 1–36, a flat CRT is obtained by initially projecting the electron beam parallel to the screen and then reflecting it through 90°. Reflecting the electron beam significantly reduces the depth of the CRT bottle and consequently of the display. The flat CRT has all the performance advantages of the conventional CRT. Currently, flat CRTs are only available in relatively small sizes. The length of the 'neck' may limit their utility in larger sizes. The utility of vacuum fluorescent displays is also currently size limited.

Plasma-gas discharge, electroluminescent and liquid crystal displays have several operating characteristics in common. Each consists of a matrix of individual pixel locations on a raster. Each pixel must contain some mechanism, or material, activated by application of either a voltage or a current, that either emits light or modulates incident light. The required voltage or current is supplied to the pixel using an individual electronic switching device, e.g., a thin

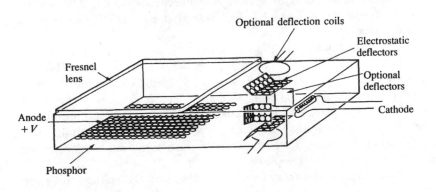

**Figure 1–36**    Flat CRT schematic.

film transistor, diode or metal-insulator-metal nonlinear resistor, located at each pixel. Displays using this technology are called active matrix displays.

An alternate, and more common, technique that significantly reduces the number of switches or drivers, uses row-column addressing of the raster. This technique requires that the display material have a switching threshold. Only when the switching threshold is exceeded does emission or modification of light occur. Part of the voltage or current required to activate an individual pixel is applied through the appropriate row and the other part through the appropriate column. The individual row or column voltage or current supplied is below the switching threshold. Together, it is above the switching threshold. Consequently, unwanted pixels along either the row or column are not activated. Only the desired pixel at the intersection of the row and column receives enough voltage or current to exceed the switching threshold and hence is activated.

When using row-column addressing, bistable pixel memory is highly desirable. With bistable memory, once activated a pixel remains activated until explicitly turned off. Bistable pixel memory eliminates the necessity of constantly refreshing pixels. Consequently, no external memory is required to refresh the display. In addition, the display controller is simplified.

The basic technology of a plasma or gas discharge display is quite simple. Essentially the display consists of a matrix of cells (the raster) in a glass envelope. Each cell is filled with a gas (usually neon or a neon/argon mixture) at low pressure (below atmospheric). When a sufficiently high voltage is applied, the gas dissociates, i.e., electrons are stripped from the atoms. The dissociated gas is called a plasma, hence the name — plasma display. When the electrons recombine, energy is released in the form of photons; and the gas glows with the characteristic bright orange-red hue. A typical plasma display is shown in Fig. 1-37.

Plasma displays can be AC or DC or combined AC/DC activated. AC, DC and hybrid AC/DC activated plasma displays are shown schematically in Figs. 1-38 a, b and c, respectively. The DC activated display is simpler than the AC display. It consists of a dielectric spacer plate containing the gas cavities sandwiched between plates containing the row-column conductors. The electric field is applied directly to the gas. A DC activated plasma display requires continuous refreshing.

In the AC activated plasma display a dielectric layer is placed between the conductors and the gas. Thus, the only coupling between the gas and the conductors is capacitive. Hence, an AC voltage is required to dissociate the gas. AC activated plasma displays have bistable memory. Thus, the necessity to continuously refresh the display is eliminated. Bistable memory is obtained by using a low AC keep alive voltage. The characteristic capacitive coupling provides enough voltage to maintain the activity in the conducting pixels, but not enough to activate nonconducting pixels.

A hybrid AC/DC plasma display (see Fig. 1-38c) uses DC voltage to 'prime' the gas and make it more easily activated by the AC voltage. The principal advantage of the hybrid AC/DC plasma display is reduced driver circuitry. Large

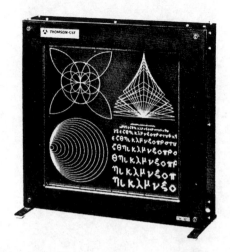

**Figure 1–37**    Typical plasma display. (Courtesy of Thomson–CSF Electron Tubes and Devices Corp.)

size ($3 \times 3$ meters at $4096 \times 4096$ pixels) plasma displays are available as are high resolution (100 pixels/inch) displays. Gray scale and color systems are possible.

In an electroluminescent display a phosphorescent material emits light when excited by either an AC or DC electric field. Because the phosphorescent material is typically zinc sulfide doped with manganese, electroluminescent displays have a yellow color. Pixel addressing uses the row-column technique discussed above for plasma displays. When the applied voltage exceeds the switching threshold, the manganese dopant electrons are excited. When an excited atom returns to a lower energy state, it emits a photon which causes the characteristic yellow color. Good 'gray' scale is obtainable since the luminescence varies with the voltage and frequency of the applied electric field. By using alternate dopants other colors are possible. Consequently, using multiple phosphorescent layers yields a color display. The phosphorescent material is either deposited macroscopically as a powder yielding a thick film or as molecular scale particles yielding a thin film. An AC or DC excited thin film electroluminescent display is most frequently used in computer graphics applications. The basic structure of an electroluminescent display is shown in Fig. 1–39. A typical display is shown in Fig. 1–40. Reasonable sized displays with resolutions of approximately 100 pixels/inch are currently available.

While plasma and electroluminescent displays are examples of active flat panel technologies, the liquid crystal display is an example of a passive technology. A liquid crystal display either transmits or reflects incident light. The polarizing characteristics of certain organic compounds are used to modify the characteristics of the incident light.

The basic principles of polarized light are shown in Fig. 1–41. In Fig. 1–41a noncoherent light is passed through the first (left) polarizer. The resulting transmitted light is polarized in the $xy$ plane. Since the polarizing axis of the second

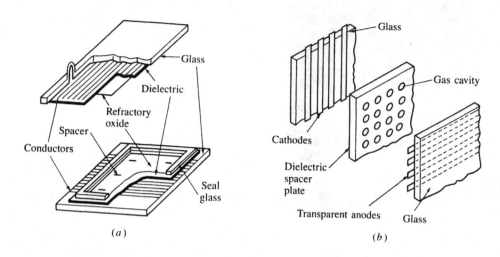

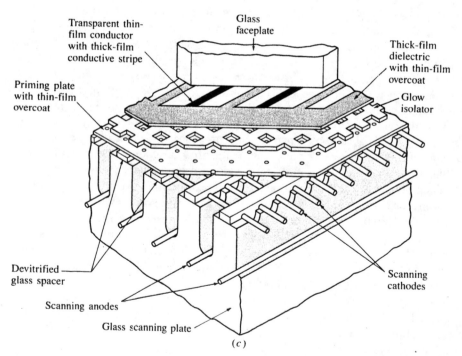

**Figure 1–38**    Basic structure of gas discharge-plasma displays. (a) AC activated; (b) DC activated; (c) AC/DC activated.

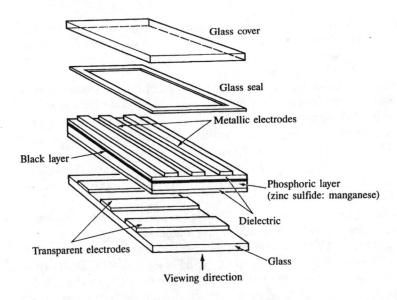

Glass cover

Glass seal

Metallic electrodes

Black layer

Phosphoric layer
(zinc sulfide: manganese)

Dielectric

Transparent electrodes

Glass

Viewing direction

**Figure 1–39**   Basic structure of an AC excited electroluminescent display.

**Figure 1–40**   Electroluminescent display. (Courtesy of Hewlett Packard Company)

polarizer is also aligned with the $xy$ plane, the light continues through the second polarizer. In Fig. 1–41b the polarizing axis of the second polarizer is rotated 90° to that of the first. Consequently, the plane polarized light that passed through the first polarizer is absorbed by the second.

Certain organic compounds which exist in the mesophase are stable at temperatures between the liquid and solid phases, hence the name liquid crystal. Liquid crystals exhibit three types of mesophase: smetic, nematic and cholesteric. In the nematic phase, the long axis of the liquid crystal molecules align parallel to each other. The alignment direction is sensitive to temperature, surface tension, pressure and, most important for display technology, electric and magnetic fields. The optical characteristics of the liquid crystal are also sensitive to these effects.

The key to one type of liquid crystal display technology is the creation of a twisted nematic crystal sandwich in which the alignment axis of the crystals rotates or twists through 90° from one face of the sandwich to the other. The basic structure of a reflective twisted nematic liquid crystal display is shown in Fig. 1–42. The two plates at the top and bottom of the liquid crystal sandwich are grooved. The top plate is grooved in one direction and the bottom at ninety degrees to that direction. The liquid crystals adjacent to the plate surface align with the grooves as shown in Fig. 1–42.

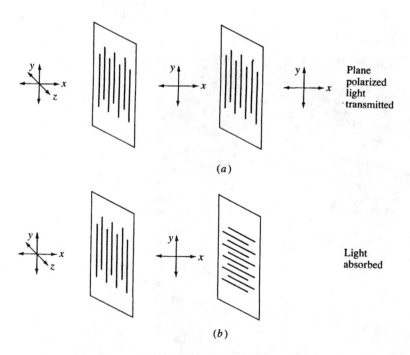

**Figure 1–41**   Polarization of light.

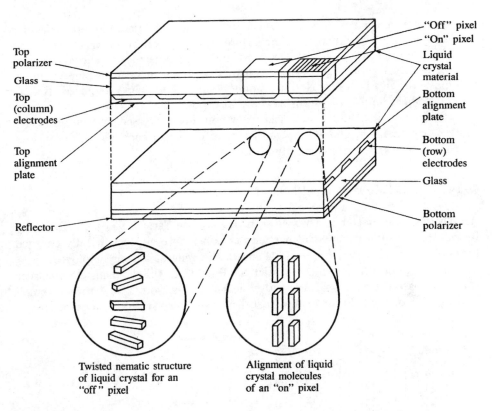

Top polarizer

Glass

Top (column) electrodes

Top alignment plate

Reflector

"Off" pixel
"On" pixel

Liquid crystal material

Bottom alignment plate

Bottom (row) electrodes

Glass

Bottom polarizer

Twisted nematic structure of liquid crystal for an "off" pixel

Alignment of liquid crystal molecules of an "on" pixel

**Figure 1–42**    Basic structure of a twisted nematic liquid crystal display.

The display contains two plane polarizers, one on each side of the sandwich aligned at 90° to each other. With a display pixel in its off or twisted state, light entering the display is plane polarized by the first polarizer, passes through the liquid crystal sandwich where it is twisted through 90°, passes through the second polarizer and is reflected back out the display. The pixel appears light.

Turning the pixel on by applying an electric field to the liquid crystal sandwich causes the crystal to untwist. Now light entering the display is plane polarized by the first polarizer, passes through the liquid crystal sandwich where it is *not* twisted and hence is absorbed by the second polarizer. The pixel appears dark. Twisted nematic liquid crystal displays require constant refreshing.

A bistable liquid crystal display using smetic liquid crystals is also possible. Two stable orientations of the smetic liquid crystal molecules have different optical properties, e.g., absorption. This difference in optical properties produces an optical contrast. A voltage pulse causes the molecules to change state. Bistable liquid crystal displays do not require refreshing.

Color liquid crystal displays are possible using colored filters or phosphors with twisted-nematic technology or using guest-host (dye) technology. Guest-host liquid crystal displays combine dichroic-dye guest molecules with the host liquid crystal molecules. The spectral characteristics of different guest molecules are used to produce different colors. Here, the application of an electric field realigns the orientation of both the guest and host molecules to allow transmission of light. A typical guest-host transmissive liquid crystal display is shown schematically in Fig. 1–43. Note that only a single polarizer is required. Reflective guest-host liquid crystal displays are also possible.

Liquid crystal displays are either row-column addressed or contain active matrix elements, e.g., individual transistors or diodes at each pixel. Resolutions up to 100 pixels/inch are currently available.

## 1–14 ELECTROSTATIC PLOTTERS

An electrostatic plotter is a raster scan device (see Secs. 1-9, 1-12). Basically it operates by depositing small particles of toner onto electrostatically charged areas of a special paper. Figure 1–44 shows the general scheme employed.

In more detail, a specially coated medium that will hold an electrostatic charge is passed over a writing head which contains from 1 to 3 rows of small writing nibs or styli. From 72 to 400 styli per inch are typical. Higher densities

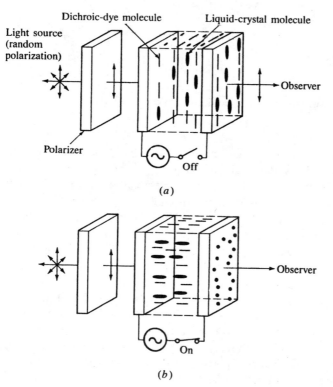

**Figure 1–43**   Guest-host liquid crystal display dye and molecules aligned to (a) block transmission and (b) allow transmission.

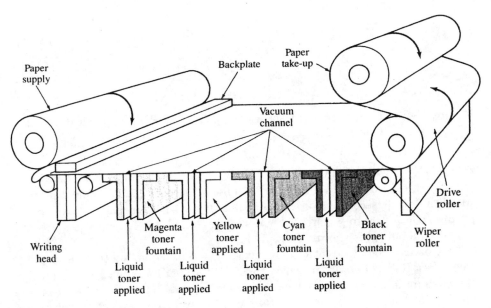

**Figure 1–44**  Conceptual description of multiple pass color electrostatic plotter.

require multiple rows of styli. As the medium is passed over the styli, an individual dot of negative electrostatic charge is deposited by each stylus. The medium is then passed over a toner applicator, where positively charged particles of liquid toner are attracted to the negatively charged dots on the medium, making them visible. The carbon toner particles are subsequently dried and fixed to the medium to make them permanent. Available plotting media include opaque and translucent vellum paper, and clear and matte polyester films.

Electrostatic plotters are available in widths up to 72 inches. The length of the plot is limited only by the length of the media roll (500 feet). The resolution of an electrostatic plotter is given by the number of styli or dots per inch (dpi). Accuracy is defined in a somewhat different way. Assuming that the direction of media movement can be reversed, accuracy is defined as the error that occurs in the position of two dots made by the same stylus on two successive passes of the medium.

An electrostatic plotter is a raster device, consequently aliasing occurs (see Ref. 1–1). High resolution devices attempt to minimize the effects of aliasing by overlapping the individual dots. Figure 1–45 shows typical dot patterns. Typical dot overlap is 30 to 50 percent. Since an electrostatic plotter is a raster scan device, picture elements, e.g., lines and polygons, must be rasterized and the picture organized into raster scan order: top to bottom, left to right. Although preparation of the picture in raster format can be accomplished by the host computer, it poses severe computational requirements. Further, communication of the rasterized picture to the plotter at sufficient speed to fully utilize the plotter's capability requires a very high speed interface. For example, consider

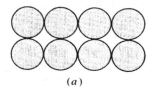 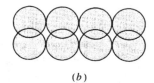 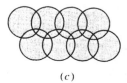

*(a)*        *(b)*        *(c)*

**Figure 1–45**    Dot patterns. (a) Nonoverlapping; (b) overlapping $y$ only; (c) overlapping $x$ and $y$.

that a 36-inch-wide plotter with a resolution of 400 dpi requires a sustained data transfer rate from host to plotter of 360 kilobytes/second at a nominal plotting speed of 1 inch/second. Consequently, many electrostatic plotters use special purpose controllers to perform these functions (Ref. 1–6). A typical electrostatic plotter and output is shown in Fig. 1–46.

Color electrostatic plotters are available. The three subtractive primary colors (see Ref. 1–1) cyan, magenta and yellow (CMY) and black are applied to the medium in either a single pass or in four successive passes. If the colors are applied in a single pass, separate rows of nibs are used for each of the colors. If the colors are applied in successive passes, the medium is rewound between application of each color. A typical plotter provides 7 line colors. Color shading of filled polygons is accomplished using dither and patterning (see Ref. 1–1). The number of available colors depends on both the size of the pattern used, e.g., $2 \times 2$, $3 \times 3$ or $4 \times 4$, and the resolution of the plotter. Typically high resolution plotters are capable of displaying a few thousand colors. Color electrostatic plotters are currently available in widths up to 42 inches and resolutions of up to 400 dpi.

## 1–15   LASER PRINTERS

Although originally designed for printing and typographic applications, laser printers are used extensively for computer graphics output. This is particularly true in publishing, where systems for combining print and graphics on the same output page are important (see for example Ref. 1–7). These systems are capable of combining near-typeset-quality text, line art and halftone pictures on a single page. Figure 1–47 shows a typical example.

A laser printer is a raster scan device. The basic process, shown schematically in Fig. 1–48, is similar to xerography. The print engine contains a drum that is coated with a photoconductive material. The drum is scanned by either a gas or semiconductor diode laser. As the drum rotates the coating is electrically charged. The drum remains charged until struck by the highly coherent light from the laser. The laser light selectively discharges areas (dots) on the drum to form a negative image, i.e., the charge is removed from dots that do *not* appear in the final image.† Positioning of the laser beam on the drum is accomplished

---

†This description is for a write-black print engine. Write-white engines reverse the process.

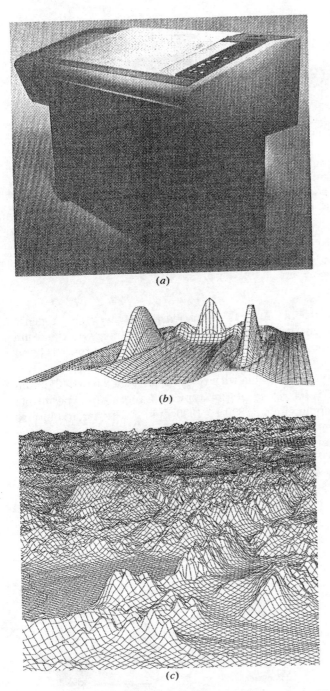

(a)

(b)

(c)

**Figure 1–46**     Electrostatic plotter (a). (Courtesy of Versatec Corp.) Typical output: (b) low resolution 100 dpi; (c) high resolution 400 dpi. (Courtesy of Versatec Corp.)

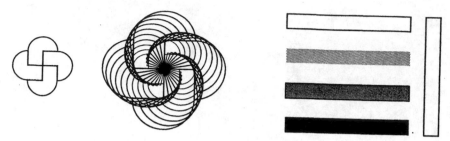

The picture (top left) was made with the rlineto command and the arc command. Then by scaling and rotating the picture we can make other interesting and different designs.

By defining a variable called box, we can print it in many different ways. Using the stroke, the setgray, and the fill commands, we can print the same box in many other shades and positions.

**Figure 1-47**    Laser printer-generated page showing a combination of text, line art and halftone picture. (Courtesy of QMS, Inc.)

using a rotating polygonal mirror. A black plastic-based powder called toner is attracted to the remaining charged areas on the drum. The image on the drum is then transferred to the oppositely precharged paper. Finally, the toner is fused to the paper, using heat and pressure to form the permanent image.

Laser printers are currently available with resolutions from $240 \times 240$ dpi up to $600 \times 600$ dpi with a $300 \times 300$ dpi resolution typical. Laboratory experiments indicate that a practical upper limit is 800 to 1000 dpi. At higher resolutions the toner particles fuse together. Although extensively used for typesetting, the resolution of typical laser printers is considerably less than that of good quality phototypesetters (1200 to 5000 dpi). Current laser printers are limited to a single dot size. Laboratory experiments with variable dot sizes are encouraging.

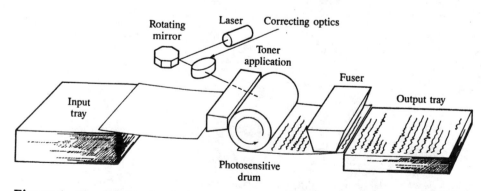

**Figure 1-48**    Schematic of a laser print engine.

Variable dot size allows increased flexibility in generating halftone images (see Ref. 1–1). Although laser printers typically produce correspondence-sized pages, they are available in up to 36 inch widths at 400 dpi that produce D-size (22 × 44 inch) and E-size (34 × 44 inch) drawings.

Laser printing is a continuous process. Once printing of a page starts it must continue at a constant speed. Because of the high resolution, very high continuous data rates are required. For example, a 300 × 300 dpi printer producing a $7\frac{1}{2} \times 10\frac{1}{2}$ inch printed area on an $8\frac{1}{2} \times 11$ inch page at 8 pages/minute requires a sustained data rate to the laser print engine of 1 megabit/second. Because of these high data rates the laser printer, like the electrostatic plotter, uses a separate controller. The general scheme is shown in Fig. 1–49. Here, the host computer provides a description of the page using a higher level page description language (see for example Ref. 1–7). The image processor-controller takes care of generating individual font characters, lines or half tone patterns and sending the required bit (dot) stream to the print engine.

Figure 1–50 shows a typical laser printer. Figure 1–51 shows examples of typical laser printer generated line drawings and halftones.

## 1–16   DOT MATRIX PLOTTERS

Printers have been used for computer graphics from the very beginning of the field. Initially the standard line printer, which is a raster scan device, was used. Line drawings, plots and even patterned halftoned pictures were generated. With a resolution of 1/6 inch vertically and 1/10 inch horizontally the results, by current standards, were crude.

A number of current mechanical printer technologies, e.g., band or belt printers, drum printers, train printers or chain printers, and daisy wheel printers are used for computer graphics. However, the most popular and versatile is the dot matrix printer.

In a dot matrix printer the printing mechanism is a matrix of thin nibs or wires arranged on a print head that moves horizontally across the paper. The basic print mechanism involves the electromagnetic release of one or more of the spring steel mounted wires or hammers. In a captured hammer design the hammers are drawn away from the ribbon by a permanent magnet. An electromagnet is used to neutralize the field of the permanent magnet. When this happens the spring steel hammer flies forward, causing the wire to impact the ribbon, which prints a dot on the paper held between the ribbon and the

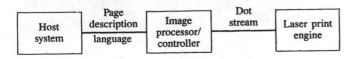

**Figure 1–49**    Laser printer system schematic.

**Figure 1–50**   Laser printer. (Courtesy of Toshiba America, Inc.)

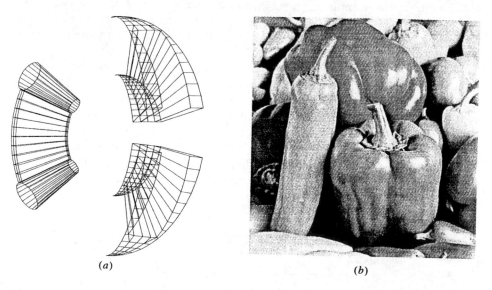

(a)                                                 (b)

**Figure 1–51**   Laser printer output. (a) Line drawing; (b) patterned halftone.

platen. The electromagnet is then disabled so that the hammer is captured by the permanent magnet when it rebounds. In a noncaptured hammer design, the hammer is both pulled back to energize it and released using an electromagnet.

Various configurations of the wires are used as shown in Fig. 1–52. For lower wire densities the typical wire size is 0.012 to 0.013 inch, which yields a dot size of 0.014 to 0.015 inch. These configurations yield a dot density or resolution of 60 to 85 dpi. The highest wire densities use 0.008 inch wires which yield a 0.009 to 0.010 inch dot. For graphics applications these configurations yield a dot density of 180-dpi. From these numbers, it is easy to see that for high wire densities dots are printed in overlapping patterns. From 20 to 50 percent overlap is used depending on the dot density. Since printing overlapping dots reduces aliasing or stair stepping (see Ref. 1–1), image quality is improved. Typical output from a 70-dpi and a 180-dpi dot matrix printer, shown in Fig. 1–53, illustrates this effect.

Color with dot matrix printers is obtained by using multicolored ribbons. Because paper is a reflective medium, a four-color ribbon containing the subtractive primaries cyan, magenta and yellow (CMY) and black is used. Use of dither and patterning techniques (see Refs. 1–1 and 1–8) allows the production of many shades of color.

## 1–17    INK JET PLOTTERS

Ink jet printers are raster scan devices. They are particularly suited for generating low cost color output. The basic idea is to shoot tiny droplets of ink onto a medium. There are basically two types of ink jet printers, continuous flow and drop-on-demand.

The continuous flow ink jet produces a stream of droplets by spraying ink out of a nozzle. The stream of ink from the nozzle is broken up into droplets by ultrasonic waves. If ink is desired on the medium, selected droplets are electrostatically charged. Deflection plates are used to then direct the droplet onto the medium. If not, the droplet is deflected into a gutter where the ink is returned to the reservoir. Paper and transparency film are typical media. This system is shown schematically in Fig. 1–54a.

Drop-on-demand technology, as its name implies, fires ink at the medium only if a dot is required at a particular location. Here, ink from a reservoir is

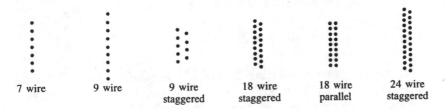

7 wire      9 wire      9 wire       18 wire      18 wire      24 wire
                        staggered    staggered    parallel     staggered

**Figure 1–52**    Selected dot matrix print wire geometries.

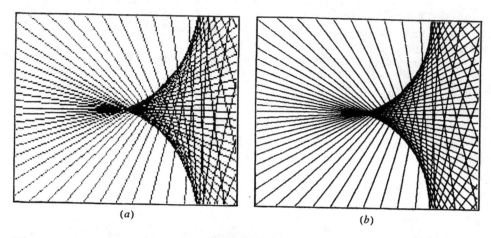

(a)　　　　　　　　　　　(b)

**Figure 1–53**　Comparison of dot matrix printer graphics output. (a) 9-pin printer at 70 dpi; (b) 24-pin printer at 180 dpi.

supplied to a nozzle under pressure. The ink is fired on demand by applying an electric voltage to a piezoelectric crystal as the head makes a pass across the medium. When a voltage is applied, the piezoelectric crystal expands, decreasing the volume of the ink chamber. This causes a drop of ink to squirt out of the nozzle. Release of the voltage causes the piezoelectric crystal to contract, decreasing the volume of the reservoir and sucking the ink back into the nozzle. A typical arrangement is shown schematically in Fig. 1–54b.

The resolution of ink jet printers is determined by the size of the droplet and hence of the nozzle. Because of the extremely small nozzle size required, nozzle clogging, ink contamination and air bubbles in the ink are significant problems. Typical resolutions are from 120 to 400 dpi. Laboratory experiments show that resolutions of up to 1000 dpi are possible.

Color ink jet printers typically use four nozzles, three for the subtractive primary colors cyan, magenta and yellow and one for black. One of the advantages of color ink jet technology is its ability to blend colors. Because liquid droplets of ink are used in a single pass across the medium, the droplets blend together before drying. This gives ink jet colors a depth and vibrancy not found in other reflective technologies. Again, patterning and dither techniques are used to produce several thousand colors (see Refs. 1–1 and 1–8).

## 1–18   THERMAL PLOTTERS

There are basically two thermal printing or plotting techniques, direct thermal transfer and indirect thermal transfer. The direct thermal transfer technique uses a temperature sensitive paper that changes color when heated. The image is formed by print head elements that selectively heat dots on the paper as the head moves across it. Either dot matrix print heads or full row nib heads similar

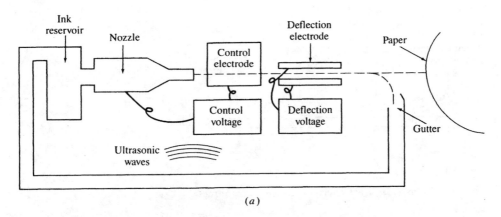

(a)

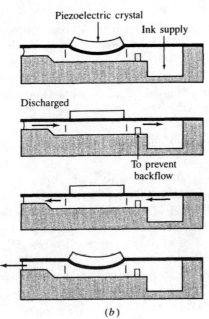

(b)

**Figure 1-54** Schematics of various ink jet printer technologies. (a) Continuous; (b) drop-on-demand.

to those in electrostatic plotters are used. Resolutions of 400 dpi are available. The chief and most serious limitation of the direct thermal transfer technique is the special paper that unfortunately fades with time.

The indirect thermal transfer technique uses a thin film or paper ribbon coated with a wax-based ink. Heating elements which are usually located behind the ribbon melt the wax coating. The pigmented ink is then rolled onto the paper. Either dot matrix print heads that move across the medium or a full row of nib heads are used. Figure 1-55 schematically illustrates this technique.

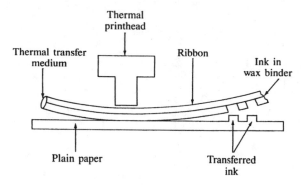

**Figure 1–55**  Indirect thermal transfer technique.

The medium is ordinary paper. Color is obtained by using multicolored ribbons. Typically seven colors are obtained directly by combining the CMY primaries from the ribbon, plus black. Patterning and dither are used to expand the color palette (see Refs. 1–1 and 1–8). Since the inks are not absorbed by the paper, quite brilliant colors are obtained. Typical resolutions are from 100 to 400 dpi. Indirect thermal transfer inks have excellent longevity.

## 1–19  PEN AND INK PLOTTERS

Digital pen and ink plotters are of three basic types, flatbed, drum and pinch roller. The basic mechanisms are shown schematically in Fig. 1–56.

In a moving-arm flatbed plotter (see Fig. 1–56a) the medium is fixed in position on the bed of the plotter. Two-dimensional motion of the plotting head is obtained by movement of an arm suspended across the width of the plotter bed. This provides motion in one direction. Motion in the second direction is obtained by moving the plotting head along the suspended arm. Figure 1–57 shows a typical moving arm flatbed plotter.

A moving head flatbed plotter (see Fig. 1–56b) uses a plotting tool carriage suspended above the bed by magnetic forces that are counterbalanced by an air bearing. This arrangement provides nearly frictionless movement. Movement of the head in two dimensions is controlled electromagnetically, using the Sawyer motor principle. Figure 1–58 shows an example.

Large flatbed plotters usually fix the medium to the plotter bed using vacuum. Large flatbed plotters have resolutions and plotting speeds as high as 0.0004 inch and 3600 inch/minute, respectively. Flatbed plotters are available in sizes from $8\,1/2 \times 11$ inches up to several tens of feet in length and width. A large variety of plotting media can be used, e.g., paper, vellum, Mylar, photographic film, scribe coat, sheet metal and cloth. Combined with this large variety of media is an accompanying variety of plotting tools including ballpoint, felt tip and wet ink pens, photographic and laser light beams, engraving tools, scribe and cloth cutters and laser cutting beams. As the wide variety of available media

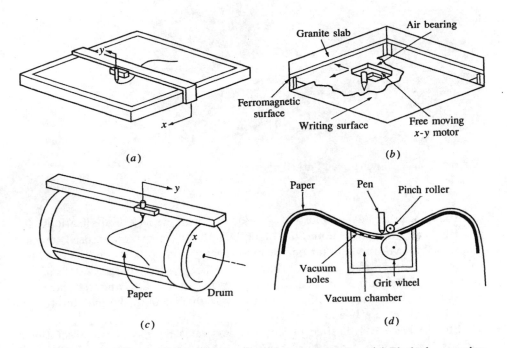

**Figure 1–56**    Schematic diagrams of pen and ink plotter types. (a) Flatbed — moving arm; (b) flatbed — moving head; (c) drum; (d) pinch roller.

**Figure 1–57**    Moving arm flatbed plotter. (Courtesy Xynetics, Inc.)

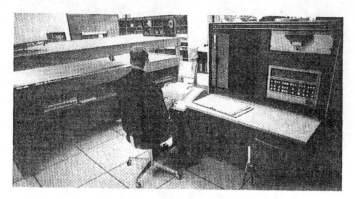

**Figure 1–58**  Moving-head flatbed plotter.

and tools suggests, flatbed plotters are used in a wide variety of applications. In addition to traditional pen and ink plots, large flatbed plotters are used to generate masks for printed circuit boards and integrated circuits. Here, the plotting medium is photographic film, and the plotting tool is a light beam. Adaptations of flatbed plotters are also used to cut out men's and ladies' apparel and even sailboat sails. Here, the medium is an appropriate cloth and the plotting tool a knife or laser cutting beam.

Smaller lower cost flatbed plotters are less versatile, have lower resolutions and lower plotting speeds. They also typically use an electrostatic hold-down system for the media, which are generally limited to paper, vellum and transparency film.

Drum plotters (see Fig. 1–56c) are mechanically more complex than flatbed plotters. Here, the plotting head moves along a fixed arm to provide one dimension. The medium itself is rolled back and forth under the fixed arm to provide the second dimension.

The medium is fixed to the drum using either a vacuum or tensioned supply and takeup rollers. Media types are limited to those that are easily rolled. Typically, the drum plotter medium is either paper or vellum. Only the width of the medium is fixed. The length of a plot is limited only by the length of the medium roll. Although resolutions are similar to those for flatbed plotters (0.0005 inch), plotting speeds are typically considerably lower.

The pinch roller plotter is a hybrid of the flatbed and drum plotters. The drawing medium is held at each edge between a pinch wheel and the plotting surface (see Fig. 1–56d). The plotting surface is cylindrical. As the pinch wheel rotates, the medium moves back and forth under a fixed arm on which the plotting head moves. These plotters use either cut or roll stock, which is usually limited to paper, vellum or transparency film. Typical resolutions are 0.001 inch, with plotting speeds of 180 inches/minute. A pinch roll plotter is shown in Fig. 1–59.

**Figure 1-59**   Pinch roll plotter. (Courtesy of Hewlett-Packard Co.)

Most pen and ink plotters operate in an incremental mode driven by stepping motors. The plotting tool moves across the plotting surface in a series of small steps. The number of movement directions is limited to eight, horizontal, vertical and diagonal, as shown in Fig. 1-60. This results in lines other than those in the directions shown in Fig. 1-60, appearing as a series of stair steps. This stair-step, or jaggies, effect is a manifestation of a fundamental phenomenon called aliasing (see Ref. 1-1). The algorithm usually chosen to select the one of eight movement directions that most nearly approximates the direction of the line is

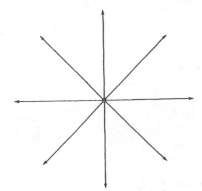

**Figure 1-60**   Directions for incremental plotters.

Bresenham's algorithm (see Ref. 1–1). Although Bresenham's algorithm is most often associated with raster scan displays, it was originally developed for digital incremental plotters.

True motion directions are obtained by using servomotors to drive the plotting head. In this case, a feedback servocircuit constantly modulates both drive motors simultaneously to yield smooth lines.

Although speed is important in a plotter, the acceleration of the plotting head is generally more important for overall throughput. Fundamentally this is because the typical drawing is made up of short straight line segments. Consequently, the plotter must start and stop between segments. High acceleration allows the plotter to attain full speed more quickly. Accelerations of up to 4g are currently possible. Many plotter controllers are also equipped with look-ahead software designed to prevent the plotter from unnecessarily stopping, e.g., when a series of short connected straight line segments is used to represent a curve.

Pen and ink plotters produce the highest quality line drawing output of any graphics device. An example is shown in Fig. 1–61.

## 1–20    COLOR FILM CAMERAS

With the advent of high quality color raster displays coupled with full color frame buffers (see Sec. 1–9) capable of displaying over 16 million colors, the need arose for a technique for preserving these results. Currently the only available techniques are based on color photographic film. In computer graphics the most frequently used device is a color camera.

Conceptually, a color camera, shown schematically in Fig. 1–62, is quite simple. The technique is called field sequential recording. A small (5-inch-diameter) precision flat-faced monochrome (white) CRT is used. First a red

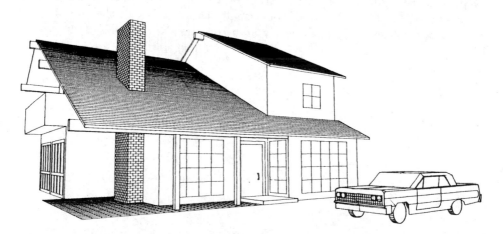

**Figure 1–61**    Typical output from a digital incremental plotter.

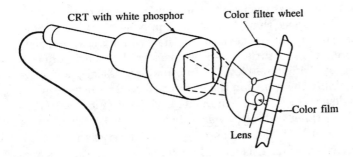

CRT with white phosphor    Color filter wheel

Color film

Lens

**Figure 1-62**    Schematic of a color camera.

photographic filter is placed in the optical path from a camera to the CRT. Then only the red intensity signal for the picture is fed to the CRT. The film is exposed. The CRT is erased, the red filter removed and a green filter rotated into position. Then only the green intensity signal for the picture is fed to the CRT. Without advancing, the film is exposed a second time. Finally, the process is repeated for the blue component of the picture. This triply exposed film now contains the complete picture.

The quality of the CRT is critical to the success of the technique (see Ref. 1-1). A flat-faced CRT is used, rather than the curved CRT used in most monitors, to eliminate distortions. The glass used in the CRT must also be of high quality, free of bubbles, striations and other defects. To allow nearly equal response to all three signals (RGB) a broadband phosphor is used. The phosphor layer must be free of blemishes and patterns, fine grained and smoothly textured. The CRT beam spot size must be as small as practical for increased resolution and the electromagnetic focusing system must be of highest quality.

With care, practical resolutions of 3000 to 5000 dpi per side on a 5-inch monitor are possible. Note that resolution and addressability are not the same. Resolution measures the number of separately distinguishable spots, whereas addressability measures the number of distinct positions at which the electron beam can be placed. Because of the characteristics of the eye, a picture made with higher addressability than resolvability will look better, even though the points are not resolved.

## 1-21    ACTIVE AND PASSIVE GRAPHICS DEVICES

Let's consider the difference between a passive and an active graphics device. A passive graphics device simply draws pictures under computer control; i.e., it allows the computer to communicate graphically with the user. Examples are dot matrix printers, an electrostatic plotter, pen and ink plotters, film recorders and storage tube refresh and raster CRT displays. Examples of some of these devices and the typical pictures that they might generate are shown in Figs. 1-17, 1-22, 1-37, 1-40, 1-46, 1-50, 1-51, 1-53, 1-57, 1-58, 1-59 and 1-61.

An active graphics device allows the user to communicate with the computer graphically. Generally, this implies that the user is supplying coordinate information in some indirect manner, i.e., by means other than typing the appropriate numbers. Since a picture, curve or surface can be considered a matrix of coordinate data, the user is supplying true pictorial information. Usually an active graphics device has the ability to reposition the cursor and read its new position. Typical active graphics devices include alphanumeric keyboards (Fig. 1–6), function buttons (Fig. 1–13) or thumb wheels, control dials (Fig. 1–12), digitizer or analog tablets (Figs. 1–7 and 1–8), light pens (Fig. 1–15), joysticks (Fig. 1–9), trackball (Fig. 1–10) or mouse (Fig. 1–11). Although these devices may sometimes be used alone, they usually require some type of passive graphics device for support. This support graphics device is frequently based on a CRT.

## 1–22  COMPUTER GRAPHICS SOFTWARE .

The totality of computer graphics software encompasses not only the concepts presented in this book and in Ref. 1–1, but also concepts from data structures, from data base design and management, from the psychology and ergonometrics of the man-machine interface and from programming languages and operating systems. These topics are well beyond the scope of this book. However, they are considerations in the design of computer graphics systems.

Numerous computer graphics standards have been and will be developed and considered. In general, these standards can currently be grouped into three general categories. First is the graphics application interface, where ideas are translated into a form understandable by a computer system. Current representative standards are the Graphical Kernel System (GKS), GKS-3D, the Programmer's Hierarchical Interactive Graphics Standard (PHIGS) and PHIGS+ (see Appendix A).

The second is concerned with the storage and transmission of data between graphics systems and between graphics-based computer aided design and computer aided manufacturing systems. The current standard in this area is the Initial Graphics Exchange Specification (IGES).

Third is a standard for defining an interface between the graphics software system or the data storage and transmission system and the requirements of the device-dependent hardware drivers. Current standards in this area are the Computer Graphics Metafile (CGM) and the Virtual Device Interface (VDI).

These standards are extremely important. They attempt to insure portability of programs, programmers and data. A more complete but not extensive discussion of these standards is given in Appendix A. Figure 1–63 shows the general layout of a computer graphics software system and how each standard fits into it. However, the purpose of this book and of Ref. 1–1 is not to discuss standards but to develop the underlying concepts and mathematical and procedural elements of computer graphics. Consequently, the view taken of computer graphics software is fundamental and minimal. A computer graphics software system that embodies these concepts is given in Appendices A and G. With

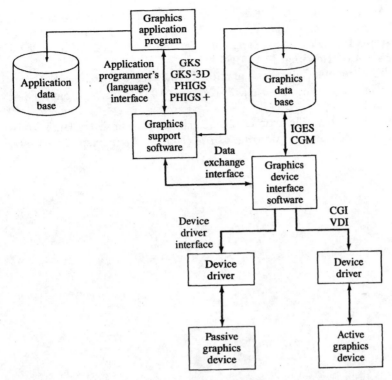

**Figure 1–63** Schematic of a computer graphics software system.

those concepts and the ones subsequently discussed in this book and in Ref. 1–1, along with appropriate concepts from data structures and data base design, a complete computer graphics software system can be designed and built or an existing system understood.

## 1–23 REFERENCES

1–1 Rogers, D.F., *Procedural Elements for Computer Graphics*, McGraw-Hill Book Co., New York, 1985.

1–2 Foley, J.D., and Wallace, V.L., "The Art of Natural Man-Machine Conversation," *Proc. IEEE*, Vol. 62, pp. 462–471, 1974.

1–3 Wallace, V.L., "The Semantics of Graphic Input Devices," *Comp. Graph.*, Vol. 10, pp. 61–65, 1976.

1–4 Ohlson, M., "System Design Considerations for Graphics Input Devices," *Computer*, pp. 9–18, Nov. 1978.

1–5 Davis, M.R., and Ellis, T.O., "The RAND Tablet: A Man-Machine Graphical Communication Device," *AFIPS Conf. Proc.*, Vol. 26, Part I, 1964 FJCC, pp. 325–332, 1964.

1-6 Ben-Dor, A., and Jones, B., "New Graphics Controller for Electrostatic Plotting," *IEEE Comp. Graph. & Appl.*, Vol. 6, No. 1, pp. 16–25, 1986.

1-7 Adobe Systems Inc., *Postscript Language Reference Manual*, Addison-Wesley Publishing Co., Reading, MA, 1985.

1-8 Kubo, S., "Continuous Color Presentation Using a Low-Cost Ink Jet Printer," *Proc. Comp. Graph. Tokyo 84*, 24-27 Apr. 1984, Tokyo, Japan, T3-6, pp. 1–10, 1984.

1-9 Constantine, J.M., Jr., "Electron Optical Technique for an Ultra High Resolution Color Film Recorder," *Journal of Photooptical Instrument Engineers*, 1984.

## TWO-DIMENSIONAL TRANSFORMATIONS

## 2–1  INTRODUCTION

We begin our study of the fundamentals of the mathematics underlying computer graphics by considering the representation and transformation of points and lines. Points and the lines which join them, along with an appropriate drawing algorithm, are used to represent objects or to display information graphically. The ability to transform these points and lines is basic to computer graphics. When visualizing an object, it may be desirable to scale, rotate, translate, distort or develop a perspective view of the object. All of these transformations can be accomplished using the mathematical techniques discussed in this and the next chapter.

## 2–2  REPRESENTATION OF POINTS

A point is represented in two dimensions by its coordinates. These two values are specified as the elements of a 1-row, 2-column matrix:

$$[\, x \quad y \,]$$

In three dimensions a $1 \times 3$ matrix

$$[\, x \quad y \quad z \,]$$

is used. Alternately, a point is represented by a 2-row, 1-column matrix

$$\begin{bmatrix} x \\ y \end{bmatrix}$$

in two dimensions or by

$$\begin{bmatrix} x \\ y \\ z \end{bmatrix}$$

**61**

in three dimensions. Row matrices like

$$[\, x \quad y \,]$$

or column matrices like

$$\begin{bmatrix} x \\ y \end{bmatrix}$$

are frequently called position vectors. In this book a row matrix formulation of the position vectors is used.

A series of points, each of which is a position vector relative to some coordinate system, is stored in a computer as a matrix or array of numbers. The position of these points is controlled by manipulating the matrix which defines the points. Lines are drawn between the points to generate lines, curves or pictures.


## 2–3   TRANSFORMATIONS AND MATRICES

Matrix elements can represent various quantities, such as a number store, a network or the coefficients of a set of equations. The rules of matrix algebra define allowable operations on these matrices (see Appendix B). Many physical problems lead to a matrix formulation. For models of physical systems, the problem is formulated as: given the matrices $[\,A\,]$ and $[\,B\,]$ find the solution matrix $[\,T\,]$, i.e., $[\,A\,][\,T\,] = [\,B\,]$. In this case the solution is $[\,T\,] = [\,A\,]^{-1}[\,B\,]$, where $[\,A\,]^{-1}$ is the inverse of the square matrix $[\,A\,]$ (see Ref. 2–1).

An alternate interpretation is to treat the matrix $[\,T\,]$ as a geometric operator. Here matrix multiplication is used to perform a geometrical transformation on a set of points represented by the position vectors contained in $[\,A\,]$. The matrices $[\,A\,]$ and $[\,T\,]$ are assumed known. It is required to determine the elements of the matrix $[\,B\,]$. The interpretation of the matrix $[\,T\,]$ as a geometrical operator is the foundation of mathematical transformations useful in computer graphics.


## 2–4   TRANSFORMATION OF POINTS

Consider the results of the multiplication of a matrix $[\, x \quad y \,]$ containing the coordinates of a point $P$ and a general $2 \times 2$ transformation matrix:

$$[\,X\,][\,T\,] = [\, x \quad y \,] \begin{bmatrix} a & b \\ c & d \end{bmatrix} = [\, (ax + cy) \quad (bx + dy) \,] = [\, x^* \quad y^* \,] \quad (2-1)$$

This mathematical notation means that the initial coordinates $x$ and $y$ are transformed to $x^*$ and $y^*$, where $x^* = (ax+cy)$ and $y^* = (bx+dy)$.† We are interested

---

†See Appendix B for the details of matrix multiplication.

in the implications of considering $x^*$ and $y^*$ as the transformed coordinates of the point $P$. We begin by investigating several special cases.

Consider the case where $a = d = 1$ and $c = b = 0$. The transformation matrix $[T]$ then reduces to the identity matrix. Thus,

$$[X][T] = [x \quad y] \begin{bmatrix} 1 & 0 \\ 0 & 1 \end{bmatrix} = [x \quad y] = [x^* \quad y^*] \qquad (2-2)$$

and no change in the coordinates of the point $P$ occurs. Since in matrix algebra multiplying by the identity matrix is equivalent to multiplying by 1 in ordinary algebra, this result is expected.

Next consider $d = 1$, $b = c = 0$, i.e.,

$$[X][T] = [x \quad y] \begin{bmatrix} a & 0 \\ 0 & 1 \end{bmatrix} = [ax \quad y] = [x^* \quad y^*] \qquad (2-3)$$

which, since $x^* = ax$, produces a scale change in the $x$ component of the position vector. The effect of this transformation is shown in Fig. 2–1a. Now consider $b = c = 0$, i.e.,

$$[X][T] = [x \quad y] \begin{bmatrix} a & 0 \\ 0 & d \end{bmatrix} = [ax \quad dy] = [x^* \quad y^*] \qquad (2-4)$$

This yields a scaling of both the $x$ and $y$ coordinates of the original position vector $P$, as shown in Fig. 2–1b. If $a \neq d$, then the scalings are not equal. If $a = d > 1$, then a pure enlargement or scaling of the coordinates of $P$ occurs. If $0 < a = d < 1$, then a compression of the coordinates of $P$ occurs.

If $a$ and/or $d$ are negative, reflections through an axis or plane occur. To see this, consider $b = c = 0$, $d = 1$ and $a = -1$. Then

$$[X][T] = [x \quad y] \begin{bmatrix} -1 & 0 \\ 0 & 1 \end{bmatrix} = [-x \quad y] = [x^* \quad y^*] \qquad (2-5)$$

and a reflection through the $y$-axis results, as shown in Fig. 2–1c. If $b = c = 0$, $a = 1$, and $d = -1$, then a reflection through the $x$-axis occurs. If $b = c = 0$, $a = d < 0$, then a reflection through the origin occurs. This is shown in Fig. 2–1d, with $a = -1$, $d = -1$. Note that both reflection and scaling of the coordinates involve only the diagonal terms of the transformation matrix.

Now consider the effects of the off-diagonal terms. First consider $a = d = 1$ and $c = 0$. Thus,

$$[X][T] = [x \quad y] \begin{bmatrix} 1 & b \\ 0 & 1 \end{bmatrix} = [x \quad (bx + y)] = [x^* \quad y^*] \qquad (2-6)$$

Note that the $x$ coordinate of the point $P$ is unchanged, while $y^*$ depends linearly on the original coordinates. This effect is called shear, as shown in Fig. 2–1e.

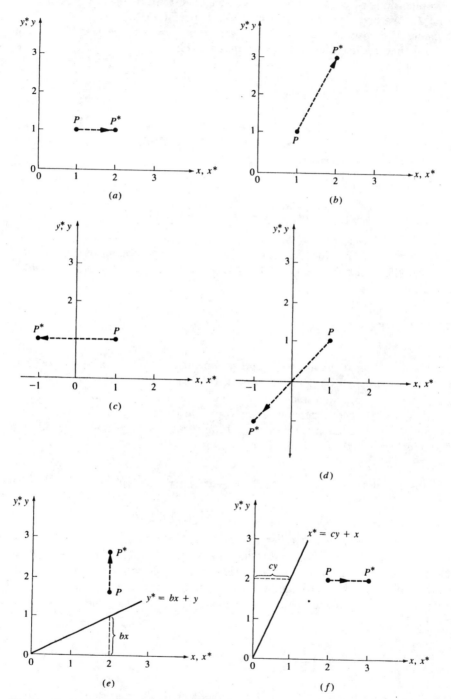

**Figure 2-1** Transformation of points.

Similarly, when $a = d = 1$, $b = 0$, the transformation produces shear proportional to the $y$ coordinate, as shown in Fig. 2–1f. Thus, we see that the off-diagonal terms produce a shearing effect on the coordinates of the position vector for $P$.

Before completing our discussion of the transformation of points, consider the effect of the general $2 \times 2$ transformation given by Eq. (2–1) when applied to the origin, i.e.,

$$[ x \quad y ] \begin{bmatrix} a & b \\ c & d \end{bmatrix} = [ (ax + cy) \quad (bx + dy) ] = [ x^* \quad y^* ]$$

or for the origin,

$$[ 0 \quad 0 ] \begin{bmatrix} a & b \\ c & d \end{bmatrix} = [ 0 \quad 0 ] = [ x^* \quad y^* ]$$

Here we see that the origin is invariant under a general $2 \times 2$ transformation. This is a limitation which will be overcome by the use of homogeneous coordinates.

## 2–5    TRANSFORMATION OF STRAIGHT LINES

A straight line can be defined by two position vectors which specify the coordinates of its end points. The position and orientation of the line joining these two points can be changed by operating on these two position vectors. The actual operation of drawing a line between two points depends on the display device used. Here, we consider only the mathematical operations on the position vectors of the end points.

A straight line between two points $A$ and $B$ in a two-dimensional plane is drawn in Fig. 2–2. The position vectors of points $A$ and $B$ are $[ A ] = [ 0 \quad 1 ]$ and $[ B ] = [ 2 \quad 3 ]$, respectively. Now consider the transformation matrix

$$[ T ] = \begin{bmatrix} 1 & 2 \\ 3 & 1 \end{bmatrix} \qquad (2 - 7)$$

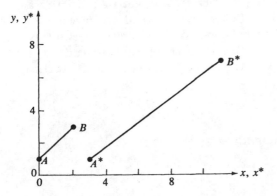

Figure 2–2    Transformation of straight lines.

which we recall from our previous discussion produces a shearing effect. Transforming the position vectors for $A$ and $B$ using $[T]$ produces new transformed position vectors $A^*$ and $B^*$ given by

$$[A][T] = [0 \quad 1]\begin{bmatrix} 1 & 2 \\ 3 & 1 \end{bmatrix} = [3 \quad 1] = [A^*] \qquad (2-8)$$

and

$$[B][T] = [2 \quad 3]\begin{bmatrix} 1 & 2 \\ 3 & 1 \end{bmatrix} = [11 \quad 7] = [B^*] \qquad (2-9)$$

Thus, the resulting coordinates for $A^*$ are $x^* = 3$ and $y^* = 1$. Similarly, $B^*$ is a new point with coordinates $x^* = 11$ and $y^* = 7$. More compactly the line $AB$ may be represented by the $2 \times 2$ matrix

$$[L] = \begin{bmatrix} 0 & 1 \\ 2 & 3 \end{bmatrix}$$

Matrix multiplication by $[T]$ then yields

$$[L][T] = \begin{bmatrix} 0 & 1 \\ 2 & 3 \end{bmatrix}\begin{bmatrix} 1 & 2 \\ 3 & 1 \end{bmatrix} = \begin{bmatrix} 3 & 1 \\ 11 & 7 \end{bmatrix} = [L^*] \qquad (2-10)$$

where the components of $[L^*]$ represent the transformed position vectors $[A^*]$ and $[B^*]$. The transformation of $A$ to $A^*$ and $B$ to $B^*$ is shown in Fig. 2–2. The initial axes are $x, y$ and the transformed axes are $x^*, y^*$. Figure 2–2 shows that the shearing transformation $[T]$ increased the length of the line and changed its orientation.

## 2–6   MIDPOINT TRANSFORMATION

Figure 2–2 shows that the $2 \times 2$ transformation matrix (see Eq. 2–7) transforms the straight line $y = x + 1$, between points $A$ and $B$, into another straight line $y = (3/4)x - 5/4$, between $A^*$ and $B^*$. In fact a $2 \times 2$ matrix transforms any straight line into a second straight line. Points on the second line have a one-to-one correspondence with points on the first line. We have already shown this to be true for the end points of the line. To further confirm this we consider the transformation of the midpoint of the straight line between $A$ and $B$. Letting

$$[A] = [x_1 \quad y_1] \qquad [B] = [x_2 \quad y_2] \qquad \text{and} \qquad [T] = \begin{bmatrix} a & b \\ c & d \end{bmatrix}$$

and transforming both end points simultaneously yields

$$\begin{bmatrix} A \\ B \end{bmatrix}[T] = \begin{bmatrix} x_1 & y_1 \\ x_2 & y_2 \end{bmatrix}\begin{bmatrix} a & b \\ c & d \end{bmatrix}$$

$$= \begin{bmatrix} ax_1 + cy_1 & bx_1 + dy_1 \\ ax_2 + cy_2 & bx_2 + dy_2 \end{bmatrix} = \begin{bmatrix} A^* \\ B^* \end{bmatrix} \qquad (2-11)$$

Hence, the end points of the transformed line $A^*B^*$ are

$$[ A^* ] = [ ax_1 + cy_1 \quad bx_1 + dy_1 ] = [ x_1^* \quad y_1^* ]$$

$$[ B^* ] = [ ax_2 + cy_2 \quad bx_2 + dy_2 ] = [ x_2^* \quad y_2^* ] \tag{2-12}$$

The midpoint of the transformed line $A^*B^*$ calculated from the transformed end points is

$$
\begin{aligned}
[ x_m^* \quad y_m^* ] &= \left[ \frac{x_1^* + x_2^*}{2} \quad \frac{y_1^* + y_2^*}{2} \right] \\
&= \left[ \frac{(ax_1 + cy_1) + (ax_2 + cy_2)}{2} \quad \frac{(bx_1 + dy_1) + (bx_2 + dy_2)}{2} \right] \\
&= \left[ a\frac{(x_1 + x_2)}{2} + c\frac{(y_1 + y_2)}{2} \quad b\frac{(x_1 + x_2)}{2} + d\frac{(y_1 + y_2)}{2} \right]
\end{aligned}
\tag{2-13}
$$

Returning to the original line $AB$ the midpoint is

$$[ x_m \quad y_m ] = \left[ \frac{x_1 + x_2}{2} \quad \frac{y_1 + y_2}{2} \right] \tag{2-14}$$

Using $[ T ]$ the transformation of the midpoint of $AB$ is

$$
\begin{aligned}
[ x_m \quad y_m ][ T ] &= \left[ \frac{x_1 + x_2}{2} \quad \frac{y_1 + y_2}{2} \right] \begin{bmatrix} a & b \\ c & d \end{bmatrix} \\
&= \left[ a\frac{(x_1 + x_2)}{2} + c\frac{(y_1 + y_2)}{2} \quad b\frac{(x_1 + x_2)}{2} + d\frac{(y_1 + y_2)}{2} \right]
\end{aligned}
\tag{2-15}
$$

Comparing Eqs. (2–13) and (2–15) shows that they are identical. Consequently, the midpoint of the line $AB$ transforms into the midpoint of the line $A^*B^*$. This process can be applied recursively to segments of the divided line. Thus, a one-to-one correspondence between points on the line $AB$ and $A^*B^*$ is assured.

---

### Example 2–1    Midpoint of a Line

Consider the line $AB$ shown in Fig. 2–2. The position vectors of the end points are

$$[ A ] = [ 0 \quad 1 ] \qquad [ B ] = [ 2 \quad 3 ]$$

The transformation

$$[ T ] = \begin{bmatrix} 1 & 2 \\ 3 & 1 \end{bmatrix}$$

yields the position vectors of the end points of the transformed line $A^*B^*$ as

$$\begin{bmatrix} A \\ B \end{bmatrix} [ T ] = \begin{bmatrix} 0 & 1 \\ 2 & 3 \end{bmatrix} \begin{bmatrix} 1 & 2 \\ 3 & 1 \end{bmatrix} = \begin{bmatrix} 3 & 1 \\ 11 & 7 \end{bmatrix} = \begin{bmatrix} A^* \\ B^* \end{bmatrix}$$

The midpoint of $A^*B^*$ is

$$[\, x_m^* \quad y_m^* \,] = \left[\, \frac{3+11}{2} \quad \frac{1+7}{2} \,\right] = [\, 7 \quad 4\, ]$$

The midpoint of the original untransformed line $AB$ is

$$[\, x_m \quad y_m \,] = \left[\, \frac{0+2}{2} \quad \frac{1+3}{2} \,\right] = [\, 1 \quad 2\, ]$$

Transforming this midpoint yields

$$[\, x_m \quad y_m \,][\, T\, ] = [\, 1 \quad 2\, ]\begin{bmatrix} 1 & 2 \\ 3 & 1 \end{bmatrix} = [\, 7 \quad 4\, ] = [\, x_m^* \quad y_m^* \,]$$

which is the same as our previous result.

---

For computer graphics applications these results show that any straight line can be transformed into any other straight line in any position by simply transforming its end points and redrawing the line between the end points.

## 2–7  TRANSFORMATION OF PARALLEL LINES

When a $2 \times 2$ matrix is used to transform a pair of parallel lines, the result is a second pair of parallel lines. To see this, consider a line between $[\, A\, ] = [\, x_1 \quad y_1\, ]$ and $[\, B\, ] = [\, x_2 \quad y_2\, ]$ and a line parallel to $AB$ between $E$ and $F$. To show that these lines and any transformation of them are parallel, examine the slopes of $AB$, $EF$, $A^*B^*$ and $E^*F^*$. Since they are parallel, the slope of both $AB$ and $EF$ is

$$m = \frac{y_2 - y_1}{x_2 - x_1} \tag{2-16}$$

Transforming the end points of $AB$ using a general $2 \times 2$ transformation yields the end points of $A^*B^*$:

$$\begin{bmatrix} A \\ B \end{bmatrix}[\, T\, ] = \begin{bmatrix} x_1 & y_1 \\ x_2 & y_2 \end{bmatrix}\begin{bmatrix} a & b \\ c & d \end{bmatrix}$$

$$= \begin{bmatrix} ax_1 + cy_1 & bx_1 + dy_1 \\ ax_2 + cy_2 & bx_2 + dy_2 \end{bmatrix}$$

$$= \begin{bmatrix} x_1^* & y_1^* \\ x_2^* & y_2^* \end{bmatrix} = \begin{bmatrix} A^* \\ B^* \end{bmatrix} \tag{2-17}$$

Using the transformed end points, the slope of $A^*B^*$ is then

$$m^* = \frac{(bx_2 + dy_2) - (bx_1 + dy_1)}{(ax_2 + cy_2) - (ax_1 + cy_1)} = \frac{b(x_2 - x_1) + d(y_2 - y_1)}{a(x_2 - x_1) + c(y_2 - y_1)}$$

or

$$m^* = \frac{b + d\dfrac{(y_2 - y_1)}{(x_2 - x_1)}}{a + c\dfrac{(y_2 - y_1)}{(x_2 - x_1)}} = \frac{b + dm}{a + cm} \qquad (2-18)$$

Since the slope $m^*$ is independent of $x_1, x_2, y_1$ and $y_2$, and since $m$, $a$, $b$, $c$ and $d$ are the same for $EF$ and $AB$, it follows that $m^*$ is the same for both $E^*F^*$ and $A^*B^*$. Thus, parallel lines remain parallel after transformation. This means that parallelograms transform into other parallelograms when operated on by a general $2 \times 2$ transformation matrix. These simple results begin to show the power of using matrix multiplication to produce graphical effects.

## 2–8   TRANSFORMATION OF INTERSECTING LINES

When a general $2 \times 2$ matrix is used to transform a pair of intersecting straight lines, the result is also a pair of intersecting straight lines. To see this consider a pair of lines, e.g., the dashed lines in Fig. 2–3, represented by

$$y = m_1 x + b_1$$
$$y = m_2 x + b_2$$

Reformulating these equations in matrix notation yields

$$[\, x \quad y \,] \begin{bmatrix} -m_1 & -m_2 \\ 1 & 1 \end{bmatrix} = [\, b_1 \quad b_2 \,]$$
$$[\, X \,][\, M \,] = [\, B \,] \qquad (2-19)$$

or

If a solution to this pair of equations exists, then the lines intersect. If not, then they are parallel. A solution can be obtained by matrix inversion. Specifically,

$$[\, X_i \,] = [\, x_i \quad y_i \,] = [\, B \,][\, M \,]^{-1} \qquad (2-20)$$

The inverse of $[\, M \,]$ is

$$[\, M \,]^{-1} = \begin{bmatrix} \dfrac{1}{m_2 - m_1} & \dfrac{m_2}{m_2 - m_1} \\ \dfrac{-1}{m_2 - m_1} & \dfrac{-m_1}{m_2 - m_1} \end{bmatrix} \qquad (2-21)$$

since $[\, M \,][\, M \,]^{-1} = [\, I \,]$, the identity matrix. Hence, the intersection of the two lines is

$$[\, X_i \,] = [\, x_i \quad y_i \,] = [\, b_1 \quad b_2 \,] \begin{bmatrix} \dfrac{1}{m_2 - m_1} & \dfrac{m_2}{m_2 - m_1} \\ \dfrac{-1}{m_2 - m_1} & \dfrac{-m_1}{m_2 - m_1} \end{bmatrix}$$

$$[\, X_i \,] = [\, x_i \quad y_i \,] = \begin{bmatrix} \dfrac{b_1 - b_2}{m_2 - m_1} & \dfrac{b_1 m_2 - b_2 m_1}{m_2 - m_1} \end{bmatrix} \qquad (2-22)$$

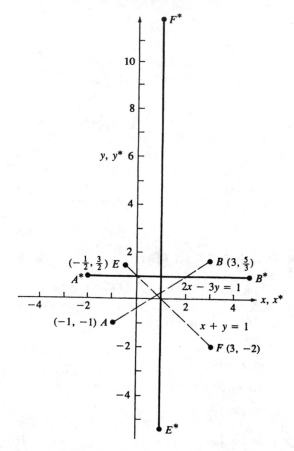

**Figure 2–3** Transformation of intersecting lines.

If these two lines are now transformed using a general $2 \times 2$ transformation matrix given by

$$[T] = \begin{bmatrix} a & b \\ c & d \end{bmatrix}$$

then they have the form

$$y^* = m_1^* x^* + b_1^*$$
$$y^* = m_2^* x^* + b_2^*$$

It is relatively easy to show that

$$m_i^* = \frac{b + dm_i}{a + cm_i} \tag{2-23}$$

and

$$b_i^* = b_i(d - cm_i^*) = b_i \frac{ad - bc}{a + cm_i} \qquad i = 1, 2 \tag{2-24}$$

The intersection of the transformed lines is obtained in the same manner as that for the untransformed lines. Thus,

$$[\,X_i^*\,] = [\,x_i^*\quad y_i^*\,]$$

$$= \begin{bmatrix} \dfrac{b_1^* - b_2^*}{m_2^* - m_1^*} & \dfrac{b_1^* m_2^* - b_2^* m_1^*}{m_2^* - m_1^*} \end{bmatrix}.$$

Rewriting the components of the intersection point using Eqs. (2–23) and (2–24) yields

$$[\,X_i^*\,] = [\,x_i^*\quad y_i^*\,]$$

$$= \begin{bmatrix} \dfrac{a(b_1 - b_2) + c(b_1 m_2 - b_2 m_1)}{m_2 - m_1} & \dfrac{b(b_1 - b_2) + d(b_1 m_2 - b_2 m_1)}{m_2 - m_1} \end{bmatrix}$$

$$(2-25)$$

Returning now to the untransformed intersection point $[\,x_i\quad y_i\,]$ and applying the same general $2 \times 2$ transformation we have

$$[\,x_i^*\quad y_i^*\,] = [\,x_i\quad y_i\,][\,T\,]$$

$$= \begin{bmatrix} \dfrac{b_1 - b_2}{m_2 - m_1} & \dfrac{b_1 m_2 - b_2 m_1}{m_2 - m_1} \end{bmatrix}\begin{bmatrix} a & b \\ c & d \end{bmatrix}$$

$$= \begin{bmatrix} \dfrac{a(b_1 - b_2) + c(b_1 m_2 - b_2 m_1)}{m_2 - m_1} & \dfrac{b(b_1 - b_2) + d(b_1 m_2 - b_2 m_1)}{m_2 - m_1} \end{bmatrix}$$

$$(2-26)$$

Comparing Eqs. (2–25) and (2–26) shows that they are identical. Consequently, the intersection point transforms into the intersection point.

---

### Example 2–2    Intersecting Lines

Consider the two dashed lines $AB$ and $EF$ shown in Fig. 2–3 with end points

$$[\,A\,] = [\,-1\quad -1\,] \qquad [\,B\,] = [\,3\quad 5/3\,]$$

and

$$[\,E\,] = [\,-1/2\quad 3/2\,] \quad [\,F\,] = [\,3\quad -2\,]$$

The equation of the line $AB$ is $-(2/3)x + y = -(1/3)$ and of the line $EF$, $x + y = 1$. In matrix notation the pair of lines is represented by

$$[\,x\quad y\,]\begin{bmatrix} -2/3 & 1 \\ 1 & 1 \end{bmatrix} = [\,-1/3\quad 1\,]$$

Using matrix inversion (see Eq. 2–21) the intersection of these lines is

$$[\,x_i\quad y_i\,] = [\,-1/3\quad 1\,]\begin{bmatrix} -3/5 & -3/5 \\ 3/5 & 2/5 \end{bmatrix}$$

$$= [\,4/5\quad 1/5\,]$$

Now consider the transformation of these lines using

$$[T] = \begin{bmatrix} 1 & 2 \\ 1 & -3 \end{bmatrix} \ .$$

The resulting lines are shown as $A^*B^*$ and $E^*F^*$ in Fig. 2–3. In matrix form the equations of the transformed lines are

$$[x^* \quad y^*] \begin{bmatrix} 1 & 0 \\ 0 & 1 \end{bmatrix} = [1 \quad 1]$$

with intersection point at $[x_i^* \quad y_i^*] = [1 \quad 1]$.

Transforming the intersection point of the untransformed lines yields

$$[x_i^* \quad y_i^*] = [x_i \quad y_i][T]$$

$$= [4/5 \quad 1/5] \begin{bmatrix} 1 & 2 \\ 1 & -3 \end{bmatrix} = [1 \quad 1]$$

which is identical to the intersection point of the transformed lines.

---

Examination of Fig. 2–3 and Ex. 2–2 shows that the original pair of untransformed dashed lines $AB$ and $EF$ are *not* perpendicular. However, the transformed solid lines $A^*B^*$ and $E^*F^*$ *are* perpendicular. Thus, the transformation $[T]$ changed a pair of intersecting nonperpendicular lines into a pair of intersecting perpendicular lines. By implication, $[T]_i^{-1}$ the inverse of the transformation, changes a pair of intersecting perpendicular lines into a pair of intersecting nonperpendicular lines. This effect can have disastrous geometrical consequences. It is thus of considerable interest to determine under what conditions perpendicular lines transform into perpendicular lines. We will return to this question in Sec. 2–14 when a little more background has been presented.

Additional examination of Fig. 2–3 and Ex. 2–2 shows that the transformation $[T]$ involved a rotation, a reflection and a scaling. Let's consider each of these effects individually.

## 2–9   ROTATION

Consider the plane triangle $ABC$ shown in Fig. 2–4. The triangle $ABC$ is rotated through 90° about the origin in a counterclockwise sense by the transformation

$$[T] = \begin{bmatrix} 0 & 1 \\ -1 & 0 \end{bmatrix}$$

If we use a 3 × 2 matrix containing the $x$ and $y$ coordinates of the triangle's vertices, then

$$\begin{bmatrix} 3 & -1 \\ 4 & 1 \\ 2 & 1 \end{bmatrix} \begin{bmatrix} 0 & 1 \\ -1 & 0 \end{bmatrix} = \begin{bmatrix} 1 & 3 \\ -1 & 4 \\ -1 & 2 \end{bmatrix}$$

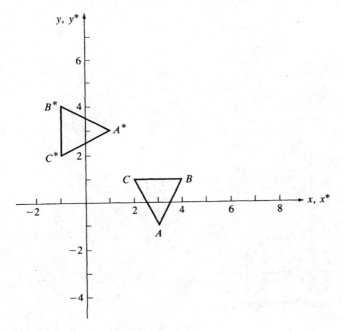

**Figure 2–4**    Rotation.

which produces the triangle $A^*B^*C^*$. A 180° rotation about the origin is obtained by using the transformation

$$[T] = \begin{bmatrix} -1 & 0 \\ 0 & -1 \end{bmatrix}$$

and a 270° rotation about the origin by using

$$[T] = \begin{bmatrix} 0 & -1 \\ 1 & 0 \end{bmatrix}$$

Of course, the identity matrix

$$[T] = \begin{bmatrix} 1 & 0 \\ 0 & 1 \end{bmatrix}$$

corresponds to a rotation about the origin of either 0° or 360°. Note that neither scaling nor reflection has occurred in these examples.

These example transformations produce specific rotations about the origin: 0°, 90°, 180°, 270°. What about rotation about the origin by an arbitrary angle $\theta$ ? To obtain this result consider the position vector from the origin to the point $P$ shown in Fig. 2–5. The length of the vector is $r$ at an angle $\phi$ to the $x$-axis. The position vector $P$ is rotated about the origin by the angle $\theta$ to $P^*$.

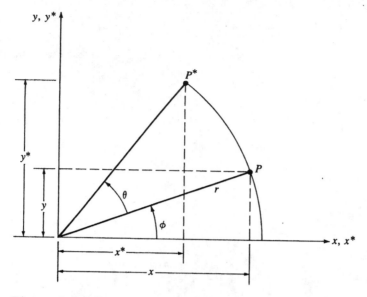

**Figure 2-5**  Rotation of a position vector.

Writing the position vectors for $P$ and $P^*$ we have

$$P = [\, x \quad y \,] = [\, r\cos\phi \quad r\sin\phi \,]$$

and
$$P^* = [\, x^* \quad y^* \,] = [\, r\cos(\phi + \theta) \quad r\sin(\phi + \theta) \,]$$

Using the sum of the angles formulas† allows writing $P^*$ as

$$P^* = [\, x^* \quad y^* \,] = [\, r(\cos\phi\cos\theta - \sin\phi\sin\theta) \quad r(\cos\phi\sin\theta + \sin\phi\cos\theta) \,]$$

Using the definitions of $x$ and $y$ allows rewriting $P^*$ as

$$P^* = [\, x^* \quad y^* \,] = [\, x\cos\theta - y\sin\theta \quad x\sin\theta + y\cos\theta \,]$$

Thus, the transformed point has components

$$x^* = x\cos\theta - y\sin\theta \qquad\qquad (2-27a)$$
$$y^* = x\sin\theta + y\cos\theta \qquad\qquad (2-27b)$$

In matrix form

$$[\, X^* \,] = [\, X \,][\, T \,] = [\, x^* \quad y^* \,]$$

$$= [\, x \quad y \,]\begin{bmatrix} \cos\theta & \sin\theta \\ -\sin\theta & \cos\theta \end{bmatrix} \qquad\qquad (2-28)$$

---

†$\cos(\phi \pm \theta) = \cos\phi\cos\theta \mp \sin\phi\sin\theta$
$\sin(\phi \pm \theta) = \cos\phi\sin\theta \pm \sin\phi\cos\theta$

Thus, the transformation for a general rotation about the origin by an arbitrary angle $\theta$ is

$$[T] = \begin{bmatrix} \cos\theta & \sin\theta \\ -\sin\theta & \cos\theta \end{bmatrix} \qquad (2-29)$$

Rotations are positive counterclockwise about the origin, as shown in Fig. 2–5.
Evaluation of the determinant of the general rotation matrix yields

$$\det[T] = \cos^2\theta + \sin^2\theta = 1 \qquad (2-30)$$

In general, transformations with a determinant identically equal to +1 yield pure rotations.

Suppose now that we wish to rotate the point $P^*$ back to $P$, i.e., perform the inverse transformation. The required rotation angle is obviously $-\theta$. From Eq. (2–29) the required transformation matrix is

$$[T]^{-1} = \begin{bmatrix} \cos(-\theta) & \sin(-\theta) \\ -\sin(-\theta) & \cos(-\theta) \end{bmatrix} = \begin{bmatrix} \cos\theta & -\sin\theta \\ \sin\theta & \cos\theta \end{bmatrix} \qquad (2-31)$$

since $\cos(-\theta) = \cos\theta$ and $\sin(-\theta) = -\sin\theta$. $[T]^{-1}$ is a formal way of writing 'the inverse of' $[T]$. We can show that $[T]^{-1}$ is the inverse of $[T]$ by recalling that the product of a matrix and its inverse yields the identity matrix. Here,

$$[T][T]^{-1} = \begin{bmatrix} \cos\theta & \sin\theta \\ -\sin\theta & \cos\theta \end{bmatrix} \begin{bmatrix} \cos\theta & -\sin\theta \\ \sin\theta & \cos\theta \end{bmatrix}$$

$$= \begin{bmatrix} \cos^2\theta + \sin^2\theta & -\cos\theta\sin\theta + \cos\theta\sin\theta \\ -\cos\theta\sin\theta + \cos\theta\sin\theta & \cos^2\theta + \sin^2\theta \end{bmatrix}$$

$$= \begin{bmatrix} 1 & 0 \\ 0 & 1 \end{bmatrix} = [I]$$

where $[I]$ is the identity matrix.

Examining Eqs. (2–29) and (2–31) reveals another interesting and useful result. Recall that the transpose of a matrix is obtained by interchanging its rows and columns. Forming the transpose of $[T]$, i.e., $[T]^T$, and comparing it with $[T]^{-1}$ shows that

$$[T]^T = \begin{bmatrix} \cos\theta & -\sin\theta \\ \sin\theta & \cos\theta \end{bmatrix} = [T]^{-1} \qquad (2-32)$$

The inverse of the general rotation matrix $[T]$ is its transpose. Since formally determining the inverse of a matrix is more computationally expensive than determining its transpose, Eq. (2–32) is an important and useful result. In general, the inverse of any pure rotation matrix, i.e., one with a determinant identically equal to +1, is its transpose.[†]

---

[†]Such matrices are said to be orthogonal.

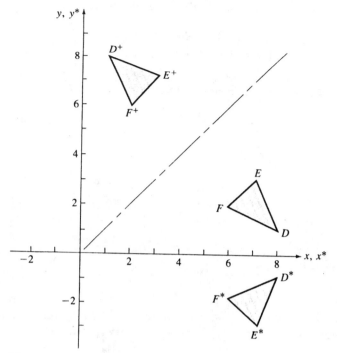

**Figure 2–6**   Reflection.

## 2–10   REFLECTION

Whereas a pure two-dimensional rotation in the $xy$ plane occurs entirely in the two-dimensional plane about an axis normal to the $xy$ plane, a reflection is a 180° rotation out into three space and back into two space about an axis in the $xy$ plane.  Two reflections of the triangle $DEF$ are shown in Fig. 2–6.  A reflection about $y = 0$, the $x$-axis, is obtained by using

$$[T] = \begin{bmatrix} 1 & 0 \\ 0 & -1 \end{bmatrix}$$

(2 – 33)

In this case the new vertices $D^*E^*F^*$ for the triangle are given by

$$\begin{bmatrix} 8 & 1 \\ 7 & 3 \\ 6 & 2 \end{bmatrix} \begin{bmatrix} 1 & 0 \\ 0 & -1 \end{bmatrix} = \begin{bmatrix} 8 & -1 \\ 7 & -3 \\ 6 & -2 \end{bmatrix}$$

Similarly reflection about $x = 0$, the $y$-axis, is given by

$$[T] = \begin{bmatrix} -1 & 0 \\ 0 & 1 \end{bmatrix}$$

(2 – 34)

A reflection about the line $y = x$ occurs for

$$[T] = \begin{bmatrix} 0 & 1 \\ 1 & 0 \end{bmatrix} \qquad (2-35)$$

The transformed, new vertices $D^+E^+F^+$ are given by

$$\begin{bmatrix} 8 & 1 \\ 7 & 3 \\ 6 & 2 \end{bmatrix} \begin{bmatrix} 0 & 1 \\ 1 & 0 \end{bmatrix} = \begin{bmatrix} 1 & 8 \\ 3 & 7 \\ 2 & 6 \end{bmatrix}$$

Similarly, a reflection about the line $y = -x$ is given by

$$[T] = \begin{bmatrix} 0 & -1 \\ -1 & 0 \end{bmatrix} \qquad (2-36)$$

Each of these reflection matrices has a determinant that is identically $-1$. In general, if the determinant of a transformation matrix is identically $-1$, then the transformation produces a pure reflection.

If two pure reflection transformations about lines passing through the origin are applied successively, the result is a pure rotation about the origin. To see this, consider the following example.

---

### Example 2-3    Reflection and Rotation

Consider the triangle $ABC$ shown in Fig. 2-7, first reflected about the $x$ axis (see Eq. 2-33) and then about the line $y = -x$ (see Eq. 2-36). Specifically, the result of the reflection about the $x$-axis is

$$[X^*] = [X][T_1] = \begin{bmatrix} 4 & 1 \\ 5 & 2 \\ 4 & 3 \end{bmatrix} \begin{bmatrix} 1 & 0 \\ 0 & -1 \end{bmatrix} = \begin{bmatrix} 4 & -1 \\ 5 & -2 \\ 4 & -3 \end{bmatrix}$$

Reflecting the triangle $A^*B^*C^*$ about the line $y = -x$ yields

$$[X^+] = [X^*][T_2] = \begin{bmatrix} 4 & -1 \\ 5 & -2 \\ 4 & -3 \end{bmatrix} \begin{bmatrix} 0 & -1 \\ -1 & 0 \end{bmatrix} = \begin{bmatrix} 1 & -4 \\ 2 & -5 \\ 3 & -4 \end{bmatrix}$$

Rotation about the origin by an angle $\theta = 270°$ (see Eq. 2-29) yields the identical result, i.e.,

$$[X^+] = [X][T_3] = \begin{bmatrix} 4 & 1 \\ 5 & 2 \\ 4 & 3 \end{bmatrix} \begin{bmatrix} 0 & -1 \\ 1 & 0 \end{bmatrix} = \begin{bmatrix} 1 & -4 \\ 2 & -5 \\ 3 & -4 \end{bmatrix}$$

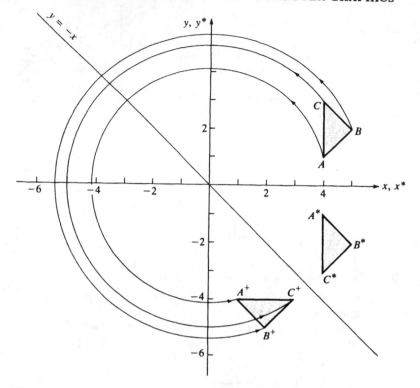

**Figure 2-7** Combined reflections yield rotations.

Note that the reflection matrices given above in Eqs. (2–33) and (2–36) are orthogonal; i.e., the transpose is also the inverse. For example,

$$\begin{bmatrix} 0 & -1 \\ -1 & 0 \end{bmatrix} = \begin{bmatrix} 0 & -1 \\ -1 & 0 \end{bmatrix}^{T} = \begin{bmatrix} 0 & -1 \\ -1 & 0 \end{bmatrix}^{-1}$$

## 2-11  SCALING

Recalling our discussion of the transformation of points, we see that scaling is controlled by the magnitude of the two terms on the primary diagonal of the matrix. If the matrix

$$[T] = \begin{bmatrix} 2 & 0 \\ 0 & 2 \end{bmatrix}$$

is used as an operator on the vertices of a triangle, a '2-times' enlargement, or uniform scaling, occurs about the origin. If the magnitudes are unequal, a distortion occurs. These effects are shown in Fig. 2–8. Triangle $ABC$ is transformed by

$$[T] = \begin{bmatrix} 2 & 0 \\ 0 & 2 \end{bmatrix}$$

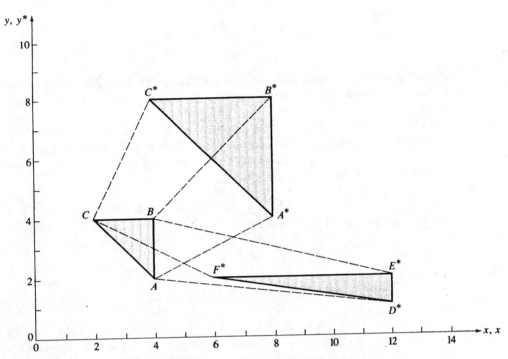

**Figure 2–8**    Uniform and nonuniform scaling or distortion.

to yield $A^*B^*C^*$, where a uniform scaling occurs. Transforming triangle $ABC$ by

$$\begin{bmatrix} 1/2 & 0 \\ 0 & 3 \end{bmatrix}$$

to $D^*E^*F^*$ shows distortion due to the nonuniform scale factors.

In general, if

$$[T] = \begin{bmatrix} a & b \\ c & d \end{bmatrix} \qquad\qquad (2-37)$$

with $a = d$, $b = c = 0$, a uniform scaling occurs; and if $a \neq d$, $b = c = 0$, a nonuniform scaling occurs. For a uniform scaling, if $a = d > 1$, a uniform expansion occurs; i.e., the figure gets larger. If $a = d < 1$, then a uniform compression occurs; i.e., the figure gets smaller. Nonuniform expansions and compressions occur, depending on whether $a$ and $d$ are individually $> 1$ or $< 1$.

Figure 2–8 also reveals what at first glance is an apparent translation of the transformed triangles. This apparent translation is easily understood if we recall that the *position vectors*, not the *points*, are scaled with respect to the origin.

To see this more clearly examine the transformation of $ABC$ to $D^*E^*F^*$ more closely. Specifically,

$$[\,X^*\,] = [\,X\,][\,T\,] = \begin{bmatrix} 4 & 2 \\ 4 & 4 \\ 2 & 4 \end{bmatrix} \begin{bmatrix} 1/2 & 0 \\ 0 & 3 \end{bmatrix} = \begin{bmatrix} 2 & 6 \\ 2 & 12 \\ 1 & 12 \end{bmatrix}$$

Note that each of the $x$ components of the *position vectors* of $DEF$ is increased by a scale factor of 3 and the $y$ components of the *position vectors* by a scale factor of 2.

To obtain a pure scaling without apparent translation, the centroid of the figure must be at the origin. This effect is shown in Fig. 2–9, where the triangle $ABC$ with the centroid coordinates (1/3 the base and 1/3 the height) at the origin is scaled by a factor of 2. Specifically,

$$[\,X^*\,] = [\,X\,][\,T\,] = \begin{bmatrix} -1 & -1 \\ 2 & -1 \\ -1 & 2 \end{bmatrix} \begin{bmatrix} 2 & 0 \\ 0 & 2 \end{bmatrix} = \begin{bmatrix} -2 & -2 \\ 4 & -2 \\ -2 & 4 \end{bmatrix}$$

## 2–12 COMBINED TRANSFORMATIONS

The power of the matrix methods described in the previous sections is clear. By performing matrix operations on the position vectors which define the vertices, the shape and position of the surface can be controlled. However, a desired orientation may require more than one transformation. Since matrix multiplication is noncommutative, the order of application of the transformations is important.

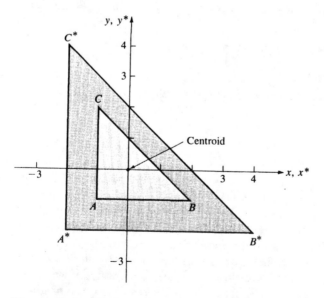

**Figure 2–9**  Uniform scaling without apparent translation.

In order to illustrate the effect of noncommutative matrix multiplication, consider the operations of rotation and reflection on the position vector $[\, x \quad y \,]$. If a 90° rotation, $[\, T_1 \,]$, is followed by reflection through the line $y = -x$, $[\, T_2 \,]$, these two consecutive transformations give

$$[\, X' \,] = [\, X \,][\, T_1 \,] = [\, x \quad y \,] \begin{bmatrix} 0 & 1 \\ -1 & 0 \end{bmatrix} = [\, -y \quad x \,]$$

and then

$$[\, X^* \,] = [\, X' \,][\, T_2 \,] = [\, -y \quad x \,] \begin{bmatrix} 0 & -1 \\ -1 & 0 \end{bmatrix} = [\, -x \quad y \,]$$

On the other hand, if reflection is followed by rotation, the results given by

$$[\, X' \,] = [\, X \,][\, T_2 \,] = [\, x \quad y \,] \begin{bmatrix} 0 & -1 \\ -1 & 0 \end{bmatrix} = [\, -y \quad -x \,]$$

and

$$[\, X^* \,] = [\, X' \,][\, T_1 \,] = [\, -y \quad -x \,] \begin{bmatrix} 0 & 1 \\ -1 & 0 \end{bmatrix} = [\, x \quad -y \,]$$

are obtained. The results are different, confirming that the order of application of matrix transformations is important.

Another important point is illustrated by the above results and by the example given below. Above, the individual transformation matrices were successively applied to the successively obtained position vectors, e.g.,

$$[\, x \quad y \,][\, T_1 \,] \rightarrow [\, x' \quad y' \,]$$

and

$$[\, x' \quad y' \,][\, T_2 \,] \rightarrow [\, x^* \quad y^* \,]$$

In the example below the individual transformations are first combined or concatenated and then the *concatenated* transformation is applied to the original position vector, e.g., $[\, T_1 \,][\, T_2 \,] \rightarrow [\, T_3 \,]$ and $[\, x \quad y \,][\, T_3 \,] \rightarrow [\, x^* \quad y^* \,]$.

---

### Example 2–4    Combined Two-Dimensional Transformations

Consider the triangle $ABC$ shown in Fig. 2–10. The two transformations are a +90° rotation about the origin:

$$[\, T_1 \,] = \begin{bmatrix} 0 & 1 \\ -1 & 0 \end{bmatrix}$$

and a reflection through the line $y = -x$

$$[\, T_2 \,] = \begin{bmatrix} 0 & -1 \\ -1 & 0 \end{bmatrix}$$

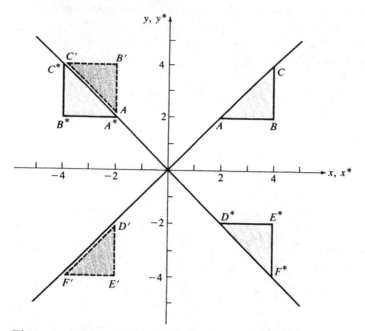

**Figure 2–10**    Combined two-dimensional transformations.

The effect of the combined transformation $[T_3] = [T_1][T_2]$ on the triangle $ABC$ is

$$[X^*] = [X][T_1][T_2] = [X][T_3]$$

or

$$\begin{bmatrix} 2 & 2 \\ 4 & 2 \\ 4 & 4 \end{bmatrix} \begin{bmatrix} 0 & 1 \\ -1 & 0 \end{bmatrix} \begin{bmatrix} 0 & -1 \\ -1 & 0 \end{bmatrix} = \begin{bmatrix} 2 & 2 \\ 4 & 2 \\ 4 & 4 \end{bmatrix} \begin{bmatrix} -1 & 0 \\ 0 & 1 \end{bmatrix} = \begin{bmatrix} -2 & 2 \\ -4 & 2 \\ -4 & 4 \end{bmatrix}$$

The final result is shown as $A^*B^*C^*$ and the intermediate result as $A'B'C'$ in Fig. 2–10.

Reversing the order of application of the transformations yields

$$[X^*] = [X][T_2][T_1] = [X][T_4]$$

or

$$\begin{bmatrix} 2 & 2 \\ 4 & 2 \\ 4 & 4 \end{bmatrix} \begin{bmatrix} 0 & -1 \\ -1 & 0 \end{bmatrix} \begin{bmatrix} 0 & 1 \\ -1 & 0 \end{bmatrix} = \begin{bmatrix} 2 & 2 \\ 4 & 2 \\ 4 & 4 \end{bmatrix} \begin{bmatrix} 1 & 0 \\ 0 & -1 \end{bmatrix} = \begin{bmatrix} 2 & -2 \\ 4 & -2 \\ 4 & -4 \end{bmatrix}$$

The final result is shown as $D^*E^*F^*$ and the intermediate result as $D'E'F'$ in Fig. 2–10.

The results are different, again confirming that the order of application of the transformations is important.   Note also that $\det [T_3] = -1$ and $\det [T_4] = -1$, indicating that both results can be obtained by a single reflection.  $A^*B^*C^*$ can be obtained from $ABC$ by reflection through the $y$-axis (see $[T_3]$ and Eq. 2–34).  $D^*E^*F^*$ can be obtained from $ABC$ by reflection through the $x$-axis (see $[T_4]$ and Eq. 2–33).

---

## 2–13    TRANSFORMATION OF THE UNIT SQUARE

So far we have concentrated on the behavior of points and lines to determine the effect of simple matrix transformations.  However, the matrix is correctly considered to operate on *every* point in the plane. As has been shown, the only point that remains invariant under a $2 \times 2$ matrix transformation is the origin. All other points within the plane are transformed. This transformation may be interpreted as a stretching of the original plane and coordinate system into a new shape.  More formally, we say that the transformation causes a mapping from one coordinate space into a second.

Consider a square-grid network consisting of unit squares in the $xy$ plane as shown in Fig. 2–11. The four position vectors of a unit square with one corner at the origin of the coordinate system are

$$\begin{bmatrix} 0 & 0 \\ 1 & 0 \\ 1 & 1 \\ 0 & 1 \end{bmatrix} \begin{array}{l} \text{origin of the coordinates } - A \\ \text{unit point on the } x\text{-axis } - B \\ \text{outer corner } - C \\ \text{unit point on the } y\text{-axis } - D \end{array}$$

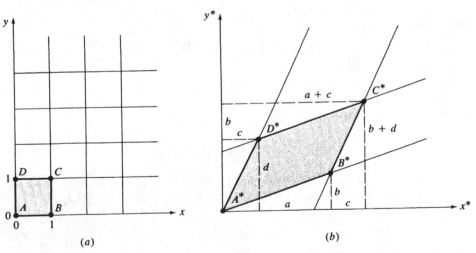

**Figure 2–11**    General transformation of unit square. (a) Before transformation; (b) after transformation.

This unit square is shown in Fig. 2–11a. Application of a general $2 \times 2$ matrix transformation to the unit square yields

$$
\begin{matrix} A \\ B \\ C \\ D \end{matrix}
\begin{bmatrix} 0 & 0 \\ 1 & 0 \\ 1 & 1 \\ 0 & 1 \end{bmatrix}
\begin{bmatrix} a & b \\ c & d \end{bmatrix}
=
\begin{bmatrix} 0 & 0 \\ a & b \\ a+c & b+d \\ c & d \end{bmatrix}
\begin{matrix} A^* \\ B^* \\ C^* \\ D^* \end{matrix}
\qquad (2-38)
$$

The results of this transformation are shown in Fig. 2–11b. First notice from Eq. (2–38) that the origin is not affected by the transformation, i.e., $[A] = [A^*] = [0 \ 0]$. Further, notice that the coordinates of $B^*$ are equal to the first row in the general transformation matrix, and the coordinates of $D^*$ are equal to the second row in the general transformation matrix. Thus, once the coordinates of $B^*$ and $D^*$ (the transformed unit vectors $[1 \ 0]$ and $[0 \ 1]$, respectively) are known, the general transformation matrix is determined. Since the sides of the unit square are originally parallel, and since we have previously shown that parallel lines transform into parallel lines, the transformed figure is a parallelogram.

The effect of the terms $a, b, c$ and $d$ in the $2 \times 2$ matrix can be identified separately. The terms $b$ and $c$ cause a shearing (see Sec. 2–4) of the initial square in the $y$ and $x$ directions, respectively, as can be seen in Fig. 2–11b. The terms $a$ and $d$ act as scale factors, as noted earlier. Thus, the general $2 \times 2$ matrix produces a combination of shearing and scaling.

It is also possible to easily determine the area of $A^*B^*C^*D^*$, the parallelogram shown in Fig. 2–11b. The area within the parallelogram can be calculated as follows:

$$
A_p = (a+c)(b+d) - \frac{1}{2}(ab) - \frac{1}{2}(cd) - \frac{c}{2}(b+b+d) - \frac{b}{2}(c+a+c)
$$

which yields

$$
A_p = ad - bc = \det \begin{bmatrix} a & b \\ c & d \end{bmatrix}
\qquad (2-39)
$$

It can be shown that the area of any parallelogram $A_p$, formed by transforming a square, is a function of the transformation matrix determinant and is related to the area of the initial square $A_s$ by the simple relationship

$$
A_p = A_s(ad - bc) = A_s \det [T]
\qquad (2-40)
$$

In fact, since the area of a general figure is the sum of unit squares, the area of any transformed figure $A_t$ is related to the area of the initial figure $A_i$ by

$$
A_t = A_i(ad - bc)
\qquad (2-41)
$$

This is a useful technique for determining the areas of arbitrary shapes.

### Example 2–5    Area Scaling

The triangle $ABC$ with position vectors $[\,1\quad 0\,]$, $[\,0\quad 1\,]$ and $[\,-1\quad 0\,]$, is transformed by

$$[\,T\,] = \begin{bmatrix} 3 & 2 \\ -1 & 2 \end{bmatrix}$$

to create a second triangle $A^*B^*C^*$ as shown in Fig. 2–12.

The area of the triangle $ABC$ is

$$A_i = \frac{1}{2}(base)(height) = \frac{1}{2}(2)(1) = 1$$

Using Eq. (2–41) the area of the transformed triangle $A^*B^*C^*$ is

$$A_t = A_i(ad - bc) = 1(6 + 2) = 8$$

Now the vertices of the transformed triangle $A^*B^*C^*$ are

$$\begin{bmatrix} 1 & 0 \\ 0 & 1 \\ -1 & 0 \end{bmatrix} \begin{bmatrix} 3 & 2 \\ -1 & 2 \end{bmatrix} = \begin{bmatrix} 3 & 2 \\ -1 & 2 \\ -3 & -2 \end{bmatrix}$$

Calculating the area from the transformed vertices yields

$$A_t = \frac{1}{2}(base)(height) = \frac{1}{2}(4)(4) = 8$$

which confirms the previous result.

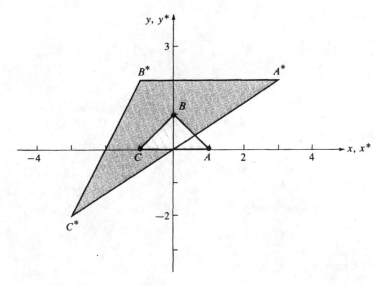

**Figure 2–12**    Area scaling.

## 2–14   SOLID BODY TRANSFORMATIONS

We now return to the question posed in Sec. 2–8, i.e., when do perpendicular lines transform as perpendicular lines? First consider the somewhat more general question of when is the angle between intersecting lines preserved?

Recall that the dot or scalar product of two vectors is

$$\bar{V}_1 \cdot \bar{V}_2 = V_{1x} V_{2x} + V_{1y} V_{2y} = |\bar{V}_1| |\bar{V}_2| \cos \theta \qquad (2-42)$$

and the cross product of two vectors confined to the two-dimensional $xy$ plane is

$$\bar{V}_1 \times \bar{V}_2 = (V_{1x} V_{2y} - V_{2x} V_{1y})\bar{k} = |\bar{V}_1||\bar{V}_2|\bar{k} \sin \theta \qquad (2-43)$$

where the subscripts $x, y$ refer to the $x$ and $y$ components of the vector, $\theta$ is the acute angle between the vectors and $\bar{k}$ is the unit vector perpendicular to the $xy$ plane.

Transforming $\bar{V}_1$ and $\bar{V}_2$ using a general $2 \times 2$ transformation yields

$$\begin{bmatrix} \bar{V}_1 \\ \bar{V}_2 \end{bmatrix} [T] = \begin{bmatrix} V_{1x} & V_{1y} \\ V_{2x} & V_{2y} \end{bmatrix} \begin{bmatrix} a & b \\ c & d \end{bmatrix}$$

$$= \begin{bmatrix} aV_{1x} + cV_{1y} & bV_{1x} + dV_{1y} \\ aV_{2x} + cV_{2y} & bV_{2x} + dV_{2y} \end{bmatrix} = \begin{bmatrix} \bar{V}_1^* \\ \bar{V}_2^* \end{bmatrix} \qquad (2-44)$$

The cross product of $\bar{V}_1^*$ and $\bar{V}_2^*$ is

$$\bar{V}_1^* \times \bar{V}_2^* = (ad - cb)(V_{1x} V_{2y} - V_{2x} V_{1y})\bar{k} = |\bar{V}_1^*||\bar{V}_2^*|\bar{k} \sin \theta \qquad (2-45)$$

Similarly the scalar product is

$$\bar{V}_1^* \cdot \bar{V}_2^* = (a^2 + b^2)V_{1x} V_{2x} + (c^2 + d^2)V_{1y} V_{2y} + (ac + bd)(V_{1x} V_{2y} + V_{1y} V_{2x})$$
$$= |\bar{V}_1^*||\bar{V}_2^*| \cos \theta \qquad (2-46)$$

Requiring that the magnitude of the vectors, as well as the angle between them, remains unchanged, comparing Eqs. (2–42) and (2–46) and Eqs. (2–43) and (2–45) and equating coefficients of like terms yields

$$a^2 + b^2 = 1 \qquad (2-47a)$$
$$c^2 + d^2 = 1 \qquad (2-47b)$$
$$ac + bd = 0 \qquad (2-47c)$$

$$ad - bc = +1 \qquad (2-48)$$

Equations (2–47a,b,c) correspond to the conditions that a matrix be orthogonal, i.e.,

$$[T][T]^{-1} = [T][T]^T = [I]$$

or

$$\begin{bmatrix} a & b \\ c & d \end{bmatrix} \begin{bmatrix} a & c \\ b & d \end{bmatrix} = \begin{bmatrix} a^2 + b^2 & ac + bd \\ ac + bd & c^2 + d^2 \end{bmatrix} = \begin{bmatrix} 1 & 0 \\ 0 & 1 \end{bmatrix}$$

Equation (2–48) requires that the determinant of the transformation matrix be +1.

Thus, the angles between intersecting lines are preserved by pure rotation. Since reflective transformations are also orthogonal with a determinant of −1, these results are easily extended. In this case the magnitude of the vectors is preserved, but the angle between the transformed vectors is technically $2\pi - \theta$. Hence, the angle is technically not preserved. Still, perpendicular lines transform as perpendicular lines. Since $\sin(2\pi - \theta) = -\sin\theta$, $ad - bc = -1$. Pure rotations and reflections are called rigid body transformations. In addition, a few minutes' thought or experimentation reveals that uniform scalings also preserve the angle between intersecting lines but not the magnitudes of the transformed vectors.[†]

## 2–15    TRANSLATIONS AND HOMOGENEOUS COORDINATES

A number of transformations governed by the general $2 \times 2$ transformation matrix, e.g., rotation, reflection, scaling, shearing etc., were discussed in the previous sections. As noted previously, the origin of the coordinate system is invariant with respect to all of these transformations. However, it is necessary to be able to modify the position of the origin, i.e., to transform every point in the two-dimensional plane. This can be accomplished by translating the origin or any other point in the two-dimensional plane, i.e.,

$$x^* = ax + cy + m$$
$$y^* = bx + dy + n$$

Unfortunately, it is not possible to introduce the constants of translation $m, n$ into the general $2 \times 2$ transformation matrix; there is no room!

This difficulty can be overcome by introducing homogeneous coordinates. The homogeneous coordinates of a nonhomogeneous position vector $[\, x \quad y \,]$ are $[\, x' \quad y' \quad h \,]$ where $x = x'/h$ and $y = y'/h$ and $h$ is any real number. Note that $h = 0$ has special meaning. One set of homogeneous coordinates is always of the form $[\, x \quad y \quad 1 \,]$. We choose this form to represent the position vector $[\, x \quad y \,]$ in the physical $xy$ plane. All other homogeneous coordinates are of the form $[\, hx \quad hy \quad h \,]$. There is no unique homogeneous coordinate representation, e.g., $[\, 6 \quad 4 \quad 2 \,], [\, 12 \quad 8 \quad 4 \,], [\, 3 \quad 2 \quad 1 \,]$ all represent the physical point $(3, 2)$.

The general transformation matrix is now $3 \times 3$. Specifically,

$$[\,T\,] = \begin{bmatrix} a & b & 0 \\ c & d & 0 \\ m & n & 1 \end{bmatrix} \tag{2-49}$$

---

[†]Since an orthogonal matrix preserves *both* the angle between the vectors and their magnitudes, the uniform scaling transformation matrix is *not* orthogonal.

where the elements $a, b, c, d$ of the upper left $2 \times 2$ submatrix have exactly the same effects revealed by our previous discussions. $m, n$ are the translation factors in the $x$ and $y$ directions, respectively. The pure two-dimensional translation matrix is

$$[\, x^* \quad y^* \quad 1 \,] = [\, x \quad y \quad 1 \,] \begin{bmatrix} 1 & 0 & 0 \\ 0 & 1 & 0 \\ m & n & 1 \end{bmatrix} = [\, x + m \quad y + n \quad 1 \,] \qquad (2-50)$$

Notice that now every point in the two-dimensional plane, even the origin ($x = y = 0$), can be transformed.

## 2-16    ROTATION ABOUT AN ARBITRARY POINT

Previously we have considered rotations as occurring about the origin. Homogeneous coordinates provide a mechanism for accomplishing rotations about points other than the origin. In general, a rotation about an arbitrary point can be accomplished by first translating the point to the origin, performing the required rotation, and then translating the result back to the original center of rotation. Thus, rotation of the position vector $[\, x \quad y \quad 1 \,]$ about the point $m, n$ through an arbitrary angle can be accomplished by

$$[\, x^* \quad y^* \quad 1 \,] = [\, x \quad y \quad 1 \,] \begin{bmatrix} 1 & 0 & 0 \\ 0 & 1 & 0 \\ -m & -n & 1 \end{bmatrix} \begin{bmatrix} \cos \theta & \sin \theta & 0 \\ -\sin \theta & \cos \theta & 0 \\ 0 & 0 & 1 \end{bmatrix} \begin{bmatrix} 1 & 0 & 0 \\ 0 & 1 & 0 \\ m & n & 1 \end{bmatrix}$$

$$(2-51)$$

By carrying out the two interior matrix products we can write

$$[\, x^* \quad y^* \quad 1 \,] = [\, x \quad y \quad 1 \,] \begin{bmatrix} \cos \theta & \sin \theta & 0 \\ -\sin \theta & \cos \theta & 0 \\ \left\{ \begin{array}{c} -m(\cos \theta - 1) \\ +n \sin \theta \end{array} \right\} & \left\{ \begin{array}{c} -n(\cos \theta - 1) \\ -m \sin \theta \end{array} \right\} & 1 \end{bmatrix}$$

$$(2-52)$$

An example illustrates this result.

---

**Example 2-6    Rotation About an Arbitrary Point.**

Suppose the center of an object is at $[\, 4 \quad 3 \,]$ and it is desired to rotate the object $90°$ counterclockwise about its center. Using the matrix

$$\begin{bmatrix} 0 & 1 & 0 \\ -1 & 0 & 0 \\ 0 & 0 & 1 \end{bmatrix}$$

causes a rotation about the origin, not the object center. The necessary procedure is to first translate the object so that the desired center of rotation is at the origin by using the translation matrix

$$\begin{bmatrix} 1 & 0 & 0 \\ 0 & 1 & 0 \\ -4 & -3 & 1 \end{bmatrix}$$

Next apply the rotation matrix, and finally translate the results of the rotation back to the original center by means of the inverse translation matrix. The entire operation

$$[\,x^* \quad y^* \quad 1\,] = [\,x \quad y \quad 1\,] \begin{bmatrix} 1 & 0 & 0 \\ 0 & 1 & 0 \\ -4 & -3 & 1 \end{bmatrix} \begin{bmatrix} 0 & 1 & 0 \\ -1 & 0 & 0 \\ 0 & 0 & 1 \end{bmatrix} \begin{bmatrix} 1 & 0 & 0 \\ 0 & 1 & 0 \\ 4 & 3 & 1 \end{bmatrix}$$

can be combined into one matrix operation by concatenating the transformation matrices, i.e.,

$$[\,x^* \quad y^* \quad 1\,] = [\,x \quad y \quad 1\,] \begin{bmatrix} 0 & 1 & 0 \\ -1 & 0 & 0 \\ 7 & -1 & 1 \end{bmatrix}$$

---

## 2–17    REFLECTION THROUGH AN ARBITRARY LINE

Previously (see Sec. 2–10) reflection through lines that passed through the origin was discussed. Occasionally reflection of an object through a line that does not pass through the origin is required. This can be accomplished using a procedure similar to that for rotation about an arbitrary point. Specifically,

Translate the line and the object so that the line passes through the origin.

Rotate the line and the object about the origin until the line is coincident with one of the coordinate axes.

Reflect through the coordinate axis.

Apply the inverse rotation about the origin.

Translate back to the original location.

In matrix notation the resulting concatenated matrix is

$$[\,T\,] = [\,T'\,][\,R\,][\,R'\,][\,R\,]^{-1}[\,T'\,]^{-1} \qquad\qquad (2-53)$$

where

$T'$ is the translation matrix
$R$ is the rotation matrix about the origin
$R'$ is the reflection matrix

The translations, rotations and reflections are also applied to the figure to be transformed. An example is given below.

**Example 2–7    Reflection Through an Arbitrary Line**

Consider the line $L$ and the triangle $ABC$ shown in Fig. 2–13a. The equation of the line $L$ is

$$y = \frac{1}{2}(x + 4)$$

The position vectors $[\,2\quad 4\quad 1\,]$, $[\,4\quad 6\quad 1\,]$ and $[\,2\quad 6\quad 1\,]$ describe the vertices of the triangle $ABC$.

The line $L$ will pass through the origin by translating it $-2$ units in the $y$ direction. The resulting line can be made coincident with the $x$-axis by rotating it by $-\tan^{-1}(\frac{1}{2}) = -26.57°$ about the origin. Equation (2–33) is then used to reflect the triangle through the $x$-axis. The transformed position vectors of the triangle are then rotated and translated back to the original orientation. The combined transformation is

$$[T] = \begin{bmatrix} 1 & 0 & 0 \\ 0 & 1 & 0 \\ 0 & -2 & 1 \end{bmatrix} \begin{bmatrix} 2/\sqrt{5} & -1/\sqrt{5} & 0 \\ 1/\sqrt{5} & 2/\sqrt{5} & 0 \\ 0 & 0 & 1 \end{bmatrix} \begin{bmatrix} 1 & 0 & 0 \\ 0 & -1 & 0 \\ 0 & 0 & 1 \end{bmatrix} \times$$

$$\begin{bmatrix} 2/\sqrt{5} & 1/\sqrt{5} & 0 \\ -1/\sqrt{5} & 2/\sqrt{5} & 0 \\ 0 & 0 & 1 \end{bmatrix} \begin{bmatrix} 1 & 0 & 0 \\ 0 & 1 & 0 \\ 0 & 2 & 1 \end{bmatrix}$$

$$[T] = \begin{bmatrix} 3/5 & 4/5 & 0 \\ 4/5 & -3/5 & 0 \\ -8/5 & 16/5 & 1 \end{bmatrix}$$

and the transformed position vectors for the triangle $A^*B^*C^*$ are

$$\begin{bmatrix} 2 & 4 & 1 \\ 4 & 6 & 1 \\ 2 & 6 & 1 \end{bmatrix} \begin{bmatrix} 3/5 & 4/5 & 0 \\ 4/5 & -3/5 & 0 \\ -8/5 & 16/5 & 1 \end{bmatrix} = \begin{bmatrix} 14/5 & 12/5 & 1 \\ 28/5 & 14/5 & 1 \\ 22/5 & 6/5 & 1 \end{bmatrix}$$

as shown in Fig. 2–13a. Figures 2–13b through 2–13e show the various steps in the transformation.

## 2–18    PROJECTION – A GEOMETRIC INTERPRETATION OF HOMOGENEOUS COORDINATES

The general $3 \times 3$ transformation matrix for two-dimensional homogeneous coordinates can be subdivided into four parts:

$$[T] = \begin{bmatrix} a & b & \vdots & p \\ c & d & \vdots & q \\ \cdots & \cdots & \cdots & \cdots \\ m & n & \vdots & s \end{bmatrix} \tag{2 – 54}$$

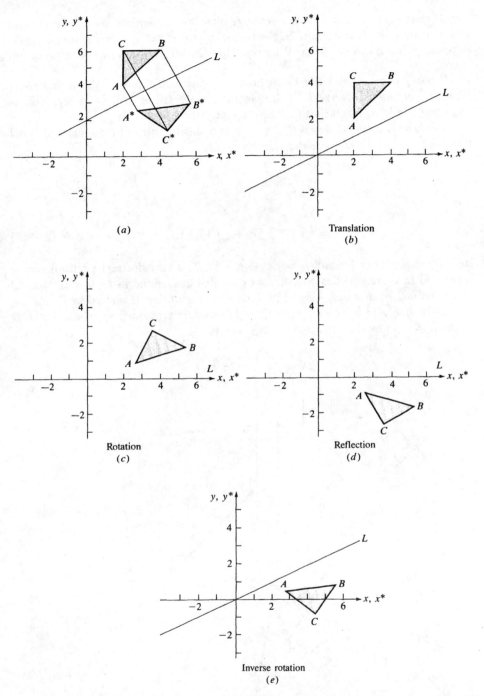

**Figure 2–13**  Reflection through an arbitrary line. (a) Original and final position; (b) translate line through origin; (c) rotate line to $x$-axis; (d) reflect about $x$-axis; (e) undo rotation; (a) undo translation.

Recall that $a, b, c$ and $d$ produce scaling, rotation, reflection and shearing; and $m$ and $n$ produce translation. In the previous two sections $p = q = 0$ and $s = 1$. Suppose $p$ and $q$ are not zero. What are the effects? A geometric interpretation is useful.

When $p = q = 0$ and $s = 1$, the homogeneous coordinate of the transformed position vectors is always $h = 1$. Geometrically this result is interpreted as confining the transformation to the $h = 1$ physical plane.

To show the effect of $p \neq 0$, $q \neq 0$ in the third column in the general $3 \times 3$ transformation matrix, consider the following:

$$[X \quad Y \quad h] = [hx \quad hy \quad h] = [x \quad y \quad 1]\begin{bmatrix} 1 & 0 & p \\ 0 & 1 & q \\ 0 & 0 & 1 \end{bmatrix}$$

$$= [x \quad y \quad (px + qy + 1)] \tag{2-55}$$

Here $X = hx$, $Y = hy$ and $h = px + qy + 1$. The transformed position vector expressed in homogeneous coordinates now lies in a plane in three-dimensional space defined by $h = px + qy + 1$. This transformation is shown in Fig. 2–14, where the line $AB$ in the physical ($h = 1$) plane is transformed to the line $CD$ in the $h \neq 1$ plane, i.e., $pX + qY - h + 1 = 0$.

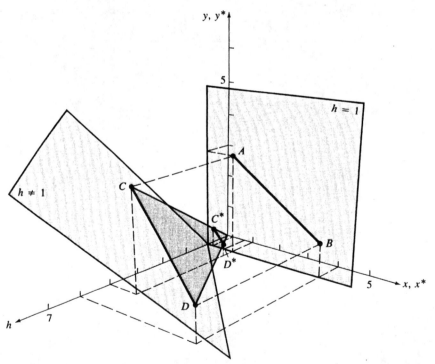

**Figure 2–14** Transformation from the physical ($h = 1$) plane into the $h \neq 1$ plane and projection from the $h \neq 1$ plane back into the physical plane.

However, the results of interest are those in the physical plane corresponding to $h = 1$. These results can be obtained by geometrically projecting $CD$ from the $h \neq 1$ plane back onto the $h = 1$ plane using a pencil of rays through the origin. From Fig. 2–14, using similar triangles,

$$x^* = \frac{X}{h} \qquad y^* = \frac{Y}{h}$$

or in homogeneous coordinates

$$[\, x^* \quad y^* \quad 1\,] = \left[\frac{X}{h} \quad \frac{Y}{h} \quad 1\right]$$

Now, normalizing Eq. (2–55) by dividing through by the homogeneous coordinate value $h$ yields

$$[\, x^* \quad y^* \quad 1\,] = \left[\frac{X}{h} \quad \frac{Y}{h} \quad 1\right] = \left[\frac{x}{px + qy + 1} \quad \frac{y}{px + qy + 1} \quad 1\right] \qquad (2-56)$$

or

$$x^* = \frac{X}{h} = \frac{x}{px + qy + 1} \qquad\qquad (2-57a)$$

$$y^* = \frac{Y}{h} = \frac{y}{px + qy + 1} \qquad\qquad (2-57b)$$

The details are given in the example below.

---

## Example 2–8   Projection in Homogeneous Coordinates

For the line $AB$ in Fig. 2–14 we have, with $p = q = 1$, $[\, A\,] = [\,1 \quad 3 \quad 1\,]$ and $[\, B\,] = [\,4 \quad 1 \quad 1\,]$,

$$\begin{bmatrix} C \\ D \end{bmatrix} = \begin{bmatrix} A \\ B \end{bmatrix}[T] = \begin{bmatrix} 1 & 3 & 1 \\ 4 & 1 & 1 \end{bmatrix}\begin{bmatrix} 1 & 0 & 1 \\ 0 & 1 & 1 \\ 0 & 0 & 1 \end{bmatrix} = \begin{bmatrix} 1 & 3 & 5 \\ 4 & 1 & 6 \end{bmatrix}$$

Thus, $[\, C\,] = [\,1 \quad 3 \quad 5\,]$ and $[\, D\,] = [\,4 \quad 1 \quad 6\,]$ in the plane $h = x + y + 1$. Projecting back onto the $h = 1$ physical plane by dividing through by the homogeneous coordinate factor yields the two-dimensional transformed points

$$[\, C^*\,] = [\,1 \quad 3 \quad 5\,] = [\,1/5 \quad 3/5 \quad 1\,]$$
$$[\, D^*\,] = [\,4 \quad 1 \quad 6\,] = [\,2/3 \quad 1/6 \quad 1\,]$$

The result is shown in Fig. 2–14.

## 2–19  OVERALL SCALING

The remaining unexplained element in the general $3 \times 3$ transformation matrix (see Eq. 2–54), $s$, produces overall scaling; i.e., all components of the position vector are equally scaled. To show this, consider the transformation

$$[X \quad Y \quad h] = [x \quad y \quad 1] \begin{bmatrix} 1 & 0 & 0 \\ 0 & 1 & 0 \\ 0 & 0 & s \end{bmatrix} = [x \quad y \quad s] \qquad (2-58)$$

Here, $X = x$, $Y = y$ and $h = s$. After normalizing, this yields

$$X^* = \frac{x}{s} \qquad \text{and} \qquad Y^* = \frac{y}{s}$$

Thus, the transformation is $[x \quad y \quad 1][T] = [\frac{x}{s} \quad \frac{y}{s} \quad 1]$, a uniform scaling of the position vector. If $s < 1$, then an expansion occurs; and if $s > 1$, a compression occurs.

Note that this is also a transformation out of the $h = 1$ plane. Here, $h = s =$ constant. Hence, the $h \neq 1$ plane is parallel to the $h = 1$ plane. A geometric interpretation of this effect is shown in Fig. 2–15. If $s < 1$, then the $h =$ constant plane lies between the $h = 1$ and $h = 0$ planes. Consequently, when the transformed line $AB$ is projected back onto the $h = 1$ plane to $A^*B^*$, it becomes larger. Similarly, if $s > 1$, then the $h =$ constant plane lies beyond the $h = 1$ plane along the $h$-axis. When the transformed line $CD$ is projected back onto the $h = 1$ plane to $C^*D^*$, it becomes smaller.

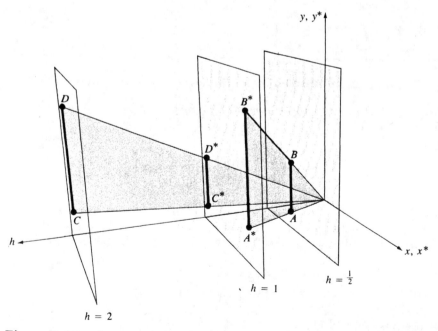

**Figure 2–15**  A geometric interpretation of overall scaling.

## 2–20    POINTS AT INFINITY

Homogeneous coordinates provide a convenient and efficient technique for mapping a set of points from one coordinate system into a corresponding set in an alternate coordinate system. Frequently, an infinite range in one coordinate system is mapped into a finite range in an alternate coordinate system. Unless the mappings are carefully chosen, parallel lines may not map into parallel lines. However, intersection points map into intersection points. This property is used to determine the homogeneous coordinate representation of a point at infinity.

We begin by considering the pair of intersecting lines given by

$$x + y = 1$$
$$2x - 3y = 0$$

which have an intersection point at $x = 3/5$, $y = 2/5$. Writing the equations as $x + y - 1 = 0$ and $2x - 3y = 0$ and casting them in matrix form yields

$$[ x \quad y \quad 1 ] \begin{bmatrix} 1 & 2 \\ 1 & -3 \\ -1 & 0 \end{bmatrix} = [ 0 \quad 0 ]$$

or

$$[ X ][ M' ] = [ R ]$$

If $[ M' ]$ were square, the intersection could be obtained by matrix inversion. This can be accomplished by slightly rewriting the system of original equations. Specifically,

$$x + y - 1 = 0$$
$$2x - 3y = 0$$
$$1 = 1$$

In matrix form this is

$$[ X ][ M ] = [ R ]$$

i.e.,

$$[ x \quad y \quad 1 ] \begin{bmatrix} 1 & 2 & 0 \\ 1 & -3 & 0 \\ -1 & 0 & 1 \end{bmatrix} = [ 0 \quad 0 \quad 1 ]$$

The inverse of this square matrix is [†]

$$[ M ]^{-1} = \begin{bmatrix} 3/5 & 2/5 & 0 \\ 1/5 & -1/5 & 0 \\ 3/5 & 2/5 & 1 \end{bmatrix} = \frac{1}{5} \begin{bmatrix} 3 & 2 & 0 \\ 1 & -1 & 0 \\ 3 & 2 & 5 \end{bmatrix}$$

---

[†]Matrix inversion techniques are discussed in Ref. 2–1 or any good linear algebra book.

Multiplying both sides of the equation by $[\,M\,]^{-1}$ and noting that $[\,M\,][\,M\,]^{-1}$ $= [\,I\,]$, the identity matrix, yields

$$[x \quad y \quad 1] = \frac{1}{5}[0 \quad 0 \quad 1]\begin{bmatrix} 3 & 2 & 0 \\ 1 & -1 & 0 \\ 3 & 2 & 5 \end{bmatrix} = [3/5 \quad 2/5 \quad 1]$$

Thus, the intersection point is again $x = 3/5$ and $y = 2/5$.

Now consider two parallel lines defined by

$$x + y = 1$$
$$x + y = 0$$

By definition, in Euclidean (common) geometric space, the intersection point of this pair of parallel lines occurs at infinity. Proceeding, as above, to calculate the intersection point of these lines leads to the matrix formulation

$$[x \quad y \quad 1]\begin{bmatrix} 1 & 1 & 0 \\ 1 & 1 & 0 \\ -1 & 0 & 1 \end{bmatrix} = [0 \quad 0 \quad 1]$$

However, even though the matrix is square it does not have an inverse, since two rows are identical. The matrix is said to be singular. Another alternate formulation is possible which does have an invertible matrix. This is obtained by rewriting the system of equations as

$$x + y - 1 = 0$$
$$x + y = 0$$
$$x = x$$

In matrix form this is

$$[x \quad y \quad 1]\begin{bmatrix} 1 & 1 & 1 \\ 1 & 1 & 0 \\ -1 & 0 & 0 \end{bmatrix} = [0 \quad 0 \quad x]$$

Here, the matrix is not singular; the inverse exists and is

$$[\,M\,]^{-1} = \begin{bmatrix} 0 & 0 & -1 \\ 0 & 1 & 1 \\ 1 & -1 & 0 \end{bmatrix}$$

Multiplying both sides of the equation by the inverse yields

$$[x \quad y \quad 1] = [0 \quad 0 \quad x]\begin{bmatrix} 0 & 1 & -1 \\ 0 & 1 & 1 \\ 1 & -1 & 0 \end{bmatrix} = [x \quad -x \quad 0] = x[1 \quad -1 \quad 0]$$

The resulting homogeneous coordinates $[\,1 \quad -1 \quad 0\,]$ represent the 'point of intersection' for the two parallel lines, i.e., a point at infinity. Specifically it represents the point at infinity in the direction $[\,1 \quad -1\,]$ in the two-dimensional plane. In general, the two-dimensional homogeneous vector $[\,a \quad b \quad 0\,]$ represents the point at infinity on the line $ay - bx = 0$. Some examples are:

$[\,1 \quad 0 \quad 0\,]$     on the positive $x$-axis
$[\,-1 \quad 0 \quad 0\,]$   on the negative $x$-axis
$[\,0 \quad 1 \quad 0\,]$     on the positive $y$-axis
$[\,0 \quad -1 \quad 0\,]$   on the negative $y$-axis
$[\,1 \quad 1 \quad 0\,]$     along the line $y = x$ in the direction $[\,1 \quad 1\,]$

The fact that a vector with the homogeneous component $h = 0$ does indeed represent a point at infinity can also be illustrated by the limiting process shown in Table 2-1. Consider the line $y^* = (3/4)x^*$ and the point $[\,X \quad Y \quad h\,] = [\,4 \quad 3 \quad 1\,]$. Recalling that a unique representation of a position vector does not exist in homogeneous coordinates, the point $[\,4 \quad 3 \quad 1\,]$ is represented in homogeneous coordinates in all the ways shown in Table 2-1. Note that in Table 2-1 as $h \rightarrow 0$, the ratio of $y^*/x^*$ remains at $3/4$, as is required by the governing equation. Further, note that successive pairs of $(x^*,y^*)$ all of which fall on the line $y^* = (3/4)x^*$, become closer to infinity. Thus, in the limit as $h \rightarrow 0$, the point at infinity is given by $[\,X \quad Y \quad h\,] = [\,4 \quad 3 \quad 0\,]$ in homogeneous coordinates.

By recalling Fig. 2-15, a geometrical interpretation of the limiting process as $h \rightarrow 0$ is also easily illustrated. Consider a line of unit length from $x = 0$, $y = 0$ in the direction $[\,1 \quad 0\,]$, in the plane $h = s$ ($s < 1$). As $s \rightarrow 0$ the projection of this line back onto the $h = 1$ physical plane by a pencil of rays through the origin becomes of infinite length. Consequently, the end point of the line must represent the point at infinity on the $x$-axis.

### Table 2-1 Homogeneous Coordinates for the Point $[\,4 \quad 3\,]$

| $h$ | $x^*$ | $y^*$ | $X$ | $Y$ |
|-----|-------|-------|-----|-----|
| 1 | 4 | 3 | 4 | 3 |
| 1/2 | 8 | 6 | 4 | 3 |
| 1/3 | 12 | 9 | 4 | 3 |
| . | | | | |
| . | | | | |
| . | | | | |
| 1/10 | 40 | 30 | 4 | 3 |
| . | | | | |
| . | | | | |
| 1/100 | 400 | 300 | 4 | 3 |
| . | | | | |
| . | | | | |

## 2–21 TRANSFORMATION CONVENTIONS

Various conventions are used to represent data and to perform transformations with matrix multiplication. Extreme care is necessary in defining the problem and interpreting the results. For example, before performing a rotation the following decisions must be made:

Are the position vectors (vertices) to be rotated defined relative to a right-hand coordinate or a left-hand coordinate system?

Is the object or the coordinate system being rotated?

How are positive and negative rotations defined?

Are the position vectors stored as a row matrix or as a column matrix?

About what line, or axis, is rotation to occur?

In this text a right-hand coordinate system is used, the object is rotated in a fixed coordinate system, positive rotation is defined using the right-hand rule, i.e., clockwise about an axis as seen by an observer at the origin looking outward along the positive axis, and position vectors are represented as row matrices.

Equation (2–29) gives the transformation for positive rotation about the origin or about the $z$-axis. Since position vectors are represented as row matrices, the transformation matrix appears *after* the data or position vector matrix. This is a post-multiplication transformation. Using homogeneous coordinates for positive rotation by an angle $\theta$ of an object about the origin ($z$-axis) using a post-multiplication transformation gives

$$[X^*] = [X][R]$$

$$[x^* \quad y^* \quad 1] = [x \quad y \quad 1] \begin{bmatrix} \cos\theta & \sin\theta & 0 \\ -\sin\theta & \cos\theta & 0 \\ 0 & 0 & 1 \end{bmatrix} \qquad (2-59)$$

If we choose to represent the position vectors in homogeneous coordinates as a column matrix, then the same rotation is performed using

$$[X^*] = [R]^{-1}[X]$$

$$\begin{bmatrix} x^* \\ y^* \\ 1 \end{bmatrix} = \begin{bmatrix} \cos\theta & -\sin\theta & 0 \\ \sin\theta & \cos\theta & 0 \\ 0 & 0 & 1 \end{bmatrix} \begin{bmatrix} x \\ y \\ 1 \end{bmatrix} \qquad (2-60)$$

Equation (2–60) is called a premultiplication transformation because the transformation matrix appears *before* the column position vector or data matrix. Notice that the $3 \times 3$ matrix in Eq. (2–60) is also the transpose of the $3 \times 3$ matrix in Eq. (2–59). That is, the rows and columns have been interchanged.

To rotate the coordinate system and keep the position vectors fixed, simply replace $\theta$ with $-\theta$ in Eq. (2–59). Recall that $\sin\theta = -\sin(-\theta)$ and $\cos\theta = \cos(-\theta)$. Equation (2–59) is then

$$[\, x^* \quad y^* \quad 1\,] = [\, x \quad y \quad 1\,]\begin{bmatrix} \cos\theta & -\sin\theta & 0 \\ \sin\theta & \cos\theta & 0 \\ 0 & 0 & 1 \end{bmatrix} \qquad (2-61)$$

Notice that the $3 \times 3$ matrix is again the inverse and also the transpose of that in Eq. (2–59).

If the coordinate system is rotated *and* a left-hand coordinate system used, then the replacement of $\theta$ with $-\theta$ is made *twice* and Eq. (2–59) is again valid, assuming a post-multiplication transformation is used on a row data matrix.

Note that, as shown in Fig. 2–16, a counterclockwise rotation of the vertices which represent an object is identical to a clockwise rotation of the coordinate axes for a fixed object. Again, no change occurs in the $3 \times 3$ transformation

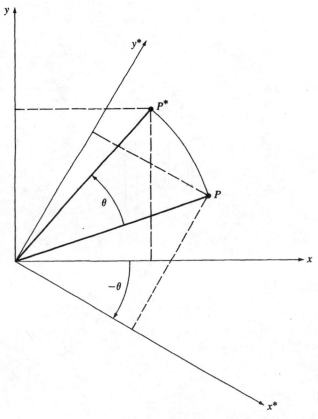

**Figure 2–16**   Equivalence of position vector and coordinate system rotation.

matrix *if* no other options are modified. These few examples show how careful we must be when performing matrix transformations.

## 2-22 REFERENCES

2-1 Fox, L., *An Introduction to Numerical Linear Algebra*, Oxford University Press, London, 1964.

2-2 Forrest, A. R., "Co-ordinates, Transformations, and Visualization Techniques," CAD Group Document No. 23, Cambridge University, June 1969.

## THREE-DIMENSIONAL TRANSFORMATIONS AND PROJECTIONS

### 3–1 INTRODUCTION

The ability to represent or display a three-dimensional object is fundamental to the understanding of the shape of that object. Furthermore, the ability to rotate, translate, and project views of that object is also, in many cases, fundamental to the understanding of its shape. This is easily demonstrated by picking up a relatively complex unfamiliar object. Immediately it is rotated, held at arm's length, moved up and down, back and forth, etc., in order to obtain an understanding of its shape. To do this with a computer we must extend our previous two-dimensional analysis to three dimensions. Based on our previous experience, we immediately introduce homogeneous coordinates. Hence, a point in three-dimensional space $[\,x \quad y \quad z\,]$ is represented by a four-dimensional position vector

$$[\,x' \quad y' \quad z' \quad h\,] = [\,x \quad y \quad z \quad 1\,][\,T\,]$$

where $[\,T\,]$ is some transformation matrix. Again, the transformation from homogeneous coordinates to ordinary coordinates is given by

$$[\,x^* \quad y^* \quad z^* \quad 1\,] = \left[\,\frac{x'}{h} \quad \frac{y'}{h} \quad \frac{z'}{h} \quad 1\,\right] \qquad (3-1)$$

The generalized $4 \times 4$ transformation matrix for three-dimensional homogeneous coordinates is

$$[\,T\,] = \begin{bmatrix} a & b & c & p \\ d & e & f & q \\ g & i & j & r \\ l & m & n & s \end{bmatrix} \qquad (3-2)$$

**101**

The $4 \times 4$ transformation matrix in Eq. (3–2) can be partitioned into four separate sections:

$$
\begin{bmatrix}
 & & & \vdots & 3 \\
 & 3 \times 3 & & \vdots & \times \\
 & & & \vdots & 1 \\
\cdots & \cdots & \cdots & \vdots & \cdots \\
 & 1 \times 3 & & \vdots & 1 \times 1
\end{bmatrix}
$$

The upper left $3 \times 3$ submatrix produces a linear transformation[†] in the form of scaling, shearing, reflection and rotation. The $1 \times 3$ lower left submatrix produces translation, and the upper right $3 \times 1$ submatrix produces a perspective transformation. The final lower right-hand $1 \times 1$ submatrix produces overall scaling. The total transformation obtained after operating on a homogeneous position vector with this $4 \times 4$ matrix and obtaining the ordinary coordinate is called a bilinear transformation.[‡] In general, this transformation yields a combination of shearing, local scaling, rotation, reflection, translation, perspective and overall scaling.

## 3–2 THREE-DIMENSIONAL SCALING

The diagonal terms of the general $4 \times 4$ transformation produce local and overall scaling. To illustrate this, consider the transformation

$$
[X][T] = [x \quad y \quad z \quad 1]
\begin{bmatrix}
a & 0 & 0 & 0 \\
0 & e & 0 & 0 \\
0 & 0 & j & 0 \\
0 & 0 & 0 & 1
\end{bmatrix}
$$

$$
= [ax \quad ey \quad jz \quad 1] = [x^* \quad y^* \quad z^* \quad 1] \qquad (3-3)
$$

which shows the local scaling effect. An example follows.

---

### Example 3–1    Local Scaling

Consider the rectangular parallelepiped ($RPP$) shown in Fig. 3–1a with homogeneous position vectors:

$$
[X] =
\begin{bmatrix}
0 & 0 & 1 & 1 \\
2 & 0 & 1 & 1 \\
2 & 3 & 1 & 1 \\
0 & 3 & 1 & 1 \\
0 & 0 & 0 & 1 \\
2 & 0 & 0 & 1 \\
2 & 3 & 0 & 1 \\
0 & 3 & 0 & 1
\end{bmatrix}
$$

---

[†]A linear transformation is one which transforms an initial linear combination of vectors into the same linear combination of transformed vectors.

[‡]A bilinear transformation results from two sequential linear transformations.

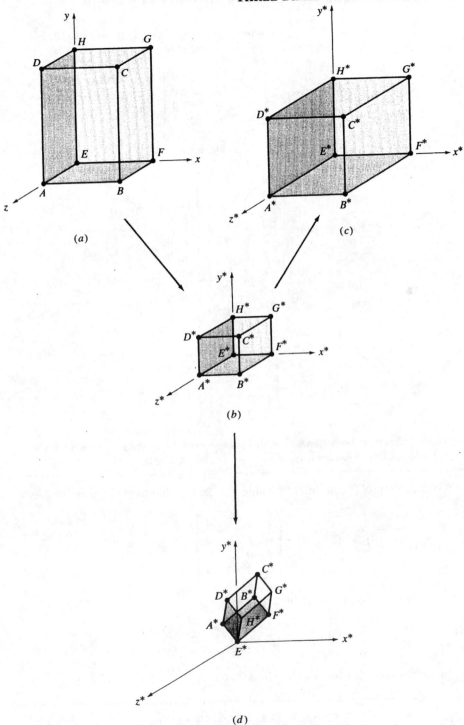

**Figure 3–1**   Three-dimensional scale transformations.

Locally scaling the $RPP$ to yield a unit cube requires scale factors of $1/2$, $1/3$, 1 along the $x, y, z$ axes, respectively. The local scaling transformation is

$$[T] = \begin{bmatrix} 1/2 & 0 & 0 & 0 \\ 0 & 1/3 & 0 & 0 \\ 0 & 0 & 1 & 0 \\ 0 & 0 & 0 & 1 \end{bmatrix}$$

The resulting cube has homogeneous position vectors

$$[X^*] = [X][T] = \begin{bmatrix} 0 & 0 & 1 & 1 \\ 2 & 0 & 1 & 1 \\ 2 & 3 & 1 & 1 \\ 0 & 3 & 1 & 1 \\ 0 & 0 & 0 & 1 \\ 2 & 0 & 0 & 1 \\ 2 & 3 & 0 & 1 \\ 0 & 3 & 0 & 1 \end{bmatrix} \begin{bmatrix} 1/2 & 0 & 0 & 0 \\ 0 & 1/3 & 0 & 0 \\ 0 & 0 & 1 & 0 \\ 0 & 0 & 0 & 1 \end{bmatrix}$$

$$= \begin{bmatrix} 0 & 0 & 1 & 1 \\ 1 & 0 & 1 & 1 \\ 1 & 1 & 1 & 1 \\ 0 & 1 & 1 & 1 \\ 0 & 0 & 0 & 1 \\ 1 & 0 & 0 & 1 \\ 1 & 1 & 0 & 1 \\ 0 & 1 & 0 & 1 \end{bmatrix}$$

Notice that the homogeneous coordinate factor $h$ is unity for each of the transformed position vectors. The result is shown in Fig. 3–1b.

---

Overall scaling is obtained by using the fourth diagonal element, i.e.,

$$[X][T] = \begin{bmatrix} x & y & z & 1 \end{bmatrix} \begin{bmatrix} 1 & 0 & 0 & 0 \\ 0 & 1 & 0 & 0 \\ 0 & 0 & 1 & 0 \\ 0 & 0 & 0 & s \end{bmatrix} = \begin{bmatrix} x' & y' & z' & s \end{bmatrix} \qquad (3-4)$$

The ordinary or physical coordinates are

$$\begin{bmatrix} x^* & y^* & z^* & 1 \end{bmatrix} = \begin{bmatrix} \dfrac{x'}{s} & \dfrac{y'}{s} & \dfrac{z'}{s} & 1 \end{bmatrix}$$

Again, an example illustrates the effect.

---

### Example 3–2    Overall Scaling

Uniformly scaling the unit cube shown in Fig. 3–1b by a factor of two (doubling the size) requires the transformation (see Eq. 3–4)

$$[T] = \begin{bmatrix} 1 & 0 & 0 & 0 \\ 0 & 1 & 0 & 0 \\ 0 & 0 & 1 & 0 \\ 0 & 0 & 0 & 1/2 \end{bmatrix}$$

The resulting $RPP$ has homogeneous position vectors given by

$$[X'] = [X^*][T] = \begin{bmatrix} 0 & 0 & 1 & 1 \\ 1 & 0 & 1 & 1 \\ 1 & 1 & 1 & 1 \\ 0 & 1 & 1 & 1 \\ 0 & 0 & 0 & 1 \\ 1 & 0 & 0 & 1 \\ 1 & 1 & 0 & 1 \\ 0 & 1 & 0 & 1 \end{bmatrix} \begin{bmatrix} 1 & 0 & 0 & 0 \\ 0 & 1 & 0 & 0 \\ 0 & 0 & 1 & 0 \\ 0 & 0 & 0 & 1/2 \end{bmatrix}$$

$$= \begin{bmatrix} 0 & 0 & 1 & 0.5 \\ 1 & 0 & 1 & 0.5 \\ 1 & 1 & 1 & 0.5 \\ 0 & 1 & 1 & 0.5 \\ 0 & 0 & 0 & 0.5 \\ 1 & 0 & 0 & 0.5 \\ 1 & 1 & 0 & 0.5 \\ 0 & 1 & 0 & 0.5 \end{bmatrix}$$

Notice that the homogeneous coordinate factor for each of the transformed position vectors is $h = 0.5$. Thus, to obtain the ordinary or physical coordinates each position vector must be divided by $h$. The result, shown in Fig. 3–1c, is

$$[X^*] = \begin{bmatrix} 0 & 0 & 2 & 1 \\ 2 & 0 & 2 & 1 \\ 2 & 2 & 2 & 1 \\ 0 & 2 & 2 & 1 \\ 0 & 0 & 0 & 1 \\ 2 & 0 & 0 & 1 \\ 2 & 2 & 0 & 1 \\ 0 & 2 & 0 & 1 \end{bmatrix}$$

Notice here, as in the two-dimensional overall scaling transformation, that the homogeneous coordinate factor is not unity. By analogy with the previous discussion (see Sec. 2–18) this represents transformation out of the physical $h = 1$ volume into another volume in 4-space. The transformed physical coordinates are obtained by projecting back into the physical $h = 1$ volume through the center of the 4-space coordinate system. Again, if $s < 1$, a uniform expansion of the position vectors occurs. If $s > 1$, a uniform compression of the position vectors occurs.

The same effect can be obtained by means of equal local scalings. In this case the transformation matrix is

$$[\,T\,] = \begin{bmatrix} 1/s & 0 & 0 & 0 \\ 0 & 1/s & 0 & 0 \\ 0 & 0 & 1/s & 0 \\ 0 & 0 & 0 & 1 \end{bmatrix}$$

Notice that here the homogeneous coordinate factor is unity, i.e., $h = 1$. Thus, the entire transformation takes place in the $h = 1$ physical volume.

## 3–3  THREE-DIMENSIONAL SHEARING

The off-diagonal terms in the upper left $3 \times 3$ submatrix of the generalized $4 \times 4$ transformation matrix produce shear in three dimensions, i.e.,

$$[\,X\,][\,T\,] = [\,x \quad y \quad z \quad 1\,] \begin{bmatrix} 1 & b & c & 0 \\ d & 1 & f & 0 \\ g & i & 1 & 0 \\ 0 & 0 & 0 & 1 \end{bmatrix}$$

$$= [\,x + yd + gz \quad bx + y + iz \quad cx + fy + z \quad 1\,] \qquad (3-5)$$

An example clarifies these results.

---

### Example 3–3  Shearing

Again consider the unit cube shown in Fig. 3–1b. Applying the shearing transformation

$$[\,T\,] = \begin{bmatrix} 1 & -0.85 & 0.25 & 0 \\ -0.75 & 1 & 0.7 & 0 \\ 0.5 & 1 & 1 & 0 \\ 0 & 0 & 0 & 1 \end{bmatrix}$$

yields

$$[\,X^*\,] = [\,X\,][\,T\,] = \begin{bmatrix} 0 & 0 & 1 & 1 \\ 1 & 0 & 1 & 1 \\ 1 & 1 & 1 & 1 \\ 0 & 1 & 1 & 1 \\ 0 & 0 & 0 & 1 \\ 1 & 0 & 0 & 1 \\ 1 & 1 & 0 & 1 \\ 0 & 1 & 0 & 1 \end{bmatrix} \begin{bmatrix} 1 & -0.85 & 0.25 & 0 \\ -0.75 & 1 & 0.7 & 0 \\ 0.5 & 1 & 1 & 0 \\ 0 & 0 & 0 & 1 \end{bmatrix}$$

$$= \begin{bmatrix} 0.5 & 1 & 1 & 1 \\ 1.5 & 0.15 & 1.25 & 1 \\ 0.75 & 1.15 & 1.95 & 1 \\ -0.25 & 2 & 1.7 & 1 \\ 0 & 0 & 0 & 1 \\ 1 & -0.85 & 0.25 & 1 \\ 0.25 & 0.15 & 0.95 & 1 \\ -0.75 & 1 & 0.7 & 1 \end{bmatrix}$$

The result is shown in Fig. 3–1d. Notice that in all three examples the origin is unaffected by the transformation.

---

## 3–4    THREE-DIMENSIONAL ROTATION

Before considering three-dimensional rotation about an arbitrary axis, we examine rotation about each of the coordinate axes. For rotation about the $x$-axis, the $x$ coordinates of the position vectors do not change. In effect, the rotation occurs in planes perpendicular to the $x$-axis. Similarly, rotation about the $y$- and $z$-axes occurs in planes perpendicular to the $y$- and $z$-axes, respectively. The transformation of the position vectors in each of these planes is governed by the general two-dimensional rotation matrix given in Eq. (2–29). Recalling that matrix, and again noting that for rotation about the $x$-axis the $x$ coordinate of the transformed position vectors does not change, allows writing down the $4 \times 4$ homogeneous coordinate transformation by the angle $\theta$ as

$$[T] = \begin{bmatrix} 1 & 0 & 0 & 0 \\ 0 & \cos\theta & \sin\theta & 0 \\ 0 & -\sin\theta & \cos\theta & 0 \\ 0 & 0 & 0 & 1 \end{bmatrix} \qquad (3-6)$$

Rotation is assumed positive in a right-hand sense, i.e., clockwise as one looks outward from the origin in the positive direction along the rotation axis.[†] The block shown in Fig. 3–2b is the result of a $-90°$ rotation about the $x$-axis of the block shown in Fig. 3–2a.

In a similar manner, the transformation matrix for rotation by an angle $\psi$ about the $z$-axis is

$$[T] = \begin{bmatrix} \cos\psi & \sin\psi & 0 & 0 \\ -\sin\psi & \cos\psi & 0 & 0 \\ 0 & 0 & 1 & 0 \\ 0 & 0 & 0 & 1 \end{bmatrix} \qquad (3-7)$$

For rotation by an angle $\phi$ about the $y$-axis, the transformation is

$$[T] = \begin{bmatrix} \cos\phi & 0 & -\sin\phi & 0 \\ 0 & 1 & 0 & 0 \\ \sin\phi & 0 & \cos\phi & 0 \\ 0 & 0 & 0 & 1 \end{bmatrix} \qquad (3-8)$$

Note that in Eq. 3–8 the signs of the sine terms are reversed from those of Eqs. (3–6) and (3–7). This is required to maintain the positive right-hand rule convention.

Examining Eqs. (3–6) to (3–8) shows that the determinant of each transformation matrix is $+1$ as required for pure rotation. An example more fully illustrates these results.

---

[†] The right-hand rule for rotation is stated as follows: align the thumb of the right hand with the positive direction of the rotation axis. The natural curl of the fingers gives the positive rotation direction.

### Example 3–4    Rotation

Consider the rectangular parallelepiped shown in Fig. 3–2a. The matrix of position vectors $[\,X\,]$ is

$$[\,X\,] = \begin{bmatrix} 0 & 0 & 1 & 1 \\ 3 & 0 & 1 & 1 \\ 3 & 2 & 1 & 1 \\ 0 & 2 & 1 & 1 \\ 0 & 0 & 0 & 1 \\ 3 & 0 & 0 & 1 \\ 3 & 2 & 0 & 1 \\ 0 & 2 & 0 & 1 \end{bmatrix} \begin{matrix} \\ \\ A \\ \\ \\ \\ \\ \end{matrix}$$

Here, the row labeled $A$ in the position matrix $[\,X\,]$ corresponds to the point $A$ in Fig. 3–2. For rotation by $\theta = -90°$ about the $x$-axis Eq. (3–6) yields

$$[\,T\,] = \begin{bmatrix} 1 & 0 & 0 & 0 \\ 0 & 0 & -1 & 0 \\ 0 & 1 & 0 & 0 \\ 0 & 0 & 0 & 1 \end{bmatrix}$$

Applying the transformation gives the new position vectors

$$[\,X^*\,] = [\,X\,][\,T\,] = \begin{bmatrix} 0 & 0 & 1 & 1 \\ 3 & 0 & 1 & 1 \\ 3 & 2 & 1 & 1 \\ 0 & 2 & 1 & 1 \\ 0 & 0 & 0 & 1 \\ 3 & 0 & 0 & 1 \\ 3 & 2 & 0 & 1 \\ 0 & 2 & 0 & 1 \end{bmatrix} \begin{bmatrix} 1 & 0 & 0 & 0 \\ 0 & 0 & -1 & 0 \\ 0 & 1 & 0 & 0 \\ 0 & 0 & 0 & 1 \end{bmatrix}$$

$$= \begin{bmatrix} 0 & 1 & 0 & 1 \\ 3 & 1 & 0 & 1 \\ 3 & 1 & -2 & 1 \\ 0 & 1 & -2 & 1 \\ 0 & 0 & 0 & 1 \\ 3 & 0 & 0 & 1 \\ 3 & 0 & -2 & 1 \\ 0 & 0 & -2 & 1 \end{bmatrix} \begin{matrix} \\ \\ A^* \\ \\ \\ \\ \\ \end{matrix}$$

Notice that the $x$ components of $[\,X\,]$ and $[\,X^*\,]$ are identical as required. The result is shown in Fig. 3–2b.

For rotation by $\phi = 90°$ about the $y$-axis, Eq. (3–7) yields

$$[\,T'\,] = \begin{bmatrix} 0 & 0 & -1 & 0 \\ 0 & 1 & 0 & 0 \\ 1 & 0 & 0 & 0 \\ 0 & 0 & 0 & 1 \end{bmatrix}$$

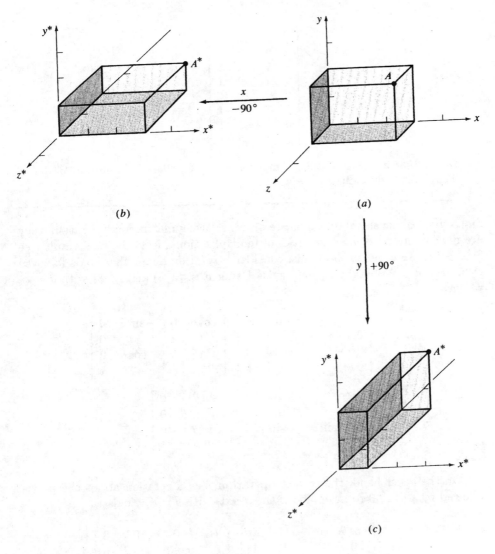

**Figure 3–2**    Three-dimensional rotations.

Again applying the transformation to the original block yields the new position vectors, i.e.,

$$[X^{*'}] = [X][T'] = \begin{bmatrix} 0 & 0 & 1 & 1 \\ 3 & 0 & 1 & 1 \\ 3 & 2 & 1 & 1 \\ 0 & 2 & 1 & 1 \\ 0 & 0 & 0 & 1 \\ 3 & 0 & 0 & 1 \\ 3 & 2 & 0 & 1 \\ 0 & 2 & 0 & 1 \end{bmatrix} \begin{bmatrix} 0 & 0 & -1 & 0 \\ 0 & 1 & 0 & 0 \\ 1 & 0 & 0 & 0 \\ 0 & 0 & 0 & 1 \end{bmatrix}$$

$$
= \begin{bmatrix}
1 & 0 & 0 & 1 \\
1 & 0 & -3 & 1 \\
1 & 2 & -3 & 1 \\
1 & 2 & 0 & 1 \\
0 & 0 & 0 & 1 \\
0 & 0 & -3 & 1 \\
0 & 2 & -3 & 1 \\
0 & 2 & 0 & 1
\end{bmatrix} A^*
$$

Notice that in this case the $y$ components of $[\,X\,]$ and $[\,X^{*\prime}\,]$ are identical. The result is shown in Fig. 3–2c.

---

Since three-dimensional rotations are obtained using matrix multiplication, they are noncommutative; i.e., the order of multiplication affects the final result (see Sec. 2–12). In order to show this, consider a rotation about the $x$-axis followed by an equal rotation about the $y$-axis. Using Eqs. (3–6) and (3–8) with $\theta = \phi$, we have

$$
[\,T\,] = \begin{bmatrix}
1 & 0 & 0 & 0 \\
0 & \cos\theta & \sin\theta & 0 \\
0 & -\sin\theta & \cos\theta & 0 \\
0 & 0 & 0 & 1
\end{bmatrix}
\begin{bmatrix}
\cos\theta & 0 & -\sin\theta & 0 \\
0 & 1 & 0 & 0 \\
\sin\theta & 0 & \cos\theta & 0 \\
0 & 0 & 0 & 1
\end{bmatrix}
$$

$$
= \begin{bmatrix}
\cos\theta & 0 & -\sin\theta & 0 \\
\sin^2\theta & \cos\theta & \cos\theta\sin\theta & 0 \\
\cos\theta\sin\theta & -\sin\theta & \cos^2\theta & 0 \\
0 & 0 & 0 & 1
\end{bmatrix} \tag{3–9}
$$

On the other hand, the reverse operation, i.e., a rotation about the $y$-axis followed by an equal rotation about the $x$-axis with $\theta = \phi$, yields

$$
[\,T\,] = \begin{bmatrix}
\cos\theta & 0 & -\sin\theta & 0 \\
0 & 1 & 0 & 0 \\
\sin\theta & 0 & \cos\theta & 0 \\
0 & 0 & 0 & 1
\end{bmatrix}
\begin{bmatrix}
1 & 0 & 0 & 0 \\
0 & \cos\theta & \sin\theta & 0 \\
0 & -\sin\theta & \cos\theta & 0 \\
0 & 0 & 0 & 1
\end{bmatrix}
$$

$$
= \begin{bmatrix}
\cos\theta & \sin^2\theta & -\cos\theta\sin\theta & 0 \\
0 & \cos\theta & \sin\theta & 0 \\
\sin\theta & -\cos\theta\sin\theta & \cos^2\theta & 0 \\
0 & 0 & 0 & 1
\end{bmatrix} \tag{3–10}
$$

Comparison of the right-hand sides of Eqs. (3–9) and (3–10) shows that they are not the same. The fact that three-dimensional rotations are noncommutative must be kept in mind when more than one rotation is to be made.

The result of transformation of the object in Fig. 3–3a consisting of two 90° rotations using the matrix product given in Eq. (3–9) is shown dashed in Figs. 3–3c and 3–3d. When the opposite order of rotation as specified by Eq. (3–10) is used, the solid figures shown in Figs. 3–3b and 3–3d graphically demonstrate that different results are obtained by changing the order of rotation. A numerical example further illustrates this concept.

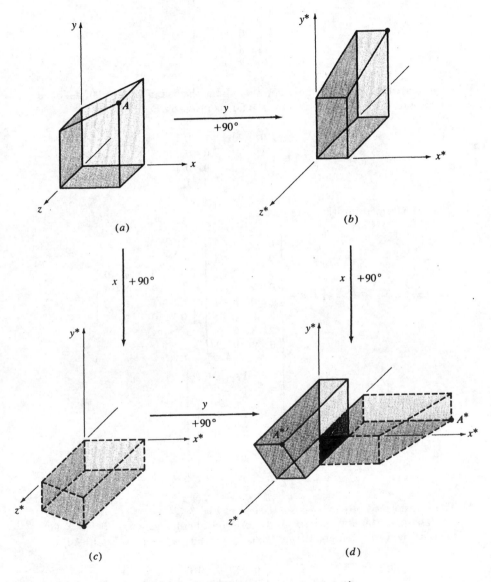

**Figure 3–3**   Three-dimensional rotations are noncommutative.

### Example 3–5    Combined Rotations

The object in Fig. 3–3a has position vectors

$$[X] = \begin{bmatrix} 0 & 0 & 1 & 1 \\ 2 & 0 & 1 & 1 \\ 2 & 3 & 1 & 1 \\ 0 & 2 & 1 & 1 \\ 0 & 0 & 0 & 1 \\ 2 & 0 & 0 & 1 \\ 2 & 3 & 0 & 1 \\ 0 & 2 & 0 & 1 \end{bmatrix} A$$

The concatenated matrix for a rotation about the $x$-axis by $\theta = 90°$ followed by a rotation about the $y$-axis by $\phi = 90°$ is given by Eq. (3–9) as

$$[T] = \begin{bmatrix} 0 & 0 & -1 & 0 \\ 1 & 0 & 0 & 0 \\ 0 & -1 & 0 & 0 \\ 0 & 0 & 0 & 1 \end{bmatrix}$$

The transformed position vectors are

$$[X^*] = [X][T] = \begin{bmatrix} 0 & 0 & 1 & 1 \\ 2 & 0 & 1 & 1 \\ 2 & 3 & 1 & 1 \\ 0 & 2 & 1 & 1 \\ 0 & 0 & 0 & 1 \\ 2 & 0 & 0 & 1 \\ 2 & 3 & 0 & 1 \\ 0 & 2 & 0 & 1 \end{bmatrix} \begin{bmatrix} 0 & 0 & -1 & 0 \\ 1 & 0 & 0 & 0 \\ 0 & -1 & 0 & 0 \\ 0 & 0 & 0 & 1 \end{bmatrix}$$

$$= \begin{bmatrix} 0 & -1 & 0 & 1 \\ 0 & -1 & -2 & 1 \\ 3 & -1 & -2 & 1 \\ 2 & -1 & 0 & 1 \\ 0 & 0 & 0 & 1 \\ 0 & 0 & -2 & 1 \\ 3 & 0 & -2 & 1 \\ 2 & 0 & 0 & 1 \end{bmatrix} A^*$$

The transformed object is shown dashed in Fig. 3–3d.

The concatenated matrix for a rotation about the y-axis by $\phi = 90°$ followed by a rotation about the $x$-axis by $\theta = 90°$ is given by Eq. (3–10) as

$$[T'] = \begin{bmatrix} 0 & 1 & 0 & 0 \\ 0 & 0 & 1 & 0 \\ 1 & 0 & 0 & 0 \\ 0 & 0 & 0 & 1 \end{bmatrix}$$

Here, the resulting transformed position vectors are

$$[X^{*\prime}] = [X][T^\prime] = \begin{bmatrix} 0 & 0 & 1 & 1 \\ 2 & 0 & 1 & 1 \\ 2 & 3 & 1 & 1 \\ 0 & 2 & 1 & 1 \\ 0 & 0 & 0 & 1 \\ 2 & 0 & 0 & 1 \\ 2 & 3 & 0 & 1 \\ 0 & 2 & 0 & 1 \end{bmatrix} \begin{bmatrix} 0 & 1 & 0 & 0 \\ 0 & 0 & 1 & 0 \\ 1 & 0 & 0 & 0 \\ 0 & 0 & 0 & 1 \end{bmatrix} = \begin{bmatrix} 1 & 0 & 0 & 1 \\ 1 & 2 & 0 & 1 \\ 1 & 2 & 3 & 1 \\ 1 & 0 & 2 & 1 \\ 0 & 0 & 0 & 1 \\ 0 & 2 & 0 & 1 \\ 0 & 2 & 3 & 1 \\ 0 & 0 & 2 & 1 \end{bmatrix} \begin{matrix} \\ \\ \\ A^{*\prime} \\ \\ \\ \\ \end{matrix}$$

The transformed object is shown by solid lines in Fig. 3–3d.

Comparing the two numerical results also clearly shows that the orientation of the transformed objects is considerably different. Hence, the order of matrix multiplication is important.

---

## 3–5   THREE DIMENSIONAL REFLECTION

Some orientations of a three-dimensional object cannot be obtained using pure rotations; they require reflections. In three dimensions, reflections occur through a plane. By analogy with the previous discussion of two-dimensional reflection (see Sec. 2–10), three-dimensional reflection through a plane is equivalent to rotation about an axis in three-dimensional space out into four-dimensional space and back into the original three-dimensional space. For a pure reflection the determinant of the reflection matrix is identically −1.

In a reflection through the $xy$ plane, only the $z$ coordinate values of the object's position vectors change. In fact, they are reversed in sign. Thus, the transformation matrix for a reflection through the $xy$ plane is

$$[T] = \begin{bmatrix} 1 & 0 & 0 & 0 \\ 0 & 1 & 0 & 0 \\ 0 & 0 & -1 & 0 \\ 0 & 0 & 0 & 1 \end{bmatrix} \tag{3 – 11}$$

The reflection of a unit cube through the $xy$ plane is shown in Fig. 3–4. For a reflection through the $yz$ plane,

$$[T] = \begin{bmatrix} -1 & 0 & 0 & 0 \\ 0 & 1 & 0 & 0 \\ 0 & 0 & 1 & 0 \\ 0 & 0 & 0 & 1 \end{bmatrix} \tag{3 – 12}$$

and for a reflection through the $xz$ plane,

$$[T] = \begin{bmatrix} 1 & 0 & 0 & 0 \\ 0 & -1 & 0 & 0 \\ 0 & 0 & 1 & 0 \\ 0 & 0 & 0 & 1 \end{bmatrix} \tag{3 – 13}$$

A numerical example further illustrates these results.

## Example 3–6　Reflection

The block $ABCDEFGH$ shown in Fig. 3–4 has position vectors

$$[X] = \begin{bmatrix} 1 & 0 & -1 & 1 \\ 2 & 0 & -1 & 1 \\ 2 & 1 & -1 & 1 \\ 1 & 1 & -1 & 1 \\ 1 & 0 & -2 & 1 \\ 2 & 0 & -2 & 1 \\ 2 & 1 & -2 & 1 \\ 1 & 1 & -2 & 1 \end{bmatrix}$$

The transformation matrix for reflection through the $xy$ plane is given by Eq. (3–11). After reflection the transformed position vectors are

$$[X^*] = [X][T] = \begin{bmatrix} 1 & 0 & -1 & 1 \\ 2 & 0 & -1 & 1 \\ 2 & 1 & -1 & 1 \\ 1 & 1 & -1 & 1 \\ 1 & 0 & -2 & 1 \\ 2 & 0 & -2 & 1 \\ 2 & 1 & -2 & 1 \\ 1 & 1 & -2 & 1 \end{bmatrix} \begin{bmatrix} 1 & 0 & 0 & 0 \\ 0 & 1 & 0 & 0 \\ 0 & 0 & -1 & 0 \\ 0 & 0 & 0 & 1 \end{bmatrix} = \begin{bmatrix} 1 & 0 & 1 & 1 \\ 2 & 0 & 1 & 1 \\ 2 & 1 & 1 & 1 \\ 1 & 1 & 1 & 1 \\ 1 & 0 & 2 & 1 \\ 2 & 0 & 2 & 1 \\ 2 & 1 & 2 & 1 \\ 1 & 1 & 2 & 1 \end{bmatrix}$$

The result $A^*B^*C^*D^*E^*F^*G^*H^*$ is shown in Fig. 3–4.

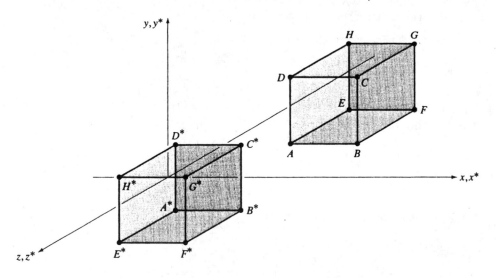

**Figure 3–4**　Three-dimensional reflection through the $xy$ plane.

## 3–6  THREE DIMENSIONAL TRANSLATION

The three-dimensional translation matrix is

$$[T] = \begin{bmatrix} 1 & 0 & 0 & 0 \\ 0 & 1 & 0 & 0 \\ 0 & 0 & 1 & 0 \\ l & m & n & 1 \end{bmatrix} \qquad (3-14)$$

The translated homogeneous coordinates are obtained by writing

$$[x' \quad y' \quad z' \quad h] = [x \quad y \quad z \quad 1] \begin{bmatrix} 1 & 0 & 0 & 0 \\ 0 & 1 & 0 & 0 \\ 0 & 0 & 1 & 0 \\ l & m & n & 1 \end{bmatrix}$$

When expanded this yields

$$[x' \quad y' \quad z' \quad h] = [(x+l) \quad (y+m) \quad (z+n) \quad 1] \qquad (3-15)$$

It follows that the transformed physical coordinates are

$$x^* = x + l$$
$$y^* = y + m$$
$$z^* = z + n$$

## 3–7  MULTIPLE TRANSFORMATIONS

Successive transformations can be combined or concatenated into a single $4 \times 4$ transformation that yields the same result. Since matrix multiplication is noncommutative, the order of application is important (in general $[A][B] \neq [B][A]$). The proper order is determined by the position of the individual transformation matrix relative to the position vector matrix. The matrix nearest the position vector matrix generates the first individual transformation, and the farthest, the last individual transformation. Mathematically this is expressed as

$$[X][T] = [X][T_1][T_2][T_3][T_4] \cdots$$

where

$$[T] = [T_1][T_2][T_3][T_4] \cdots$$

and the $[T_i]$ are any combination of scaling, shearing, rotation, reflection, translation, perspective and projective matrices. Since perspective transformations distort geometric objects (see Sec. 3–15) and projective transformations result in lost information (see Sec. 3–12), if these matrices are included, they must occur next to last and last in the order, respectively.

The example below explicitly illustrates this concept.

### Example 3–7    Multiple Transformations

Consider the effect of a translation in the $x, y, z$ directions by $-1$, $-1$, $-1$, respectively, followed successively by a $+30°$ rotation about the $x$-axis, and a $+45°$ rotation about the $y$-axis on the homogeneous coordinate position vector $[3\ \ 2\ \ 1\ \ 1]$.

First derive the concatenated transformation matrix. Using Eqs. (3–14), (3–6) and (3–8) yields

$$[T] = [Tr][R_x][R_y]$$

$$= \begin{bmatrix} 1 & 0 & 0 & 0 \\ 0 & 1 & 0 & 0 \\ 0 & 0 & 1 & 0 \\ l & m & n & 1 \end{bmatrix} \begin{bmatrix} 1 & 0 & 0 & 0 \\ 0 & \cos\theta & \sin\theta & 0 \\ 0 & -\sin\theta & \cos\theta & 0 \\ 0 & 0 & 0 & 1 \end{bmatrix} \begin{bmatrix} \cos\phi & 0 & -\sin\phi & 0 \\ 0 & 1 & 0 & 0 \\ \sin\phi & 0 & \cos\phi & 0 \\ 0 & 0 & 0 & 1 \end{bmatrix}$$

$$= \begin{bmatrix} 1 & 0 & 0 & 0 \\ 0 & 1 & 0 & 0 \\ 0 & 0 & 1 & 0 \\ l & m & n & 1 \end{bmatrix} \begin{bmatrix} \cos\phi & 0 & -\sin\phi & 0 \\ \sin\phi\sin\theta & \cos\theta & \cos\phi\sin\theta & 0 \\ \sin\phi\cos\theta & -\sin\theta & \cos\phi\cos\theta & 0 \\ 0 & 0 & 0 & 1 \end{bmatrix}$$

$$= \begin{bmatrix} \cos\phi & 0 & -\sin\phi & 0 \\ \sin\phi\sin\theta & \cos\theta & \cos\phi\sin\theta & 0 \\ \sin\phi\cos\theta & -\sin\theta & \cos\phi\cos\theta & 0 \\ \begin{array}{c} l\cos\phi \\ +m\sin\phi\sin\theta \\ +n\sin\phi\cos\theta \end{array} & m\cos\theta \\ -n\sin\theta & \begin{array}{c} -l\sin\phi \\ +m\cos\phi\sin\theta \\ +n\cos\phi\cos\theta \end{array} & 1 \end{bmatrix}$$

$$(3-16)$$

where $\theta$, $\phi$ are the rotation angles about the $x$- and $y$-axes, respectively; and $l, m, n$ are the translation factors in the $x, y, z$ directions, respectively.

For a general position vector we have

$$[X][T] = [x\ \ y\ \ z\ \ 1] \begin{bmatrix} \cos\phi & 0 & -\sin\phi & 0 \\ \sin\phi\sin\theta & \cos\theta & \cos\phi\sin\theta & 0 \\ \sin\phi\cos\theta & -\sin\theta & \cos\phi\cos\theta & 0 \\ \begin{array}{c} l\cos\phi \\ +m\sin\phi\sin\theta \\ +n\sin\phi\cos\theta \end{array} & \begin{array}{c} m\cos\theta \\ -n\sin\theta \end{array} & \begin{array}{c} -l\sin\phi \\ +m\cos\phi\sin\theta \\ +n\cos\phi\cos\theta \end{array} & 1 \end{bmatrix}$$

$$= \begin{bmatrix} \begin{array}{c} (x+l)\cos\phi \\ +(y+m)\sin\phi\sin\theta \\ +(z+n)\sin\phi\cos\theta \end{array} & \begin{array}{c} (y+m)\cos\theta \\ -(z+n)\sin\theta \end{array} & \begin{array}{c} -(x+l)\sin\phi \\ +(y+m)\cos\phi\sin\theta \\ +(z+n)\cos\phi\cos\theta \end{array} & 1 \end{bmatrix}$$

For specific values of $\theta = +30°$, $\phi = +45°$, $l = -1$, $m = -1$, $n = -1$ the transformed position vector is $[3\ \ 2\ \ 1\ \ 1]$.

$$[X][T] = [3 \quad 2 \quad 1 \quad 1] \begin{bmatrix} 0.707 & 0 & -0.707 & 0 \\ 0.354 & 0.866 & 0.354 & 0 \\ 0.612 & -0.5 & 0.612 & 0 \\ -1.673 & -0.366 & -0.259 & 1 \end{bmatrix}$$

$$[X][T] = [1.768 \quad 0.866 \quad -1.061 \quad 1]$$

To confirm that the concatenated matrix yields the same result as individually applied matrices consider

$$[X'] = [X][Tr]$$

$$= [3 \quad 2 \quad 1 \quad 1] \begin{bmatrix} 1 & 0 & 0 & 0 \\ 0 & 1 & 0 & 0 \\ 0 & 0 & 1 & 0 \\ -1 & -1 & -1 & 1 \end{bmatrix}$$

$$= [2 \quad 1 \quad 0 \quad 1]$$

$$[X''] = [X'][R_x] = [2 \quad 1 \quad 0 \quad 1] \begin{bmatrix} 1 & 0 & 0 & 0 \\ 0 & 0.866 & 0.5 & 0 \\ 0 & -0.5 & 0.866 & 0 \\ 0 & 0 & 0 & 1 \end{bmatrix}$$

$$= [2 \quad 0.866 \quad 0.5 \quad 1]$$

$$[X'''] = [X''][R_y] = [2 \quad 0.866 \quad .5 \quad 1] \begin{bmatrix} 0.707 & 0 & -0.707 & 0 \\ 0 & 1 & 0 & 0 \\ 0.707 & 0 & 0.707 & 0 \\ 0 & 0 & 0 & 1 \end{bmatrix}$$

$$[X'''] = [1.768 \quad 0.866 \quad -1.061 \quad 1]$$

which confirms our previous result.

---

## 3–8   ROTATIONS ABOUT AN AXIS PARALLEL TO A COORDINATE AXIS

The transformations given in Eqs. (3–6) to (3–8) cause rotation about the $x, y$ and $z$ coordinate axes. Often it is necessary to rotate an object about an axis other than these. Here, the special case of an axis that is parallel to one of the $x$, $y$ or $z$ coordinate axes is considered. Figure 3–5 shows a body with a local axis system $x'y'z'$ parallel to the fixed global axis system $xyz$. Rotation of the body about any of the individual $x'$, $y'$ or $z'$ local axes is accomplished using the following procedure:

Translate the body until the local axis is coincident with the coordinate axis in the same direction.

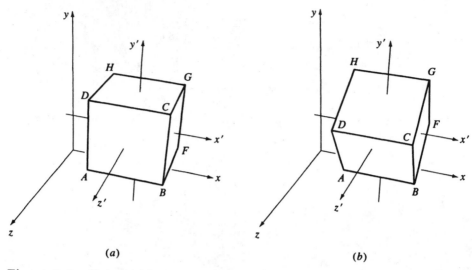

**Figure 3–5**    Rotation about an axis parallel to one of the coordinate axes.

Rotate about the specified axis.

Translate the transformed body back to its original position.

Mathematically

$$[\, X^* \,] = [\, X \,][\, Tr \,][\, R_x \,][\, Tr \,]^{-1}$$

where

| | |
|---|---|
| $[\, X^* \,]$ | represents the transformed body |
| $[\, X \,]$ | is the untransformed body |
| $[\, Tr \,]$ | is the translation matrix |
| $[\, R_x \,]$ | is the appropriate rotation matrix |
| $[\, Tr \,]^{-1}$ | is the inverse of the translation matrix |

An illustrative example is given below.

---

**Example 3–8    Single Relative Rotation**

Consider the block in Fig. 3–5a defined by the position vectors

$$[X] = \begin{bmatrix} 1 & 1 & 2 & 1 \\ 2 & 1 & 2 & 1 \\ 2 & 2 & 2 & 1 \\ 1 & 2 & 2 & 1 \\ 1 & 1 & 1 & 1 \\ 2 & 1 & 1 & 1 \\ 2 & 2 & 1 & 1 \\ 1 & 2 & 1 & 1 \end{bmatrix} \begin{matrix} A \\ B \\ C \\ D \\ E \\ F \\ G \\ H \end{matrix}$$

relative to the global $xyz$-axis system. Let's rotate the block $\theta = +30°$ about the local $x'$-axis passing through the centroid of the block. The origin of the local axis system is assumed to be the centroid of the block.

The centroid of the block is $[\ x_c\quad y_c\quad z_c\quad 1\ ] = [\ 3/2\quad 3/2\quad 3/2\quad 1\ ]$. The rotation is accomplished by

$$[\ X^*\ ] = [\ X\ ][\ Tr\ ][\ R\ ][\ Tr\ ]^{-1}$$

where

$$[\ Tr\ ] = \begin{bmatrix} 1 & 0 & 0 & 0 \\ 0 & 1 & 0 & 0 \\ 0 & 0 & 1 & 0 \\ 0 & -y_c & -z_c & 1 \end{bmatrix} = \begin{bmatrix} 1 & 0 & 0 & 0 \\ 0 & 1 & 0 & 0 \\ 0 & 0 & 1 & 0 \\ 0 & -3/2 & -3/2 & 1 \end{bmatrix}$$

$$[\ R_x\ ] = \begin{bmatrix} 1 & 0 & 0 & 0 \\ 0 & \cos\theta & \sin\theta & 0 \\ 0 & -\sin\theta & \cos\theta & 0 \\ 0 & 0 & 0 & 1 \end{bmatrix} = \begin{bmatrix} 1 & 0 & 0 & 0 \\ 0 & 0.866 & 0.5 & 0 \\ 0 & -0.5 & 0.866 & 0 \\ 0 & 0 & 0 & 1 \end{bmatrix}$$

and

$$[\ Tr\ ]^{-1} = \begin{bmatrix} 1 & 0 & 0 & 0 \\ 0 & 1 & 0 & 0 \\ 0 & 0 & 1 & 0 \\ 0 & y_c & z_c & 1 \end{bmatrix} = \begin{bmatrix} 1 & 0 & 0 & 0 \\ 0 & 1 & 0 & 0 \\ 0 & 0 & 1 & 0 \\ 0 & 3/2 & 3/2 & 1 \end{bmatrix}$$

The first matrix $[\ Tr\ ]$ translates the block parallel to the $x = 0$ plane until the $x'$-axis is coincident with the $x$-axis. The second matrix $[\ R_x\ ]$ performs the required rotation about the $x$-axis, and the third matrix $[\ Tr\ ]^{-1}$ translates the $x'$-axis and hence the rotated block back to its original position. Concatenating these three matrices yields

$$[\ T\ ] = [\ Tr\ ][\ R_x\ ][\ Tr\ ]^{-1}$$

$$= \begin{bmatrix} 1 & 0 & 0 & 0 \\ 0 & \cos\theta & \sin\theta & 0 \\ 0 & -\sin\theta & \cos\theta & 0 \\ 0 & y_c(1 - \cos\theta) + z_c\sin\theta & z_c(1 - \cos\theta) - y_c\sin\theta & 1 \end{bmatrix}$$

After substituting numerical values the transformed coordinates are

$$[\ X'\ ] = [\ X\ ][\ T\ ] = \begin{bmatrix} 1 & 1 & 2 & 1 \\ 2 & 1 & 2 & 1 \\ 2 & 2 & 2 & 1 \\ 1 & 2 & 2 & 1 \\ 1 & 1 & 1 & 1 \\ 2 & 1 & 1 & 1 \\ 2 & 2 & 1 & 1 \\ 1 & 2 & 1 & 1 \end{bmatrix} \begin{bmatrix} 1 & 0 & 0 & 0 \\ 0 & 0.866 & 0.5 & 0 \\ 0 & -0.5 & 0.866 & 0 \\ 0 & 0.951 & -0.549 & 1 \end{bmatrix}$$

$$[X'] = \begin{bmatrix} 1 & 0.817 & 1.683 & 1 \\ 2 & 0.817 & 1.683 & 1 \\ 2 & 1.683 & 2.183 & 1 \\ 1 & 1.683 & 2.183 & 1 \\ 1 & 1.317 & 0.817 & 1 \\ 2 & 1.317 & 0.817 & 1 \\ 2 & 2.183 & 1.317 & 1 \\ 1 & 2.183 & 1.317 & 1 \end{bmatrix} \begin{matrix} A \\ B \\ C \\ D \\ E \\ F \\ G \\ H \end{matrix}$$

The result is shown in Fig. 3–5b.

In the previous example only rotation about a single axis parallel to one of the coordinate axes was required. Thus, it was only necessary to make the rotation axis coincident with the corresponding coordinate axis. If multiple rotations in a local axis system parallel to the global axis system are required, then the origin of the local axis system must be made coincident with that of the global axis system. Specifically, the rotations can be accomplished with the following procedure:

Translate the origin of the local axis system to make it coincident with that of the global coordinate system.

Perform the required rotations.

Translate the local axis system back to its original position.

The example below illustrates this procedure.

### Example 3–9    Multiple Relative Rotations

Again consider the block shown on Fig. 3–5a. To rotate the block $\phi = -45°$ about the $y'$-axis, followed by a rotation of $\theta = +30°$ about the $x'$-axis, requires that the origin of the $x'y'z'$-axis system be made coincident with the origin of the $xyz$-axis system, the rotations performed and then the result translated back to the original position.

The combined transformation is

$$[X'] = [X][T] = [X][Tr][R_y][R_x][Tr]^{-1}$$

Specifically,

$$[T] = \begin{bmatrix} 1 & 0 & 0 & 0 \\ 0 & 1 & 0 & 0 \\ 0 & 0 & 1 & 0 \\ -x_c & -y_c & -z_c & 1 \end{bmatrix} \begin{bmatrix} \cos\phi & 0 & -\sin\phi & 0 \\ 0 & 1 & 0 & 0 \\ \sin\phi & 0 & \cos\phi & 0 \\ 0 & 0 & 0 & 1 \end{bmatrix} \times$$

$$\begin{bmatrix} 1 & 0 & 0 & 0 \\ 0 & \cos\theta & \sin\theta & 0 \\ 0 & -\sin\theta & \cos\theta & 0 \\ 0 & 0 & 0 & 1 \end{bmatrix} \begin{bmatrix} 1 & 0 & 0 & 0 \\ 0 & 1 & 0 & 0 \\ 0 & 0 & 1 & 0 \\ x_c & y_c & z_c & 1 \end{bmatrix}$$

where $\phi$ and $\theta$ represent the rotation angle about the $y'$- and $x'$-axes respectively. Concatenating these matrices yields

$$[T] = \begin{bmatrix} \cos\phi & \sin\phi\sin\theta & -\sin\phi\cos\theta & 0 \\ 0 & \cos\theta & \sin\theta & 0 \\ \sin\phi & -\cos\phi\sin\theta & \cos\phi\cos\theta & 0 \\ \begin{array}{l} x_c(1-\cos\phi) \\ -z_c\sin\phi \end{array} & \begin{array}{l} -x_c\sin\phi\sin\theta \\ +y_c(1-\cos\theta) \\ +z_c\cos\phi\sin\theta \end{array} & \begin{array}{l} x_c\sin\phi\cos\theta \\ -y_c\sin\theta \\ +z_c(1-\cos\phi\cos\theta) \end{array} & 1 \end{bmatrix}$$

$$(3-17)$$

The transformed position vectors are then

$$[X'] = \begin{bmatrix} 1 & 1 & 2 & 1 \\ 2 & 1 & 2 & 1 \\ 2 & 2 & 2 & 1 \\ 1 & 2 & 2 & 1 \\ 1 & 1 & 1 & 1 \\ 2 & 1 & 1 & 1 \\ 2 & 2 & 1 & 1 \\ 1 & 2 & 1 & 1 \end{bmatrix} \begin{bmatrix} 0.707 & -0.354 & 0.612 & 0 \\ 0 & 0.866 & 0.5 & 0 \\ -0.707 & -0.354 & 0.612 & 0 \\ 1.5 & 1.262 & -1.087 & 1 \end{bmatrix}$$

$$[X'] = \begin{bmatrix} 0.793 & 1.067 & 1.25 & 1 \\ 1.5 & 0.713 & 1.862 & 1 \\ 1.5 & 1.579 & 2.362 & 1 \\ 0.793 & 1.933 & 1.75 & 1 \\ 1.5 & 1.421 & 0.638 & 1 \\ 2.207 & 1.067 & 1.25 & 1 \\ 2.207 & 1.933 & 1.75 & 1 \\ 1.5 & 2.287 & 1.138 & 1 \end{bmatrix}$$

The result is shown in Fig. 3-6.

## 3-9    ROTATION ABOUT AN ARBITRARY AXIS IN SPACE

The general case of rotation about an arbitrary axis in space frequently occurs, e.g., in robotics, animation, and simulation. Following the previous discussion, rotation about an arbitrary axis in space is accomplished with a procedure using translations and simple rotations about the coordinate axes. Since the technique for rotation about a coordinate axis is known, the underlying procedural idea is to make the arbitrary rotation axis coincident with one of the coordinate axes.

Assume an arbitrary axis in space passing through the point $(x_0, y_0, z_0)$ with direction cosines $(c_x, c_y, c_z)$. Rotation about this axis by some angle $\delta$ is accomplished using the following procedure:

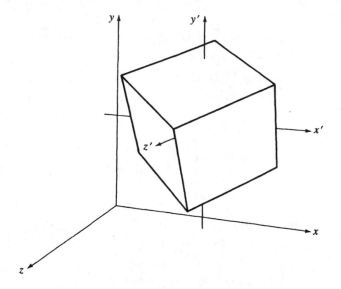

**Figure 3–6**   Multiple rotations about a local axis system.

Translate so that the point $(x_0, y_0, z_0)$ is at the origin of the coordinate system.

Perform appropriate rotations to make the axis of rotation coincident with the $z$-axis.[†]

Rotate about the $z$-axis by the angle $\delta$.

Perform the inverse of the combined rotation transformation.

Perform the inverse of the translation.

In general, making an arbitrary axis passing through the origin coincident with one of the coordinate axes requires two successive rotations about the other two coordinate axes. To make the arbitrary rotation axis coincident with the $z$-axis, first rotate about the $x$-axis and then about the $y$-axis. To determine the rotation angle, $\alpha$, about the $x$-axis used to place the arbitrary axis in the $xz$ plane, first project the unit vector along the axis onto the $yz$ plane as shown in Fig. 3–7a. The $y$ and $z$ components of the projected vector are $c_y$ and $c_z$, the direction cosines of the unit vector along the arbitrary axis. From Fig. 3–7a we have that

$$d = \sqrt{c_y{}^2 + c_z{}^2} \qquad (3-18)$$

and

$$\cos\alpha = \frac{c_z}{d} \qquad \sin\alpha = \frac{c_y}{d} \qquad (3-19)$$

---

[†]The choice of the $z$-axis is arbitrary.

After rotation about the $x$-axis into the $xz$ plane, the $z$ component of the unit vector is $d$, and the $x$ component is $c_x$, the direction cosine in the $x$ direction as shown in Fig. 3–7b. The length of the unit vector is, of course, 1. Thus, the rotation angle $\beta$ about the $y$-axis required to make the arbitrary axis coincident with the $z$-axis is

$$\cos\beta = d \qquad \sin\beta = c_x \qquad\qquad (3-20)$$

The complete transformation is then

$$[\,M\,] = [\,T\,][\,R_x\,][\,R_y\,][\,R_b\,][\,R_y\,]^{-1}[\,R_x\,]^{-1}[\,T\,]^{-1} \qquad (3-21)$$

where the required translation matrix is

$$[\,T\,] = \begin{bmatrix} 1 & 0 & 0 & 0 \\ 0 & 1 & 0 & 0 \\ 0 & 0 & 1 & 0 \\ -x_0 & -y_0 & -z_0 & 1 \end{bmatrix} \qquad (3-22)$$

the transformation matrix for rotation about the $x$-axis is

$$[\,R_x\,] = \begin{bmatrix} 1 & 0 & 0 & 0 \\ 0 & \cos\alpha & \sin\alpha & 0 \\ 0 & -\sin\alpha & \cos\alpha & 0 \\ 0 & 0 & 0 & 1 \end{bmatrix} = \begin{bmatrix} 1 & 0 & 0 & 0 \\ 0 & c_z/d & c_y/d & 0 \\ 0 & -c_y/d & c_z/d & 0 \\ 0 & 0 & 0 & 1 \end{bmatrix} \qquad (3-23)$$

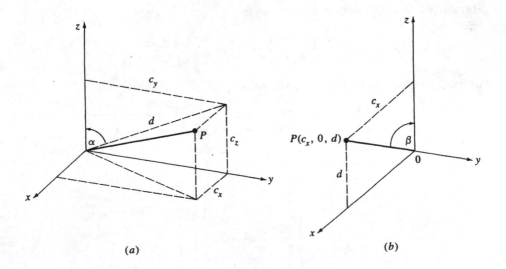

**Figure 3–7**   Rotations required to make the unit vector $OP$ coincident with the $z$-axis. (a) Rotation about $x$; (b) rotation about $y$.

and about the $y$-axis

$$[R_y] = \begin{bmatrix} \cos(-\beta) & 0 & -\sin(-\beta) & 0 \\ 0 & 1 & 0 & 0 \\ \sin(-\beta) & 0 & \cos(-\beta) & 0 \\ 0 & 0 & 0 & 1 \end{bmatrix} = \begin{bmatrix} d & 0 & c_x & 0 \\ 0 & 1 & 0 & 0 \\ -c_x & 0 & d & 0 \\ 0 & 0 & 0 & 1 \end{bmatrix} \qquad (3-24)$$

Finally, the rotation about the arbitrary axis is given by a $z$-axis rotation matrix

$$[R_\delta] = \begin{bmatrix} \cos\delta & \sin\delta & 0 & 0 \\ -\sin\delta & \cos\delta & 0 & 0 \\ 0 & 0 & 1 & 0 \\ 0 & 0 & 0 & 1 \end{bmatrix} \qquad (3-25)$$

In practice, the angles $\alpha$ and $\beta$ are not explicitly calculated. The elements of the rotation matrices $[R_x]$ and $[R_y]$ in Eq. (3–21) are obtained from Eqs. (3–18) to (3–20) at the expense of two divisions and a square root calculation. Although developed with the arbitrary axis in the first quadrant, these results are applicable in all quadrants.

If the direction cosines of the arbitrary axis are not known, they can be obtained knowing a second point on the axis $(x_1, y_1, z_1)$ by normalizing the vector from the first to the second point. Specifically, the vector along the axis from $(x_0, y_0, z_0)$ to $(x_1, y_1, z_1)$ is

$$[V] = [(x_1 - x_0) \quad (y_1 - y_0) \quad (z_1 - z_0)]$$

Normalized, it yields the direction cosines

$$[c_x \quad c_y \quad c_z] = \frac{[(x_1 - x_0) \quad (y_1 - y_0) \quad (z_1 - z_0)]}{[(x_1 - x_0)^2 + (y_1 - y_0)^2 + (z_1 - z_0)^2]^{\frac{1}{2}}} \qquad (3-26)$$

An example more fully illustrates the procedure.

---

### Example 3–10    Rotation About an Arbitrary Axis

Consider the cube with one corner removed shown in Fig. 3–8a. Position vectors for the vertices are

$$[X] = \begin{bmatrix} 2 & 1 & 2 & 1 \\ 3 & 1 & 2 & 1 \\ 3 & 1.5 & 2 & 1 \\ 2.5 & 2 & 2 & 1 \\ 2 & 2 & 2 & 1 \\ 2 & 1 & 1 & 1 \\ 3 & 1 & 1 & 1 \\ 3 & 2 & 1 & 1 \\ 2 & 2 & 1 & 1 \\ 3 & 2 & 1.5 & 1 \end{bmatrix} \begin{matrix} A \\ B \\ C \\ D \\ E \\ F \\ G \\ H \\ I \\ J \end{matrix}$$

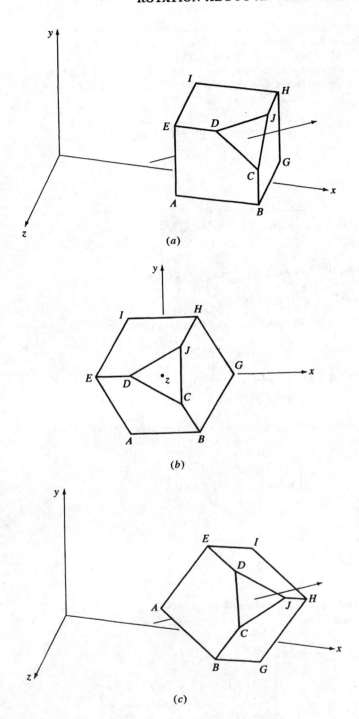

(a)

(b)

(c)

**Figure 3–8**    Rotation about an arbitrary axis.

The cube is to be rotated by $-45°$ about a local axis passing through the point $F$ and the diagonally opposite corner. The axis is directed from $F$ to the opposite corner and passes through the center of the corner face.

First, determine the direction cosines of the rotation axis. Observing that the corner cut off by the triangle $CDJ$ also lies on the axis, Eq. (3–26) yields

$$[\, c_x \quad c_y \quad c_z \,] = \frac{[\, (3-2) \quad (2-1) \quad (2-1) \,]}{((3-2)^2 + (2-1)^2 + (2-1)^2)^{\frac{1}{2}}}$$

$$= [\, 1/\sqrt{3} \quad 1/\sqrt{3} \quad 1/\sqrt{3} \,]$$

Using Eqs. (3–18) to (3–20) yields

$$d = \sqrt{(1/\sqrt{3})^2 + (1/\sqrt{3})^2} = \sqrt{2/3}$$

and

$$\alpha = \cos^{-1}(1/\sqrt{3} \Big/ \sqrt{2/3}) = \cos^{-1}(1/\sqrt{2}) = 45°$$

$$\beta = \cos^{-1}(\sqrt{2/3}) = 35.26°$$

Since the point $F$ lies on the rotation axis, the translation matrix is

$$[\,T\,] = \begin{bmatrix} 1 & 0 & 0 & 0 \\ 0 & 1 & 0 & 0 \\ 0 & 0 & 1 & 0 \\ -2 & -1 & -1 & 1 \end{bmatrix}$$

The rotation matrices to make the arbitrary axis coincident with the $z$-axis are then

$$[\,R_x\,] = \begin{bmatrix} 1 & 0 & 0 & 0 \\ 0 & 1/\sqrt{2} & 1/\sqrt{2} & 0 \\ 0 & -1/\sqrt{2} & 1/\sqrt{2} & 0 \\ 0 & 0 & 0 & 1 \end{bmatrix}$$

and

$$[\,R_y\,] = \begin{bmatrix} 2/\sqrt{6} & 0 & 1/\sqrt{3} & 0 \\ 0 & 1 & 0 & 0 \\ -1/\sqrt{3} & 0 & 2/\sqrt{6} & 0 \\ 0 & 0 & 0 & 1 \end{bmatrix}$$

$[\,R_x\,]^{-1}$, $[\,R_y\,]^{-1}$, and $[\,T\,]^{-1}$ are obtained by substituting $-\alpha$, $-\beta$ and $(x_0, y_0, z_0)$ for $\alpha$, $\beta$ and $(-x_0, -y_0, -z_0)$, respectively, in Eqs. (3–22) to (3–24).

Concatenating $[\,T\,][\,R_x\,][\,R_y\,]$ yields

$$[\,M\,] = [\,T\,][\,R_x\,][\,R_y\,] = \begin{bmatrix} 2/\sqrt{6} & 0 & 1/\sqrt{3} & 0 \\ -1/\sqrt{6} & 1/\sqrt{2} & 1/\sqrt{3} & 0 \\ -1/\sqrt{6} & -1/\sqrt{2} & 1/\sqrt{3} & 0 \\ -2/\sqrt{6} & 0 & -4/\sqrt{3} & 1 \end{bmatrix}$$

The transformed intermediate position vectors are

$$[X][M] = \begin{bmatrix} -0.408 & -0.707 & 0.577 & 1 \\ 0.408 & -0.707 & 1.155 & 1 \\ 0.204 & -0.354 & 1.443 & 1 \\ -0.408 & 0 & 1.443 & 1 \\ -0.816 & 0 & 1.155 & 1 \\ 0 & 0 & 0 & 1 \\ 0.816 & 0 & 0.577 & 1 \\ 0.408 & 0.707 & 1.155 & 1 \\ -0.408 & 0.707 & 0.577 & 1 \\ 0.204 & 0.354 & 1.443 & 1 \end{bmatrix}$$

This intermediate result is shown in Fig. 3–8b. Notice that point $F$ is at $(0,0,0)$.

The rotation about the arbitrary axis is now given by the equivalent rotation about the $z$-axis. Hence (see Eq. 3–7)

$$[R_\delta] = \begin{bmatrix} \sqrt{2}/2 & -\sqrt{2}/2 & 0 & 0 \\ \sqrt{2}/2 & \sqrt{2}/2 & 0 & 0 \\ 0 & 0 & 1 & 0 \\ 0 & 0 & 0 & 1 \end{bmatrix}$$

The transformed object is returned to its 'original' position in space, using

$$[M]^{-1} = [R_y]^{-1}[R_x]^{-1}[T]^{-1} = \begin{bmatrix} 2/\sqrt{6} & -1/\sqrt{6} & -1/\sqrt{6} & 0 \\ 0 & 1/\sqrt{2} & -1/\sqrt{2} & 0 \\ 1/\sqrt{3} & 1/\sqrt{3} & 1/\sqrt{3} & 0 \\ 2 & 1 & 1 & 1 \end{bmatrix}$$

This result can be obtained either by concatenating the inverses of the individual component matrices of $[M]$ or by formally taking the inverse of $[M]$. Incidentally, notice that $[R_x][R_y]$ is a pure rotation. The upper left $3 \times 3$ submatrix of $[M]^{-1}$ is just the transpose of the upper left $3 \times 3$ submatrix of $[M]$.

The resulting position vectors are

$$[X][M][R_\delta][M]^{-1} = \begin{bmatrix} 1.689 & 1.506 & 1.805 & 1 \\ 2.494 & 1.195 & 2.311 & 1 \\ 2.747 & 1.598 & 2.155 & 1 \\ 2.598 & 2.155 & 1.747 & 1 \\ 2.195 & 2.311 & 1.494 & 1 \\ 2 & 1 & 1 & 1 \\ 2.805 & 0.689 & 1.506 & 1 \\ 3.311 & 1.494 & 1.195 & 1 \\ 2.506 & 1.805 & 0.689 & 1 \\ 3.155 & 1.747 & 1.598 & 1 \end{bmatrix}$$

where

$$[\,M\,][\,R_\delta\,][\,M\,]^{-1} = \begin{bmatrix} 0.805 & -0.311 & 0.506 & 0 \\ 0.506 & 0.805 & -0.311 & 0 \\ -0.311 & 0.506 & 0.805 & 0 \\ 0.195 & 0.311 & -0.506 & 1 \end{bmatrix} .$$

The transformed object is shown in Fig. 3–8c.

---

## 3–10   REFLECTION THROUGH AN ARBITRARY PLANE

The transformations given in Eqs. (3–11) to (3–13) cause reflection through the $x = 0$, $y = 0$, $z = 0$ coordinate planes, respectively. Often it is necessary to reflect an object through a plane other than one of these. Again, this can be accomplished using a procedure incorporating the previously defined simple transformations. One possible procedure is:

Translate a known point $P$, that lies in the reflection plane, to the origin of the coordinate system.

Rotate the normal vector to the reflection plane at the origin until it is coincident with the $+z$-axis (see Sec. 3–9, Eqs. 3–23 and 3–24); this makes the reflection plane the $z = 0$ coordinate plane.

After also applying the above transformations to the object, reflect the object through the $z = 0$ coordinate plane (see Eq. 3–11).

Perform the inverse transformations to those given above to achieve the desired result.

The general transformation is then

$$[\,M\,] = [\,T\,][\,R_x\,][\,R_y\,][\,Rflt_z\,][\,R_y\,]^{-1}[\,R_x\,]^{-1}[\,T\,]^{-1}$$

where the matrices $[\,T\,]$, $[\,R_x\,]$, $[\,R_y\,]$ are given by Eqs. (3–22) to (3–24), respectively. $(x_0, y_0, z_0) = (P_x, P_y, P_z)$, the components of point $P$ in the reflection plane; and $(c_x, c_y, c_z)$ are the direction cosines of the normal to the reflection plane.[†]

An example more fully illustrates the procedure.

---

#### Example 3–11    Reflection

Again consider the cube with one corner removed shown in Fig. 3–8a. Reflect the cube through the plane containing the triangle $CDJ$.

---

[†]If the equation of the reflection plane $ax + by + cz + d = 0$ is known, then the unit normal to the plane is

$$[\,\hat{n}\,] = [\,c_x \quad c_y \quad c_z\,] = \frac{[\,a \quad b \quad c\,]}{\sqrt{a^2 + b^2 + c^2}}$$

See Ref. 3–1 for more details.

Recalling the position vectors for the cube, and choosing to translate the point $C$ to the origin, yields the translation matrix

$$[T] = \begin{bmatrix} 1 & 0 & 0 & 0 \\ 0 & 1 & 0 & 0 \\ 0 & 0 & 1 & 0 \\ -3 & -3/2 & -2 & 1 \end{bmatrix}$$

The normal to the reflection plane is obtained using the position vectors $C$, $D$, $J$ (see Ref. 3-1). Specifically, taking the cross product of the vectors $CJ$ and $CD$ prior to translation yields

$$n = ([\,J\,] - [\,C\,]) \times ([\,D\,] - [\,C\,])$$
$$= [\,(3-3) \quad (2-1.5) \quad (1.5-2)\,] \times [\,(2.5-3) \quad (2-1.5) \quad (2-2)\,]$$
$$= [\,0 \quad 1/2 \quad -1/2\,] \times [\,-1/2 \quad 1/2 \quad 0\,]$$
$$= [\,1/4 \quad 1/4 \quad 1/4\,]$$

Normalizing yields
$$\hat{n} = [\,1/\sqrt{3} \quad 1/\sqrt{3} \quad 1/\sqrt{3}\,]$$

Using Eqs. (3-19) and (3-20) gives

$$d = \sqrt{n_y^2 + n_z^2} = \sqrt{(1/\sqrt{3})^2 + (1/\sqrt{3})^2} = \sqrt{2/3}$$

and
$$\alpha = 45° \qquad \beta = 35.26°$$

The rotation matrices to make the normal at $C$ coincide with the $z$-axis are (see Eqs. 3-23 and 3-24)

$$[R_x] = \begin{bmatrix} 1 & 0 & 0 & 0 \\ 0 & 1/\sqrt{2} & 1/\sqrt{2} & 0 \\ 0 & -1/\sqrt{2} & 1/\sqrt{2} & 0 \\ 0 & 0 & 0 & 1 \end{bmatrix}$$

$$[R_y] = \begin{bmatrix} 2/\sqrt{6} & 0 & 1/\sqrt{3} & 0 \\ 0 & 1 & 0 & 0 \\ -1/\sqrt{3} & 0 & 2/\sqrt{6} & 0 \\ 0 & 0 & 0 & 1 \end{bmatrix}$$

The matrices $[R_x]^{-1}$, $[R_y]^{-1}$ and $[T]^{-1}$ are obtained by substituting $-\alpha$, $-\beta$, and $[\,x_0 \quad y_0 \quad z_0\,] = [\,C\,]$ into Eqs. (3-22) to (3-24).
Concatenating $[T]$, $[R_x]$ and $[R_y]$ yields

$$[M] = [T][R_x][R_y] = \begin{bmatrix} 2/\sqrt{6} & 0 & 1/\sqrt{3} & 0 \\ -1/\sqrt{6} & 1/\sqrt{2} & 1/\sqrt{3} & 0 \\ -1/\sqrt{6} & -1/\sqrt{2} & 1/\sqrt{3} & 0 \\ -5/2\sqrt{6} & 1/2\sqrt{2} & -13/2\sqrt{3} & 1 \end{bmatrix}$$

The transformed intermediate position vectors are

$$[X][M] = \begin{bmatrix} -0.612 & -0.354 & -0.876 & 1 \\ 0.204 & -0.354 & -0.287 & 1 \\ 0 & 0 & 0 & 1 \\ -0.612 & 0.354 & 0 & 1 \\ -1.021 & 0.354 & -0.287 & 1 \\ -0.204 & 0.354 & -1.443 & 1 \\ 0.612 & 0.354 & -0.876 & 1 \\ 0.204 & 1.061 & -0.287 & 1 \\ -0.612 & 1.061 & -0.876 & 1 \\ 0 & 0.707 & 0 & 1 \end{bmatrix}$$

This intermediate result is shown in Fig. 3–9b. Notice that the point $C$ is at the origin and the $z$-axis points out of the page.

Reflection through the arbitrary plane is now given by reflection through the $z = 0$ plane. Hence (see Eq. 3–11)

$$[Rflt] = \begin{bmatrix} 1 & 0 & 0 & 0 \\ 0 & 1 & 0 & 0 \\ 0 & 0 & -1 & 0 \\ 0 & 0 & 0 & 1 \end{bmatrix}$$

Returning the transformed object to its 'original' position in space requires

$$[M]^{-1} = [R_y]^{-1}[R_x]^{-1}[T]^{-1} = \begin{bmatrix} 2/\sqrt{6} & -1/\sqrt{6} & -1/\sqrt{6} & 0 \\ 0 & 1/\sqrt{2} & -1/\sqrt{2} & 0 \\ 1/\sqrt{3} & 1/\sqrt{3} & 1/\sqrt{3} & 0 \\ 3 & 3/2 & 2 & 1 \end{bmatrix}$$

The resulting position vectors are

$$[X][M][Rflt][M]^{-1} = \begin{bmatrix} 3 & 2 & 3 & 1 \\ 10/3 & 4/3 & 7/3 & 1 \\ 3 & 3/2 & 2 & 1 \\ 5/2 & 2 & 2 & 1 \\ 7/3 & 7/3 & 7/3 & 1 \\ 11/3 & 8/3 & 8/3 & 1 \\ 4 & 2 & 2 & 1 \\ 10/3 & 7/3 & 4/3 & 1 \\ 3 & 3 & 2 & 1 \\ 3 & 2 & 3/2 & 1 \end{bmatrix}$$

where

$$[M][Rflt][M]^{-1} = \begin{bmatrix} 1/3 & -2/3 & -2/3 & 0 \\ -2/3 & 1/3 & -2/3 & 0 \\ -2/3 & -2/3 & 1/3 & 0 \\ 13/3 & 13/3 & 13/3 & 1 \end{bmatrix}$$

The transformed object is shown in Fig. 3–9c.

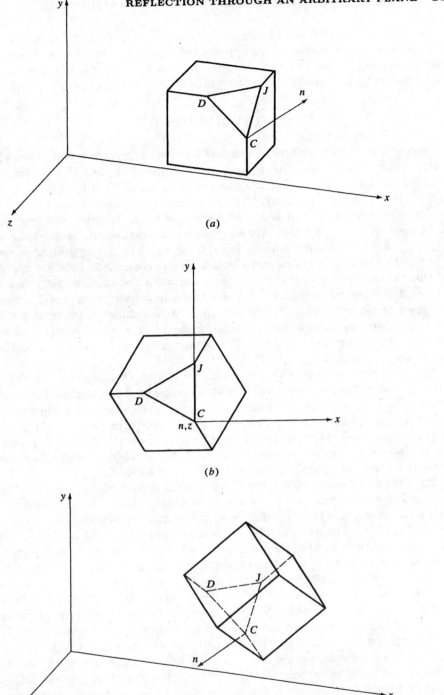

(a)

(b)

(c)

**Figure 3-9**   Reflection through an arbitrary plane.

As this and the previous section show, complex manipulative transformations can easily be constructed using procedures involving simple single-action transformations. This is the recommended approach. Generally it is less error prone and is computationally more efficient than a direct mathematical approach.

## 3–11    AFFINE AND PERSPECTIVE GEOMETRY

Geometric theorems have been developed for both perspective and affine geometry. The theorems of affine geometry are identical to those for Euclidean geometry. In both affine and Euclidean geometry parallelism is an important concept. In perspective geometry, lines are generally nonparallel.

An affine transformation is a combination of linear transformations, e.g., rotation followed by translation. For an affine transformation, the last column in the general $4 \times 4$ transformation matrix is $[\,0 \quad 0 \quad 0 \quad 1\,]^T$. Otherwise, as shown in Sec. 3–15 below, the transformed homogeneous coordinate $h$ is not unity; and there is not a one-to-one correspondence between the affine transformation and the $4 \times 4$ matrix operator. Affine transformations form a useful subset of bilinear transformations, since the product of two affine transformations is also affine. This allows the general transformation of a set of points relative to an arbitrary coordinate system while maintaining a value of unity for the homogeneous coordinate $h$.

Since Euclidean geometry has been taught in schools for many years, drawing and sketching techniques based on Euclidean geometry have become standard methods for graphical communication. Although perspective views are often used by artists and architects to yield more realistic pictures, because of the difficulty of manual construction they are seldom used in technical work. However, with the use of homogeneous coordinates to define an object, both affine and perspective transformations are obtained with equal ease.

Both affine and perspective transformations are three-dimensional, i.e., they are transformations from one three space to another three space. However, viewing the results on a two-dimensional surface requires a projection from three space to two space. The result is called a plane geometric projection. Figure 3–10 illustrates the hierarchy of plane geometric projections. The projection matrix from three space to two space always contains a column of zeros. Consequently the determinant of a projective transformation is always zero.

Plane geometric projections of objects are formed by the intersection of lines called projectors with a plane called the projection plane. Projectors are lines from an arbitrary point called the center of projection, through each point in an object. If the center of projection is located at a finite point in three space, the result is a perspective projection. If the center of projection is located at infinity, all the projectors are parallel and the result is a parallel projection. Plane geometric projections provide the basis for descriptive geometry. Nonplanar and nongeometric projections are also useful; e.g., they are used extensively in cartography.

In developing the various transformations shown in Fig. 3–10 two alternate approaches can be used. The first assumes that the center of projection or eye

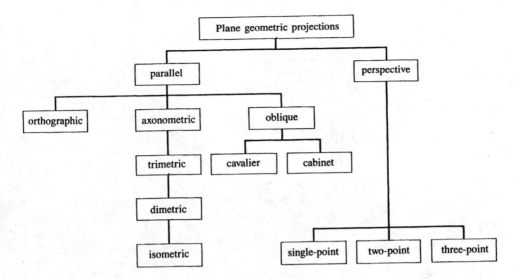

**Figure 3-10**    Hierarchy of plane geometric projections.

point is fixed and that the plane of projection is perpendicular to the viewing direction as shown in Fig. 3-11a. The object is manipulated to obtain any required view. The second assumes that the object is fixed, that the center of projection is free to move anywhere in three space, and that the plane of projection is not necessarily perpendicular to the viewing direction. An example is shown in Fig. 3-11b. Both approaches are *mathematically equivalent.*

By analogy the first approach is similar to the actions of a human observer when asked to describe a small object, e.g., a book. The object is picked up, rotated and translated in order to view all sides and aspects of the object. The center of projection is fixed and the object is manipulated. The second approach is similar to the actions of the human observer when asked to describe a large object, e.g., an automobile. The observer walks around the object to view the various sides, climbs up on a ladder to view the top, and kneels down to look at the bottom. Here the object is fixed, and the center of projection and eye point are moved.

When designing or viewing an object on a computer graphics display the location of the eye is typically fixed and the plane of projection, i.e., the face of the CRT, is typically perpendicular to the viewing direction. Hence, the first approach is generally more appropriate. However, if the graphics display is used to simulate the motion of a vehicle or of an observer moving through a computer generated model, as is the case for vehicle simulators, or for an observer strolling through an architectured model, then the second approach is more appropriate.

A fixed center of projection, movable object approach is used in this book. The fixed object, movable center of projection approach is nicely developed by Carlbom and Paciorek (Ref. 3-2).

We begin our discussion of plane geometric projections (see Fig. 3-10) by first considering the parallel projections.

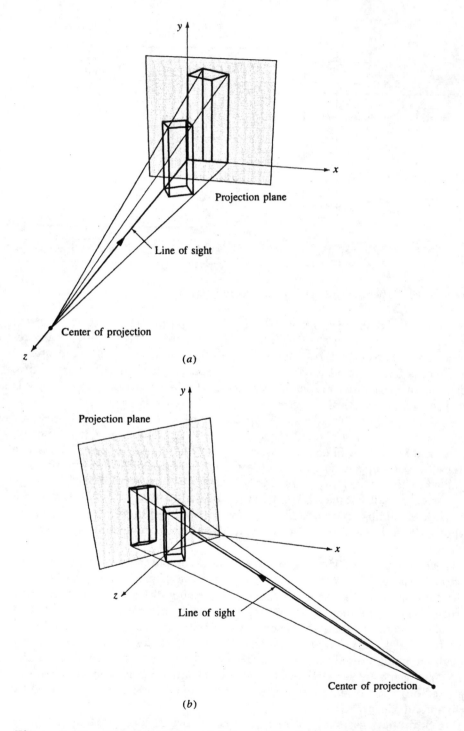

**Figure 3–11**   Plane projections. (a) Center of projection fixed; (b) object fixed.

## 3–12   ORTHOGRAPHIC PROJECTIONS

The simplest of the parallel projections is the orthographic projection, commonly used for engineering drawings. They accurately show the correct or 'true' size and shape of a single plane face of an object. Orthographic projections are projections onto one of the coordinate planes $x = 0$, $y = 0$ or $z = 0$. The matrix for projection onto the $z = 0$ plane is

$$[\,P_z\,] = \begin{bmatrix} 1 & 0 & 0 & 0 \\ 0 & 1 & 0 & 0 \\ 0 & 0 & 0 & 0 \\ 0 & 0 & 0 & 1 \end{bmatrix} \qquad (3-27)$$

Notice that the third column (the $z$ column) is all zeros. Consequently, the effect of the transformation is to set the $z$ coordinate of a position vector to zero.

Similarly, the matrices for projection onto the $x = 0$ and $y = 0$ planes are

$$[\,P_x\,] = \begin{bmatrix} 0 & 0 & 0 & 0 \\ 0 & 1 & 0 & 0 \\ 0 & 0 & 1 & 0 \\ 0 & 0 & 0 & 1 \end{bmatrix} \qquad (3-28)$$

and

$$[\,P_y\,] = \begin{bmatrix} 1 & 0 & 0 & 0 \\ 0 & 0 & 0 & 0 \\ 0 & 0 & 1 & 0 \\ 0 & 0 & 0 & 1 \end{bmatrix} \qquad (3-29)$$

Orthographic projections of the object in Fig. 3–12a onto the $x = 0$, $y = 0$ and $z = 0$ planes from centers of projection at infinity on the $+x$-, $+y$- and $+z$-axes are shown in Figs. 3–12b, 3–12c and 3–12d respectively.

A single orthographic projection does not provide sufficient information to visually and practically reconstruct the shape of an object. Consequently, multiple orthographic projections are necessary. These multiview orthographic projections are by convention† arranged as shown in Fig. 3–13. The front, right side and top views are obtained by projection onto the $z = 0$, $x = 0$ and $y = 0$ planes from centers of projection at infinity on the $+z$-, $+x$- and $+y$-axes. The rear, left side and bottom view projections are obtained by projection onto the $z = 0$, $x = 0$, $y = 0$ planes from centers of projection at infinity on the $-z$-, $-x$- and $-y$-axes. The coordinate axes are not normally shown on the views.

As shown in Fig. 3–13, by convention hidden lines are shown dashed. All six views are normally not required to adequately convey the shape of an object. The front, top and right side views are most frequently used. Even when all six views are not used, the ones that are used appear in the locations shown. The

---

†This is the convention used in the United States.

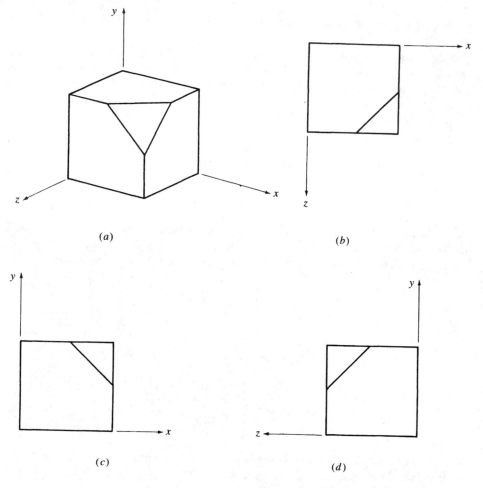

$(a)$ $\qquad$ $(b)$

$(c)$ $\qquad$ $(d)$

**Figure 3–12** Orthographic projections onto (b) $y = 0$, (c) $z = 0$ and (d) $x = 0$ planes.

front and side views are sometimes called the front and side elevations. The top view is sometimes called the plan view.

It is interesting and important to note that all six views can be obtained by combinations of reflection, rotation and translation, followed by projection onto the $z = 0$ plane from a center of projection at infinity on the $+z$-axis. For example, the rear view is obtained by reflection through the $z = 0$ plane, followed by projection onto the $z = 0$ plane. Similarly, the left side view is obtained by rotation about the $y$-axis by $+90°$, followed by projection onto the $z = 0$ plane.

For objects with planes that are not parallel to one of the coordinate planes, the standard orthographic views do not show the correct or true shape of these planes. Auxiliary views are used for this purpose. An auxiliary view is formed by rotating and translating the object so that the normal to the auxiliary plane

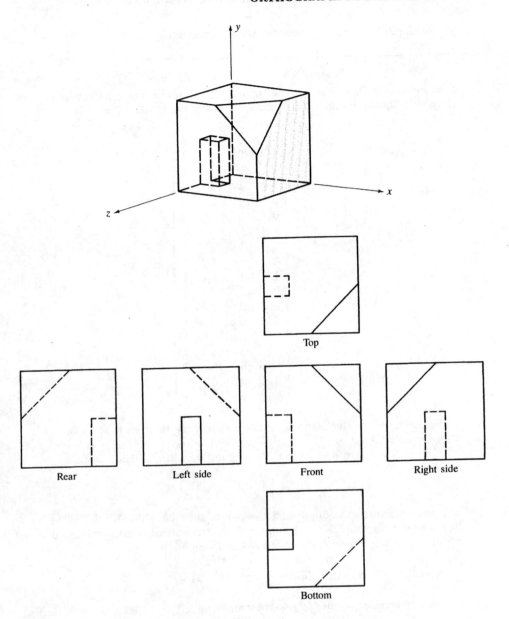

**Figure 3–13**   Multiview orthographic projection.

is coincident with one of the coordinate axes (see Sec. 3–9). The result is then projected onto the coordinate plane perpendicular to that axis. Figure 3–14c shows an auxiliary plane illustrating the true shape of the triangular corner of the block shown in Fig. 3–13.

An example more fully illustrates these constructions.

### Example 3–12    Auxiliary View

Develop an auxiliary view showing the true shape of the triangular corner for the object shown in Fig. 3–14a. The position vectors for the object are

$$[X] = \begin{bmatrix} 0 & 0 & 1 & 1 \\ 1 & 0 & 1 & 1 \\ 1 & 0.5 & 1 & 1 \\ 0.5 & 1 & 1 & 1 \\ 0 & 1 & 1 & 1 \\ 0 & 0 & 0 & 1 \\ 1 & 0 & 0 & 1 \\ 1 & 1 & 0 & 1 \\ 0 & 1 & 0 & 1 \\ 1 & 1 & 0.5 & 1 \\ 0 & 0 & 0.6 & 1 \\ 0.25 & 0 & 0.6 & 1 \\ 0.25 & 0.5 & 0.6 & 1 \\ 0 & 0.5 & 0.6 & 1 \\ 0 & 0 & 0.4 & 1 \\ 0.25 & 0 & 0.4 & 1 \\ 0.25 & 0.5 & 0.4 & 1 \\ 0 & 0.5 & 0.4 & 1 \end{bmatrix}$$

The vertex numbers shown in Fig. 3–14 correspond to the rows in the position vector matrix $[X]$.

The unit outward normal to the triangular face has direction cosines

$$[c_x \quad c_y \quad c_z] = [1/\sqrt{3} \quad 1/\sqrt{3} \quad 1/\sqrt{3}]$$

and passes through the origin and the point $[0.83333 \quad 0.83333 \quad 0.83333]$. Recalling the results of Sec. 3–9 and Ex. 3–10, the normal is made coincident with the z-axis by rotation about the x-axis by an angle

$$\alpha = \cos^{-1}(c_z/d) = \cos^{-1}(1/\sqrt{2}) = +45°$$

followed by rotation about the y-axis by an angle

$$\beta = \cos^{-1}(d) = \cos^{-1}(2/\sqrt{6}) = +35.26°$$

Here, the concatenated transformation matrix is

$$[T] = \begin{bmatrix} 2/\sqrt{6} & 0 & 1/\sqrt{3} & 0 \\ -1/\sqrt{6} & 1/\sqrt{2} & 1/\sqrt{3} & 0 \\ -1/\sqrt{6} & -1/\sqrt{2} & 1/\sqrt{3} & 0 \\ 0 & 0 & 0 & 1 \end{bmatrix}$$

The transformed position vectors are

$$[X'] = [X][T] = \begin{bmatrix} -0.408 & -0.707 & 0.577 & 1 \\ 0.408 & -0.707 & 1.155 & 1 \\ 0.204 & -0.354 & 1.443 & 1 \\ -0.408 & 0 & 1.443 & 1 \\ -0.816 & 0 & 1.155 & 1 \\ 0 & 0 & 0 & 1 \\ 0.816 & 0 & 0.577 & 1 \\ 0.408 & 0.707 & 1.155 & 1 \\ -0.408 & 0.707 & 0.577 & 1 \\ 0.204 & 0.354 & 1.443 & 1 \\ -0.245 & -0.424 & 0.354 & 1 \\ -0.041 & -0.424 & 0.491 & 1 \\ -0.245 & -0.071 & 0.779 & 1 \\ -0.449 & -0.071 & 0.635 & 1 \\ -0.163 & -0.283 & 0.231 & 1 \\ 0.041 & -0.283 & 0.375 & 1 \\ -0.163 & 0.071 & 0.664 & 1 \\ -0.367 & 0.071 & 0.52 & 1 \end{bmatrix}$$

The result is shown in Fig. 3–14b. The auxiliary view is created by projecting this intermediate result onto the $z = 0$ plane using Eq. (3–27), i.e.,

$$[P_z] = \begin{bmatrix} 1 & 0 & 0 & 0 \\ 0 & 1 & 0 & 0 \\ 0 & 0 & 0 & 0 \\ 0 & 0 & 0 & 1 \end{bmatrix}$$

The transformation matrices $[T]$ and $[P_z]$ are concatenated to yield

$$[T'] = [T][P_z] = \begin{bmatrix} 2/\sqrt{6} & 0 & 0 & 0 \\ -1/\sqrt{6} & 1/\sqrt{2} & 0 & 0 \\ -1/\sqrt{3} & -1/\sqrt{2} & 0 & 0 \\ 0 & 0 & 0 & 1 \end{bmatrix}$$

Notice the column of zeros. The auxiliary view is then created by

$$[X''] = [X][T']$$

$[X'']$ is the same as $[X']$ except that the third column is all zeros, i.e., the effect of the projection is to neglect the $z$ coordinate. The result is shown in Fig. 3–14c. Hidden lines are shown solid. Notice that the true shape of the triangle, which is equilateral, is shown.

---

For complex objects it is frequently necessary to show details of the interior. This is accomplished using a sectional view. A sectional view is constructed by passing a plane, called the section or 'cutting' plane, through the object,

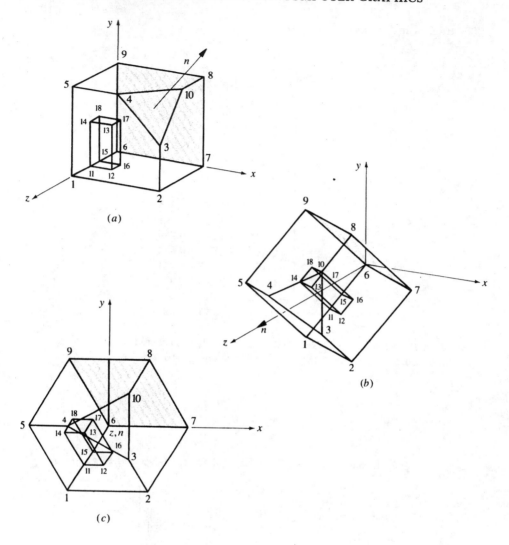

**Figure 3–14** Development of an auxiliary view. (a) Trimetric view; (b) normal coincident with the z-axis; (c) projected onto the z = 0 plane.

removing the part of the object on one side of the plane and projecting the remainder onto the section plane. Again, a sectional view can be constructed by making the normal to the section plane coincident with one of the coordinate axes (see Sec. 3–9), clipping the object to one side of the section plane (see Ref. 3–1), and finally projecting the result onto the coordinate plane perpendicular to the axis.

Figure 3–15 shows a section plane passing through the notch on the left side of the object of Fig. 3–13. The arrows are used to show the section plane and the viewing direction.

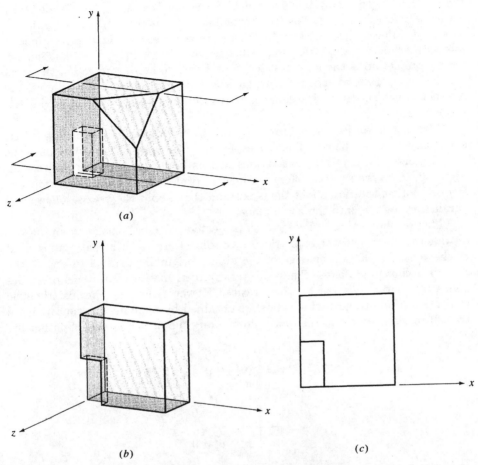

**Figure 3–15**   Development of a sectional view.  (a) Complete object; (b) portion between the section plane and the center of projection removed; (c) projected onto the $z = 0$ plane.

## 3–13   AXONOMETRIC PROJECTIONS

A single orthographic projection fails to illustrate the general three-dimensional shape of an object.  Axonometric projections overcome this limitation.  An axonometric projection is constructed by manipulating the object, using rotations and translations, such that at least three adjacent faces are shown.[†]  The result is then projected from a center of projection at infinity onto one of the coordinate planes, usually the $z = 0$ plane.  Unless a face is parallel to the plane of projection, an axonometric projection does not show its true shape.  However,

---

[†]The minimal number of faces occurs for simple cuboidal objects such as are used in most illustrations in this chapter.

the relative lengths of originally parallel lines remain constant, i.e., parallel lines are equally foreshortened. The foreshortening factor is the ratio of the projected length of a line to its true length. There are three axonometric projections of interest: trimetric, dimetric, and isometric, as shown in Fig. 3–10. The trimetric projection is the least restrictive and the isometric projection the most restrictive. In fact, as shown below, an isometric projection is a special case of a dimetric projection, and a dimetric projection is a special case of a trimetric projection.

A trimetric projection is formed by arbitrary rotations, in arbitrary order, about any or all of the coordinate axes, followed by parallel projection onto the $z = 0$ plane. Most of the illustrations in this book are trimetric projections. Figure 3–16 shows several different trimetric projections. Each projection was formed by first rotating about the $y$-axis and then about the $x$-axis, followed by parallel projection onto the $z = 0$ plane.

The foreshortening ratios for each projected principal axis ($x$, $y$ and $z$) are all different in a general trimetric projection. Here, a principal axis is used in the sense of an axis or edge of the object originally parallel to one of the $x$, $y$ or $z$ coordinate axes. The wide variety of trimetric projections precludes giving a general equation for these ratios. However, for any specific trimetric projection, the foreshortening ratios are obtained by applying the concatenated transformation matrix to the unit vectors along the principal axes. Specifically,

$$[U][T] = \begin{bmatrix} 1 & 0 & 0 & 1 \\ 0 & 1 & 0 & 1 \\ 0 & 0 & 1 & 1 \end{bmatrix} [T]$$

$$= \begin{bmatrix} x_x^* & y_x^* & 0 & 1 \\ x_y^* & y_y^* & 0 & 1 \\ x_z^* & y_z^* & 0 & 1 \end{bmatrix} \qquad (3-30)$$

where $[U]$ is the matrix of unit vectors along the untransformed $x$, $y$ and $z$ axes, respectively, and $[T]$ is the concatenated trimetric projection matrix. The foreshortening factors along the projected principal axes are then

$$f_x = \sqrt{x_x^{*2} + y_x^{*2}} \qquad (3-31a)$$

$$f_y = \sqrt{x_y^{*2} + y_y^{*2}} \qquad (3-31b)$$

$$f_z = \sqrt{x_z^{*2} + y_z^{*2}} \qquad (3-31c)$$

Example 3–13 provides the details of a trimetric projection.

---

### Example 3–13   Trimetric Projection

Consider the center illustration of Fig. 3–16 formed by a $\phi = 30°$ rotation about the $y$-axis, followed by a $\theta = 45°$ rotation about the $x$-axis, and then

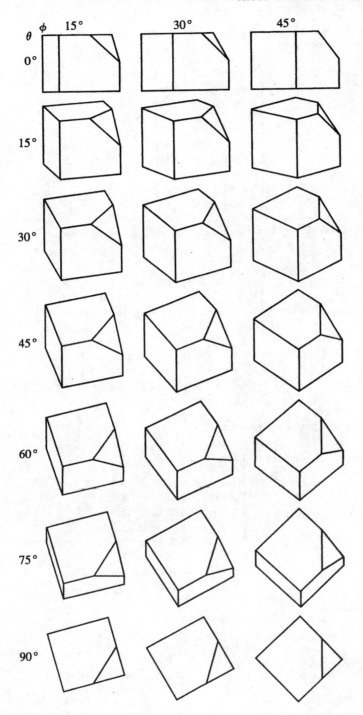

**Figure 3–16**   Trimetric projections.

parallel projection onto the $z = 0$ plane. The position vectors for the cube with one corner removed are

$$[X] = \begin{bmatrix} 0 & 0 & 1 & 1 \\ 1 & 0 & 1 & 1 \\ 1 & 0.5 & 1 & 1 \\ 0.5 & 1 & 1 & 1 \\ 0 & 1 & 1 & 1 \\ 0 & 0 & 0 & 1 \\ 1 & 0 & 0 & 1 \\ 1 & 1 & 0 & 1 \\ 0 & 1 & 0 & 1 \\ 1 & 1 & 0.5 & 1 \end{bmatrix}$$

The concatenated trimetric projection is (see Eqs. 3–8, 3–6, and 3–27)

$$[T] = [R_y][R_x][P_z]$$

$$= \begin{bmatrix} \cos\phi & 0 & -\sin\phi & 0 \\ 0 & 1 & 0 & 0 \\ \sin\phi & 0 & \cos\phi & 0 \\ 0 & 0 & 0 & 1 \end{bmatrix} \begin{bmatrix} 1 & 0 & 0 & 0 \\ 0 & \cos\theta & \sin\theta & 0 \\ 0 & -\sin\theta & \cos\theta & 0 \\ 0 & 0 & 0 & 1 \end{bmatrix} \begin{bmatrix} 1 & 0 & 0 & 0 \\ 0 & 1 & 0 & 0 \\ 0 & 0 & 0 & 0 \\ 0 & 0 & 0 & 1 \end{bmatrix}$$

$$= \begin{bmatrix} \cos\phi & \sin\phi\sin\theta & 0 & 0 \\ 0 & \cos\theta & 0 & 0 \\ \sin\phi & -\cos\phi\sin\theta & 0 & 0 \\ 0 & 0 & 0 & 1 \end{bmatrix} = \begin{bmatrix} \sqrt{3}/2 & \sqrt{2}/4 & 0 & 0 \\ 0 & \sqrt{2}/2 & 0 & 0 \\ 1/2 & -\sqrt{6}/4 & 0 & 0 \\ 0 & 0 & 0 & 1 \end{bmatrix}$$

Thus, the transformed position vectors are

$$[X^*] = [X][T] = \begin{bmatrix} 0.5 & -0.612 & 0 & 1 \\ 1.366 & -0.259 & 0 & 1 \\ 1.366 & 0.095 & 0 & 1 \\ 0.933 & 0.272 & 0 & 1 \\ 0.5 & 0.095 & 0 & 1 \\ 0 & 0 & 0 & 1 \\ 0.866 & 0.354 & 0 & 1 \\ 0.866 & 1.061 & 0 & 1 \\ 0 & 0.707 & 0 & 1 \\ 1.116 & 0.754 & 0 & 1 \end{bmatrix}$$

The foreshortening ratios are

$$[U][T] = \begin{bmatrix} 1 & 0 & 0 & 1 \\ 0 & 1 & 0 & 1 \\ 0 & 0 & 1 & 1 \end{bmatrix} \begin{bmatrix} \sqrt{3}/2 & \sqrt{2}/4 & 0 & 0 \\ 0 & \sqrt{2}/2 & 0 & 0 \\ 1/2 & -\sqrt{6}/4 & 0 & 0 \\ 0 & 0 & 0 & 1 \end{bmatrix}$$

$$= \begin{bmatrix} \sqrt{3}/2 & \sqrt{2}/4 & 0 & 1 \\ 0 & \sqrt{2}/2 & 0 & 1 \\ 1/2 & -\sqrt{6}/4 & 0 & 1 \end{bmatrix}$$

and

$$f_x = \sqrt{(\sqrt{3}/2)^2 + (\sqrt{2}/4)^2} = 0.935$$

$$f_y = \sqrt{2}/2 \qquad\qquad\qquad = 0.707$$

$$f_z = \sqrt{(1/2)^2 + (-\sqrt{6}/4)^2} = 0.791$$

---

A dimetric projection is a trimetric projection with two of the three fore-shortening factors equal; the third is arbitrary. A dimetric projection is constructed by a rotation about the $y$-axis through an angle $\phi$ followed by rotation about the $x$-axis through an angle $\theta$ and projection from a center of projection at infinity onto the $z = 0$ plane. The specific rotation angles are as yet unknown. Using Eqs. (3–8), (3–6) and (3–27), the resulting transformation is

$$[T] = [R_y][R_x][P_z]$$

$$= \begin{bmatrix} \cos\phi & 0 & -\sin\phi & 0 \\ 0 & 1 & 0 & 0 \\ \sin\phi & 0 & \cos\phi & 0 \\ 0 & 0 & 0 & 1 \end{bmatrix} \begin{bmatrix} 1 & 0 & 0 & 0 \\ 0 & \cos\theta & \sin\theta & 0 \\ 0 & -\sin\theta & \cos\theta & 0 \\ 0 & 0 & 0 & 1 \end{bmatrix} \begin{bmatrix} 1 & 0 & 0 & 0 \\ 0 & 1 & 0 & 0 \\ 0 & 0 & 0 & 0 \\ 0 & 0 & 0 & 1 \end{bmatrix}$$

Concatenation yields

$$[T] = \begin{bmatrix} \cos\phi & \sin\phi\sin\theta & 0 & 0 \\ 0 & \cos\theta & 0 & 0 \\ \sin\phi & -\cos\phi\sin\theta & 0 & 0 \\ 0 & 0 & 0 & 1 \end{bmatrix} \qquad (3-32)$$

The unit vectors on the $x, y,$ and $z$ principal axes transform to

$$[U^*] = [U][T] = \begin{bmatrix} 1 & 0 & 0 & 1 \\ 0 & 1 & 0 & 1 \\ 0 & 0 & 1 & 1 \end{bmatrix} \begin{bmatrix} \cos\phi & \sin\phi\sin\theta & 0 & 0 \\ 0 & \cos\theta & 0 & 0 \\ \sin\phi & -\cos\phi\sin\theta & 0 & 0 \\ 0 & 0 & 0 & 1 \end{bmatrix}$$

$$[U^*] = \begin{bmatrix} \cos\phi & \sin\phi\sin\theta & 0 & 1 \\ 0 & \cos\theta & 0 & 1 \\ \sin\phi & -\cos\phi\sin\theta & 0 & 1 \end{bmatrix} \qquad (3-33)$$

The square of the length of the original unit vector along the $x$-axis, i.e., the square of the foreshortening factor, is now

$$f_x^2 = (x_x^{*2} + y_x^{*2}) = \cos^2\phi + \sin^2\phi\sin^2\theta \qquad (3-34)$$

Similarly, the squares of the lengths of the original unit vectors along the $y$-

and $z$-axes are given by

$$f_y^2 = (x_y^{*2} + y_y^{*2}) = \cos^2 \theta \tag{3-35}$$

$$f_z^2 = (x_z^{*2} + y_z^{*2}) = \sin^2 \phi + \cos^2 \phi \sin^2 \theta \tag{3-36}$$

Equating the foreshortening factors along the $x$ and $y$ principal axes† yields one equation in the two unknown rotation angles $\phi$ and $\theta$. Specifically,

$$\cos^2 \phi + \sin^2 \phi \sin^2 \theta = \cos^2 \theta$$

Using the identities $\cos^2 \phi = 1 - \sin^2 \phi$ and $\cos^2 \theta = 1 - \sin^2 \theta$ yields

$$\sin^2 \phi = \frac{\sin^2 \theta}{1 - \sin^2 \theta} \tag{3-37}$$

A second relation between $\phi$ and $\theta$ is obtained by choosing the foreshortening factor along the $z$ principal axis $f_z$. Combining Eqs. (3–36) and (3–37) using $\cos^2 \phi = 1 - \sin^2 \phi$ yields

$$2\sin^2 \theta - 2\sin^4 \theta - (1 - \sin^2 \theta)f_z^2 = 0$$

or

$$2\sin^4 \theta - (2 + f_z^2)\sin^2 \theta + f_z^2 = 0 \tag{3-38}$$

After letting $u = \sin^2 \theta$, solution yields

$$\sin^2 \theta = f_z^2/2,\ 1$$

Since the $\sin^2 \theta = 1$ solution yields an infinite result when substituted into Eq. (3–37), it is discarded. Hence,

$$\theta = \sin^{-1}\left( \pm f_z/\sqrt{2} \right) \tag{3-39}$$

Substituting into Eq. (3–37) yields

$$\phi = \sin^{-1}\left( \pm f_z/\sqrt{2 - f_z^2} \right) \tag{3-40}$$

This result shows that the range of foreshortening factors is $0 \le f_z \le 1$.‡ Further, note that each foreshortening factor $f_z$ yields four possible dimetric projections.

Figure 3–17 shows dimetric projections for various foreshortening factors. For each foreshortening factor, the dimetric projection corresponding to a positive rotation about the $y$-axis followed by a positive rotation about the $x$-axis was chosen.

---

†Any two of the three principal axes could have been used.
‡Negative foreshortening factors are not sensible.

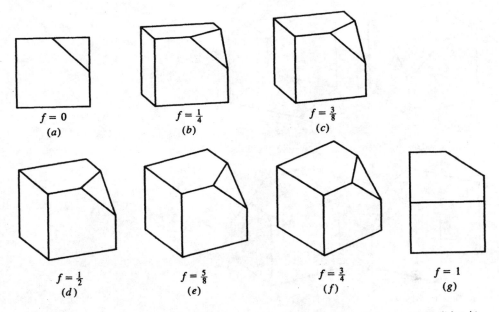

$f = 0$
(a)

$f = \frac{1}{4}$
(b)

$f = \frac{3}{8}$
(c)

$f = \frac{1}{2}$
(d)

$f = \frac{5}{8}$
(e)

$f = \frac{3}{4}$
(f)

$f = 1$
(g)

**Figure 3–17**   Dimetric projections for various foreshortening factors. (a) 0; (b) 1/4; (c) 3/8; (d) 1/2; (e) 5/8; (f) 3/4; (g) 1.

Figure 3–18 shows the four possible dimetric projections for a foreshortening factor of 5/8.

An example illustrates specific results.

---

### Example 3–14    Dimetric Projections

For the cube with the corner cut off, determine the dimetric projection for a foreshortening factor along the $z$-axis of 1/2.

From Eq. (3–39)

$$\theta = \sin^{-1}\left(\pm f_z/\sqrt{2}\right)$$

$$= \sin^{-1}\left(\pm 1/2\sqrt{2}\right)$$

$$= \sin^{-1}(\pm 0.35355)$$

$$= \pm 20.705°$$

From Eq. (3–40)

$$\phi = \sin^{-1}\left(\pm f_z/\sqrt{2 - f_z^2}\right)$$

$$= \sin^{-1}\left(\pm 1/2/\sqrt{7/4}\right)$$

$$= \sin^{-1}(\pm 0.378)$$

$$= \pm 22.208°$$

Choosing $\phi = +22.208°$ and $\theta = +20.705°$, Eq. (3–32) yields the dimetric

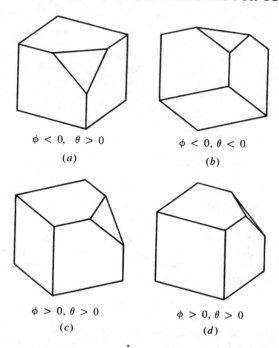

$\phi < 0, \quad \theta > 0$

(a)

$\phi < 0, \theta < 0$

(b)

$\phi > 0, \theta > 0$

(c)

$\phi > 0, \theta > 0$

(d)

**Figure 3–18**   Four possible dimetric projections for a foreshortening factor of 5/8 and rotation angles $\phi = \pm 29.52°$, $\theta = \pm 26.23°$. (a) $\phi = -29.52°$, $\theta = +26.23°$; (b)$\phi = -29.52°$, $\theta = -26.23°$; (c) $\phi = +29.52°$, $\theta = +26.23°$; (d) $\phi = +29.52°$, $\theta = -26.23°$.

projection matrix

$$[T] = \begin{bmatrix} 0.926 & 0.134 & 0 & 0 \\ 0 & 0.935 & 0 & 0 \\ 0.378 & -0.327 & 0 & 0 \\ 0 & 0 & 0 & 1 \end{bmatrix}$$

Recalling the position vectors for the cube with the corner cut off $[X]$ (see Ex. 3–13), the transformed position vectors are

$$[X^*] = [X][T] = \begin{bmatrix} 0.378 & -0.327 & 0 & 1 \\ 1.304 & -0.194 & 0 & 1 \\ 1.304 & 0.274 & 0 & 1 \\ 0.841 & 0.675 & 0 & 1 \\ 0.378 & 0.608 & 0 & 1 \\ 0 & 0 & 0 & 1 \\ 0.926 & 0.134 & 0 & 1 \\ 0.926 & 1.069 & 0 & 1 \\ 0 & 0.935 & 0 & 1 \\ 1.115 & 0.905 & 0 & 1 \end{bmatrix}$$

The result is shown in Fig. 3–17d.

A dimetric projection allows two of the three transformed principal axes to be measured with the same scale factor. Measurements along the third transformed principal axis require a different scale factor. If accurate scaling of the dimensions of the projected object is required, this can lead to both confusion and error. An isometric projection eliminates this problem.

In an isometric projection all three foreshortening factors are equal. Recalling Eqs. (3–34) to (3–36) and equating Eqs. (3–34) and (3–35) again yields Eq. (3–37), i.e.,

$$\sin^2 \phi = \frac{\sin^2 \theta}{1 - \sin^2 \theta} \tag{3 – 37}$$

Equating Eqs. (3–35) and (3–36) yields

$$\sin^2 \phi = \frac{1 - 2\sin^2 \theta}{1 - \sin^2 \theta} \tag{3 – 41}$$

From Eqs. (3–37) and (3–41) it follows that $\sin^2 \theta = 1/3$ or $\sin \theta = \pm\sqrt{1/3}$ and $\theta = \pm 35.26°$. Then

$$\sin^2 \phi = \frac{1/3}{1 - 1/3} = 1/2$$

and $\phi = \pm 45°$. Again note that there are four possible isometric projections. These are shown in Fig. 3–19. The foreshortening factor for an isometric projection is (see Eq. 3–35)

$$f = \sqrt{\cos^2 \theta} = \sqrt{2/3} = 0.8165$$

In fact, an isometric projection is a special case of a dimetric projection with $f_z = 0.8165$.

The angle that the projected $x$-axis makes with the horizontal is important in manual construction of isometric projections. Transforming the unit vector along the $x$-axis using the isometric projection matrix yields

$$[U_x^*] = [1 \quad 0 \quad 0 \quad 1] \begin{bmatrix} \cos\phi & \sin\phi\sin\theta & 0 & 0 \\ 0 & \cos\theta & 0 & 0 \\ \sin\phi & -\cos\phi\sin\theta & 0 & 0 \\ 0 & 0 & 0 & 1 \end{bmatrix}$$

$$= [\cos\phi \quad \sin\phi\sin\theta \quad 0 \quad 1]$$

The angle between the projected $x$-axis and the horizontal is then

$$\tan\alpha = \frac{y_x^*}{x_x^*} = \frac{\sin\phi\sin\theta}{\cos\phi} = \pm\sin\theta \tag{3 – 42}$$

since $\sin\phi = \cos\phi$ for $\phi = 45°$. Alpha is then

$$\alpha = \tan^{-1}(\pm\sin 35.26439°) = \pm 30°$$

A plastic right triangle with included angles of 30° and 60° is a commonly used tool for manually constructing isometric projections. An example illustrates the details.

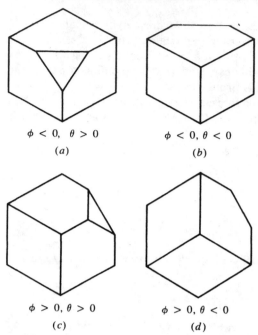

$\phi < 0, \ \theta > 0$

(a)

$\phi < 0, \theta < 0$

(b)

$\phi > 0, \theta > 0$

(c)

$\phi > 0, \theta < 0$

(d)

**Figure 3–19**   Four possible isometric projections with rotation angles $\phi = \pm 45°$, $\theta = \pm 35.26°$. (a) $\phi = -45°$, $\theta = +35.26°$; (b) $\phi = -45°$, $\theta = -35.26°$; (c) $\phi = +45°$, $\theta = +35.26°$; (d) $\phi = +45°$, $\theta = -35.26°$.

---

### Example 3–15     Isometric Projection

Again considering the cube with the corner cut off (see Ex. 3–13), determine the isometric projection for $\phi = -45°$ and $\theta = +35.26439°$. From Eq. (3–32) the isometric projection transformation is

$$[T] = \begin{bmatrix} 0.707 & -0.408 & 0 & 0 \\ 0 & 0.816 & 0 & 0 \\ -0.707 & -0.408 & 0 & 0 \\ 0 & 0 & 0 & 1 \end{bmatrix}$$

Recalling the position vectors $[X]$, the transformed position vectors are

$$[X^*] = [X][T] = \begin{bmatrix} -0.707 & -0.408 & 0 & 1 \\ 0 & -0.816 & 0 & 1 \\ 0 & -0.408 & 0 & 1 \\ -0.354 & 0.204 & 0 & 1 \\ -0.707 & 0.408 & 0 & 1 \\ 0 & 0 & 0 & 1 \\ 0.707 & -0.408 & 0 & 1 \\ 0.707 & 0.408 & 0 & 1 \\ 0 & 0.816 & 0 & 1 \\ 0.354 & 0.204 & 0 & 1 \end{bmatrix}$$

The result is shown in Fig. 3–19a.

---

### 3–14    OBLIQUE PROJECTIONS

In contrast to the orthographic and axonometric projections for which the projectors are perpendicular to the plane of projection, an oblique projection is formed by parallel projectors from a center of projection at infinity that intersect the plane of projection at an oblique angle. The general scheme is shown in Fig. 3–20.

Oblique projections illustrate the general three-dimensional shape of the object. However, only faces of the object parallel to the plane of projection are shown at their true size and shape, i.e., angles and lengths are preserved for these faces only. In fact, the oblique projection of these faces is equivalent to an orthographic front view. Faces not parallel to the plane of projection are distorted.

Two oblique projections, cavalier and cabinet, are of particular interest. A cavalier projection is obtained when the angle between the oblique projectors and the plane of projection is 45°. In a cavalier projection the foreshortening factors for all three principal directions are equal. The resulting figure appears too thick. A cabinet projection is used to 'correct' this deficiency.

An oblique projection for which the foreshortening factor for edges perpendicular to the plane of projection is one-half is called a cabinet projection. As is shown below, for a cabinet projection the angle between the projectors and the plane of projection is $\cot^{-1}(1/2) = 63.43°$.

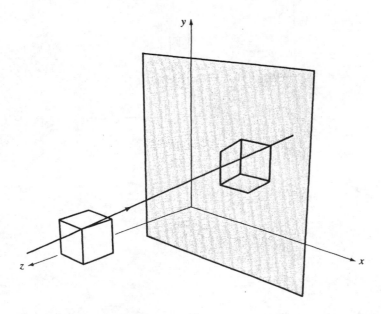

**Figure 3–20**    Oblique projection.

To develop the transformation matrix for an oblique projection, consider the unit vector $[\,0 \quad 0 \quad 1\,]$ along the $z$-axis shown in Fig. 3–21. For an orthographic or axonometric projection onto the $z = 0$ plane the vector $PO$ gives the direction of projection. For an oblique projection, the projectors make an angle with the plane of projection. Typical oblique projectors, $P_1O$ and $PP_2$, are shown in Fig. 3–21. $P_1O$ and $PP_2$ make an angle $\beta$ with the plane of projection $z = 0$. Note that all possible projectors through $P$ or $O$ making an angle $\beta$ with the $z = 0$ plane lie on the surface of a cone with apex at $P$ or $O$. Thus, there are an infinite number of oblique projections for a given angle $\beta$.

The projector $P_1O$ can be obtained from $PO$ by translating the point $P$ to the point $P_1$ at $[\,-a \quad -b \quad 1\,]$. In the two-dimensional plane through $P$ perpendicular to the $z$-axis, the $3 \times 3$ transformation matrix is

$$[\,T'\,] = \begin{bmatrix} 1 & 0 & 0 \\ 0 & 1 & 0 \\ -a & -b & 1 \end{bmatrix}$$

In three dimensions this two-dimensional translation is equivalent to a shearing of the vector $PO$ in the $x$ and $y$ directions. The required transformation to accomplish this is

$$[\,T''\,] = \begin{bmatrix} 1 & 0 & 0 & 0 \\ 0 & 1 & 0 & 0 \\ -a & -b & 1 & 0 \\ 0 & 0 & 0 & 1 \end{bmatrix}$$

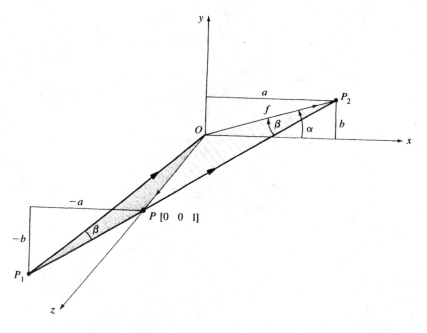

**Figure 3–21**   Direction of the oblique projection matrix.

Projection onto the $z = 0$ plane yields

$$[T] = \begin{bmatrix} 1 & 0 & 0 & 0 \\ 0 & 1 & 0 & 0 \\ -a & -b & 0 & 0 \\ 0 & 0 & 0 & 1 \end{bmatrix}$$

From Fig. 3–21

$$a = f \cos \alpha$$
$$b = f \sin \alpha$$

where $f$ is the projected length of the $z$-axis unit vector, i.e., the foreshortening factor, and $\alpha$ is the angle between the horizontal and the projected $z$-axis. Figure 3–21 also shows that $\beta$, the angle between the oblique projectors and the plane of projection, is

$$\beta = \cot^{-1}(f) \tag{3 – 43}$$

Thus, the transformation for an oblique projection is

$$[T] = \begin{bmatrix} 1 & 0 & 0 & 0 \\ 0 & 1 & 0 & 0 \\ -f \cos \alpha & -f \sin \alpha & 0 & 0 \\ 0 & 0 & 0 & 1 \end{bmatrix} \tag{3 – 44}$$

If $f = 0$, $\beta = 90°$, then an orthographic projection results. If $f = 1$, the edges perpendicular to the projection plane are not foreshortened. This is the condition for a cavalier projection. From Eq. (3–43)

$$\beta = \cot^{-1}(1) = 45°$$

For a cavalier projection, notice that $\alpha$ is still a free parameter. Figure 3–22 shows cavalier projections for several values of $\alpha$. Commonly used values of $\alpha$ are 30° and 45°. Values of $180° - \alpha$ are also acceptable.

A cabinet projection is obtained when the foreshortening factor $f = 1/2$. Here

$$\beta = \cot^{-1}(1/2) = 63.435°$$

Again, as shown in Fig. 3–23, $\alpha$ is variable. Common values are 30° and 45°. Values of $180° - \alpha$ are also acceptable. Figure 3–24 shows oblique projections for foreshortening factors $f = 1, 7/8, 3/4, 5/8, 1/2$, with $\alpha = 45°$.

Because one face is shown in its true shape, oblique projections are particularly suited for illustration of objects with circular or otherwise curved faces. Faces with these characteristics should be parallel to the plane of projection to avoid unwanted distortions. Similarly, as in all parallel projections, objects with one dimension significantly larger than the others suffer significant distortion unless the long dimension is parallel to the projection plane. These effects are illustrated in Fig. 3–25.

A detailed example is given below.

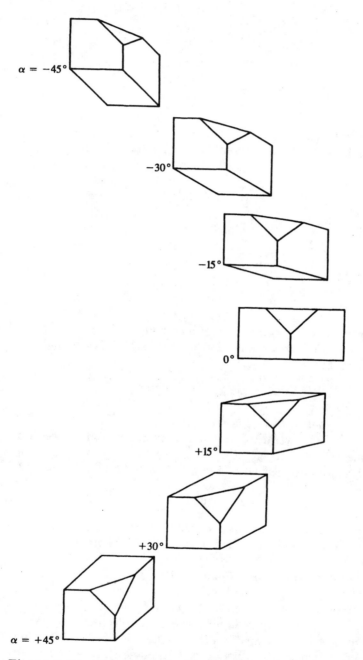

$\alpha = -45°$

$-30°$

$-15°$

$0°$

$+15°$

$+30°$

$\alpha = +45°$

**Figure 3–22**  Cavalier projections. Top to bottom, $\alpha = -45°$ to $+45°$ at 15° intervals with $\beta = 45°$.

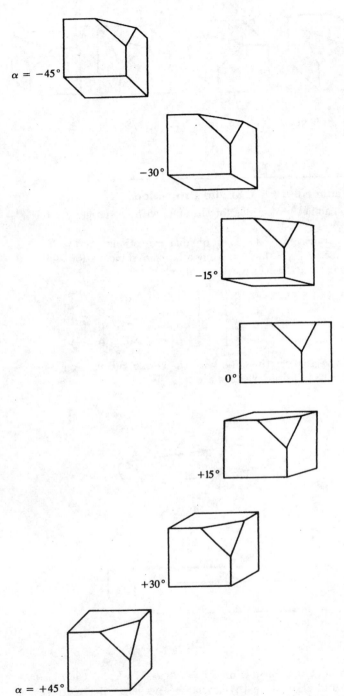

$\alpha = -45°$

$-30°$

$-15°$

$0°$

$+15°$

$+30°$

$\alpha = +45°$

**Figure 3-23**    Cabinet projections. Top to bottom, $\alpha = -45°$ to $+45°$ at 15° intervals
with $f = 0.5$.

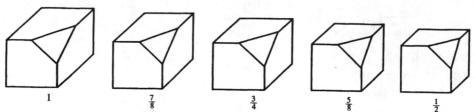

**Figure 3–24**  Oblique projections. Left to right, $f = 1$, 7/8, 3/4, 5/8, 1/2, with $\alpha = 45°$.

---

### Example 3–16    Oblique Projections

Develop cavalier and cabinet projections for the cube with one corner cut off (see Ex. 3–13).

Recalling that a cavalier projection is an oblique projection with $\beta = 45°$, i.e., a foreshortening factor $f = 1$, and choosing a horizontal inclination angle $\alpha = 30°$, Eq. (3–44) yields the transformation matrix

$$[T] = \begin{bmatrix} 1 & 0 & 0 & 0 \\ 0 & 1 & 0 & 0 \\ -f\cos\alpha & -f\sin\alpha & 0 & 0 \\ 0 & 0 & 0 & 1 \end{bmatrix} = \begin{bmatrix} 1 & 0 & 0 & 0 \\ 0 & 1 & 0 & 0 \\ -0.866 & -0.5 & 0 & 0 \\ 0 & 0 & 0 & 1 \end{bmatrix}$$

Recalling the position vectors for the cube with the corner cut off $[X]$ (see Ex. 3–13), the transformed position vectors are

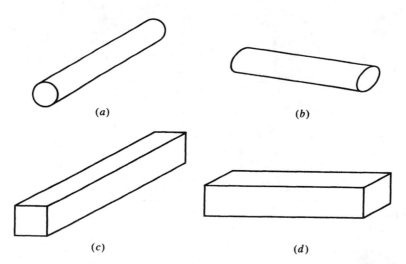

(a)

(b)

(c)

(d)

**Figure 3–25**  Distortion in oblique projections, $f = 5/8$, $\alpha = 45°$. (a) Circular face parallel to projection plane; (b) circular face perpendicular to projection plane; (c) long dimension perpendicular to projection plane; (d) long dimension parallel to projection plane.

$$[X^*] = [X][T] = \begin{bmatrix} -0.866 & -0.5 & 0 & 1 \\ 0.134 & -0.5 & 0 & 1 \\ 0.134 & 0 & 0 & 1 \\ -0.366 & 0.5 & 0 & 1 \\ -0.866 & 0.5 & 0 & 1 \\ 0 & 0 & 0 & 1 \\ 1 & 0 & 0 & 1 \\ 1 & 1 & 0 & 1 \\ 0 & 1 & 0 & 1 \\ 0.567 & 0.75 & 0 & 1 \end{bmatrix}$$

The result is shown in Fig. 3–22.

Turning now to the cabinet projection, and recalling that the foreshortening factor is 1/2, Eq. (3–43) yields

$$\beta = \cot^{-1}(1/2) = \tan^{-1}(2) = 63.435°$$

Again choosing $\alpha = 30°$ Eq. (3–44) becomes

$$[T] = \begin{bmatrix} 1 & 0 & 0 & 0 \\ 0 & 1 & 0 & 0 \\ -f\cos\alpha & -f\sin\alpha & 0 & 0 \\ 0 & 0 & 0 & 1 \end{bmatrix} = \begin{bmatrix} 1 & 0 & 0 & 0 \\ 0 & 1 & 0 & 0 \\ -0.433 & -0.25 & 0 & 0 \\ 0 & 0 & 0 & 1 \end{bmatrix}$$

The transformed position vectors for the cabinet projection of the cube with the corner cut off are

$$[X^*] = [X][T] = \begin{bmatrix} -0.433 & -0.25 & 0 & 1 \\ 0.567 & -0.25 & 0 & 1 \\ 0.567 & 0.25 & 0 & 1 \\ 0.067 & 0.75 & 0 & 1 \\ -0.433 & 0.75 & 0 & 1 \\ 0 & 0 & 0 & 1 \\ 1 & 0 & 0 & 1 \\ 1 & 1 & 0 & 1 \\ 0 & 1 & 0 & 1 \\ 0.783 & 0.875 & 0 & 1 \end{bmatrix}$$

The result is shown in Fig. 3–23.

Notice that for both the cavalier and cabinet projections the triangular corner is *not* shown either true size or true shape because it is *not* parallel to the plane of projection ($z = 0$).

## 3–15   PERSPECTIVE TRANSFORMATIONS

When any of the first three elements of the fourth column of the general $4 \times 4$ homogeneous coordinate transformation matrix is nonzero, a perspective transformation results. As previously mentioned (see Sec. 3–11), a perspective transformation is a transformation from one three space to another three space. In contrast to the parallel transformations previously discussed, in perspective transformations parallel lines converge, object size is reduced with increasing distance from the center of projection, and nonuniform foreshortening of lines in the object as a function of orientation and distance of the object from the center of projection occurs. All of these effects aid the depth perception of the human visual system, but the shape of the object is not preserved.

A single-point perspective transformation is given by

$$[\, x \quad y \quad z \quad 1\,] \begin{bmatrix} 1 & 0 & 0 & 0 \\ 0 & 1 & 0 & 0 \\ 0 & 0 & 1 & r \\ 0 & 0 & 0 & 1 \end{bmatrix} = [\, x \quad y \quad z \quad rz+1\,] \qquad (3-45)$$

Here $h = rz + 1 \neq 1$. The ordinary coordinates are obtained by dividing through by $h$, to yield

$$[\, x^* \quad y^* \quad z^* \quad 1\,] = \left[\, \frac{x}{rz+1} \quad \frac{y}{rz+1} \quad \frac{z}{rz+1} \quad 1\,\right] \qquad (3-46)$$

A perspective projection onto some two-dimensional viewing plane is obtained by concatenating an orthographic projection with the perspective transformation. For example, a perspective projection onto the $z = 0$ plane is given by

$$[\,T\,] = [\,P_r\,][\,P_z\,]$$

$$= \begin{bmatrix} 1 & 0 & 0 & 0 \\ 0 & 1 & 0 & 0 \\ 0 & 0 & 1 & r \\ 0 & 0 & 0 & 1 \end{bmatrix} \begin{bmatrix} 1 & 0 & 0 & 0 \\ 0 & 1 & 0 & 0 \\ 0 & 0 & 0 & 0 \\ 0 & 0 & 0 & 1 \end{bmatrix} = \begin{bmatrix} 1 & 0 & 0 & 0 \\ 0 & 1 & 0 & 0 \\ 0 & 0 & 0 & r \\ 0 & 0 & 0 & 1 \end{bmatrix} \qquad (3-47)$$

and

$$[\, x \quad y \quad z \quad 1\,] \begin{bmatrix} 1 & 0 & 0 & 0 \\ 0 & 1 & 0 & 0 \\ 0 & 0 & 0 & r \\ 0 & 0 & 0 & 1 \end{bmatrix} = [\, x \quad y \quad 0 \quad rz+1\,] \qquad (3-48)$$

The ordinary coordinates are

$$[\, x^* \quad y^* \quad z^* \quad 1\,] = \left[\, \frac{x}{rz+1} \quad \frac{y}{rz+1} \quad 0 \quad 1\,\right] \qquad (3-49)$$

To show that Eq. (3–47) produces a perspective projection onto the $z = 0$ plane, consider Fig. 3–26, which illustrates the geometry for a perspective projection of the three-dimensional point $P$ onto a $z = z^* = 0$ plane at $P^*$ from a center of projection at $z_c$ on the $z$-axis. The coordinates of the projected point $P^*$ are obtained using similar triangles. From Fig. 3–26

$$\frac{x^*}{z_c} = \frac{x}{z_c - z}$$

or

$$x^* = \frac{x}{1 - \dfrac{z}{z_c}}$$

and

$$\frac{y^*}{\sqrt{x^{*2} + z_c^2}} = \frac{y}{\sqrt{x^2 + (z_c - z)^2}}$$

or

$$y^* = \frac{y}{1 - \dfrac{z}{z_c}}$$

$z^*$ is, of course, zero.

Letting $r = -1/z_c$ yields results identical to those obtained using Eq. (3–47). Thus, Eq. (3–47) produces a perspective projection onto the $z = 0$ plane from a center of projection at $(-1/r)$ on the $z$-axis. Notice that as $z_c$ approaches infinity, $r$ approaches zero and an axonometric projection onto the $z = 0$ plane results. Further, notice that for points in the plane of projection, i.e., $z = 0$, the perspective transformation has no effect. Also note that the origin ($x = y = z = 0$) is unaffected. Consequently, if the plane of projection ($z = 0$) passes through an object, then that section of the object is shown at true size and true shape. All other parts of the object are distorted.

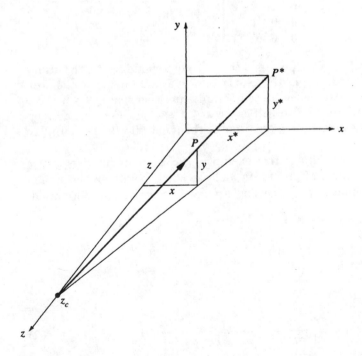

**Figure 3–26**   Perspective projection of a point.

To help understand the effects of a perspective transformation consider Fig. 3–27. Figure 3–27 shows the perspective projection onto the $z = 0$ plane of the line $AB$ originally parallel to the $z$-axis, into the line $A^*B^*$ in the $z = 0$ plane, from a center of projection at $-1/r$ on the $z$-axis. The transformation can be considered in two steps (see Eq. 3–47). First, the perspective transformation of the line $AB$ yields the three-dimensional transformed line $A'B'$ (see Fig. 3–27 below). Subsequent orthographic projection of the line $A'B'$ in three-dimensional perspective space onto the $z = 0$ plane from a center of projection at infinity on the $z$-axis yields the line $A^*B^*$.

Examination of Fig. 3–27 shows that the line $A'B'$ intersects the $z = 0$ plane at the same point as the line $AB$. It also intersects the $z$-axis at $z = +1/r$. Effectively then, the perspective transformation (see Eqs. 3–45 and 3–46) has transformed the intersection point at infinity of the line $AB$ parallel to the $z$-axis and the $z$-axis itself into the finite point at $z = 1/r$ on the $z$-axis. This point is called the vanishing point† Notice that the vanishing point lies an equal distance on the opposite side of the plane of projection from the center of projection, e.g., if $z = 0$ is the projection plane and the center of projection is at $z = -1/r$, the vanishing point is at $z = +1/r$.

To confirm this observation consider the perspective transformation of the point at infinity on the $+z$-axis, i.e.,

$$[\,0 \quad 0 \quad 1 \quad 0\,] \begin{bmatrix} 1 & 0 & 0 & 0 \\ 0 & 1 & 0 & 0 \\ 0 & 0 & 1 & r \\ 0 & 0 & 0 & 1 \end{bmatrix} = [\,0 \quad 0 \quad 1 \quad r\,] \qquad (3-50)$$

The point $[\,x^* \quad y^* \quad z^* \quad 1\,] = [\,0 \quad 0 \quad 1/r \quad 1\,]$, corresponding to the transformed point at infinity on the positive $z$-axis, is now a finite point on the positive $z$-axis. This means that the entire semi-infinite positive space $(0 \le z \le \infty)$ is transformed to the finite positive half space $0 \le z^* \le 1/r$. Further, all lines originally parallel to the $z$-axis now pass through the point $[\,0 \quad 0 \quad 1/r \quad 1\,]$, the vanishing point.

Before presenting some illustrative examples the single-point perspective transformations with centers of projection and vanishing points on the $x$- and $y$-axes are given for completeness. The single-point perspective transformation

$$[\,x \quad y \quad z \quad 1\,] \begin{bmatrix} 1 & 0 & 0 & p \\ 0 & 1 & 0 & 0 \\ 0 & 0 & 1 & 0 \\ 0 & 0 & 0 & 1 \end{bmatrix} = [\,x \quad y \quad z \quad (px+1)\,] \qquad (3-51)$$

with ordinary coordinates

$$[\,x^* \quad y^* \quad z^* \quad 1\,] = \left[\, \frac{x}{px+1} \quad \frac{y}{px+1} \quad \frac{z}{px+1} \quad 1 \,\right] \qquad (3-52)$$

---

†Intuitively the vanishing point is that point in the 'distance' to which parallel lines 'appear' to converge and 'vanish'. A practical example is a long straight railroad track.

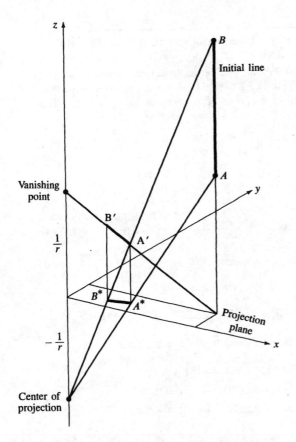

**Figure 3–27** Projection of a line parallel to the z-axis.

has a center of projection at $[\,-1/p \quad 0 \quad 0 \quad 1\,]$ and a vanishing point located on the x-axis at $[\,1/p \quad 0 \quad 0 \quad 1\,]$.

The single-point perspective transformation

$$[\,x \quad y \quad z \quad 1\,]\begin{bmatrix} 1 & 0 & 0 & 0 \\ 0 & 1 & 0 & q \\ 0 & 0 & 1 & 0 \\ 0 & 0 & 0 & 1 \end{bmatrix} = [\,x \quad y \quad z \quad (qy+1)\,] \qquad (3-53)$$

with ordinary coordinates

$$[\,x^* \quad y^* \quad z^* \quad 1\,] = \left[\, \frac{x}{qy+1} \quad \frac{y}{qy+1} \quad \frac{z}{qy+1} \quad 1 \,\right] \qquad (3-54)$$

has a center of projection at $[\,0 \quad -1/q \quad 0 \quad 1\,]$ and a vanishing point located on the y-axis at $[\,0 \quad 1/q \quad 0 \quad 1\,]$.

**Example 3–17    Perspective Transformation of a Line Parallel to the $z$-Axis**

Consider the line segment $AB$ in Fig. 3–27 parallel to the $z$-axis with end points $A\,[\,3\quad 2\quad 4\quad 1\,]$ and $B\,[\,3\quad 2\quad 8\quad 1\,]$. Perform a perspective projection onto the $z = 0$ plane from a center of projection at $z_c = -2$. The perspective transformation of $AB$ to $A'B'$ with $r = 0.5$ is

$$\begin{matrix} A \\ B \end{matrix} \begin{bmatrix} 3 & 2 & 4 & 1 \\ 3 & 2 & 8 & 1 \end{bmatrix} \begin{bmatrix} 1 & 0 & 0 & 0 \\ 0 & 1 & 0 & 0 \\ 0 & 0 & 1 & 0.5 \\ 0 & 0 & 0 & 1 \end{bmatrix} = \begin{bmatrix} 3 & 2 & 4 & 3 \\ 3 & 2 & 8 & 5 \end{bmatrix}$$

$$= \begin{bmatrix} 1 & 0.667 & 1.333 & 1 \\ 0.6 & 0.4 & 1.6 & 1 \end{bmatrix} \begin{matrix} A' \\ B' \end{matrix}$$

The parametric equation of the line segment $A'B'$ is

$$P(t) = [\,A'\,] + [\,B' - A'\,]t \quad 0 \le t \le 1$$

or    $P(t) = [\,1\quad 0.667\quad 1.333\quad 1\,] + [\,-0.4\quad -0.267\quad 0.267\quad 0\,]t$

Intersection of this line with the $x = 0$, $y = 0$ and $z = 0$ planes yields

$$\begin{aligned} x(t) = 0 &= 1 - 0.4t & \rightarrow \quad t &= 2.50 \\ y(t) = 0 &= 0.667 - 0.267t & \rightarrow \quad t &= 2.50 \\ z(t) = 0 &= 1.333 + 0.267t & \rightarrow \quad t &= -5.0 \end{aligned}$$

Substituting $t = 2.5$ into the parametric equation of the line $A'B'$ yields

$$z(2.5) = 1.333 + (0.267)(2.5) = 2.0$$

which represents the intersection of the line $A'B'$ with the $z$-axis at $z = +1/r$, the vanishing point. Now substituting $t = -5.0$ into the $x$ and $y$ component equations yields the intersection with the $z = 0$ plane, i.e.,

$$x(-5.0) = 1 - (0.4)(-5.0) = 3.0$$
$$y(-5.0) = 0.667 - (0.267)(-5.0) = 2.0$$

which is the same as the intersection of the line $AB$ with the $z = 0$ plane.
  Projection of line $A'B'$ into the line $A^*B^*$ in the $z = 0$ plane is given by

$$\begin{matrix} A' \\ B' \end{matrix} \begin{bmatrix} 1 & 0.667 & 1.333 & 1 \\ 0.6 & 0.4 & 1.6 & 1 \end{bmatrix} \begin{bmatrix} 1 & 0 & 0 & 0 \\ 0 & 1 & 0 & 0 \\ 0 & 0 & 0 & 0 \\ 0 & 0 & 0 & 1 \end{bmatrix} = \begin{bmatrix} 1 & 0.667 & 0 & 1 \\ 0.6 & 0.4 & 0 & 1 \end{bmatrix} \begin{matrix} A^* \\ B^* \end{matrix}$$

An example using a simple cube is given below.

**Example 3–18    Single-Point Perspective Transformation of a Cube**

Perform a perspective projection onto the $z = 0$ plane of the unit cube shown in Fig. 3–28a from a center of projection at $z_c = 10$ on the $z$-axis.

The single-point perspective factor $r$ is

$$r = -1/z_c = -1/10 = -0.1$$

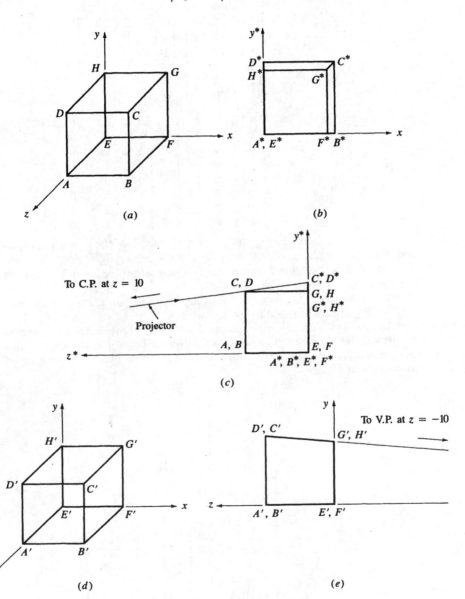

**Figure 3–28**    Single-point perspective projection of a unit cube.

From Eq. (3–48) the transformation is

$$[T] = \begin{bmatrix} 1 & 0 & 0 & 0 \\ 0 & 1 & 0 & 0 \\ 0 & 0 & 0 & -0.1 \\ 0 & 0 & 0 & 1 \end{bmatrix}$$

$$[X^*] = [X][T] = \begin{bmatrix} 0 & 0 & 1 & 1 \\ 1 & 0 & 1 & 1 \\ 1 & 1 & 1 & 1 \\ 0 & 1 & 1 & 1 \\ 0 & 0 & 0 & 1 \\ 1 & 0 & 0 & 1 \\ 1 & 1 & 0 & 1 \\ 0 & 1 & 0 & 1 \end{bmatrix} \begin{bmatrix} 1 & 0 & 0 & 0 \\ 0 & 1 & 0 & 0 \\ 0 & 0 & 0 & -0.1 \\ 0 & 0 & 0 & 1 \end{bmatrix}$$

$$= \begin{bmatrix} 0 & 0 & 0 & 0.9 \\ 1 & 0 & 0 & 0.9 \\ 1 & 1 & 0 & 0.9 \\ 0 & 1 & 0 & 0.9 \\ 0 & 0 & 0 & 1 \\ 1 & 0 & 0 & 1 \\ 1 & 1 & 0 & 1 \\ 0 & 1 & 0 & 1 \end{bmatrix} = \begin{bmatrix} 0 & 0 & 0 & 1 \\ 1.11 & 0 & 0 & 1 \\ 1.11 & 1.11 & 0 & 1 \\ 0 & 1.11 & 0 & 1 \\ 0 & 0 & 0 & 1 \\ 1 & 0 & 0 & 1 \\ 1 & 1 & 0 & 1 \\ 0 & 1 & 0 & 1 \end{bmatrix}$$

The result is shown in Fig. 3–28b. Notice that since the center of projection is on the positive $z$-axis the front face of the cube $ABCD$ projects larger than the back face. Figure 3–28c, which is a parallel projection of the original cube onto the $x = 0$ plane, shows why.

Notice also that because the vanishing point lies on the $z$-axis the line $C^*G^*$ in Fig. 3–28b passes through the origin.

An alternate and equivalent approach to that above is to first perform the perspective transformation to obtain a distorted object in three space and then to orthographically project the result onto some plane. The distorted object is obtained by

$$[X'] = [X][P_r] = \begin{bmatrix} 0 & 0 & 1 & 1 \\ 1 & 0 & 1 & 1 \\ 1 & 1 & 1 & 1 \\ 0 & 1 & 1 & 1 \\ 0 & 0 & 0 & 1 \\ 1 & 0 & 0 & 1 \\ 1 & 1 & 0 & 1 \\ 0 & 1 & 0 & 1 \end{bmatrix} \begin{bmatrix} 1 & 0 & 0 & 0 \\ 0 & 1 & 0 & 0 \\ 0 & 0 & 1 & -0.1 \\ 0 & 0 & 0 & 1 \end{bmatrix}$$

$$= \begin{bmatrix} 0 & 0 & 1 & 0.9 \\ 1 & 0 & 1 & 0.9 \\ 1 & 1 & 1 & 0.9 \\ 0 & 1 & 1 & 0.9 \\ 0 & 0 & 0 & 1 \\ 1 & 0 & 0 & 1 \\ 1 & 1 & 0 & 1 \\ 0 & 1 & 0 & 1 \end{bmatrix} = \begin{bmatrix} 0 & 0 & 1.11 & 1 \\ 1.11 & 0 & 1.11 & 1 \\ 1.11 & 1.11 & 1.11 & 1 \\ 0 & 1.11 & 1.11 & 1 \\ 0 & 0 & 0 & 1 \\ 1 & 0 & 0 & 1 \\ 1 & 1 & 0 & 1 \\ 0 & 1 & 0 & 1 \end{bmatrix}$$

The result is shown using an oblique projection in Fig. 3–28d. Notice that the 'front' face ($A'B'C'D'$) is larger than the 'rear' face ($E'F'G'H'$). Subsequent orthographic projection onto the $z = 0$ plane yields the same result for $[\,X^*\,]$ as given above and illustrated in Fig. 3–28c.

Figure 3–28e, which is an orthographic projection of the distorted object of Fig. 3–28d onto the $x = 0$ plane, shows that the edges of the distorted object originally parallel to the $z$-axis now converge to the vanishing point at $z = -10$.

---

Figure 3–28b does not convey the three-dimensional character of the cube. A more satisfactory result is obtained by centering the cube. This is illustrated in the next example.

---

**Example 3–19   Single-Point Perspective Transformation of a Centered Cube**

The cube shown in Fig. 3–28a can be centered on the $z$-axis by translating it $-1/2$ unit in the $x$ and $y$ directions. The resulting transformation is

$$[T] = [Tr_{xy}][P_{rz}] = \begin{bmatrix} 1 & 0 & 0 & 0 \\ 0 & 1 & 0 & 0 \\ 0 & 0 & 1 & 0 \\ -0.5 & -0.5 & 0 & 1 \end{bmatrix} \begin{bmatrix} 1 & 0 & 0 & 0 \\ 0 & 1 & 0 & 0 \\ 0 & 0 & 0 & -0.1 \\ 0 & 0 & 0 & 1 \end{bmatrix}$$

$$= \begin{bmatrix} 1 & 0 & 0 & 0 \\ 0 & 1 & 0 & 0 \\ 0 & 0 & 0 & -0.1 \\ -0.5 & -0.5 & 0 & 1 \end{bmatrix}$$

The translated cube is shown in Fig. 3–29a.

The transformed ordinary coordinates are

$$[X^*] = [X][T] = \begin{bmatrix} 0 & 0 & 1 & 1 \\ 1 & 0 & 1 & 1 \\ 1 & 1 & 1 & 1 \\ 0 & 1 & 1 & 1 \\ 0 & 0 & 0 & 1 \\ 1 & 0 & 0 & 1 \\ 1 & 1 & 0 & 1 \\ 0 & 1 & 0 & 1 \end{bmatrix} \begin{bmatrix} 1 & 0 & 0 & 0 \\ 0 & 1 & 0 & 0 \\ 0 & 0 & 0 & -0.1 \\ -0.5 & -0.5 & 0 & 1 \end{bmatrix}$$

$$= \begin{bmatrix} -0.5 & -0.5 & 0 & 0.9 \\ 0.5 & -0.5 & 0 & 0.9 \\ 0.5 & 0.5 & 0 & 0.9 \\ -0.5 & 0.5 & 0 & 0.9 \\ -0.5 & -0.5 & 0 & 1 \\ 0.5 & -0.5 & 0 & 1 \\ 0.5 & 0.5 & 0 & 1 \\ -0.5 & 0.5 & 0 & 1 \end{bmatrix} = \begin{bmatrix} -0.56 & -0.56 & 0 & 1 \\ 0.56 & -0.56 & 0 & 1 \\ 0.56 & 0.56 & 0 & 1 \\ -0.56 & 0.56 & 0 & 1 \\ -0.5 & -0.5 & 0 & 1 \\ 0.5 & -0.5 & 0 & 1 \\ 0.5 & 0.5 & 0 & 1 \\ -0.5 & 0.5 & 0 & 1 \end{bmatrix}$$

The result is shown in Fig. 3–29b. Notice that the lines originally parallel to the z-axis connecting the corners of the front and rear faces now converge to intersect the z-axis ($x = 0$, $y = 0$) in Fig. 3–29b.

Unfortunately, the resulting display still does not provide an adequate perception of the three-dimensional shape of the object. Consequently, we turn our attention to more complex perspective transformations.

If two terms in the first three rows of the fourth column of the $4 \times 4$ transformation matrix are nonzero, the result is called a two-point perspective transformation. The two-point perspective transformation

$$
[ x \quad y \quad z \quad 1 ]
\begin{bmatrix}
1 & 0 & 0 & p \\
0 & 1 & 0 & q \\
0 & 0 & 1 & 0 \\
0 & 0 & 0 & 1
\end{bmatrix}
= [ x \quad y \quad z \quad (px + qy + 1) ] \tag{3-55}
$$

with ordinary coordinates,

$$
[ x^* \quad y^* \quad z^* \quad 1 ] = \left[ \frac{x}{px + qy + 1} \quad \frac{y}{px + qy + 1} \quad \frac{z}{px + qy + 1} \quad 1 \right] \tag{3-56}
$$

has two centers of projection: one on the $x$-axis at $[ -1/p \quad 0 \quad 0 \quad 1 ]$ and one on the $y$-axis at $[ 0 \quad -1/q \quad 0 \quad 1 ]$, and two vanishing points: one on the $x$-axis at $[ 1/p \quad 0 \quad 0 \quad 1 ]$ and one on the $y$-axis at $[ 0 \quad 1/q \quad 0 \quad 1 ]$. Note that the two-point perspective transformation given by Eq. (3–55) can be obtained by concatenation of two single-point perspective transformations. Specifically,

$$
[ P_{pq} ] = [ P_p ][ P_q ]
$$

$$
= [ P_q ][ P_p ]
$$

where $[ P_{pq} ]$ is given by Eq. (3–55), $[ P_p ]$ by Eq. (3–53) and $[ P_q ]$ by Eq. (3–51). The next example shows the details of a two-point perspective projection.

---

**Example 3–20   Two-Point Perspective Projections**

Again consider the cube described in Ex. 3–18 transformed by a two-point perspective transformation with centers of projection at $x = -10$ and $y = -10$ projected onto the $z = 0$ plane. The transformation is obtained by concatenating Eqs. (3–55) and (3–27). Specifically,

$$
[ T ] = [ P_{pq} ][ P_z ] =
\begin{bmatrix}
1 & 0 & 0 & p \\
0 & 1 & 0 & q \\
0 & 0 & 1 & 0 \\
0 & 0 & 0 & 1
\end{bmatrix}
\begin{bmatrix}
1 & 0 & 0 & 0 \\
0 & 1 & 0 & 0 \\
0 & 0 & 0 & 0 \\
0 & 0 & 0 & 1
\end{bmatrix}
$$

$$
=
\begin{bmatrix}
1 & 0 & 0 & p \\
0 & 1 & 0 & q \\
0 & 0 & 0 & 0 \\
0 & 0 & 0 & 1
\end{bmatrix}
$$

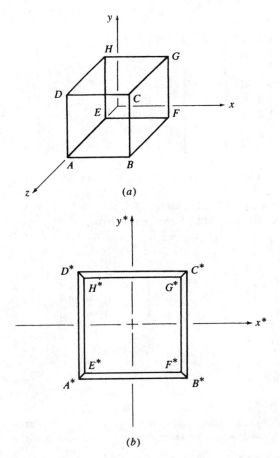

**Figure 3–29** Single-point perspective projection of a centered unit cube.

Here $p$ and $q$ are

$$p = -1/(-10) = 0.1 \qquad q = -1/(-10) = 0.1$$

The transformed coordinates of the cube are

$$[X^*] = [X][T] = \begin{bmatrix} 0 & 0 & 1 & 1 \\ 1 & 0 & 1 & 1 \\ 1 & 1 & 1 & 1 \\ 0 & 1 & 1 & 1 \\ 0 & 0 & 0 & 1 \\ 1 & 0 & 0 & 1 \\ 1 & 1 & 0 & 1 \\ 0 & 1 & 0 & 1 \end{bmatrix} \begin{bmatrix} 1 & 0 & 0 & 0.1 \\ 0 & 1 & 0 & 0.1 \\ 0 & 0 & 0 & 0 \\ 0 & 0 & 0 & 1 \end{bmatrix}$$

$$
=
\begin{bmatrix}
0 & 0 & 0 & 1 \\
1 & 0 & 0 & 1.1 \\
1 & 1 & 0 & 1.2 \\
0 & 1 & 0 & 1.1 \\
0 & 0 & 0 & 1 \\
1 & 0 & 0 & 1.1 \\
1 & 1 & 0 & 1.2 \\
0 & 1 & 0 & 1.1
\end{bmatrix}
=
\begin{bmatrix}
0 & 0 & 0 & 1 \\
0.909 & 0 & 0 & 1 \\
0.833 & 0.833 & 0 & 1 \\
0 & 0.909 & 0 & 1 \\
0 & 0 & 0 & 1 \\
0.909 & 0 & 0 & 1 \\
0.833 & 0.833 & 0 & 1 \\
0 & 0.909 & 0 & 1
\end{bmatrix}
$$

The results are shown in Fig. 3–30a. The two vanishing points are at $x = 10$ and $y = 10$.

Centering the cube on the $z$-axis by translating $-0.5$ in $x$ and $y$ as was done in Ex. 3–18 yields the concatenated transformation matrix

$$
[\,T\,] = [\,T_{xy}\,][\,P_{pq}\,][\,P_z\,]
$$

$$
=
\begin{bmatrix}
1 & 0 & 0 & 0 \\
0 & 1 & 0 & 0 \\
0 & 0 & 1 & 0 \\
-0.5 & -0.5 & 0 & 1
\end{bmatrix}
\begin{bmatrix}
1 & 0 & 0 & 0.1 \\
0 & 1 & 0 & 0.1 \\
0 & 0 & 1 & 0 \\
0 & 0 & 0 & 1
\end{bmatrix}
\begin{bmatrix}
1 & 0 & 0 & 0 \\
0 & 1 & 0 & 0 \\
0 & 0 & 0 & 0 \\
0 & 0 & 0 & 1
\end{bmatrix}
$$

$$
=
\begin{bmatrix}
1 & 0 & 0 & 0.1 \\
0 & 1 & 0 & 0.1 \\
0 & 0 & 0 & 0 \\
-0.5 & -0.5 & 0 & 0.9
\end{bmatrix}
$$

where projection onto the $z = 0$ plane has been assumed. Notice that here the overall scaling factor (see Eq. 3–4) is no longer unity, i.e., there is an apparent scaling of the cube caused by translation. The transformed coordinates are

$$
[\,X^*\,] = [\,X\,][\,T\,] =
\begin{bmatrix}
0 & 0 & 1 & 1 \\
1 & 0 & 1 & 1 \\
1 & 1 & 1 & 1 \\
0 & 1 & 1 & 1 \\
0 & 0 & 0 & 1 \\
1 & 0 & 0 & 1 \\
1 & 1 & 0 & 1 \\
0 & 1 & 0 & 1
\end{bmatrix}
\begin{bmatrix}
1 & 0 & 0 & 0.1 \\
0 & 1 & 0 & 0.1 \\
0 & 0 & 0 & 0 \\
-0.5 & -0.5 & 0 & 0.9
\end{bmatrix}
$$

$$
=
\begin{bmatrix}
-0.5 & -0.5 & 0 & 0.9 \\
0.5 & -0.5 & 0 & 1 \\
0.5 & 0.5 & 0 & 1.1 \\
-0.5 & 0.5 & 0 & 1 \\
-0.5 & -0.5 & 0 & 0.9 \\
0.5 & -0.5 & 0 & 1 \\
0.5 & 0.5 & 0 & 1.1 \\
-0.5 & 0.5 & 0 & 1
\end{bmatrix}
=
\begin{bmatrix}
-0.56 & -0.56 & 0 & 1 \\
0.5 & -0.5 & 0 & 1 \\
0.46 & 0.46 & 0 & 1 \\
-0.5 & 0.5 & 0 & 1 \\
-0.56 & -0.56 & 0 & 1 \\
0.5 & -0.5 & 0 & 1 \\
0.46 & 0.46 & 0 & 1 \\
-0.5 & 0.5 & 0 & 1
\end{bmatrix}
$$

The results are shown in Fig. 3–30b.

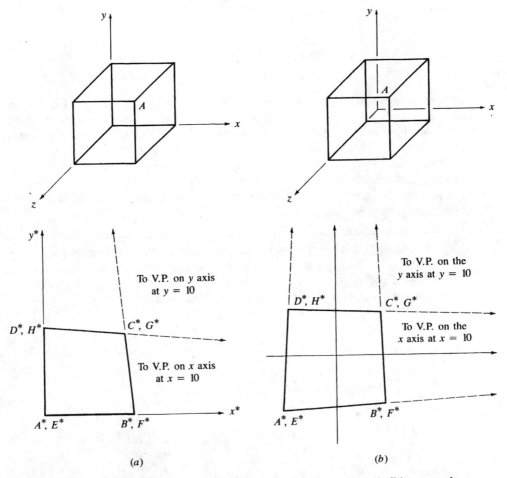

**Figure 3–30**  Two-point perspective projections. (a) Non-centered; (b) centered.

Again the resulting display does not provide an adequate perception of the three-dimensional shape of the object. Hence we turn our attention to three-point perspective transformations.

If three terms in the first three rows of the fourth column of the 4 × 4 transformation matrix are nonzero, then a three-point perspective is obtained. The three-point perspective transformation

$$[\,x \quad y \quad z \quad 1\,] \begin{bmatrix} 1 & 0 & 0 & p \\ 0 & 1 & 0 & q \\ 0 & 0 & 1 & r \\ 0 & 0 & 0 & 1 \end{bmatrix} = [\,x \quad y \quad z \quad (px + qy + rz + 1)\,] \quad (3-57)$$

with ordinary coordinates

$$[x^* \quad y^* \quad z^* \quad 1] = \left[ \frac{x}{px+qy+rz+1} \quad \frac{y}{px+qy+rz+1} \quad \frac{z}{px+qy+rz+1} \quad 1 \right]$$

$$(3-58)$$

has three centers of projection: one on the $x$-axis at $[-1/p \quad 0 \quad 0 \quad 1]$, one on the $y$-axis at $[0 \quad -1/q \quad 0 \quad 1]$, and one on the $z$-axis at $[0 \quad 0 \quad -1/r \quad 1]$, and three vanishing points: one on the $x$-axis at $[1/p \quad 0 \quad 0 \quad 1]$, one on the $y$-axis at $[0 \quad 1/q \quad 0 \quad 1]$, and one on the $z$-axis at $[0 \quad 0 \quad 1/r \quad 1]$.

Again, note that the three-point perspective transformation given by Eq. (3–57) can be obtained by concatenation of three single-point perspective transformations, one for each of the coordinate axes. An example illustrates the generation of a three-point perspective.

---

**Example 3–21    Three-Point Perspective Transformation**

Consider the cube described in Ex. 3–18 transformed by a three-point perspective transformation with centers of projection at $x = -10$, $y = -10$ and $z = 10$ projected onto the $z = 0$ plane. Vanishing points are at $x = 10$, $y = 10$ and $z = -10$. The transformation matrix is

$$[T] = \begin{bmatrix} 1 & 0 & 0 & 0.1 \\ 0 & 1 & 0 & 0.1 \\ 0 & 0 & 0 & -0.1 \\ 0 & 0 & 0 & 1 \end{bmatrix}$$

The transformed coordinates of the cube are

$$[X^*] = [X][T] = \begin{bmatrix} 0 & 0 & 1 & 1 \\ 1 & 0 & 1 & 1 \\ 1 & 1 & 1 & 1 \\ 0 & 1 & 1 & 1 \\ 0 & 0 & 0 & 1 \\ 1 & 0 & 0 & 1 \\ 1 & 1 & 0 & 1 \\ 0 & 1 & 0 & 1 \end{bmatrix} \begin{bmatrix} 1 & 0 & 0 & 0.1 \\ 0 & 1 & 0 & 0.1 \\ 0 & 0 & 0 & -0.1 \\ 0 & 0 & 0 & 1 \end{bmatrix}$$

$$= \begin{bmatrix} 0 & 0 & 0 & 0.9 \\ 1 & 0 & 0 & 1 \\ 1 & 1 & 0 & 1.1 \\ 0 & 1 & 0 & 1 \\ 0 & 0 & 0 & 1 \\ 1 & 0 & 0 & 1.1 \\ 1 & 1 & 0 & 1.2 \\ 0 & 1 & 0 & 1.1 \end{bmatrix} = \begin{bmatrix} 0 & 0 & 0 & 1 \\ 1 & 0 & 0 & 1 \\ 0.909 & 0.909 & 0 & 1 \\ 0 & 1 & 0 & 1 \\ 0 & 0 & 0 & 1 \\ 0.909 & 0 & 0 & 1 \\ 0.833 & 0.833 & 0 & 1 \\ 0 & 0.909 & 0 & 1 \end{bmatrix}$$

The result is shown in Fig. 3–31b. The distorted object, after perspective transformation, is shown in Fig. 3–31c. Note the convergence of the edges.

---

Again, although mathematically correct the resulting view is not informative. Appropriate techniques for generating perspective views are discussed in Sec. 3–16.

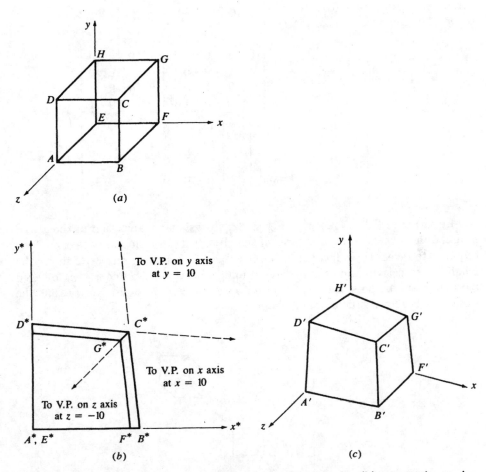

**Figure 3–31**    Three-point perspective. (a) The original cube; (b) perspective projection onto the $z = 0$ plane; (c) the distorted cube.

## 3–16    TECHNIQUES FOR GENERATING PERSPECTIVE VIEWS

The perspective projection views shown in the previous section were uninformative because in each case only one face of the cube was visible from each center of projection. For an observer to perceive the three-dimensional shape of an object from a single view, it is necessary that multiple faces of the object be visible. For simple cuboidal objects, a minimum of three faces must be visible. For a fixed center of projection with the projection plane perpendicular to the viewing direction, a single-point perspective projection, preceded by translation and/or rotation of the object, provides the required multiple face view. Then, provided the center of projection is not too close to the object, a realistic view is obtained.

First, consider simple translation of the object followed by a single-point perspective projection from a center of projection at $z = z_c$ onto the $z = 0$ plane. The required transformation is

$$[T] = [Tr_{xyz}][P_{rz}] = \begin{bmatrix} 1 & 0 & 0 & 0 \\ 0 & 1 & 0 & 0 \\ 0 & 0 & 1 & 0 \\ l & m & n & 1 \end{bmatrix} \begin{bmatrix} 1 & 0 & 0 & 0 \\ 0 & 1 & 0 & 0 \\ 0 & 0 & 0 & r \\ 0 & 0 & 0 & 1 \end{bmatrix}$$

$$= \begin{bmatrix} 1 & 0 & 0 & 0 \\ 0 & 1 & 0 & 0 \\ 0 & 0 & 0 & r \\ l & m & 0 & 1+rn \end{bmatrix} = \begin{bmatrix} 1 & 0 & 0 & 0 \\ 0 & 1 & 0 & 0 \\ 0 & 0 & 0 & -1/z_c \\ l & m & 0 & 1-n/z_c \end{bmatrix} \qquad (3-59)$$

where $r = -1/z_c$.

Equation (3–59), along with Fig. 3–32, shows that translation in the $x$ and $y$ directions reveals additional faces of the object. Translation in both $x$ and $y$ is required to reveal three faces of a simple cuboidal object. Figure 3–32 shows the results of translating an origin-centered unit cube along the line $y = x$, followed by a single-point perspective projection onto the $z = 0$ plane. Notice that the front face is shown true size and shape.

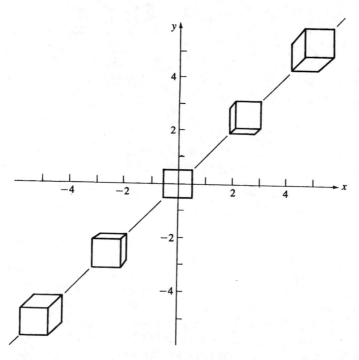

**Figure 3–32**   Single-point perspective projection with $x$ and $y$ translations.

Equation (3–59) also shows that translation in the $z$ direction, i.e., toward or away from the center of projection, results in an apparent scale change (as shown by the term $1 - n/z_c$). This effect corresponds to physical reality, since objects that are farther away from an observer appear smaller. Notice that as the center of projection approaches infinity the scale effect disappears. Figure 3–33 schematically illustrates the effect. As shown in Fig. 3–33, the object can be on either side of the center of projection. If the object and the plane of projection are on the same side of the center of projection, as shown in Fig. 3–33, then an upright image results. However, if the object and the plane of projection are on opposite sides of the center of projection an inverted image results.

Figure 3–34 illustrates the effects of translation in all three directions. Here, a cube is translated along the three-dimensional line from $-x = -y = -z$ to $x = y = z$. Notice the apparent size increase. Also notice that the true shape but *not* the true size of the front face is shown in all views.

An example more fully illustrates these concepts.

---

**Example 3–22    Single-Point Perspective Projection with Translation**

Consider an origin-centered unit cube with position vectors given by

$$[X] = \begin{bmatrix} -0.5 & -0.5 & 0.5 & 1 \\ 0.5 & -0.5 & 0.5 & 1 \\ 0.5 & 0.5 & 0.5 & 1 \\ -0.5 & 0.5 & 0.5 & 1 \\ -0.5 & -0.5 & -0.5 & 1 \\ 0.5 & -0.5 & -0.5 & 1 \\ 0.5 & 0.5 & -0.5 & 1 \\ -0.5 & 0.5 & -0.5 & 1 \end{bmatrix}$$

Translate the cube 5 units in the $x$ and $y$ directions and perform a single-point perspective projection onto the $z = 0$ plane from a center of projection at $z = z_c = 10$.

From Eq. (3–59) the concatenated transformation matrix is

$$[T] = \begin{bmatrix} 1 & 0 & 0 & 0 \\ 0 & 1 & 0 & 0 \\ 0 & 0 & 0 & -0.1 \\ 5 & 5 & 0 & 1 \end{bmatrix}$$

The resulting transformed position vectors are

$$[X^*] = [X][T] = \begin{bmatrix} 4.5 & 4.5 & 0 & 0.95 \\ 5.5 & 4.5 & 0 & 0.95 \\ 5.5 & 5.5 & 0 & 0.95 \\ 4.5 & 5.5 & 0 & 0.95 \\ 4.5 & 4.5 & 0 & 1.05 \\ 5.5 & 4.5 & 0 & 1.05 \\ 5.5 & 5.5 & 0 & 1.05 \\ 4.5 & 5.5 & 0 & 1.05 \end{bmatrix} = \begin{bmatrix} 4.737 & 4.737 & 0 & 1 \\ 5.789 & 4.737 & 0 & 1 \\ 5.789 & 5.789 & 0 & 1 \\ 4.737 & 5.789 & 0 & 1 \\ 4.286 & 4.286 & 0 & 1 \\ 5.238 & 4.286 & 0 & 1 \\ 5.238 & 5.238 & 0 & 1 \\ 4.286 & 5.238 & 0 & 1 \end{bmatrix}$$

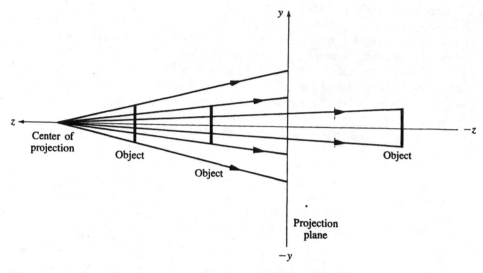

**Figure 3–33**  Scale effect of $z$ translation for a single-point perspective projection.

The result is shown as the upper right hand object in Fig. 3–32.

If the original object is translated by 5 units in the $x$, $y$ and $z$ directions and a single-point perspective projection onto the $z = 0$ plane from a center of projection at $z = z_c = 20$ is performed, then from Eq. (3–59) the concatenated transformation matrix is

$$[T] = \begin{bmatrix} 1 & 0 & 0 & 0 \\ 0 & 1 & 0 & 0 \\ 0 & 0 & 0 & -0.05 \\ 5 & 5 & 0 & 0.75 \end{bmatrix}$$

Notice the overall scaling indicated by the value of 0.75 in the lower right hand element of the transformation matrix.

The resulting transformed position vectors are

$$[X^*] = [X][T] = \begin{bmatrix} 4.5 & 4.5 & 0 & 0.725 \\ 5.5 & 4.5 & 0 & 0.725 \\ 5.5 & 5.5 & 0 & 0.725 \\ 4.5 & 5.5 & 0 & 0.725 \\ 4.5 & 4.5 & 0 & 0.775 \\ 5.5 & 4.5 & 0 & 0.775 \\ 5.5 & 5.5 & 0 & 0.775 \\ 4.5 & 5.5 & 0 & 0.775 \end{bmatrix} = \begin{bmatrix} 6.207 & 6.207 & 0 & 1 \\ 7.586 & 6.207 & 0 & 1 \\ 7.586 & 7.586 & 0 & 1 \\ 6.207 & 7.586 & 0 & 1 \\ 5.806 & 5.806 & 0 & 1 \\ 7.097 & 5.806 & 0 & 1 \\ 7.097 & 7.097 & 0 & 1 \\ 5.806 & 7.097 & 0 & 1 \end{bmatrix}$$

The result is shown as the upper right hand object in Fig. 3–34.

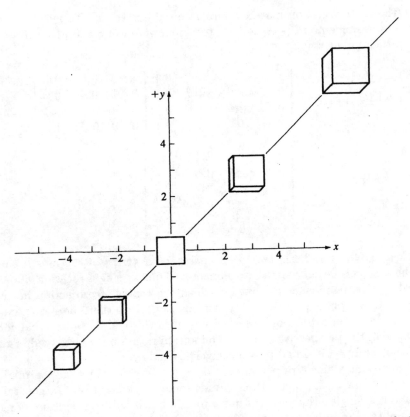

**Figure 3–34**  Single-point perspective projection with $x$, $y$ and $z$ translations.

Multiple faces of an object are also revealed by rotation of the object. A single rotation reveals at least two faces of an object, while two or more rotations about separate axes reveal a minimum of three faces.

The transformation matrix for rotation about the $y$-axis by an angle $\phi$, followed by a single-point perspective projection onto the $z = 0$ plane from a center of projection at $z = z_c$, is given by

$$[T] = [R_y][P_{rz}] = \begin{bmatrix} \cos\phi & 0 & -\sin\phi & 0 \\ 0 & 1 & 0 & 0 \\ \sin\phi & 0 & \cos\phi & 0 \\ 0 & 0 & 0 & 1 \end{bmatrix} \begin{bmatrix} 1 & 0 & 0 & 0 \\ 0 & 1 & 0 & 0 \\ 0 & 0 & 0 & -1/z_c \\ 0 & 0 & 0 & 1 \end{bmatrix}$$

$$= \begin{bmatrix} \cos\phi & 0 & 0 & \dfrac{\sin\phi}{z_c} \\ 0 & 1 & 0 & 0 \\ \sin\phi & 0 & 0 & -\dfrac{\cos\phi}{z_c} \\ 0 & 0 & 0 & 1 \end{bmatrix} \qquad (3-60)$$

Similarly, the transformation matrix for rotation about the $x$-axis by an angle $\theta$, followed by a single-point perspective projection onto the $z = 0$ plane from a center of projection at $z = z_c$, is

$$[T] = [R_x][P_{rz}] = \begin{bmatrix} 1 & 0 & 0 & 0 \\ 0 & \cos\theta & \sin\theta & 0 \\ 0 & -\sin\theta & \cos\theta & 0 \\ 0 & 0 & 0 & 1 \end{bmatrix} \begin{bmatrix} 1 & 0 & 0 & 0 \\ 0 & 1 & 0 & 0 \\ 0 & 0 & 0 & -1/z_c \\ 0 & 0 & 0 & 1 \end{bmatrix}$$

$$= \begin{bmatrix} 1 & 0 & 0 & 0 \\ 0 & \cos\theta & 0 & -\dfrac{\sin\theta}{z_c} \\ 0 & -\sin\theta & 0 & -\dfrac{\cos\theta}{z_c} \\ 0 & 0 & 0 & 1 \end{bmatrix} \qquad (3-61)$$

In both Eqs. (3–60) and (3–61) two of the perspective terms in the fourth column of the transformation matrix are nonzero. Thus, a single rotation about a principal axis perpendicular to that on which the center of projection lies is equivalent to a two-point perspective transformation. Rotation about the axis on which the center of projection lies does not have this effect. Notice that for a single rotation the perspective term for the axis of rotation is unchanged, e.g., in Eqs. (3–60) and (3–61) $q$ and $p$, respectively, remain zero.

Rotation about a single principal axis does not in general reveal the minimum three faces for an adequate three-dimensional representation. In general, rotation about a single principal axis must be combined with translation along the axis to obtain an adequate three-dimensional representation. The next example illustrates this.

---

**Example 3–23    Two-Point Perspective Projection Using Rotation About a Single Principal Axis**

Consider the cube shown in Fig. 3–35a rotated about the $y$-axis by $\phi = 60°$ to reveal the left-hand face and translated $-2$ units in $y$ to reveal the top face projected onto the $z = 0$ plane from a center of projection at $z = z_c = 2.5$.

Using Eq. (3–38) with $\phi = 60°$, Eq. (3–47) with $z_c = 2.5$ and Eq. (3–14) with $n = l = 0$, $m = -2$ yields

$$[T] = [R_y][Tr][P_{rz}]$$

$$= \begin{bmatrix} 0.5 & 0 & -0.866 & 0 \\ 0 & 1 & 0 & 0 \\ 0.866 & 0 & 0.5 & 0 \\ 0 & 0 & 0 & 1 \end{bmatrix} \begin{bmatrix} 1 & 0 & 0 & 0 \\ 0 & 1 & 0 & 0 \\ 0 & 0 & 1 & 0 \\ 0 & -2 & 0 & 1 \end{bmatrix} \begin{bmatrix} 1 & 0 & 0 & 0 \\ 0 & 1 & 0 & 0 \\ 0 & 0 & 0 & -0.4 \\ 0 & 0 & 0 & 1 \end{bmatrix}$$

$$= \begin{bmatrix} 0.5 & 0 & 0 & 0.346 \\ 0 & 1 & 0 & 0 \\ 0.866 & 0 & 0 & -0.2 \\ 0 & -2 & 0 & 1 \end{bmatrix}$$

The transformed position vectors are

$$[X^*] = [X][T] = \begin{bmatrix} 0 & 0 & 1 & 1 \\ 1 & 0 & 1 & 1 \\ 1 & 1 & 1 & 1 \\ 0 & 1 & 1 & 1 \\ 0 & 0 & 0 & 1 \\ 1 & 0 & 0 & 1 \\ 1 & 1 & 0 & 1 \\ 0 & 1 & 0 & 1 \end{bmatrix} \begin{bmatrix} 0.5 & 0 & 0 & 0.346 \\ 0 & 1 & 0 & 0 \\ 0.866 & 0 & 0 & -0.2 \\ 0 & -2 & 0 & 1 \end{bmatrix}$$

$$= \begin{bmatrix} 0.866 & -2 & 0 & 0.8 \\ 1.366 & -2 & 0 & 1.146 \\ 1.366 & -1 & 0 & 1.146 \\ 0.866 & -1 & 0 & 0.8 \\ 0 & -2 & 0 & 1 \\ 0.5 & -2 & 0 & 1.346 \\ 0.5 & -1 & 0 & 1.346 \\ 0 & -1 & 0 & 1 \end{bmatrix} = \begin{bmatrix} 1.083 & -2.5 & 0 & 1 \\ 1.192 & -1.745 & 0 & 1 \\ 1.192 & -0.872 & 0 & 1 \\ 1.083 & -1.25 & 0 & 1 \\ 0 & -2 & 0 & 1 \\ 0.371 & -1.485 & 0 & 1 \\ 0.371 & -0.743 & 0 & 1 \\ 0 & -1 & 0 & 1 \end{bmatrix}$$

The result is shown in Fig. 3–35b. The distortion is the result of the center of projection being very close to the cube. Notice the convergence of lines originally parallel to the $x$ and $z$ axes to vanishing points that lie on the $x$-axis. These vanishing points are determined in Ex. 3–25 in Sec. 3–17.

---

Similarly, a three-point perspective transformation is obtained by rotating about two or more of the principal axes and then performing a single-point perspective transformation. For example, rotation about the $y$-axis followed by rotation about the $x$-axis and a perspective projection onto the $z = 0$ plane from a center of projection at $z = z_c$ yields the concatenated transformation matrix

$$[T] = [R_y][R_x][P_{rz}]$$

$$= \begin{bmatrix} \cos\phi & 0 & -\sin\phi & 0 \\ 0 & 1 & 0 & 0 \\ \sin\phi & 0 & \cos\phi & 0 \\ 0 & 0 & 0 & 1 \end{bmatrix} \begin{bmatrix} 1 & 0 & 0 & 0 \\ 0 & \cos\theta & \sin\theta & 0 \\ 0 & -\sin\theta & \cos\theta & 0 \\ 0 & 0 & 0 & 1 \end{bmatrix} \begin{bmatrix} 1 & 0 & 0 & 0 \\ 0 & 1 & 0 & 0 \\ 0 & 0 & 0 & -1/z_c \\ 0 & 0 & 0 & 1 \end{bmatrix}$$

$$= \begin{bmatrix} \cos\phi & \sin\phi\sin\theta & 0 & \dfrac{\sin\phi\cos\theta}{z_c} \\ 0 & \cos\theta & 0 & -\dfrac{\sin\theta}{z_c} \\ \sin\phi & -\cos\phi\sin\theta & 0 & -\dfrac{\cos\phi\cos\theta}{z_c} \\ 0 & 0 & 0 & 1 \end{bmatrix} \qquad (3-62)$$

Notice the three nonzero perspective terms. The object may also be translated. If translation occurs after rotation, then the resulting concatenated transformation

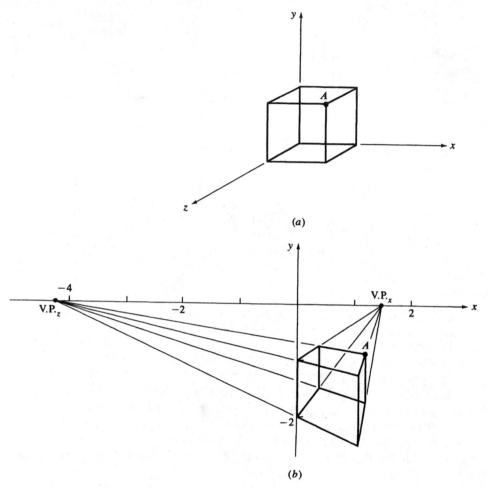

**Figure 3–35** Two-point perspective projection with rotation about a single axis.

matrix is

$$[T] = [R_y][R_x][Tr][P_{rz}]$$

$$= \begin{bmatrix} \cos\phi & \sin\phi\sin\theta & 0 & \dfrac{\sin\phi\cos\theta}{z_c} \\[2mm] 0 & \cos\theta & 0 & -\dfrac{\sin\theta}{z_c} \\[2mm] \sin\phi & -\cos\phi\sin\theta & 0 & -\dfrac{\cos\phi\cos\theta}{z_c} \\[2mm] l & m & 0 & 1 - \dfrac{n}{z_c} \end{bmatrix} \qquad (3-63)$$

Here, note the apparent scaling effect of translation in $z$. If the order of the rotations is reversed or if translation occurs before rotation, the results are different.

**Example 3–24    Three-Point Perspective Projection with Rotation About Two Axes**

Consider the cube shown in Fig. 3–35a rotated about the $y$-axis by $\phi = -30°$, about the $x$-axis by $\theta = 45°$ and projected onto the $z = 0$ plane from a center of projection at $z = z_c = 2.5$.

Using Eq. (3–62) yields

$$[T] = \begin{bmatrix} 0.866 & -0.354 & 0 & -0.141 \\ 0 & 0.707 & 0 & -0.283 \\ -0.5 & -0.612 & 0 & -0.245 \\ 0 & 0 & 0 & 1 \end{bmatrix}$$

The transformed position vectors are

$$[X^*] = [X][T] = \begin{bmatrix} 0 & 0 & 1 & 1 \\ 1 & 0 & 1 & 1 \\ 1 & 1 & 1 & 1 \\ 0 & 1 & 1 & 1 \\ 0 & 0 & 0 & 1 \\ 1 & 0 & 0 & 1 \\ 1 & 1 & 0 & 1 \\ 0 & 1 & 0 & 1 \end{bmatrix} \begin{bmatrix} 0.866 & -0.354 & 0 & -0.141 \\ 0 & 0.707 & 0 & -0.283 \\ -0.5 & -0.612 & 0 & -0.245 \\ 0 & 0 & 0 & 1 \end{bmatrix}$$

$$= \begin{bmatrix} -0.5 & -0.612 & 0 & 0.755 \\ 0.366 & -0.966 & 0 & 0.614 \\ 0.366 & -0.259 & 0 & 0.331 \\ -0.5 & 0.095 & 0 & 0.472 \\ 0 & 0 & 0 & 1 \\ 0.866 & -0.354 & 0 & 0.859 \\ 0.866 & 0.354 & 0 & 0.576 \\ 0 & 0.707 & 0 & 0.717 \end{bmatrix} = \begin{bmatrix} -0.662 & -0.811 & 0 & 1 \\ 0.596 & -1.574 & 0 & 1 \\ 1.107 & -0.782 & 0 & 1 \\ -1.059 & 0.201 & 0 & 1 \\ 0 & 0 & 0 & 1 \\ 1.009 & -0.412 & 0 & 1 \\ 1.504 & 0.614 & 0 & 1 \\ 0 & 0.986 & 0 & 1 \end{bmatrix}$$

The result is shown in Fig. 3–36.

From these results it is clear that one-, two- or three-point perspective transformations can be constructed using rotations and translations about and along the principal axes, followed by a single-point perspective transformation from a center of projection on one of the principal axes. These results also follow for rotation about a general axis in space. Consequently, in implementing a graphics system using a fixed center of projection object manipulation paradigm, it is only necessary to provide for a single-point perspective projection onto the $z = 0$ plane from a center of projection on the $z$-axis.

## 3–17  VANISHING POINTS

When a perspective view of an object is created a horizontal reference line, normally at eye level, as shown in Fig. 3–37a is used. Principal vanishing points

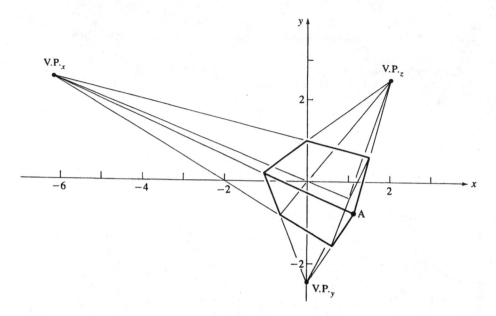

**Figure 3–36**   Three-point perspective projection with rotation about two axes.

are points on the horizontal reference line at which lines originally parallel to the untransformed principal axes converge. In general, different sets of parallel lines have different principal vanishing points. This is illustrated in Fig. 3–37b. For planes of an object which are tilted relative to the untransformed principal axes, the vanishing points fall above or below the horizontal reference line. These are often called trace points, as shown in Fig. 3–37c.

Two methods for determining vanishing points are of general interest. The first simply calculates the intersection point of a pair of transformed projected parallel lines. The second is more complex but numerically more accurate. Here, an object with sides originally parallel to the principal axes is transformed to the desired position and orientation. A single-point perspective projection is applied. The final concatenated transformation matrix (see Eq. 3–63) is then used to transform the points at infinity on the principal axes. The resulting ordinary coordinates are the principal vanishing points for that object. For trace points resulting from inclined planes, the points at infinity in the directions of the edges of the inclined plane are first found and then transformed.

Several examples illustrate these techniques. The first uses intersection of the transformed lines to find the vanishing points.

---

**Example 3–25    Principal Vanishing Points by Line Intersection**

Recalling Ex. 3–23, the transformed position vectors for the pair of line segments with one line through the point $A$ (see Fig. 3–35a) originally parallel to

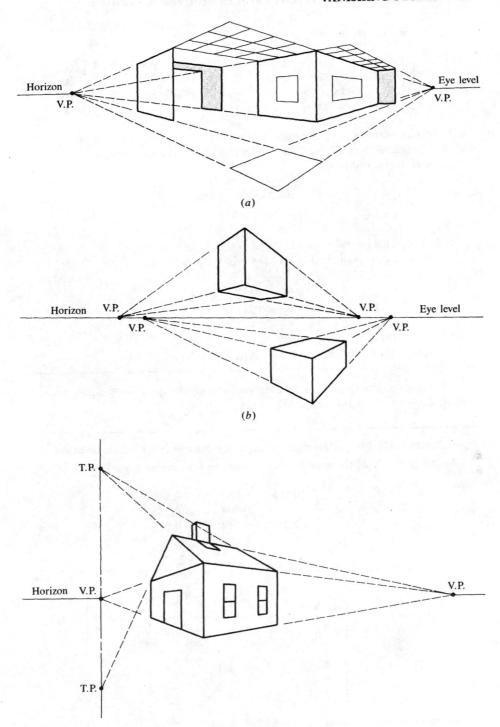

(a)

(b)

**Figure 3–37**   Trace points and vanishing points.

the $x$- and $z$-axes, respectively, are

$$
\begin{array}{c}
④ \\ ③ \\ ⑧ \\ ⑦
\end{array}
\begin{bmatrix}
1.083 & -1.25 & 0 & 1 \\
1.192 & -0.872 & 0 & 1 \\
0 & -1 & 0 & 1 \\
0.371 & 0.743 & 0 & 1
\end{bmatrix}
\quad \text{and} \quad
\begin{bmatrix}
1.192 & -0.872 & 0 & 1 \\
0.371 & -0.743 & 0 & 1 \\
1.083 & -1.25 & 0 & 1 \\
0 & -1 & 0 & 1
\end{bmatrix}
\begin{array}{c}
③ \\ ⑦ \\ ④ \\ ⑧
\end{array}
$$

Here, the numbers in circles refer to the rows in the original and transformed data matrices given in Ex. 3-23. The equations of the pair of lines originally parallel to the $x$-axis are

$$y = 3.468x - 5.006$$
$$y = 0.693x - 1$$

Solution yields $[\,VP_x\,] = [\,1.444 \quad 0\,]$.

The equations of the pair of lines originally parallel to the $z$-axis are

$$y = -0.157x - 0.685$$
$$y = -0.231x - 1$$

Solution yields $[\,VP_z\,] = [\,-4.333 \quad 0\,]$.

These vanishing points are shown in Fig. 3-35b.

---

The second example uses transformation of the points at infinity on the principal axes to find the vanishing point.

---

**Example 3-26    Principal Vanishing Points by Transformation**

Recalling Ex. 3-24 the concatenated complete transformation was

$$
[\,T\,] =
\begin{bmatrix}
0.866 & -0.354 & 0 & -0.141 \\
0 & 0.707 & 0 & -0.283 \\
-0.5 & -0.612 & 0 & -0.245 \\
0 & 0 & 0 & 1
\end{bmatrix}
$$

Transforming the points at infinity on the $x$-, $y$- and $z$-axes yields

$$
[\,VP\,][\,T\,] =
\begin{bmatrix}
1 & 0 & 0 & 0 \\
0 & 1 & 0 & 0 \\
0 & 0 & 1 & 0
\end{bmatrix}
\begin{bmatrix}
0.866 & -0.354 & 0 & -0.141 \\
0 & 0.707 & 0 & -0.283 \\
-0.5 & -0.612 & 0 & -0.245 \\
0 & 0 & 0 & 1
\end{bmatrix}
$$

$$
=
\begin{bmatrix}
-6.142 & 2.5 & 0 & 1 \\
0 & -2.5 & 0 & 1 \\
2.04 & 2.5 & 0 & 1
\end{bmatrix}
$$

These vanishing points are shown in Fig. 3-36.

---

This third example uses transformation of the points at infinity for skew planes to find trace points.

---

### Example 3–27    Trace Points by Transformation

Consider the simple triangular prism shown in Fig. 3–38a. The position vectors for the prism are

$$[X] = \begin{bmatrix} 0 & 0 & 1 & 1 \\ 1 & 0 & 1 & 1 \\ 0.5 & 0.5 & 1 & 1 \\ 0 & 0 & 0 & 1 \\ 1 & 0 & 0 & 1 \\ 0.5 & 0.5 & 0 & 1 \end{bmatrix}$$

Applying the concatenated transformation of Ex. 3–24 yields transformed position vectors

$$[X^*] = [X][T]$$

$$= \begin{bmatrix} 0 & 0 & 1 & 1 \\ 1 & 0 & 1 & 1 \\ 0.5 & 0.5 & 1 & 1 \\ 0 & 0 & 0 & 1 \\ 1 & 0 & 0 & 1 \\ 0.5 & 0.5 & 0 & 1 \end{bmatrix} \begin{bmatrix} 0.866 & -0.354 & 0 & -0.141 \\ 0 & 0.707 & 0 & -0.283 \\ -0.5 & -0.612 & 0 & -0.245 \\ 0 & 0 & 0 & 1 \end{bmatrix}$$

$$= \begin{bmatrix} -0.5 & -0.612 & 0 & 0.755 \\ 0.366 & -0.966 & 0 & 0.614 \\ -0.067 & -0.436 & 0 & 0.543 \\ 0 & 0 & 0 & 1 \\ 0.866 & -0.354 & 0 & 0.859 \\ 0.433 & 0.177 & 0 & 0.788 \end{bmatrix}$$

$$= \begin{bmatrix} -0.662 & -0.811 & 0 & 1 \\ 0.596 & -1.574 & 0 & 1 \\ -0.123 & -0.802 & 0 & 1 \\ 0 & 0 & 0 & 1 \\ 1.009 & -0.412 & 0 & 1 \\ 0.55 & 0.224 & 0 & 1 \end{bmatrix}$$

The transformed prism is shown in Fig. 3–38b.

The direction cosines for the inclined edges of the left-hand plane forming the top of the untransformed prism are $[0.5 \quad 0.5 \quad 0]$. Thus, the point at infinity in this direction is $[1 \quad 1 \quad 0 \quad 0]$.

Similarly, $[-0.5 \quad 0.5 \quad 0]$ are the direction cosines for the inclined edges of the right-hand plane forming the top of the untransformed prism. Thus, the point at infinity in this direction is $[-1 \quad 1 \quad 0 \quad 0]$.

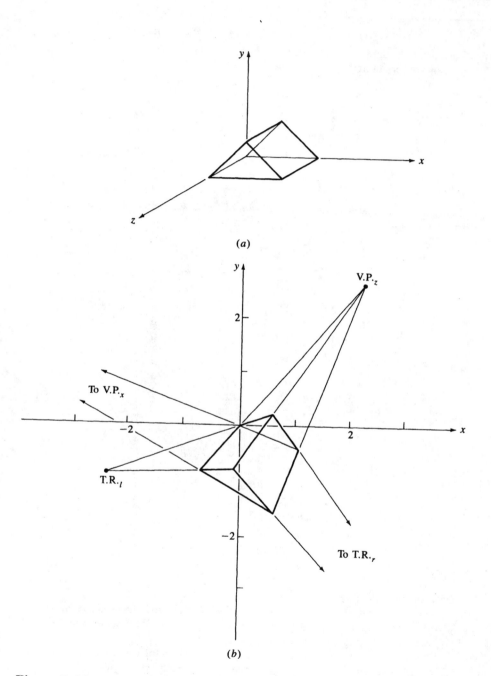

(a)

(b)

**Figure 3-38**   Trace points.

Transforming these infinite points along with those for the principal axes yields

$$[VP][T] = \begin{bmatrix} 1 & 0 & 0 & 0 \\ 0 & 1 & 0 & 0 \\ 0 & 0 & 1 & 0 \\ 1 & 1 & 0 & 0 \\ -1 & 1 & 0 & 0 \end{bmatrix} \begin{bmatrix} 0.866 & -0.354 & 0 & -0.141 \\ 0 & 0.707 & 0 & -0.283 \\ -0.5 & -0.612 & 0 & -0.245 \\ 0 & 0 & 0 & 1 \end{bmatrix}$$

$$= \begin{bmatrix} 0.866 & -0.354 & 0 & -0.141 \\ 0 & 0.707 & 0 & -0.283 \\ -0.5 & -0.612 & 0 & -0.245 \\ 0.866 & 0.354 & 0 & -0.424 \\ -0.866 & 1.061 & 0 & -0.141 \end{bmatrix}$$

$$= \begin{bmatrix} -6.142 & 2.5 & 0 & 1 \\ 0 & -2.5 & 0 & 1 \\ 2.041 & 2.5 & 0 & 1 \\ -2.041 & -0.833 & 0 & 1 \\ 6.142 & -7.5 & 0 & 1 \end{bmatrix} \begin{matrix} VP_x \\ VP_y \\ VP_z \\ TP_l \\ TP_r \end{matrix}$$

The vanishing and trace points are also shown in Fig. 3–38b. Notice that as expected $VP_x$, $VP_y$ and $VP_z$ are the same as found in Ex. 3–26.

---

## 3–18 PHOTOGRAPHY AND THE PERSPECTIVE TRANSFORMATION

A photograph is a perspective projection. The general case for a pinhole camera is illustrated in Fig. 3–39. The center of projection is the focal point of the camera lens. It is convenient to consider the creation of the original photographic negative and of a print from that negative as two separate cases.

Figure 3–40a illustrates the geometry for creation of the original negative. Here it is convenient to place the negative at the $z = 0$ plane with the center of projection and the scene located in the negative half space $z < 0$. Perspective

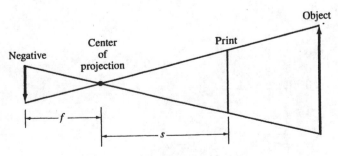

**Figure 3–39** A photograph as a perspective projection.

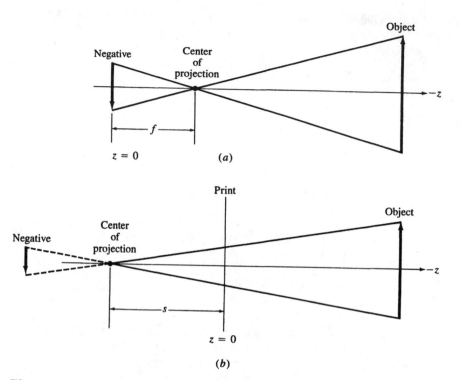

**Figure 3–40**   Photographic perspective geometry. (a) Creation of the original negative; (b) creation of a print.

projection onto the $z = 0$ plane (the negative) yields the transformation

$$[\,T_n\,] = \begin{bmatrix} 1 & 0 & 0 & 0 \\ 0 & 1 & 0 & 0 \\ 0 & 0 & 0 & 1/f \\ 0 & 0 & 0 & 1 \end{bmatrix} \qquad (3-64)$$

where $f$ is the focal length of the lens. Note that an inverted image of the object is formed on the negative. Specifically,

$$[\,x \quad y \quad z \quad 1\,] \begin{bmatrix} 1 & 0 & 0 & 0 \\ 0 & 1 & 0 & 0 \\ 0 & 0 & 0 & 1/f \\ 0 & 0 & 0 & 1 \end{bmatrix} = [\,x \quad y \quad 0 \quad 1+z/f\,]$$

and

$$x^* = \frac{xf}{f+z} \qquad y^* = \frac{yf}{f+z}$$

Here, for $f + z < 0$, $x^*$ and $y^*$ are of opposite sign to $x$ and $y$, and an inverted image is formed on the negative.

Figure 3–40b illustrates the geometry for creation of a print from a photographic negative. Here $s$ is the distance from the focal point of the enlarger lens to the paper. The paper is assumed to be located at $z = 0$. The perspective projection transformation is then

$$[\, T_p \,] = \begin{bmatrix} 1 & 0 & 0 & 0 \\ 0 & 1 & 0 & 0 \\ 0 & 0 & 0 & -1/s \\ 0 & 0 & 0 & 1 \end{bmatrix} \tag{3-65}$$

Note that an upright image of the object is formed on the print. Specifically,

$$\begin{bmatrix} x & y & z & 1 \end{bmatrix} \begin{bmatrix} 1 & 0 & 0 & 0 \\ 0 & 1 & 0 & 0 \\ 0 & 0 & 0 & -1/s \\ 0 & 0 & 0 & 1 \end{bmatrix} = \begin{bmatrix} x & y & z & 1 - \dfrac{z}{s} \end{bmatrix}$$

and

$$x^* = \frac{xs}{s - z} \qquad y^* = \frac{ys}{s - z}$$

For the object $z < 0$, $s - z > 0$ and $x^* y^*$ are of the same sign as $x, y$, i.e., an upright image is formed.

## 3–19   STEREOGRAPHIC PROJECTION

Increasing the perception of three-dimensional depth in a scene is important in many applications. There are two basic types of depth perception cues used by the eye-brain system: monocular and binocular, depending on whether they are apparent when one or two eyes are used. The principal monocular cues are:

Perspective — convergence of parallel lines.

Movement parallax — when the head is moved laterally, near objects appear to move more against a projection plane than far objects.

Relative size of known objects.

Overlap — a closer object overlaps and appears in front of a more distant object.

Highlights and shadows.

Atmospheric attenuation of, and the inability of the eye to resolve, fine detail in distant objects.

Focusing accommodation — objects at different distances require different tension in the focusing muscles of the eye.

The principal binocular cues are:

The convergence angles of the optical axes of the eyes.

Retinal disparity — the different location of objects projected on the eye's retina is interpreted as differences in distance from the eye.

The monocular cues produce only weak perceptions of three-dimensional depth. However, because the eye-brain system fuses the two separate and distinct images produced by each eye into a single image, the binocular cues produce very strong three-dimensional depth perceptions. Stereography attempts to produce an image with characteristics analogous to those for true binocular vision. There are several techniques for generating stereo images (see Refs. 3–4 and 3–5). All depend upon supplying the left and right eyes with separate images.

Two methods, called chromatic anaglyphic and polarized anaglyphic, use filters to insure reception of correct and separate images by the left and right eyes. Briefly, the chromatic anaglyphic technique creates two images in two different colors, one for the left eye and one for the right eye. When viewed through corresponding filters the left eye sees only the left image and the right eye only the right image. The eye-brain system combines both two-dimensional images into a single three-dimensional image with the correct colors. The polarized anaglyphic method uses polarizing filters instead of color filters.

A third technique uses a flicker system to alternately project a left and a right eye view. An associated viewing device is synchronized to block the light to the opposite eye.

A fourth method, autostereoscopy, does not require any special viewing equipment. The method depends on the use of line or lenticular screens. The images are called parallax stereograms, parallax panoramagrams and panoramic parallax stereograms. The details are given in Ref. 3–5.

All of these techniques require projection of an object onto a plane from two different centers of projection, one for the right eye and one for the left eye. Figure 3–41 shows a projection of the point $P$ onto the $z = 0$ plane from centers of projection at $E_L(-e, 0, d_e)$ and $E_R(e, 0, d_e)$ corresponding to the left and right eye, respectively.

For convenience, the center of projection for the left eye is translated so that it lies on the $z$-axis as shown in Fig. 3–41b. Using similar triangles then yields

$$\frac{x_L^{*\prime}}{d_e} = \frac{x'}{d_e - z}$$

and

$$x_L^{*\prime} = \frac{x'}{1 - z/d_e} = \frac{x'}{1 + rz}$$

where

$$r = -1/d_e$$

Similarly, translating the center of projection for the right eye so that it lies on the $z$-axis as shown in Fig. 3–41c, and again using similar triangles, yields

$$\frac{x_R^{*\prime\prime}}{d_e} = \frac{x''}{d_e - z}$$

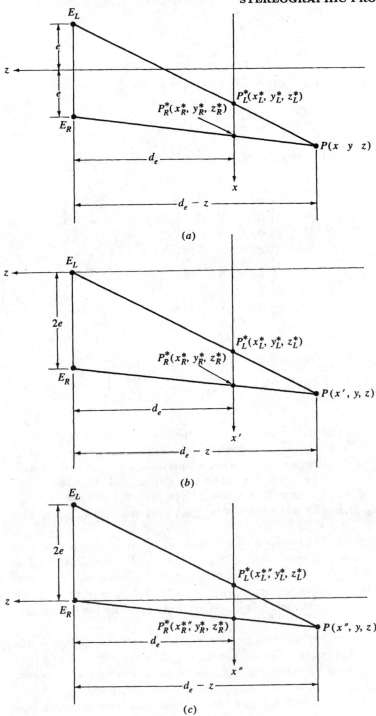

*(a)*

*(b)*

*(c)*

**Figure 3–41**  Stereographic projection onto $z = 0$.

and

$$x_R^{*''} = \frac{x''}{1 - z/d_e} = \frac{x''}{1 + rz}$$

Since each eye is at $y = 0$, the projected values of $y$ are both

$$y^* = \frac{y}{1 - z/d_e} = \frac{y}{1 + rz}$$

The equivalent $4 \times 4$ transformation matrices for the left and right eye views are

$$[S_L] = [Tr_x][P_{rz}] = \begin{bmatrix} 1 & 0 & 0 & 0 \\ 0 & 1 & 0 & 0 \\ 0 & 0 & 1 & 0 \\ e & 0 & 0 & 1 \end{bmatrix} \begin{bmatrix} 1 & 0 & 0 & 0 \\ 0 & 1 & 0 & 0 \\ 0 & 0 & 0 & -1/d_e \\ 0 & 0 & 0 & 1 \end{bmatrix}$$

$$= \begin{bmatrix} 1 & 0 & 0 & 0 \\ 0 & 1 & 0 & 0 \\ 0 & 0 & 0 & -1/d_e \\ e & 0 & 0 & 1 \end{bmatrix} \tag{3-66}$$

and

$$[S_R] = [Tr_x][P_{rz}] = \begin{bmatrix} 1 & 0 & 0 & 0 \\ 0 & 1 & 0 & 0 \\ 0 & 0 & 0 & -1/d_e \\ -e & 0 & 0 & 1 \end{bmatrix} \tag{3-67}$$

Consequently, a stereographic projection is obtained by transforming the scene using Eqs. (3–66) and (3–67) and displaying both images.

Stereographic projections are displayed in a number of ways. For many individuals a stereo image can be created without any viewing aid. One technique, which takes a bit of practice, is to first focus the eyes at infinity; then, without changing the focus, gradually move the stereo pairs, held at about arm's length, into view.

Binocular fusion of the stereo pairs is improved by using a small opaque mask, e.g., a strip of black cardboard about an inch wide. As illustrated in Fig. 3–42, the mask is placed between the eyes and the stereo pair and moved back and forth until it is in the position shown. When the mask is in the position shown, the left eye sees only the left image and the right eye only the right image of the stereo pair.

Two more formal devices for viewing stereo pairs are shown in Figs. 3–43a and 3–43b. Figure 3–43a shows a Brewster stereopticon popular in the early part of this century. Figure 3–43b shows a typical modern laboratory stereoscope. Both devices are examples of simple focal plane lens stereoscopes.

Although Eqs. (3–66) and (3–67) provide the basic transformation for generating stereo pairs, it is necessary to modify this basic transformation to accommodate the geometry of various stereo viewing devices. The geometry for a simple focal plane stereoscope is shown in Fig. 3–44. Here the stereo pairs are

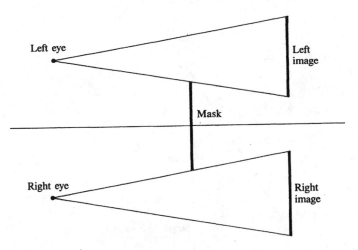

**Figure 3–42**    Simple stereo pair viewing method.

located at the focal distance $f$ of the lenses. The stereo image is reconstructed at a distance $I$ from the lenses. As mentioned previously, the stereo convergence angle $\gamma$, which is one of the strongest binocular fusion cues, is associated with the convergence of the optical axes of the eyes. For a normal human the inter-pupil distance of the eyes is about 60 millimeters. Experiments (Ref. 3–4) have shown that the strongest stereo effect occurs at a normal viewing distance of about 600 millimeters. Consequently, the strongest stereo effect occurs for $\tan(\gamma/2) = 1/5$. If, as shown in Fig. 3–44, the stereo pairs are located at the focal distance $f$, they must be separated by an amount $2w$ to achieve binocular fusion.

From Fig. 3–44 with $2D$ as the distance between the lenses of the stereoscope, similar triangles show that

$$\frac{D - w}{f} = \frac{D}{I} = \frac{1}{5}$$

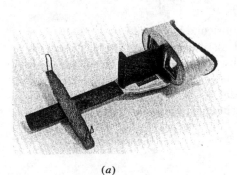

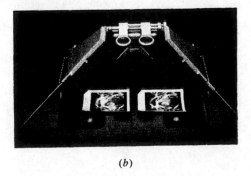

(a)                                    (b)

**Figure 3–43**    Stereoscopes. (a) Brewster stereopticon; (b) typical laboratory instrument.

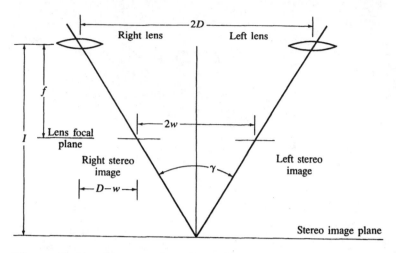

**Figure 3–44**  Geometry for a focal plane stereoscope.

Thus, a separation of

$$w = D - \frac{f}{5} \qquad (3-68)$$

yields the strongest stereo effect. For a stereo pair to be viewed with a simple lens stereoscope, Eqs. (3–66) and (3–67) become

$$[\,S_L\,] = \begin{bmatrix} 1 & 0 & 0 & 0 \\ 0 & 1 & 0 & 0 \\ 0 & 0 & 0 & -1/f \\ w & 0 & 0 & 1 \end{bmatrix} \qquad (3-69a)$$

and

$$[\,S_R\,] = \begin{bmatrix} 1 & 0 & 0 & 0 \\ 0 & 1 & 0 & 0 \\ 0 & 0 & 0 & -1/f \\ -w & 0 & 0 & 1 \end{bmatrix} \qquad (3-69b)$$

A typical stereo pair for a simple lens stereoscope is shown in Fig. 3–45.

The separations obtained from Eq. (3–68) for typical values of $D$ and $f$ are quite small. Thus, only small stereo pair images are viewable. To allow viewing larger images, mirrors or prisms are used to increase the separation distance. A typical mirrored stereoscope is shown in Fig. 3–43b. The associated geometry is shown in Fig. 3–46. Again using similar triangles, the stereo pair separation is

$$\frac{w_0 - w}{f} = \frac{D}{I} = \frac{1}{5}$$

and

$$w = \frac{w_0 - f}{5} \qquad (3-70)$$

An example illustrates the generation of a typical stereo pair.

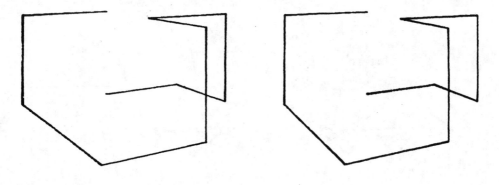

**Figure 3–45**    Stereo pair.

---

### Example 3–28    Stereo Pair Generation

Consider a simple three-dimensional wire frame image with position vectors

$$[X] = \begin{bmatrix} 0 & 0 & 0 & 1 \\ 1 & 0 & 0 & 1 \\ 1 & 0 & 1 & 1 \\ 1 & 1 & 1 & 1 \\ 0 & 1 & 1 & 1 \\ 0 & 1 & 2 & 1 \\ 0 & 0 & 2 & 1 \\ -1 & 0 & 2 & 1 \\ -1 & 0 & 0 & 1 \\ -1 & 0 & 0 & 1 \\ -1 & 1 & 0 & 1 \end{bmatrix}$$

as shown in Fig. 3–45. The figure is first rotated about the $y$-axis by 20° and then translated $-1.5$ units in the $z$ direction for viewing purposes. The resulting transformation is

$$[V] = [R_y][T_z] = \begin{bmatrix} 0.94 & 0 & -0.342 & 0 \\ 0 & 1 & 0 & 0 \\ 0.342 & 0 & 0.94 & 0 \\ 0 & 0 & 0 & 1 \end{bmatrix} \begin{bmatrix} 1 & 0 & 0 & 0 \\ 0 & 1 & 0 & 0 \\ 0 & 0 & 1 & 0 \\ 0 & 0 & -1.5 & 1 \end{bmatrix}$$

$$= \begin{bmatrix} 0.94 & 0 & -0.342 & 0 \\ 0 & 1 & 0 & 0 \\ 0.342 & 0 & 0.94 & 0 \\ 0 & 0 & -1.5 & 1 \end{bmatrix}$$

A stereo pair is constructed for viewing through a simple lens focal plane stereoscope. The lens separation $2D = 4$ inches and the focal length is also 4 inches. From Eq. (3–68) the stereo pair separation is

$$w = 2 - 4/5 = 1.2''$$

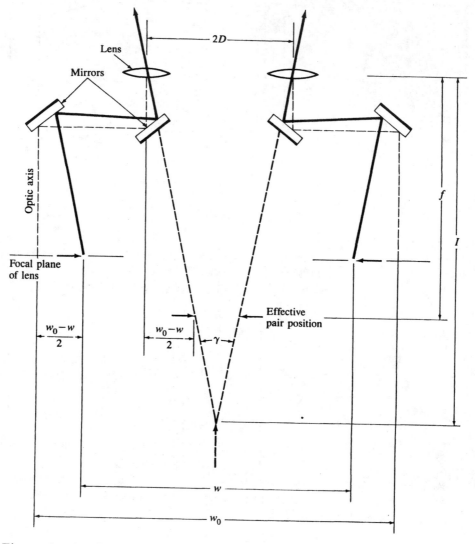

**Figure 3–46**   Geometry for a mirrored stereoscope.

Using Eq. (3–69), the right and left stereo image transformations are

$$[S_L] = \begin{bmatrix} 1 & 0 & 0 & 0 \\ 0 & 1 & 0 & 0 \\ 0 & 0 & 0 & -0.25 \\ 1.2 & 0 & 0 & 1 \end{bmatrix} \quad \text{and} \quad [S_R] = \begin{bmatrix} 1 & 0 & 0 & 0 \\ 0 & 1 & 0 & 0 \\ 0 & 0 & 0 & -0.25 \\ -1.2 & 0 & 0 & 1 \end{bmatrix}$$

The combined viewing and left and right image transformations are

$$[C_L] = [V][S_L] \quad \text{and} \quad [C_R] = [V][S_R]$$

$$[C_L] = \begin{bmatrix} 0.94 & 0 & 0 & 0.086 \\ 0 & 1 & 0 & 0 \\ 0.342 & 0 & 0 & -0.235 \\ 1.2 & 0 & 0 & 1.38 \end{bmatrix}$$

and

$$[C_R] = \begin{bmatrix} 0.94 & 0 & 0 & 0.086 \\ 0 & 1 & 0 & 0 \\ 0.342 & 0 & 0 & -0.235 \\ -1.2 & 0 & 0 & 1.375 \end{bmatrix}$$

The transformed position vectors for the left and right images are

$$[X_L^*] = [X][C_L] \quad \text{and} \quad [X_R^*] = [X][C_R]$$

$$[X_L^*] = \begin{bmatrix} 0.873 & 0 & 0 & 1 \\ 1.465 & 0 & 0 & 1 \\ 2.025 & 0 & 0 & 1 \\ 2.025 & 0.816 & 0 & 1 \\ 1.353 & 0.877 & 0 & 1 \\ 2.081 & 1.105 & 0 & 1 \\ 2.081 & 0 & 0 & 1 \\ 1.152 & 0 & 0 & 1 \\ 0.202 & 0 & 0 & 1 \\ 0.202 & 0 & 0 & 1 \\ 0.202 & 0.775 & 0 & 1 \end{bmatrix} \quad \text{and} \quad [X_R^*] = \begin{bmatrix} -0.873 & 0 & 0 & 1 \\ -0.178 & 0 & 0 & 1 \\ 0.067 & 0 & 0 & 1 \\ 0.067 & 0.816 & 0 & 1 \\ -0.753 & 0.877 & 0 & 1 \\ -0.57 & 1.105 & 0 & 1 \\ -0.57 & 0 & 0 & 1 \\ -1.776 & 0 & 0 & 1 \\ -1.659 & 0 & 0 & 1 \\ -1.659 & 0 & 0 & 1 \\ -1.659 & 0.775 & 0 & 1 \end{bmatrix}$$

The result is shown in Fig. 3-45. Note that in generating the final image the results must be scaled for each particular output device to yield the correct physical dimensions for $w$.

## 3-20    COMPARISON OF OBJECT FIXED AND CENTER OF PROJECTION FIXED PROJECTIONS

An object fixed movable center of projection technique is easily converted to the movable object fixed center of projection technique previously discussed. There are two cases of interest. The first and simpler assumes that the projection plane is perpendicular to the sight vector from the center of projection into the scene. The second eliminates the perpendicular projection plane assumption. Only the first is discussed here.

When the projection plane is perpendicular to the sight vector, the following procedure yields the equivalent movable object fixed center of projection transformation:

Determine the intersection of the sight vector and the projection plane.

Translate the intersection point to the origin.

Rotate the sight vector so that it is coincident with the $+z$-axis and pointed towards the origin (see Sec. 3–9).

Apply the concatenated transformations to the scene.

Perform a single-point perspective projection onto the $z = 0$ plane from the transformed center of projection on the $z$-axis.

A relatively simple example serves to illustrate the technique.

---

**Example 3–29    Object Fixed Perspective Projection onto a Perpendicular Projection Plane**

Consider the cube with one corner removed, previously discussed in Ex. 3–10. Project the cube from a center of projection at $[\,10 \quad 10 \quad 10\,]$ onto the plane passing through the point $[\,-1 \quad -1 \quad -1\,]$ and perpendicular to the sight vector as shown in Fig. 3–47.

The equation for the projection plane can be obtained from its normal (see Ref. 3–1 for alternate techniques). Here the normal is in the opposite direction to the sight vector.

The direction of the sight vector is given by

$$[\,s\,] = [\,-1 \quad -1 \quad -1\,]$$

The normal to the projection plane through $[\,-1 \quad -1 \quad -1\,]$ perpendicular to the sight vector is then

$$[\,n\,] = [\,1 \quad 1 \quad 1\,]$$

The general form of a plane equation is

$$ax + by + cz + d = 0$$

The normal to the general plane is given by

$$[\,n\,] = [\,a \quad b \quad c\,]$$

The value of $d$ in the plane equation is obtained from any point in the plane. The equation for the projection plane through $[\,-1 \quad -1 \quad -1\,]$ is then

$$x + y + z + d = 0$$

and

$$d = -x - y - z = 1 + 1 + 1 = 3$$

Hence,

$$x + y + z + 3 = 0$$

is the equation for the projection plane.

The intersection of the sight vector and the projection plane is obtained by writing the parametric equation of the sight vector, substituting into the plane equation, and solving for the parameter value.

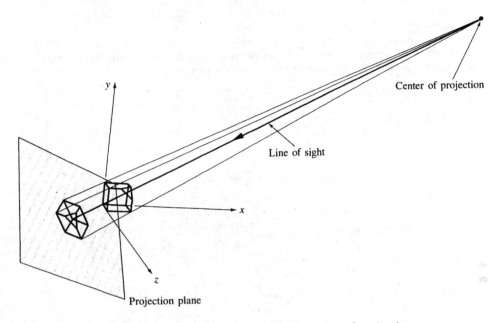

**Figure 3-47**    Perspective projection from movable center of projection.

The parametric equation of the sight vector is

$$[ S(t) ] = [ x(t) \quad y(t) \quad z(t) ]$$
$$= [ 10 \quad 10 \quad 10 ] + [ -11 \quad -11 \quad -11 ] t \qquad 0 \le t \le 1$$

Substituting into the plane equation yields

$$x(t) + y(t) + z(t) + 3 = (10 - 11t) + (10 - 11t) + (10 - 11t) + 3 = 0$$

Solving for $t$ yields the parameter value for the intersection point, i.e.,

$$-33t + 33 = 0 \quad \rightarrow \quad t = 1.0$$

The intersection is obtained by substituting $t$ into $[ S(t) ]$. Specifically,

$$[ I ] = [ S(1) ] = [ 10 \quad 10 \quad 10 ] + [ -11 \quad -11 \quad -11 ] (1.0)$$
$$= [ -1 \quad -1 \quad -1 ]$$

The intersection point is at $x = y = z = -1$ as expected from simple geometric considerations.

The required translation matrix is

$$[ Tr ] = \begin{bmatrix} 1 & 0 & 0 & 0 \\ 0 & 1 & 0 & 0 \\ 0 & 0 & 1 & 0 \\ 1 & 1 & 1 & 1 \end{bmatrix}$$

After translation the center of projection is at $[\,11 \quad 11 \quad 11\,]$ and the sight vector passes through the origin.

Using the results of Sec. 3–9, a rotation about the $x$-axis of $\alpha = 45°$ followed by a rotation about the $y$-axis by $\beta = 35.26°$ makes the sight vector coincident with the $z$-axis. The rotation matrices are

$$[\,R_x\,] = \begin{bmatrix} 1 & 0 & 0 & 0 \\ 0 & 1/\sqrt{2} & 1/\sqrt{2} & 0 \\ 0 & -1/\sqrt{2} & 1/\sqrt{2} & 0 \\ 0 & 0 & 0 & 1 \end{bmatrix} \quad \text{and} \quad [\,R_y\,] = \begin{bmatrix} 2/\sqrt{6} & 0 & 1/\sqrt{3} & 0 \\ 0 & 1 & 0 & 0 \\ -1/\sqrt{3} & 0 & 2/\sqrt{6} & 0 \\ 0 & 0 & 0 & 1 \end{bmatrix}$$

and the concatenated transformation matrix is

$$[\,M\,] = [\,Tr\,][\,R_x\,][\,R_y\,] = \begin{bmatrix} 2/\sqrt{6} & 0 & 1/\sqrt{3} & 0 \\ -1/\sqrt{6} & 1/\sqrt{2} & 1/\sqrt{3} & 0 \\ -1/\sqrt{6} & -1/\sqrt{2} & 1/\sqrt{3} & 0 \\ 0 & 0 & 3/\sqrt{3} & 1 \end{bmatrix}$$

Transforming the center of projection yields

$$[\,C_p\,][\,M\,] = [\,10 \quad 10 \quad 10 \quad 1\,] \begin{bmatrix} 2/\sqrt{6} & 0 & 1/\sqrt{3} & 0 \\ -1/\sqrt{6} & 1/\sqrt{2} & 1/\sqrt{3} & 0 \\ -1/\sqrt{6} & -1/\sqrt{2} & 1/\sqrt{3} & 0 \\ 0 & 0 & 3/\sqrt{3} & 1 \end{bmatrix}$$

$$= [\,0 \quad 0 \quad 33/\sqrt{3} \quad 1\,]$$

The transformation for a single-point perspective projection from a center of projection at $z = 33/\sqrt{3}$ onto the $z = 0$ plane is

$$[\,P_{rz}\,] = \begin{bmatrix} 1 & 0 & 0 & 0 \\ 0 & 1 & 0 & 0 \\ 0 & 0 & 0 & -\sqrt{3}/33 \\ 0 & 0 & 0 & 1 \end{bmatrix}$$

Concatenation with $[\,M\,]$ yields

$$[\,T\,] = [\,M\,][\,P_{rz}\,] = \begin{bmatrix} 2/\sqrt{6} & 0 & 1/\sqrt{3} & 0 \\ -1/\sqrt{6} & 1/\sqrt{2} & 1/\sqrt{3} & 0 \\ -1/\sqrt{6} & -1/\sqrt{2} & 1/\sqrt{3} & 0 \\ 0 & 0 & 3/\sqrt{3} & 1 \end{bmatrix} \begin{bmatrix} 1 & 0 & 0 & 0 \\ 0 & 1 & 0 & 0 \\ 0 & 0 & 0 & -\sqrt{3}/33 \\ 0 & 0 & 0 & 1 \end{bmatrix}$$

$$= \begin{bmatrix} 2/\sqrt{6} & 0 & 0 & -1/33 \\ -1/\sqrt{6} & 1/\sqrt{2} & 0 & -1/33 \\ -1/\sqrt{6} & -1/\sqrt{2} & 0 & -1/33 \\ 0 & 0 & 0 & 30/33 \end{bmatrix}$$

The transformed ordinary coordinates of the projected object are

$$[X^*] = [X][T] = \begin{bmatrix} 0 & 0 & 1 & 1 \\ 1 & 0 & 1 & 1 \\ 1 & 0.5 & 1 & 1 \\ 0.5 & 1 & 1 & 1 \\ 0 & 1 & 1 & 1 \\ 0 & 0 & 0 & 1 \\ 1 & 0 & 0 & 1 \\ 1 & 1 & 0 & 1 \\ 0 & 1 & 0 & 1 \\ 1 & 1 & 0.5 & 1 \end{bmatrix} \begin{bmatrix} 0.816 & 0 & 0 & -0.030 \\ -0.408 & 0.707 & 0 & -0.030 \\ -0.408 & -0.707 & 0 & -0.030 \\ 0 & 0 & 0 & 0.909 \end{bmatrix}$$

$$= \begin{bmatrix} -0.408 & -0.707 & 0 & 0.879 \\ 0.408 & -0.707 & 0 & 0.848 \\ 0.204 & -0.354 & 0 & 0.833 \\ -0.408 & 0 & 0 & 0.833 \\ -0.816 & 0 & 0 & 0.848 \\ 0 & 0 & 0 & 0.909 \\ 0.816 & 0 & 0 & 0.879 \\ 0.408 & 0.707 & 0 & 0.848 \\ -0.408 & 0.707 & 0 & 0.879 \\ 0.204 & 0.354 & 0 & 0.833 \end{bmatrix}$$

$$= \begin{bmatrix} -0.465 & -0.805 & 0 & 1 \\ 0.481 & -0.833 & 0 & 1 \\ 0.245 & -0.424 & 0 & 1 \\ -0.490 & 0 & 0 & 1 \\ -0.962 & 0 & 0 & 1 \\ 0 & 0 & 0 & 1 \\ 0.929 & 0 & 0 & 1 \\ 0.481 & 0.833 & 0 & 1 \\ -0.465 & 0.805 & 0 & 1 \\ 0.245 & 0.424 & 0 & 1 \end{bmatrix}$$

The result is shown in Fig. 3–48.

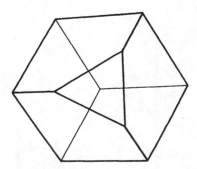

**Figure 3–48**   Result for Ex. 3–29.

## 3–21 RECONSTRUCTION OF THREE-DIMENSIONAL IMAGES

The reconstruction of a three-dimensional object or position in space is a common problem. For example, it occurs continuously in utilizing mechanical drawings which are orthographic projections. The method of reconstructing a three-dimensional object or position from two or more views (orthographic projections) given on a mechanical drawing is well known. However, the technique of reconstructing a three-dimensional position vector from two perspective projections, for example, two photographs, is not as well known. Of course, if the method is valid for perspective projections, then it is also valid for the simpler orthographic projections, and in fact for all the projections mentioned in previous sections. Further, as is shown below, if certain other information is available, then no direct knowledge about the transformation is required.

Before considering the more general problem we consider the special case of reconstruction of the three-dimensional coordinates of a point from two or more orthographic projections. Front, right-side and top orthographic views (projections) of an object are shown in Fig. 3–49. In determining the three-dimensional coordinates of point $A$, the front view yields values for $x$ and $y$, the right-side view for $y$ and $z$, and the top view for $x$ and $z$, i.e.,

$$\text{front} : x_f \quad y_f$$
$$\text{right side} : \quad y_r \quad z_r$$
$$\text{top} : x_t \quad \quad z_t$$

Notice that two values are obtained for each coordinate. In any measurement system, in general $x_f \neq x_t$, $y_f \neq y_r$, $z_r \neq z_t$.[†] Since neither value is necessarily correct, the most reasonable solution is to average the values. Mathematically, the problem is said to be overspecified. Here only three independent values need be determined, but six conditions (equations) determining those values are available.

Turning now to reconstruction of three-dimensional coordinates from perspective projections, recall that the general perspective transformation is represented as a $4 \times 4$ matrix. Thus,

$$[\, x \quad y \quad z \quad 1 \,][\, T' \,] = [\, x' \quad y' \quad z' \quad h \,]$$

where

$$[\, T' \,] = \begin{bmatrix} T'_{11} & T'_{12} & T'_{13} & T'_{14} \\ T'_{21} & T'_{22} & T'_{23} & T'_{24} \\ T'_{31} & T'_{32} & T'_{33} & T'_{34} \\ T'_{41} & T'_{42} & T'_{43} & T'_{44} \end{bmatrix}$$

---

[†]For this reason mechanical drawings are explicitly dimensioned.

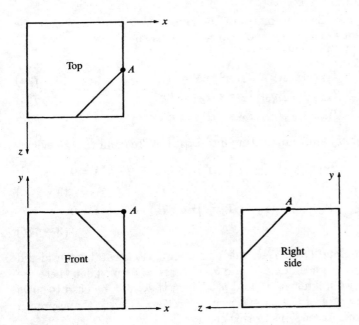

**Figure 3–49**    Three-dimensional reconstruction from orthographic projections.

The results can be projected onto a two-dimensional plane, say $z = 0$, using

$$[T''] = \begin{bmatrix} 1 & 0 & 0 & 0 \\ 0 & 1 & 0 & 0 \\ 0 & 0 & 0 & 0 \\ 0 & 0 & 0 & 1 \end{bmatrix}$$

Concatenation of the two matrices yields

$$[T] = [T''][T'] = \begin{bmatrix} T_{11} & T_{12} & 0 & T_{14} \\ T_{21} & T_{22} & 0 & T_{24} \\ T_{31} & T_{32} & 0 & T_{34} \\ T_{41} & T_{42} & 0 & T_{44} \end{bmatrix}$$

It is useful to write the transformation as

$$[x \quad y \quad z \quad 1] \begin{bmatrix} T_{11} & T_{12} & 0 & T_{14} \\ T_{21} & T_{22} & 0 & T_{24} \\ T_{31} & T_{32} & 0 & T_{34} \\ T_{41} & T_{42} & 0 & T_{44} \end{bmatrix} = [x' \quad y' \quad 0 \quad h]$$

$$= h[x^* \quad y^* \quad 0 \quad 1] \quad (3-71)$$

Note that $x^*$ and $y^*$ are the coordinates of the perspective projection onto the $z = 0$ plane. Projections onto the $x = 0$ or $y = 0$ planes could also be used.

Writing out Eq. (3–71) yields

$$T_{11}x + T_{21}y + T_{31}z + T_{41} = hx^* \qquad (3-72a)$$

$$T_{12}x + T_{22}y + T_{32}z + T_{42} = hy^* \qquad (3-72b)$$

$$T_{14}x + T_{24}y + T_{34}z + T_{44} = h \qquad (3-72c)$$

Using $h$ from Eq. (3–72c) and substituting into Eqs. (3–72a) and (3–72b) yields

$$(T_{11} - T_{14}x^*)x + (T_{21} - T_{24}x^*)y + (T_{31} - T_{34}x^*)z + (T_{41} - T_{44}x^*) = 0$$
$$(3-73a)$$

$$(T_{12} - T_{14}y^*)x + (T_{22} - T_{24}y^*)y + (T_{32} - T_{34}y^*)z + (T_{42} - T_{44}y^*) = 0$$
$$(3-73b)$$

As suggested by Sutherland (Ref. 3–4), this pair of equations can be considered in three different ways. First assume $T$ and $x$, $y$, $z$ are known. Then there are two equations in the two unknowns $x^*$ and $y^*$. Thus, they may be used to solve directly for the coordinates of the perspective projection. This is the approach taken in all the previous discussions in this chapter.

Alternately $T$, $x^*$, $y^*$ can be assumed known. In this case two equations in the three unknown space coordinates $x$, $y$, $z$ result. The system of equations cannot be solved. However, if two perspective projections, say two photographs, are available, then Eq. (3–73) can be written for both projections. This yields

$$(T_{11}^1 - T_{14}^1 x^{*1})x + (T_{21}^1 - T_{24}^1 x^{*1})y + (T_{31}^1 - T_{34}^1 x^{*1})z + (T_{41}^1 - T_{44}^1 x^{*1}) = 0$$

$$(T_{12}^1 - T_{14}^1 y^{*1})x + (T_{22}^1 - T_{24}^1 y^{*1})y + (T_{32}^1 - T_{34}^1 y^{*1})z + (T_{42}^1 - T_{44}^1 y^{*1}) = 0$$

$$(T_{11}^2 - T_{14}^2 x^{*2})x + (T_{21}^2 - T_{24}^2 x^{*2})y + (T_{31}^2 - T_{34}^2 x^{*2})z + (T_{41}^2 - T_{44}^2 x^{*2}) = 0$$

$$(T_{12}^2 - T_{14}^2 y^{*2})x + (T_{22}^2 - T_{24}^2 y^{*2})y + (T_{32}^2 - T_{34}^2 y^{*2})z + (T_{42}^2 - T_{44}^2 y^{*2}) = 0$$

where the superscripts 1 and 2 indicate the first and second perspective projections. Note that the transformations $[T^1]$ and $[T^2]$ need not be the same. These equations can be rewritten in matrix form as

$$[A][X] = [B] \qquad (3-74)$$

where

$$[A] = \begin{bmatrix} T_{11}^1 - T_{14}^1 x^{*1} & T_{21}^1 - T_{24}^1 x^{*1} & T_{31}^1 - T_{34}^1 x^{*1} \\ T_{12}^1 - T_{14}^1 y^{*1} & T_{22}^1 - T_{24}^1 y^{*1} & T_{32}^1 - T_{34}^1 y^{*1} \\ T_{11}^2 - T_{14}^2 x^{*2} & T_{21}^2 - T_{24}^2 x^{*2} & T_{31}^2 - T_{34}^2 x^{*2} \\ T_{12}^2 - T_{14}^2 y^{*2} & T_{22}^2 - T_{24}^2 y^{*2} & T_{32}^2 - T_{34}^2 y^{*2} \end{bmatrix}$$

$$[X]^T = \begin{bmatrix} x & y & z \end{bmatrix}$$

$$[B]^T = \begin{bmatrix} T_{44}^1 x^{*1} - T_{41}^1 & T_{44}^1 y^{*1} - T_{42}^1 & T_{44}^2 x^{*2} - T_{41}^2 & T_{44}^2 y^{*2} - T_{42}^2 \end{bmatrix}$$

Equation (3–74) represents four equations in the three unknown space coordinates $x$, $y$, $z$. $[A]$ is not a square matrix and consequently cannot be inverted to obtain the solution for $[X]$. Again, as in the case of reconstructing three-dimensional coordinates from orthographic projections, the problem is overspecified and thus can be solved only in some mean or best-fit sense.

A mean solution is computed by recalling that a matrix times its transpose is always square. Thus, multiplying both sides of Eq. (3–74) by $[A]^T$ yields

$$[A]^T[A][X] = [A]^T[B]$$

Taking the inverse of $[[A]^T[A]]$ yields a mean solution for $[X]$, i.e.,

$$[X] = [[A]^T[A]]^{-1}[A]^T[B] \qquad (3-75)$$

If no solution for $[X]$ results, then the imposed conditions are redundant and no unique solution which yields a least error condition exists. An example illustrates this technique.

---

## Example 3–30    Three-Dimensional Reconstruction

Assume that the measured position of a point in one perspective projection is $[0.836 \quad -1.836 \quad 0 \quad 1]$ and is $[0.6548 \quad 0 \quad 0.2886 \quad 1]$ in a second perspective projection. The first perspective projection transformation is known to be the result of a 60° rotation about the $y$-axis, followed by a translation of 2 units in the negative $y$ direction. The point of projection is at $z = -1$, and the result is projected onto the $z = 0$ plane. This is effectively a two-point perspective projection. The second perspective projection is the result of a 30° rotation about each of the $x$- and $y$-axes. The point of projection is at $y = -1$ and the result is projected onto the $y = 0$ plane, i.e., effectively a three-point perspective projection. $[T^1]$ and $[T^2]$ are thus

$$[T^1] = \begin{bmatrix} 0.5 & 0 & 0 & -0.87 \\ 0 & 1 & 0 & 0 \\ 0.87 & 0 & 0 & 0.5 \\ 0 & -2 & 0 & 1 \end{bmatrix} \text{ and } [T^2] = \begin{bmatrix} 0.87 & 0 & -0.5 & 0 \\ 0.25 & 0 & 0.43 & 0.87 \\ 0.43 & 0 & 0.75 & -0.5 \\ 0 & 0 & 0 & 1 \end{bmatrix}$$

First noting that the last two rows of $[A]$ and $[B]$ must be rewritten to account for $[T^2]$ being a projection onto the $y = 0$ plane, the $A$-matrix is

$$[A] = \begin{bmatrix} 1.22 & 0 & 0.45 \\ -1.59 & 1 & 0.92 \\ 0.87 & -0.32 & 0.76 \\ -0.5 & 0.18 & 0.89 \end{bmatrix}$$

and $$[B]^T = [0.84 \quad 0.16 \quad 0.65 \quad 0.29]$$

Solution yields $[X] = [0.5 \quad 0.5 \quad 0.5]$, i.e., the center of the unit cube.

As a third way of considering Eq. (3–73) note that if the location of several points which appear in the perspective projection are known in object space *and* in the perspective projection, then it is possible to determine the transformation elements, i.e., the $T_{ij}$'s. These transformation elements can subsequently be used to determine the location of unknown points using the second technique described above. To see this, rewrite Eq. (3–73) as

$$T_{11}x + T_{21}y + T_{31}z + T_{41} - T_{14}xx^* - T_{24}yx^* - T_{34}zx^* - T_{44}x^* = 0 \qquad (3-76a)$$

$$T_{12}x + T_{22}y + T_{32}z + T_{42} - T_{14}xy^* - T_{24}yy^* - T_{34}zy^* - T_{44}y^* = 0 \qquad (3-76b)$$

Assuming that $x^*$ and $y^*$ as well as $x$, $y$, $z$ are known, Eqs. (3–76a) and (3–76b) represent two equations in the 12 unknown transformation elements $T_{ij}$. Applying these equations to 6 noncoplanar known locations in object space and in the perspective projection yields a system of 12 equations in 12 unknowns. These equations can be solved exactly for the $T_{ij}$'s. Thus, the transformation that produced the perspective projection, for example, a photograph, is determined. Notice that in this case no prior knowledge of the transformation is required. If, for example, the perspective projections are photographs, neither the location nor the orientation of the camera is required. In matrix form the system of 12 equations is written as

$$
\begin{bmatrix}
x_1 & 0 & -x_1x_1^* & y_1 & 0 & -y_1x_1^* & z_1 & 0 & -z_1x_1^* & 1 & 0 & -x_1^* \\
0 & x_1 & -x_1y_1^* & 0 & y_1 & -y_1y_1^* & 0 & z_1 & -z_1y_1^* & 0 & 1 & -y_1^* \\
x_2 & 0 & -x_2x_2^* & y_2 & 0 & -y_2x_2^* & z_2 & 0 & -z_2x_2^* & 1 & 0 & -x_2^* \\
0 & x_2 & -x_2y_2^* & 0 & y_2 & -y_2y_2^* & 0 & z_2 & -z_2y_2^* & 0 & 1 & -y_2^* \\
x_3 & 0 & -x_3x_3^* & y_3 & 0 & -y_3x_3^* & z_3 & 0 & -z_3x_3^* & 1 & 0 & -x_3^* \\
0 & x_3 & -x_3y_3^* & 0 & y_3 & -y_3y_3^* & 0 & z_3 & -z_3y_3^* & 0 & 1 & -y_3^* \\
x_4 & 0 & -x_4x_4^* & y_4 & 0 & -y_4x_4^* & z_4 & 0 & -z_4x_4^* & 1 & 0 & -x_4^* \\
0 & x_4 & -x_4y_4^* & 0 & y_4 & -y_4y_4^* & 0 & z_4 & -z_4y_4^* & 0 & 1 & -y_4^* \\
x_5 & 0 & -x_5x_5^* & y_5 & 0 & -y_5x_5^* & z_5 & 0 & -z_5x_5^* & 1 & 0 & -x_5^* \\
0 & x_5 & -x_5y_5^* & 0 & y_5 & -y_5y_5^* & 0 & z_5 & -z_5y_5^* & 0 & 1 & -y_5^* \\
x_6 & 0 & -x_6x_6^* & y_6 & 0 & -y_6x_6^* & z_6 & 0 & -z_6x_6^* & 1 & 0 & -x_6^* \\
0 & x_6 & -x_6y_6^* & 0 & y_6 & -y_6y_6^* & 0 & z_6 & -z_6y_6^* & 0 & 1 & -y_6^*
\end{bmatrix}
\begin{bmatrix}
T_{11} \\ T_{12} \\ T_{14} \\ T_{21} \\ T_{22} \\ T_{24} \\ T_{31} \\ T_{32} \\ T_{34} \\ T_{41} \\ T_{42} \\ T_{44}
\end{bmatrix} = 0
$$

$$(3-77)$$

where the subscripts correspond to points with known locations. Equations (3–77) are written in more compact form as

$$[A'][T] = 0$$

Since Eqs. (3–77) are homogeneous, they contain an arbitrary scale factor. Hence $T_{44}$ may, for example, be defined as unity and the resulting transformation normalized. This reduces the requirement to 11 equations or 5 1/2 points. If the transformation is normalized, then the last column in $[A']$ is moved to the right-hand side and the nonhomogeneous matrix equation is solved. An example is given below.

### Example 3–31    Elements for Reconstruction

As a specific example, consider the unit cube with the six known corner points in the physical plane given by

$$[P] = \begin{bmatrix} 0 & 0 & 0 \\ 0 & 0 & 1 \\ 0 & 1 & 1 \\ 0 & 1 & 0 \\ 1 & 0 & 0 \\ 1 & 0 & 1 \end{bmatrix}$$

The corresponding points in the transformed view are marked by a dot as shown in Fig. 3–50.  The corresponding transformed coordinates of these points are

$$\begin{bmatrix} 0 & -1 \\ 0.34 & -0.8 \\ 0.34 & -0.4 \\ 0 & -0.5 \\ 0.44 & -1.75 \\ 0.83 & -1.22 \end{bmatrix}$$

Equation (3–77) then becomes

$$\begin{bmatrix} 0 & 0 & 0 & 0 & 0 & 0 & 0 & 0 & 0 & 1 & 0 & 0 \\ 0 & 0 & 0 & 0 & 0 & 0 & 0 & 0 & 0 & 0 & 1 & 1 \\ 0 & 0 & 0 & 0 & 0 & 0 & 1 & 0 & -0.34 & 1 & 0 & -0.34 \\ 0 & 0 & 0 & 0 & 0 & 0 & 0 & 1 & 0.8 & 0 & 1 & 0.8 \\ 0 & 0 & 0 & 1 & 0 & -0.34 & 1 & 0 & -0.34 & 1 & 0 & -0.34 \\ 0 & 0 & 0 & 0 & 1 & 0.4 & 0 & 1 & 0.4 & 0 & 1 & 0.4 \\ 0 & 0 & 0 & 1 & 0 & 0 & 0 & 0 & 0 & 1 & 0 & 0 \\ 0 & 0 & 0 & 0 & 1 & 0.5 & 0 & 0 & 0 & 0 & 1 & 0.5 \\ 1 & 0 & -0.44 & 0 & 0 & 0 & 0 & 0 & 0 & 1 & 0 & -0.44 \\ 0 & 1 & 1.75 & 0 & 0 & 0 & 0 & 0 & 0 & 0 & 1 & 1.75 \\ 1 & 0 & -0.83 & 0 & 0 & 0 & 1 & 0 & -0.83 & 1 & 0 & -0.83 \\ 0 & 1 & 1.22 & 0 & 0 & 0 & 0 & 1 & 1.22 & 0 & 1 & 1.22 \end{bmatrix} \begin{bmatrix} T_{11} \\ T_{12} \\ T_{14} \\ T_{21} \\ T_{22} \\ T_{24} \\ T_{31} \\ T_{32} \\ T_{34} \\ T_{41} \\ T_{42} \\ T_{44} \end{bmatrix} = 0$$

Solution for the 12 unknown $T_{ij}$'s yields

$$\begin{bmatrix} T_{11} \\ T_{12} \\ T_{14} \\ T_{21} \\ T_{22} \\ T_{24} \\ T_{31} \\ T_{32} \\ T_{34} \\ T_{41} \\ T_{42} \\ T_{44} \end{bmatrix} = \begin{bmatrix} 0.25 \\ 0 \\ -0.43 \\ 0 \\ 0.5 \\ 0 \\ 0.43 \\ 0 \\ 0.25 \\ 0 \\ -1 \\ 1 \end{bmatrix}$$

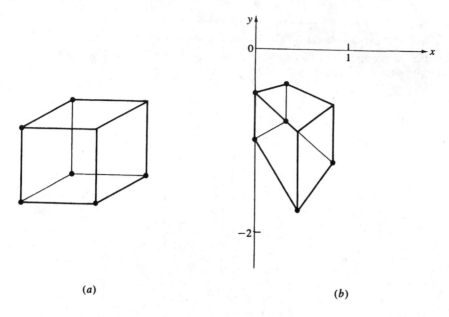

(a)                                                                    (b)

**Figure 3–50**    Determining the transformation from a perspective projection.

Substituting these results into the $4 \times 4$ $[T]$ matrix yields

$$[T] = \begin{bmatrix} 0.25 & 0 & 0 & -0.43 \\ 0 & 0.5 & 0 & 0 \\ 0.43 & 0 & 0 & 0.25 \\ 0 & -1 & 0 & 1 \end{bmatrix}$$

## 3–22    REFERENCES

3–1 Rogers, D.F., *Procedural Elements for Computer Graphics*, McGraw-Hill Book Co., New York, 1985.

3–2 Carlbom, I., and Paciorek, J., "Planar Geometric Projections and Viewing Transformations," *ACM Comp. Surv.*, Vol. 10, No.4, pp. 465–502, 1978.

3–3 Sutherland, I.E., "Three Dimensional Data Input by Tablet," *Proc. IEEE*, Vol. 62, No. 2, pp. 453–461, 1974.

3–4 Slama, C. (ed.), *Manual of Photogrammetry*, American Society of Photogrammetry, 1980.

3–5 Kingslake, R. (ed.), *Applied Optics and Optical Engineering*, Vol. 2, Academic Press, New York, 1965.

## FOUR

## PLANE CURVES

## 4-1   INTRODUCTION

A multitude of techniques are available for drawing and designing curves manually. A wide variety of pencils, pens, brushes, knives, etc., along with straight-edges, French curves, compasses, splines, templates, etc., are used to aid the designer. Each tool has its function and use. No single tool is sufficient for all tasks. Similarly, a variety of techniques and tools are useful for curve design and generation in computer graphics. Two-dimensional curve generation techniques are discussed in this chapter. A curve is two-dimensional if it lies in its entirety in a single plane. Here, the discussion is limited to the conic sections.

## 4-2   CURVE REPRESENTATION

The previous two chapters treated the transformation of points. A curve may be represented as a collection of points. Provided the points are properly spaced, connection of the points by short straight line segments yields an adequate visual representation of the curve. Figure 4-1 shows two alternate point representations of the same plane curve. Points along the curve in Fig. 4-1a are equally spaced along the curve length. Notice that connection of the points by short straight

|     |     |
| :-: | :-: |
| (a) | (b) |

**Figure 4-1**   Point representations of curves. (a) Equal point density along the curve length; (b) point density increases with decreasing radius of curvature.

line segments yields a poor representation of the curve. The representation is especially poor where the radius of curvature is small. Increasing the point density in these regions, as shown in Fig. 4–1b, improves the representation.

Although, as shown above, curves can be adequately represented as a collection of points, an analytical representation has several advantages. Some of these are precision, compact storage and ease of calculation of intermediate points. With an analytical representation, curve properties such as slope and radius of curvature are easily determined. However, with a point representation, numerical differentiation, a notably inaccurate procedure, is required. Contrast the storage required for a point representation of a circle with 32 points on its circumference, to that for the center coordinates and the radius required by an analytical representation. Any point on an analytically represented curve can be precisely determined. When represented by a collection of points, intermediate points must be obtained using interpolation. In general, the resulting point does not actually lie on the curve.

Experience has shown that drawings of analytically represented curves are more easily produced. An analytical representation has also proven more useful when continuous alteration of curve shape is required to meet design criteria. Various techniques for analytically representing two-dimensional curves are considered below.

Analytical representations of curves originally defined by points are frequently required. From a mathematical point of view, the problem of analytically defining a curve from a known set of data points is one of interpolation. A curve that passes through all known data points is said to *fit* the data. One common technique for curve fitting is piecewise polynomial approximation. This technique requires determining the coefficients of a polynomial of some degree. The actual shape between data points depends on the degree of the polynomial and the imposed boundary conditions. Piecewise polynomial approximation is discussed in Chapter 5.

Alternately, if the data points are only approximations to some unknown true values, e.g., values obtained from experimental measurement or observed data, then a curve that shows the correct *trend* of the data is required. In general, the curve may not actually pass through any of the data points. The curve is said to *fair* the data.

One common curve fairing technique is the method of least squares approximation (Ref. 4–1). The method of least squares approximation produces a curve of the form $y = f(x)$ that minimizes the sum of the $y$-squared deviations between the data and the derived curve. The chosen form $y = f(x)$ is usually based on a knowledge of the phenomenon that produced the data.

The curve forms used in the least squares technique are typically power, exponential and polynomial functions, e.g., $y = ax^b$, $y = ae^{bx}$ or $y = c_1 + c_2x + c_3x^2 + \cdots + c_{n+1}x^n$, where $a$, $b$ and the $c_i$'s are constants. Regardless of the chosen curve form the least squares technique requires solving a set of simultaneous, linear algebraic equations to determine the unknown constants. More details are given in Ref. 4–1 and in standard numerical analysis books.

## 4–3   NONPARAMETRIC CURVES

Mathematically, either a parametric or a nonparametric form is used to represent a curve. A nonparametric representation is either explicit or implicit. For a plane curve, an explicit, nonparametric form is given by

$$y = f(x)$$

An example is the equation of a straight line, $y = mx + b$. In this form, for each $x$-value only one $y$-value is obtained. Consequently, closed or multiple-value curves, e.g., a circle, cannot be represented explicitly. Implicit representations of the form

$$f(x, y) = 0$$

do not have this limitation.

A general second-degree implicit equation written as

$$ax^2 + 2bxy + cy^2 + 2dx + 2ey + f = 0$$

provides a variety of two-dimensional curve forms called conic sections. The three types of conic sections are the parabola, the hyperbola and the ellipse, as shown in Fig. 4–2. A circle is a special case of an ellipse. By defining the constant coefficients $a$, $b$, $c$, $d$, $e$ and $f$, several different types of conic sections are produced. If the conic section is defined relative to a local coordinate system and passes through the origin, then $f = 0$. Geometric boundary conditions are used to establish a particular curve through specific points.

If $c = 1.0$ in the general equation, then, to define a curve segment between two points, five independent conditions must be specified to determine the values of the remaining five coefficients $a$, $b$, $c$, $d$, $e$ and $f$. One choice is to specify the position of the two end points, the slope of the curve segment at each end point, and an intermediate point through which the curve must pass.

If instead $b = 0$ and $c = 1.0$, then the analytical description of the resulting curve is fixed by specifying only four additional conditions, e.g., the two end points and the two end slopes. An even simpler curve is defined by first setting $a = 1.0$, $b = 0$ and $c = 1.0$. Then the form of the curve is

$$x^2 + y^2 + 2dx + 2ey + f = 0$$

The three conditions required to fix $d$, $e$ and $f$ are, e.g., the two end points and either the slope at the beginning or the slope at the end of the curve segment. An alternate choice is to specify the two end points and a third internal point through which the curve must pass.

A straight line is obtained by setting $a = b = c = 0$. The equation is then

$$dx + ey + f = 0$$

or

$$y = -\left(\frac{d}{e}\right)x - \frac{f}{e} = mx + b'$$

where, as usual, $m$ is the slope of the line and $b'$ is its $y$ intercept.

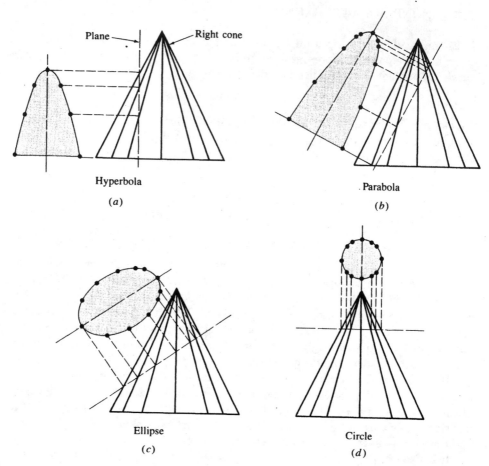

**Figure 4–2**   Conic sections.

Both explicit and implicit nonparametric curve representations are axis-dependent. Thus, the choice of coordinate system affects the ease of use. For example, if, in the chosen coordinate system, an infinite slope is required as a boundary condition, difficulties arise. This infinite slope cannot be directly used as a numerical boundary condition. Either the chosen coordinate system must be changed or the infinite slope numerically represented by a large positive or negative value.

Further, when points on an axis-dependent nonparametric curve are calculated at equal increments in $x$ or $y$, they are not evenly distributed along the curve length. This unequal distribution of points affects the quality and accuracy of graphical representation. In spite of these limitations, nonparametric representations are useful. However, their limitations lead to an interest in parametric curve representations.

## 4-4   PARAMETRIC CURVES

In parametric form each coordinate of a point on a curve is represented as a function of a single parameter. The position vector of a point on the curve is fixed by the value of the parameter. For a two-dimensional curve with $t$ as the parameter, the Cartesian coordinates of a point on the curve are

$$x = x(t)$$
$$y = y(t)$$

The position vector of a point on the curve is then

$$P(t) = [\, x(t) \quad y(t) \,]$$

The nonparametric form is obtained from the parametric form by eliminating the parameter to obtain a single equation in terms of $x$ and $y$.

The parametric form is suitable for representing closed and multiple valued curves. The derivative or tangent vector on a parametric curve is given by

$$P'(t) = [\, x'(t) \quad y'(t) \,]$$

where the $'$ denotes differentiation with respect to the parameter. The slope of the curve, $dy/dx$, is

$$\frac{dy}{dx} = \frac{dy/dt}{dx/dt} = \frac{y'(t)}{x'(t)}$$

Note that when $x'(t) = 0$ the slope is infinite. Hence an infinite slope is specified by letting one component of the tangent vector be zero. Thus, computational difficulties are avoided by using the parametric derivative.

Since a point on a parametric curve is specified by a single value of the parameter, the parametric form is axis-independent. The curve end points and length are fixed by the parameter range. Often it is convenient to normalize the parameter range for the curve segment of interest to $0 \le t \le 1$. Because a parametric curve is axis-independent, it is easily manipulated using the affine manipulation transformations discussed in Chapters 2 and 3.

The simplest parametric 'curve' representation is for a straight line. For two position vectors $P_1$ and $P_2$, a parametric representation of the straight line segment between them is

$$P(t) = P_1 + (P_2 - P_1)t \qquad 0 \le t \le 1$$

Since $P(t)$ is a position vector, each of the components of $P(t)$ has a parametric representation $x(t)$ and $y(t)$ between $P_1$ and $P_2$, i.e.,

$$x(t) = x_1 + (x_2 - x_1)t \qquad 0 \le t \le 1$$
$$y(t) = y_1 + (y_2 - y_1)t$$

**Example 4–1    Parametric Representation of a Straight Line**

For the position vectors $P_1 [ 1 \quad 2 ]$ and $P_2 [ 4 \quad 3 ]$ determine the parametric representation of the line segment between them. Also determine the slope and tangent vector of the line segment.

A parametric representation is

$$P(t) = P_1 + (P_2 - P_1)t = [ 1 \quad 2 ] + ( [ 4 \quad 3 ] - [ 1 \quad 2 ] )t \qquad 0 \le t \le 1$$
$$P(t) = [ 1 \quad 2 ] + [ 3 \quad 1 ]t \qquad 0 \le t \le 1$$

Parametric representations of the $x$ and $y$ components are

$$x(t) = x_1 + (x_2 - x_1)t = 1 + 3t \qquad 0 \le t \le 1$$
$$y(t) = y_1 + (y_2 - y_1)t = 2 + t$$

The tangent vector is obtained by differentiating $P(t)$. Specifically,

$$P'(t) = [ \, x'(t) \quad y'(t) \, ] = [ 3 \quad 1 ]$$

or

$$\bar{V}_t = 3\mathbf{i} + \mathbf{j}$$

where $\bar{V}_t$ is the tangent vector and $\mathbf{i}, \mathbf{j}$ are unit vectors in the $x, y$ directions, respectively.

The slope of the line segment is

$$\frac{dy}{dx} = \frac{dy/dt}{dx/dt} = \frac{y'(t)}{x'(t)} = \frac{1}{3}$$

A comparison of nonparametric and parametric representations for a circle in the first quadrant are shown in Fig. 4–3. The nonparametric representation of the unit circle in the first quadrant given by

$$y = +\sqrt{1 - x^2} \qquad 0 \le x \le 1 \tag{4 – 1}$$

is shown in Fig. 4–3a. Equal increments in $x$ were used to obtain the points on the arc. Notice that the resulting arc lengths along the curve are unequal. A poor visual representation of the circle results. Further, calculation of the square root is computationally expensive.

The standard parametric form for a unit circle is

$$x = \cos\theta \qquad 0 \le \theta \le 2\pi$$
$$y = \sin\theta$$

or

$$P(\theta) = [ \, x \quad y \, ] = [ \cos\theta \quad \sin\theta \, ] \qquad 0 \le \theta \le 2\pi \tag{4 – 2}$$

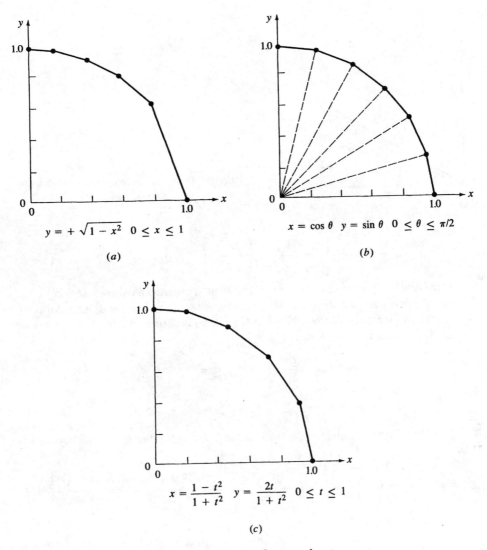

**Figure 4–3**    Circle representations for the first quadrant.

where the *parameter* $\theta$ is associated with the geometric angle measured counter-clockwise from the positive $x$-axis. Equal increments in the parameter $\theta$ for the range $0 \leq \theta \leq \pi/2$ were used to obtain points on the arc shown in Fig. 4–3b. Since for this parametric representation equal parameter increments produce equal arc lengths along the circumference of the circle, the appearance is quite good. However, computation of the trigonometric functions is expensive. (A computationally less expensive technique is described below in Sec. 4–5.)

There is no unique parametric representation for a curve. For example,

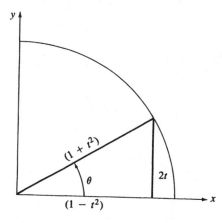

**Figure 4–4**   A correlation between parametric representations.

$$P(t) = \left[ \begin{array}{cc} \dfrac{(1-t^2)}{(1+t^2)} & \dfrac{2t}{(1+t^2)} \end{array} \right] \qquad 0 \leq t \leq 1 \qquad\qquad (4-3)$$

also represents the unit circular arc in the first quadrant as shown in Fig. 4–3c. The correlation between the parametric representation of Eq. (4–3) and the standard parametric representation given in Eq. (4–2) is shown in Fig. 4–4. Referring to Fig. 4–4 shows that for a unit circle

$$x = \cos\theta = \frac{1-t^2}{1+t^2} \qquad 0 \leq \theta \leq \pi/2 \qquad 0 \leq t \leq 1$$

$$y = \sin\theta = \frac{2t}{1+t^2} \qquad 0 \leq \theta \leq \pi/2 \qquad 0 \leq t \leq 1$$

The fact that Eq. 4–3 represents a unit circular arc is further confirmed by noting that

$$r^2 = x^2 + y^2 = \left(\frac{1-t^2}{1+t^2}\right)^2 + \left(\frac{2t}{1+t^2}\right)^2 = \frac{1-2t^2+t^4+4t^2}{(1+t^2)^2} = \frac{(1+t^2)^2}{(1+t^2)^2} = 1$$

where $r$ is the unit radius.

Figure 4–3c illustrates results for equal increments in $t$. Here, unequal perimeter lengths along the circumference result. The results are better than for the explicit representation (Eq. 4–1) but not as good as the standard parametric representation (Eq. 4–2). However, Eq. (4–3) is computationally less expensive, i.e., it is a compromise.

---

**Example 4–2**   **Determination of a Point on a Parametric Curve**

Consider the problem of determining the value of $y$ for a given value of $x$. As an example, assume that $x = 0.5$ and that it is required to determine $y$ on a unit circle. For the explicit representation (Eq. 4–1) this is straightforward.

$$y = \sqrt{1-x^2} = \sqrt{1-(0.5)^2} = \sqrt{0.75} = 0.866$$

For the parametric representation it is first necessary to solve for the parameter $t$ in terms of $x$ and then use this value to obtain $y$. Specifically, the parametric representation of Eq. (4–2) is

$$x = \cos\theta$$
$$y = \sin\theta$$

Thus,

$$\theta = \cos^{-1}(x) = \cos^{-1}(0.5) = 60°$$
$$y = \sin(60°) = 0.866$$

Alternately, from Eq. (4–3)

$$x = \frac{1 - t^2}{1 + t^2}$$
$$y = \frac{2t}{1 + t^2}$$

Solving the first of these equations for $t$ yields

$$t = \left(\frac{1 - x}{1 + x}\right)^{1/2} = \frac{1}{\sqrt{3}} = 0.57735$$

and thus

$$y = \frac{2/\sqrt{3}}{4/3} = \frac{\sqrt{3}}{2} = 0.866$$

---

For more complex parametric representations, an iterative technique may be more convenient for finding the unknown value of an explicit variable.

Parametric representations of the conic sections are axis-independent and yield visually more acceptable representations than nonparametric representations. However, neither parametric nor nonparametric representations are a panacea. Both have advantages and disadvantages, and both find useful applications in computer graphics.

## 4–5    PARAMETRIC REPRESENTATION OF A CIRCLE

An origin-centered circle of radius $r$ is parametrically represented by

$$x = r\cos\theta \qquad 0 \leq \theta \leq 2\pi$$
$$y = r\sin\theta \tag{4 - 4}$$

where $\theta$ is the parameter. Previously we remarked that although equal increments in $\theta$ produced excellent visual output, the algorithm was inefficient because it required repeated calculation of the trigonometric functions. By eliminating this requirement (Ref. 4–2) an efficient algorithm is obtained.

Noting that a circle is completely swept out for a range of the parameter $\theta$ from 0 to $2\pi$, and assuming that a fixed number of uniformly spaced points on the circumference are calculated, then $\delta\theta$, the parameter increment between points, is a constant. The Cartesian coordinates of any point on an origin-centered circle are then

$$x_{i+1} = r\cos(\theta_i + \delta\theta)$$
$$y_{i+1} = r\sin(\theta_i + \delta\theta)$$

where $\theta_i$ is the value of the parameter that yields the point at $x_i$, $y_i$.

Using the sum of the angles formulas yields

$$x_{i+1} = r(\cos\theta_i \cos\delta\theta - \sin\theta_i \sin\delta\theta)$$
$$y_{i+1} = r(\cos\theta_i \sin\delta\theta + \cos\delta\theta \sin\theta_i)$$

But recalling Eq. (4–4) with $\theta = \theta_i$

$$x_i = r\cos\theta_i$$
$$y_i = r\sin\theta_i$$

gives the recursion equations

$$x_{i+1} = x_i \cos\delta\theta - y_i \sin\delta\theta$$
$$y_{i+1} = x_i \sin\delta\theta + y_i \cos\delta\theta \qquad\qquad (4-5)$$

which represent the rotation of the point $x_i, y_i$ by an amount $\delta\theta$.

Since $\delta\theta$ is constant and equal to $2\pi/(n-1)$ where $n$ is the number of uniformly spaced points on the circle, the values of $\sin\delta\theta$ and $\cos\delta\theta$ need to be calculated only once. The resulting algorithm requires only four multiplies, an add and a subtract in the inner loop. It is very efficient.[†] The results, shown in Fig. 4–5, are identical to those given by Eq. (4–4).

A non-origin-centered circle is obtained by translating an origin-centered circle of the appropriate radius. For some applications a further simplification is possible. Here a single origin-centered *unit* circle is generated. Circles of arbitrary radius $r$ and center $(h, k)$ are obtained by combined scaling and translation.

---

### Example 4–3    Parametric Circle Generation

Generate a circle of radius 2 with center located at $(2, 2)$. Two approaches are considered. First, generate an origin-centered circle of radius 2 and then translate the result 2 units in $x$ and $y$. Alternately, an origin-centered unit circle is generated, then scaled by a factor of 2 and finally translated by 2 units in $x$ and $y$. The second approach is illustrated here. To conserve space only eight unique points on the circle are calculated. Normally a much larger

---

[†]A note of caution: As with any recursive algorithm, the results for large $n$ may be numerically sensitive.

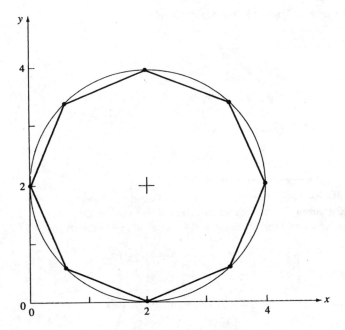

**Figure 4–5**    Parametric unit circle with $n = 8$.

number of points is required. In fact, for display purposes, the number of points depends on the radius of the circle.

Since a circle is a closed curve, the first point ($\theta = 0$) and the last point ($\theta = 2\pi$) coincide. Thus, to obtain $n$ unique points on the circle it is necessary to calculate $n + 1$ points. For open curves this is not necessary.

Thus, $\delta\theta$ is

$$\delta\theta = \frac{2\pi}{(n + 1 - 1)} = \frac{2\pi}{n} = \frac{2\pi}{8} = \frac{\pi}{4}$$

Using Eq. (4–4) and starting at $\theta = 0$ yields initial values for $x$ and $y$. Specifically,

$$x_1 = r\cos\theta_1 = (1)\cos(0) = 1$$
$$y_1 = r\sin\theta_1 = (1)\sin(0) = 0$$

Now using Eq. (4–5) the other seven unique points are obtained. First

$$\sin\delta\theta = \sin\frac{\pi}{4} = \frac{\sqrt{2}}{2}$$

$$\cos\delta\theta = \cos\frac{\pi}{4} = \frac{\sqrt{2}}{2}$$

and

$$x_2 = x_1\cos\delta\theta - y_1\sin\delta\theta = (1)(\sqrt{2}/2) - 0(\sqrt{2}/2) = (\sqrt{2}/2)$$
$$y_2 = x_1\sin\delta\theta + y_1\cos\delta\theta = (1)(\sqrt{2}/2) + 0(\sqrt{2}/2) = (\sqrt{2}/2)$$

Results for the other points are shown in Table 4–1.

Table 4–1 Results for Unit Circle

| $i$ | $x_i$ | $y_i$ |
|---|---|---|
| 1 | 1 | 0 |
| 2 | $\sqrt{2}/2$ | $\sqrt{2}/2$ |
| 3 | 0 | 1 |
| 4 | $-\sqrt{2}/2$ | $\sqrt{2}/2$ |
| 5 | $-1$ | 0 |
| 6 | $-\sqrt{2}/2$ | $-\sqrt{2}/2$ |
| 7 | 0 | $-1$ |
| 8 | $\sqrt{2}/2$ | $-\sqrt{2}/2$ |
| 9 | 1 | 0 |

Recalling the results for two-dimensional transformations previously derived in Chapter 2, the combined $3 \times 3$ transformation that first locally scales these results by a factor of 2 and then translates the center of the circle to the point $(2,2)$ is

$$[T] = [S][Tr_{xy}] = \begin{bmatrix} 2 & 0 & 0 \\ 0 & 2 & 0 \\ 0 & 0 & 1 \end{bmatrix} \begin{bmatrix} 1 & 0 & 0 \\ 0 & 1 & 0 \\ 2 & 2 & 1 \end{bmatrix} = \begin{bmatrix} 2 & 0 & 0 \\ 0 & 2 & 0 \\ 2 & 2 & 1 \end{bmatrix}$$

Applying the first of these transformations to the point $(x, y)$ yields

$$[x_1 \quad y_1 \quad 1][T] = [1 \quad 0 \quad 1] \begin{bmatrix} 2 & 0 & 0 \\ 0 & 2 & 0 \\ 2 & 2 & 1 \end{bmatrix} = [4 \quad 2 \quad 1]$$

as expected. The complete results are shown in Table 4–2 and in Fig. 4–5.

Table 4–2 Results for Circle of Radius 2 with Center at (2,2)

| $i$ | $x_i$ | $y_i$ |
|---|---|---|
| 1 | 4 | 2 |
| 2 | 3.414 | 3.414 |
| 3 | 2 | 4 |
| 4 | 0.586 | 3.414 |
| 5 | 0 | 2 |
| 6 | 0.586 | 0.586 |
| 7 | 2 | 0 |
| 8 | 3.414 | 0.586 |
| 9 | 4 | 2 |

By restricting the range of the parameter $\theta$, the algorithm generates circular arcs. For example, for $0 \leq \theta \leq \pi/2$, the quarter circle in the first quadrant is obtained. Similarly, $\pi \leq 0 \leq 3\pi/2$ yields the quarter circle in the third quadrant.

## 4–6   PARAMETRIC REPRESENTATION OF AN ELLIPSE

For the circle, a fixed number of uniformly spaced points provides a good visual representation when connected by short straight lines. With a circle, the

distribution of that fixed number of points is obvious, i.e., equal angle increments. However, for an ellipse, if equal angle increments are used to calculate
the display points, an unacceptable result is obtained as shown by the dashed
lines in Fig. 4–6. Here, the ends are not adequately represented. This is because
near the ends of the ellipse the curvature is too large to be represented by a few
points.

An alternate method is to use equal increments along the perimeter. For a
sufficient number of increments this gives a better representation. However, the
ellipse is overspecified along the sides, where the curvature is small. Further,
determination of the equal perimeter lengths involves calculation of a computationally expensive elliptic integral. What is required is small increments in
perimeter length near the ends, where the curvature is large, and larger perimeter increments along the sides, where the curvature is small.

The desired point distribution is obtained by considering the parametric representation of an origin-centered ellipse of semimajor axis $a$ and semiminor axis
$b$ given by

$$x = a\cos\theta$$
$$y = b\sin\theta \qquad\qquad (4-6)$$

where $\theta$ is the parameter. Varying $\theta$ between 0 and $2\pi$ sweeps out the entire

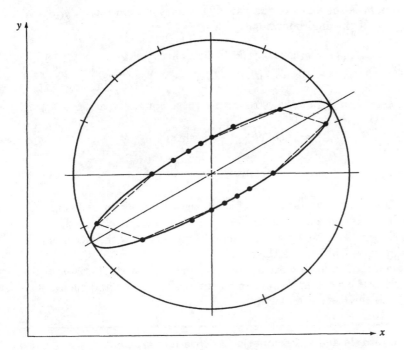

**Figure 4–6**    Equal-angle representation of a high-eccentricity ellipse.

ellipse. A specified number of points along the perimeter of the ellipse is obtained by taking uniform increments in the parameter $\theta$.

Examining the derivatives of $x$ and $y$

$$dx = -a \sin \theta d\theta$$
$$dy = b \cos \theta d\theta \qquad (4-7)$$

shows that the desired perimeter increments are automatically obtained. When $\theta$ is near 0 or $\pi$, i.e., near the ends, $|dx| \approx 0$ and $|dy| \approx bd\theta$. When $\theta$ is near $\pi/2$ or $3\pi/2$, i.e., along the sides, $|dx| \approx ad\theta$ and $|dy| \approx 0$. Thus, near the ends, where the curvature is high, more points are generated; while along the sides, where the curvature is low, fewer points are generated. In fact, the ratio of the perimeter increment size at the ends to that along the sides is approximately $b/a$. Further, note that in the case of a circle where $b = a$ the optimum representation results, i.e., equal perimeter or equal angle increments.

Again assuming a fixed number of points on the ellipse perimeter allows development of an efficient algorithm using the sum of the angles formulas (Ref. 4–2). The Cartesian coordinates of any point on an origin-centered ellipse are then

$$x_{i+1} = a \cos(\theta_i + \delta\theta)$$
$$y_{i+1} = b \sin(\theta_i + \delta\theta)$$

where $\delta\theta = 2\pi/(n-1)$ is the fixed increment in $\theta$, $n$ is the number of points on the perimeter and $\theta_i$ is the value of the parameter for the point at $x_i$, $y_i$.

Using the sum of the angles formulas yields

$$x_{i+1} = a(\cos \theta_i \cos \delta\theta - \sin \theta_i \sin \delta\theta)$$
$$y_{i+1} = b(\cos \theta_i \sin \delta\theta + \cos \delta\theta \sin \theta_i)$$

Recalling Eq. (4–4) with $\theta = \theta_i$ allows rewriting these equations as

$$x_{i+1} = x_i \cos \delta\theta - \left(\frac{a}{b}\right) y_i \sin \delta\theta$$
$$y_{i+1} = \left(\frac{b}{a}\right) x_i \sin \delta\theta + y_i \cos \delta\theta \qquad (4-8)$$

Since $\delta\theta$ and $a$ and $b$ are constant, an efficient algorithm, again utilizing only four multiplies, an add and a subtract within the inner loop, is obtained. Smith (Ref. 4–2) has shown that the algorithm yields the polygon with maximum inscribed area. Figure 4–7 illustrates the results.

Non-origin-centered ellipses with major axes inclined to the horizontal are obtained by first rotating about the origin to the desired angle and then translating the origin to the desired location.

---

### Example 4–4    Parametric Ellipse Generation

Generate an ellipse with semimajor axis $a = 4$ and semiminor axis $b = 1$ inclined 30° to the horizontal with center at $(2, 2)$.

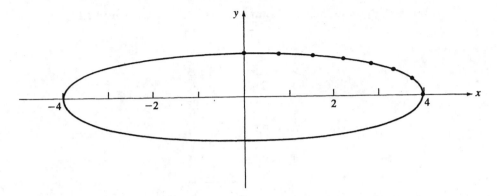

**Figure 4–7**    Parametric representation of an ellipse.

First an origin-centered ellipse is generated. To illustrate the results, 32 unique points on the ellipse are generated requiring $n = 33$ because the first and last points are coincident. However, to conserve space only points in the first quadrant are illustrated here. Thus, the parameter range is $0 \le \theta \le \pi/2$.

First

$$\delta\theta = \frac{2\pi}{(n-1)} = \frac{2\pi}{32} = \frac{\pi}{16}$$

Using Eq. (4–6) and starting at $\theta = 0$, initial values for $x$ and $y$ are

$$x_1 = a\cos\theta_1 = (4)\cos(0) = 4$$

$$y_1 = b\sin\theta_1 = (1)\sin(0) = 0$$

Then, $a/b = 4$, $b/a = 1/4$ and

$$\sin\delta\theta = \sin\frac{\pi}{16} = 0.195$$

$$\cos\delta\theta = \cos\frac{\pi}{16} = 0.981$$

Now using Eq. (4–8) the second point is

$$x_2 = x_1 \cos\delta\theta - \left(\frac{a}{b}\right) y_1 \sin\delta\theta = (4)(0.981) - (4)(0)(0.195) = 3.92$$

$$y_2 = \left(\frac{b}{a}\right) x_1 \sin\delta\theta + y_1 \cos\delta\theta = (1/4)(4)(0.195) + (0)(0.981) = 0.195$$

Results for the other points in the first quadrant are shown in Table 4–3 and in Fig. 4–7.

Recalling the results for the two-dimensional transformations derived in Chapter 2 yields the combined $3 \times 3$ transformation that first rotates about the origin by $\alpha = 30°$ and then translates the center to the point $(2, 2)$.

### Table 4–3 First Quadrant Points for an Origin-Centered Ellipse

| $i$ | $x_i$ | $y_i$ |
|---|---|---|
| 1 | 4.0 | 0 |
| 2 | 3.923 | 0.195 |
| 3 | 3.696 | 0.383 |
| 4 | 3.326 | 0.556 |
| 5 | 2.828 | 0.707 |
| 6 | 2.222 | 0.831 |
| 7 | 1.531 | 0.924 |
| 8 | 0.780 | 0.981 |
| 9 | 0 | 1.0 |

Specifically,

$$[T] = [R][Tr_{xy}] = \begin{bmatrix} \cos\alpha & \sin\alpha & 0 \\ -\sin\alpha & \cos\alpha & 0 \\ 0 & 0 & 1 \end{bmatrix} \begin{bmatrix} 1 & 0 & 0 \\ 0 & 1 & 0 \\ m & n & 1 \end{bmatrix}$$

$$= \begin{bmatrix} 0.866 & 0.5 & 0 \\ -0.5 & 0.866 & 0 \\ 0 & 0 & 1 \end{bmatrix} \begin{bmatrix} 1 & 0 & 0 \\ 0 & 1 & 0 \\ 2 & 2 & 1 \end{bmatrix}$$

$$= \begin{bmatrix} 0.866 & 0.5 & 0 \\ -0.5 & 0.866 & 0 \\ 2 & 2 & 1 \end{bmatrix}$$

Applying this transformation to $(x_1, y_1)$ and $(x_2, y_2)$ yields

$$\begin{bmatrix} x_1 & y_1 & 1 \\ x_2 & y_2 & 1 \end{bmatrix} [T] = \begin{bmatrix} 4 & 0 & 1 \\ 3.923 & 0.195 & 1 \end{bmatrix} \begin{bmatrix} 0.866 & 0.5 & 0 \\ -0.5 & 0.866 & 0 \\ 2 & 2 & 1 \end{bmatrix}$$

$$= \begin{bmatrix} 5.464 & 4 & 1 \\ 5.3 & 4.131 & 1 \end{bmatrix}$$

Results are shown in Table 4–4 and Fig. 4–8.

### Table 4–4 Results for Rotated and Translated Ellipse

| $i$ | $x_i$ | $y_i$ |
|---|---|---|
| 1 | 5.464 | 4.0 |
| 2 | 5.3 | 4.131 |
| 3 | 5.009 | 4.179 |
| 4 | 4.603 | 4.144 |
| 5 | 4.096 | 4.027 |
| 6 | 3.509 | 3.831 |
| 7 | 2.864 | 3.565 |
| 8 | 2.185 | 3.240 |
| 9 | 1.5 | 2.866 |

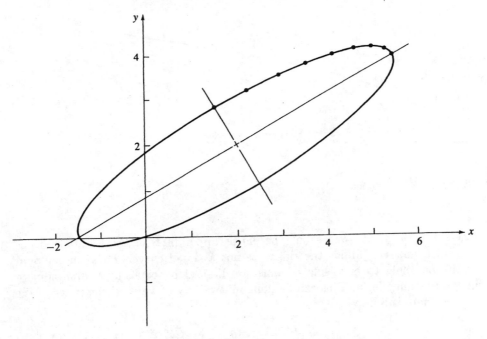

**Figure 4–8**   Rotated and translated ellipse.

## 4–7   PARAMETRIC REPRESENTATION OF A PARABOLA

Consider an origin-centered parabola opening to the right, i.e., with the axis of symmetry the positive $x$-axis. The upper limb of such a parabola is shown in Fig. 4–9. In rectangular coordinates the parabola is represented in nonparametric form by

$$y^2 = 4ax$$

A parametric representation is given by

$$x = \tan^2 \phi$$

$$y = \pm 2\sqrt{a} \tan \phi$$

where $0 \le \phi \le \pi/2$. Although this provides an adequate representation of a parabola, Smith (Ref. 4–2) points out that it does not yield a figure with maximum inscribed area and thus is not the most efficient visual representation. An alternate parametric representation which does yield maximum inscribed area is

$$x = a\theta^2$$

$$y = 2a\theta \qquad\qquad (4-9)$$

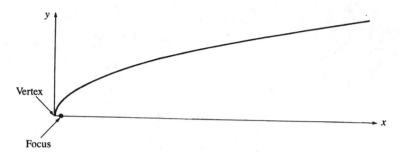

**Figure 4–9**　Parabola.

where $0 \le \theta \le \infty$ sweeps out the entire upper limb of the parabola. The parabola, however, unlike the ellipse, is not a closed curve. Thus, the amount of the parabola to be displayed must be limited by choosing a minimum or maximum value for $\theta$. This can be done in a variety of ways. If the range of the $x$ coordinate is limited, then

$$\theta_{\min} = \sqrt{\frac{x_{\min}}{a}} \qquad \theta_{\max} = \sqrt{\frac{x_{\max}}{a}} \qquad (4-10)$$

If the range of the $y$ coordinate is limited, then

$$\theta_{\min} = \frac{y_{\min}}{2a} \qquad \theta_{\max} = \frac{y_{\max}}{2a} \qquad (4-11)$$

Having established $\theta_{\min}$ and/or $\theta_{\max}$, the parabola in the first quadrant is generated. Parabolas in other quadrants with displaced centers or at other orientations are obtained using reflection, rotation and translation.

This parabola can also be generated incrementally. Assuming a fixed number of points on the parabola yields a fixed increment in $\theta$. For $\theta_{i+1} = \theta_i + \delta\theta$, Eqs. (4–9) become

$$x_{i+1} = a\theta_i^2 + 2a\theta_i\delta\theta + a(\delta\theta)^2$$
$$y_{i+1} = 2a\theta_i + 2a\delta\theta$$

Using Eqs. (4–9) with $\theta = \theta_i$ allows rewriting these equations as

$$x_{i+1} = x_i + y_i\delta\theta + a(\delta\theta)^2$$
$$y_{i+1} = y_i + 2a\delta\theta \qquad (4-12)$$

Here a new point on the parabola is obtained at the cost of three adds and a multiply within the algorithm's inner loop. Figure 4–10 shows an example of a parabola generated using the recursion relations in Eqs. (4–12).

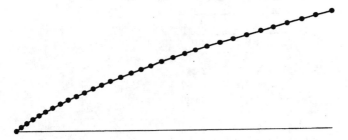

**Figure 4–10**   Parametrically generated parabola.

### Example 4–5    Parametric Parabola Generation

Generate the parabolic segment in the first quadrant for $1 \le x \le 4$ for the parabola given by

$$x = a\theta^2 = \theta^2 \qquad y = 2a\theta = 2\theta$$

i.e., for $a = 1$.

First it is necessary to determine the limits of $\theta$. Using Eq. (4–10) to determine both $\theta_{min}$ and $\theta_{max}$ yields

$$\theta_{min} = \sqrt{\frac{x_{min}}{a}} = \sqrt{\frac{1}{1}} = 1$$

$$\theta_{max} = \sqrt{\frac{x_{max}}{a}} = \sqrt{\frac{4}{1}} = 2$$

For 10 points on the parabolic segment

$$\delta\theta = \frac{\theta_{max} - \theta_{min}}{n - 1} = \frac{2 - 1}{10 - 1} = \frac{1}{9}$$

Starting at $\theta_1 = \theta_{min}$, $x_1 = 1$, Eq. (4–9) yields

$$y_1 = 2a\theta_1 = (2)(1) = 2$$

From Eqs. (4–12)

$$x_2 = x_1 + y_1\delta\theta + (\delta\theta)^2 = 1 + (2)\left(\frac{1}{9}\right) + \left(\frac{1}{9}\right)^2 = 1.235$$

$$y_2 = y_1 + 2\delta\theta = 2 + (2)\left(\frac{1}{9}\right) = 2.222$$

Complete results are shown in Table 4–5 and Fig. 4–11.

Table 4–5 Results for Parabolic Segment

| $i$ | $x_i$ | $y_i$ |
|---|---|---|
| 1 | 1.0 | 2.0 |
| 2 | 1.235 | 2.222 |
| 3 | 1.494 | 2.444 |
| 4 | 1.778 | 2.667 |
| 5 | 2.086 | 2.889 |
| 6 | 2.420 | 3.111 |
| 7 | 2.778 | 3.333 |
| 8 | 3.160 | 3.556 |
| 9 | 3.568 | 3.778 |
| 10 | 4.0 | 4.0 |

For specific purposes, other parametric representations may be more useful. The specific representation depends on the application and the information specified by the user. For example, if a parabolic arc is to be drawn between two points, and control of the end slopes is necessary, then the following form is suggested:

$$x(t) = (Q_x - 2R_x + P_x)t^2 + 2(R_x - P_x)t + P_x$$
$$y(t) = (Q_y - 2R_y + P_y)t^2 + 2(R_y - P_y)t + P_y \qquad 0 \le t \le 1.0 \qquad (4-13)$$

Here the parameter is $t$, and the two end points of the parabola are $P = [\, P_x \quad P_y \,]$ and $Q = [\, Q_x \quad Q_y \,]$. The point $R = [\, R_x \quad R_y \,]$ is the point of intersection of the two end tangents. The three vertices $P, Q, R$ define the parabola

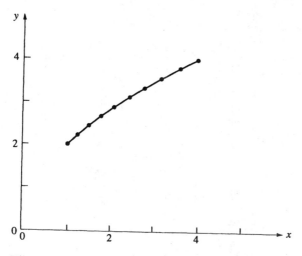

**Figure 4–11**   Parabolic segment.

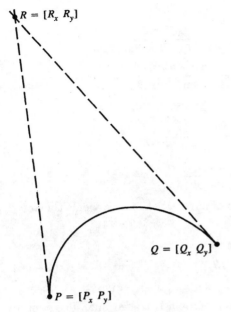

$R = [R_x \ R_y]$

$Q = [Q_x \ Q_y]$

$P = [P_x \ P_y]$

**Figure 4–12**   The vertex definition of a parametric parabola.

as shown in Fig. 4–12. A more general method of defining a curve by use of the vertices of an open polygon was developed by Bézier and is discussed in the next chapter.

## 4–8   PARAMETRIC REPRESENTATION OF A HYPERBOLA

An origin-centered hyperbola with the $x$-axis as the axis of symmetry is to be generated. The rectangular nonparametric coordinate representation of this hyperbola is

$$\frac{x^2}{a^2} - \frac{y^2}{b^2} = 1$$

which implies that the vertex is at $(a, 0)$ and the asymptotic slopes are $\pm b/a$. A parametric representation is given by

$$x = \pm a \sec \theta$$
$$y = \pm b \tan \theta \qquad\qquad (4-14)$$

where $0 \le \theta \le \pi/2$ yields the desired hyperbola. Smith (Ref. 4–2) points out that with this parametric representation the inscribed polygon is not of maximum area. However, it is of nearly maximum area, and the sum of the angles formulas can be used to yield an efficient algorithm. To see this, recall that

$$\sec(\theta + \delta\theta) = \frac{1}{\cos(\theta + \delta\theta)} = \frac{1}{\cos\theta \cos\delta\theta - \sin\theta \sin\delta\theta}$$

and
$$\tan(\theta + \delta\theta) = \frac{(\tan\theta + \tan\delta\theta)}{1 - \tan\theta \tan\delta\theta}$$

Substituting into Eqs. (4–14) yields

$$x_{i+1} = \pm a\sec(\theta + \delta\theta) = \pm\frac{ab/\cos\theta}{b\cos\delta\theta - b\tan\theta\sin\delta\theta}$$

$$y_{i+1} = \pm b\tan(\theta + \delta\theta) = \pm\frac{b\tan\theta + b\tan\delta\theta}{1 - \tan\theta\tan\delta\theta}$$

Using Eqs. (4–14) with $\theta = \theta_i$ allows rewriting these equations as

$$x_{i+1} = \pm\frac{bx_i}{b\cos\delta\theta - y_i\sin\delta\theta}$$

$$y_{i+1} = \pm\frac{b(y_i + b\tan\delta\theta)}{b - y_i\tan\delta\theta} \tag{4–15}$$

An alternate parametric representation of a hyperbola which yields the polygon with maximum inscribed area is

$$x = a\cosh\theta$$

$$y = b\sinh\theta \tag{4–16}$$

The hyperbolic functions are defined as $\cosh\theta = (e^\theta + e^{-\theta})/2$ and $\sinh\theta = (e^\theta - e^{-\theta})/2$. As $\theta$ varies from 0 to $\infty$ the hyperbola is traced out. The sum of the angles formulas for cosh and sinh are

$$\cosh(\theta + \delta\theta) = \cosh\theta\cosh\delta\theta + \sinh\theta\sinh\delta\theta$$

$$\sinh(\theta + \delta\theta) = \sinh\theta\cosh\delta\theta + \cosh\theta\sinh\delta\theta$$

These allow writing Eqs. (4–16) as

$$x_{i+1} = a(\cosh\theta\cosh\delta\theta + \sinh\theta\sinh\delta\theta)$$

$$y_{i+1} = b(\sinh\theta\cosh\delta\theta + \cosh\theta\sinh\delta\theta)$$

or

$$x_{i+1} = x_i\cosh\delta\theta + \left(\frac{a}{b}\right)y_i\sinh\delta\theta$$

$$y_{i+1} = \left(\frac{b}{a}\right)x_i\sinh\delta\theta + y_i\cosh\delta\theta \tag{4–17}$$

Again the maximum and minimum values of $\theta$ must be set in order to limit the extent of the hyperbola. Considering the branch of the hyperbola in the first and fourth quadrants and plotting the portion of the hyperbola for $x_{min} \leq x \leq x_{max}$, then

$$\theta_{min} = \cosh^{-1}\left(\frac{x_{min}}{a}\right)$$

$$\theta_{max} = \cosh^{-1}\left(\frac{x_{max}}{a}\right) \tag{4–18}$$

where the inverse hyperbolic cosine is obtained from

$$\cosh^{-1}x = \ln(x + \sqrt{x^2 - 1}) \tag{4–19}$$

Other limits are similarly determined. An example of the first quadrant portion of a hyperbola generated using this technique is shown in Fig. 4–13.

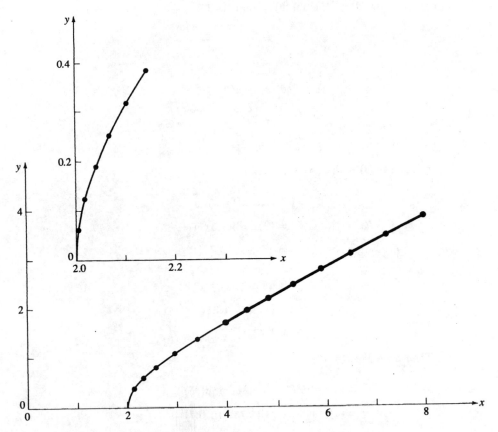

**Figure 4–13**    Parametric hyperbola.

---

### Example 4–6    Parametric Hyperbola

Use the parametric representation given in Eqs. (4–16) to generate eight points on the hyperbolic segment in the first quadrant with $a = 2, b = 1$ for $4 \le x \le 8$.

First, the parameter limits are determined. Using Eqs. (4–18) and (4–19) yields

$$\theta_{max} = \cosh^{-1}\left(\frac{x_{max}}{a}\right) = \ln\left(\frac{x_{max}}{a} + \sqrt{\left(\frac{x_{max}}{a}\right)^2 - 1}\right)$$

$$= \ln(4 + \sqrt{16 - 1})$$

$$= 2.063$$

Similarly,     $\theta_{min} = 1.317$

Thus,     $$\delta\theta = \frac{\theta_{max} - \theta_{min}}{n - 1} = \frac{2.063 - 1.317}{7} = 0.107$$

and
$$\sinh(\delta\theta) = \sinh(0.107)$$
$$= \frac{e^{0.107} - e^{-0.107}}{2}$$
$$= 0.107$$

$$\cosh(\delta\theta) = \cosh(0.107)$$
$$= \frac{e^{0.107} + e^{-0.107}}{2}$$
$$= 1.006$$

Using Eqs. (4–16) with $\theta_1 = \theta_{min}$ yields

$$x_1 = a\cosh(\theta_{min})$$
$$= (2)\cosh(1.317)$$
$$= 4.000$$

$$y_1 = b\sinh(\theta_{min})$$
$$= (1)\sinh(1.317)$$
$$= 1.732$$

Then from Eqs. (4–17)

$$x_2 = x_1\cosh(\delta\theta) + (a/b)y_1\sinh(\delta\theta)$$
$$= (4)(1.006) + (2)(1.732)(0.107)$$
$$= 4.393$$

$$y_2 = (b/a)x_1\sinh(\delta\theta) + y_1\cosh(\delta\theta)$$
$$= (1/2)(4)(0.107) + (1.732)(1.006) = 1.956$$

Complete results are shown in Table 4–6 and as the heavy line in Fig. 4–13.

## Table 4–6 Results for Hyperbolic Segment

| $i$ | $x_i$ | $y_i$ |
|---|---|---|
| 1 | 4 | 1.732 |
| 2 | 4.393 | 1.956 |
| 3 | 4.836 | 2.201 |
| 4 | 5.334 | 2.472 |
| 5 | 5.892 | 2.771 |
| 6 | 6.518 | 3.102 |
| 7 | 7.218 | 3.468 |
| 8 | 8 | 3.873 |

## 4–9  A PROCEDURE FOR USING CONIC SECTIONS

A number of common applications in computer graphics involve planar geometric constructions. Examples are machine part design and computer aided drafting systems. Problems of particular concern are determining the location of a conic section and its intersection and/or point of tangency with another conic section or with a line. At first glance the problems appear to be trivial or relatively simple. However, if the geometric elements are arbitrarily located in the two-dimensional plane, multiple solutions may exist, selection of the appropriate solution may not be obvious, and the resulting mathematics is frequently nonlinear. The techniques discussed below eliminate the nonlinear mathematics and simplify the resulting linear mathematics. Further, when multiple solutions exist, the logic structure required to select a particular solution is clarified.

The underlying philosophy is to use computer graphics manipulation techniques, in particular, two-dimensional rotations and translations, to place the geometry into the first quadrant in a standard configuration. If the geometry involves conic sections, the center of one (in the case of a parabola or hyperbola, the vertex) is placed at the origin of the coordinate system. In general, nonparametric forms of the equations are used to solve for the unknown centers, vertices, tangency or intersection points. A parametric form is used to draw the conic sections. This divorces the calculation procedure from the drawing procedure, thus utilizing the most efficient aspects of both representations.

The philosophy and power of the technique is best illustrated by a detailed example. One of the simplest and most common geometric requirements is to draw a circle through three points. The geometry is shown in Fig. 4–14, where $P_1(x_1, y_1)$, $P_2(x_2, y_2)$, $P_3(x_3, y_3)$ are the specified points. The location of the center and the radius of the circle through the three points are to be determined. A direct solution technique is to write the three simultaneous nonlinear equations in $h, k$, the $x$ and $y$ coordinates of the center of the circle, and $R$, the radius, i.e.,

$$(x_1 - h)^2 + (y_1 - k)^2 = R^2 \qquad (4 - 20a)$$

$$(x_2 - h)^2 + (y_2 - k)^2 = R^2 \qquad (4 - 20b)$$

$$(x_3 - h)^2 + (y_3 - k)^2 = R^2 \qquad (4 - 20c)$$

A solution algorithm which first subtracts Eq. (4–20b) from Eqs. (4–20a) and (4–20c) reduces the solution to a linear problem. Specifically, the solution algorithm is $[(a) - (b)](x_3 - x_2) - [(c) - (b)](x_1 - x_2)$ where the letters in brackets refer to Eqs. (4–20). The resulting equation in the unknown $k$ is

$$k = \frac{[(x_1^2 - x_2^2) + (y_1^2 - y_2^2)](x_3 - x_2)}{2[(y_1 - y_2)(x_3 - x_2) - (y_3 - y_2)(x_1 - x_2)]}$$

$$- \frac{[(x_3^2 - x_2^2) + (y_3^2 - y_2^2)](x_1 - x_2)}{2[(y_1 - y_2)(x_3 - x_2) - (y_3 - y_2)(x_1 - x_2)]} \qquad (4 - 21)$$

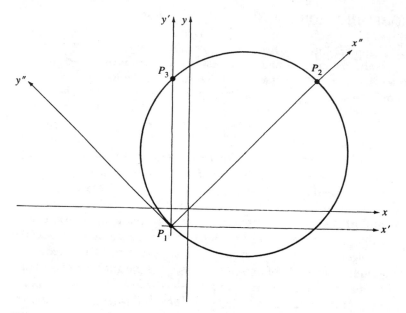

**Figure 4–14**   Circle through three points.

Similarly, $h$ is calculated from $[(a) - (b)]$ and Eq. (4–21) as

$$h = \frac{(x_1^2 - x_2^2) + (y_1^2 - y_2^2) - 2k(y_1 - y_2)}{2(x_1 - x_2)} \qquad (4-22)$$

$R$ is determined from any of Eqs. 4–20 .

Examination of Eqs. (4–21) and (4–22) reveals some difficulties. In particular, if the denominator of either equation is zero, then alternate methods must be used. Further, the condition to check for an infinite radius or for colinear points is not immediately obvious.

The complexity of the resulting equations for $h$ and $k$ is reduced by first translating the three points such that $P_1$ lies at the origin of the coordinate system (see Fig. 4–14). Here, the governing equations are

$$h'^2 + k'^2 = R^2 \qquad (4-23a)$$

$$(x_2' - h')^2 + (y_2' - k')^2 = R^2 \qquad (4-23b)$$

$$(x_3' - h')^2 + (y_3' - k')^2 = R^2 \qquad (4-23c)$$

Subtracting $(a)$ from $(b)$ and $(c)$ yields two simultaneous linear equations. The solution algorithm is $[(b) - (a)]x_3' - [(c) - (a)]x_2'$, which yields

$$k' = \frac{[x_3' x_2'(x_2' - x_3') + y_2'^2 x_3' - y_3'^2 x_2']}{2(y_2' x_3' - y_3' x_2')} \qquad (4-24)$$

$$h' = \frac{x_2'^2 + y_2'^2 - 2y_2' k'}{2x_2'} \qquad (4-25)$$

$$R = (h'^2 + k'^2)^{\frac{1}{2}} \tag{4-26}$$

Translating $h', k'$ back to the original coordinate system yields $h, k$. This technique again has difficulties if the denominator of either Eq. (4–24) or (4–25) is zero. In addition, the condition for an infinite radius or for colinear points is again not immediately obvious. To overcome these difficulties the following solution procedure is adopted:

Translate such that one of the points is at the origin of the coordinate system.

Rotate about the origin such that one of the other points lies on the positive $x$-axis.

Check for colinear points.

Solve in the translated and rotated coordinate system for the center and radius of the circle.

Rotate about the origin back to the intermediate coordinate system.

Translate back to the original coordinate system to get the center of the circle in the original coordinate system.

Figure 4–14 illustrates this technique where $P_1$ has been translated to the origin and $P_2$ rotated to the positive $x$-axis. The governing equations in the $(x'', y'')$ coordinate system are

$$h''^2 + k''^2 = R^2 \tag{4-27a}$$

$$(x_2'' - h'')^2 + k''^2 = R^2 \tag{4-27b}$$

$$(x_3'' - h'')^2 + (y_3'' - k'')^2 = R^2 \tag{4-27c}$$

Subtracting Eq. (4–27a) from Eq. (4–27b) yields

$$x_2''^2 - 2x_2'' h'' = 0$$

$$h'' = x_2''/2 \tag{4-28}$$

or

Subtracting Eq. (4–27a) from Eq. (4–27c) and substituting Eq. (4–28) yields

$$k'' = \frac{x_3''}{2y_3''}(x_3'' - x_2'') + \frac{y_3''}{2} \tag{4-29}$$

and from Eq. (4–27a)

$$R = (h''^2 + k''^2)^{1/2} \tag{4-30}$$

Examination of Eq. 4–29 reveals that if $y_3'' = 0$ then $k$ is infinite. However, $y_3''$ can only be zero if the three points are colinear. Thus, there is a simple obvious check for the colinear case.

The circle through three points is a simple example. No decision tree is required to select the desired solution from among multiple solutions. However, most geometric constructions involving the conic sections and lines have multiple solutions. A technique for distinguishing among the solutions is suggested by Rogers (Ref. 4-3).

Following Rogers, in the context of the solution technique discussed here, left, right, near, far, inside, outside are used to distinguish among multiple solutions. Left and right are used with respect to a direction established by looking from one known point to another. Near and far are established with respect to a crossing line. Inside and outside are established with respect to a circle.

These concepts remain the same, both in the user orientation, i.e., any arbitrary location in space, and in the standard solution configuration in the first quadrant. A simple example illustrating the concepts of left-right and near-far is to determine the location of the center and the tangency points for a circle of known radius $R$ tangent to two intersecting lines $P$ and $L$. In practice this problem arises when a fillet or radius corner is required. There are four solutions, all of which are possible for any given radius. The solution strategy is:

Solve for the intersection point of the two lines. If there is no solution, the lines are parallel.

Translate such that the center of the coordinate system is at the intersection point.

Rotate about the new origin such that one of the lines is coincident with the $x$-axis.

Determine the angle between the other line and the positive $x$-axis.

Rotate about the new origin such that the positive $x$-axis is the bisector of the intersecting lines.

Solve for the center and tangency points.

Transform back to the original location.

Figure 4-15 shows this case in the standard configuration. The two intersecting lines are $P$ and $L$ with end points designated as $P_1$, $P_2$, $L_1$, $L_2$, respectively. For each of the possible solutions one of the center coordinates of the circle $(h, k)$ lies on one of the coordinate axes. The appropriate solution is selected by designating whether it is to the left or right of the line $P$ looking from $P_1$ to $P_2$ and whether it is on the near or far side of the line $L$ looking from $P_1$ to $P_2$. In Fig. 4-15 $C_1$ is *right* and *far* and $C_3$ is *left* and *near*. From the geometry shown in Fig. 4-15 the center of $C_1$ is

$$h = R/\sin\theta$$
$$k = 0$$

where $\theta$ is the acute angle between the positive $x$-axis and $P$. The tangency points with the lines $P$ and $L$ are

$$x_t = h - R\sin\theta$$
$$y_t = \pm R\cos\theta$$

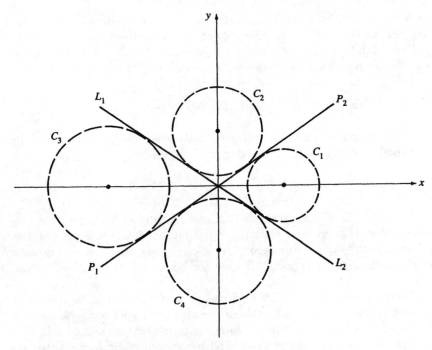

**Figure 4–15**    Circle tangent to two intersecting lines.

### Table 4–7 Circle Tangent to Two Intersecting Lines

| Orientation with respect to line $P$ | Orientation with respect to line $L$ | Center location | Tangency points |
|---|---|---|---|
| Left | Far | $h = 0$ $\phantom{}$ $k = R/\sin(90 - \theta)$ $= R/\cos(\theta)$ | $x_t = \pm R\cos(90 - \theta)$ $= \pm R\sin(\theta)$ $y_t = k - R\cos(\theta)$ |
| Left | Near | $h = -R/\sin(\theta)$ $k = 0$ | $x_t = h + R\sin(\theta)$ $y_t = \pm R\cos(\theta)$ |
| Right | Far | $h = -R/\sin(\theta)$ $k = 0$ | $x_t = h - R\sin(\theta)$ $y_t = \pm R\cos(\theta)$ |
| Right | Near | $h = 0$ $\phantom{}$ $k = -R/\sin(90 - \theta)$ $= -R/\cos(\theta)$ | $x_t = \pm R\cos(90 - \theta)$ $= \pm R\sin(\theta)$ $y_t = k + R\cos(\theta)$ |

Complete results are given in Table 4–7. More complex circle-line constructions illustrating the application of the concepts of inside and outside are given in Ref. 4–3. Extension to other conic sections is possible. An alternate formulation of this and similar problems using a vector approach is given in Ref. 4–4.

## 4–10    THE GENERAL CONIC EQUATIONS

The conic curves discussed in the previous sections are each special cases of the curves described by the general second-degree equation

$$Ax^2 + Bxy + Cy^2 + Dx + Ey + F = 0 \qquad (4-31)$$

where $A$, $B$, $C$, $D$, $E$, $F$ are constants.[†] A conic is any plane curve that satisfies this equation. The general equation is not only of interest itself, but also as background for subsequent discussions of rational conic curves and of quadric surfaces. A matrix algebra approach is used for both completeness and convenience.

Conic curves or sections are either central or noncentral. The central forms are those with a center, specifically the ellipse and the hyperbola. (A circle is a special case of an ellipse.) The parabola is the only noncentral conic. It does not have a center. In addition to these well-recognized conic forms there are several degenerate forms. All of the degenerate forms are central. The objective here is to determine, for specific values of the constants $A$ through $F$, whether Eq. (4–31) represents a central or noncentral conic, i.e., whether it represents an ellipse, a hyperbola or a parabola. Identification of all the degenerate forms is also required.

To begin, notice that Eq. (4–31) can be written in matrix form as

$$\begin{bmatrix} x & y & 1 \end{bmatrix} \begin{bmatrix} A & B/2 & D/2 \\ B/2 & C & E/2 \\ D/2 & E/2 & F \end{bmatrix} \begin{bmatrix} x \\ y \\ 1 \end{bmatrix} = 0$$

that is

$$[\,X\,][\,S\,][\,X\,]^T = 0 \qquad (4-32)$$

Notice also that $[\,S\,]$ is symmetric about the main diagonal.

The first task is to transform the conic into standard form. For a central conic (ellipse or hyperbola) the standard form places the center of the conic at the origin with its axes aligned with the coordinate axes. For a noncentral conic (parabola) the standard form is with the axis of symmetry of the parabola coincident with the positive $x$-axis, with the vertex at the origin and the parabola opening to the right. Translations and rotations are used to transform the general conic into the standard form.

---

[†]Equation (4–31) is a modified version of the second-degree implicit equation given in Sec. 4–3 with $A = a$, $B = 2b$, $C = c$, $D = 2d$, $E = 2e$ and $F = f$.

If the conic is central, the linear terms are eliminated from Eqs. (4–31) or (4–32) by translating the center of the conic to the origin. After translation Eq. (4–32) becomes

$$[X][Tr][S][Tr]^T[X]^T = 0 \qquad (4-33)$$

where the translation matrix $[Tr]$ is

$$[Tr] = \begin{bmatrix} 1 & 0 & 0 \\ 0 & 1 & 0 \\ m & n & 1 \end{bmatrix}$$

After concatenating the translation and coefficient matrices, the transformed equation becomes

$$[X][S'][X]^T = 0 \qquad (4-34)$$

where

$$[S'] = [Tr][S][Tr]^T = \left(\frac{1}{2}\right) \begin{bmatrix} 2A' & B' & D' \\ B' & 2C' & E' \\ D' & E' & 2F' \end{bmatrix} \qquad (4-35)$$

and

$$A' = A$$
$$B' = B$$
$$C' = C$$
$$D' = 2Am + Bn + D$$
$$E' = Bm + 2Cn + E$$
$$2F' = mD' + nE' + (Dm + En + 2F)$$

Note that $[S']$ is also symmetric.
   Hence Eq. (4–31) transforms to

$$A'x^2 + B'xy + C'y^2 + D'x + E'y + F' = 0$$

The translation factors $m$ and $n$ required to eliminate the linear terms are obtained by setting $D' = E' = 0$. Hence

$$2Am + Bn + D = 0$$
$$Bm + 2Cn + E = 0$$

or in matrix form

$$[m \quad n] \begin{bmatrix} 2A & B \\ B & 2C \end{bmatrix} = \begin{bmatrix} -D \\ -E \end{bmatrix} \qquad (4-36)$$

which may be written as $[M][L] = [Q]$.
   If $[L]$ is invertible, a solution for $[M]$ exists and the conic is central, i.e., an ellipse or a hyperbola. If $[L]$ is not invertible, i.e., singular, a solution for $[M]$

does not exist and the conic is noncentral, i.e., a parabola. If $[L]$ is singular, its determinant is zero. Hence

$$\det[L] = |L| = \begin{vmatrix} 2A & B \\ B & 2C \end{vmatrix} = 0 \qquad (4-37)$$

or
$$B^2 - 4AC = 0$$

Thus, Eq. (4–31) represents a parabola if $B^2 - 4AC = 0$ and a central conic if $B^2 - 4AC \neq 0$. If the conic is central and if $B^2 - 4AC < 0$, then Eq. (4–31) represents an ellipse, and if $B^2 - 4AC > 0$, a hyperbola.

Whether $[L]$ is invertible or not, the axes of the conic can be made parallel to the coordinate axes by rotation. Returning to Eq. (4–32) and applying a general two-dimensional homogeneous coordinate rotation matrix $[R]$ yields

$$[X][R][S][R]^T[X]^T = 0 \qquad (4-38)$$

where for a rotation angle $\theta$

$$[R] = \begin{bmatrix} \cos\theta & \sin\theta & 0 \\ -\sin\theta & \cos\theta & 0 \\ 0 & 0 & 1 \end{bmatrix}$$

Concatenating the matrices yields

$$[X][S''][X]^T = 0 \qquad (4-39)$$

where

$$[S''] = [R][S][R]^T = \left(\frac{1}{2}\right)\begin{bmatrix} 2A'' & B'' & D'' \\ B'' & 2C'' & E'' \\ D'' & E'' & 2F'' \end{bmatrix}$$

and

$$A'' = A\cos^2\theta + B\cos\theta\sin\theta + C\sin^2\theta$$
$$B'' = 2(C - A)\cos\theta\sin\theta + B(\cos^2\theta - \sin^2\theta)$$
$$C'' = A\sin^2\theta - B\cos\theta\sin\theta + C\cos^2\theta$$
$$D'' = D\cos\theta + E\sin\theta$$
$$E'' = E\cos\theta - D\sin\theta$$
$$F'' = F$$

Again note that $[S'']$ is symmetric. If the axes of the conic are parallel to the coordinate axes, then the cross-product term $Bxy$ in Eq. (4–31) is not present. Thus, setting the coefficient $B'' = 0$ yields the required rotation angle. Specifically,

$$2(C - A)\cos\theta\sin\theta + B(\cos^2\theta - \sin^2\theta) = 0$$

or
$$(C - A)\sin 2\theta + B\cos 2\theta = 0$$

Solving for $\theta$, the rotation angle, gives

$$\theta = \frac{1}{2} \tan^{-1} \left( \frac{B}{A-C} \right) \tag{4-40}$$

For this rotation angle, $[\,S''\,]$ becomes

$$[\,S''\,] = \left( \frac{1}{2} \right) \begin{bmatrix} 2A'' & 0 & D'' \\ 0 & 2C'' & E'' \\ D'' & E'' & 2F'' \end{bmatrix}_{\theta = \frac{1}{2}\tan^{-1}(\frac{B}{A-C})}$$

Equation (4–37) allows determining whether the conic is central or not. If the conic is central, then it is placed in the standard form by a combination of translation and rotation. Translation followed by rotation yields

$$[\,X\,][\,Tr\,][\,R\,][\,S\,][\,R\,]^T\,[\,Tr\,]^T\,[\,X\,]^T = 0 \tag{4-41}$$

Concatenating the central matrices yields

$$[\,S'''\,] = [\,Tr\,][\,R\,][\,S\,][\,R\,]^T\,[\,Tr\,]^T$$

$$= \left( \frac{1}{2} \right) \begin{bmatrix} 2A''' & B''' & D''' \\ B''' & 2C''' & E''' \\ D''' & E''' & 2F''' \end{bmatrix}$$

$$= \begin{bmatrix} A''' & 0 & 0 \\ 0 & C''' & 0 \\ 0 & 0 & F''' \end{bmatrix} = \begin{bmatrix} \alpha & 0 & 0 \\ 0 & \beta & 0 \\ 0 & 0 & -\kappa \end{bmatrix} \tag{4-42}$$

with

$$A''' = A\cos^2\theta + B\cos\theta\sin\theta + C\sin^2\theta \tag{4-43a}$$
$$B''' = 2(C - A)\cos\theta\sin\theta + B(\cos^2\theta - \sin^2\theta) \tag{4-43b}$$
$$C''' = A\sin^2\theta - B\cos\theta\sin\theta + C\cos^2\theta \tag{4-43c}$$
$$D''' = \xi\cos\theta + \eta\sin\theta \tag{4-43d}$$
$$E''' = \eta\cos\theta - \xi\sin\theta \tag{4-43e}$$
$$F''' = (m\xi + \eta n + \zeta)/2 \tag{4-43f}$$

where

$$\xi = 2Am + Bn + D \tag{4-43g}$$
$$\eta = Bm + 2Cn + E \tag{4-43h}$$
$$\zeta = Dm + En + 2F \tag{4-43i}$$

Notice that this is a diagonal matrix, i.e., all the off-diagonal terms are zero. The explanation is that rotation eliminated the cross-product term ($B''' = 0$) and subsequent translation eliminated the linear terms ($D''' = E''' = 0$) from the central conic.

The rotation angle is given by Eq. (4–40). As above, the translation factors $m, n$ are obtained by setting $D''' = E''' = 0$. $D'''$ and $E'''$ are zero if $\xi = \eta = 0$, i.e., if

$$2Am + Bn + D = 0$$
$$Bm + 2Cn + E = 0$$

Solution yields

$$m = \frac{2CD - BE}{B^2 - 4AC} \qquad (4 - 44a)$$

$$n = \frac{2AE - BD}{B^2 - 4AC} \qquad (4 - 44b)$$

Recall that for a central conic $B^2 - 4AC \neq 0$.

Writing out Eq. (4–41) using Eq. (4–42) yields

$$\alpha x^2 + \beta y^2 = \kappa \qquad (4 - 45)$$

which is the standard form for a central conic. It remains to systematically investigate the results for various values of $\alpha$ and $\beta$.

Assuming that $\kappa$ is nonzero and positive, then if $\alpha$ and $\beta$ are both positive the conic is an ellipse.

If $\alpha$ and $\beta$ are of opposite sign and neither is zero, then the conic is a hyperbola.

If both $\alpha$ and $\beta$ are negative, Eq. (4–45) cannot be satisfied. There are no solutions.

Both $\alpha$ and $\beta$ cannot simultaneously be zero since Eq. (4–45) would then contain no second-degree terms. However, either $\alpha$ or $\beta$ can be zero. Assume $\beta = 0$ (if $\alpha = 0$ then interchange $x$ and $y$ to obtain $\beta = 0$ instead). Equation (4–45) then becomes

$$\alpha x^2 = -\kappa$$

Solution yields a pair of parallel lines at $x = \pm\sqrt{-\kappa/\alpha}$ provided $-\kappa/\alpha > 0$. If $-\kappa/\alpha < 0$, then there are no solutions, i.e., the conic is the empty set.

If $\kappa = 0$, there are two possibilities; $\alpha$ and $\beta$ have the same or opposite signs. Both yield degenerate solutions. If $\alpha$ and $\beta$ have the same sign, then only the origin, i.e., $x = y = 0$, satisfies Eq. (4–45). This result might be considered as a limiting case of an ellipse.

If $\alpha$ and $\beta$ have opposite signs, then Eq. (4–45) becomes

$$y^2 = -\frac{\alpha}{\beta}x^2$$

or

$$y = \pm\sqrt{-\frac{\alpha}{\beta}}\, x$$

which represents a pair of lines intersecting at the origin. This result is the limiting case of an hyperbola.

Finally, if $\beta = 0$ (if $\alpha = 0$ interchange $x$ and $y$ to get $\beta = 0$), then the solution is the $y$-axis for all values of $\alpha$, i.e., the $y$-axis 'repeated.'

If the conic is noncentral, i.e., a parabola, then as previously mentioned the linear terms cannot both be eliminated. However, one of the linearly dependent terms along with one of the quadratic terms either in $x$ or $y$ can be eliminated. Returning to Eq. (4–39), which represents the quadratic equation after a general rotation, then applying a general translation yields

$$[S^+] = \frac{1}{2} \begin{bmatrix} 2A^+ & 0 & D^+ \\ 0 & 2C^+ & E^+ \\ D^+ & E^+ & 2F^+ \end{bmatrix} \qquad (4-46)$$

where

$$A^+ = A'' \qquad\qquad (4-47a)$$
$$C^+ = C'' \qquad\qquad (4-47b)$$
$$D^+ = 2A''m + D'' \qquad\qquad (4-47c)$$
$$E^+ = 2C''n + E'' \qquad\qquad (4-47d)$$
$$F^+ = (m/2)D^+ + (n/2)E^+ + (mD'' + nE'' + 2F'') \qquad (4-47e)$$

The rotation angle given by Eq. (4–40) is assumed. Here either $A^+ = A''$ or $C^+ = C''$ will be zero. Either the linear terms in $x$ or $y$ can be eliminated by setting either $D^+$ or $E^+$ equal to zero. Setting $D^+ = 0$ yields

$$m = \frac{-D''}{2A''} \qquad\qquad (4-48a)$$

Setting $E^+ = 0$ yields

$$n = \frac{-E''}{2C''} \qquad\qquad (4-48b)$$

Note that if $A'' = 0$, then $m$ cannot be determined. Thus, only the linear terms in $y$ are eliminated. If $C'' = 0$, then $n$ cannot be determined and only the linear terms in $x$ are eliminated.

Assuming that the linear terms in $y$ ($E^+ = 0$) and the quadratic terms in $x$ ($A^+ = 0$) are eliminated (if $\beta = 0$, interchange $x$ and $y$ to get $\gamma = 0$), $[S^+]$ becomes

$$[S^+] = \begin{bmatrix} 0 & 0 & 0 \\ 0 & \beta & 0 \\ \gamma & 0 & -\kappa \end{bmatrix}$$

Writing out the equation for the conic yields

$$\beta y^2 + 2\gamma x = \kappa \qquad\qquad (4-49)$$

The parabola can be placed in standard form with the vertex at the origin by translating in $x$ by $\kappa$

$$y^2 = -\frac{2\gamma}{\beta} x' = ax'$$

All the degenerate forms are central conics. Hence the parabola is the only noncentral conic. Table 4–8 summarizes the results.

### Table 4–8 Summary of Conic Sections †

| Name | Equation | Conditions | Type | Sketch |
|---|---|---|---|---|
| Ellipse | $\alpha x^2 + \beta y^2 = \kappa$ | $\kappa,\ \alpha,\ \beta > 0$ | Central | |
| Hyperbola | $\alpha x^2 + \beta y^2 = \kappa$ | $\beta < 0 < \kappa,\ \alpha$ | Central | |
| Parabola | $\alpha y^2 + \beta x = 0$ <br> $\beta x^2 + \alpha y = 0$ | | .Noncentral | |
| Empty set | $\alpha x^2 + \beta y^2 = \kappa$ | $\alpha,\ \beta < 0 < \kappa$ | (Central) | (No sketch) |
| Point | $\alpha x^2 + \beta y^2 = 0$ | $\alpha,\ \beta > 0$ | Central | |
| Pair of lines | $\alpha x^2 + \beta y^2 = 0$ | $\beta < 0 < \alpha$ | Central | |
| Parallel lines | $\alpha x^2 = \kappa$ | $\alpha,\ \kappa > 0$ | Central | |
| Empty set | $\alpha x^2 = \kappa$ | $\alpha < 0 < \kappa$ | (Central) | (No sketch) |
| 'Repeated' line | $\alpha x^2 = 0$ | | Central | |

†The ellipse, hyperbola and parabola are the nondegenerate conics, all the rest being called degenerate.

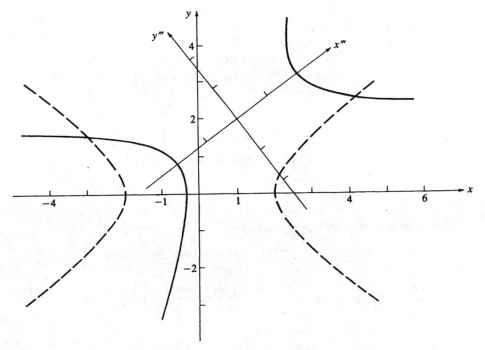

**Figure 4–16**   Hyperbola $2x^2 - 72xy + 23y^2 + 140x - 20y + 50 = 0$. Solid lines in original position. Dashed lines in standard position.

An example more fully illustrates these concepts.

---

### Example 4–7   Hyperbolic Segment

Determine the type of conic described by

$$2x^2 - 72xy + 23y^2 + 140x - 20y + 50 = 0$$

and shown as a solid line in Fig. 4–16. Draw the segment for $3 < x < 5$ for $y_{min}$. Here, the conic segment is to be drawn using the parametric representations developed in previous sections. The techniques discussed in the current section are used to determine the appropriate values for the parametric representation.

First determine the type of conic.

$$B^2 - 4AC = (-72)^2 - (4)(2)(23) = 5000 > 0$$

and the conic is a hyperbola.

Using Eqs. (4–40) to (4–44) to transform the hyperbola into standard form yields

$$\theta = \frac{1}{2}\tan^{-1}\left(\frac{B}{A-C}\right) = \frac{1}{2}\tan^{-1}\left(\frac{-72}{2-23}\right) = \frac{1}{2}\tan^{-1}\left(\frac{24}{7}\right) = 36.87°$$

for the rotation angle.

Noting that $\cos\theta = 4/5$, $\sin\theta = 3/5$ yields

$$
\begin{aligned}
A''' &= A\cos^2\theta + B\cos\theta\sin\theta + C\sin^2\theta \\
&= (2)(4/5)^2 + (-72)(4/5)(3/5) + (23)(3/5)^2 \\
&= -625/25 \\
&= -25
\end{aligned}
$$

$$
\begin{aligned}
C''' &= A\sin^2\theta - B\cos\theta\sin\theta + C\cos^2\theta \\
&= (2)(3/5)^2 - (-72)(4/5)(3/5) + (23)(4/5)^2 \\
&= 1250/25 \\
&= 50
\end{aligned}
$$

The translation factors $m$ and $n$ are then

$$
m = \frac{2CD - BE}{B^2 - 4AC} = \frac{(2)(23)(140) - (-72)(-20)}{5000} = \frac{5000}{5000} = 1
$$

$$
n = \frac{2AE - BD}{B^2 - 4AC} = \frac{(2)(2)(-20) - (-72)(140)}{5000} = \frac{10000}{5000} = 2
$$

Since $\xi = \eta = 0$, the constant term is

$$
\begin{aligned}
F''' = \frac{\zeta}{2} &= \frac{(Dm + En + 2F)}{2} \\
&= \frac{(140)(1) + (-20)(2) + (2)(50)}{2} = \frac{200}{2} = 100
\end{aligned}
$$

The equation of the hyperbola is then

$$
-25x^2 + 50y^2 + 100 = 0
$$

In standard form $\alpha x^2 + \beta y^2 + \kappa = 0$ the result is

$$
-x^2 + 2y^2 + 4 = 0 \quad \Rightarrow \quad x^2 - 2y^2 = 4
$$

In the form

$$
\left(\frac{x}{a}\right)^2 - \left(\frac{y}{b}\right)^2 = 1
$$

we have

$$
\frac{x^2}{4} - \frac{y^2}{2} = 1
$$

which yields $a = 2$, $b = \sqrt{2}$.

Parametrically the hyperbola is represented by (see Eq. 4–16)

$$
x = a\cosh(t)
$$
$$
y = b\sinh(t)
$$

where here $t$ is the parameter. Drawing the hyperbola parametrically requires determining the values of $t$ corresponding to $x = 3, 5$. Noting that the transformations used to place the conic in the standard form transform the axes rather than the conic itself, the corresponding transformed $x$ values are obtained by using the *inverse* of these transformations. The resulting concatenated transformation is

$$[TR] = [T][R] = \begin{bmatrix} 1 & 0 & 0 \\ 0 & 1 & 0 \\ -m & -n & 1 \end{bmatrix} \begin{bmatrix} \cos\theta & \sin(-\theta) & 0 \\ -\sin(-\theta) & \cos\theta & 0 \\ 0 & 0 & 1 \end{bmatrix}$$

$$= \begin{bmatrix} \cos\theta & -\sin\theta & 0 \\ \sin\theta & \cos\theta & 0 \\ -(m\cos\theta + n\sin\theta) & m\sin\theta - n\cos\theta & 1 \end{bmatrix}$$

$$= \begin{bmatrix} 4/5 & -3/5 & 0 \\ 3/5 & 4/5 & 0 \\ -2 & -1 & 1 \end{bmatrix}$$

The transformed $x$ coordinates are

$$\begin{bmatrix} 3 & 2.871 & 1 \\ 5 & 2.476 & 1 \end{bmatrix} \begin{bmatrix} 4/5 & -3/5 & 0 \\ 3/5 & 4/5 & 0 \\ -2 & -1 & 1 \end{bmatrix} = \begin{bmatrix} 2.123 & -0.503 & 1 \\ 3.486 & -2.019 & 1 \end{bmatrix}$$

where the $y$ coordinates have also been included. The parametric values are then

$$t_{min} = t|_{x=3} = \cosh^{-1}\left(\frac{x}{2}\right) = \cosh^{-1}\left(\frac{2.123}{2}\right) = 0.3486$$

$$t_{max} = t|_{x=5} = \cosh^{-1}\left(\frac{x}{2}\right) = \cosh^{-1}\left(\frac{3.486}{2}\right) = 1.1539$$

Using these parametric values for $t_{min}$ and $t_{max}$ yielded the results shown in Table 4–9 and in Fig. 4–16.

### Table 4–9 Hyperbolic Segment in the Standard Position

| $t$ | $x$ | $y$ |
|---|---|---|
| 0.349 | 2.123 | −0.503 |
| 0.438 | 2.195 | −0.640 |
| 0.528 | 2.285 | −0.781 |
| 0.617 | 2.393 | −0.929 |
| 0.706 | 2.520 | −1.084 |
| 0.796 | 2.668 | −1.248 |
| 0.885 | 2.837 | −1.422 |
| 0.975 | 3.028 | −1.608 |
| 1.064 | 3.244 | −1.806 |
| 1.153 | 3.486 | −2.019 |

These results are then transformed to the original position using the inverse transformation

$$[TR]^{-1} = \begin{bmatrix} 4/5 & 3/5 & 0 \\ -3/5 & 4/5 & 0 \\ 1 & 2 & 1 \end{bmatrix}$$

The results are shown in Table 4–10 and in Fig. 4–16.

### Table 4–10 Hyperbolic Segment in Original Position

| $t$ | $x$ | $y$ |
|-------|-------|-------|
| 0.349 | 3.000 | 2.871 |
| 0.438 | 3.140 | 2.805 |
| 0.528 | 3.297 | 2.746 |
| 0.617 | 3.472 | 2.693 |
| 0.706 | 3.667 | 2.645 |
| 0.796 | 3.883 | 2.602 |
| 0.885 | 4.123 | 2.564 |
| 0.975 | 4.387 | 2.531 |
| 1.064 | 4.679 | 2.502 |
| 1.153 | 5.000 | 2.476 |

## 4–11 REFERENCES

4–1 Lancaster, P., and Salkauskas, K., *Curve and Surface Fitting, An Introduction*, Academic Press, 1987.

4–2 Smith, L.B., "Drawing Ellipses, Hyperbolas, or Parabolas With a Fixed Number of Points and Maximum Inscribed Area," *Comp. J.*, Vol. 14, pp. 81–86, 1969.

4–3 Rogers, D.F., "Interactive Graphics and Numerical Control," *Comp. Aid. Des.*, Vol. 12, pp. 253–261, 1980.

4–4 Middleditch, A.E., and Stacey, T.W., "Robust Computation of Tangent Lines and Circles," *Comp. Aid. Des.*, Vol. 19, pp. 503–507, 1987.

# FIVE

## SPACE CURVES

## 5–1   INTRODUCTION

Three-dimensional, or space, curves and surfaces play an important role in the engineering, design and manufacture of a diverse range of products, e.g., automobiles, ship hulls, aircraft fuselages and wings, propeller blades, shoes, bottles, buildings, etc.. They also play an important role in the description and interpretation of physical phenomena, e.g., in geology, physics and medical science.

Prior to the development of mathematical and computer models to support engineering, design and manufacturing, descriptive geometry was used. Many of these geometric design techniques have been carried over into computer aided geometric design.

Surfaces are frequently described by a net of curves lying in orthogonal cutting planes plus three-dimensional feature or detail lines. An example is shown in Fig. 5–1. These section curves are obtained by digitizing a physical model or a drawing and then fitting a mathematical curve to the digitized data. Two techniques for obtaining a mathematical curve model from digitized data are discussed in this chapter: cubic spline and parabolically blended curves. Many others exist (see, for example, Ref. 5–1). These methods are generally referred to as curve *fitting* techniques. They are characterized by the fact that the derived mathematical curve *passes* through each and every data point.

Alternatively, the mathematical description of a space curve is generated *ab initio*, i.e., without any prior knowledge of the curve shape or form. Again two techniques are discussed in this chapter: Bézier curves, and their powerful generalization to *B*-spline curves. These two techniques are characterized by the fact that few if any points on the curve pass through the control points used to define the curve. These methods are frequently referred to as curve *fairing* techniques.

Although generally used to obtain a mathematical curve description from

**247**

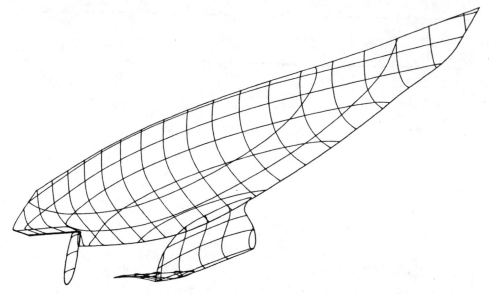

**Figure 5–1**   A surface described as a net of orthogonal planar curves. (Courtesy of George Hazen.)

known data, curve fitting techniques can be and are used for *ab initio* design. Curve fairing techniques, as we shall show, can also be used to fit a mathematical curve to known data.

## 5–2   REPRESENTATION OF SPACE CURVES

Three-dimensional space curves are represented nonparametrically or parametrically. An explicit nonparametric representation is

$$x = x$$
$$y = f(x)$$
$$z = g(x)$$

Alternatively, a nonparametric implicit representation of the curve as the intersection of two surfaces is given by

$$f(x, y, z) = 0$$
$$g(x, y, z) = 0$$

---

### Example 5–1   A Space Curve

Determine the curve described by the intersection of the two second-degree surfaces described by

$$f(x, y, z) = y - z^2 = 0$$
$$g(x, y, z) = zx - y^2 = 0$$

Provided that

$$\det \begin{vmatrix} \dfrac{\partial f}{\partial x} & \dfrac{\partial f}{\partial y} \\[2ex] \dfrac{\partial g}{\partial x} & \dfrac{\partial g}{\partial y} \end{vmatrix} \neq 0$$

and provided that $z \neq 0$, $x$ and $y$ can be expressed in terms of $z$ to obtain the explicit form of the intersection curve

$$y = z^2$$

$$x = \frac{y^2}{z} = z^3$$

Notice that the intersection of two second-degree surfaces yields a third-degree curve. The surfaces and the intersection curve are shown in Fig. 5–2.

---

In general, a parametric space curve is expressed as

$$x = x(t)$$
$$y = y(t)$$
$$z = z(t)$$

where the parameter $t$ varies over a given range $t_1 \leq t \leq t_2$. Reconsidering the explicit nonparametric representation above we note that $x$ itself can be considered a parameter, $x = t$, and the same curve is then expressed in parametric form by

$$x = t$$
$$y = f(t)$$
$$z = g(t)$$

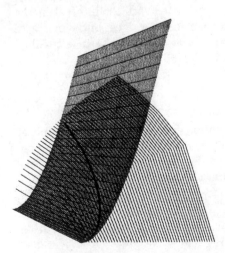

**Figure 5–2**    The intersection of second-degree surfaces.

Further, if the nonparametric implicit representation given in Ex. 5–1 is reconsidered, we see that by letting $z = t$ the parametric equations for that curve are

$$x = t^3$$

$$y = t^2$$

$$z = t$$

Some useful parametric space curves have known analytic solutions. For example, the curve that describes the seam on a tennis or baseball is given by

$$x = \lambda[a\cos(\theta + \frac{\pi}{4}) - b\cos 3(\theta + \frac{\pi}{4})]$$

$$y = \mu[a\sin(\theta + \frac{\pi}{4}) - b\sin 3(\theta + \frac{\pi}{4})]$$

$$z = c\sin(2\theta)$$

where

$$\lambda = 1 + d\sin(2\theta) = 1 + d(\frac{z}{c})$$

$$\mu = 1 - d\sin(2\theta) = 1 - d(\frac{z}{c})$$

and the parameter $\theta = 2\pi t$, and $0 \leq t \leq 1.0$. If $d = 0$ and $c^2 = 4ab$, then the curve lies on a sphere of radius $a + b$. An example for $a = 1$, $b = 1$, $c = 2$, and $d = 0$, where the curve lies on a sphere of radius 2 is shown in Fig. 5–3a.

Another example of a parametric space curve is the circular helix. The parametric equations are given by

$$x = r\cos t$$

$$y = r\sin t$$

$$z = bt$$

for $r$ and $b \neq 0$ and $-\infty < t < \infty$. This curve lies on the surface of a right circular cylinder of radius $|r|$. The effect of the equation $z = bt$ is to move the points of the curve infinitely in the $z$ direction. After each $2\pi$ interval in the parameter $t$, the variables $x$ and $y$ return to their initial values, but $z$ increases or decreases by $2\pi|b|$, depending upon the sign of $b$. This change in $z$ is called the pitch of the helix. An example is shown in Fig. 5–3b.

## 5–3  CUBIC SPLINES

In many industries, e.g., shipbuilding, automotive and aircraft, the final full or nearly full size shape is determined by a process called lofting.† Early in the development of mathematical tools for computer aided geometric design there was considerable interest in developing a mathematical model of this process. As a

---

†In the shipbuilding industry, as well as others, it is necessary to determine the shape of the ship with more accuracy than possible on a small 'paper' drawing. Thus, it is common practice to redraw the ship's lines at full or nearly full size on a large wooden floor located in the 'mold loft'. The skilled craftsmen who perform this task are known as 'loftsmen' and the process as 'lofting'.

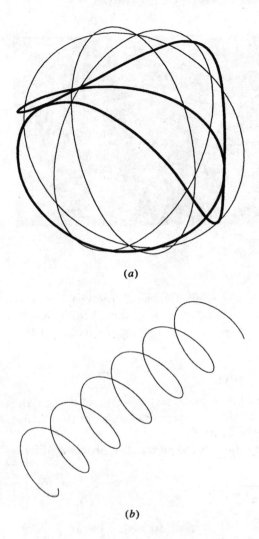

(a)

(b)

**Figure 5–3**   Examples of parametric space curves. (a) Baseball seam; (b) circular helix.

result, the form of the mathematical spline is derived from its physical counterpart — the loftsman's spline (Fig. 5–4). A physical spline is a long, narrow strip of wood or plastic used to fit curves through specified data points. The splines are shaped by lead weights called 'ducks'. By varying the number and position of the lead weights the spline is made to pass through the specified data such that the resulting curve appears 'smooth,' or 'fair,' and 'pleasing to the eye'.[†]

---

[†]There is no commonly agreed definition of the 'fairness,' 'smoothness' or 'sweetness' of a curve. Here it is used in the qualitative sense of 'pleasing to the eye'. No attempt at a mathematical definition is made. Any such attempt would lead to 'howls of protest' from at least half the interested scientific community!

**Figure 5–4**  Physical spline and ducks.

Considering the physical spline as a thin elastic beam, the shape of the spline, corresponding to the deflection of the beam $y$, is obtained from Euler's equation (see Ref. 5–2) for the bending moment $M(x)$ along the length of the beam. Specifically,

$$M(x) = \frac{EI}{R(x)}$$

where $E$ is Young's modulus (determined by the material properties of the beam), $I$ is the moment of inertia (determined by the cross-sectional shape of the beam) and $R(x)$ is the radius of curvature of the beam.

For small deflections ($y' \ll 1$) the radius of curvature is approximated by

$$\frac{1}{R(x)} = \frac{y''}{(1 + y'^2)^{3/2}} \approx y''$$

where the prime denotes differentiation with respect to $x$, the distance along the beam, and $y$ represents the deflection of the beam. Euler's equation then becomes

$$y'' = \frac{M(x)}{EI}$$

Assuming that the ducks act as simple supports, the bending moment $M(x)$ is known to vary linearly between supports. Substituting $M(x) = Ax + B$, Euler's equation becomes

$$y'' = \frac{Ax + B}{EI}$$

Integrating twice yields

$$y = A_1 x^3 + B_1 x^2 + C_1 x + D_1$$

for the deflection of the beam. This result shows that the shape of the physical spline between ducks is mathematically described by cubic polynomials. Thus we consider a mathematical spline modeled using cubic polynomials.

In general, the mathematical spline is a piecewise polynomial of degree $K$ with continuity of derivatives of order $K - 1$ at the common joints between segments. Thus, the cubic spline has second-order or $C^2$ continuity at the joints. Piecewise splines of low-degree polynomials are most useful for curve fitting because low-degree polynomials both reduce the computational requirements and also reduce numerical instabilities that arise with higher degree curves. These instabilities cause undesirable oscillations when several points are joined in a common curve. However, since low-degree polynomials cannot span an arbitrary series of points, adjacent polynomial segments are used. Based on these considerations and the analogy with the physical spline, a common technique is to use a series of cubic spline segments with each segment spanning only two points. Further, the cubic spline is advantageous since it is the lowest degree curve which allows a point of inflection and which has the ability to twist through space.

The equation for a single parametric cubic spline segment is given by

$$P(t) = \sum_{i=1}^{4} B_i \, t^{i-1} \qquad t_1 \le t \le t_2 \tag{5-1}$$

where $t_1$ and $t_2$ are the parameter values at the beginning and end of the segment. $P(t)$ is the position vector of any point on the cubic spline segment. $P(t) = [\, x(t) \quad y(t) \quad z(t) \,]$ is a vector valued function. The three components of $P(t)$ are the Cartesian coordinates of the position vector.† Each component has a similar formulation to $P(t)$, i.e.,

$$x(t) = \sum_{i=1}^{4} B_{i_x} \, t^{i-1} \qquad t_1 \le t \le t_2$$

$$y(t) = \sum_{i=1}^{4} B_{i_y} \, t^{i-1} \qquad t_1 \le t \le t_2$$

$$z(t) = \sum_{i=1}^{4} B_{i_z} \, t^{i-1} \qquad t_1 \le t \le t_2$$

The constant coefficients $B_i$ are determined by specifying four boundary conditions for the spline segment. Writing out Eq. (5–1) yields

$$P(t) = B_1 + B_2 t + B_3 t^2 + B_4 t^3 \qquad t_1 \le t \le t_2 \tag{5-2}$$

Let $P_1$ and $P_2$ be the position vectors at the ends of the spline segment (see

---

†$P(t) = [\, r(t) \quad \theta(t) \quad z(t) \,]$, where $r(t), \theta(t), z(t)$ are considered components of a cylindrical coordinate system, is also perfectly acceptable, as are representations in other coordinate systems. (See Prob. 5–8.)

Fig. 5–5). Also let $P_1'$ and $P_2'$, the derivatives with respect to $t$, be the tangent vectors at the ends of the spline segment. Differentiating Eq. (5–1) yields

$$P'(t) = [\, x'(t) \quad y'(t) \quad z'(t)\,] = \sum_{i=1}^{4} B_i\,(i-1)t^{i-2} \qquad t_1 \le t \le t_2 \qquad (5-3)$$

Writing this result out gives

$$P'(t) = B_2 + 2B_3 t + 3B_4 t^2 \qquad t_1 \le t \le t_2 \qquad (5-4)$$

Assuming, without loss of generality, that $t_1 = 0$, and applying the four boundary conditions,

$$P(0) = P_1 \qquad\qquad (5-5a)$$

$$P(t_2) = P_2 \qquad\qquad (5-5b)$$

$$P'(0) = P_1' \qquad\qquad (5-5c)$$

$$P'(t_2) = P_2' \qquad\qquad (5-5d)$$

yields four equations for the unknown $B_i$'s. Specifically,

$$P(0) = B_1 = P_1 \qquad\qquad (5-6a)$$

$$P'(0) = \sum_{i=1}^{4} (i-1)\,t^{i-2}B_i\Big|_{t=0} = B_2 = P_1' \qquad\qquad (5-6b)$$

$$P(t_2) = \sum_{i=1}^{4} B_i\,t^{i-1}\Big|_{t=t_2} = B_1 + B_2 t_2 + B_3 t_2^2 + B_4 t_2^3 \qquad\qquad (5-6c)$$

$$P'(t_2) = \sum_{i=1}^{4} (i-1)t^{i-2}B_i\Big|_{t=t_2} = B_2 + 2B_3 t_2 + 3B_4 t_2^2 \qquad\qquad (5-6d)$$

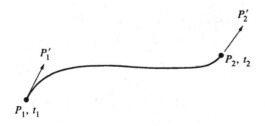

**Figure 5–5**   Single cubic spline segment.

Solving for $B_3$ and $B_4$ yields

$$B_3 = \frac{3(P_2 - P_1)}{t_2^2} - \frac{2P_1'}{t_2} - \frac{P_2'}{t_2} \qquad (5-7a)$$

and

$$B_4 = \frac{2(P_1 - P_2)}{t_2^3} + \frac{P_1'}{t_2^2} + \frac{P_2'}{t_2^2} \qquad (5-7b)$$

These values of $B_1$, $B_2$, $B_3$ and $B_4$ determine the cubic spline segment. Note that the shape of the segment depends on the position and tangent vectors at the ends of the segment. Further, notice that the value of the parameter $t = t_2$ at the end of the segment occurs in the results. Since each of the end position and tangent vectors has three components, the parametric equation for a cubic space curve depends on twelve vector components and the parameter value $t_2$ at the end of the segment.

Substituting Eqs. (5–6) and (5–7) into Eq. (5–1) yields the equation for a single cubic spline segment:

$$P(t) = P_1 + P_1't + \left[\frac{3(P_2 - P_1)}{t_2^2} - \frac{2P_1'}{t_2} - \frac{P_2'}{t_2}\right]t^2$$

$$+ \left[\frac{2(P_1 - P_2)}{t_2^3} + \frac{P_1'}{t_2^2} + \frac{P_2'}{t_2^2}\right]t^3 \qquad (5-8)$$

Equation (5–8) is for a single cubic spline segment. However, to represent a complete curve, multiple segments are joined together. Two adjacent segments are shown in Fig. 5–6. Provided that the position vectors $P_1$, $P_2$, $P_3$, the tangent vectors $P_1'$, $P_2'$, $P_3'$ and the parameter values $t_2$, $t_3$ are known, then Eq. (5–8), applied to each of the two segments, yields their shapes. However, it is unlikely that the tangent vector $P_2'$ at the internal joint between the two segments is known. Fortunately, the internal tangent vector $P_2'$ can be determined by imposing a continuity condition at the internal joint.

Recall that a piecewise spline of degree $K$ has continuity of order $K-1$ at the internal joints. Thus, a cubic spline has second-order continuity at the internal joints. This means that the second derivative $P_2''(t)$ is continuous across the joint; i.e., the curvature is continuous across the joint. Differentiating Eq. (5–1) twice yields

$$P''(t) = \sum_{i=1}^{4}(i-1)(i-2)B_i\, t^{i-3} \qquad t_1 \le t \le t_2 \qquad (5-9)$$

Noting that for the first cubic spline segment the parameter range is $0 \le t \le t_2$, evaluating Eq. (5–9) at the end of the segment where $t = t_2$ gives

$$P'' = 6B_4t_2 + 2B_3$$

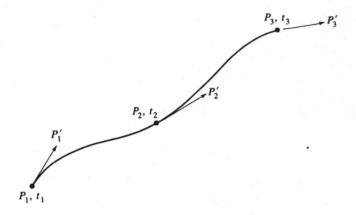

**Figure 5–6**   Two piecewise cubic spline segments.

For the second cubic spline segment the parameter range is $0 \leq t \leq t_3$. Evaluating Eq. (5–9) at the beginning of this second segment where $t = 0$ yields

$$P'' = 2B_3$$

Equating these two results and using Eqs. (5–6a, b) and (5–7a) yields

$$6t_2 \left[ \frac{2(P_1 - P_2)}{t_2^3} + \frac{P_1'}{t_2^2} + \frac{P_2'}{t_2^2} \right] + 2 \left[ \frac{3(P_2 - P_1)}{t_2^2} - \frac{2P_1'}{t_2} - \frac{P_2'}{t_2} \right]$$

$$= 2 \left[ \frac{3(P_3 - P_2)}{t_3^2} - \frac{2P_2'}{t_3} - \frac{P_3'}{t_3} \right]$$

Here the left-hand side of the equation represents the curvature at the end of the first segment and the right-hand side the curvature at the beginning of the second segment. Multiplying by $t_2 t_3$ and collecting terms gives

$$t_3 P_1' + 2(t_3 + t_2)P_2' + t_2 P_3' = \frac{3}{t_2 t_3} [t_2^2(P_3 - P_2) + t_3^2(P_2 - P_1)] \qquad (5 - 10)$$

which can be solved for $P_2'$, the unknown tangent vector at the internal joint. Again notice that the end values of the parameter $t$, i.e., $t_2$ and $t_3$, occur in the resulting equation.

These results can be generalized for $n$ data points to give $n - 1$ piecewise cubic spline segments with position, slope and curvature, i.e., $C^2$ continuity at the internal joints. Using the notation shown in Fig. 5–7 the generalized equations for any two adjacent cubic spline segments $P_k(t)$ and $P_{k+1}(t)$[†] are:

---

[†]Rather than introduce additional notation, the following convention is adopted: $P_k(t)$ refers to the parametric curve between the position vectors $P_k$ and $P_{k+1}$; i.e., the functional parametric notation is used in referring to the curve and is not used when referring to position vectors.

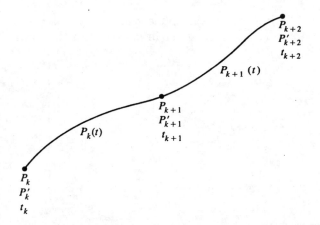

**Figure 5–7**   Notation for multiple piecewise cubic spline segments.

$$P_k(t) = P_k + P'_k t + \left[ \frac{3(P_{k+1} - P_k)}{t_{k+1}^2} - \frac{2P'_k}{t_{k+1}} - \frac{P'_{k+1}}{t_{k+1}} \right] t^2$$

$$+ \left[ \frac{2(P_k - P_{k+1})}{t_{k+1}^3} + \frac{P'_k}{t_{k+1}^2} + \frac{P'_{k+1}}{t_{k+1}^2} \right] t^3 \qquad (5-11)$$

for the first segment, and

$$P_{k+1}(t) = P_{k+1} + P'_{k+1} t + \left[ \frac{3(P_{k+2} - P_{k+1})}{t_{k+2}^2} - \frac{2P'_{k+1}}{t_{k+2}} - \frac{P'_{k+2}}{t_{k+2}} \right] t^2$$

$$+ \left[ \frac{2(P_{k+1} - P_{k+2})}{t_{k+2}^3} + \frac{P'_{k+1}}{t_{k+2}^2} + \frac{P'_{k+2}}{t_{k+2}^2} \right] t^3 \qquad (5-12)$$

for the second segment. Recalling that the parameter range begins at zero for each segment, for the first segment $0 \le t \le t_{k+1}$ and for the second $0 \le t \le t_{k+2}$.

For any two adjacent spline segments, equating the second derivatives at the common internal joint, i.e., letting $P''_k(t_k) = P''_{k+1}(0)$, yields the generalized result, equivalent to Eq. (5–10), i.e.,

$$t_{k+2} P'_k + 2(t_{k+1} + t_{k+2}) P'_{k+1} + t_{k+1} P'_{k+2}$$

$$= \frac{3}{t_{k+1} t_{k+2}} \left[ t_{k+1}^2 (P_{k+2} - P_{k+1}) + t_{k+2}^2 (P_{k+1} - P_k) \right] \qquad 1 \le k \le n-2$$

$$(5-13)$$

for determining the tangent vector at the internal joint between any two spline segments $P_k$ and $P_{k+1}$.

Applying Eq. (5–13) recursively over all the spline segments yields $n-2$ equations for the tangent vectors $P'_k$, $2 \le k \le n-1$. In matrix form the result is

$$
\begin{bmatrix}
t_3 & 2(t_2 + t_3) & t_2 & 0 & \cdot & \cdot & & \cdot & & \cdot \\
0 & t_4 & 2(t_3 + t_4) & t_3 & 0 & \cdot & & \cdot & & \cdot \\
0 & 0 & t_5 & 2(t_4 + t_5) & t_4 & 0 & & \cdot & & \cdot \\
\cdot & \cdot & \cdot & \cdot & \cdot & \cdot & \cdot & \cdot & & \cdot \\
\cdot & \cdot & \cdot & \cdot & \cdot & \cdot & \cdot & \cdot & & \cdot \\
\cdot & \cdot & \cdot & \cdot & & 0 & t_n & 2(t_n + t_{n-1}) & t_{n-1}
\end{bmatrix} \times
$$

$$
\begin{bmatrix} P'_1 \\ P'_2 \\ P'_3 \\ \cdot \\ \cdot \\ P'_n \end{bmatrix} =
\begin{bmatrix}
\dfrac{3}{t_2 t_3}\{t_2^2(P_3 - P_2) + t_3^2(P_2 - P_1)\} \\[2mm]
\dfrac{3}{t_3 t_4}\{t_3^2(P_4 - P_3) + t_4^2(P_3 - P_2)\} \\[2mm]
\cdot \\ \cdot \\ \cdot \\[2mm]
\dfrac{3}{t_{n-1} t_n}\{t_{n-1}^2(P_n - P_{n-1}) + t_n^2(P_{n-1} - P_{n-2})\}
\end{bmatrix}
\tag{5-14}
$$

or

$$[M^*][P'] = [R]$$

Since there are only $n-2$ equations for the $n$ tangent vectors, $[M^*]$ is not square and thus cannot be inverted to obtain the solution for $[P']$; i.e., the problem is indeterminate. By assuming that the end tangent vectors $P'_1$ and $P'_n$ are known, the problem becomes determinant. The matrix formulation is now

$$
\begin{bmatrix}
1 & 0 & \cdot & & \cdot & \cdot & \cdot & & \cdot & & \cdot \\
t_3 & 2(t_2 + t_3) & t_2 & 0 & \cdot & \cdot & & \cdot & & \cdot \\
0 & t_4 & 2(t_3 + t_4) & t_3 & 0 & \cdot & & \cdot & & \cdot \\
0 & 0 & t_5 & 2(t_4 + t_5) & t_4 & 0 & & \cdot & & \cdot \\
\cdot & \cdot & \cdot & \cdot & \cdot & \cdot & \cdot & \cdot & & \cdot \\
\cdot & \cdot & \cdot & \cdot & \cdot & \cdot & \cdot & \cdot & & \cdot \\
\cdot & \cdot & \cdot & \cdot & \cdot & 0 & t_n & 2(t_n + t_{n-1}) & t_{n-1} \\
\cdot & \cdot & \cdot & \cdot & & & \cdot & \cdot & 0 & 1
\end{bmatrix} \times
$$

$$
\begin{bmatrix}
P_1' \\
P_2' \\
P_3' \\
\cdot \\
\cdot \\
\cdot \\
P_n'
\end{bmatrix}
=
\begin{bmatrix}
P_1' \\
\dfrac{3}{t_2 t_3}\{t_2^2(P_3 - P_2) + t_3^2(P_2 - P_1)\} \\
\dfrac{3}{t_3 t_4}\{t_3^2(P_4 - P_3) + t_4^2(P_3 - P_2)\} \\
\cdot \\
\cdot \\
\cdot \\
\cdot \\
\cdot \\
\dfrac{3}{t_{n-1}t_n}\{t_{n-1}^2(P_n - P_{n-1}) + t_n^2(P_{n-1} - P_{n-2})\} \\
P_n'
\end{bmatrix}
\qquad (5-15)
$$

or
$$ [M][P'] = [R] $$

where $[M]$ is now square and invertible. Notice also that $[M]$ is tridiagonal,[†] which reduces the computational work required to invert it. Further, $[M]$ is diagonally dominant.[‡] Hence it is nonsingular, and inversion yields a unique solution. The solution for $[P']$ is thus

$$ [P'] = [M]^{-1}[R] \qquad (5-16) $$

Once the $P_k'$'s are known, the $B_i$ coefficients for each spline segment can be determined. Generalizing Eqs. (5-6) – (5-11) yields

$$ B_{1k} = P_k $$

$$ B_{2k} = P_k' $$

$$ B_{3k} = \frac{3(P_{k+1} - P_k)}{t_{k+1}^2} - \frac{2P_k'}{t_{k+1}} - \frac{P_{k+1}'}{t_{k+1}} $$

$$ B_{4k} = \frac{2(P_k - P_{k+1})}{t_{k+1}^3} + \frac{P_k'}{t_{k+1}^2} + \frac{P_{k+1}'}{t_{k+1}^2} $$

Recalling that the $P_k$'s and $P_k'$'s are vector valued confirms that the $B_i$'s are also vector valued; i.e., if the $P_k$'s and $P_k'$'s have $x$, $y$, $z$ components then the $B_i$'s also have $x$, $y$, $z$ components.

---

[†] A tridiagonal matrix is one in which coefficients appear only on the main, first upper and first lower diagonals.

[‡] In a diagonally dominant matrix the magnitude of the terms on the main diagonal exceed that of the off-diagonal terms on the same row.

In matrix form these equations for any spline segment $k$ are

$$[B] = \begin{bmatrix} B_{1k} \\ B_{2k} \\ B_{3k} \\ B_{4k} \end{bmatrix}$$

$$= \begin{bmatrix} 1 & 0 & 0 & 0 \\ 0 & 1 & 0 & 0 \\ -\dfrac{3}{t_{k+1}^2} & -\dfrac{2}{t_{k+1}} & \dfrac{3}{t_{k+1}^2} & -\dfrac{1}{t_{k+1}} \\ \dfrac{2}{t_{k+1}^3} & \dfrac{1}{t_{k+1}^2} & -\dfrac{2}{t_{k+1}^3} & \dfrac{1}{t_{k+1}^2} \end{bmatrix} \begin{bmatrix} P_k \\ P_k' \\ P_{k+1} \\ P_{k+1}' \end{bmatrix} \qquad (5-17)$$

To generate a piecewise cubic spline through $n$ given position vectors $P_k$, $1 \le k \le n$, with end tangent vectors $P_1'$ and $P_n'$, Eq. (5–16) is used to determine the internal tangent vectors $P_k'$, $2 \le k \le n-1$. Then for each piecewise cubic spline segment the end position and tangent vectors for that segment are used to determine the $B_{ik}$'s, $1 \le i \le 4$ for that segment using Eq. (5–17). Finally the generalization of Eq. (5–1)

$$P_k(t) = \sum_{i=1}^{4} B_{ik} t^{i-1} \qquad 0 \le t \le t_{k+1}, \ 1 \le k \le n-1 \qquad (5-18)$$

is used to determine points on the spline segment.
   In matrix form Eq. (5–18) becomes

$$P_k(t) = [\,1 \quad t \quad t^2 \quad t^3\,] \begin{bmatrix} B_{1k} \\ B_{2k} \\ B_{3k} \\ B_{4k} \end{bmatrix} \qquad 0 \le t \le t_{k+1} \qquad (5-19)$$

Substituting Eq. (5–17) and rearranging yields

$$P_k(\tau) = [\, F_1(\tau) \quad F_2(\tau) \quad F_3(\tau) \quad F_4(\tau)\,] \begin{bmatrix} P_k \\ P_{k+1} \\ P_k' \\ P_{k+1}' \end{bmatrix} \qquad \begin{array}{l} 0 \le \tau \le 1 \\ 1 \le k \le n-1 \end{array}$$

$$(5-20)$$

where

$$\tau = (t/t_{k+1})$$

$$F_{1k}(\tau) = 2\tau^3 - 3\tau^2 + 1 \qquad\qquad (5-21a)$$

$$F_{2k}(\tau) = -2\tau^3 + 3\tau^2 \qquad\qquad (5-21b)$$

$$F_{3k}(\tau) = \tau(\tau^2 - 2\tau + 1)t_{k+1} \qquad\qquad (5-21c)$$

$$F_{4k}(\tau) = \tau(\tau^2 - \tau)t_{k+1} \qquad\qquad (5-21d)$$

are called blending or weighting functions.

Using the definitions of the blending functions, Eq. (5–20) is written in matrix form as

$$P_k(\tau) = [F][G] \qquad\qquad (5-22)$$

where $[F]$ is a blending function matrix given by

$$[F] = [\, F_1(\tau) \quad F_2(\tau) \quad F_3(\tau) \quad F_4(\tau) \,] \qquad\qquad (5-23)$$

and

$$[G]^T = [\, P_k \quad P_{k+1} \quad P'_k \quad P'_{k+1} \,] \qquad\qquad (5-24)$$

contains the geometric information. As we shall see, equations of the form of Eqs. (5–22), i.e., a matrix of blending functions times a matrix of geometric conditions, frequently appear in curve and surface descriptions.

Notice from Eqs. (5–21) that each of the blending functions is a cubic. Any point on a cubic spline segment is a weighted sum of the end position and tangent vectors. The $F_{ik}$'s act as the blending or weighting functions. Figure 5–8 shows

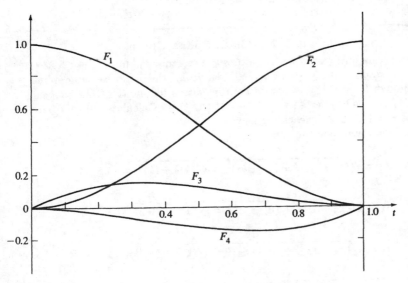

**Figure 5–8**   Cubic spline blending functions for $t_{k+1} = 1.0$.

the $F_i$'s for $t_{k+1} = 1.0$. Notice from Fig. 5–8 that $F_1(0) = 1$ and $F_2(0) = F_3(0) = F_4(0) = 0$. Thus, the curve passes through the end position vector $P_1$. Similarly $F_2(1) = 1$ and $F_1(1) = F_3(1) = F_4(1) = 0$. Thus, the curve also passes through the end position vector $P_2$. Further, note the symmetry of $F_1$ and $F_2$ and of $F_3$ and $F_4$. In fact, $F_2(\tau) = 1 - F_1(\tau)$. Finally, note the relative magnitudes of $F_1$ and $F_2$ and of $F_3$ and $F_4$. This significant difference in magnitude shows that in general the end position vectors have relatively more influence than the end tangent vectors.

Recall that a piecewise cubic spline curve is determined by the position vectors, tangent vectors *and* the parameter values, i.e., the $t_k$'s at the end of each segment. The choice of the $t_k$'s affects the curve smoothness.

Continuity of the second derivatives at the internal joints does not in itself produce a fair or smooth cubic spline curve in the sense of minimum curvature along the curve. To obtain minimum curvature and hence maximum smoothness, the coefficients $B_3$ and $B_4$ must be minimized for each segment by choosing appropriate values for the $t_k$'s for each segment. This additional computational effort is normally not required. Simpler methods, such as those described here, are used to generate curves smooth and fair enough for most practical purposes.

One approach used to determine the $t_k$'s is to set the parameter values equal to the chord lengths between successive data points. Acceptably smooth curves for most practical purposes are obtained using this technique. A second approach is to normalize the variation by choosing $t_k = 1.0$ for each cubic segment. This choice simplifies the computational requirements (see Sec. 5–4). As can be seen from the previous equations, each choice of $t_k$ produces different coefficient values and, hence, different curves through the given data points.

An example more fully illustrates the procedure.†

---

### Example 5–2　　Cubic Spline Curve

Considering the four two-dimensional position vectors $P_1 [\, 0 \quad 0 \,]$, $P_2 [\, 1 \quad 1 \,]$, $P_3 [\, 2 \quad -1 \,]$ and $P_4 [\, 3 \quad 0 \,]$ (see Fig. 5–9), determine the piecewise cubic spline curve through them using the chord approximation for the $t_k$'s. The tangent vectors at the ends are $P_1' [\, 1 \quad 1 \,]$ and $P_4' [\, 1 \quad 1 \,]$. Calculate intermediate points at $\tau = 1/3,\ 2/3$ for each segment.

To begin, determine the $t_k$'s:

$$t_2 = \sqrt{(x_2 - x_1)^2 + (y_2 - y_1)^2} = \sqrt{(1)^2 + (1)^2} = \sqrt{2}$$

$$t_3 = \sqrt{(x_3 - x_2)^2 + (y_3 - y_2)^2} = \sqrt{(1)^2 + (-2)^2} = \sqrt{5}$$

$$t_4 = \sqrt{(x_4 - x_3)^2 + (y_4 - y_3)^2} = \sqrt{(1)^2 + (1)^2} = \sqrt{2}$$

---

†Two-dimensional examples are used throughout this chapter to simplify the calculations and the presentation of results. Three dimensions is a simple extension (see the problems for Chapter 5).

The internal tangent vectors $P_2'$ and $P_3'$ are found using Eq. (5–15). Specifically,

$$
\begin{bmatrix}
1 & 0 & 0 & 0 \\
t_3 & 2(t_2 + t_3) & t_2 & 0 \\
0 & t_4 & 2(t_3 + t_4) & t_3 \\
0 & 0 & 0 & 1
\end{bmatrix}
\begin{bmatrix}
P_1' \\
P_2' \\
P_3' \\
P_4'
\end{bmatrix}
=
$$

$$
\begin{bmatrix}
P_1' \\[4pt]
\dfrac{3}{t_2 t_3}\{t_2^2(P_3 - P_2) + t_3^2(P_2 - P_1)\} \\[8pt]
\dfrac{3}{t_3 t_4}\{t_3^2(P_4 - P_3) + t_4^2(P_3 - P_2)\} \\[4pt]
P_4'
\end{bmatrix}
$$

Substituting yields

$$
\begin{bmatrix}
1 & 0 & 0 & 0 \\
\sqrt{5} & 2(\sqrt{2} + \sqrt{5}) & \sqrt{2} & 0 \\
0 & \sqrt{2} & 2(\sqrt{5} + \sqrt{2}) & \sqrt{5} \\
0 & 0 & 0 & 1
\end{bmatrix}
\begin{bmatrix}
P_1' \\
P_2' \\
P_3' \\
P_4'
\end{bmatrix}
$$

$$
=
\begin{bmatrix}
[\,1 \quad 1\,] \\[4pt]
\dfrac{3}{\sqrt{2}\sqrt{5}}\{2([\,2 \quad -1\,] - [\,1 \quad 1\,]) + 5([\,1 \quad 1\,] - [\,0 \quad 0\,])\} \\[8pt]
\dfrac{3}{\sqrt{5}\sqrt{2}}\{5([\,3 \quad 0\,] - [\,2 \quad -1\,]) + 2([\,2 \quad -1\,] - [\,1 \quad 1\,])\} \\[4pt]
[\,1 \quad 1\,]
\end{bmatrix}
$$

$$
=
\begin{bmatrix}
[\,1 \quad 1\,] \\[4pt]
\dfrac{3}{\sqrt{2}\sqrt{5}}\{[\,2 \quad -4\,] + [\,5 \quad 5\,]\} \\[8pt]
\dfrac{3}{\sqrt{5}\sqrt{2}}\{[\,5 \quad 5\,] + [\,2 \quad -4\,]\} \\[4pt]
[\,1 \quad 1\,]
\end{bmatrix}
=
\begin{bmatrix}
[\,1 \quad 1\,] \\
0.949\,[\,7 \quad 1\,] \\
0.949\,[\,7 \quad 1\,] \\
[\,1 \quad 1\,]
\end{bmatrix}
$$

or

$$
\begin{bmatrix}
1 & 0 & 0 & 0 \\
2.236 & 7.300 & 1.414 & 0 \\
0 & 1.414 & 7.300 & 2.236 \\
0 & 0 & 0 & 1
\end{bmatrix}
\begin{bmatrix}
P_1' \\
P_2' \\
P_3' \\
P_4'
\end{bmatrix}
=
\begin{bmatrix}
1 & 1 \\
6.641 & 0.949 \\
6.641 & 0.949 \\
1 & 1
\end{bmatrix}
$$

Inverting and premultiplying yields the tangent vectors

$$
\begin{bmatrix} P_1' \\ P_2' \\ P_3' \\ P_4' \end{bmatrix} = \begin{bmatrix} 1 & 0 & 0 & 0 \\ -0.318 & 0.142 & -0.028 & 0.062 \\ 0.062 & -0.028 & 0.142 & -0.318 \\ 0 & 0 & 0 & 1 \end{bmatrix} \begin{bmatrix} 1 & 1 \\ 6.641 & 0.949 \\ 6.641 & 0.949 \\ 1 & 1 \end{bmatrix}
$$

$$
= \begin{bmatrix} 1 & 1 \\ 0.505 & -0.148 \\ 0.505 & -0.148 \\ 1 & 1 \end{bmatrix}
$$

Recalling Eqs. (5–21)the blending functions for the first segment are

$$
F_1(1/3) = 2(1/3)^3 - 3(1/3)^2 + 1 = \frac{20}{27} = 0.741
$$

$$
F_2(1/3) = -2(1/3)^3 + 3(1/3)^2 = \frac{7}{27} = 0.259
$$

$$
F_3(1/3) = (1/3)[(1/3)^2 - 2(1/3) + 1]\sqrt{2} = \frac{4\sqrt{2}}{27} = 0.210
$$

$$
F_4(1/3) = (1/3)[(1/3)^2 - 1/3]\sqrt{2} = -\frac{2\sqrt{2}}{27} = -0.105
$$

and at $\tau = 2/3$

$$
F_1(2/3) = 2(2/3)^3 - 3(2/3)^2 + 1 = \frac{7}{27} = 0.259
$$

$$
F_2(2/3) = -2(2/3)^3 + 3(2/3)^2 = \frac{20}{27} = 0.741
$$

$$
F_3(2/3) = (2/3)[(2/3)^2 - 2(2/3) + 1]\sqrt{2} = \frac{2\sqrt{2}}{27} = 0.105
$$

$$
F_4(2/3) = (2/3)[(2/3)^2 - 2/3]\sqrt{2} = \frac{-4\sqrt{2}}{27} = -0.210
$$

The point on the first spline segment at $\tau = 1/3$ is given by Eq. (5–22), $P(\tau) = [\,F\,][\,G\,]$, where here

$$
P(1/3) = [\,0.741 \quad 0.259 \quad 0.210 \quad -0.105\,] \begin{bmatrix} 0 & 0 \\ 1 & 1 \\ 1 & 1 \\ 0.505 & -0.148 \end{bmatrix}
$$

$$
= [\,0.416 \quad 0.484\,]
$$

and at $\tau = 2/3$ by

$$
P(2/3) = [\,0.259 \quad 0.741 \quad 0.105 \quad -0.210\,] \begin{bmatrix} 0 & 0 \\ 1 & 1 \\ 1 & 1 \\ 0.505 & -0.148 \end{bmatrix}
$$

$$
= [\,0.740 \quad 0.876\,]
$$

### Table 5–1 Results for Cubic Spline Curve

| Segment | $\tau$ | $P_x(\tau)$ | $P_y(\tau)$ |
|---------|--------|-------------|-------------|
| 1 | 1/3 | 0.416 | 0.484 |
|   | 2/3 | 0.740 | 0.876 |
| 2 | 1/3 | 1.343 | 0.457 |
|   | 2/3 | 1.657 | −0.457 |
| 3 | 1/3 | 2.260 | −0.876 |
|   | 2/3 | 2.584 | −0.484 |

Complete results are shown in Table 5–1. The cubic spline curve is shown in Fig. 5–9.

---

Although the blending functions (see Eq. 5–21) indicate that the end tangent vectors have less influence than the end position vectors on the shape of the spline segment, the effect can still be significant. Figure 5–10 shows a single plane symmetric spline segment with constant tangent vector directions and varying magnitudes. The tangent vector directions are indicated by the angle $\alpha$, and the relative magnitudes by the length of the vectors. When the magnitude is a small fraction of the chord length $l$, the curve is convex at the ends and lies

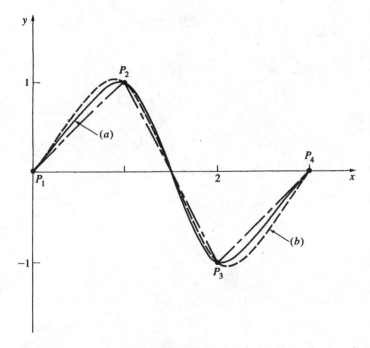

**Figure 5–9**   Piecewise cubic spline. (a) $t_k$ determined using the chord approximation; (b) $t_k$ normalized to 1.

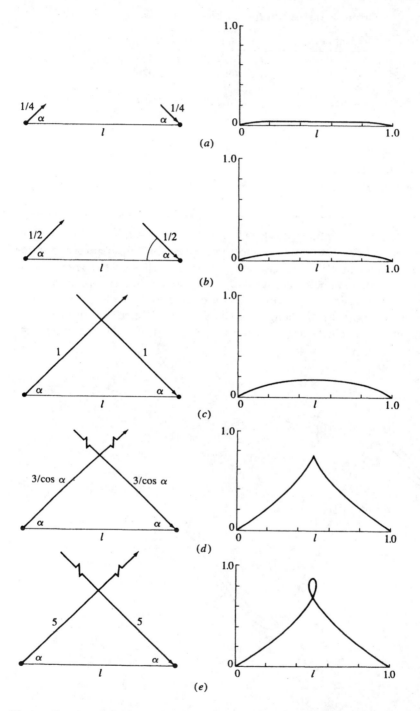

**Figure 5–10**   Effect of tangent vector magnitude on cubic spline segment shape, $\alpha = \pi/4$. (a) 1/4; (b) 1/2; (c) 1; (d) 3/$\cos \alpha$; (e) 3/2.

within the triangle formed by the chord and the tangent vector directions. As the magnitude increases, the curve eventually becomes concave at the ends and lies outside the triangle. For this special case, an apex in the curve is formed when the tangent vector magnitude is $3/\cos\alpha$ (see Fig. 5–10d). For magnitudes larger than this value a loop is formed as shown in Fig. 5–10e. A heuristic approach, sometimes used to improve the shape of the curve, is to restrict the tangent vector magnitude to less than or equal to the chord length.

## 5–4    NORMALIZED CUBIC SPLINES

An alternate approximation for the $t_k$ spline segment parameter values to that previously suggested is to normalize them to unity. Thus, $0 \le t \le 1$ for all segments.

The blending functions (see Eq. 5–21) now become[†]

$$F_1(t) = 2t^3 - 3t^2 + 1 \tag{5–25a}$$

$$F_2(t) = -2t^3 + 3t^2 \tag{5–25b}$$

$$F_3(t) = t^3 - 2t^2 + t \tag{5–25c}$$

$$F_4(t) = t^3 - t^2 \tag{5–25d}$$

For the normalized cubic spline the blending function matrix is now written as

$$[F] = [T][N] = \begin{bmatrix} t^3 & t^2 & t & 1 \end{bmatrix} \begin{bmatrix} 2 & -2 & 1 & 1 \\ -3 & 3 & -2 & -1 \\ 0 & 0 & 1 & 0 \\ 1 & 0 & 0 & 0 \end{bmatrix} \tag{5–26}$$

The matrix equation for a cubic spline segment (see Eq. 5–22) can now be written as

$$P(t) = [F][G] = [T][N][G] \tag{5–27}$$

Notice that $[T]$ and $[N]$ are constant for all cubic spline segments. Only the geometry matrix $[G]$ changes from segment to segment.

Equation (5–15), used to determine the internal tangent vectors required in $[G]$, now becomes

$$\begin{bmatrix} 1 & 0 & \cdot & \cdot & \cdot & \cdot \\ 1 & 4 & 1 & 0 & \cdot & \cdot \\ 0 & 1 & 4 & 1 & 0 & \cdot \\ \cdot & \cdot & \cdot & \cdot & \cdot & \cdot \\ \cdot & \cdot & 0 & 1 & 4 & 1 \\ \cdot & \cdot & \cdot & \cdot & 0 & 1 \end{bmatrix} \begin{bmatrix} P_1' \\ P_2' \\ \cdot \\ \cdot \\ \cdot \\ P_n' \end{bmatrix} = \begin{bmatrix} 3\{(P_3 - P_2) + (P_2 - P_1)\} \\ 3\{(P_4 - P_3) + (P_3 - P_2)\} \\ \cdot \\ \cdot \\ \cdot \\ 3\{(P_n - P_{n-1}) + (P_{n-1} - P_{n-2})\} \end{bmatrix} \tag{5–28}$$

---

[†]These blending functions are the cubic Hermite polynomial blending functions on the interval $0 \le t \le 1$.

The solution is again given by Eq. (5–16). However, here $[\,M\,]$ is constant and need only be inverted once. When the number of position vectors is large, this represents a considerable savings in computational expense.

An example illustrates these results.

---

### Example 5–3    Normalized Cubic Spline Curve

Again consider the four two-dimensional position vectors of Ex. 5–2, i.e., $P_1[\,0\ \ 0\,]$, $P_2[\,1\ \ 1\,]$, $P_3[\,2\ \ -1\,]$ and $P_4[\,3\ \ 0\,]$ with tangent vectors $P_1'[\,1\ \ 1\,]$ and $P_4'[\,1\ \ 1\,]$. Determine the normalized piecewise cubic spline curve through them.

Here the $t_k$ parameter values are $t_2 = t_3 = t_4 = 1.0$.

The internal tangent vectors are obtained using Eq. (5–28), i.e.,

$$
\begin{bmatrix} 1 & 0 & 0 & 0 \\ 1 & 4 & 1 & 0 \\ 0 & 1 & 4 & 1 \\ 0 & 0 & 0 & 1 \end{bmatrix}
\begin{bmatrix} P_1' \\ P_2' \\ P_3' \\ P_4' \end{bmatrix}
=
\begin{bmatrix}
[\,1\ \ 1\,] \\
3\{[\,2\ \ -1\,] - [\,1\ \ 1\,] + [\,1\ \ 1\,] - [\,0\ \ 0\,]\} \\
3\{[\,3\ \ 0\,] - [\,2\ \ -1\,] + [\,2\ \ -1\,] - [\,1\ \ 1\,]\} \\
[\,1\ \ 1\,]
\end{bmatrix}
$$

$$
=
\begin{bmatrix} 1 & 1 \\ 6 & -3 \\ 6 & -3 \\ 1 & 1 \end{bmatrix}
$$

Inverting and premultiplying yields

$$
\begin{bmatrix} P_1' \\ P_2' \\ P_3' \\ P_4' \end{bmatrix}
=
\begin{bmatrix}
1 & 0 & 0 & 0 \\
-0.267 & 0.267 & -0.067 & 0.067 \\
0.067 & -0.067 & 0.267 & -0.267 \\
0 & 0 & 0 & 1
\end{bmatrix}
\begin{bmatrix} 1 & 1 \\ 6 & -3 \\ 6 & -3 \\ 1 & 1 \end{bmatrix}
$$

$$
=
\begin{bmatrix} 1 & 1 \\ 1 & -0.8 \\ 1 & -0.8 \\ 1 & 1 \end{bmatrix}
$$

Notice that here the internal tangent vectors $P_2'$, $P_3'$ are considerably different from those determined with the chord approximation used in Ex. 5–2.

Using Eq. (5–26) the blending function matrix for the first segment at $t = 1/3$ is

$$
[\,F\,] = [\,T\,][\,N\,] = [\,1/27\ \ \ 1/9\ \ \ 1/3\ \ \ 1\,]
\begin{bmatrix}
2 & -2 & 1 & 1 \\
-3 & 3 & -2 & -1 \\
0 & 0 & 1 & 0 \\
1 & 0 & 0 & 0
\end{bmatrix}
$$

$$
= [\,20/27\ \ \ 7/27\ \ \ 4/27\ \ \ -2/27\,]
$$

and at $t = 2/3$,

$$[F] = [\, 7/27 \quad 20/27 \quad 2/27 \quad -4/27 \,]$$

The point on the first spline segment at $t = 1/3$ is

$$P(t) = [\,F\,][\,G\,] = [\, 20/27 \quad 7/27 \quad 4/27 \quad -2/27 \,] \begin{bmatrix} 0 & 0 \\ 1 & 1 \\ 1 & 1 \\ 1 & -0.8 \end{bmatrix}$$

$$= [\, 1/3 \quad 63/135 \,] = [\, 0.333 \quad 0.467 \,]$$

and at $t = 2/3$,

$$P(t) = [\,F\,][\,G\,] = [\, 7/27 \quad 20/27 \quad 2/27 \quad -4/27 \,] \begin{bmatrix} 0 & 0 \\ 1 & 1 \\ 1 & 1 \\ 1 & -0.8 \end{bmatrix}$$

$$= [\, 2/3 \quad 126/135 \,]$$

Complete results are shown in Table 5–2.

**Table 5–2 Results for Normalized Cubic Spline Curve**

| Segment | $t$ | $P_x(t)$ | $P_y(t)$ |
|---------|-----|----------|----------|
| 1 | 1/3 | 0.333 | 0.467 |
|   | 2/3 | 0.667 | 0.933 |
| 2 | 1/3 | 1.333 | 0.422 |
|   | 2/3 | 1.667 | −0.422 |
| 3 | 1/3 | 2.333 | −0.933 |
|   | 2/3 | 2.667 | −0.467 |

The cubic spline curve is shown in Fig. 5–9 along with that of Ex. 5–1. Notice that the two curves are different, thus confirming that the parameterization does affect the results.

If the position vectors for a given set of data are not uniformly distributed, experience shows that the resulting normalized curve is not as smooth as that obtained using the chord length approximation for the $t_k$'s. This is illustrated in Fig. 5–11. Figure 5–11a shows a set of ordered data points representing the outline of a rooster. Figure 5–11b connects the points with short straight lines. Figures 5–11c and d represent normalized and chord length cubic spline approximations, respectively. Notice in particular the representation of the feet and the comb in Figs. 5–11c and d. The chord length approximation significantly reduces the looping evident in the feet in Fig. 5–11c and provides a smoother, more rounded representation of the comb. Regardless of these shortcomings the

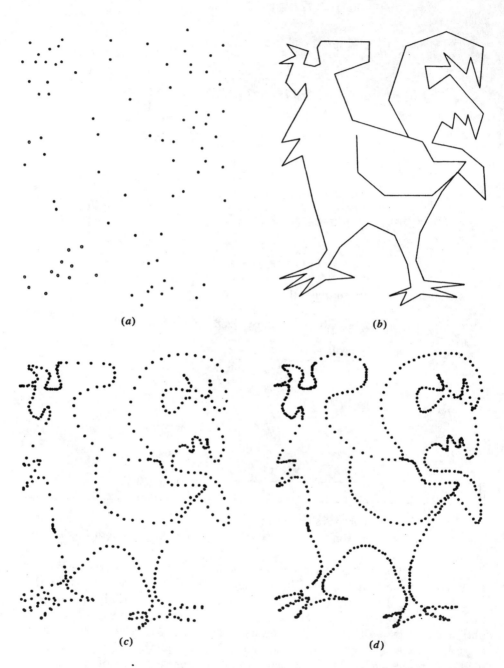

Figure 5–11   Comparison of cubic spline approximations. (a) Data; (b) connected
with straight lines; (c) normalized approximation for $t_k$'s; (d) chord
length approximation for $t_k$'s.

normalized formulation finds use in creating cubic boundary curves for three-dimensional surface patches as discussed in Chapter 6.

One final point is of interest. If, for the normalized spline, the matrix $[B]^T = [B_1 \quad B_2 \quad B_3 \quad B_4]$ is known, then the geometry matrix for the spline segment, i.e., $[G]$, is given by

$$[G] = [N]^{-1}[B]^T$$

where $[N]^{-1}$, the inverse of $[N]$, is

$$[N]^{-1} = \begin{bmatrix} 0 & 0 & 0 & 1 \\ 1 & 1 & 1 & 1 \\ 0 & 0 & 1 & 0 \\ 3 & 2 & 1 & 0 \end{bmatrix} \qquad (5-29)$$

Points along the spline segment are again obtained using Eq. (5–27).

## 5–5    ALTERNATE CUBIC SPLINE END CONDITIONS

In the previous discussions the tangent vectors $P_1'$ and $P_n'$ at the ends of the piecewise cubic spline curve were assumed known. This boundary condition is called the *clamped* end condition. Solution for the unknown internal tangent vectors is given by inversion of the tridiagonal matrix $[M]$ described in Eq. (5–15).

If only a few data points are known, or if physical constraints require accurate control of the curve shape at the ends, alternate boundary conditions may be desired. One alternative is to specify the curvature at the ends of the spline curve. When the curvature is zero, a *relaxed* or *natural* end condition is obtained. Approximating the curvature by the second derivative and recalling Eq. (5–9) yields

$$P''(t) = \sum_{i=1}^{4} (i-1)(i-2)B_i t^{i-3} \qquad 0 \le t \le t_{k+1}$$

At the beginning of the first spline segment $t = 0$. Here, note that only the $i = 3$ term contributes to the result. Using Eq. (5–17)

$$P''(0) = 2B_3 = 2\left(\frac{3(P_2 - P_1)}{t_2^2} - \frac{2P_1'}{t_2} - \frac{P_2'}{t_2}\right) = 0$$

Rearranging yields

$$P_1' + \frac{P_2'}{2} = \frac{3}{2t_2}(P_2 - P_1) \qquad (5-30)$$

The first row in the matrices $[M]$ and $[R]$ (see Eq. 5–15) is now

$$\begin{bmatrix} 1 & 1/2 & 0 & \cdots \end{bmatrix}[P_1'] = \left[\frac{3}{2t_2}(P_2 - P_1)\right]$$

At the end of the last segment $t = t_n$, $k = n - 1$. Here, both the $i = 3$ and $i = 4$ terms in Eq. (5–9) contribute to the result. Specifically,

$$P''(t_n) = 2B_3 + 6B_4 t_n = 0$$

or using Eq. (5–17),

$$\frac{6}{t_n^2}(P_{n-1} - P_n) + \frac{2P'_{n-1}}{t_n} + \frac{4P'_n}{t_n} = 0$$

Rearranging yields

$$2P'_{n-1} + 4P'_n = \frac{6}{t_n}(P_n - P_{n-1}) \tag{5-31}$$

The last row of the matrices $[\,M\,]$ and $[\,R\,]$ (see Eq. 5–15) is now

$$\lfloor \cdots \quad 0 \quad 2 \quad 4 \,\rfloor \lfloor\, P'_n \,\rfloor = \left| \frac{6}{t_n}(P_n - P_{n-1}) \right|$$

Note that clamped and relaxed end conditions can be mixed for a given piecewise cubic spline curve, e.g., an initial relaxed end condition and a final clamped end condition or vice versa. An example more fully illustrates these results.

---

### Example 5–4   Cubic Spline with Relaxed End Conditions

Assume that the three position vectors $P_1[\,0 \quad 0\,]$, $P_2[\,1 \quad 2\,]$ and $P_3[\,3 \quad 2\,]$ are known. Determine the cubic spline curve through these points using relaxed end conditions. Use the chord length approximation for the $t_k$'s.
The $t_k$'s are

$$t_2 = \sqrt{(x_2 - x_1)^2 + (y_2 - y_1)^2} = \sqrt{(1)^2 + (2)^2} = \sqrt{5}$$

$$t_3 = \sqrt{(x_3 - x_2)^2 + (y_3 - y_2)^2} = \sqrt{(3-1)^2 + (0)^2} = 2$$

Using Eqs. (5–30) and (5–31) for relaxed end conditions to modify the matrices $[\,M\,]$ and $[\,R\,]$ of Eq. (5–15) yields the equation of the internal tangent vector at $P'_2$. Specifically,

$$\begin{bmatrix} 1 & 0.5 & 0 \\ 2 & 8.472 & 2.236 \\ 0 & 2 & 4 \end{bmatrix} \begin{bmatrix} P'_1 \\ P'_2 \\ P'_3 \end{bmatrix}$$

$$= \begin{bmatrix} \dfrac{3}{2\sqrt{5}}([\,1 \quad 2\,] - [\,0 \quad 0\,]) \\[2mm] \dfrac{3}{2\sqrt{5}}\{5([\,3 \quad 2\,] - [\,1 \quad 2\,]) + 4([\,1 \quad 2\,] - [\,0 \quad 0\,])\} \\[2mm] 3([\,3 \quad 2\,] - [\,1 \quad 2\,]) \end{bmatrix}$$

$$= \begin{bmatrix} 0.671 & 1.342 \\ 9.391 & 5.367 \\ 6 & 0 \end{bmatrix}$$

Solving for the derivatives by inverting the $3 \times 3$ matrix and premultiplying yields

$$\begin{bmatrix} P_1' \\ P_2' \\ P_3' \end{bmatrix} = \begin{bmatrix} 1.157 & -0.079 & 0.044 \\ -0.315 & 0.157 & -0.088 \\ 0.157 & -0.079 & 0.294 \end{bmatrix} \begin{bmatrix} 0.671 & 1.342 \\ 9.391 & 5.367 \\ 6 & 0 \end{bmatrix}$$

$$= \begin{bmatrix} 0.301 & 1.131 \\ 0.739 & 0.422 \\ 1.131 & -0.211 \end{bmatrix}$$

Using Eq. (5–21) the blending functions at $\tau = 1/3,\ 2/3$ for the first segment are

$$[\,F\,]_{\tau=1/3} = [\,0.741 \quad 0.259 \quad 0.331 \quad -0.166\,]$$

$$[\,F\,]_{\tau=2/3} = [\,0.259 \quad 0.741 \quad 0.166 \quad -0.331\,]$$

Equation (5–22) then yields the points on the first segment, i.e.,

$$P(1/3) = [\,0.741 \quad 0.259 \quad 0.331 \quad -0.166\,] \begin{bmatrix} 0 & 0 \\ 1 & 2 \\ 0.301 & 1.131 \\ 0.739 & 0.422 \end{bmatrix}$$

$$= [\,0.237 \quad 0.823\,]$$

Similarly

$$P(2/3) = [\,0.546 \quad 1.529\,]$$

The blending functions at $\tau = 1/3,\ 2/3$ for the second segment are

$$[\,F\,]_{\tau=1/3} = [\,0.741 \quad 0.259 \quad 0.296 \quad -0.148\,]$$

$$[\,F\,]_{\tau=2/3} = [\,0.259 \quad 0.741 \quad 0.148 \quad -0.296\,]$$

and Eq. (5–22) yields

$$P(1/3) = [\,1.570 \quad 2.156\,]$$

$$P(2/3) = [\,2.256 \quad 2.125\,]$$

The results are shown in Fig. 5–12.

---

Two other boundary conditions of interest are the cyclic and anticyclic end conditions. A cyclic spline is used to produce a closed curve or a portion of a curve that repeats at intervals. The cyclic end condition requires that both the tangent vector and the curvature at the two ends be equal, i.e.,

$$P_1'(0) = P_n'(t_n) \tag{5 – 32}$$

$$P_1''(0) = P_n''(t_n) \tag{5 – 33}$$

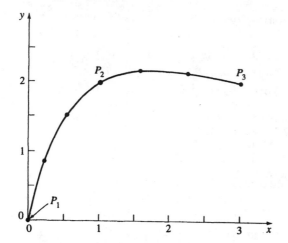

**Figure 5–12** Cubic spline fit for Ex. 5–4.

Recalling Eqs. (5–3) and (5–9) and using Eqs. (5–17), Eq. (5–32) becomes

$$P_1' - P_{n-1}' = 2t_n\left[\frac{3(P_n - P_{n-1})}{t_n^2} - \frac{2P_{n-1}'}{t_n} - \frac{P_n'}{t_n}\right]$$

$$+ 3t_n\left[\frac{2(P_{n-1} - P_n)}{t_n^3} + \frac{P_{n-1}'}{t_n^2} + \frac{P_n'}{t_n^2}\right] \qquad (5-34)$$

Similarly, Eq. (5–33) becomes

$$2\left[\frac{3(P_2 - P_1)}{t_2^2} - \frac{2P_1'}{t_2} - \frac{P_2'}{t_2}\right] = 2\left[\frac{3(P_n - P_{n-1})}{t_n^2} - \frac{2P_{n-1}'}{t_n} - \frac{P_n'}{t_n}\right]$$

$$+ 6t_n\left[\frac{2(P_{n-1} - P_n)}{t_n^3} + \frac{P_{n-1}'}{t_n^2} + \frac{P_n'}{t_n^2}\right]$$

$$(5-35)$$

Combining Eqs. (5–34) and (5–35) by multiplying Eq. (5–35) by $t_n$ and subtracting it from Eq. (5–34) yields

$$P_1' - P_{n-1}' - 2t_n\left[\frac{3(P_2 - P_1)}{t_2^2} - \frac{2P_1'}{t_2} - \frac{P_2'}{t_2}\right]$$

$$= 3t_n^2\left[\frac{2(P_{n-1} - P_n)}{t_n^3} + \frac{P_{n-1}'}{t_n^2} + \frac{P_n'}{t_n^2}\right]$$

$$- 6t_n^2\left[\frac{2(P_{n-1} - P_n)}{t_n^3} + \frac{P_{n-1}'}{t_n^2} + \frac{P_n'}{t_n^2}\right]$$

Recalling that $P_1' = P_n'$ and rearranging the terms gives

$$2(1 + \frac{t_n}{t_2})P_1' + \frac{t_n}{t_2}P_2' + P_{n-1}' = 3\frac{t_n}{t_2^2}(P_2 - P_1) - \frac{3}{t_n}(P_{n-1} - P_n) \qquad (5-36)$$

The tangent vectors at the internal joints are again obtained using Eq. (5–15). However, because all the tangent vectors are no longer independent (recall $P_1' = P_n'$), $[M]$ is now $(n-1) \times (n-1)$ with the first row given by the coefficients of Eq. (5–36); i.e.,

$$
\begin{bmatrix}
2(1 + \frac{t_n}{t_2}) & \frac{t_n}{t_2} & 0 & 0 & \cdot & 1 \\
t_3 & 2(t_2 + t_3) & t_2 & \cdot & \cdot & \cdot \\
\cdot & \cdot & \cdot & \cdot & \cdot & \cdot \\
\cdot & \cdot & \cdot & \cdot & \cdot & \cdot \\
\cdot & \cdot & 0 & t_n & 2(t_n + t_{n-1}) & t_{n-1}
\end{bmatrix}
\begin{bmatrix}
P_1' \\ P_2' \\ P_3' \\ \cdot \\ \cdot \\ P_{n-1}'
\end{bmatrix}
$$

$$
=
\begin{bmatrix}
3\frac{t_n}{t_2^2}(P_2 - P_1) - \frac{3}{t_n}(P_{n-1} - P_n) \\[2mm]
\frac{3}{t_2 t_3}\{t_2^2(P_3 - P_2) + t_3^2(P_2 - P_1)\} \\[2mm]
\frac{3}{t_3 t_4}\{t_3^2(P_4 - P_3) + t_4^2(P_3 - P_2)\} \\[2mm]
\cdot \\ \cdot \\
\frac{3}{t_{n-1}t_n}\{t_{n-1}^2(P_n - P_{n-1}) + t_n^2(P_{n-1} - P_{n-2})\}
\end{bmatrix}
\qquad (5-37)
$$

Note that the matrix is no longer tridiagonal.

The anticyclic spline is similar to the cyclic spline except that

$$P_1'(0) = -P_n'(t_n) \qquad (5-38)$$

$$P_1''(0) = -P_n''(t_n) \qquad (5-39)$$

Following the same procedure used for the cyclic end conditions yields

$$2(1 + \frac{t_n}{t_2})P_1' + \frac{t_n}{t_2}P_2' - P_{n-1}' = 3\frac{t_n}{t_2^2}(P_2 - P_1) + \frac{3}{t_n}(P_{n-1} - P_n) \qquad (5-40)$$

Equation (5–40) shows that the only effect of imposing the anticyclic end condition is to change the sign of the 1 at $M(1, n-1)$ in the $[M]$ matrix and to change the sign of the second term at $R(1,1)$ in Eq. (5–37). Anticyclic splines are useful for producing parallel end spans with end tangent vectors that are equal in magnitude but opposite in direction. A practical example is a laminated wooden tennis racket. Table 5–3 summarizes end conditions for cubic splines.

## Table 5–3 Cubic Spline End Conditions

| End Condition | Nonzero Elements in the First and Last Rows of $[\,M\,]$ | First and Last Rows of $[\,R\,]$ |
|---|---|---|
| Clamped | $M(1,1) = 1$ <br> $M(n,n) = 1$ | $R(1,1) = P_1'$ <br> $R(n,1) = P_n'$ |
| Relaxed | $M(1,1) = 1$ <br><br> $M(1,2) = 1/2$ <br><br> $M(n,n-1) = 2$ <br><br> $M(n,n) = 4$ | $R(1,1) = \dfrac{3}{2t_2}(P_2 - P_1)$ <br><br><br> $R(n,1) = \dfrac{6}{t_n}(P_n - P_{n-1})$ |
| Cyclic | $M(1,1) = 2\left(1 + \dfrac{t_n}{t_2}\right)$ <br><br> $M(1,2) = \dfrac{t_n}{t_2}$ <br><br> $M(1,n-1) = 1$ | $R(1,1) = 3\left(\dfrac{t_n}{t_2^2}\right)(P_2 - P_1)$ <br><br> $\qquad -\dfrac{3}{t_n}(P_{n-1} - P_n)$ <br><br> $R(n,1)$ undefined |
| Anticyclic | $M(1,1) = 2\left(1 + \dfrac{t_n}{t_2}\right)$ <br><br> $M(1,2) = \dfrac{t_n}{t_2}$ <br><br> $M(1,n-1) = -1$ | $R(1,1) = 3\left(\dfrac{t_n}{t_2^2}\right)(P_2 - P_1)$ <br><br> $\qquad +\dfrac{3}{t_n}(P_{n-1} - P_n)$ <br><br> $R(n,1)$ undefined |

Cubic spline curves have continuous first and second derivatives with any type of end conditions. However, if the number of data points is large, the computation time required to invert the tangent vector matrix can be excessive.

Figure 5–13 shows two cubic spline curves through the same five data points, one with clamped end conditions and the other with relaxed end conditions. The specified end tangent vectors for the two clamped ends are $[\,-1 \quad 1\,]$ and $[\,1 \quad 1\,]$, respectively. For this case not a great deal of difference exists between the two curves. Other end tangent vectors significantly modify the shape of the curve with clamped ends, e.g., $[\,1 \quad 1\,]$ and $[\,1 \quad 1\,]$.

Figure 5–14 shows the effect of changing the magnitude, but not the direction, of the end tangent vectors for a closed, cubic spline curve through five points, where the first and last points are identical. These cubic spline curves are symmetrical since the square matrix in Eq. (5–15) is tridiagonal.

Figure 5–15 shows a relaxed and a cyclic spline curve for the same five points used in Fig. 5–14. Notice that the relaxed spline curve is symmetrical but the cyclic spline curve is not.

Figure 5–16 compares a relaxed end condition to a cyclic end condition. This illustrates that a cyclic end condition can be used with an open curve. Here,

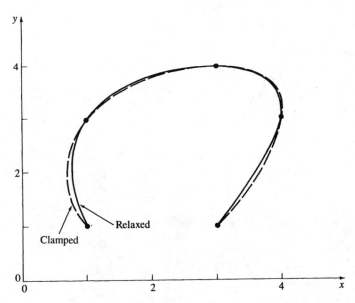

**Figure 5–13**    Comparison of clamped and relaxed end conditions for normalized, piecewise cubic splines.

even though the curve is open, the direction of the initial end tangent vector on the curve with cyclic end conditions is the same as the direction of the final end tangent vector.

Although parametric piecewise cubic spline curves have proven useful in a number of applications, e.g., in the automotive, shipbuilding and aircraft industries, a number of disadvantages exist. Specifically, parametric cubics never reduce exactly to a conic section; they poorly approximate asymptotic curves; and, if not carefully controlled, they frequently exhibit spurious oscillations. Oscillations occur since the cubic spline is influenced locally by each data point along the curve, and the third derivative is only piecewise constant. Discontinuities in third derivatives can thus induce unwanted inflection points at certain locations along the curve. Although such an oscillating curve is $C^2$ continuous, it is *not* fair.

One attempt to reduce the occurrence of oscillations yields a mathematical analog to the physical phenomenon of adding tension along the direction of the spline curve. To see this, consider a physical spline supported by ducks at certain points. If the thin, flexible beam has small oscillations, one way to remove them is to apply tension to the ends of the beam to smooth out the spline. A discussion of splines under tension is beyond the scope of this text. However, a few remarks are in order. The earliest attempts by Schwiekert (Ref. 5–6) and Cline (Ref. 5–7) resulted in exponentially based alternatives to the natural spline. These exponential splines were expensive to calculate. Nielson (Ref. 5–8) developed a polynomial alternative which he called the $\nu$-spline. The effect of adding tension to a cubic spline is shown in Fig. 5–17.

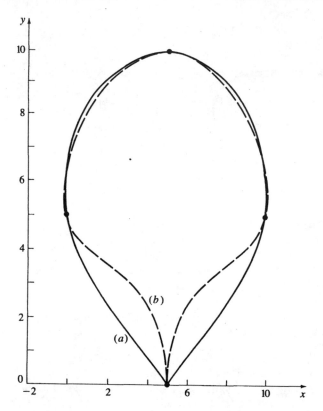

**Figure 5–14**   The effect of tangent vector magnitude on normalized, piecewise cubic spline curves. (a) $P_1'[0 \quad 1], P_2'[0 \quad -1]$; (b) $P_1'[0 \quad 10], P_2'[0 \quad -10]$.

## 5–6   PARABOLIC BLENDING

Although cubic spline curves have proven both powerful and useful, they do have certain disadvantages. Among these disadvantages are the nonintuitive effects of varying tangent vector direction and magnitude, the necessity of prespecifying all the data points on the curve before it is drawn, and a lack of local control of the curve shape. The lack of local control is particularly important for interactive design. Because cubic spline fitting requires inversion of a large matrix dependent upon *all* the spline segments, a change in any one segment affects all segments. Although these effects diminish as the distance along the curve away from the perturbed point increases, the subtle effects that remain are a problem. Parabolically blended curves solve most of these problems at the expense of being only $C^1$ continuous, i.e., only first-derivative continuity is maintained at the internal joints. However, $C^1$ continuity is sufficient for many applications. Further, a parabolically blended curve is computationally inexpensive.

Parabolic blending was first presented by A. W. Overhauser[†] (Ref. 5–9).

---

[†]Overhauser's original derivation was basically repeated in the first edition of this book.

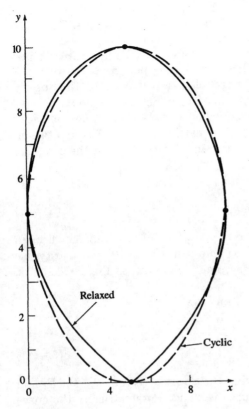

**Figure 5–15**    Comparison of relaxed and cyclic end conditions for normalized, piece-wise cubic spline curves.

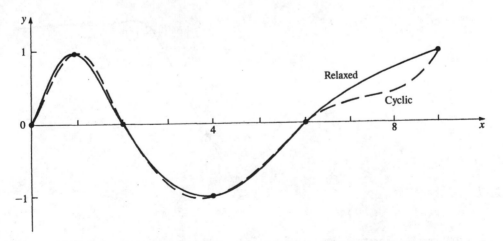

**Figure 5–16**    Comparison of relaxed and cyclic end conditions for open curves.

Overhauser used geometric considerations to derive the blended curve. The basic idea is to linearly blend the overlapping portion of two parabolas defined by a set of four consecutive points. The first parabola is defined by the first three points; the second, by the last three points. The overlapping portion is between the second and third points. Although each parabola is a planar curve, the linearly blended curve is a cubic which may twist in space, as Fig. 5–18 shows.

Brewer and Anderson (Ref. 5–10) provided an alternate derivation for *one* of a family of parabolically blended curves using matrix methods. A computationally more efficient algorithm resulted. A generalized derivation for the complete family is given here.

A parabolically blended curve is given by

$$C(t) = (1 - t)p(r) + tq(s) \qquad (5-41)$$

where $r$, $s$ and $t$ are parameters. $p(r)$, $q(s)$ are parametric parabolas through $P_1$, $P_2$, $P_3$ and $P_2$, $P_3$, $P_4$, respectively, as shown in Fig. 5–19. For clarity the parabolas in Fig. 5–19 both lie in the same plane. However, as Fig. 5–18 shows, this is not necessary.

The parametric representation of $p(r)$ and $q(s)$ is

$$p(r) = [\, r^2 \quad r \quad 1 \,][\, B \,] \qquad (5-42)$$

$$q(s) = [\, s^2 \quad s \quad 1 \,][\, D \,] \qquad (5-43)$$

where $[\, B \,]$ and $[\, D \,]$ are matrices involving the position vectors $P_1$, $P_2$, $P_3$ and $P_2$, $P_3$, $P_4$, respectively. The blended curve is cubic. Parametrically the curve $C(t)$ is

$$C(t) = [\, t^3 \quad t^2 \quad t \quad 1 \,][\, A \,][\, G \,] = [\, T \,][\, A \,][\, G \,] \qquad (5-44)$$

where $[\, T \,][\, A \,]$ is a blending function matrix and $[\, G \,]$ is a geometry matrix involving the position vectors $P_1$, $P_2$, $P_3$, $P_4$. To determine $[\, B \,]$ and $[\, D \,]$ and

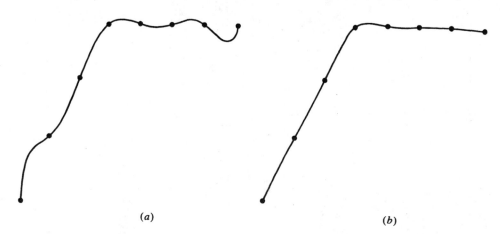

(*a*)

(*b*)

**Figure 5–17**   Effect of adding tension to a piecewise cubic spline curve. (a) No tension; (b) with tension.

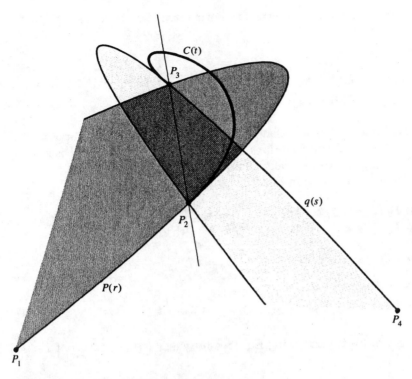

**Figure 5–18**    Parabolic blending.

hence $[A]$ and $[G]$ it is necessary to establish a relationship between the parameters $r$, $s$ and $t$. Looking at Fig. 5–19, and noting that $r$ varies from 0 to 1
from $P_1$ to $P_3$ along $p(r)$, $s$ varies from 0 to 1 from $P_2$ to $P_4$ along $q(s)$ and $t$
varies from 0 to 1 from $P_2$ to $P_3$ along $C(t)$, it seems reasonable to assume that
$r$ and $t$ and $s$ and $t$ are linearly related. Hence, assume

$$r = k_1 t + k_2 \qquad s = k_3 t + k_4 \qquad\qquad (5-45)$$

where the $k_i$ are constants determined from boundary conditions at $P_1$, $P_2$,
$P_3$ and $P_4$. Noting that data is frequently evenly or nearly evenly spaced and

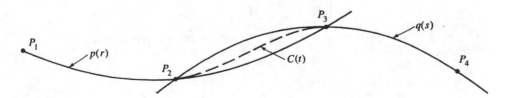

**Figure 5–19**    Notation for parabolic blending.

assuming that the parameter ranges are normalized, i.e., $0 \leq r, s, t \leq 1$, it is reasonable to assume that

$$p(0) = P_1 \qquad p(1/2) = P_2 \qquad p(1) = P_3 \qquad (5-46a)$$
$$q(0) = P_2 \qquad q(1/2) = P_3 \qquad q(1) = P_4 \qquad (5-46b)$$
$$C(0) = P_2 \qquad\qquad\qquad\qquad C(1) = P_3 \qquad (5-46c)$$

The key assumptions here are that for $r = 1/2$, $p(r) = P_2$ and for $s = 1/2$, $q(s) = P_3$. These are the assumptions made in Ref. 5–10. The result is a single member of a family of parabolically blended curves as shown below.

Using these assumptions in Eqs. (5–45) yields

$$
\begin{aligned}
@ \ P_2: & \quad r = 1/2, \ t = 0 & \Rightarrow \quad k_2 = 1/2 \\
@ \ P_3: & \quad r = 1, \ t = 1 & \Rightarrow \quad k_1 + k_2 = 1 & \quad \Rightarrow \quad k_1 = 1/2 \\
@ \ P_2: & \quad s = 0, \ t = 0 & \Rightarrow \quad k_4 = 0 \\
@ \ P_3: & \quad s = 1/2, \ t = 1 & \Rightarrow \quad k_3 = 1/2
\end{aligned}
$$

Thus,
$$r(t) = \frac{1}{2}(1+t) \qquad s(t) = \frac{1}{2}t \qquad\qquad (5-47)$$

Recalling Eq. (5–42) and using Eq. (5–46a) yields $[\,B\,]$ in terms of $P_1$, $P_2$, $P_3$. Specifically,

$$p(0) = P_1 = [\,0 \quad 0 \quad 1\,][\,B\,] \qquad\qquad (5-48a)$$
$$p(1/2) = P_2 = [\,1/4 \quad 1/2 \quad 1\,][\,B\,] \qquad\qquad (5-48b)$$
$$p(1) = P_3 = [\,1 \quad 1 \quad 1\,][\,B\,] \qquad\qquad (5-48c)$$

Rewriting as a single matrix gives

$$
\begin{bmatrix} P_1 \\ P_2 \\ P_3 \end{bmatrix} =
\begin{bmatrix} 0 & 0 & 1 \\ 1/4 & 1/2 & 1 \\ 1 & 1 & 1 \end{bmatrix} [\,B\,] = [\,M\,][\,B\,]
$$

Hence
$$
[\,B\,] = [\,M\,]^{-1}
\begin{bmatrix} P_1 \\ P_2 \\ P_3 \end{bmatrix} =
\begin{bmatrix} 2 & -4 & 2 \\ -3 & 4 & -1 \\ 1 & 0 & 0 \end{bmatrix}
\begin{bmatrix} P_1 \\ P_2 \\ P_3 \end{bmatrix} \qquad (5-49)
$$

$[\,D\,]$ is found in terms of $P_2$, $P_3$, $P_4$ in exactly an analogous manner. Hence using Eq. (5–46b)

$$q(0) = P_2 = [\,0 \quad 0 \quad 1\,][\,D\,] \qquad\qquad (5-50a)$$
$$q(1/2) = P_3 = [\,1/4 \quad 1/2 \quad 1\,][\,D\,] \qquad\qquad (5-50b)$$
$$q(1) = P_4 = [\,1 \quad 1 \quad 1\,][\,D\cdot] \qquad\qquad (5-50c)$$

Comparing with Eqs. (5–48) immediately yields

$$[D] = [M]^{-1} \begin{bmatrix} P_2 \\ P_3 \\ P_4 \end{bmatrix} = \begin{bmatrix} 2 & -4 & 2 \\ -3 & 4 & -1 \\ 1 & 0 & 0 \end{bmatrix} \begin{bmatrix} P_2 \\ P_3 \\ P_4 \end{bmatrix} \qquad (5-51)$$

Recalling Eq. (5–41) and substituting Eqs. (5–42) and (5–43) results in

$$C(t) = (1-t)[\, r^2 \quad r \quad 1\,][B] + t[\, s^2 \quad s \quad 1\,][D]$$

Using Eqs. (5–47) to rewrite this in terms of the parameter $t$ only gives

$$C(t) = [\, -\tfrac{1}{4}(t^3 + t^2 - t - 1) \quad -\tfrac{1}{2}(t^2 - 1) \quad 1-t\,][B] + \left[ \dfrac{t^3}{4} \quad \dfrac{t^2}{2} \quad t \right][D]$$

Substituting for $[B]$ and $[D]$ using Eqs. (5–49) and (5–51) yields

$$C(t) = \left[ -\dfrac{t^3}{2} + t^2 - \dfrac{t}{2} \quad t^3 - t^2 - t + 1 \quad -\dfrac{t^3}{2} + \dfrac{t}{2} \right] \begin{bmatrix} P_1 \\ P_2 \\ P_3 \end{bmatrix}$$

$$+ \left[ \dfrac{t^3}{2} - \dfrac{3}{2}t^2 + t \quad -t^3 + 2t^2 \quad \dfrac{t^3}{2} - \dfrac{t^2}{2} \right] \begin{bmatrix} P_2 \\ P_3 \\ P_4 \end{bmatrix}$$

Rewriting to include all four points $P_1$, $P_2$, $P_3$, $P_4$,

$$C(t) = \left[ -\dfrac{t^3}{2} + t^2 - \dfrac{t}{2} \quad t^3 - t^2 - t + 1 \quad -\dfrac{t^3}{2} + \dfrac{t}{2} \quad 0 \right] \begin{bmatrix} P_1 \\ P_2 \\ P_3 \\ P_4 \end{bmatrix}$$

$$+ \left[ 0 \quad \dfrac{t^3}{2} - \dfrac{3}{2}t^2 + t \quad -t^3 + 2t^2 \quad \dfrac{t^3}{2} - \dfrac{t^2}{2} \right] \begin{bmatrix} P_1 \\ P_2 \\ P_3 \\ P_4 \end{bmatrix}$$

Finally, rewriting this result in the form of Eq. (5–44) yields

$$C(t) = [\, t^3 \quad t^2 \quad t \quad 1\,][A][G] = [T][A][G] \qquad (5-44)$$

where

$$[A] = \left( \dfrac{1}{2} \right) \begin{bmatrix} -1 & 3 & -3 & 1 \\ 2 & -5 & 4 & -1 \\ -1 & 0 & 1 & 0 \\ 0 & 2 & 0 & 0 \end{bmatrix} \qquad (5-52)$$

and

$$[G]^T = [\, P_1 \quad P_2 \quad P_3 \quad P_4\,] \qquad (5-53)$$

Notice that again (see Sec. 5–3 and Eq. 5–22) the form of the result is given as a blending function matrix times a geometry matrix. The blending functions $[F] = [T][A]$ are shown in Fig. 5–20. The resulting algorithm is very simple to implement. An example illustrates the details.

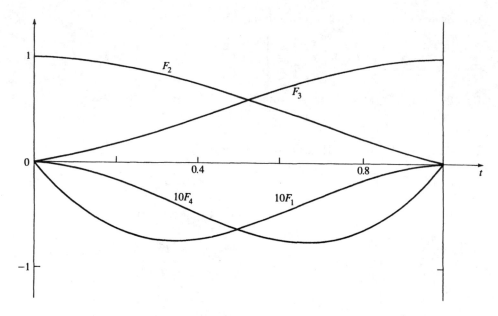

**Figure 5–20** Blending functions for parabolically blended curves $\alpha = \beta = 0.5$.

---

### Example 5–5    Parabolic Blending

Again consider the four two-dimensional position vectors $P_1 [\,0 \quad 0\,]$, $P_2 [\,1 \quad 1\,]$, $P_3 [\,2 \quad -1\,]$ and $P_4 [\,3 \quad 0\,]$ previously used in Exs. 5–2 and 5–3 (see Fig. 5–21). Determine the parabolically blended curve between $P_2$ and $P_3$. Calculate intermediate points at $t = 1/3$, 2/3.

Using Eqs. (5–44), (5–52) and (5–53) for $t = 1/3$ yields

$$C\left(\frac{1}{3}\right) = \left(\frac{1}{2}\right) \begin{bmatrix} \frac{1}{27} & \frac{1}{9} & \frac{1}{3} & 1 \end{bmatrix} \begin{bmatrix} -1 & 3 & -3 & 1 \\ 2 & -5 & 4 & -1 \\ -1 & 0 & 1 & 0 \\ 0 & 2 & 0 & 0 \end{bmatrix} \begin{bmatrix} 0 & 0 \\ 1 & 1 \\ 2 & -1 \\ 3 & 0 \end{bmatrix}$$

$$= \begin{bmatrix} \frac{4}{3} & \frac{4}{9} \end{bmatrix}$$

Similarly at $t = 2/3$, $C(2/3) = [\,5/3 \quad -4/9\,]$. The resulting curve is shown in Fig. 5–21.

---

## 5–7    GENERALIZED PARABOLIC BLENDING

The parabolically blended curve developed in Sec. 5–6 assumed a specific value of 1/2 for the parameters $r$ and $s$ at $P_2$ and $P_3$, respectively. If the position

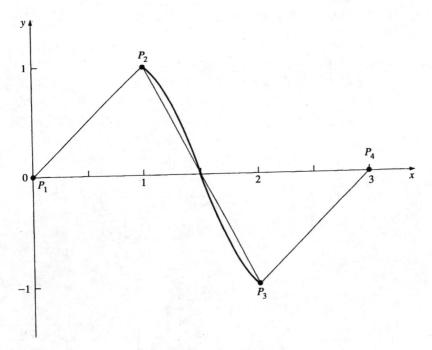

**Figure 5–21**    Parabolic blended curve for Ex. 5–5.

vectors (data) to be fit are not nearly evenly spaced, the smoothness or fairness of the resulting curve is decreased. A more reasonable assumption is to use a normalized chord length approximation. Thus, let

$$\alpha = \frac{||[\,P_2\,]-[\,P_1\,]||}{||[\,P_3\,]-[\,P_2\,]||+||[\,P_2\,]-[\,P_1\,]||} \qquad 0 < \alpha < 1 \qquad (5-54)$$

and

$$\beta = \frac{||[\,P_3\,]-[\,P_2\,]||}{||[\,P_4\,]-[\,P_3\,]||+||[\,P_3\,]-[\,P_2\,]||} \qquad 0 < \beta < 1 \qquad (5-55)$$

Then Eqs. (5–46) become

$$p(0) = P_1 \qquad p(\alpha) = P_2 \qquad p(1) = P_3 \qquad (5-56a)$$
$$q(0) = P_2 \qquad q(\beta) = P_3 \qquad q(1) = P_4 \qquad (5-56b)$$
$$C(0) = P_2 \qquad\qquad C(1) = P_3 \qquad (5-56c)$$

Using these assumptions the linear relations $r(t)$ and $s(t)$ (see Eq. 5–47) become

$$r(t) = (1-\alpha)t + \alpha \qquad s(t) = \beta t \qquad (5-57)$$

Proceeding to find $[\,B\,]$ by recalling Eq. (5–42) and now using Eq. (5–56a) yields

$$\begin{bmatrix} P_1 \\ P_2 \\ P_3 \end{bmatrix} = \begin{bmatrix} 0 & 0 & 1 \\ \alpha^2 & \alpha & 1 \\ 1 & 1 & 1 \end{bmatrix} [\,B\,] = [\,M\,][\,B\,]$$

Hence, here

$$[\,B\,] = [\,M\,]^{-1} \begin{bmatrix} P_1 \\ P_2 \\ P_3 \end{bmatrix} = \begin{bmatrix} \dfrac{1}{\alpha} & \dfrac{-1}{\alpha(1-\alpha)} & \dfrac{1}{1-\alpha} \\ \dfrac{-(1+\alpha)}{\alpha} & \dfrac{1}{\alpha(1-\alpha)} & \dfrac{-\alpha}{1-\alpha} \\ 1 & 0 & 0 \end{bmatrix} \begin{bmatrix} P_1 \\ P_2 \\ P_3 \end{bmatrix} \qquad (5-58)$$

Similarly,

$$[\,D\,] = \begin{bmatrix} \dfrac{1}{\beta} & \dfrac{-1}{\beta(1-\beta)} & \dfrac{1}{1-\beta} \\ \dfrac{-(1+\beta)}{\beta} & \dfrac{1}{\beta(1-\beta)} & \dfrac{-\beta}{1-\beta} \\ 1 & 0 & 0 \end{bmatrix} \begin{bmatrix} P_2 \\ P_3 \\ P_4 \end{bmatrix} \qquad (5-59)$$

Recalling Eq. (5–41) and substituting Eqs. (5–58) and (5–59) yields

$$C(t) = (1-t)\,[\,\{(1-\alpha)t+\alpha\}^2 \quad (1-\alpha)t+\alpha \quad 1\,] \quad \times$$

$$\begin{bmatrix} \dfrac{1}{\alpha} & \dfrac{-1}{\alpha(1-\alpha)} & \dfrac{1}{1-\alpha} \\ \dfrac{-(1+\alpha)}{\alpha} & \dfrac{1}{\alpha(1-\alpha)} & \dfrac{-\alpha}{1-\alpha} \\ 1 & 0 & 0 \end{bmatrix} \begin{bmatrix} P_1 \\ P_2 \\ P_3 \end{bmatrix}$$

$$+ \; t\,[\,(\beta t)^2 \quad \beta t \quad 1\,] \begin{bmatrix} \dfrac{1}{\beta} & \dfrac{-1}{\beta(1-\beta)} & \dfrac{1}{1-\beta} \\ \dfrac{-(1+\beta)}{\beta} & \dfrac{1}{\beta(1-\beta)} & \dfrac{-\beta}{1-\beta} \\ 1 & 0 & 0 \end{bmatrix} \begin{bmatrix} P_2 \\ P_3 \\ P_4 \end{bmatrix}$$

Following the procedure in the previous section this may be rewritten in matrix form as

$$C(t) = [\,t^3 \quad t^2 \quad t \quad 1\,][\,A\,][\,G\,] = [\,T\,][\,A\,][\,G\,] \qquad (5-44)$$

where here

$$[A] = \begin{bmatrix} \dfrac{-(1-\alpha)^2}{\alpha} & \dfrac{(1-\alpha)+\alpha\beta}{\alpha} & \dfrac{-(1-\alpha)-\alpha\beta}{1-\beta} & \dfrac{\beta^2}{1-\beta} \\[2mm] \dfrac{2(1-\alpha)^2}{\alpha} & \dfrac{-2(1-\alpha)-\alpha\beta}{\alpha} & \dfrac{2(1-\alpha)-\beta(1-2\alpha)}{(1-\beta)} & \dfrac{-\beta^2}{1-\beta} \\[2mm] \dfrac{-(1-\alpha)^2}{\alpha} & \dfrac{(1-2\alpha)}{\alpha} & \alpha & 0 \\[2mm] 0 & 1 & 0 & 0 \end{bmatrix}$$

$$(5-60)$$

and again $\qquad\qquad [G]^T = [\,P_1 \quad P_2 \quad P_3 \quad P_4\,] \qquad\qquad (5-53)$

$$F_1(t) = \frac{(1-\alpha)^2}{\alpha}(-t^3 + 2t^2 - t) \tag{5-61a}$$

$$F_2(t) = \frac{[(1-\alpha)+\alpha\beta]}{\alpha}t^3 + \frac{[-2(1-\alpha)-\alpha\beta]}{\alpha}t^2 + \frac{(1-2\alpha)}{\alpha}t + 1 \tag{5-61b}$$

$$F_3(t) = \frac{[-(1-\alpha)-\alpha\beta]}{1-\beta}t^3 + \frac{[2(1-\alpha)-\beta(1-2\alpha)]}{\alpha}t^2 + \alpha t \tag{5-61c}$$

$$F_4(t) = \frac{\beta^2}{1-\beta}(t^3 - t^2) \tag{5-61d}$$

Figure 5–22 shows the blending functions $F_i(t)$ for the special case of $\beta = 1 - \alpha$, which implies that the chord distance from $P_1$ to $P_2$ be equal to that from $P_3$ to $P_4$; i.e., $||\,P_2 - P_1\,|| = ||\,P_4 - P_3\,||$.
An example illustrates these results.

---

### Example 5–6   Generalized Parabolic Blending

Again consider the four two-dimensional position vectors $P_1[\,0 \quad 0\,]$, $P_2[\,1 \quad 1\,]$, $P_3[\,2 \quad -1\,]$ and $P_4[\,3 \quad 0\,]$ previously used in Exs. 5–2, 5–3 and 5–5 (see Fig. 5–22). Determine the parabolically blended curve between $P_2$ and $P_3$ using the generalized formulation. Calculate intermediate points at $t = 1/3$, $t = 2/3$.

First calculating $\alpha$ and $\beta$ using Eqs. (5–54) and (5–55).

$$c_{21} = ||\,[P_2\,] - [\,P_1\,]\,|| = \sqrt{(x_2 - x_1)^2 + (y_2 - y_1)^2}$$
$$= \sqrt{(1-0)^2 + (1-0)^2} = \sqrt{2}$$

$$c_{32} = ||\,[P_3\,] - [\,P_2\,]\,|| = \sqrt{(x_3 - x_2)^2 + (y_3 - y_2)^2}$$
$$= \sqrt{(2-1)^2 + (-1-1)^2} = \sqrt{5}$$

$$c_{43} = ||\,[P_4\,] - [\,P_3\,]\,|| = \sqrt{(x_4 - x_3)^2 + (y_4 - y_3)^2}$$
$$= \sqrt{(3-2)^2 + (0+1)^2} = \sqrt{2}$$

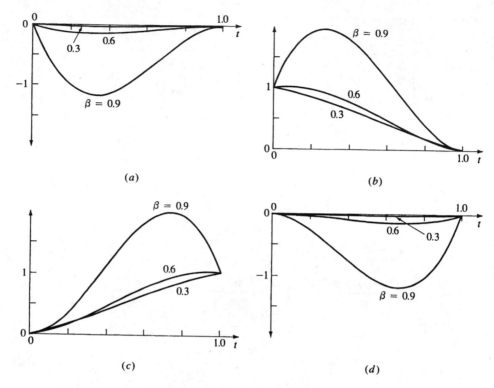

**Figure 5-22**    Generalized parabolic blending functions, $\alpha = 1 - \beta$. (a) $F_1$; (b) $F_2$; (c) $F_3$; (d) $F_4$.

Thus

$$\alpha = \frac{c_{21}}{c_{32} + c_{21}} = \frac{\sqrt{2}}{\sqrt{5} + \sqrt{2}} = 0.387$$

$$\beta = \frac{c_{32}}{c_{43} + c_{32}} = \frac{\sqrt{5}}{\sqrt{2} + \sqrt{5}} = 0.613$$

Note that here $\beta = 1 - \alpha$.
    From Eq. (5-60),

$$[A] = \begin{bmatrix} -0.969 & 2.194 & -2.194 & 0.969 \\ 1.937 & -3.775 & 2.806 & -0.969 \\ -0.969 & 0.581 & 0.387 & 0 \\ 0 & 1 & 0 & 0 \end{bmatrix}$$

and from Eq. (5-44),

$$C\left(\frac{1}{3}\right) = \begin{bmatrix} \frac{1}{27} & \frac{1}{9} & \frac{1}{3} & 1 \end{bmatrix} [A] \begin{bmatrix} 0 & 0 \\ 1 & 1 \\ 2 & -1 \\ 3 & 0 \end{bmatrix} = \begin{bmatrix} 1.360 & 0.496 \end{bmatrix}$$

Similarly at $t = 2/3$, $C(2/3) = [\ 1.640 \quad -0.496\ ]$. The resulting curve along with that from Ex. 5–5 is shown in Fig. 5–23. Note the additional fullness near the data points.

Figure 5–24 illustrates the local control exhibited by parabolically blended curves. Here there are 11 data points or position vectors and 9 parabolic blended segments. The center point has been moved to three positions. Notice that the influence of moving the point on the curve shape is limited to ±2 segments.

Although the results presented here are a generalization of those in Sec. 5–6, they are not the same as those originally derived by Overhauser in Ref. (5–9). A further generalization using the chord distance for the maximum parameter value is required to reproduce those results. The details are left to the problems (see Probs 5–10 and 5–11).

## 5–8    BÉZIER CURVES

The previously discussed techniques for curve generation constrained the curves to pass through *existing* data points; i.e., they are curve fitting techniques. In many cases excellent results are achieved with these methods. They are particularly suited to shape description, where the basic shape is arrived at by experimental evaluation or mathematical calculation. Examples are aircraft wings,

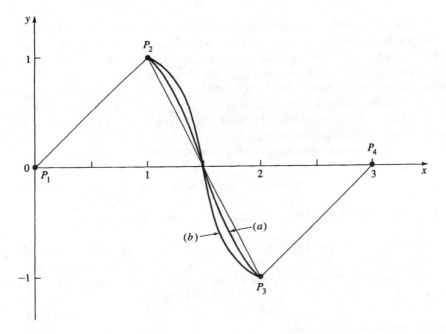

**Figure 5–23**    Comparison of results for parabolically blended curves. (a) Ex. 5–5, $\alpha = \beta = 1/2$; (b) Ex. 5–6, $\alpha = 1 - \beta$.

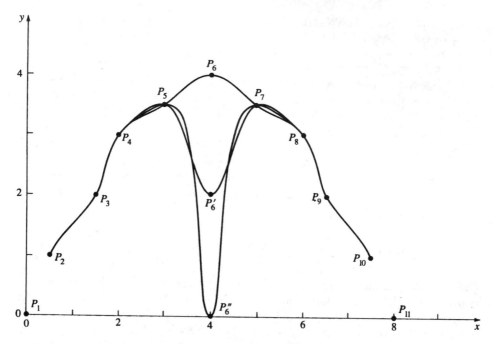

**Figure 5–24** Local control with parabolically blended curves.

engine manifolds, mechanical and/or structural parts. However, there is another class of shape design problems that depends on *both* aesthetic *and* functional requirements. These problems are frequently termed *ab initio* design. Examples are the 'skin' of car bodies, aircraft fuselages, ship hulls, furniture and glassware. *Ab initio* design problems cannot be formulated entirely in terms of quantitative criteria but must be resolved by a judicious combination of computational and heuristic methods. These methods are most effective when implemented in a real time interactive graphics environment.

The curve fitting techniques, e.g., the cubic spline fitting method previously discussed, are rendered ineffective for interactive *ab initio* design. Numerical specification of both direction and magnitude of tangent derivatives to control the shape does not provide the intuitive 'feel' required for *ab initio* design. An obvious relationship between the numbers and the curve shape does not always exist.

An alternate method of shape description suitable for *ab initio* design of free-form curves and surfaces was developed by Pierre Bézier. Although Bézier originally derived the mathematical basis of the technique from geometrical considerations (Refs. 5–11 to 5–13), Forrest (Ref. 5–14) and Gordon and Riesenfeld (Ref. 5–15) have shown that the result is equivalent to the Bernstein basis or polynomial approximation function.

A Bézier curve is determined by a defining polygon, e.g., that shown in Fig. 5–25. Because the Bézier basis is also the Bernstein basis, several properties

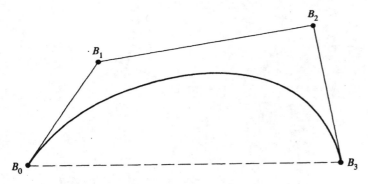

**Figure 5–25**   A Bézier curve and its defining polygon.

of Bézier curves are immediately known. For example:

The basis functions are real.

The degree of the polynomial defining the curve segment is one less than the number of defining polygon points.

The curve generally follows the shape of the defining polygon.

The first and last points on the curve are coincident with the first and last points of the defining polygon.

The tangent vectors at the ends of the curve have the same direction as the first and last polygon spans, respectively.

The curve is contained within the convex hull of the defining polygon, i.e., within the largest convex polygon defined by the polygon vertices. In Fig. 5–25, the convex hull is shown by the polygon and the dashed line.

The curve exhibits the variation diminishing property. Basically this means that the curve does not oscillate about any straight line more often than the defining polygon.

The curve is invariant under an affine transformation.

Several four-point Bézier polygons and the resulting cubic curves are shown in Fig. 5–26. With just the information given above a user quickly learns to predict the shape of a curve generated by a Bézier polygon.

Mathematically a parametric Bézier curve is defined by

$$P(t) = \sum_{i=0}^{n} B_i \, J_{n,i}(t) \qquad 0 \le t \le 1 \qquad (5-62)$$

where the Bézier or Bernstein basis or blending function is

$$J_{n,i}(t) = \binom{n}{i} t^i (1-t)^{n-i} \qquad (5-63)$$

with

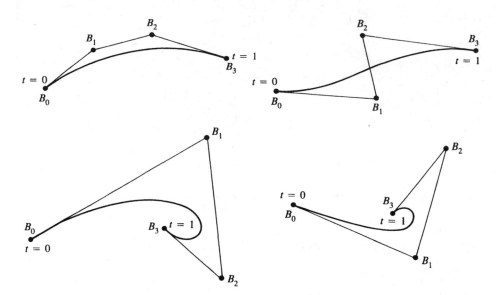

**Figure 5–26**   Bézier polygons for cubics.

$$\binom{n}{i} = \frac{n!}{i!\,(n-i)!} \qquad (5-64)$$

$J_{n,i}(t)$ is the $i$th $n$th-order Bernstein basis function. Here $n$, the degree of the defining Bernstein basis function and thus of the polynomial curve segment, is one less than the number of points in the defining Bézier polygon. The vertices of the Bézier polygon are numbered from 0 to $n$ as shown in Fig. 5–25.† Also $(0)^0 \equiv 1$ and $0! \equiv 1$.

Figure 5–27 shows the blending functions for several values of $n$. Notice the symmetry of the functions. Each of the blending functions is of degree $n$. For

---

†This notation and polygon numbering scheme is chosen to be consistent with the vast body of existing literature on Bézier curves and Bernstein basis functions. For programming purposes an alternate formulation is somewhat more convenient, i.e.,

$$P(t) = \sum_{I=1}^{N} B_I J_{N,I}(t)$$

where

$$J_{N,I} = \binom{N-1}{I-1} t^{I-1} (1-t)^{N-I}$$

and

$$\binom{N-1}{I-1} = \frac{(N-1)!}{(I-1)!\,(N-I)!}$$

The polygon points are numbered from 1 to $N$. The transformations $n = N - 1$ and $i = I - 1$ convert between the two notations.

example, each of the four blending functions shown in Fig. 5–27b for $n = 3$ is a cubic. The maximum value of each blending function occurs at $t = i/n$ and is given in Ref. 5–14 by

$$J_{n,i}\left(\frac{i}{n}\right) = \binom{n}{i}\frac{i^i(n-i)^{n-i}}{n^n} \qquad (5-65)$$

For example, for a cubic $n = 3$. The maximum values for $J_{3,1}$ and $J_{3,2}$ occur at $1/3$ and $2/3$, respectively, with values

$$J_{3,1}\left(\frac{1}{3}\right) = \frac{4}{9} \qquad \text{and} \qquad J_{3,2}\left(\frac{2}{3}\right) = \frac{4}{9}$$

Figure 5–27b illustrates this result.

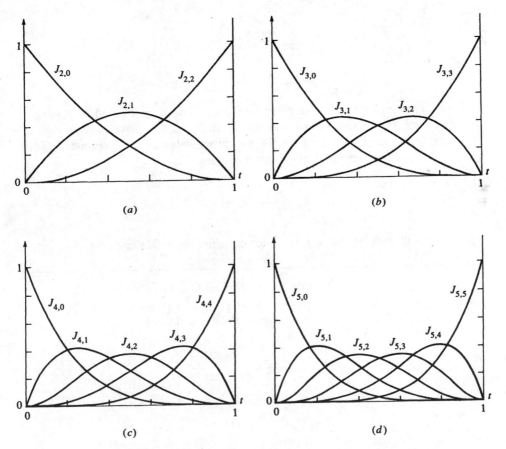

(a)

(b)

(c)

(d)

**Figure 5–27**  Bézier/Bernstein blending functions. (a) Three polygon points, $n = 2$; (b) four polygon points, $n = 3$; (c) five polygon points, $n = 4$; (d) six polygon points, $n = 5$.

Examining Eqs. (5–62) to (5–64) for the first point on the curve, i.e., at $t = 0$, shows that

$$J_{n,0}(0) = \frac{n! \ (1)(1-0)^{n-0}}{n!} = 1 \qquad i = 0$$

and

$$J_{n,i}(0) = \frac{n! \ (0)^i(1-0)^{n-i}}{i! \ (n-i)!} = 0 \qquad i \neq 0$$

Thus, $\qquad\qquad P(0) = B_0 J_{n,0}(0) = B_0$

and the first point on the Bézier curve and on its defining polygon are coincident as previously claimed.

Similarly, for the last point on the curve, i.e., at $t = 1$,

$$J_{n,n}(1) = \frac{n! \ (1)^n(0)^{n-n}}{n! \ (1)} = 1 \qquad i = n$$

$$J_{n,i}(1) = \frac{n!}{i! \ (n-i)!} t^i(1-1)^{n-i} = 0 \qquad i \neq n$$

Thus, $\qquad\qquad P(1) = B_n J_{n,n}(1) = B_n$

and the last point on the Bézier curve and the last point on its defining polygon are coincident. The blending functions shown in Fig. 5–27 illustrate these results.

Further, it can be shown that for any given value of the parameter $t$, the summation of the basis functions is precisely one; i.e.,

$$\sum_{i=0}^{n} J_{n,i}(t) = 1 \qquad\qquad (5-66)$$

An example illustrates the technique for determining a Bézier curve.

---

### Example 5–7  Bézier Curve

Given $B_0 [ 1 \quad 1 ]$, $B_1 [ 2 \quad 3 ]$, $B_2 [ 4 \quad 3 ]$ and $B_3 [ 3 \quad 1 ]$ the vertices of a Bézier polygon (see Fig. 5–28), determine seven points on the Bézier curve.

Recall Eqs. (5–62) to (5–64):

$$P(t) = \sum_{i=0}^{n} B_i J_{n,i}(t)$$

where

$$J_{n,i}(t) = \binom{n}{i} t^i(1-t)^{n-i}$$

and

$$\binom{n}{i} = \frac{n!}{i! \ (n-i)!}$$

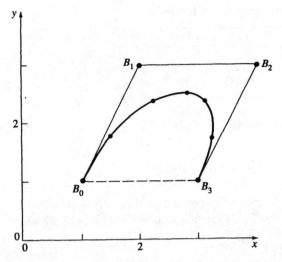

**Figure 5–28**   Results for Bézier curve segment for Ex. 5–7.

Here $n = 3$, since there are four vertices. Hence

$$\binom{n}{i} = \binom{3}{i} = \frac{6}{i!\,(3-i)!}$$

and
$$J_{3,0}(t) = (1)t^0(1-t)^3 = (1-t)^3$$
$$J_{3,1}(t) = 3t(1-t)^2$$
$$J_{3,2}(t) = 3t^2(1-t)$$
$$J_{3,3}(t) = t^3$$

Thus,      $P(t) = B_0 J_{3,0} + B_1 J_{3,1} + B_2 J_{3,2} + B_3 J_{3,3}$
$$= (1-t)^3 P_0 + 3t(1-t)^2 P_1 + 3t^2(1-t)P_2 + t^3 P_3$$

A table of $J_{n,i}$ for various values of $t$ is given below.
The points on the curve are then

$$P(0) = B_0 = [\,1 \quad 1\,]$$
$$P(0.15) = 0.614 B_0 + 0.325 B_1 + 0.058 B_2 + 0.003 B_3 = [\,1.5 \quad 1.765\,]$$
$$P(0.35) = 0.275 B_0 + 0.444 B_1 + 0.239 B_2 + 0.042 B_3 = [\,2.248 \quad 2.367\,]$$
$$P(0.5) = 0.125 B_0 + 0.375 B_1 + 0.375 B_2 + 0.125 B_3 = [\,2.75 \quad 2.5\,]$$
$$P(0.65) = 0.042 B_0 + 0.239 B_1 + 0.444 B_2 + 0.275 B_3 = [\,3.122 \quad 2.367\,]$$
$$P(0.85) = 0.003 B_0 + 0.058 B_1 + 0.325 B_2 + 0.614 B_3 = [\,3.248 \quad 1.765\,]$$
$$P(1) = B_3 = [\,3 \quad 1\,]$$

**Table 5-4 Coefficients for a Bézier curve**

| $t$ | $J_{3,0}$ | $J_{3,1}$ | $J_{3,2}$ | $J_{3,3}$ |
|------|-----------|-----------|-----------|-----------|
| 0 | 1 | 0 | 0 | 0 |
| 0.15 | 0.614 | 0.325 | 0.058 | 0.003 |
| 0.35 | 0.275 | 0.444 | 0.239 | 0.042 |
| 0.5 | 0.125 | 0.375 | 0.375 | 0.125 |
| 0.65 | 0.042 | 0.239 | 0.444 | 0.275 |
| 0.85 | 0.003 | 0.058 | 0.325 | 0.614 |
| 1 | 0 | 0 | 0 | 1 |

These points are shown along with the defining polygon in Fig. 5–28.

---

The equation for a Bézier curve can be expressed in a matrix form similar to those for cubic splines and parabolically blended curves (see Eqs. 5–27 and 5–44), i.e., as

$$P(t) = [\,T\,][\,N\,][\,G\,] = [\,F\,][\,G\,] \tag{5–67}$$

Here $[\,F\,] = [\,J_{n,0} \quad J_{n,1} \quad \cdots \quad J_{n,n}\,]$ and $[\,G\,]^T = [\,B_0 \quad B_1 \quad \cdots \quad B_n\,]$.

The specific matrix forms for low values of $n$ are of interest. For four defining polygon points ($n = 3$), the cubic Bézier curve is given by

$$P(t) = [\,(1-t)^3 \quad 3t(1-t)^2 \quad 3t^2(1-t) \quad t^3\,]\begin{bmatrix} B_o \\ B_1 \\ B_2 \\ B_3 \end{bmatrix}$$

Collecting the coefficients of the parameter terms allows rewriting this as

$$P(t) = [\,T\,][\,N\,][\,G\,] = [\,t^3 \quad t^2 \quad t \quad 1\,]\begin{bmatrix} -1 & 3 & -3 & 1 \\ 3 & -6 & 3 & 0 \\ -3 & 3 & 0 & 0 \\ 1 & 0 & 0 & 0 \end{bmatrix}\begin{bmatrix} B_o \\ B_1 \\ B_2 \\ B_3 \end{bmatrix} \tag{5–68}$$

Similarly, the quartic ($n = 4$) Bézier curve corresponding to five Bézier polygon points is

$$P(t) = [\,t^4 \quad t^3 \quad t^2 \quad t \quad 1\,]\begin{bmatrix} 1 & -4 & 6 & -4 & 1 \\ -4 & 12 & -12 & 4 & 0 \\ 6 & -12 & 6 & 0 & 0 \\ -4 & 4 & 0 & 0 & 0 \\ 1 & 0 & 0 & 0 & 0 \end{bmatrix}\begin{bmatrix} B_o \\ B_1 \\ B_2 \\ B_3 \\ B_4 \end{bmatrix} \tag{5–69}$$

Cohen and Riesenfeld (Ref. 5–19) have generalized this representation to

$$P(t) = [\,T\,][\,N\,][\,G\,]$$

where here

$$[T] = [\, t^n \quad t^{n-1} \quad \cdots \quad t \quad 1 \,]$$

$$[N] = \begin{bmatrix} \binom{n}{0}\binom{n}{n}(-1)^n & \binom{n}{1}\binom{n-1}{n-1}(-1)^{n-1} & \cdots & \binom{n}{n}\binom{n-n}{n-n}(-1)^0 \\ \binom{n}{0}\binom{n}{n-1}(-1)^{n-1} & \binom{n}{1}\binom{n-1}{n-2}(-1)^{n-2} & \cdots & 0 \\ \vdots & \vdots & \vdots & \vdots \\ \binom{n}{0}\binom{n}{1}(-1)^1 & \binom{n}{1}\binom{n-1}{0}(-1)^0 & \cdots & 0 \\ \binom{n}{0}\binom{n}{0}(-1)^0 & 0 & \cdots & 0 \end{bmatrix}$$

$$(5-70)$$

$[G]^T$ is again $[\, B_0 \quad B_1 \quad \cdots \quad B_n \,]$. The individual terms in $[N]$ are given by

$$(N_{i+1,j+1})_{i,j=0}^n = \begin{cases} \binom{n}{j}\binom{n-j}{n-i-j}(-1)^{n-i-j} & 0 \le i+j \le n \\ 0 & \text{otherwise} \end{cases}$$

Equation (5–70) can be decomposed into a sometimes more convenient form,

$$[N] = [C][D] \qquad\qquad (5-71)$$

where

$$[C] = \begin{bmatrix} \binom{n}{n}(-1)^n & \binom{n}{1}\binom{n-1}{n-1}(-1)^{n-1} & \cdots & \binom{n}{n}\binom{n-n}{n-n}(-1)^0 \\ \binom{n}{n-1}(-1)^{n-1} & \binom{n}{1}\binom{n-1}{n-2}(-1)^{n-2} & & 0 \\ \vdots & \vdots & \ddots & \vdots \\ \binom{n}{1}(-1)^1 & \binom{n}{1}\binom{n-1}{0}(-1)^0 & & 0 \\ \binom{n}{0}(-1)^0 & 0 & \cdots & 0 \end{bmatrix}$$

$$[D] = \begin{bmatrix} \binom{n}{0} & & \cdots & 0 \\ \vdots & \binom{n}{1} & & \vdots \\ \vdots & & \ddots & \vdots \\ 0 & \cdots & & \binom{n}{n} \end{bmatrix}$$

Equation (5–70) or (5–71) is more convenient to evaluate for arbitrary values of $n$. Notice that for each value of $n$ the matrix $[\,N\,]$ is symmetrical about the main diagonal and that the lower right triangular corner is all zeros.

Although it is not necessary to numerically specify the tangent vectors at the ends of an individual Bézier curve, maintaining slope and curvature continuity when joining Bézier curves, determining surface normals for lighting or numerical control tool path calculation, or local curvature for smoothness or fairness calculations requires a knowledge of both the first and second derivatives of a Bézier curve.

Recalling Eq. (5–62), the first derivative of a Bézier curve is

$$P'(t) = \sum_{i=0}^{n} B_i J'_{n,i}(t) \qquad (5-72)$$

The second derivative is given by

$$P''(t) = \sum_{i=0}^{n} B_i J''_{n,i}(t) \qquad (5-73)$$

The derivatives of the basis function are obtained by formally differentiating Eq. (5–63). Specifically,

$$
\begin{aligned}
J'_{n,i}(t) &= \binom{n}{i} \{i\, t^{i-1}(1-t)^{n-i} - (n-i)t^i(1-t)^{n-i-1}\} \\
&= \binom{n}{i} t^i(1-t)^{n-i}\left\{\frac{i}{t} - \frac{(n-i)}{(1-t)}\right\} \\
&= \frac{(i-nt)}{t(1-t)} J_{n,i}(t)
\end{aligned}
\qquad (5-74)
$$

Similarly the second derivative is

$$J''_{n,i}(t) = \left\{\frac{(i-nt)^2 - nt^2 - i(1-2t)}{t^2(1-t)^2}\right\} J_{n,i}(t) \qquad (5-75)$$

At the beginning and the ends of a Bézier curve, i.e., at $t = 0$ and $t = 1$, *numerical* evaluation of Eqs. (5–74) and (5–75) creates difficulties.[†]

An alternate evaluation for the $r$th derivative at $t = 0$ is given by

$$P^r(0) = \frac{n!}{(n-r)!} \sum_{i=0}^{r} (-1)^{r-i} \binom{r}{i} B_i \qquad (5-76)$$

---

[†]Algebraic evaluation of $J_{n,i}(t)$ and substitution *before* numerical evaluation yields correct results (see Ex. 5–8).

and at $t = 1$ by

$$P^r(1) = \frac{n!}{(n-r)!} \sum_{i=0}^{r} (-1)^i \binom{r}{i} B_{n-i} \qquad (5-77)$$

Thus, the first derivatives at the ends are

$$P'(0) = n(B_1 - B_0) \qquad (5-78)$$

and

$$P'(1) = n(B_n - B_{n-1}) \qquad (5-79)$$

This illustrates that the tangent vector for a Bézier curve at the initial and final points has the same direction as the initial and final polygon spans.

Similarly the second derivatives at the ends are

$$P''(0) = n(n-1)(B_0 - 2B_1 + B_2) \qquad (5-80a)$$

and

$$P''(1) = n(n-1)(B_n - 2B_{n-1} + B_{n-2}) \qquad (5-80b)$$

Thus, the second derivative of the Bézier curve at the initial and final points depends on the two nearest polygon spans, i.e., on the nearest three polygon vertices. In general, the $r$th derivative at an end point or starting point is determined by the end or starting point and its $r$ neighboring polygon vertices. An example provides a more explicit illustration.

---

### Example 5–8    Derivatives of Bézier Curves

Consider a four-point Bézier polygon as shown, for example, in Figs. 5–26 and 5–28. Recall that the Bézier curve is given by

$$P(t) = B_0 J_{3,0}(t) + B_1 J_{3,1}(t) + B_2 J_{3,2}(t) + B_3 J_{3,3}(t)$$

Hence the first derivative is

$$P(t) = B_0 J'_{3,0}(t) + B_1 J'_{3,1}(t) + B_2 J'_{3,2}(t) + B_3 J'_{3,3}(t)$$

Recalling Ex. 5–7 and differentiating the basis functions directly yields

$$
\begin{aligned}
J_{3,0}(t) &= (1-t)^3 & \Rightarrow && J'_{3,0}(t) &= -3(1-t)^2 \\
J_{3,1}(t) &= 3t(1-t)^2 & \Rightarrow && J'_{3,1}(t) &= 3(1-t)^2 - 6t(1-t) \\
J_{3,2}(t) &= 3t^2(1-t) & \Rightarrow && J'_{3,2}(t) &= 6t(1-t) - 3t^2 \\
J_{3,3}(t) &= t^3 & \Rightarrow && J'_{3,3}(t) &= 3t^2
\end{aligned}
$$

Evaluating these results at $t = 0$ yields

$$J'_{3,0}(0) = -3 \qquad J'_{3,1}(0) = 3 \qquad J'_{3,2}(0) = 0 \qquad J'_{3,3}(0) = 0$$

Substituting yields

$$P'(0) = -3P_0 + 3P_1 = 3(P_1 - P_0)$$

Thus, the direction of the tangent vector at the beginning of the curve is the same as that of the first polygon span (see Fig. 5–28).

At the end of the curve, $t = 1$ and

$$J'_{3,0}(1) = 0 \qquad J'_{3,1}(1) = 0 \qquad J'_{3,2}(1) = -3 \qquad J'_{3,3}(1) = 3$$

Substituting yields

$$P'(1) = -3P_2 + 3P_3 = 3(P_3 - P_2)$$

Thus, the direction of the tangent vector at the end of the curve is the same as that of the last polygon span.

The basis functions given above along with Eqs. (5–74) and (5–75) can be used to evaluate the derivatives along the curve. Specifically, the first derivatives are

$$J'_{3,0}(t) = \frac{(0 - 3t)}{t(1 - t)}(1 - t)^3 = -3(1 - t)^2$$

$$J'_{3,1}(t) = \frac{(1 - 3t)}{t(1 - t)}(3t)(1 - t)^2 = 3(1 - 3t)(1 - t) = 3(1 - 4t + 3t^2)$$

$$J'_{3,2}(t) = \frac{(2 - 3t)}{t(1 - t)}(3t^2)(1 - t) = 3t(2 - 3t)$$

$$J'_{3,3}(t) = \frac{3(1 - t)}{t(1 - t)}t^3 = 3t^2$$

Notice that there is no difficulty in evaluating these results at either $t = 0$ or $t = 1$. Substituting into Eq. (5–72) yields the first derivative at any point on the curve. For example, at $t = 1/2$,

$$P'\left(\frac{1}{2}\right) = -3\left(1 - \frac{1}{2}\right)^2 B_0 + 3\left(1 - \frac{3}{2}\right)\left(1 - \frac{1}{2}\right)B_1 + \left(\frac{3}{2}\right)\left(2 - \frac{3}{2}\right)B_2 + \frac{3}{4}B_3$$

$$= -\frac{3}{4}B_0 - \frac{3}{4}B_1 + \frac{3}{4}B_2 + \frac{3}{4}B_3 = -\frac{3}{4}(B_0 + B_1 - B_2 - B_3)$$

Complete results for $B_0$, $B_1$, $B_2$, $B_3$ given in Ex. 5–7 are shown in Fig. 5–29. Similarly, the second derivatives are

$$J''_{3,0}(t) = \frac{\{(-3t)^2 - 3t^2\}}{t^2(1 - t)^2}(1 - t)^3 = 6(1 - t)$$

$$J''_{3,1}(t) = \frac{\{(1 - 3t)^2 - 3t^2 - (1 - 2t)\}}{t^2(1 - t)^2}(3t)(1 - t)^2 = -6(2 - 3t)$$

$$J''_{3,2}(t) = \frac{\{(2 - 3t)^2 - 3t^2 - 2(1 - 2t)\}}{t^2(1 - t)^2}(3t^2)(1 - t) = 6(1 - 3t)$$

$$J''_{3,3}(t) = \frac{\{(3 - 3t)^2 - 3t^2 - 3(1 - 2t)\}}{t^2(1 - t)^2}t^3 = 6t$$

Using Eq. (3–73) for $t = 1/2$, these results yield

$$P''\left(\frac{1}{2}\right) = 6\left(1 - \frac{1}{2}\right)B_0 - 6\left(2 - \frac{3}{2}\right)B_1 + 6\left(1 - \frac{3}{2}\right)B_2 + 3B_3$$

$$= 3B_0 - 3B_1 - 3B_2 + 3B_3 = 3(B_0 - B_1 - B_2 + B_3)$$

Complete results for $(B_0, B_1, B_2, B_3)$ given in Ex. 5–7 are also shown in Fig. 5–29. Notice that a vector from the origin to any point on each of these curves represents the direction and magnitude of the position, tangent and approximate curvature, respectively, of that point on the curve.

---

Continuity conditions between adjacent Bézier curves are simply specified. If one Bézier curve $P(t)$ of degree $n$ is defined by vertices $B_i$ and an adjacent Bézier curve $Q(s)$ of degree $m$ by vertices $C_i$, then first-derivative continuity at the joint between the curves is given by

$$P'(1) = gQ'(0)$$

where $g$ is a scalar. Using Eqs. (5–78) and (5–79) yields

$$C_1 - C_0 = \frac{n}{m}(B_n - B_{n-1})$$

Since positional continuity is implied at the joint, $C_0 = B_n$ and

$$C_1 = \frac{n}{m}(B_n - B_{n-1}) + B_n$$

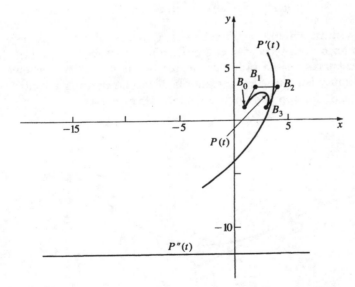

Figure 5–29    Bézier curve and its derivatives. (a) $P(t)$; (b) $P'(t)$; (c) $P''(t)$.

Thus, the tangent vector directions at the joint are the same if the three vertices $B_{n-1}$, $B_n = C_0$, $C_1$ are colinear; i.e., $B_n$ need only lie somewhere on the line between $B_{n-1}$ and $C_1$. If both direction *and* magnitude of the tangent vectors at the joint are to be equal, then, for equal degree curves ($n = m$), $B_n = C_0$ must be the midpoint of the line joining $B_{n-1}$ and $C_1$, i.e.,

$$C_1 - C_0 = B_n - B_{n-1} = C_0 - B_{n-1}$$

or
$$C_1 + B_{n-1} = 2C_0 = 2B_n$$

Figure 5–30 illustrates this for $n = m = 3$, i.e., for two cubic Bézier curves. Second-derivative continuity between adjacent Bézier curves is given by

$$m(m-1)(C_0 - 2C_1 + C_2) = n(n-1)(B_{n-2} - 2B_{n-1} + B_n)$$

Using the conditions for $C^0$ and $C^1$ continuity at the joint given above yields

$$C_2 = \frac{n(n-1)}{m(m-1)}B_{n-2} - 2\left\{\frac{n(n-1)}{m(m-1)} + \frac{n}{m}\right\}B_{n-1} + \left\{1 + 2\frac{n}{m} + \frac{n(n-1)}{m(m-1)}\right\}B_n$$

the position of the third defining vertex in the second defining polygon in terms of the last three defining vertices in the first defining polygon. This result shows that the polygon vertices $B_{n-2}$, $B_{n-1}$, $B_n = C_0$, $C_1$, $C_2$ must either form a convex polygon or be colinear to maintain $C^2$ continuity across the joint. For cubic Bézier curves ($n = m = 3$) this result reduces to

$$C_2 = B_{n-1} - 4(B_{n-1} - B_n)$$

A few minutes' work with pencil and paper shows that this requirement places significant restrictions on overall piecewise curve design. Consequently, practical design using Bézier curves results in higher degree polynomial curves when second-derivative continuity is required. An example of second-derivative continuity is shown in Fig. 5–31 for two five point adjacent Bézier curves.

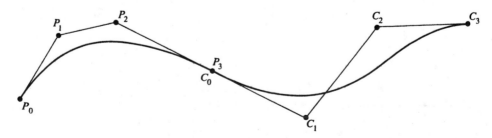

**Figure 5–30**    First-derivative continuity between cubic Bézier curves.

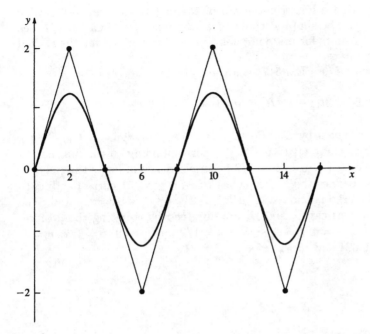

**Figure 5–31**    Second-derivative continuity between quartic Bézier curves.

If a Bézier curve with additional flexibility is required, the degree of the defining polynomial can be increased by increasing the number of defining polygon points. For every point on a Bézier curve with $n$ defining polygon vertices $B_0, \cdots, B_n$ the same point on a new Bézier curve with $n + 1$ defining polygon vertices $B_0^*, \cdots, B_{n+1}^*$ is given by

$$P(t) = \sum_{i=0}^{n} B_i J_{n,i}(t) = \sum_{i=0}^{n+1} B_i^* J_{n+1,i}(t) \qquad (5-81)$$

where     $B_0^* = B_0$

$$B_i^* = \alpha_i B_{i-1} + (1 - \alpha_i) B_i \qquad \alpha_i = \frac{i}{n+1} \qquad i = 1, \cdots, n$$

$B_{n+1}^* = B_n$

This technique, given in Ref. 5–14, can be applied successively. In the limit the polygon converges to the curve. Additional flexibility can also be obtained by subdividing a Bézier curve into two new Bézier curves that, combined, are identical with the original curve. The task is to determine the defining polygons for the two new curves in terms of those for the original curve. Barsky (Refs. 5–16 and 5–18) has shown that a Bézier curve can be divided at any parameter value in the range $0 \leq t \leq 1$. The simplest choice is at the midpoint, i.e., $t = 1/2$ (see Ref. 5–18). Here the results for midpoint subdivision are derived for the special case of cubic Bézier curves.

A cubic Bézier curve (see Ex. 5–7) is given by

$$P(t) = (1 - t)^3 B_0 + 3t(1 - t)^2 B_1 + 3t^2(1 - t)B_2 + t^3 B_3 \qquad 0 \leq t \leq 1$$

with defining polygon given by $B_0$, $B_1$, $B_2$, $B_3$. The polygon $C_0$, $C_1$, $C_2$, $C_3$ then defines the Bézier curve $Q(u)$, $0 \leq u \leq 1$ corresponding to the first half of the original curve; i.e., $P(t)$, $0 \leq t \leq 1/2$ is required . Similarly, the polygon $D_0$, $D_1$, $D_2$, $D_3$ that defines the Bézier curve $R(v)$, $0 \leq v \leq 1$ corresponding to the second half of the original curve; i.e., $P(t)$, $1/2 \leq t \leq 1$ is also required. The new defining polygon vertices $C_i$ and $D_i$ are obtained by equating the position and tangent vectors at $u = 0$, $t = 0$; $u = 1$, $t = 1/2$ and $v = 0$, $t = 1/2$; $v = 1$, $t = 1$. Using Eqs. (5–62) and (5–72) yields

$$C_0 = B_0$$

$$3(C_1 - C_0) = \frac{3}{2}(B_1 - B_0)$$

$$3(C_3 - C_2) = \frac{3}{8}(B_3 + B_2 - B_1 - B_0)$$

$$C_3 = \frac{1}{8}(B_3 + 3B_2 + 3B_1 + B_0)$$

Solution of these equations gives

$$C_0 = B_0$$

$$C_1 = \frac{1}{2}(B_1 + B_0)$$

$$C_2 = \frac{1}{4}(B_2 + 2B_1 + B_0)$$

$$C_3 = \frac{1}{8}(B_3 + 3B_2 + 3B_1 + B_0)$$

Similarly,

$$D_0 = \frac{1}{8}(B_3 + 3B_2 + 3B_1 + B_0)$$

$$D_1 = \frac{1}{4}(B_3 + 2B_2 + B_1)$$

$$D_2 = \frac{1}{2}(B_3 + B_2)$$

$$D_3 = B_3$$

These results generalize to

$$C_i = \sum_{j=0}^{i} \binom{i}{j} \frac{B_j}{2^i} \qquad i = 0, 1, \cdots, n \qquad\qquad (5 - 82a)$$

$$D_i = \sum_{j=i}^{n} \binom{n - i}{n - j} \frac{B_j}{2^{n-i}} \qquad i = 0, 1, \cdots, n \qquad\qquad (5 - 82b)$$

Applied successively, the defining polygons converge to the Bézier curve itself.

## 5–9   B-SPLINE CURVES

From a mathematical point of view, a curve generated by using the vertices of a defining polygon is dependent on some interpolation or approximation scheme to establish the relationship between the curve and the polygon. This scheme is provided by the choice of basis function. As noted in Sec. 5–8, the Bernstein basis produces Bézier curves generated by Eq. (5–62). Two characteristics of the Bernstein basis, however, limit the flexibility of the resulting curves. First the number of specified polygon vertices fixes the order of the resulting polynomial which defines the curve. For example, a cubic curve must be defined by a polygon with four vertices and three spans. A polygon with six vertices always produces a fifth-degree curve. The only way to reduce the degree of the curve is to reduce the number of vertices, and conversely the only way to increase the degree of the curve is to increase the number of vertices.

The second limiting characteristic is due to the global nature of the Bernstein basis. This means that the value of the blending function $J_{n,i}(t)$ given by Eq. (5–63) is nonzero for all parameter values over the entire curve. Since any point on a Bézier curve is a result of blending the values of all defining vertices, a change in one vertex is felt throughout the entire curve. This eliminates the ability to produce a local change within a curve.

For example, since the end slopes of a Bézier curve are established by the directions of the first and last polygon spans, it is possible to change the middle vertex of a five-point polygon without changing the *direction* of the end slopes. However, the shape of the total curve is affected due to the global nature of the Bernstein basis. This lack of local control is detrimental in some applications.

There is another basis, called the B-spline basis (from Basis spline), which contains the Bernstein basis as a special case. This basis is generally nonglobal. The nonglobal behavior of B-spline curves is due to the fact that each vertex $B_i$ is associated with a unique basis function. Thus, each vertex affects the shape of a curve only over a range of parameter values where its associated basis function is nonzero. The B-spline basis also allows the order of the basis function and hence the degree of the resulting curve to be changed without changing the number of defining polygon vertices. The theory for B-splines was first suggested by Schoenberg (Ref. 5–20). A recursive definition useful for numerical computation was independently discovered by Cox (Ref. 5–21) and by de Boor (Ref. 5–22). Gordon and Riesenfeld (Refs. 5–15 and 5–23) applied the B-spline basis to curve definition.

Again letting $P(t)$ be the position vectors along the curve as a function of the parameter $t$, a B-spline curve is given by

$$P(t) = \sum_{i=1}^{n+1} B_i N_{i,k}(t) \qquad t_{min} \le t < t_{max}, \quad 2 \le k \le n+1 \qquad (5-83)$$

where the $B_i$ are the position vectors of the $n+1$ defining polygon vertices and the $N_{i,k}$ are the normalized B-spline basis functions.

For the $i$th normalized B-spline basis function of order $k$ (degree $k-1$), the basis functions $N_{i,k}(t)$ are defined by the Cox-deBoor recursion formulas. Specifically,

$$N_{i,1}(t) = \begin{cases} 1 & \text{if } x_i \le t < x_{i+1} \\ 0 & \text{otherwise} \end{cases} \qquad (5-84a)$$

and

$$N_{i,k}(t) = \frac{(t - x_i)N_{i,k-1}(t)}{x_{i+k-1} - x_i} + \frac{(x_{i+k} - t)N_{i+1,k-1}(t)}{x_{i+k} - x_{i+1}} \qquad (5-84b)$$

The values of $x_i$ are elements of a knot vector satisfying the relation $x_i \le x_{i+1}$. The parameter $t$ varies from $t_{min}$ to $t_{max}$ along the curve $P(t)$.[†] The convention $0/0 = 0$ is adopted.

Formally a B-spline curve is defined as a polynomial spline function of order $k$ (degree $k-1$) since it satisfies the following two conditions:

The function $P(t)$ is a polynomial of degree $k-1$ on each interval $x_i \le t < x_{i+1}$.

$P(t)$ and its derivatives of order $1, 2, \cdots, k-2$ are all continuous over the entire curve.

Thus, for example, a fourth-order B-spline curve is a piecewise cubic curve.

Because a B-spline basis is used to describe a B-spline curve, several properties in addition to those already mentioned above are immediately known:

The sum of the B-spline basis functions for any parameter value $t$ can be shown (see Refs. 5–15 and 5–22) to be

$$\sum_{i=1}^{n+1} N_{i,k}(t) \equiv 1 \qquad (5-85)$$

Each basis function is positive or zero for all parameter values, i.e., $N_{i,k} \ge 0$.

Except for $k = 1$ each basis function has precisely one maximum value.

---

[†] Here note that, in contrast to the Bézier curve, the defining polygon vertices or points are numbered from 1 to $n+1$.

The maximum order of the curve is equal to the number of defining polygon vertices.

The curve exhibits the variation diminishing property. Thus the curve does not oscillate about any straight line more often than its defining polygon.

The curve generally follows the shape of the defining polygon.

Any affine transformation can be applied to the curve by applying it to the defining polygon vertices; i.e., the curve is transformed by transforming the defining polygon vertices.

The curve lies within the convex hull of its defining polygon.

In fact, the convex hull property of B-spline curves is stronger than that for Bézier curves. For a B-spline curve of order $k$ (degree $k - 1$) a point on the curve lies within the convex hull of $k$ neighboring points. Thus, all points on a B-spline curve must lie within the union of *all* such convex hulls formed by taking $k$ successive defining polygon vertices. Figure 5–32, where the convex hulls are shown shaded, illustrates this effect for different values of $k$. Notice in particular that for $k = 2$ the convex hull is just the defining polygon itself. Hence, the B-spline curve is also just the defining polygon itself.

Using the convex hull property it is easy to see that if all the defining polygon vertices are colinear, then the resulting B-spline curve is a straight line for all orders $k$. Further, if $l$ colinear polygon vertices occur in a noncolinear defining polygon, then the straight portions of the defining curve (if any) start and end at least $k - 2$ spans from the beginning and end of the series of colinear polygon vertices. If the series of colinear polygon vertices is completely contained within a noncolinear defining polygon, then the number of colinear curve spans is at least $l - 2k + 3$. If the series of colinear polygon vertices occurs at the end of a noncolinear defining polygon, then the number of colinear curve spans is at least $l - k + 1$. Figure 5–33 illustrates these results.

If at least $k - 1$ coincident defining polygon vertices occur, i.e., $B_i = B_{i+1} \cdots = B_{i+k-2}$, then the convex hull of $B_i$ to $B_{i+k-2}$ is the vertex itself. Hence, the resulting B-spline curve must pass through the vertex $B_i$. Figure 5–34 illustrates this point for $k = 3$. Further, since a B-spline curve is everywhere $C^{k-2}$ continuous, it is $C^{k-2}$ continuous at $B_i$.

Finally, note that because of these continuity properties B-spline curves smoothly transition, with $C^{k-2}$ continuity, into embedded straight segments as shown in Fig. 5–35.

Equations (5–84) clearly show that the choice of knot vector has a significant influence on the B-spline basis functions $N_{i,k}(t)$ and hence on the resulting B-spline curve. The only requirement for a knot vector is that it satisfy the relation $x_i \leq x_{i+1}$; i.e., it is a monotonically increasing series of real numbers. Fundamentally three types of knot vector are used: uniform, open uniform (or open) and nonuniform.

In a uniform knot vector, individual knot values are evenly spaced. Examples are

$$[0 \quad 1 \quad 2 \quad 3 \quad 4]$$

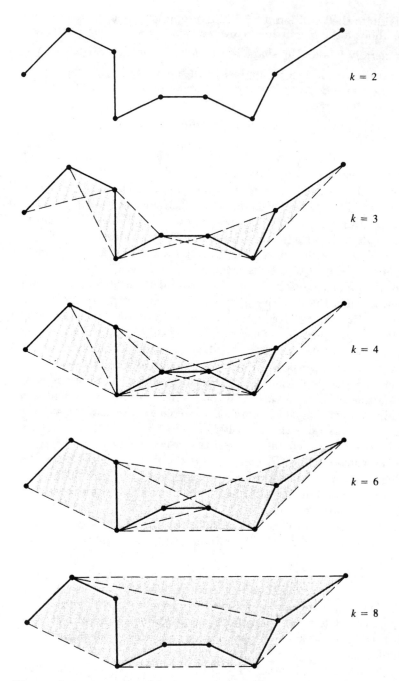

$k = 2$

$k = 3$

$k = 4$

$k = 6$

$k = 8$

**Figure 5–32**   Convex hull properties of B-spline curves.

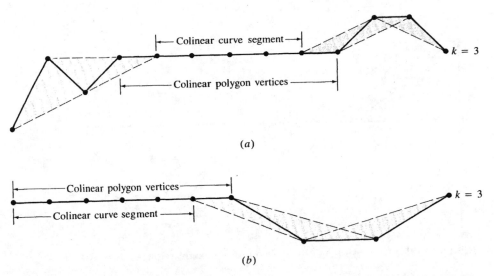

(a)

Colinear polygon vertices

Colinear curve segment

$k = 3$

(b)

**Figure 5-33**    B-spline convex hull properties for colinear curve segments. (a) Within the defining polygon vertices; (b) at the end of the defining polygon vertices.

$$[\,-0.2 \quad -0.1 \quad 0 \quad 0.1 \quad 0.2\,]$$

In practice, uniform knot vectors generally begin at zero and are incremented by 1 to some maximum value or are normalized in the range between 0 and 1, i.e., equal decimal intervals, e.g.,

$$[\,0 \quad 0.25 \quad 0.5 \quad 0.75 \quad 1.0\,]$$

For a given order $k$, uniform knot vectors yield periodic uniform basis functions for which

$$N_{i,k}(t) = N_{i-1,k}(t-1) = N_{i+1,k}(t+1)$$

Thus each basis function is a translate of the other. Figure 5–36 illustrates this.

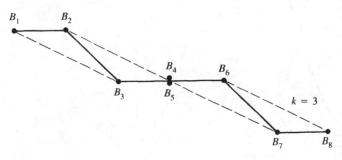

**Figure 5-34**    Convex hull for coincident polygon vertices, $k = 3$.

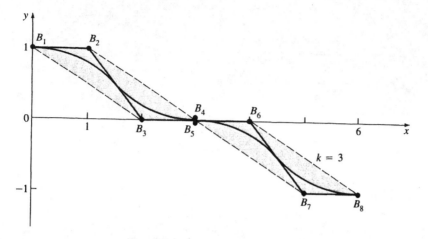

**Figure 5–35** Smooth $(C^{k-2})$ transition into straight segments.

An open uniform knot vector has multiplicity of knot values at the ends equal to the order $k$ of the B-spline basis function. Internal knot values are evenly spaced. Some examples using integer increments are

$$k = 2 \qquad [\,0 \quad 0 \quad 1 \quad 2 \quad 3 \quad 4 \quad 4\,]$$

$$k = 3 \qquad [\,0 \quad 0 \quad 0 \quad 1 \quad 2 \quad 3 \quad 3 \quad 3\,]$$

$$k = 4 \qquad [\,0 \quad 0 \quad 0 \quad 0 \quad 1 \quad 2 \quad 2 \quad 2 \quad 2\,]$$

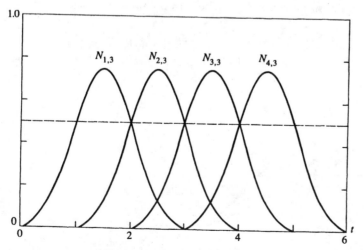

**Figure 5–36** Periodic uniform B-spline basis functions, $[\,X\,] = [\,0 \quad 1 \quad 2 \quad 3 \quad 4 \quad 5 \quad 6\,]$, $n + 1 = 4$, $k = 3$.

or for normalized increments

$$k = 2 \qquad [0 \quad 0 \quad 1/4 \quad 1/2 \quad 3/4 \quad 1 \quad 1]$$
$$k = 3 \qquad [0 \quad 0 \quad 0 \quad 1/3 \quad 2/3 \quad 1 \quad 1 \quad 1]$$
$$k = 4 \qquad [0 \quad 0 \quad 0 \quad 0 \quad 1/2 \quad 1 \quad 1 \quad 1 \quad 1]$$

Formally, an open uniform knot vector is given by

$$x_i = 0 \qquad 1 \le i \le k$$
$$x_i = i - k \qquad k+1 \le i \le n+1$$
$$x_i = n - k + 2 \qquad n+2 \le i \le n+k+1$$

The resulting open uniform basis functions yield curves that behave most nearly like Bézier curves. In fact, when the number of defining polygon vertices is equal to the order of the B-spline basis and an open uniform knot vector is used, the B-spline basis reduces to the Bernstein basis. Hence, the resulting B-spline curve is a Bézier curve. In that case, the knot vector is just $k$ zeros followed by $k$ ones. For example, for four polygon vertices the fourth order ($k = 4$) open uniform knot vector is

$$[0 \quad 0 \quad 0 \quad 0 \quad 1 \quad 1 \quad 1 \quad 1]$$

A cubic Bézier/B-spline curve results. The corresponding open uniform basis functions are shown in Fig. 5-27b. Additional open uniform basis functions are shown in Fig. 5-37.

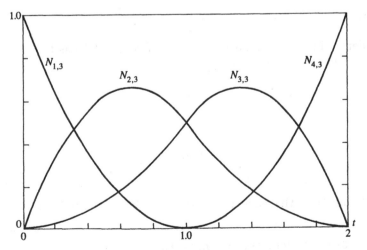

**Figure 5-37**  Open uniform B-spline basis functions, $[X] = [0 \quad 0 \quad 0 \quad 1 \quad 2 \quad 2 \quad 2]$, $k = 3$, $n + 1 = 4$.

for $N_{i,3}$ are given by the following diagram:

$$
\begin{array}{cccccc}
N_{1,3} & N_{2,3} & N_{3,3} & N_{4,3} & & \\
N_{1,2} & N_{2,2} & N_{3,2} & N_{4,2} & N_{5,2} & \\
N_{1,1} & N_{2,1} & N_{3,1} & N_{4,1} & N_{5,1} & N_{6,1}
\end{array}
$$

The inverse dependencies for $i \geq 1$ are given by

$$
\begin{array}{cccccc}
N_{1,3} & N_{2,3} & N_{3,3} & N_{4,3} & N_{5,3} & N_{6,3} \\
N_{1,2} & N_{2,2} & N_{3,2} & N_{4,2} & N_{5,2} & \\
N_{1,1} & N_{2,1} & N_{3,1} & N_{4,1} & &
\end{array}
$$

Now, what is the knot vector range needed for this calculation? Equation (5–84) shows that the calculation of $N_{6,1}$ requires knot values $x_6$ and $x_7$, while calculation of $N_{1,1}$ requires $x_1$ and $x_2$. Thus, knot values from 0 to $n + k$ are required. The number of knot values is thus $n + k + 1$. Hence the knot vector for these periodic basis functions is

$$[\,X\,] = [\,0 \quad 1 \quad 2 \quad 3 \quad 4 \quad 5 \quad 6\,]$$

where $x_1 = 0, \cdots, x_7 = 6$. The parameter range is $0 \leq t \leq 6$. Using Eq. (5–84) and the dependency diagram above, the basis functions for various parameter ranges are

$0 \leq t < 1$

$$N_{1,1}(t) = 1; \qquad N_{i,1}(t) = 0, \quad i \neq 1$$
$$N_{1,2}(t) = t; \qquad N_{i,2}(t) = 0, \quad i \neq 1$$
$$N_{1,3}(t) = \frac{t^2}{2}; \qquad N_{i,3}(t) = 0, \quad i \neq 1$$

$1 \leq t < 2$

$$N_{2,1}(t) = 1; \qquad N_{i,1}(t) = 0, \quad i \neq 2$$
$$N_{1,2}(t) = (2 - t); \qquad N_{2,2}(t) = (t - 1); \qquad N_{i,2}(t) = 0, \quad i \neq 1, 2$$
$$N_{1,3}(t) = \frac{t}{2}(2 - t) + \left(\frac{3 - t}{2}\right)(t - 1);$$
$$N_{2,3}(t) = \frac{(t - 1)^2}{2}; \qquad N_{i,3}(t) = 0, \quad i \neq 1, 2, 3$$

$2 \leq t < 3$

$$N_{3,1}(t) = 1; \qquad N_{i,1}(t) = 0, \quad i \neq 3$$
$$N_{2,2}(t) = (3 - t); \qquad N_{3,2}(t) = (t - 2); \qquad N_{i,2}(t) = 0, \quad i \neq 2, 3$$
$$N_{1,3}(t) = \frac{(3 - t)^2}{2};$$
$$N_{2,3}(t) = \frac{(t - 1)(3 - t)}{2} + \frac{(4 - t)(t - 2)}{2};$$
$$N_{3,3}(t) = \frac{(t - 2)^2}{2}; \qquad N_{i,3}(t) = 0, \quad i \neq 1, 2, 3$$

$3 \le t < 4$

$$N_{4,1}(t) = 1; \qquad N_{i,1}(t) = 0, \quad i \ne 4$$

$$N_{3,2}(t) = (4 - t); \qquad N_{4,2}(t) = (t - 3); \qquad N_{i,2}(t) = 0, \quad i \ne 3, 4$$

$$N_{2,3}(t) = \frac{(4 - t)^2}{2}; \qquad N_{3,3}(t) = \frac{(t - 2)(4 - t)}{2} + \frac{(5 - t)(t - 3)}{2};$$

$$N_{4,3}(t) = \frac{(t - 3)^2}{2}; \qquad N_{i,3}(t) = 0, \quad i \ne 2, 3, 4$$

$4 \le t < 5$

$$N_{5,1}(t) = 1; \qquad N_{i,1}(t) = 0, \quad i \ne 5$$

$$N_{4,2}(t) = (5 - t); \qquad N_{5,2}(t) = (t - 4); \qquad N_{i,2}(t) = 0, \quad i \ne 4, 5$$

$$N_{3,3}(t) = \frac{(5 - t)^2}{2};$$

$$N_{4,3}(t) = \frac{(t - 3)(5 - t)}{2} + \frac{(6 - t)(t - 4)}{2};$$

$$N_{i,3}(t) = 0, \quad i \ne 3, 4$$

$5 \le t < 6$

$$N_{6,1}(t) = 1; \qquad N_{i,1}(t) = 0, \quad i \ne 6$$

$$N_{5,2}(t) = (6 - t); \qquad N_{i,2}(t) = 0, \quad i \ne 5$$

$$N_{4,3}(t) = \frac{(6 - t)^2}{2}; \qquad N_{i,3}(t) = 0, \quad i \ne 4$$

Note that because of the $<$ sign in the definition of $N_{i,1}$, all basis functions are precisely zero at $t = 6$.

These results are shown in Fig. 5–36 and Fig. 5–39c. Note that each one of the basis functions is a piecewise parabolic (quadratic) curve. Here, three piecewise parabolic segments on the intervals $x_i \to x_{i+1}$, $x_{i+1} \to x_{i+2}$, $x_{i+2} \to x_{i+3}$ are joined together to form each $N_{i,3}$ basis function. Further, note that each of the basis functions is simply a translate of the other.

---

Using the results of Ex. 5–9, the buildup of the higher order basis functions $N_{i,3}$ from lower order basis functions is easily illustrated. Figure 5–39a shows the first-order basis functions determined in Ex. 5–9, Fig. 5–39b shows the second-order basis functions and Fig. 5–39c repeats the third-order basis functions of Fig. 5–36 for completeness. Notice how the range of nonzero basis function values spreads with increasing order. The basis function is said to provide support on the interval $x_i$ to $x_{i+k}$.

Examining Fig. 5–36 closely reveals an important property of uniform basis functions. Recalling from Eq. 5–85 that $\sum N_{i,k}(t) = 1$ at any parameter value $t$ shows that a complete set of periodic basis functions for $k = 3$ is defined only in the range $2 \le t \le 4$. Outside of this range the $\sum N_{i,k}(t) \ne 1$ . For a uniform knot vector beginning at 0 with integer spacings the usable parameter range is $k - 1 \le t \le (n + k) - (k - 1) = n + 1$. For more general or normalized knot vectors, the reduction in usable parameter range corresponds to the loss of $k - 1$ knot value intervals at each end of the knot vector.

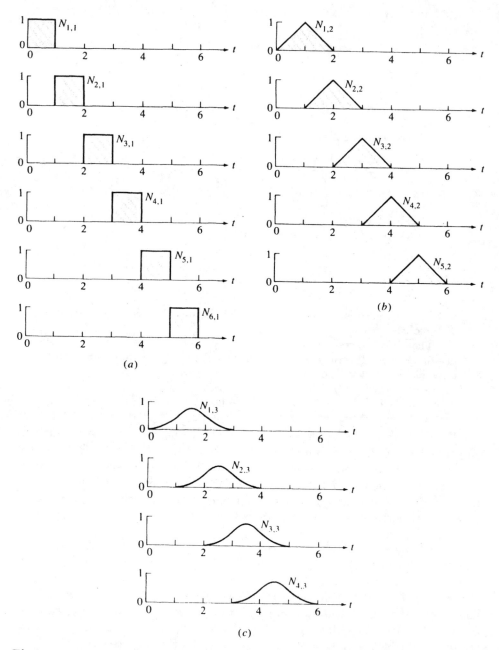

**Figure 5–39** Periodic basis function buildup $n + 1 = 4$. (a) $k = 1$; (b) $k = 2$; (c) $k = 3$.

**Example 5–10    Calculating Open Uniform Basis Functions**

Calculate the four ($n = 3$) third-order ($k = 3$) basis functions $N_{i,3}(t)$, $i = 1, 2, 3, 4$ with an open knot vector.

Recalling that formally an open knot vector with integer intervals between internal knot values is given by

$$x_i = 0 \qquad 1 \leq i \leq k$$
$$x_i = i - k \qquad k + 1 \leq i \leq n + 1$$
$$x_i = n - k + 2 \qquad n + 2 \leq i \leq n + k + 1$$

The parameter range is $0 \leq t \leq n - k + 2$, i.e., from zero to the maximum knot value. Again, as in Ex. 5–9, the number of knot values is $n + k + 1$. Using integer knot values, the knot vector for the current example is

$$[X] = [0 \quad 0 \quad 0 \quad 1 \quad 2 \quad 2 \quad 2]$$

where $x_1 = 0, \cdots, x_7 = 2$. The parameter range is from $0 \leq t \leq 2$.

Using Eqs. (5–84) and the dependency diagrams, the basis functions for various parameter ranges are

$0 \leq t < 1$
$$N_{3,1}(t) = 1; \qquad N_{i,1}(t) = 0, \quad i \neq 3$$
$$N_{2,2}(t) = 1 - t; \qquad N_{3,2}(t) = t; \qquad N_{i,2}(t) = 0, \quad i \neq 2, 3$$
$$N_{1,3}(t) = (1 - t)^2; \qquad N_{2,3}(t) = t(1 - t) + \frac{(2 - t)}{2} t;$$
$$N_{3,3}(t) = \frac{t^2}{2}; \qquad N_{i,3}(t) = 0, \quad i \neq 1, 2, 3$$

$1 \leq t < 2$
$$N_{4,1}(t) = 1; \qquad N_{i,1}(t) = 0, \quad i \neq 4$$
$$N_{3,2}(t) = (2 - t); \qquad N_{4,2}(t) = (t - 1); \qquad N_{i,2}(t) = 0, \quad i \neq 3, 4$$
$$N_{2,3}(t) = \frac{(2 - t)^2}{2}; \qquad N_{3,3}(t) = \frac{t(2 - t)}{2} + (2 - t)(t - 1);$$
$$N_{4,3}(t) = (t - 1)^2; \qquad N_{i,3}(t) = 0, \quad i \neq 2, 3, 4$$

These results are shown in Fig. 5–40.

Comparing the results from Ex. 5–10 shown in Fig. 5–40 with those from Ex. 5–9 shown in Fig. 5–39 illustrates that significantly different results are obtained when using periodic uniform or open uniform knot vectors. In particular, note that for open uniform knot vectors a complete set of basis functions is defined for the entire parameter range; i.e., $\sum N_{i,k}(t) = 1$ for all $t$, $0 \leq t \leq n - k + 2$. Notice also the reduction in parameter range compared to that for a periodic uniform knot vector.

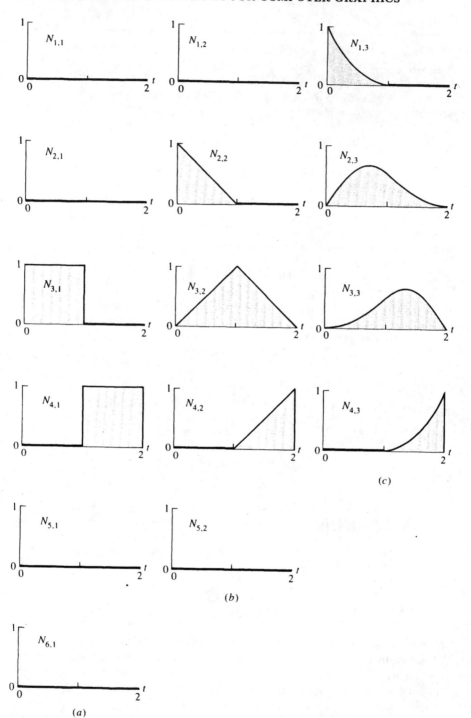

**Figure 5–40**    Open basis function buildup $n + 1 = 4$. (a) $k = 1$; (b) $k = 2$; (c) $k = 3$.

**Example 5–11    Calculating Nonuniform Basis Functions**

Calculate the five $(n + 1 = 5)$ third-order $(k = 3)$ basis functions $N_{i,3}(t)$, $i = 1, 2, 3, 4, 5$ using the knot vector $[\,X\,] = [\,0 \quad 0 \quad 0 \quad 1 \quad 1 \quad 3 \quad 3 \quad 3\,]$ which contains an interior repeated knot value. Using Eqs. (5–84) and the dependency diagrams, the basis functions are

$0 \le t < 1$

$$N_{3,1}(t) = 1; \qquad N_{i,1}(t) = 0, \quad i \ne 2$$

$$N_{2,2}(t) = 1 - t; \qquad N_{3,2}(t) = t; \qquad N_{i,2}(t) = 0, \quad i \ne 2, 3$$

$$N_{1,3}(t) = (1 - t)^2; \qquad N_{2,3}(t) = t(1 - t) + (1 - t)t = 2t(1 - t);$$

$$N_{3,3}(t) = t^2; \qquad N_{i,3}(t) = 0, \quad i \ne 1, 2, 3$$

$1 \le t < 1$

$$N_{i,1}(t) = 0, \quad \text{all } i$$

$$N_{i,2}(t) = 0, \quad \text{all } i$$

$$N_{i,3}(t) = 0, \quad \text{all } i$$

Notice specifically that as a consequence of the multiple knot value, $N_{4,1}(t) = 0$ for all $t$.

$1 \le t < 3$

$$N_{5,1}(t) = 1; \qquad N_{i,1}(t) = 0, \quad i \ne 5$$

$$N_{4,2}(t) = \frac{(3 - t)}{2}; \qquad N_{5,2}(t) = \frac{(t - 1)}{2}; \qquad N_{i,2}(t) = 0, \quad i \ne 4, 5$$

$$N_{3,3}(t) = \frac{(3 - t)^2}{4};$$

$$N_{4,3}(t) = \frac{(t - 1)(3 - t)}{4} + \frac{(3 - t)(t - 1)}{4} = \frac{(3 - t)(t - 1)}{2};$$

$$N_{5,3}(t) = \frac{(t - 1)^2}{4}; \qquad N_{i,3}(t) = 0, \quad i \ne 3, 4, 5$$

The results are shown in Fig. 5–38d.

Notice that for each value of $t$ the $\sum N_{i,k}(t) = 1.0$. For example, with $0 \le t < 1$

$$\sum_{i=1}^{5} N_{i,3}(t) = (1 - t)^2 + 2t(1 - t) + t^2 = 1 - 2t + t^2 + 2t - 2t^2 + t^2 = 1$$

Similarly, for $1 \le t < 3$

$$\sum_{i=1}^{5} N_{i,3}(t) = \frac{1}{4}[(3 - t)^2 + 2(3 - t)(t - 1) + (t - 1)^2]$$

$$= \frac{1}{4}[9 - 6t + t^2 - 6 + 8t - 2t^2 + 1 - 2t + t^2]$$

$$= \frac{4}{4} = 1$$

The above discussion shows the significant influence of the choice of knot vector on the shape of the B-spline basis functions and hence on the shape of any resulting B-spline curve.

Because of the flexibility of B-spline basis functions and hence of the resulting B-spline curves, different types of control 'handles' are used to influence the shape of the curve. Control is achieved by:

Changing the type of knot vector and hence basis function: periodic uniform, open uniform or nonuniform.

Changing the order $k$ of the basis function.

Changing the number and position of the defining polygon vertices.

Using multiple polygon vertices.

Using multiple knot values in the knot vector.

These effects are illustrated first with open B-spline curves and then with periodic B-spline curves and finally with nonuniform B-spline curves.

The behavior of an open B-spline curve is in many respects analogous to that of a Bézier curve. In fact, as has previously been mentioned, when the order of a B-spline curve is equal to the number of defining polygon vertices, the B-spline basis reduces to the Bernstein basis. Consequently, the resulting B-spline curve is identical to a Bézier curve. For an open B-spline curve of any order ($k \geq 2$) the first and last points on the curve are coincident with the first and last polygon vertices. Further, the slope of the B-spline curve at the first and last polygon vertices is equal to the slope of the first and last polygon spans.

Figure 5–41 shows three open B-spline curves of different order, each defined by the same four polygon vertices. The fourth-order curve corresponds to the Bézier curve. This curve is a single cubic polynomial segment. The third-order curve is composed of two parabolic curve segments joined at the center of the second span with $C^1$ continuity. The second-order curve reproduces the defining polygon. It consists of three linear 'curve' segments joined at the second and third polygon vertices with $C^0$ continuity. Notice that all three curves have the same end slopes, determined by the slope of the first and last spans of the defining polygon. Notice also that as the order of the curve increases, the resulting curve looks less like the defining polygon. Thus, increasing the order 'tightens' or 'smooths' the curve.

Figure 5–42 illustrates the effect of multiple or coincident vertices on the defining polygon. The B-spline curves are all of the order $k = 4$. The lowest curve is defined by four polygon vertices as shown. Here the knot vector is [0 0 0 0 1 1 1 1]. The intermediate curve is defined by five polygon vertices with two coincident vertices at the second polygon vertex, i.e., [3 9]. The knot vector for this curve is [0 0 0 0 1 2 2 2 2]. The highest curve is defined by six polygon vertices with three coincident vertices at [3 9]. The knot vector is [0 0 0 0 1 2 3 3 3 3]. Thus, the defining polygons for the three curves are $B_1, B_2, B_3, B_4$; $B_1, B_2, B_2, B_3, B_4$ and $B_1, B_2, B_2, B_2, B_3, B_4$, respectively.

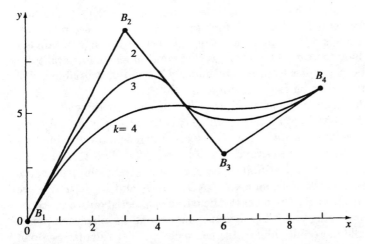

**Figure 5–41**   Effect of varying order on B-spline curves.

The lowest curve is composed of a single cubic segment. The intermediate curve is composed of two segments joined midway between $B_2$ and $B_3$. The highest curve is composed of three segments. The first is from $B_1$ to $B_2$, the second from $B_2$ to midway between $B_2$ and $B_3$. The final segment is from midway between $B_2$ and $B_3$ to $B_4$. Notice that as the number of multiple vertices at $B_2$ increases, the curve is pulled closer to $B_2$. If the number of multiple vertices is $k - 1$, then a sharp corner or cusp is created. This sharp corner is predicted by the convex hull properties of B-spline curves. Close examination of Fig. 5–42 shows that on both sides of the multiple vertex location a linear segment occurs.

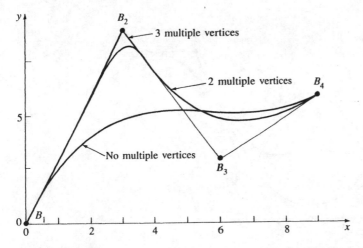

**Figure 5–42**   Effect of multiple vertices at $B_2$ on a B-spline curve , $k = 4$.

Although a cusp exists when $k - 1$ multiple vertices occur, the $C^{k-2}$ differentiability of the curve is maintained. At first glance, this might seem contradictory. However, a cusp is defined by a zero tangent vector. But a zero tangent vector does not preclude the tangent vector varying continuously. The ability to include sharp corners or cusps within a continuously $C^{k-2}$ differentiable curve is an important characteristic of B-spline curves.

Finally notice that each of the curves has the same slope at the ends.

Figure 5–43 shows three fourth-order B-spline curves. The defining polygons each have eight vertices as indicated. The three curves shown are obtained by moving the polygon vertex $B_5$ successively to $B_5'$ and $B_5''$. Note that moving $B_5$ influences the curve only over a limited region. Specifically, only the curve segments corresponding to the polygon spans $B_3 B_4$, $B_4 B_5$ and $B_5 B_6$, $B_6 B_7$ are affected by the movement of $B_5$. In general, the curve is affected only over those curve segments corresponding to $\pm k/2$ polygon spans around the displaced point.

A detailed example more fully illustrates the technique for calculating open B-spline curves.

---

**Example 5–12    Calculating an Open B-spline Curve**

Consider the same defining polygon used previously in Ex. 5–7 to determine a Bézier curve, i.e., $B_1 [\,1 \quad 1\,]$, $B_2 [\,2 \quad 3\,]$, $B_3 [\,4 \quad 3\,]$, $B_4 [\,3 \quad 1\,]$. Calculate both second- and fourth-order B-spline curves.

For $k = 2$ the open knot vector is

$$[\,0 \quad 0 \quad 1 \quad 2 \quad 3 \quad 3\,]$$

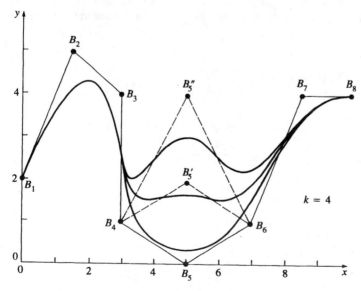

**Figure 5–43**    Local control of B-spline curves.

where $x_1 = 0$, $x_2 = 0, \cdots, x_6 = 3$. The parameter range is $0 \leq t \leq 3$. The curve is composed of three linear $(k - 1 = 1)$ segments. For $0 \leq t < 3$ the basis functions are:

$0 \leq t < 1$

$$N_{2,1}(t) = 1; \qquad N_{i,1}(t) = 0, \quad i \neq 2$$
$$N_{1,2}(t) = 1 - t; \qquad N_{2,2}(t) = t; \qquad N_{i,2}(t) = 0, \quad i \neq 1, 2$$

$1 \leq t < 2$

$$N_{3,1}(t) = 1; \qquad N_{i,1}(t) = 0, \quad i \neq 3$$
$$N_{2,2}(t) = 2 - t; \qquad N_{3,2}(t) = (t - 1); \qquad N_{i,2}(t) = 0, \quad i \neq 2, 3$$

$2 \leq t < 3$

$$N_{4,1}(t) = 1; \qquad N_{i,1}(t) = 0, \quad i \neq 4$$
$$N_{3,2}(t) = (3 - t); \qquad N_{4,2}(t) = (t - 2); \qquad N_{i,2}(t) = 0, \quad i \neq 3, 4$$

Using Eq. (5–83) the parametric B-spline curve is

$$P(t) = B_1 N_{1,2}(t) + B_2 N_{2,2}(t) + B_3 N_{3,2}(t) + B_4 N_{4,2}(t)$$

For each of these intervals the curve is given by

$$P(t) = (1 - t)B_1 + tB_2 = B_1 + (B_2 - B_1)t \qquad 0 \leq t < 1$$
$$P(t) = (2 - t)B_2 + (t - 1)B_3 = B_2 + (B_3 - B_2)t \qquad 1 \leq t < 2$$
$$P(t) = (3 - t)B_3 + (t - 2)B_4 = B_3 + (B_4 - B_3)t \qquad 2 \leq t < 3$$

In each case the result is the equation of the parametric straight line for the polygon span, i.e., the 'curve' is the defining polygon.

The last point on the curve $(t = t_{\max} = 3)$ requires special consideration. Because of the open right-hand interval in Eq. (5–84a) all the basis functions $N_{i,k}$ at $t = 3$ are zero. Consequently, the last polygon point does not technically lie on the B-spline curve. However, practically it does. Consider $t = 3 - \epsilon$ where $\epsilon$ is an infinitesimal value. Letting $\epsilon \to 0$ shows that in the limit the last point on the curve and the last polygon point are coincident. Practically, this result is incorporated by either artificially adding the last polygon point to the curve description or by defining $N(t = t_{\max}) = 1.0$.

For $k = 4$ the order of the curve is equal to the number of defining polygon vertices. Thus the B-spline curve reduces to a Bézier curve. The knot vector with $t_{\max} = n - k + 2 = 3 - 4 + 2 = 1$ is $[0 \ \ 0 \ \ 0 \ \ 0 \ \ 1 \ \ 1 \ \ 1 \ \ 1]$. The basis functions are

$0 \leq t < 1$

$$N_{4,1}(t) = 1; \qquad N_{i,1}(t) = 0, \quad i \neq 4$$
$$N_{3,2}(t) = (1 - t); \qquad N_{4,2}(t) = t; \qquad N_{i,2}(t) = 0, \quad i \neq 3, 4$$
$$N_{2,3}(t) = (1 - t)^2; \qquad N_{3,3}(t) = 2t(1 - t);$$
$$N_{4,3}(t) = t^2; \qquad N_{i,3}(t) = 0, \quad i \neq 2, 3, 4$$
$$N_{1,4}(t) = (1 - t)^3; \qquad N_{2,4}(t) = t(1 - t)^2 + 2t(1 - t)^2 = 3t(1 - t)^2;$$
$$N_{3,4}(t) = 2t^2(1 - t) + (1 - t)t^2 = 3t^2(1 - t); \qquad N_{4,4}(t) = t^3$$

Using Eq. (5–83) the parametric B-spline is

$$P(t) = B_1 N_{1,4}(t) + B_2 N_{2,4}(t) + B_3 N_{3,4}(t) + B_4 N_{4,4}(t)$$
$$P(t) = (1-t)^3 B_1 + 3t(1-t)^2 B_2 + 3t^2(1-t)B_3 + t^3 B_4$$

Thus, at $t = 0$

$$P(0) = B_1$$

and at $t = 1/2$

$$P\left(\frac{1}{2}\right) = \frac{1}{8}B_1 + \frac{3}{8}B_2 + \frac{3}{8}B_3 + \frac{1}{8}B_4$$

and

$$P\left(\frac{1}{2}\right) = \frac{1}{8}[\,1 \quad 1\,] + \frac{3}{8}[\,2 \quad 3\,] + \frac{3}{8}[\,4 \quad 3\,] + \frac{1}{8}[\,3 \quad 1\,]$$

$$= [\,11/4 \quad 5/2\,]$$

Comparison with Ex. 5–7 shows that the current results are identical. The resulting curve is shown in Fig. 5–28.

---

Turning now to periodic B-spline curves, Fig. 5–44 shows three periodic B-spline curves of different orders. Each of the curves is defined by the same polygon vertices as the open B-spline curves in Fig. 5–41. For $k = 2$ the B-spline curve again coincides with the defining polygon. However, notice that for periodic B-spline curves for $k > 2$ the first and last points on the B-spline curve do *not* correspond to the first and last defining polygon vertices. Nor in general is the slope at the first and last points the same as that of the first and last defining polygon spans. For $k = 3$ the B-spline curve starts at the midpoint of the first polygon span and ends at the midpoint of the last polygon span as indicated by the arrows. These effects are a result of the reduced parameter range for periodic B-spline basis functions. For $k = 2$ the periodic knot vector is $[\,0 \quad 1 \quad 2 \quad 3 \quad 4 \quad 5\,]$ with a parameter range of $1 \le t \le 4$. For $k = 3$ the periodic knot vector is $[\,0 \quad 1 \quad 2 \quad 3 \quad 4 \quad 5 \quad 6\,]$ with parameter range of $2 \le t \le 4$. For $k = 4$ the periodic knot vector is $[\,0 \quad 1 \quad 2 \quad 3 \quad 4 \quad 5 \quad 6 \quad 7\,]$ with parameter range of $3 \le t \le 4$. Comparing these results with those for open knot vectors in Fig. 5–41 shows that the multiple knot values at the ends of the open knot vector permit the curve to be defined over the full range of parameter values. The effect is to 'pull' the curve out to the ends of the defining polygon.

Here again the fourth-order curve consists of a single cubic polynomial segment, the third-order curve of two parabolic segments joined at the center of the second polygon span with $C^1$ continuity, and the second-order 'curve' of three linear segments joined at the second and third polygon vertices with $C^0$ continuity. Notice that again increasing order has a 'smoothing' effect on the curve, but here it also decreases the curve length.

Figure 5–45 illustrates that the effect of multiple vertices in the defining polygon is similar for periodic and open B-spline curves. The small inset shows the details near $B_2$.

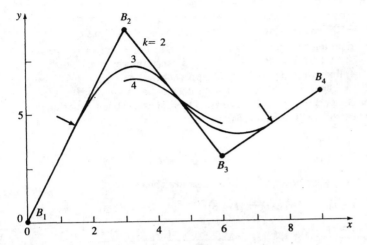

**Figure 5–44**   Effect of varying order on periodic B-spline curves.

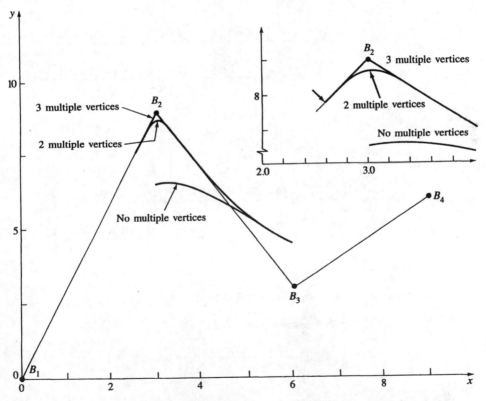

**Figure 5–45**   Effect of multiple vertices on a periodic B-spline curve, $k = 4$.

**Example 5–13    Calculating a Periodic B-spline Curve**

Again consider the defining polygon shown in Fig. 5–44. The polygon vertices are $B_1 [\,0 \quad 0\,]$, $B_2 [\,3 \quad 9\,]$, $B_3 [\,6 \quad 3\,]$, $B_4 [\,9 \quad 6\,]$. Determine the fourth-order $(k = 4)$ periodic B-spline curve defined by this polygon.

For $k = 4$, $[\,0 \quad 1 \quad 2 \quad 3 \quad 4 \quad 5 \quad 6 \quad 7\,]$ with parameter range $3 \le t < 4$ is the knot vector for the periodic basis functions. The first-order basis functions for this parameter range are (see Eq. 5–84a)

$$3 \le t < 4$$

$$N_{4,1}(t) = 1; \qquad N_{i,1}(t) = 0, \quad i \ne 4$$

From Eq. (5–84b) the higher order basis functions are then

$$N_{3,2}(t) = (4 - t); \qquad N_{4,2}(t) = (t - 3); \qquad N_{i,2}(t) = 0, \quad i \ne 3, 4$$

$$N_{2,3}(t) = \frac{(4 - t)^2}{2}; \qquad N_{3,3}(t) = \frac{(t - 2)(4 - t)}{2} + \frac{(5 - t)(t - 3)}{2};$$

$$N_{4,3}(t) = \frac{(t - 3)^2}{2}; \qquad N_{i,3}(t) = 0, \quad i \ne 2, 3, 4$$

$$N_{1,4}(t) = \frac{(4 - t)^3}{6};$$

$$N_{2,4}(t) = \frac{(t - 1)(4 - t)^2}{6} + \frac{(5 - t)(4 - t)(t - 2)}{6} + \frac{(5 - t)^2(t - 3)}{6};$$

$$N_{3,4}(t) = \frac{(t - 2)^2(4 - t)}{6} + \frac{(t - 2)(t - 3)(5 - t)}{6} + \frac{(6 - t)(t - 3)^2}{6};$$

$$N_{4,4}(t) = \frac{(t - 3)^3}{6}$$

At $t = 3$

$$N_{1,4}(3) = \frac{(4 - 3)^2}{6} = \frac{1}{6}$$

$$N_{2,4}(3) = \frac{(3 - 1)(4 - 3)^2}{6} + \frac{(5 - 3)(4 - 3)(3 - 2)}{6} + \frac{(5 - 3)^2(3 - 3)}{6} = \frac{2}{3}$$

$$N_{3,4}(3) = \frac{(3 - 2)^2(4 - 3)}{6} + \frac{(3 - 2)(3 - 3)(5 - 3)}{6} + \frac{(6 - 3)(3 - 3)^2}{6} = \frac{1}{6}$$

$$N_{4,4}(3) = \frac{(3 - 3)^3}{6} = 0$$

The point on the B-spline curve at $t = 3$ is thus

$$P(3) = \frac{1}{6}B_1 + \frac{2}{3}B_2 + \frac{1}{6}B_3 + 0B_4$$

$$= \frac{1}{6}[\,0 \quad 0\,] + \frac{2}{3}[\,3 \quad 9\,] + \frac{1}{6}[\,6 \quad 3\,] + 0[\,9 \quad 6\,]$$

$$= [\,3 \quad 6.5\,]$$

The complete curve is shown in Fig. 5–44.

Periodic B-spline curves are also useful for generating closed curves. Figure 5–46a shows a fourth-order $(k = 4)$ periodic cubic B-spline curve generated using the closed polygon $B_1 B_2 B_3 B_4 B_5 B_6 B_7 B_8 B_1$. Here the first vertex is repeated as the last vertex to close the polygon. Because of the restricted parameter range used with periodic basis functions, the resulting B-spline curve is not closed. Here the periodic uniform knot vector is $[\,0 \quad 1 \quad 2 \quad \cdot \quad \cdot \quad \cdot \quad 10 \quad 11 \quad 12\,]$ with a usable parameter range of $3 \leq t \leq 9$.

By repeating a total of $k - 2$ polygon vertices at the beginning and/or end of the defining closed polygon, a closed periodic B-spline curve is obtained. (An alternate technique using a matrix formulation is discussed later in this section.) Figure 5–46b shows the results. $B_8 B_1 B_2 B_3 B_4 B_5 B_6 B_7 B_8 B_1 B_2$ with the periodic uniform knot vector $[\,0 \quad 1 \quad 2 \quad \cdot \quad \cdot \quad \cdot \quad 12 \quad 13 \quad 14\,]$ with the usable parameter range $3 \leq t \leq 11$ is the defining polygon for Fig. 5–46b. The alternate defining polygons $B_1 B_2 B_3 B_4 B_5 B_6 B_7 B_8 B_1 B_2 B_3$ or $B_7 B_8 B_1 B_2 B_3 B_4 \ B_5 B_6 B_7 B_8 B_1$ yield the same results.

Figure 5–47 shows the effect of moving the single polygon vertex $B_4$. Again the effect is confined to those curve segments corresponding to $\pm k/2$ polygon spans on either side of the displaced point.

Figure 5–48 shows the effect of multiple vertices at $B_4$. The details near $B_4$ are shown in the inset. Again notice that the excellent local control properties of B-spline curves confine the effect to those curve segments corresponding to $\pm k/2$ polygon spans on either side of the multiple vertex location.

Turning now to nonuniform B-spline curves, Fig. 5–49 illustrates the effect of multiple interior knot values on the resulting curve. The upper third-order $(k = 3)$ curve in Fig. 5–49 was generated with the open knot vector

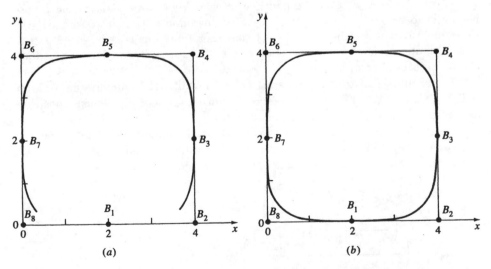

(a)                                      (b)

**Figure 5–46**   Closed periodic B-spline curve. (a) $B_1 B_2 B_3 B_4 B_5 B_6 B_7 B_8 B_1$ as the defining polygon; (b) $B_8 B_1 B_2 B_3 B_4 B_5 B_6 B_7 B_8 B_1 B_2$ as the defining polygon.

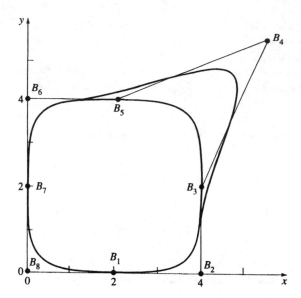

**Figure 5–47**   Effect of moving a single polygon vertex on a closed periodic B-spline curve.

$[\,0\ \ 0\ \ 0\ \ 1\ \ 2\ \ 3\ \ 3\ \ 3\,]$. The basis functions for this curve are shown in Fig. 5–38a. The lower third-order curve in Fig. 5–49 was generated with the nonuniform knot vector $[\,0\ \ 0\ \ 0\ \ 1\ \ 1\ \ 3\ \ 3\ \ 3\,]$. The basis functions are shown in Fig. 5–38d. An identical curve is obtained with the nonuniform knot vector $[\,0\ \ 0\ \ 0\ \ 2\ \ 2\ \ 3\ \ 3\ \ 3\,]$ and the basis functions shown in Fig. 5–38e.

Figure 5–49 shows that the multiple interior knot value yields a sharp corner or cusp at $B_3$. A multiple knot value introduces a span of zero length. Consequently, the width of support of the basis functions is reduced. Further, multiple interior knot values, in contrast to multiple polygon vertices, reduce the differentiability of the basis function at $x_i$ to $C^{k-m-1}$ where $m \le k-1$ is the multiplicity of the interior knot value. Locally, the nonuniform curve in Fig. 5–49 is $C^0$ ($k-m-1 = 3-2-1 = 0$) continuous near $B_3$. Thus, a position discontinuity or 'corner' in the curve occurs.

Figure 5–50 shows third-order ($k = 3$) open nonuniform B-spline curves generated using a knot vector with interior knot values proportional to the chord distances between polygon vertices. Specifically, the knot vector is given by

$$x_i = 0 \qquad 1 \le i \le k$$

$$x_{i+k} = \left( \frac{\left( \dfrac{i}{n-k+2} \right) c_{i+1} + \displaystyle\sum_{j=1}^{i} c_j}{\displaystyle\sum_{i=1}^{n} c_i} \right)(n-k+2) \qquad 1 \le i \le n-k+1$$

$$x_i = n-k+2 \qquad n+1 \le i \le n+k$$

$$(5-86)$$

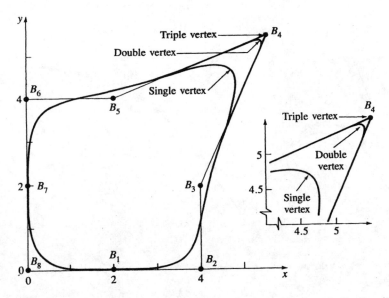

**Figure 5–48**    Effect of multiple vertices on a closed periodic B-spline curve.

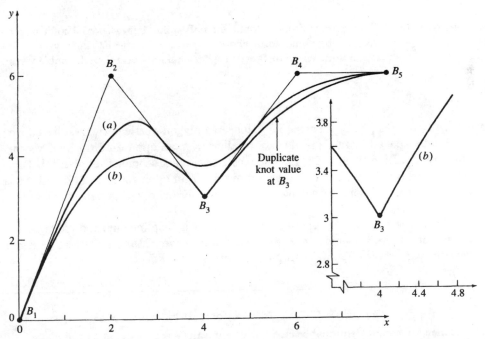

**Figure 5–49**    Nonuniform B-spline curves, $k = 3$. (a) $[X] = [0 \ 0 \ 0 \ 1 \ 2 \ 3 \ 3 \ 3]$;
(b) $[X] = [0 \ 0 \ 0 \ 1 \ 1 \ 3 \ 3 \ 3]$.

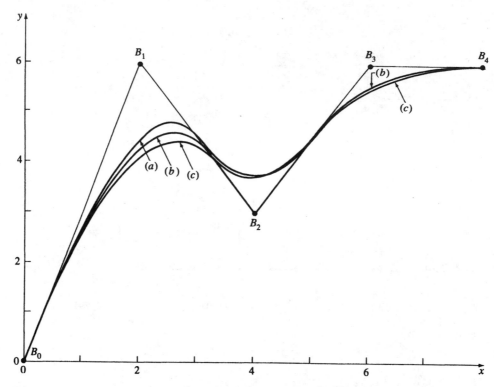

**Figure 5–50**  Comparison of open nonuniform B-spline curves. (a) Uniform knot vector; (b) nonuniform chord distance proportional knot vector; (c) nonuniform chord distance proportional knot vector with double vertex at $B_2$.

where $c_i = |B_{i+1} - B_i|$. For equally spaced polygon vertices the result reduces to equally spaced integer interior knot values, i.e., an open uniform knot vector. Hartley and Judd (Ref. 5–25) have suggested a similar scheme that yields distinct interior knot values. The curve generated with an open uniform knot vector is shown for comparison. Also shown is the curve obtained with a pair of coincident vertices at $B_2$.

From these results it appears that nonuniform B-spline curves do not greatly differ from uniform B-spline curves unless the relative distances between polygon vertices vary radically. An example illustrates these effects.

---

### Example 5–14    Nonuniform B-spline Curve

Using a nonuniform knot vector with knot values proportional to the chord distances between defining polygon vertices determine the third-order open B-spline curve defined by $B_1[0\ 0]$, $B_2[2\ 6]$, $B_3[4\ 3]$, $B_4[6\ 6]$, $B_5[8\ 6]$.

First determine the chord lengths:

$$c_1 = \sqrt{(2-0)^2 + (6-0)^2} = \sqrt{40} = 6.325$$

$$c_2 = \sqrt{(4-2)^2 + (3-6)^2} = \sqrt{13} = 3.606$$

$$c_3 = \sqrt{(6-4)^2 + (6-3)^2} = \sqrt{13} = 3.606$$

$$c_4 = \sqrt{(8-6)^2 + (6-6)^2} = \sqrt{4} = 2.0$$

The total chord length is

$$\sum_{i=1}^{4} c_i = 15.537$$

Using Eq. (5–86) the interior knot values are

$$x_4 = \left[ \frac{\dfrac{c_2}{3} + c_1}{15.537} \right] (3) = 1.453$$

$$x_5 = \left[ \frac{\dfrac{2c_3}{3} + c_1 + c_2}{15.537} \right] (3) = 2.382$$

The knot vector is thus

$$[\,x\,] = [\,0 \quad 0 \quad 0 \quad 1.45 \quad 2.382 \quad 3 \quad 3 \quad 3\,]$$

where $x_1 = 0$, $x_2 = 0, \cdots, x_8 = 3$. The parameter range is $0 \le t \le 3$. The curve is composed of three parabolic ($k - 1 = 2$) segments.

For $0 \le t < 1.453$ the basis functions are

$$N_{3,1}(t) = 1; \qquad N_{i,1}(t) = 0, \quad i \ne 3$$

$$N_{2,2}(t) = \frac{(1.453 - t)}{1.453}; \quad N_{3,2}(t) = \frac{t}{1.453}; \qquad N_{i,2}(t) = 0, \quad i \ne 2,3$$

$$N_{1,3}(t) = \frac{(1.453 - t)^2}{(1.453)^2}; \quad N_{2,3}(t) = \frac{t}{(1.453)^2}(1.453 - t) + \frac{(2.382 - t)t}{(2.382)(1.453)};$$

$$N_{3,3}(t) = \frac{t^2}{(2.382)(1.453)}; \qquad N_{i,3}(t) = 0, \quad i \ne 1,2,3$$

For $1.453 \le t < 2.382$ the basis functions are

$$N_{4,1}(t) = 1; \qquad N_{i,1}(t) = 0, \quad i \ne 4$$

$$N_{3,2}(t) = \frac{(2.382 - t)}{(2.382 - 1.453)};$$

$$N_{4,2}(t) = \frac{(t - 1.453)}{(2.382)(1.453)}; \qquad N_{i,2}(t) = 0, \quad i \ne 3,4$$

$$N_{2,3}(t) = \frac{(2.382 - t)^2}{2.382(2.382 - 1.453)};$$

$$N_{3,3}(t) = \frac{t}{2.382}\frac{(2.382 - t)}{(2.382 - 1.453)} + \frac{(3 - t)}{(3 - 1.453)}\frac{(t - 1.453)}{(2.382 - 1.453)};$$

$$N_{4,3}(t) = \frac{(t - 1.453)^2}{(3 - 1.453)(2.382 - 1.453)}; \qquad N_{i,3}(t) = 0, \quad i \ne 2,3,4$$

For $2.382 \le t < 3$

$$N_{5,1}(t) = 1; \qquad N_{i,1}(t) = 0, \quad i \ne 5$$

$$N_{4,2}(t) = \frac{(3-t)}{(3-2.382)};$$

$$N_{5,2}(t) = \frac{(t-2.382)}{(3-2.382)}; N_{i,2}(t) = 0, \quad i \ne 4,5$$

$$N_{3,3}(t) = \frac{(3-t)^2}{(3-1.453)(3-2.382)};$$

$$N_{4,3}(t) = \frac{(t-1.453)(3-t)}{(3-1.453)(3-2.382)} + \frac{(3-t)(t-2.382)}{(3-2.382)^2};$$

$$N_{5,3}(t) = \frac{(t-2.382)^2}{(3-2.382)^2}; \qquad N_{i,3}(t) = 0, \quad i \ne 3,4,5$$

Recalling that a point on the B-spline curve is given by

$$P(t) = N_{1,3}(t)B_1 + N_{2,3}(t)B_2 + N_{3,3}(t)B_3 + N_{4,3}(t)B_4 + N_{5,3}(t)B_5$$

then for $t = 1/2$

$$P\left(\frac{1}{2}\right) = 0.430B_1 + 0.498B_2 + 0.072B_3 + (0)B_4 + (0)B_5$$

$$= 0.430\,[\,0 \quad 0\,] + 0.498\,[\,2 \quad 6\,] + 0.072\,[\,4 \quad 3\,]$$

$$= [\,1.284 \quad 3.202\,]$$

and for $t = 2$

$$P(2) = (0)B_1 + 0.066B_2 + 0.726B_3 + 0.208B_4 + (0)B_5$$

$$= 0.066\,[\,2 \quad 6\,] + 0.726\,[\,4 \quad 3\,] + 0.208\,[\,6 \quad 6\,]$$

$$= [\,4.284 \quad 3.822\,]$$

Complete results are shown in Fig. 5–50.

---

The equations for B-spline curves can be expressed in a matrix form similar to those for cubic spline curves, parabolically blended curves and Bézier curves (see Eqs. 5–27, 5–44 and 5–67). The matrix form is particularly simple for periodic B-spline curves.

Recall that periodic B-spline basis functions are all translates of each other (see Fig. 5–36) and that the 'spread' or influence of a given basis function is limited to $k$ intervals. Thus, for integer knot values all periodic basis functions on the unit interval $0 \le t^* < 1$ have the same form, $N^*_{i,k}(t^*)$. Thus, it is sometimes convenient to reparameterize the basis functions to this interval. A point on a parametric B-spline curve on the reparameterized unit interval is given by

$$P_j(t^*) = \sum_{i=0}^{k-1} N^*_{i+1,k}(t^*) B_{j+i} \qquad 1 \le j \le n-k+1, \qquad 0 \le t^* < 1 \quad (5-87)$$

where $j$ counts the curve segments. Again, $n$ is one less than the number of defining polygon vertices. Notice that when written out Eq. (5–87) has only $k$ terms; i.e.,

$$P_j(t^*) = N^*_{1,k} B_j + N^*_{2,k} B_{j+1} + \cdots + N^*_{k,k} B_{j+k-1}$$

For $k = 3$ the reparameterized basis functions on the interval $0 \le t^* < 1$ are

$$N^*_{1,3}(t^*) = \frac{(1-t^*)^2}{2}$$

$$N^*_{2,3}(t^*) = \frac{-2t^{*2} + 2t^* + 1}{2}$$

$$N^*_{3,3}(t^*) = \frac{t^{*2}}{2}$$

Equation (5–87) then becomes

$$2P_j(t^*) = (1 - 2t^* + t^{*2})B_j + (-2t^{*2} + 2t^* + 1)B_{j+1} + t^{*2}B_{j+2}$$

$$\begin{aligned} = \quad & t^{*2} ( \quad B_j \ - \ 2B_{j+1} + \quad B_{j+2}) \\ + \ & t^* \ ( \ -2B_j \ + \ 2B_{j+1} + 0 \cdot B_{j+2}) \\ + \quad & ( \quad B_j \ + \ B_{j+1} + 0 \cdot B_{j+2}) \end{aligned}$$

Rewriting in matrix form yields

$$P_j(t^*) = [\,T^*\,][\,N^*\,][\,G\,]$$

$$= \frac{1}{2} [\, t^{*2} \quad t^* \quad 1 \,] \begin{bmatrix} 1 & -2 & 1 \\ -2 & 2 & 0 \\ 1 & 1 & 0 \end{bmatrix} \begin{bmatrix} B_j \\ B_{j+1} \\ B_{j+2} \end{bmatrix} \qquad (5-88)$$

Similarly, for $k = 4$ the reparameterized basis functions on the interval $0 \le t^* < 1$ are

$$N^*_{1,4}(t^*) = \frac{-t^{*3} + 3t^{*2} - 3t^* + 1}{6}$$

$$N^*_{2,4}(t^*) = \frac{3t^{*3} + 6t^{*2} + 4}{6}$$

$$N^*_{3,4}(t^*) = \frac{-t^{*3} + 3t^{*2} + 3t^* + 1}{6}$$

$$N^*_{4,4}(t^*) = \frac{t^{*3}}{6}$$

For $k = 4$ the matrix form is

$$P_j(t^*) = [\,T^*\,][\,N^*\,][\,G\,]$$

$$= \frac{1}{6}[\,t^{*3} \quad t^{*2} \quad t^* \quad 1\,] \begin{bmatrix} -1 & 3 & -3 & 1 \\ 3 & -6 & 3 & 0 \\ -3 & 0 & 3 & 0 \\ 1 & 4 & 1 & 0 \end{bmatrix} \begin{bmatrix} B_j \\ B_{j+1} \\ B_{j+2} \\ B_{j+3} \end{bmatrix} \quad (5-89)$$

Notice that Eqs. (5–87) and (5–89) are of the form of a blending function times a geometry matrix (see Eqs. 5–27, 5–44 and 5–67); i.e.,

$$P_j(t^*) = [\,T^*\,][\,N^*\,][\,G\,] = [\,F\,][\,G\,] \quad 1 \le j \le n-k+1, \quad 0 \le t^* < 1$$
$$(5-90)$$

where here

$$[\,T^*\,] = [\,t^{*k-1} \quad t^{*k-2} \quad \cdots \quad t^* \quad 1\,] \quad 0 \le t^* < 1$$

$[\,G\,]^T = [\,B_j \quad \cdots \quad B_{j+k-1}\,]$ contains the geometry represented by the defining polygon vertices, and $[\,F\,]$ is composed of the appropriate B-spline basis functions.

For periodic B-spline curves Cohen and Riesenfeld (Ref. 5–19) have shown that the generalized form of $[\,N\,]$ is

$$[\,N^*\,] = [\,N^*_{i+1,\,j+1}\,] \quad (5-91)$$

where

$$N^*_{i+1,\,j+1} = \frac{1}{(k-1)!}n^*_{i+1,j+1}$$

$$= \frac{1}{(k-1)!}\binom{k-1}{i}\sum_{l=j}^{k-1}(k-(l+1))^i(-1)^{l-j}\binom{k}{l-j} \quad 0 \le i,\, j \le k-1$$

Recall that for closed periodic B-spline curves it is necessary to repeat some of the defining polygon vertices to close the curve. A matrix formulation makes this more convenient. A closed periodic B-spline curve is given by

$$P_{j+1}(t^*) = \sum_{i=0}^{k-1}N^*_{i+1,k}(t^*)B_{((j+i)\ \mathrm{mod}\ (n+1))}+1 \quad 0 \le j \le n \quad (5-92)$$

Or in matrix form

$$P_{j+1}(t^*) = [\,T^*\,][\,N^*\,] \begin{bmatrix} B_{(j\ \mathrm{mod}\ (n+1))+1} \\ B_{((j+1)\ \mathrm{mod}\ (n+1))+1} \\ \cdot \\ \cdot \\ \cdot \\ B_{((j+1+n-k)\ \mathrm{mod}\ (n+1))+1} \end{bmatrix} \quad (5-93)$$

where $[T^*]$ and $[N^*]$ are as given in Eq. (5–90), and mod is the modulo or remainder function; e.g., 3 mod 2 = 1.

While open B-spline curves can also be represented in matrix form, the existence of multiple knot values at the ends precludes obtaining as compact a result as for periodic B-splines. In general, the matrix representation of an open B-spline curve with integer knot values is given by

$$P(t) = [F][G] = [T][N][G] \qquad (5-94)$$

where

$$[G]^T = [B_1 \quad \cdot \quad \cdot \quad \cdot \quad B_{n+1}]$$

and the elements of $[F]$ or $[N]$ are obtained using the Cox–deBoor algorithm (see Eq. 5–84) for each nonzero interval in the knot vector $[X]$. For low-order B-spline curves described by polygons with large numbers of vertices, most of the terms in $[F]$ are zero. Significant computational efficiencies result by taking advantage of this fact.[†] Cohen and Riesenfeld (Ref. 5–19) give a generalized formulation for $[N^*]$ on the reparameterized interval $0 \le t^* < 1$. However, because of the multiplicity of knot values at the ends of the knot vector, the first and last $k - 1$ $[N^*]$ matrices are special cases. The matrices for the interior intervals are given by Eq. (5–91).

An example illustrates the matrix method.

---

### Example 5–15 Calculating a Closed B-spline Curve

Determine the fourth-order $(k = 4)$ closed B-spline curve defined by the polygon shown in Fig. 5–46. Use the matrix formulation. The polygon vertices are $B_1[2 \quad 0]$, $B_2[4 \quad 0]$, $B_3[4 \quad 2]$, $B_4[4 \quad 4]$, $B_5[2 \quad 4]$, $B_6[0 \quad 4]$, $B_7[0 \quad 2]$, $B_8[0 \quad 0]$, $B_9[2 \quad 0]$. Thus $n = 8$.

For each unit interval $0 \le t^* < 1$, Eqs. (5–89) and (5–93) yield

$$P_{j+1}(t^*) = \frac{1}{6}[t^{*3} \quad t^{*2} \quad t^* \quad 1]\begin{bmatrix} -1 & 3 & -3 & 1 \\ 3 & -6 & 3 & 0 \\ -3 & 0 & 3 & 0 \\ 1 & 4 & 1 & 0 \end{bmatrix}\begin{bmatrix} B_{(j \bmod 8)+1} \\ B_{((j+1) \bmod 8)+1} \\ B_{((j+2) \bmod 8)+1} \\ B_{((j+3) \bmod 8)+1} \end{bmatrix}$$

At $t^* = 1/2$ on the first segment $(j = 0)$ of the curve the result is

$$P_1\left(\frac{1}{2}\right) = \frac{1}{6}\begin{bmatrix} \frac{1}{8} & \frac{1}{4} & \frac{1}{2} & 1 \end{bmatrix}\begin{bmatrix} -1 & 3 & -3 & 1 \\ 3 & -6 & 3 & 0 \\ -3 & 0 & 3 & 0 \\ 1 & 4 & 1 & 0 \end{bmatrix}\begin{bmatrix} B_1 \\ B_2 \\ B_3 \\ B_4 \end{bmatrix}$$

$$= \frac{1}{48}[1 \quad 23 \quad 23 \quad 1]\begin{bmatrix} 2 & 0 \\ 4 & 0 \\ 4 & 2 \\ 4 & 4 \end{bmatrix}$$

$$= \frac{1}{48}[190 \quad 50] = [3.958 \quad 1.042]$$

---

[†] See the algorithm in Appendix G.

At $t^* = 1/2$ on segment eight $(j = 7)$ the result is

$$P_8\left(\frac{1}{2}\right) = \frac{1}{48}\begin{bmatrix} 1 & 23 & 23 & 1 \end{bmatrix}\begin{bmatrix} B_8 \\ B_1 \\ B_2 \\ B_3 \end{bmatrix}$$

$$= \frac{1}{48}\begin{bmatrix} 1 & 23 & 23 & 1 \end{bmatrix}\begin{bmatrix} 0 & 0 \\ 2 & 0 \\ 4 & 0 \\ 4 & 2 \end{bmatrix}$$

$$= \frac{1}{48}\begin{bmatrix} 142 & 2 \end{bmatrix} = \begin{bmatrix} 2.958 & 0.417 \end{bmatrix}$$

Complete results are shown in Fig. 5-46b.

---

The derivatives of a B-spline curve at any point on the curve are obtained by formal differentiation. Specifically recalling Eq. (5-83), i.e.,

$$P(t) = \sum_{i=1}^{n+1} B_i N_{i,k}(t) \tag{5-83}$$

the first derivative is

$$P'(t) = \sum_{i=1}^{n+1} B_i N'_{i,k}(t) \tag{5-95}$$

while the second derivative is

$$P''(t) = \sum_{i=1}^{n+1} B_i N''_{i,k}(t) \tag{5-96}$$

Here, the primes denote differentiation with respect to the parameter $t$.

The derivatives of the basis functions are also obtained by formal differentiation. Differentiating Eqs. (5-84) once yields

$$N'_{i,k}(t) = \frac{N_{i,k-1}(t) + (t - x_i)N'_{i,k-1}(t)}{x_{i+k-1} - x_i} + \frac{(x_{i+k} - t)N'_{i+1,k-1}(t) - N_{i+1,k-1}(t)}{x_{i+k} - x_{i+1}}$$

$$\tag{5-97}$$

Note from Eq. (5-84a) that $N'_{i,1}(t) = 0$ for all $t$. Consequently, for $k = 2$, Eq. (5-97) reduces to

$$N'_{i,2}(t) = \frac{N_{i,1}(t)}{x_{i+k-1} - x_i} - \frac{N_{i+1,1}(t)}{x_{i+k} - x_{i+1}} \tag{5-98}$$

Differentiating Eq. (5–97) yields the second derivative of the basis function:

$$N''_{i,k}(t) = \frac{2N'_{i,k-1}(t) + (t - x_i)N''_{i,k-1}(t)}{x_{i+k-1} - x_i}$$

$$+ \frac{(x_{i+k} - t)N''_{i+1,k-1}(t) - 2N'_{i+1,k-1}(t)}{x_{i+k} - x_{i+1}} \qquad (5-99)$$

Here, note that both $N''_{i,1}(t) = 0$ and $N''_{i,2}(t) = 0$ for all $t$. Consequently, for $k = 3$, Eq. (5–97) reduces to

$$N''_{i,3}(t) = 2\left( \frac{N'_{i,2}(t)}{x_{i+k-1} - x_i} - \frac{N'_{i+1,2}(t)}{x_{i+k} - x_{i+1}} \right) \qquad (5-100)$$

Figure 5–51 shows several B-spline basis functions and their first and second derivatives for $k = 4$. Notice that for $k = 4$ each B-spline basis function is described by piecewise cubic equations, the first derivatives by piecewise parabolic equations and the second derivatives by piecewise linear equations. The third derivative, if shown, would be described by discontinuous constant values.

An example is instructive.

---

### Example 5–16    Calculating B-spline Curve Derivatives

Consider the defining polygon previously used in Ex. 5–12 to calculate the open B-spline curve, i.e., $B_1[1\ \ 1]$, $B_2[2\ \ 3]$, $B_3[4\ \ 3]$, $B_4[3\ \ 1]$. Determine the first derivative of the second-order curve $(k = 2)$.

For $k = 2$ the open knot vector is

$$[0\ \ 0\ \ 1\ \ 2\ \ 3\ \ 3]$$

where $x_1 = 0$, $x_2 = 0, \cdots, x_6 = 3$. The parameter range is $0 \le t \le 3$. From Eq. (5–95) the first derivative of the curve for $n = 3$, $k = 2$ is

$$P'(t) = B_1 N'_{1,2}(t) + B_2 N'_{2,2}(t) + B_3 N'_{3,2}(t) + B_4 N'_{4,2}(t)$$

From Eq. (5–98)

$$N'_{i,2}(t) = \frac{N_{i,1}(t)}{x_{i+k-1} - x_i} - \frac{N_{i+1,1}(t)}{x_{i+k} - x_{i+1}}$$

Using results from Ex. 5–12 yields for $0 \le t < 1$

$$N_{2,1}(t) = 1; \qquad N_{i,1}(t) = 0, \quad i \ne 2$$

and

$$N'_{1,2}(t) = -1; \qquad N'_{2,2}(t) = 1; \qquad N'_{i,2}(t) = 0, \quad i \ne 1, 2$$

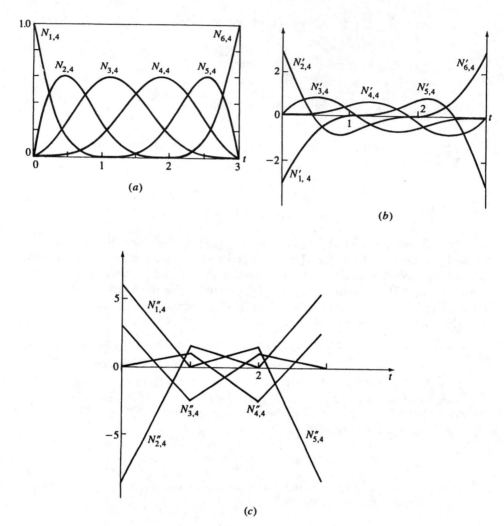

**Figure 5–51**　B-spline basis functions and their first and second derivatives, $k = 4$, $n = 6$. (a) Basis functions; (b) first derivative; (c) second derivative.

Thus,

$$P'(t) = B_2 - B_1$$

which is the slope (tangent vector) of the first polygon span as it should be. For $1 \le t < 2$

$$N_{3,1}(t) = 1; \quad N_{i,1}(t) = 0 \quad i \ne 3$$

and

$$N'_{2,2}(t) = -1; \quad N'_{3,2}(t) = 1; \quad N'_{i,2}(t) = 0 \quad i \ne 2, 3$$

which yields

$$P'(t) = B_3 - B_2$$

which is the slope (tangent vector) of the second polygon span.

Finally for $2 \le t < 3$

$$N_{4,1}(t) = 1; \quad N_{i,1}(t) = 0 \quad i \ne 4$$

and

$$N'_{3,2}(t) = -1; \quad N'_{4,2}(t) = 1; \quad N'_{i,2}(t) = 0 \quad i \ne 3,4$$

which yields

$$P'(t) = B_4 - B_3$$

the slope (tangent vector) of the last polygon span.

At $t = 3$, $N_{i,1}(3) = 0$ for all $i$. Consequently, formally $P'(3) = 0$. However, again considering the limiting result for $t = 3 - \epsilon$, $\epsilon \to 0$ shows that practically $P'(3) = (B_4 - B_3)$.

---

## 5–10    END CONDITIONS FOR PERIODIC B-SPLINE CURVES

As previously shown, periodic B-spline curves do not start and end at the first and last vertices of the defining polygon. Two questions thus occur. First, where do they start and end and what are the conditions (derivatives) at these points? Second, how can the starting and ending points and conditions at those points be controlled? Barsky (Ref. 5–24) has studied these conditions for the specific case of cubic ($k = 4$) B-spline curves. The present discussion is somewhat more general.

In general, a periodic B-spline curve starts at $P_s = P(t = x_k)$ and ends at $P_e = P(t = x_{n+1})$. For integer knot values beginning at zero $P_s = P(t = k)$ and $P_e = P(t = n)$. Recalling Eqs. (5–87) and (5–91) and that any point on a B-spline curve is affected by only $k$ defining polygon vertices, then for the reparameterized interval $0 \le t^* < 1$, the starting point occurs for $t^* = 0$. Thus,

$$P_s = \frac{1}{(k-1)!}(N^*_{k,1}B_1 + N^*_{k,2}B_2 + \cdots + N^*_{k,k}B_k)$$

Noting that $N^*_{k,k} = 0$ for all $k$ yields

$$P_s = \frac{1}{(k-1)!}(N^*_{k,1}B_1 + N^*_{k,2}B_2 + \cdots + N^*_{k,k-1}B_{k-1}) \qquad n \ge k \qquad (5-101)$$

At the end of the reparameterized interval $t^* = 1$. Noting that $\sum_{i=1}^{k} N^*_{i,1} = 0$ the end point is given by

$$P_e = \frac{1}{(k-1)!}\left(\sum_{i=1}^{k}N^*_{i,2}B_{n-k+3} + \sum_{i=1}^{k}N^*_{i,3}B_{n-k+4} + \cdots + \sum_{i=1}^{k}N^*_{i,k}B_{n+1}\right) \qquad n \ge k$$

$$(5-102)$$

For quadratic ($k = 3$) periodic B-spline curves Eqs. (5–101) and (5–102) yield

$$P_s = \frac{1}{2}(B_1 + B_2)$$

$$P_e = \frac{1}{2}(B_n + B_{n+1})$$

Thus, quadratic periodic B-spline curves start and end at the midpoint of the first and last spans of the defining polygon, respectively.

For cubic ($k = 4$) periodic B-spline curves the start and end points are

$$P_s = \frac{1}{6}(B_1 + 4B_2 + B_3)$$

$$P_e = \frac{1}{6}(B_{n-1} + 4B_n + B_{n+1})$$

Recalling Eq. (5–90) the first derivative at the starting point is

$$P_s' = [\,T^{*'}\,]_{t^*=0}\,[\,N^*\,][\,G\,]$$

$$= \frac{1}{(k-1)!}(N_{k-1,1}^* B_1 + N_{k-1,2}^* B_2 + \cdots + N_{k-1,k-1}^* B_{k-1})$$

$$(5-103)$$

since $N_{k-1,k}^* = 0$ for all $k$. The first derivative at the end point is

$$P_e' = [\,T^{*'}\,]_{t^*=1}\,[\,N^*\,][\,G\,]$$

$$= \frac{1}{(k-1)!}\left(\sum_{i=1}^{k-1}(k-i)N_{i,2}^* B_{n-k+3}\right.$$

$$\left.+ \sum_{i=1}^{k-1}(k-i)N_{i,3}^* B_{n-k+4} + \cdots + \sum_{i=1}^{k-1}(k-i)N_{i,k}^* B_{n+1}\right) \qquad (5-104)$$

where $[\,T^{*'}\,] = [\,(k-1)t^{*(k-2)} \quad (k-2)t^{*(k-3)} \quad \cdots \quad 1 \quad 0\,]$ is the derivative of the parameter vector.

For quadratic ($k = 3$) periodic B-spline curves these results reduce to

$$P_s' = \frac{1}{2}(-2B_1 + 2B_2) = B_2 - B_1$$

$$P_e' = \frac{1}{2}(-2B_n + 2B_{n+1}) = B_{n+1} - B_n$$

the tangent vectors (slopes) of the first and last polygon spans.

For cubic ($k = 4$) curves the results are

$$P_s' = \frac{1}{6}(-3B_1 + 3B_3) = \frac{1}{2}(B_3 - B_1)$$

$$P_e' = \frac{1}{6}(-3B_{n-2} + 3B_{n+1}) = \frac{1}{2}(B_{n+1} - B_{n-1})$$

Here, the tangent vectors (slopes) are given by the tangent vectors (slopes) of the lines from the first to the third and the third from last to the last defining polygon vertices.

The second derivatives at the start and end points are

$$P_s'' = [\,T^{*''}\,]_{t^*=0}[\,N^*\,][\,G\,]$$

$$= \frac{2}{(k-1)!}(N_{k-2,1}^* B_1 + N_{k-2,2}^* B_2 + \cdots + N_{k-2,k-1}^* B_{k-1})$$

$$(5-105)$$

$$P_e'' = [\,T^{*''}\,]_{t^*=1}[\,N^*\,][\,G\,]$$

$$= \frac{1}{(k-1)!}\left(\sum_{i=1}^{k-2}(k-i)(k-i-1)N_{i,2}^* B_{n-k+3}\right.$$

$$+ \sum_{i=1}^{k-2}(k-i)(k-i-1)N_{i,3}^* B_{n-k+4}$$

$$\left. + \cdots + \sum_{i=1}^{k-2}(k-i)(k-i-1)N_{i,k}^* B_{n+1}\right)$$

$$(5-106)$$

where $[\,T^{*''}\,] = [\,(k-1)t^{*(k-2)}\quad (k-2)t^{*(k-3)}\quad \cdots \quad 1\quad 0\,]$ is the second derivative of the parameter vector.

For cubic ($k = 4$) curves Eqs. (5–105) and (5–106) yield

$$P_s'' = \frac{1}{6}(6B_1 - 12B_2 + 6B_3) = B_1 - 2B_2 + B_3$$

$$P_e'' = \frac{1}{6}(6B_{n-1} - 12B_n + 6B_{n+1}) = B_{n-1} - 2B_n + B_{n+1}$$

Techniques for controlling the position of the start and end points and the conditions at those points fall into two categories: multiple vertices and pseudovertices.

Defining multiple coincident vertices at an end of a periodic B-spline curve pulls the starting and ending point of the curve closer to the vertex. When $k-1$ multiple coincident vertices are defined, then the end point of the curve is coincident with the vertices and the tangent vector (slope) of the curve is given by the direction of the adjacent nonzero length polygon span.

For example, for $k = 3$ with double vertices at the ends, i.e., with $B_1 = B_2$ and $B_n = B_{n+1}$, Eqs. (5–101) and (5–102) yield

$$P_s = \frac{1}{2}(B_1 + B_2) = \frac{1}{2}(2B_1) = B_1$$

$$P_e = \frac{1}{2}(B_n + B_{n+1}) = \frac{1}{2}(2B_{n+1}) = B_{n+1}$$

For $k = 4$ with double vertices at the ends, Eqs. (5–101) and (5–102) yield

$$P_s = \frac{1}{6}(5B_1 + B_3)$$

$$P_e = \frac{1}{6}(B_{n-1} + 5B_{n+1})$$

Thus, the starting point is one-sixth of the distance along the span from $B_1$ to $B_3$, and the end point is five-sixths of the distance along the span from $B_{n-1}$ to $B_{n+1}$.

With triple vertices at the ends, i.e., with $B_1 = B_2 = B_3$ and $B_{n-1} = B_n = B_{n+1}$, the results for $k = 4$ are

$$P_s = \frac{1}{6}(B_1 + 4B_1 + B_1) = B_1$$

$$P_e = \frac{1}{6}(B_{n+1} + 4B_{n+1} + B_{n+1}) = B_{n+1}$$

The curve starts and ends at the first and last polygon vertices. Figure 5–52 shows the effect of multiple coincident vertices at the beginning and end of the defining polygon.

With triple vertices at the ends, the first and last B-spline curve segments for $k = 4$ are given by (see Eq. 5–89)

$$P_1(t^*) = B_1 + \frac{t^{*3}}{6}[B_4 - B_1] = B_3 + \frac{t^{*3}}{6}[B_4 - B_3] \quad 0 \le t^* < 1$$

and
$$P_n(t^*) = B_{n+1} + \frac{(1 - t^{*3})}{6}(B_n - B_{n+1})$$

Inspection shows that the first and last segments are linear. The first curve segment is coincident with and extends one-sixth of the distance along the span from $B_1 = B_2 = B_3$ to $B_4$. The last segment is coincident with and extends from five-sixths of the distance along the span from $B_{n-2}$ to $B_{n-1} = B_n = B_{n+1}$.

Although this short straight curve segment can be made arbitrarily small, it can cause difficulties in certain design applications. Open B-spline curves do not exhibit this characteristic and thus may be more suitable for these design applications.

Instead of multiple vertices at the ends of a periodic B-spline curve, pseudovertices can be constructed to control both the location of, and conditions at, the start and end points. Generally these pseudovertices are neither displayed nor can a user manipulate them. Here, as shown in Fig. 5–53, $B_0$ and $B_{n+2}$ are used to designate the pseudovertices at the start and end of a B-spline curve. With this notation Eqs. (5–101) and (5–102) become

$$P_s = \frac{1}{(k-1)!}(N^*_{k,1}B_0 + N^*_{k,2}B_1 + \cdots + N^*_{k,k-1}B_{k-2}) \qquad n \ge k \qquad (5-107)$$

and

$$P_e = \frac{1}{(k-1)!}\left(\sum_{i=1}^{k} N^*_{i,2}B_{n-k+4} + \sum_{i=1}^{k} N^*_{i,3}B_{n-k+5} + \cdots + \sum_{i=1}^{k} N^*_{i,k}B_{n+2}\right) \qquad n \ge k$$

$$(5-108)$$

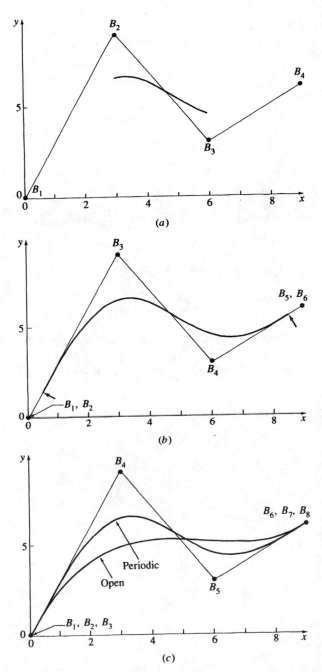

(a)

(b)

(c)

**Figure 5-52**   Effect of multiple coincident vertices at the ends of the defining polygon ($k = 4$). (a) No multiple vertices; (b) two multiple vertices; (c) three multiple vertices and the corresponding open B-spline curves.

With $P_s = B_1$ and $P_e = B_{n+1}$ these equations yield

$$B_0 = \left((k-1)! - N_{k,2}^*\right)B_1 - (N_{k,3}^* B_2 + \cdots + N_{k,k-1}^* B_{k-2}) \qquad n \geq k \quad (5-109)$$

and

$$B_{n+2} = \left((k-1)! - \sum_{i=1}^{k} N_{i,k-1}^*\right)B_{n+1}$$

$$- \left(\sum_{i=1}^{k} N_{i,2}^* B_{n-k+4} + \cdots + \sum_{i=1}^{k} N_{i,k-2}^* B_n\right) \qquad n \geq k$$

$$(5-110)$$

where the fact that $N_{k,1}^* = 1$ and $\sum_{i=1}^{k} N_{i,k}^* = 1$ has been used.

For $k = 3$ Eqs. (5–109) and (5–110) yield $B_0 = B_1$ and $B_{n+2} = B_{n+1}$, i.e., duplicate vertices at the ends!

For $k = 4$ the results are

$$B_0 = (6-4)B_1 - B_2 = 2B_1 - B_2$$

and

$$B_{n+2} = (6-4)B_{n+1} - B_n = 2B_{n+1} - B_n$$

Figure 5–53 illustrates these results.

The first and second derivatives at the ends of the curve are given by Eqs. (5–103) and (5–104) appropriately modified to account for the pseudovertices. As an example, after using the above results for $B_0$, Eqs. (5–103) and (5–104) for $k = 4$ yield

$$P_s' = \frac{1}{2}(B_2 - B_0) = \frac{1}{2}\{B_2 - (2B_1 - B_2)\} = B_2 - B_1$$

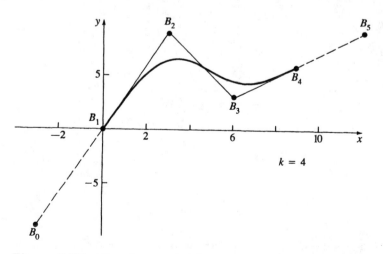

**Figure 5–53**    Pseudovertices control start and end points of periodic B-spline curves.

and

$$P'_e = \frac{1}{2}(B_{n+2} - B_n) = \frac{1}{2}\{2B_{n+1} - B_n - B_n\} = B_{n+1} - B_n$$

Thus, the curve is tangent to the first and last defining polygon spans.

Similarly, for $k = 4$, after using the above results for $B_0$ and $B_{n+2}$, Eqs. (5–105) and (5–106) yield

$$P''_s = B_0 - 2B_1 + B_2 = 2B_1 - B_2 - 2B_1 + B_2 = 0$$

$$P''_e = B_n + 2B_{n+1} + B_{n+2} = B_n - 2B_{n+1} + 2B_{n+1} - B_n = 0$$

Thus, the 'curvature' at the ends is zero.

Rewriting Eqs. (5–103) and (5–104) allows the determination of pseudovertices that yield specified tangent vectors at the ends of the curve. Specifically, Eq. (5–103) yields

$$B_0 = \frac{1}{N^*_{k-1,1}}\left\{(k-1)!\, P'_s - (N^*_{k-1,2}B_1 + \cdots + N^*_{k-1,k-1}B_{k-2})\right\} \qquad n \geq k$$

$$(5-111)$$

and Eq. (5–104) yields

$$B_{n+2} = \frac{1}{\displaystyle\sum_{i=1}^{k-1}(k-1)N^*_{i,k}}\left\{(k-1)!\, P'_e\right.$$

$$\left. - \left(\sum_{i=1}^{k-1}(k-1)N^*_{i,2}B_{n-k+4} + \cdots + \sum_{i=1}^{k-1}(k-1)N^*_{i,k-1}B_{n+1}\right)\right\} \qquad n \geq k$$

$$(5-112)$$

For $k = 4$, Eqs. (5–111) and (5–112) reduce to

$$B_0 = B_2 - 2P'_s$$

$$B_{n+2} = 2P'_e + B_n$$

Typical results are shown in Fig. 5–54. The start and end points for the resulting curve are obtained by substituting these values into Eqs. (5–107) and (5–108). Notice from Fig. 5–54 that the start and end points for the curve with specified tangent vectors at the ends, defined by $B_0B_1B_2B_3B_4B_5$, are quite different from those for the curve defined only by $B_1B_2B_3B_4$ (marked by ×'s).

The second derivative or approximate curvature at the start and end points of the curve is controlled by rewriting Eqs. (5–105) and (5–106) to yield

$$B_0 = \frac{1}{N^*_{k-2,1}}\left\{\frac{(k-1)!}{2}\, P''_s - (N^*_{k-2,2}B_1 + \cdots + N^*_{k-2,k-1}B_{k-2})\right\} \qquad n \geq k$$

$$(5-113)$$

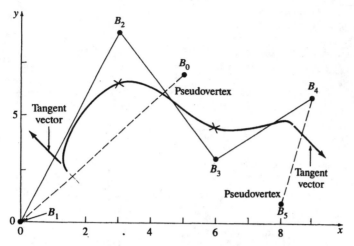

**Figure 5–54**   Tangent vector control for periodic B-spline curves, $k = 4$.

and

$$B_{n+2} = \cfrac{1}{\sum\limits_{i=1}^{k-1}(k-1)(k-i-1)N^*_{i,k}}\left\{(k-1)!\,P''_e\right.$$

$$-\left(\sum_{i=1}^{k-2}(k-1)(k-i-1)N^*_{i,2}B_{n-k+4}\right.$$

$$\left.\left.+\cdots+\sum_{i=1}^{k-2}(k-1)(k-i-1)N^*_{i,k-1}B_{n+1}\right)\right\}\qquad n \geq k$$

$$(5-114)$$

For $k = 4$, Eqs. (5–113) and (5–114) yield

$$B_0 = P''_s + 2B_1 - B_2$$

$$B_{n+2} = P''_e + 2B_{n+1} - B_n$$

Again the start and end points are obtained by substituting these values into Eqs. (5–107) and (5–108). Similarly, the tangent vectors are obtained by using Eqs. (5–103) and (5–104) rewritten in terms of $B_0$ to $B_{n+2}$.

## 5–11   B-SPLINE CURVE FIT

The previous sections discussed the generation of a B-spline curve from its defining polygon. Here, determining a polygon that generates a B-spline curve for a set of *known* data points is considered. The problem is shown schematically in Fig. 5–55.

If a data point lies on the B-spline curve, then it must satisfy Eq. (5–83). Writing Eq. (5–83) for each of $j$ data points yields

$$D_1(t_1) = N_{1,k}(t_1)B_1 + N_{2,k}(t_1)B_2 + \cdots + N_{n+1,k}(t_1)B_{n+1}$$

$$D_2(t_2) = N_{1,k}(t_2)B_1 + N_{2,k}(t_2)B_2 + \cdots + N_{n+1,k}(t_2)B_{n+1}$$

$$\vdots$$

$$D_j(t_j) = N_{1,k}(t_j)B_1 + N_{2,k}(t_j)B_2 + \cdots + N_{n+1,k}(t_j)B_{n+1}$$

where $2 \le k \le n+1 \le j$. This system of equations is more compactly written in matrix form as

$$[D] = [N][B] \tag{5-115}$$

where

$$[D]^T = [\, D_1(t_1) \quad D_2(t_2) \quad \cdots \quad D_j(t_j) \,]$$

$$[B]^T = [\, B_1 \quad B_2 \quad \cdots \quad B_{n+1} \,]$$

$$[N] = \begin{bmatrix} N_{1,k} & \cdots & \cdots & N_{n+1,k}(t_1) \\ \vdots & \ddots & & \vdots \\ \vdots & & \ddots & \vdots \\ N_{1,k}(t_j) & \cdots & \cdots & N_{n+1,k}(t_j) \end{bmatrix}$$

If $2 \le k \le n+1 = j$, then the matrix $[N]$ is square and the defining polygon is obtained directly by matrix inversion, i.e.,

$$[B] = [N]^{-1}[D] \qquad 2 \le k \le n+1 = j \tag{5-116}$$

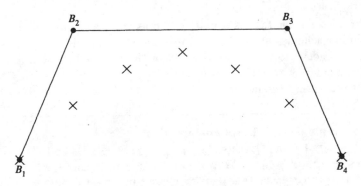

**Figure 5–55**   Determining a B-spline polygon for a known data set.

In this case, the resulting B-spline curve passes through each data point, i.e., a curve fit is obtained. Although the continuity of the resulting curve is everywhere $C^{k-2}$, it may not be 'smooth', or 'sweet' or 'fair'. The fitted curve may develop unwanted wiggles or undulations.

A fairer or smoother curve is obtained by specifying fewer defining polygon points than data points, i.e., $2 \le k \le n+1 < j$. Here, $[N]$ is no longer square, the problem is overspecified and can only be solved in a mean sense. Recalling that a matrix times its transpose is always square (see Sec. 3–21), the defining polygon vertices for a B-spline curve that fairs or smooths the data are given by

$$[D] = [N][B]$$

$$[N]^T[D] = [N]^T[N][B]$$

and
$$[B] = [[N]^T \ [N]]^{-1}[N]^T[D] \qquad (5-117)$$

Both of these techniques assume that the matrix $[N]$ is known. Provided that the order of the B-spline basis $k$, the number of defining polygon points $n+1$, and the parameter value along the curve are known, then the basis functions $N_{i,k}(t_j)$ and hence the matrix $[N]$ can be obtained. Within the restrictions $2 \le k \le n+1 \le j$, the order and number of polygon vertices are arbitrary.

The parameter value $t_j$ for each data point is a measure of the data point's distance along the B-spline curve. One useful approximation for this parameter value uses the chord length between data points. Specifically, for $j$ data points the parameter value at the $l$th data point is

$$t_1 = 0$$

$$\frac{t_l}{t_{\max}} = \frac{\sum\limits_{s=2}^{l} |D_s - D_{s-1}|}{\sum\limits_{s=2}^{j} |D_s - D_{s-1}|} \qquad l \ge 2$$

The maximum parameter value $t_{\max}$ is usually taken as the maximum value of the knot vector. Similar schemes are mentioned in Refs. (5–15) and (5–22).

For an open uniform knot vector with multiplicity of the knot values at the ends equal to $k$, a Bézier curve is obtained when $n = k$.

An example illustrates these techniques.

---

### Example 5–17    B-spline Curve Fit

For the five data points $D_1[0 \quad 0]$, $D_2[1.5 \quad 2]$, $D_3[3 \quad 2.5]$, $D_4[4.5 \quad 2]$, $D_5[6 \quad 0]$ determine the third-order ($k = 3$) defining polygons having five and four polygon vertices that generate a B-spline curve 'through' the data points. Use the chord length approximation for the parameter values along the B-spline curve corresponding to the data points.

First determine the chord lengths.

$$D_{21} = |D_2 - D_1| = \sqrt{(x_2 - x_1)^2 + (y_2 - y_1)^2} = \sqrt{(1.5)^2 + (2)^2} = \sqrt{6.25} = 2.5$$

$$D_{32} = |D_3 - D_2| = \sqrt{(1.5)^2 + (.5)^2} = 1.58$$

$$D_{43} = |D_4 - D_3| = \sqrt{(1.5)^2 + (-.5)^2} = 1.58$$

$$D_{54} = |D_5 - D_4| = \sqrt{(1.5)^2 + (-2)^2} = 2.5$$

and

$$\sum_{s=2}^{5}(D_s - D_{s-1}) = D_{51} = 8.16$$

Thus

$$t_1 = 0$$

$$\frac{t_2}{t_{max}} = \frac{D_{21}}{D_{51}} = \frac{2.5}{8.16} = 0.31$$

$$\frac{t_3}{t_{max}} = \frac{D_{31}}{D_{51}} = \frac{(2.5 + 1.58)}{8.16} = 0.5$$

$$\frac{t_4}{t_{max}} = \frac{D_{41}}{D_{51}} = \frac{(2.5 + 1.58 + 1.58)}{8.16} = 0.69$$

$$\frac{t_5}{t_{max}} = \frac{D_{51}}{D_{51}} = 1$$

For five polygon vertices, the maximum value of the knot vector for a third-order B-spline curve is $n - k + 2 = 4 - 3 + 2 = 3$. $n$ is one less than the number of polygon vertices. The knot vector with multiplicity $k$ at the ends is

$$[\,0 \quad 0 \quad 0 \quad 1 \quad 2 \quad 3 \quad 3 \quad 3\,]$$

With these values Eq. (5–115) becomes

$$[D] = [N][B]$$

$$
\begin{bmatrix}
0 & 0 \\
1.5 & 2 \\
3 & 2.5 \\
4.5 & 2 \\
6 & 0
\end{bmatrix}
=
\begin{bmatrix}
1 & 0 & 0 & 0 & 0 \\
0.007 & 0.571 & 0.422 & 0 & 0 \\
0 & 0.125 & 0.75 & 0.125 & 0 \\
0 & 0 & 0.422 & 0.571 & 0.007 \\
0 & 0 & 0 & 0 & 1
\end{bmatrix}
[B]
$$

Solving for $[B]$ yields

$$[B] = [N]^{-1}[D]$$

$$
=
\begin{bmatrix}
1 & 0 & 0 & 0 & 0 \\
-0.013 & 2.037 & -1.307 & 0.286 & -0.002 \\
0.003 & -0.387 & 1.769 & -0.387 & 0.003 \\
-0.002 & 0.286 & -1.307 & 2.037 & -0.013 \\
0 & 0 & 0 & 0 & 1
\end{bmatrix}
\begin{bmatrix}
0 & 0 \\
1.5 & 2 \\
3 & 2.5 \\
4.5 & 2 \\
6 & 0
\end{bmatrix}
$$

$$[B] = \begin{bmatrix} 0 & 0 \\ 0.409 & 1.378 \\ 3 & 2.874 \\ 5.591 & 1.377 \\ 6 & 0 \end{bmatrix}$$

Figure 5–56a shows the original data points, the calculated polygon vertices and the resulting curve.

For four polygon vertices, the knot vector with multiplicity $k$ at the ends is

$$[0 \quad 0 \quad 0 \quad 1 \quad 2 \quad 2 \quad 2]$$

$[N]$ becomes

$$[N] = \begin{bmatrix} 1 & 0 & 0 & 0 \\ 0.15 & 0.662 & 0.188 & 0 \\ 0 & 0.5 & 0.5 & 0 \\ 0 & 0.188 & 0.662 & 0.15 \\ 0 & 0 & 0 & 1 \end{bmatrix}$$

Multiplying by $[N]^T$ and taking the inverse yields

$$[[N]^T[N]]^{-1} = \begin{bmatrix} 0.995 & -0.21 & 0.106 & -0.005 \\ -0.21 & 2.684 & -1.855 & 0.106 \\ 0.106 & -1.855 & 2.684 & -0.21 \\ -0.005 & 0.106 & -0.21 & 0.995 \end{bmatrix}$$

Equation (5–117) then gives

$$[B] = [[N]^T[N]]^{-1}[N]^T[D] = \begin{bmatrix} 0 & 0 \\ 0.788 & 2.414 \\ 5.212 & 2.414 \\ 6 & 0 \end{bmatrix}$$

The original data, the calculated polygon vertices and the resulting curve are shown in Fig. 5–56b. Notice that except at the ends the curve does not pass through the original data points.

---

The above fitting technique allows each of the determined defining polygon points for the B-spline curve to be located anywhere in three space. In some design situations it is more useful to constrain the defining polygon points to lie at a particular coordinate value, say $x = $ constant. An example of such a design situation is in fitting B-spline curves to existing ships' lines. Rogers and Fog (Ref. 5–26) have developed such a technique for both curves and surfaces. Essentially, the technique iterates the parameter value of the fixed coordinate until the value on the B-spline curve at the assumed parameter value calculated with the defining polygons obtained using the above fitting technique is within some specified amount of the fixed value, i.e., $|x_{\text{fixed}} - x_{\text{calc}}| \leq$ error. The resulting fit is less accurate but more convenient for subsequent modification.

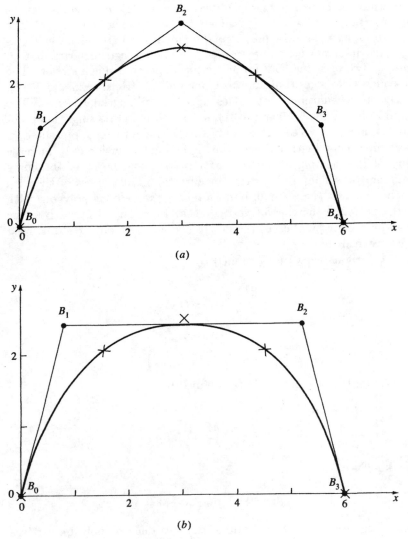

(a)

(b)

**Figure 5–56**  Results for Ex. 5–17. (a) Five polygon vertices; (b) four polygon vertices.

## 5–12   B-SPLINE CURVE SUBDIVISION

The flexibility of a Bézier curve is increased by raising the degree of the defining polynomial curve by adding an additional vertex to the defining polygon (see Sec. 5–8). The flexibility of a B-spline curve can also be increased by raising the order of the defining B-spline basis and hence of the defining polynomial segments. Cohen et al. (Ref. 5–27) provide both the theory and an algorithm for degree raising of B-spline curves.

As an alternate to degree raising, the flexibility of a B-spline curve can be increased by inserting additional knot values into the defining knot vector. The effect is to locally split a piecewise polynomial segment for a given knot value interval (parametric interval) into two piecewise polynomial segments over that interval. There are two basic methods for accomplishing knot value insertion. The first, the so-called Oslo algorithm, due to Cohen et al. (Refs. 5–28 and 5–29), simultaneously inserts multiple knot values into the defining knot vector. The second, due to Böhm (Refs. 5–30 and 5–31), sequentially inserts single knot values into the defining knot vector. Here, only the Oslo algorithm is presented.

The basic idea behind either degree raising or knot insertion is to increase the flexibility of the defining curve (or surface) basis and hence of the curve *without* changing the shape of the curve (or surface). The success of the idea depends on the fact that there are an infinite number of defining polygons with more than the minimum number of vertices that represent identical B-spline curves. Subsequent manipulation of the newly defined polygon vertices is used to change the curve shape.

Consider the original curve $P(t)$ defined by

$$P(t) = \sum_{i=1}^{n+1} B_i N_{i,k}(t)$$

with knot vector

$$[\,X\,] = [\,x_1 \quad x_2 \quad \cdots \quad x_{n+k+1}\,]$$

After knot insertion the new curve is $R(s)$ defined by

$$R(s) = \sum_{j=1}^{m+1} C_j M_{j,k}(s) \tag{5 – 118}$$

with the new knot vector

$$[\,Y\,] = [\,y_1 \quad y_2 \quad \cdots \quad y_{m+k+1}\,]$$

where $m > n$. The objective is to determine the new defining polygon vertices $C_j$ such that $P(t) = R(s)$. By the Oslo algorithm (see Ref. 5–29) the new $C_j$'s are

$$C_j = \sum_{i=1}^{n+1} \alpha_{i,j}^k B_i \qquad 1 \le i \le n, \qquad 1 \le j \le m \tag{5 – 119}$$

where the $\alpha_{i,j}^k$'s are given by the recursion relation

$$\alpha_{i,j}^1 = \begin{cases} 1 & x_i \le y_j < x_{i+1} \\ 0 & \text{otherwise} \end{cases} \tag{5 – 120a}$$

$$\alpha_{i,j}^k = \frac{y_{j+k-1} - x_i}{x_{i+k-1} - x_i} \alpha_{i,j}^{k-1} + \frac{x_{i+k} - y_{j+k-1}}{x_{i+k} - x_{i+1}} \alpha_{i+1,j}^{k-1} \tag{5 – 120b}$$

Note that $\sum_{i}^{n+1} \alpha_{i,j}^{k} = 1$.

At first glance it appears that if the original knot vector is uniform, either periodic or open, then the final knot vector, after insertion of a knot value(s), is nonuniform. However, a uniform knot vector can be maintained by inserting multiple knot values midway in each existing nonzero interval. An example serves to more fully illustrate this subdivision technique.

---

### Example 5–18    General Subdivision of a B-spline Curve

Consider an open third-order $(k = 3)$ B-spline curve initially defined by four $(n + 1 = 4)$ polygon vertices $B_1 [\, 0 \quad 0\,]$, $B_2 [\, 1 \quad 1\,]$, $B_3 [\, 2 \quad 1\,]$, $B_4 [\, 3 \quad 0\,]$. Subdivide the curve while maintaining an open uniform knot vector.

Initially the open uniform knot vector is defined by

$$[\, X'\,] = [\, 0 \quad 0 \quad 0 \quad 1 \quad 2 \quad 2 \quad 2\,]$$

where the two nonzero knot intervals $0 \rightarrow 1$ and $1 \rightarrow 2$ yield two piecewise parabolic segments comprising the B-spline curve. For convenience, a uniform knot vector with integer intervals is required after subdivision. Thus, the curve is reparameterized by multiplying each knot value in $[\, X'\,]$ by 2 to obtain

$$[\, X\,] = [\, 0 \quad 0 \quad 0 \quad 2 \quad 4 \quad 4 \quad 4\,]$$

with $x_1 = 0$, $x_2 = 0, \cdots, x_7 = 4$. The resulting curve is exactly the same.

The original curve is subdivided, while maintaining a uniform knot vector, by inserting knot values of 1 and 3 in the intervals $0 \rightarrow 2$ and $2 \rightarrow 4$ respectively. The new knot vector is

$$[\, Y\,] = [\, 0 \quad 0 \quad 0 \quad 1 \quad 2 \quad 3 \quad 4 \quad 4 \quad 4\,]$$

with $y_1 = 0$, $y_2 = 0, \cdots, y_9 = 4$.

Four piecewise parabolic segments now comprise the B-spline curve.

The six new defining polygon vertices, $C_j$, are given by Eq. (5–119). The $\alpha_{i,j}^{3}$ 's are obtained by using the recursion relations given in Eq. (5–120). Specifically, Eq. (5–120a) shows that the only nonzero first-order $(k = 1)$ $\alpha_{i,j}^{1}$ 's are

$$\alpha_{3,1}^{1} = \alpha_{3,2}^{1} = \alpha_{3,3}^{1} = \alpha_{3,4}^{1} = \alpha_{4,5}^{1} = \alpha_{4,6}^{1} = 1$$

From Eq. (5–120b) the nonzero second-order $(k = 2)$ $\alpha_{i,j}^{2}$ 's are

$j = 1$

$$\alpha_{3,1}^{2} = \frac{y_2 - x_3}{x_4 - x_3} \alpha_{3,1}^{1} = \frac{0 - 0}{2 - 0}(1) = 0$$

$$\alpha_{2,1}^{2} = \frac{x_4 - y_2}{x_4 - x_3} \alpha_{3,1}^{1} = \frac{2 - 0}{2 - 0}(1) = 1$$

$j = 2$

$$\alpha_{2,2}^{2} = \frac{x_4 - y_3}{x_4 - x_3} \alpha_{3,1}^{1} = \frac{2 - 0}{2 - 0}(1) = 1$$

$$\alpha_{3,2}^2 = \frac{y_3 - x_3}{x_4 - x_3}\alpha_{3,2}^1 = \frac{0 - 0}{2 - 0}(1) = 0$$

$j = 3$

$$\alpha_{3,3}^2 = \frac{y_4 - x_3}{x_4 - x_3}\alpha_{3,3}^1 = \frac{1 - 0}{2 - 0}(1) = \frac{1}{2}$$

$$\alpha_{2,3}^2 = \frac{x_4 - y_4}{x_4 - x_3}\alpha_{3,3}^1 = \frac{2 - 1}{2 - 0}(1) = \frac{1}{2}$$

$j = 4$

$$\alpha_{3,4}^2 = \frac{y_5 - x_3}{x_4 - x_3}\alpha_{3,4}^1 = \frac{2 - 0}{2 - 0}(1) = 1$$

$$\alpha_{2,4}^2 = \frac{x_4 - y_5}{x_4 - x_3}\alpha_{3,4}^1 = \frac{2 - 2}{2 - 0}(1) = 0$$

$j = 5$

$$\alpha_{4,5}^2 = \frac{y_6 - x_4}{x_5 - x_4}\alpha_{4,5}^1 = \frac{3 - 2}{4 - 2}(1) = \frac{1}{2}$$

$$\alpha_{3,5}^2 = \frac{x_5 - y_6}{x_5 - x_4}\alpha_{4,5}^1 = \frac{4 - 3}{4 - 2}(1) = \frac{1}{2}$$

$j = 6$

$$\alpha_{4,6}^2 = \frac{y_7 - x_4}{x_5 - x_4}\alpha_{4,6}^1 = \frac{4 - 2}{4 - 2}(1) = 1$$

$$\alpha_{3,6}^2 = \frac{x_5 - y_7}{x_5 - x_4}\alpha_{4,6}^1 = \frac{4 - 4}{4 - 2}(1) = 0$$

The required third-order $(k = 3)$ $\alpha_{i,j}^3$ 's are

$j = 1$

$$\alpha_{2,1}^3 = \frac{y_3 - x_2}{x_4 - x_2}\alpha_{2,1}^2 = \frac{0 - 0}{2 - 0}(1) = 0$$

$$\alpha_{1,1}^3 = \frac{x_4 - y_3}{x_4 - x_2}\alpha_{2,1}^2 = \frac{2 - 0}{2 - 0}(1) = 1$$

$j = 2$

$$\alpha_{1,2}^3 = \frac{x_4 - y_4}{x_4 - x_2}\alpha_{2,2}^2 = \frac{2 - 1}{2 - 0}(1) = \frac{1}{2}$$

$$\alpha_{2,2}^3 = \frac{y_4 - x_2}{x_4 - x_2}\alpha_{2,2}^2 = \frac{1 - 0}{2 - 0}(1) = \frac{1}{2}$$

$j = 3$

$$\alpha_{3,3}^3 = \frac{y_5 - x_3}{x_5 - x_3}\alpha_{3,3}^2 = \frac{2 - 0}{4 - 0}\left(\frac{1}{2}\right) = \frac{1}{4}$$

$$\alpha_{2,3}^3 = \frac{y_5 - x_2}{x_4 - x_2}\alpha_{2,3}^2 + \frac{x_5 - y_5}{x_5 - x_3}\alpha_{3,3}^2 = \frac{2-0}{2-0}\left(\frac{1}{2}\right) + \frac{4-2}{4-0}\left(\frac{1}{2}\right) = \frac{1}{2} + \frac{1}{4} = \frac{3}{4}$$

$$\alpha_{1,3}^3 = \frac{x_4 - y_5}{x_4 - x_2}\alpha_{2,3}^3 = \frac{2 - 2}{2 - 0}\left(\frac{1}{2}\right) = 0$$

$j = 4$

$$\alpha_{3,4}^3 = \frac{y_6 - x_3}{x_5 - x_3}\alpha_{3,4}^2 = \frac{3 - 0}{4 - 0}(1) = \frac{3}{4}$$

$$\alpha_{2,4}^3 = \frac{x_5 - y_6}{x_5 - x_3}\alpha_{3,4}^2 = \frac{4 - 3}{4 - 0}(1) = \frac{1}{4}$$

$j = 5$

$$\alpha_{2,5}^3 = \frac{x_5 - y_7}{x_5 - x_3}\alpha_{3,5}^2 = \frac{4 - 4}{4 - 0}\left(\frac{1}{2}\right) = 0$$

$$\alpha_{3,5}^3 = \frac{y_7 - x_3}{x_5 - x_3}\alpha_{3,5}^2 + \frac{x_6 - y_7}{x_6 - x_4}\alpha_{4,5}^2 = \frac{4 - 0}{4 - 0}\left(\frac{1}{2}\right) + \frac{4 - 4}{4 - 2}\left(\frac{1}{2}\right) = \frac{1}{2}$$

$$\alpha_{4,5}^3 = \frac{y_7 - x_4}{x_6 - x_4}\alpha_{4,5}^2 = \frac{4 - 2}{4 - 2}\left(\frac{1}{2}\right) = \frac{1}{2}$$

$j = 6$

$$\alpha_{4,6}^3 = \frac{y_8 - x_4}{x_6 - x_4}\alpha_{4,6}^2 = \frac{4 - 2}{4 - 2}(1) = 1$$

$$\alpha_{3,6}^3 = \frac{x_6 - y_8}{x_6 - x_4}\alpha_{4,6}^2 = \frac{4 - 4}{4 - 2}(1) = 0$$

The new polygon vertices are given by Eq. (5–119); e.g.,

$$C_1 = \sum_{i=1}^{n+1} \alpha_{i,1}^3 B_i = \alpha_{1,1}^3 B_1 + \alpha_{2,1}^3 B_2 + \alpha_{3,1}^3 B_3 + \alpha_{4,1}^3 B_4$$

$$= \alpha_{1,1}^3 B_1 = B_1 = [\,0 \quad 0\,]$$

Similarly,

$$C_2 = \frac{1}{2}(B_1 + B_2) = \frac{1}{2}([\,0 \quad 0\,] + [\,1 \quad 1\,]) = \left[\frac{1}{2} \quad \frac{1}{2}\right]$$

$$C_3 = \frac{3}{4}B_2 + \frac{1}{4}B_3 = \frac{3}{4}[\,1 \quad 1\,] + \frac{1}{4}[\,2 \quad 1\,] = \left[\frac{5}{4} \quad 1\right]$$

$$C_4 = \frac{1}{4}B_2 + \frac{3}{4}B_3 = \frac{1}{4}[\,1 \quad 1\,] + \frac{3}{4}[\,2 \quad 1\,] = \left[\frac{7}{4} \quad 1\right]$$

$$C_5 = \frac{1}{2}(B_3 + B_4) = \frac{1}{2}\left([\,2 \quad 1\,] + [\,3 \quad 0\,]\right) = \left[\frac{5}{2} \quad \frac{1}{2}\right]$$

$$C_6 = B_4 = [\,3 \quad 0\,]$$

The result is increased flexibility of the entire curve.

---

The next example illustrates the addition of a single knot value to an initially open uniform knot vector. The result is a nonuniform knot vector.

---

### Example 5–19    Local Subdivision of a B-spline Curve

Consider the open third-order ($k = 3$) B-spline curve of Ex. 5–18. Subdivide the curve by inserting the knot value 1 in the interval $0 \rightarrow 1$ of the knot vector:

$$[X] = [0 \quad 0 \quad 0 \quad 1 \quad 2 \quad 2 \quad 2]$$

with $x_1 = 0$, $x_2 = 0, \cdots, x_7 = 2$. The new knot vector is

$$[Y] = [0 \quad 0 \quad 0 \quad 1 \quad 1 \quad 2 \quad 2 \quad 2]$$

with $y_1 = 0$, $y_2 = 0, \cdots, y_8 = 2$. There are five new polygon vertices $C_1 \cdots C_5$.

The nonzero $\alpha_{i,j}^k$ 's required to determine the $C_j$ 's are

$$k = 1$$
$$\alpha_{3,1}^1 = \alpha_{3,2}^1 = \alpha_{3,3}^1 = \alpha_{3,4}^1 = \alpha_{4,5}^1 = 1$$

$$k = 2$$
$$\alpha_{2,1}^2 = \alpha_{2,2}^2 = \alpha_{3,3}^2 = \alpha_{3,4}^2 = \alpha_{4,5}^2 = 1$$

$$k = 3$$
$$\alpha_{1,1}^3 = \alpha_{2,2}^3 = \alpha_{3,4}^3 = \alpha_{4,5}^3 = 1, \quad \alpha_{3,3}^3 = \alpha_{2,3}^3 = \frac{1}{2}$$

The new polygon vertices are

$$C_1 = \alpha_{3,1}^3 B_1 = B_1 = [0 \quad 0]$$

$$C_2 = \alpha_{3,2}^3 B_2 = B_2 = [1 \quad 1]$$

$$C_3 = \alpha_{2,3}^3 B_2 + \alpha_{3,3}^3 B_3 = \frac{1}{2}(B_2 + B_3) = \frac{1}{2}([1 \quad 1] + [2 \quad 1]) = \left[\frac{3}{2} \quad 1\right]$$

$$C_4 = \alpha_{3,4}^3 B_3 = B_3 = [2 \quad 1]$$

$$C_5 = \alpha_{4,5}^3 B_4 = B_4 = [3 \quad 0]$$

If $C_3$ is moved to coincide with $C_2$, i.e., $C_2 = C_3 = [1 \quad 1]$, both a double vertex and a double knot value corresponding to $C_2 = C_3$ exist. The resulting B-spline curve for $k = 3$ has a cusp or sharp corner at $C_2 = C_3$ (see Prob. 5–30).

---

## 5–13   RATIONAL B-SPLINE CURVES

Rational curve and surface descriptions were first introduced into the computer graphics literature by Coons (Ref. 5–32). Rational forms of the cubic spline and Bézier curves previously discussed in this chapter are well known in the literature (see Refs. 5–33 to 5–37). Rational forms of the conic sections are also well known (see Ref. 5–38). Both because of space limitations and because they form a unifying foundation, the current discussion is limited to rational B-spline curves. Rational B-splines provide a single precise mathematical form capable of representing the common analytical shapes—lines, planes, conic curves including circles, free-form curves, quadric and sculptured surfaces—used in computer graphics and computer aided design.

Versprille (Ref. 5–39) was the first to discuss rational B-splines. The seminal papers by Tiller (Ref. 5–40) and Piegl and Tiller (Ref. 5–41) form the basis of the current discussion. Interestingly enough, nonuniform rational B-splines (NURBS) have been an Initial Graphics Exchange Specification (IGES) standard since 1983 (see Ref. 5–42). IGES is the standard for the interchange of design information between various computer aided design systems and between computer aided design and computer aided manufacturing systems. Rational B-splines have been incorporated into a number of geometric modeling systems. They have also been implemented in hardware (VLSI or microcode) by a number of graphics workstation manufacturers.

A rational B-spline curve is the projection of a nonrational (polynomial) B-spline curve defined in four-dimensional (4D) homogeneous coordinate space back into three-dimensional (3D) physical space. Specifically,

$$P(t) = \sum_{i=1}^{n+1} B_i^h N_{i,k}(t) \qquad (5-121)$$

where the $B_i^h$'s are the 4D homogeneous defining polygon vertices for the nonrational 4D B-spline curve. $N_{i,k}(t)$ is the nonrational B-spline basis function previously given in Eq. (5–84).

Projecting back into three-dimensional space by dividing through by the homogeneous coordinate yields the rational B-spline curve

$$P(t) = \frac{\sum_{i=1}^{n+1} B_i h_i N_{i,k}(t)}{\sum_{i=1}^{n+1} h_i N_{i,k}(t)} = \sum_{i=1}^{n+1} B_i R_{i,k}(t) \qquad (5-122)$$

where the $B_i$'s are the 3D defining polygon vertices for the rational B-spline curve and the

$$R_{i,k}(t) = \frac{h_i N_{i,k}(t)}{\sum_{i=1}^{n+1} h_i N_{i,k}(t)} \qquad (5-123)$$

are the rational B-spline basis functions. Here, $h_i \geq 0$ for all values of $i$.[†]

As can be seen from Eqs. (5–121) to (5–123), rational B-spline basis functions and curves are a generalization of nonrational B-spline basis functions and curves. They carry forward nearly all the analytic and geometric characteristics of their nonrational B-spline counterparts. In particular:

Each rational basis function is positive or zero for all parameter values, i.e., $R_{i,k} \geq 0$.

---

[†] Note that rational B-spline basis functions for $h_i < 0$ are valid (see Ref. 5–39) but are not convenient in terms of the current discussion.

The sum of the rational B-spline basis functions for any parameter value $t$ is one, i.e.,

$$\sum_{i=1}^{n+1} R_{i,k}(t) \equiv 1 \qquad (5-124)$$

Except for $k = 1$, each rational basis function has precisely one maximum.

A rational B-spline curve of order $k$ (degree $k - 1$) is $C^{k-2}$ continuous everywhere.

The maximum order of the rational B-spline curve is equal to the number of defining polygon vertices.

A rational B-spline curve exhibits the variation diminishing property.

A rational B-spline curve generally follows the shape of the defining polygon.

A rational B-spline curve lies within the union of convex hulls formed by $k$ successive defining polygon vertices.

Any *projective* transformation is applied to a rational B-spline curve by applying it to the defining polygon vertices; i.e., the curve is invariant with respect to a *projective* transformation. Note that this is a stronger condition than that for a nonrational B-spline which is only invariant with respect to an *affine* transformation.

From Eqs. (5–85) and (5–123) it is clear that when all $h_i = 1$, $R_{i,k}(t) = N_{i,k}(t)$. Thus, nonrational B-spline basis functions and curves are included as a special case of rational B-spline basis functions and curves. Further, it is easy to show that an open rational B-spline curve with order equal to the number of defining polygon vertices is a rational Bézier curve. For the case of all $h_i = 1$, the rational Bézier curve reduces to a nonrational Bézier curve. Thus, both rational and nonrational Bézier curves are included as special cases of rational B-spline curves.

Since rational B-splines are a four-dimensional generalization of nonrational B-splines, algorithms for degree-raising (see Ref. 5–27 and Ex. 6–18), subdivision (see Sec. 5–12 and Refs. 5–28 to 5–31) and curve fitting (see Sec. 5–11) of nonrational B-spline curves are valid for rational B-splines simply by applying them to the 4D defining polygon vertices.

Open uniform, periodic uniform and nonuniform knot vectors can be used to generate rational B-spline basis functions and rational B-spline curves.

In Eqs. (5–122) and (5–123) the homogeneous coordinates $h_i$ (occasionally called weights) provide additional blending capability. $h = 1$ is called the affine space. By convention it corresponds to physical space. The effect of the homogeneous coordinates $h$ on the rational B-spline basis functions is shown in Fig. 5–57. Here, an open uniform knot vector $[\,0 \quad 0 \quad 0 \quad 1 \quad 2 \quad 3 \quad 3 \quad 3\,]$ $(n+1 = 5, k = 3)$ is used with a homogeneous coordinate vector $h_i = 1$, $i \neq 3$. Values of $h_3$ range from 0 to 5. The rational B-spline basis functions shown in Fig. 5–57c with $h = 1$ are identical to the corresponding nonrational B-spline basis functions. The rational B-spline curve for $h_3 = 1$, shown in Fig. 5–58, is also identical

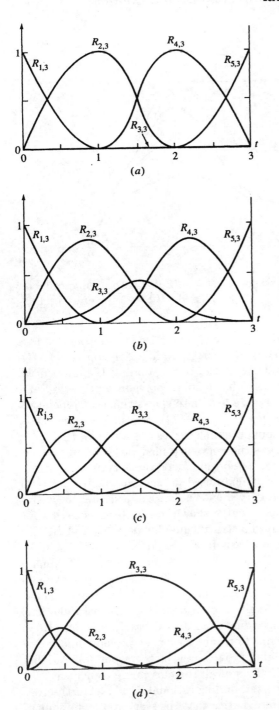

**Figure 5-57**    Rational B-spline basis functions for $n + 1 = 5$, $k = 3$ with open knot vector $[X] = [0 \ 0 \ 0 \ 1 \ 2 \ 3 \ 3 \ 3]$, $[H] = [1 \ 1 \ h_3 \ 1 \ 1]$. (a) $h_3 = 0$;  (b) $h_3 = 0.25$; (c) $h_3 = 1.0$; (d) $h_3 = 5.0$.

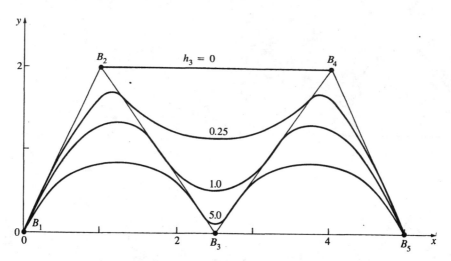

**Figure 5–58** Rational B-spline curves for $n + 1 = 5$, $k = 3$ with open knot vector $[X] = [0 \quad 0 \quad 0 \quad 1 \quad 2 \quad 3 \quad 3 \quad 3]$ and $[H] = [1 \quad 1 \quad h_3 \quad 1 \quad 1]$.

with the corresponding nonrational B-spline curve. Notice that for $h_3 = 0$ (see Fig. 5–57a) $R_{3,3} = 0$ everywhere. Thus, the corresponding polygon vertex, $B_3$, effectively has no influence on the shape of the corresponding B-spline curve. This effect is shown in Fig. 5–58 where the defining polygon vertices $B_2$ and $B_4$ are connected by a straight line. Figure 5–57 also shows that as $h_3$ increases $R_{3,3}$ also increases; but, as a consequence of Eq. (5–124), $R_{2,3}$ and $R_{4,3}$ decrease. The effects on the corresponding rational B-spline curves are shown in Fig. 5–58. Note, in particular, that as $h_3$ increases the curve is pulled closer to $B_3$. Hence, as mentioned previously, the homogeneous coordinates provide additional blending capability. Similar characteristics are exhibited for the fourth-order ($k = 4$) rational B-spline basis functions and curves shown in Figs. 5–59 and 5–60, respectively. However, for the higher order curve shown in Fig. 5–60 note that for $h_3 = 0$ the curve does not degenerate to a straight line between $B_2$ and $B_4$.

Figure 5–61 shows periodic uniform basis functions for $n + 1 = 5$, $k = 3$ for a knot vector $[X] = [0 \quad 1 \quad 2 \quad 3 \quad 4 \quad 5 \quad 6 \quad 7]$ and homogeneous coordinate vector $[H] = [1 \quad 1 \quad h_3 \quad 1 \quad 1]$ with $0 \leq h_3 \leq 5$. Here, as for nonrational B-spline basis functions, the usable parameter range is $2 \leq t \leq 5$. Only this parameter range is shown in Fig. 5–61. Again, the rational B-spline basis functions for $h_3 = 1$ are identical to the corresponding nonrational basis functions. However, note that for $h_3 \neq 1$ the basis functions are no longer periodic and hence no longer translates of each other. Figure 5–62 shows the corresponding rational B-spline curves. Notice that the end points of all the curves are coincident.

Figures 5–63 and 5–64 show the corresponding rational B-spline fourth-order ($k = 4$) basis functions and curves. Here, notice that the start and end points of the curves lie along a straight line.

Recalling the $(t_{\max} - \epsilon)_{\epsilon \to 0}$ argument of Ex. 5–12, evaluation of Eqs. (5–122) and (5–123) at the ends of the curve shows that the first and last points on

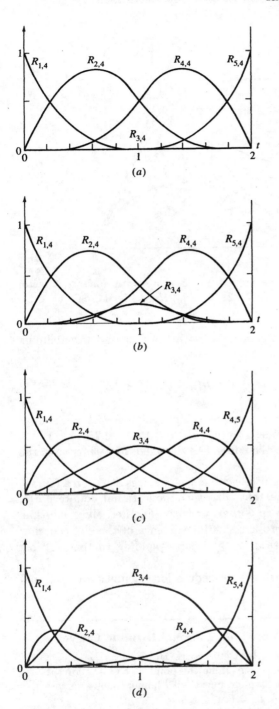

**Figure 5–59**    Rational B-spline basis functions for $n + 1 = 5$, $k = 4$ with open knot vector $[X] = [0 \; 0 \; 0 \; 0 \; 1 \; 2 \; 2 \; 2 \; 2]$, $[H] = [1 \; 1 \; h_3 \; 1 \; 1]$. (a) $h_3 = 0$; (b) $h_3 = 0.25$; (c) $h_3 = 1.0$; (d) $h_3 = 5.0$.

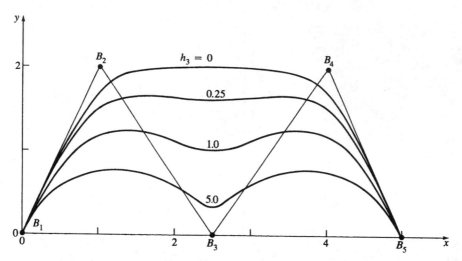

**Figure 5–60**  Rational B-spline curves for $n + 1 = 5$, $k = 4$ with open knot vector $[X] = [0 \;\; 0 \;\; 0 \;\; 0 \;\; 1 \;\; 2 \;\; 2 \;\; 2 \;\; 2]$, $[H] = [1 \;\; 1 \;\; h_3 \;\; 1 \;\; 1]$.

an open rational B-spline curve are coincident with the first and last defining polygon vertices. Specifically,

$$P(0) = B_1 \quad \text{and} \quad P(t_{\max}) = P(n - k + 2) = B_{n+1}$$

Figure 5–65 shows that the effect of moving a single polygon vertex is similar to the results for nonrational B-splines. Here, $[H] = [1 \;\; 1 \;\; 0.25 \;\; 1 \;\; 1]$. If $h_3 = 0$, moving $B_3$ has no effect on the curve. As the value of $h_3$ increases the effect of moving $B_3$ increases.

Figure 5–66 shows the effect of multiple coincident vertices at $B_3$ on a fourth-order rational B-spline curve. Note that, like their nonrational counterparts, $k - 1$ coincident vertices yield a sharp corner, or cusp. Further, since multiple coincident vertices yield spans of zero length, the existence of the sharp corner or cusp is independent of the values of $h_i \geq 0$ corresponding to the multiple vertices (see Prob. 5–33).

An example more fully illustrates the procedure for calculation of rational B-splines.

---

**Example 5–20    Calculation of Open Rational B-spline Curves**

Consider the defining polygon given by the vertices $B_1 [0 \;\; 1]$, $B_2 [1 \;\; 2]$, $B_3 [2.5 \;\; 0]$, $B_4 [4 \;\; 2]$, $B_5 [5 \;\; 0]$. Determine the point at $t = 3/2$ for the third-order ($k = 3$) open rational B-spline curve with homogeneous vectors given by $[H] = [1 \;\; 1 \;\; h_3 \;\; 1 \;\; 1]$, $h_3 = 0, 1/4, 1, 5$.

The knot vector is $[0 \;\; 0 \;\; 0 \;\; 1 \;\; 2 \;\; 3 \;\; 3 \;\; 3]$. The parameter range is $0 \leq t \leq 3$. The curves are composed of three piecewise rational quadratics, one for each of the interior intervals in the knot vector.

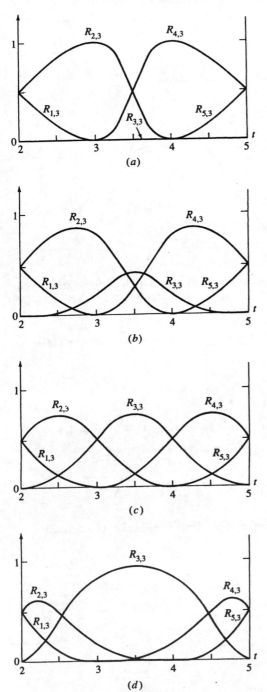

**Figure 5–61**    Rational B-spline basis functions for $n + 1 = 5$, $k = 3$ with periodic knot vector $[X] = [0 \quad 1 \quad 2 \quad 3 \quad 4 \quad 5 \quad 6 \quad 7]$ and $[H] = [1 \quad 1 \quad h_3 \quad 1 \quad 1]$. (a) $h_3 = 0$; (b) $h_3 = 0.25$; (c) $h_3 = 1.0$; (d) $h_3 = 5.0$.

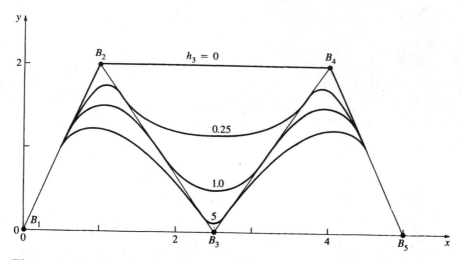

**Figure 5-62**   Rational B-spline curves for $n + 1 = 5$, $k = 4$ with periodic knot vector $[X] = [0\ \ 1\ \ 2\ \ 3\ \ 4\ \ 5\ \ 6\ \ 7]$ and $[H] = [1\ \ 1\ \ h_3\ \ 1\ \ 1]$.

Using Eq. (5–84) on the interval $1 \le t < 2$, the nonrational B-spline basis functions are

$$1 \le t < 2$$

$$N_{4,1}(t) = 1; \qquad N_{i,1}(t) = 0, \quad i \neq 4$$

$$N_{3,2}(t) = (2 - t); \qquad N_{4,2}(t) = (t - 1); \qquad N_{i,2}(t) = 0, \quad i \neq 3, 4$$

$$N_{2,3}(t) = \frac{(2 - t)^2}{2}; \qquad N_{3,3}(t) = \frac{t(2 - t)}{2} + \frac{(3 - t)(t - 1)}{2};$$

$$N_{4,3}(t) = \frac{(t - 1)^2}{2}; \qquad N_{i,3}(t) = 0, \quad i \neq 2, 3, 4$$

From Eq. (5–123) and these results, after first determining the denominator,

$$S = \sum_{i=1}^{n+1} h_i N_{i,k}(t) = h_1 N_{1,3}(t) + h_2 N_{2,3}(t) + h_4 N_{4,3}(t) + h_5 N_{5,3}(t)$$

$$= h_2 N_{2,3}(t) + h_4 N_{4,3}(t)$$

$$= \frac{(2 - t)^2}{2} + \frac{(t - 1)^2}{2} = \frac{2t^2 - 6t + 5}{2}$$

the rational B-spline basis functions are

$$1 \le t < 2$$

$$h_3 = 0$$

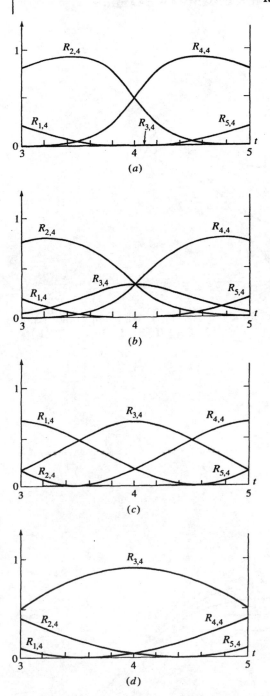

**Figure 5–63**    Rational B-spline basis functions for $n + 1 = 5$, $k = 4$ with periodic knot vector $[X] = [0 \quad 1 \quad 2 \quad 3 \quad 4 \quad 5 \quad 6 \quad 7 \quad 8]$ and $[H] = [1 \quad 1 \quad h_3 \quad 1 \quad 1]$. (a) $h_3 = 0$; (b) $h_3 = 0.25$; (c) $h_3 = 1.0$; (d) $h_3 = 5.0$.

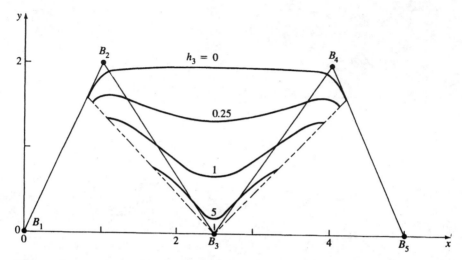

**Figure 5–64**  Rational B-spline curves for $n + 1 = 5$, $k = 4$ with periodic knot vector $[\,X\,] = [\,0 \quad 1 \quad 2 \quad 3 \quad 4 \quad 5 \quad 6 \quad 7 \quad 8\,]$, $[\,H\,] = [\,1 \quad 1 \quad h_3 \quad 1 \quad 1\,]$.

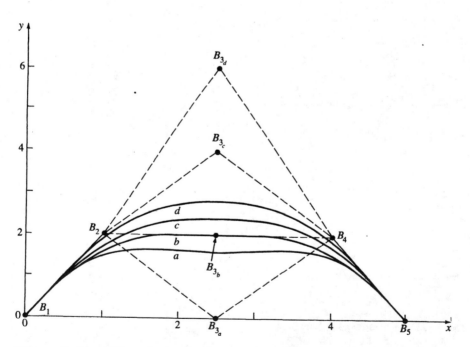

**Figure 5–65**  Effect of moving a single polygon vertex on a rational B-spline curve, $n + 1 = 5$, $k = 4$, $[\,H\,] = [\,1 \quad 1 \quad 0.25 \quad 1 \quad 1\,]$.

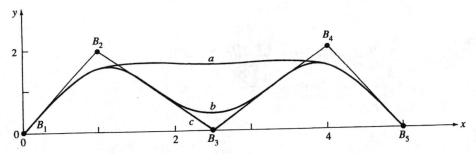

**Figure 5–66**    Effect of multiple vertices at $B_3$ on a rational B-spline curve, $n+1=5$, $k=4$.  (a) Single vertex $[\,H\,] = [\,1 \quad 1 \quad 0.25 \quad 1 \quad 1\,]$; (b) double vertex $[\,H\,] = [\,1 \quad 1 \quad 0.25 \quad 0.25 \quad 1 \quad 1\,]$; (c) triple vertex $[\,H\,] = [\,1 \quad 1 \quad 0.25 \quad 0.25 \quad 0.25 \quad 1 \quad 1\,]$.

$$R_{1,3}(t) = 0$$

$$R_{2,3}(t) = \frac{h_2 N_{2,3}(t)}{S} = \frac{(2-t)^2}{2t^2 - 6t + 5}$$

$$R_{3,3}(t) = 0$$

$$R_{4,3}(t) = \frac{h_4 N_{4,3}(t)}{S} = \frac{(t-1)^2}{2t^2 - 6t + 5}$$

$$R_{5,3}(t) = 0$$

$h_3 = 1/4$

$$S = h_2 N_{2,3}(t) + h_3 N_{3,3}(t) + h_4 N_{4,3}(t)$$

$$= \frac{(2-t)^2}{2} + \frac{t(2-t)}{8} + \frac{(3-t)(t-1)}{8} + \frac{(t-1)^2}{2}$$

$$= \frac{6t^2 - 18t + 17}{8}$$

$$R_{1,3}(t) = 0$$

$$R_{2,3}(t) = \frac{4(2-t)^2}{6t^2 - 18t + 17}$$

$$R_{3,3}(t) = \frac{t(2-t) + (3-t)(t-1)}{6t^2 - 18t + 17} = \frac{-2t^2 + 6t - 3}{6t^2 - 18t + 17}$$

$$R_{4,3}(t) = \frac{4(t-1)^2}{6t^2 - 18t + 17}$$

$$R_{5,3}(t) = 0$$

$h_3 = 1$

$$S = 1$$

$$R_{1,3}(t) = 0$$

$$R_{2,3}(t) = N_{2,3}(t) = \frac{(2-t)^2}{2}$$

$$R_{3,3}(t) = N_{3,3}(t) = \frac{t(2-t)}{2} + \frac{(3-t)(t-1)}{2}$$

$$R_{4,3}(t) = N_{4,3}(t) = \frac{(t-1)^2}{2}$$

$$R_{5,3}(t) = 0$$

$$h_3 = 5$$

$$S = \frac{(2-t)^2}{2} + \frac{5t(2-t)}{2} + \frac{5(3-t)(t-1)}{2} + \frac{(t-1)^2}{2}$$

$$= -4t^2 + 12t - 5$$

$$R_{1,3}(t) = 0$$

$$R_{2,3}(t) = \frac{(2-t)^2}{2(-4t^2 + 12t - 5)}$$

$$R_{3,3}(t) = \frac{5t(2-t) + 5(3-t)(t-1)}{2(-4t^2 + 12t - 5)} = \frac{5(-2t^2 + 6t - 3)}{2(-4t^2 + 12t - 5)}$$

$$R_{4,3}(t) = \frac{(t-1)^2}{2(-4t^2 + 12t - 5)}$$

$$R_{5,3}(t) = 0$$

Complete results are shown in Fig. 5–57.
Evaluating these results at $t = 3/2$ yields

$$h_3 = 0: \quad R_{1,3}(3/2) = 0; \quad R_{2,3}(3/2) = \frac{1}{2}; \quad R_{3,3}(3/2) = 0;$$

$$R_{4,3}(3/2) = \frac{1}{2}; \quad R_{5,3}(3/2) = 0$$

$$h_3 = \frac{1}{4}: \quad R_{1,3}(3/2) = 0; \quad R_{2,3}(3/2) = \frac{2}{7}; \quad R_{3,3}(3/2) = \frac{3}{7};$$

$$R_{4,3}(3/2) = \frac{2}{7}; \quad R_{5,3}(3/2) = 0$$

$$h_3 = 1: \quad R_{1,3}(3/2) = 0; \quad R_{2,3}(3/2) = \frac{1}{8}; \quad R_{3,3}(3/2) = \frac{3}{4};$$

$$R_{4,3}(3/2) = \frac{1}{8}; \quad R_{5,3}(3/2) = 0$$

$$h_3 = 5: \quad R_{1,3}(3/2) = 0; \quad R_{2,3}(3/2) = \frac{1}{32}; \quad R_{3,3}(3/2) = \frac{15}{16};$$

$$R_{4,3}(3/2) = \frac{1}{32}; \quad R_{5,3}(3/2) = 0$$

The corresponding points on the rational B-spline curves are

$$h_3 = 0: \quad P(3/2) = \frac{1}{2}[\,1 \quad 2\,] + \frac{1}{2}[\,4 \quad 2\,] = \begin{bmatrix} \frac{5}{2} & 2 \end{bmatrix}$$

$$h_3 = \frac{1}{4}: \quad P(3/2) = \frac{2}{7}[\,1 \quad 2\,] + \frac{3}{7}\begin{bmatrix} \frac{5}{2} & 0 \end{bmatrix} + \frac{2}{7}[\,4 \quad 2\,] = \begin{bmatrix} \frac{5}{2} & \frac{8}{7} \end{bmatrix}$$

$$h_3 = 1: \qquad P(3/2) = \frac{1}{8} \begin{bmatrix} 1 & 2 \end{bmatrix} + \frac{3}{4} \begin{bmatrix} \frac{5}{2} & 0 \end{bmatrix} + \frac{1}{8} \begin{bmatrix} 4 & 2 \end{bmatrix} = \begin{bmatrix} \frac{5}{2} & \frac{1}{2} \end{bmatrix}$$

$$h_3 = 5: \qquad P(3/2) = \frac{1}{32} \begin{bmatrix} 1 & 2 \end{bmatrix} + \frac{15}{16} \begin{bmatrix} \frac{5}{2} & 0 \end{bmatrix} + \frac{1}{32} \begin{bmatrix} 4 & 2 \end{bmatrix} = \begin{bmatrix} \frac{5}{2} & \frac{1}{8} \end{bmatrix}$$

Complete results are shown in Fig. 5–58.

---

The derivatives of rational B-spline curves are obtained by formal differentiation of Eqs. (5–122) and (5–123). Specifically,

$$P'(t) = \sum_{i=1}^{n+1} B_i R'_{i,k}(t) \qquad (5-125)$$

with

$$R'_{i,k}(t) = \frac{h_i N'_{i,k}(t)}{\displaystyle\sum_{i=1}^{n+1} h_i N_{i,k}} - \frac{h_i N_{i,k} \displaystyle\sum_{i=1}^{n+1} h_i N'_{i,k}}{\left( \displaystyle\sum_{i=1}^{n+1} h_i N_{i,k} \right)^2} \qquad (5-126)$$

Evaluating these results at $t = 0$ and $t = n - k + 2$ yields

$$P'(0) = (k-1)\frac{h_2}{h_1}(B_2 - B_1) \qquad (5-127)$$

$$P'(n-k+2) = (k-1)\frac{h_n}{h_{n+1}}(B_{n+1} - B_n) \qquad (5-128)$$

which shows that the direction of the slope is along the first and last polygon spans, respectively.

Higher order derivatives are obtained in a similar manner (see Probs. 5–35 and 5–36).

A simple example illustrates these results.

---

**Example 5–21    Derivatives of Open Rational B-spline Curves**

Consider the defining polygon previously used in Ex. 5–16. The polygon vertices were $B_1 [\, 1 \quad 1 \,]$, $B_2 [\, 2 \quad 3 \,]$, $B_3 [\, 4 \quad 3 \,]$, $B_4 [\, 3 \quad 1 \,]$. Determine the first derivative of the second order rational B-spline curve ($k = 2$) with $[\, H \,] = [\, 1 \quad 1/2 \quad 1 \quad 1 \,]$.

The knot vector is $[\, X \,] = [\, 0 \quad 0 \quad 1 \quad 2 \quad 3 \quad 3 \,]$. The parameter range is $0 \le t \le 3$. From Eq. (5–125) the first derivative is

$$P'(t) = B_1 R'_{1,2}(t) + B_2 R'_{2,2}(t) + B_3 R'_{3,2}(t) + B_4 R'_{4,3}(t)$$

From Eqs. (5–12) and (5–16) the nonrational basis functions and their derivatives are

$$0 \le t < 1$$

$$N_{1,2}(t) = 1 - t; \qquad N_{2,2}(t) = t; \qquad N_{i,2}(t) = 0, \quad i \neq 1,2$$

$$N'_{1,2}(t) = -1; \qquad N'_{2,2}(t) = 1; \qquad N'_{i,2}(t) = 0, \quad i \neq 1,2$$

Using Eq. (5–126) the rational basis functions and their derivatives are

$$\sum_{i=1}^{n+1} h_i N_{i,2} = \frac{2-t}{2}; \qquad \sum_{i=1}^{n+1} h_i N'_{i,2} = -\frac{1}{2};$$

$$R'_{1,2}(t) = \frac{2}{2-t}\left\{(-1) - (1-t)\frac{(-1)}{(2-t)}\right\} = \frac{-2}{(2-t)^2}$$

$$R'_{2,2}(t) = \left(\frac{1}{2}\right)\left(\frac{2}{2-t}\right)\left\{1 - t\frac{(-1)}{(2-t)}\right\} = \frac{2}{(2-t)^2}$$

$$R'_{i,2}(t) = 0, \quad i \neq 1,2$$

Thus
$$P'(t) = \frac{2}{(2-t)^2}(B_2 - B_1)$$

Note here, in contrast to the nonrational B-spline curve of Ex. 5–16, that although the direction is that of the first polygon span, the magnitude now varies along the curve length. At $t = 0$, the beginning of the curve,

$$P'(t) = \frac{1}{2}(B_2 - B_1)$$

which shows that the magnitude is half that found for the nonrational B-spline curve in Ex. 5–16.

For the interval

$$1 \leq t < 2$$

$$N_{2,2}(t) = 2 - t; \qquad N_{3,2}(t) = t - 1; \qquad N_{i,2}(t) = 0, \quad i \neq 2,3$$
$$N'_{2,2}(t) = -1; \qquad N'_{3,2}(t) = 1; \qquad N'_{i,2}(t) = 0, \quad i \neq 2,3$$

Here

$$\sum_{i=1}^{n+1} h_i N_{i,2} = \frac{t}{2}; \qquad \sum_{i=1}^{n+1} h_i N'_{i,2} = \frac{1}{2};$$

$$R'_{2,2}(t) = \left(\frac{1}{2}\right)\left(\frac{2}{t}\right)\left\{(-1) - (2-t)\left(\frac{1}{t}\right)\right\} = -\frac{2}{t^2}$$

$$R'_{3,2}(t) = \frac{2}{t}\left\{(1) - (t-1)\left(\frac{1}{t}\right)\right\} = \frac{2}{t^2}$$

$$R'_{i,2}(t) = 0, \quad i \neq 2,3$$

Thus
$$P'(t) = \frac{2}{t^2}(B_3 - B_2)$$

For the interval

$$2 \leq t < 3$$

$$N_{3,2}(t) = 3 - t; \qquad N_{4,2}(t) = t - 2; \qquad N_{i,2}(t) = 0, \quad i \neq 3,4$$
$$N'_{3,2}(t) = -1; \qquad N'_{4,2}(t) = 1; \qquad N'_{i,2}(t) = 0, \quad i \neq 3,4$$

With

$$\sum_{i=1}^{n+1} h_i N_{i,2} = 1; \qquad \sum_{i=1}^{n+1} h_i N'_{i,2} = 0;$$

$$R'_{3,2}(t) = N'_{3,2}(t) = -1; \qquad R'_{4,2}(t) = N'_{4,2}(t) = 1;$$

$$R'_{i,2}(t) = 0, \quad i \neq 3, 4$$

Hence

$$P'(t) = B_4 - B_3$$

Using the $t = (3 - \epsilon)$, $\epsilon \to 0$ argument yields the same result at $t = 3$.

---

As mentioned previously, rational B-spline curves can be used to represent all the conic sections. Further, they provide a single mathematical description capable of blending the conic sections into free-form curves. Since the conic sections are described by quadratic equations, it is convenient to first consider a quadratic rational B-spline ($k = 3$) defined by three polygon vertices ($n + 1 = 3$) with knot vector $[ X ] = [0 \quad 0 \quad 0 \quad 1 \quad 1 \quad 1]$. Writing this out yields

$$P(t) = \frac{h_1 N_{1,3}(t) B_1 + h_2 N_{2,3}(t) B_2 + h_3 N_{3,3}(t) B_3}{h_1 N_{1,3}(t) + h_2 N_{2,3}(t) + h_3 N_{3,3}(t)} \qquad (5-129)$$

which, in fact, is a third-order rational Bézier curve (see Fig. 5–67). It is convenient to assume $h_1 = h_3 = 1$. Equation (5–129) then reduces to

$$P(t) = \frac{N_{1,3}(t) B_1 + h_2 N_{2,3}(t) B_2 + N_{3,3}(t) B_3}{N_{1,3}(t) + h_2 N_{2,3}(t) + N_{3,3}(t)} \qquad (5-130)$$

Now, if $h_2 = 0$, a straight line between $B_1$ and $B_3$ results. If $h_2 \to \infty$, the defining polygon is reproduced. When $h_2 = 0$ and $t = 1/2$ the midpoint of the line $B_1 B_3$, labelled $M$ in Fig. 5–67, is obtained. Similarly, when $h_2 \to \infty, t = 1/2$ yields the polygon point at $B_2$. For $0 < h_2 < \infty$, the point $S$ corresponding to the point at $t = 1/2$ on the curve $P(t)$ moves along the straight line connecting $M$ and $B_2$. $S$ is called the shoulder point. The value of $h_2$ determines the type of conic section. Lee (Ref. 5–43) has shown that if

| | |
|---|---|
| $h_2 = 0$ | a straight line results. |
| $0 < h_2 < 1$ | an elliptic curve segment results. |
| $h_2 = 1$ | a parabolic curve segment results. |
| $h_2 > 1$ | a hyperbolic curve segment results. |

Using Eq. (5–84) and substituting $t = 1/2$ into Eq. (5–130) yields

$$P(t) = \frac{(1-t)^2 B_1 + 2 h_2 t (1-t) B_2 + t^2 B_3}{(1-t)^2 + 2 h_2 t (1-t) + t^2}$$

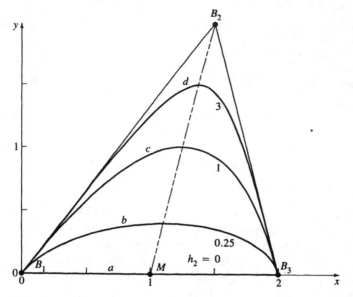

**Figure 5–67**    Conic sections defined by rational B-spline (Bézier) curves. (a) Straight line, $h_2 = 0$; (b) elliptic, $h_2 = 0.25$; (c) parabolic, $h_2 = 1$; (d) hyperbolic, $h_2 = 3$.

For $t = 1/2$, $P(t) = S$ which yields

$$S = \frac{1}{1 + h_2}\frac{B_1 + B_3}{2} + \frac{h_2}{1 + h_2}B_2 = \frac{M}{1 + h_2} + \frac{h_2}{1 + h_2}B_2 \qquad (5-131)$$

Writing the parametric equation of the straight line between $M$ and $B_2$ gives

$$S = (1 - s)M + sB_2 \qquad (5-132)$$

where $s$ is the parameter. Equating coefficients of Eqs. (5–131) and (5–132) shows that

$$s = \frac{h_2}{1 + h_2} \qquad \text{and} \qquad h_2 = \frac{s}{1 - s} = \frac{M - S}{S - B_2} \qquad (5-133)$$

The parameter $s$ controls the shape of the curve and its conic form. Hence, it is a good design tool.

Since a circle is a special case of an ellipse, for a particular value of $h_2$ Eq. (5–130) yields a circular arc. Because of symmetry $B_1$, $B_2$ and $B_3$ for a circular arc form an isosceles triangle as shown in Fig. 5–68. The required value of $h_2$ is determined from the geometry shown in Fig. 5–68.

Because the triangle $B_1 B_2 B_3$ is isosceles, $S$ is the maximum point on the curve. Hence the tangent at $S$ is parallel to the line $B_1 B_3$. The triangle $B_1 q S$ is also isosceles with equal base angles $\angle SB_1q$ and $\angle B_1Sq$, labelled $\theta/2$ in Fig. 5–68. Since the tangent at $S$ is parallel to the line $B_1B_3$ the angles $\angle qSB_1$ and $\angle SB_1M$ are equal. Thus, the angle $\angle SB_1M = \theta/2$ is half the base angle of the isosceles triangle formed by $B_1$, $B_2$ and $B_3$.

From Eq. (5–133) and these results $h_2$ is

$$h_2 = \frac{M - S}{S - B_2} = \frac{e\tan\left(\dfrac{\theta}{2}\right)}{f\sin\theta - e\tan\left(\dfrac{\theta}{2}\right)}$$

Recalling that $\tan(\theta/2) = \sin\theta/(1 + \cos\theta)$ yields

$$h_2 = \frac{\dfrac{e\sin\theta}{1 + \cos\theta}}{f\sin\theta - \dfrac{e\sin\theta}{1 + \cos\theta}} = \frac{e}{f(1 + \cos\theta) - e} = \frac{e}{f} = \cos\theta \qquad (5-134)$$

The portion of the circle subtended by the arc is twice the angle $\theta$. For an arc of 120°, $\theta = 60°$ and $h_2 = 1/2$. For this particular case the radius of the circle is $2(S - M)$.

A full circle is formed by piecing together multiple segments. Specifically, a full circle is given by the three rational quadratic B-spline curve segments, each subtending 120°. The defining polygon points form an equilateral triangle, as

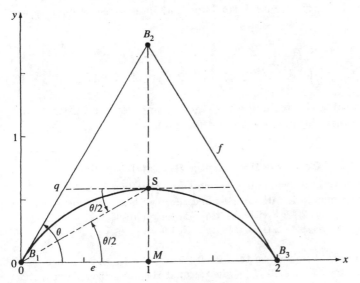

**Figure 5–68**  Circular arc formed as a rational B-spline curve.

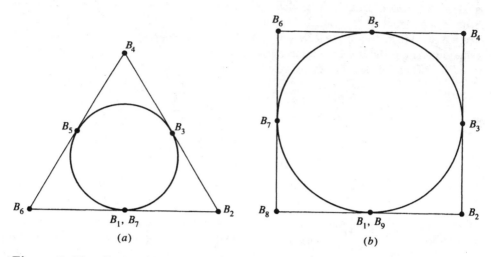

**Figure 5–69** Rational B-spline circles. (a) Three 120° segments; (b) four 90° segments.

shown in Fig. 5–69a. The nonuniform knot and homogeneous coordinate vectors are

$$[X] = [0 \quad 0 \quad 0 \quad 1 \quad 1 \quad 2 \quad 2 \quad 3 \quad 3 \quad 3]$$

$$[H] = [1 \quad 1/2 \quad 1 \quad 1/2 \quad 1 \quad 1/2 \quad 1]$$

Similarly, a full circle is also given by the four rational quadratic B-spline curve segments each subtending 90° with defining polygon points forming a square, as shown in Fig. 5–69b. Here, the nonuniform knot and homogeneous coordinate vectors are

$$[X] = [0 \quad 0 \quad 0 \quad 1 \quad 1 \quad 2 \quad 2 \quad 3 \quad 3 \quad 4 \quad 4 \quad 4]$$

$$[H] = [1 \quad \sqrt{2}/2 \quad 1 \quad \sqrt{2}/2 \quad 1 \quad \sqrt{2}/2 \quad 1 \quad \sqrt{2}/2 \quad 1]$$

An example illustrates the techniques for generating conic sections using rational B-splines and blending them with free-form curves.

---

**Example 5–22    Conic Sections Using Rational B-splines**

Construct a single third-order rational B-spline curve that blends a 90° circular arc defined by a quadratic rational B-spline curve with polygon vertices $B_1[0 \quad 0]$, $B_2[0 \quad 2]$, $B_3[2 \quad 2]$ with the third-order quadratic rational B-spline curve defined by $B_3[2 \quad 2]$, $B_4[4 \quad 2]$, $B_5[6 \quad 3]$, $B_6[7 \quad 5]$ with $h_i = 1$, $4 \le i \le 7$.

The 90° circular arc has knot vector $[0 \quad 0 \quad 0 \quad 1 \quad 1 \quad 1]$ and homogeneous coordinate vector $[1 \quad \sqrt{2}/2 \quad 1]$. The rational B-spline curve defined by $B_3, B_4, B_5, B_6$ has knot vector $[0 \quad 0 \quad 0 \quad 1 \quad 2 \quad 2 \quad 2]$ with homogeneous coordinate vector $[1 \quad 1 \quad 1 \quad 1]$.

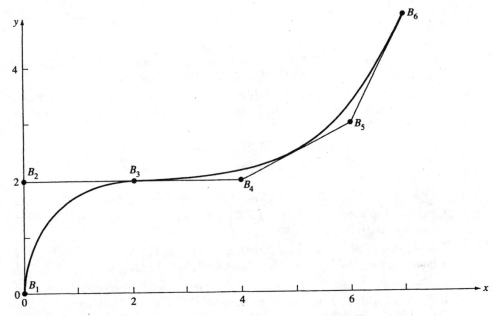

**Figure 5–70**    Blended quadratic rational B-spline curve.

$[X] = [0 \quad 0 \quad 0 \quad 1 \quad 1 \quad 2 \quad 3 \quad 3 \quad 3]$ is the nonuniform knot vector for the combined curve, with $[1 \quad \sqrt{2}/2 \quad 1 \quad 1 \quad 1 \quad 1]$ the homogeneous coordinate vector. The result is shown in Fig. 5–70.

---

## 5–14    REFERENCES

5-1 Böhm, W., Farin, G., and Kahmann, J., "A Survey of Curve and Surface Methods in CAGD," *Comp. Aid. Geom. Des.*, Vol. 1, pp. 1–60, 1984.

5-2 Higdon, A., Ohlsen, E., Stiles, W., and Weese, J., *Mechanics of Materials*, 2d ed., John Wiley & Sons, New York, 1967.

5-3 South, N.E., and Kelly, J.P., "Analytic Surface Methods," Ford Motor Company N/C Development Unit, Product Engineering Office, December 1965.

5-4 Nutbourne, A.W., "A Cubic Spline Package Part 2 – The Mathematics," *Comp. Aid. Des.*, Vol. 5, No. 1, January 1973.

5-5 Adams, J.A., "A Comparison of Methods for Cubic Spline Curve Fitting," *Comp. Aid. Des.*, Vol. 6, pp. 1–9, 1974.

5-6 Schweikert, D.C., "An Interpolation Curve Using a Spline in Tension," *J. Math. Phys.*, Vol. 45, pp. 312–317, 1966.

5-7 Cline, A.K., "Curve Fitting Using Splines Under Tension," *Atmos. Tech.*, No. 3, pp. 60–65, 1973.

5-8 Nielson, G., "Some Piecewise Polynomial Alternatives to Splines Under Tension," *Computer Aided Geometric Design*, Barnhill, R.E., and Riesenfeld, R.F. (eds.), pp. 209–235, Academic Press, New York, 1974.

5-9 Overhauser, A.W., "Analytic Definition of Curves and Surfaces by Parabolic Blending," Tech. Rep. No. SL68–40, Ford Motor Company Scientific Laboratory, May 8, 1968.

5-10 Brewer, J.A., and Anderson, D.C., "Visual Interaction with Overhauser Curves and Surfaces," *Comp. Graph.*, Vol. 11, pp. 132–137, 1977 (SIGGRAPH 77).

5-11 Bézier, P.E., "How Renault Uses Numerical Control for Car Body Design and Tooling," SAE paper 680010, Society of Automotive Engineers' Congress, Detroit, MI, 1968.

5-12 Bézier, P.E., "Example of an Existing System in the Motor Industry: The Unisurf System," *Proc. Roy. Soc. (London)*, Vol. A321, pp. 207–218, 1971.

5-13 Bézier, P.E., *Emploi des Machines à Commande Numerique*, Masson et Cie, Paris, 1970. Translated by Forrest, A.R., and Pankhurst, A.F., as Bézier, P.E., *Numerical Control Mathematics and Applications*, John Wiley & Sons, London, 1972.

5-14 Forrest, A.R., "Interactive Interpolation and Approximation by Bézier Polynomials," *Comp. J.*, Vol. 15, pp. 71–79, 1972.

5-15 Gordon, W.J., and Riesenfeld, R.F., "Bernstein-Bézier Methods for the Computer Aided Design of Free-form Curves and Surfaces," *J. ACM*, Vol. 21, pp. 293–310, 1974.

5-16 Bartels, R.H., Beatty, J.C., and Barsky, B.A., *Splines For Use in Computer Graphics & Geometric Modeling*, Morgan Kaufman, Los Altos, CA, 1987.

5-17 Barsky, B.A., "Arbitrary Subdivision of Bézier Curves," TR UCB/CSD 85/265, Comp. Sci. Div., Univ. of Cal., Berkeley, November 1985.

5-18 Clark, J.H., "A Fast Scanline Algorithm for Rendering Parametric Surfaces", *Comp. Graph.*, Vol. 14, pp. 7–12, 1979 [addendum to SIGGRAPH 79 Conf. Proc. — "papers to be published in the CACM"].

5-19 Cohen, E., and Riesenfeld, R.F., "General Matrix Representations for Bézier and B-Spline Curves," *Comp. in Indus.*, Vol. 3, pp. 9–15, 1982.

5-20 Schoenberg, I.J., "Contributions to the Problem of Approximation of Equidistant Data by Analytic Functions," *Q. Appl. Math.*, Vol. 4, pp. 45–99; pp. 112–141, 1946.

5-21 Cox, M.G., "The Numerical Evaluation of B-Splines," National Physical Laboratory DNAC 4, August 1971.

5-22 de Boor, C., "On Calculation with B-splines," *J. Approx. Theory*, Vol. 6, pp. 50–62, 1972.

5-23 Riesenfeld, R.F., "Application of B-Spline Approximation to Geometric Problems of Computer Aided Design," PhD dissertation, Syracuse Univ.,

Syracuse, NY, 1972. Also available as U. of Utah, UTEC-CSc-73-126, March 1973.

5-24 Barsky, B.A., "End Conditions and Boundary Conditions for Uniform B-Spline Curve and Surface Representations," *Comp. in Indus.*, Vol. 3, pp. 17-29, 1982.

5-25 Hartley, P.J., and Judd, C.J., "Parameterization of Bézier Type B-spline Curves and Surfaces," *Comp. Aid. Des.*, Vol. 10, pp. 130-134, 1978.

5-26 Rogers, D.F., and Fog, N.G., "Constrained B-spline Curve and Surface Fitting," *CADJ*, Vol. 21, pp. 641-648, 1989.

5-27 Cohen, E., Lyche, T., and Schumacher, L.L., "Algorithms for Degree-Raising of Splines," *ACM Trans. on Graph.*, Vol. 4, pp. 171-181, 1985.

5-28 Cohen, E., Lyche, T., and Riesenfeld, R.F., "Discrete B-Splines and Subdivision Techniques in Computer Aided Geometric Design and Computer Graphics," *Comp. Graph. Imag. Proc.*, Vol. 14, pp. 87-111, 1980.

5-29 Prautzsch, H., "A Short Proof of the Oslo Algorithm," *Comp. Aid. Geom. Des.*, Vol. 1, pp. 95-96, 1984.

5-30 Böhm, W., "Inserting New Knots into B-spline Curves," *Comp. Aid. Des.*, Vol. 12, pp. 199-201, 1980.

5-31 Böhm, W., and Prautzsch, H., "The Insertion Algorithm," *Comp. Aid. Des.*, Vol. 17, pp. 58-59, 1985.

5-32 Coons, S.A., "Surfaces for Computer Aided Design of Space Forms," MIT Project MAC-TR-41, 1967.

5-33 Farouki, R., and Hinds, J., "A Hierarchy of Geometric Forms," *IEEE Comp. Graph. & Appl.*, Vol. 5, No. 5, pp. 51-78, 1985.

5-34 Piegl, L., "A Geometric Investigation of the Rational Bézier Scheme of Computer Aided Design," *Comp. in Indust.*, Vol. 7, pp. 401-410, 1986.

5-35 Forrest, A.R., "The Twisted Cubic Curve: A Computer Aided Geometric Design Approach," *Comp. Aid. Des..*, Vol. 12, pp. 165-172, 1980.

5-36 Böhm, W., "On Cubics: A Survey," *Comp. Graph. Imag. Proc.*, Vol. 19, pp. 201-226, 1982.

5-37 Forrest, A.R., "Curves and Surfaces for Computer-Aided Design," PhD Dissertation, Cambridge Univ., 1968.

5-38 Ball, A.A., "Consurf I-III," *Comp. Aid. Des..*, Vol. 6, pp. 243-249, 1974; Vol. 7, pp. 237-242, 1975; Vol. 9, pp. 9-12, 1977.

5-39 Versprille, K.J., "Computer-Aided Design Applications of the Rational B-spline Approximation Form," PhD dissertation, Syracuse Univ., Syracuse, NY, February 1975.

5-40 Tiller, W., "Rational B-splines for Curve and Surface Representation," *IEEE Comp. Graph. & Appl.*, Vol. 3, No. 6, pp. 61-69, September 1983.

5-41 Piegl, L., and Tiller, W., "Curve and Surface Constructions Using Rational B-splines," *Comp. Aid. Des..*, Vol. 19, pp. 485-498, 1987.

5–42 IGES 'Initial Graphics Exchange Specifications, Version 3.0,' Doc. No. NB-SIR 86-3359 Nat. Bur. of Stds., Gaithersburg, MD, USA, 1986.

5–43 Lee, E., "Rational Bézier Representation for Conics," in *Geometric Modeling*, Farin, G. (ed.), SIAM, pp. 3–27, 1986.

## SURFACES

## 6–1   INTRODUCTION

Surfaces and their description play a critical role in design and manufacturing. The design and manufacture of automobile bodies, ship hulls, aircraft fuselages and wings; propeller, turbine, compressor and fan blades; glassware and bottles; furniture, and shoes are obvious examples. Surface shape or geometry is the essence of design for either functional or aesthetic reasons. Surface description also plays an important role in the representation of data obtained from medical, geological, physical and other natural phenomena.

In design and engineering the traditional way of representing a surface is to use multiple orthogonal projections. In effect, the surface is defined by a net or mesh of orthogonal plane curves lying in plane sections plus multiple orthogonal projections of certain three-dimensional 'feature' lines (see Fig. 5–1). The curves may originally be designed on paper or they may be taken (digitized) from a three-dimensional model, e.g., the clay stylist's model traditionally used in the automotive industry.

In computer graphics and computer aided design it is advantageous to develop a 'true' three-dimensional mathematical model of a surface. Such a model allows early and relatively easy analysis of surface characteristics, e.g., curvature, or of physical quantities that depend on the surface, e.g., volume, surface area, moment of inertia, etc. Visual rendering of the surface (see Ref. 6–1) for design or design verification is simplified. Further, generation of the necessary information required to fabricate the surface, e.g., numerical control codes, is also considerably simplified as compared to the traditional net of lines approach. Early work by Bézier (Ref. 6–2), Sabin (Ref. 6–3) and Peters (Ref. 6–4) among others demonstrated the feasibility of this approach. Recently surface description techniques have advanced to the point where it is 'almost' possible to abolish the traditional net of lines surface description.

There are two basic philosophies embedded in surface description techniques.

**379**

The first, mostly associated with the name of Coons, seeks to create a mathematical surface from known data. The second, mostly associated with the name of Bézier, seeks to create a mathematical surface *ab initio*. Initially, disciplines that depended upon numerical parameters, e.g., engineering, were attracted to the first approach, while disciplines that depended upon visual, tactile or aesthetic factors, e.g., stylists and graphic artists, were attracted to the *ab initio* techniques. Recent work by Rogers (Refs. 6–5 to 6–7) with real-time interactive systems for design of ship hulls and by Cohen (Ref. 6–8) for general surface design shows that the two approaches are compatible.

The elements of mathematical parametric surface representation as used in computer graphics and computer aided design are given in the following sections.

## 6–2 SURFACES OF REVOLUTION

Perhaps the simplest method for generating a three-dimensional surface is to revolve a two-dimensional entity, e.g., a line or a plane curve, about an axis in space. Such surfaces are called surfaces of revolution. For simplicity, initially the axis of rotation is assumed coincident with the $x$-axis and in the positive direction. The point, line or plane curve to be rotated is assumed to lie in the $xy$ plane. Later a procedure to remove these restrictions is developed.

The simplest entity that can be rotated about an axis is a point. Provided that the point does not lie on the axis, rotation through an angle of $2\pi$ (360°) yields a circle. Rotation through an angle less than $2\pi$ (360°) yields a circular arc.

Next in complexity is a line segment parallel to and not coincident with the axis of rotation. Rotation through an angle of $2\pi$ (360°) yields a circular cylinder. The radius of the cylinder is the perpendicular distance from the line to the rotation axis. The length of the cylinder is the length of the line segment. An example is shown in Fig. 6–1.

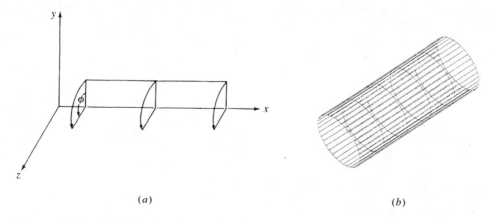

(a)

(b)

**Figure 6–1** Cylindrical surface of revolution. (a) Schematic; (b) result.

If the line segment and the axis of rotation are coplanar and the line segment is not parallel to the rotation axis, then rotation about the axis through $2\pi$ (360°) yields a truncated right circular cone. The radius of the cone at each end is the perpendicular distance from the end points of the line segment to the axis of rotation. The length of the cone is the projected length of the line segment on the rotation axis. An example is shown in Fig. 6–2.

Again if the line segment and the axis of rotation are coplanar and the line segment is perpendicular to the axis of rotation, then rotation through $2\pi$ (360°) yields a planar disc. If the line segment intersects (or touches) the axis of rotation, a solid disc results; otherwise the disc has a circular hole in it. Examples are shown in Fig. 6–3.

Finally if the line segment is skew to the axis of rotation, i.e., not coplanar, then rotation through $2\pi$ (360°) yields a hyperboloid of one sheet (see Secs. 6–4 and 6–7).

Closed or open polygons can also be used to generate surfaces of revolution. An example representing a cone with a cylindrical hole in it is shown in Fig. 6–4.

The parametric equation for a point on a surface of revolution is developed by recalling that the parametric equation of the entity to be rotated, e.g.,

$$P(t) = [\, x(t) \quad y(t) \quad z(t) \,] \qquad 0 \le t \le t_{max}$$

is a function of the single parameter $t$. Rotation about an axis causes the location of the point to also be a function of the rotation angle $\phi$. Thus, a point on a surface of revolution is specified by *two* parameters $t$ and $\phi$. It is a biparametric function as shown in Fig. 6–5.

For the specific case at hand, i.e., rotation about the $x$-axis of an entity

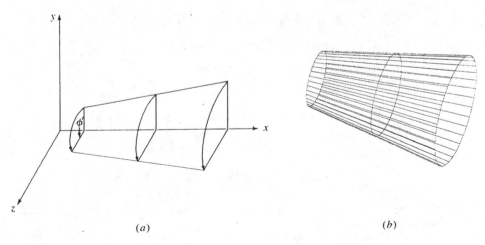

(a)    (b)

**Figure 6–2**    Conical surface of revolution. (a) Schematic; (b) result.

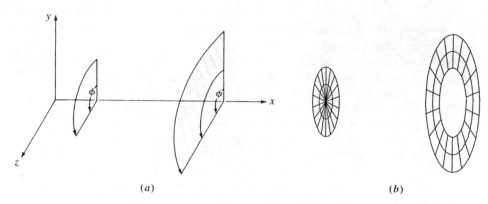

**Figure 6-3**   A disc as a surface of revolution. (a) Schematic; (b) result.

initially lying in the $xy$ plane, the surface equation is†

$$Q(t, \phi) = [\, x(t) \quad y(t) \cos \phi \quad y(t) \sin \phi \,] \qquad (6-1)$$

Note that here the $x$ coordinate does not change. An example is illustrative.

---

### Example 6-1   Simple Surface of Revolution

Consider the line segment with end points $P_1 [\, 1 \quad 1 \quad 0 \,]$ and $P_2 [\, 6 \quad 2 \quad 0 \,]$ lying in the $xy$ plane. Rotating the line about the $x$-axis yields a conical surface. Determine the point on this surface at $t = 0.5$, $\phi = \pi/3$ (60°).

The parametric equation for the line segment from $P_1$ to $P_2$ is

$$P(t) = [\, x(t) \quad y(t) \quad z(t) \,] = P_1 + (P_2 - P_1)t \qquad 0 \le t \le 1$$

with Cartesian components

$$x(t) = x_1 + (x_2 - x_1)t = 1 + 5t$$
$$y(t) = y_1 + (y_2 - y_1)t = 1 + t$$
$$z(t) = z_1 + (z_2 - z_1)t = 0$$

Using Eq. (6-1), the point $Q\,(1/2, \pi/3)$ on the surface of revolution is

$$Q(1/2, \pi/3) = [\, 1 + 5t \quad (1 + t) \cos \phi \quad (1 + t) \sin \phi \,]$$

$$= \left[\, \frac{7}{2} \quad \frac{3}{2} \cos \left( \frac{\pi}{3} \right) \quad \frac{3}{2} \sin \left( \frac{\pi}{3} \right) \,\right]$$

$$= \left[\, \frac{7}{2} \quad \frac{3}{4} \quad \frac{3\sqrt{3}}{4} \,\right] = [\, 3.5 \quad 0.75 \quad 1.3 \,]$$

---

†Note that $Q(t, \phi)$ is a vector valued function. Thus, in vector form
$$Q(t, \phi) = x(t)\mathbf{i} + y(t) \cos \phi \mathbf{j} + y(t) \sin \phi \mathbf{k}$$
where $\mathbf{i}, \mathbf{j}, \mathbf{k}$ are unit vectors in the $x, y, z$ directions, respectively.

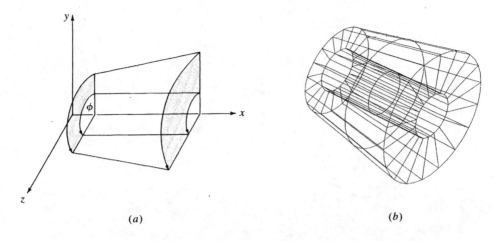

**Figure 6–4**    A surface of revolution from a closed polygon. (a) Schematic; (b) result.

Rotating plane curves also yields surfaces of revolution. A sphere is obtained by rotating an origin-centered semicircle in the $xy$ plane about the $x$-axis as shown in Fig. 6–6a. Recalling the parametric equation of the circle (see Sec. 4–5)

$$x = r \cos \theta \qquad 0 \le \theta \le \pi \qquad\qquad (4-4)$$

$$y = r \sin \theta$$

the parametric equation of the sphere is

$$Q(\theta, \phi) = [\, x(\theta) \quad y(\theta) \cos \phi \quad y(\theta) \sin \phi \,]$$

$$= [\, r \cos \theta \quad r \sin \theta \cos \phi \quad r \sin \theta \sin \phi \,] \qquad 0 \le \theta \le \pi$$

$$0 \le \phi \le 2\pi \quad (6-2)$$

An ellipsoid of revolution is obtained if the parametric equation of an origin centered semiellipse in the $xy$ plane is substituted for that of the circle. Specifically recalling the parametric equation of the semiellipse (see Sec. 4–6)

$$x = a \cos \theta \qquad 0 \le \theta \le \pi \qquad\qquad (4-6)$$

$$y = b \sin \theta$$

gives the parametric equation for any point on the ellipsoid of revolution as

$$Q(\theta, \phi) = [\, a \cos \theta \quad b \sin \theta \cos \phi \quad b \sin \theta \sin \phi \,] \qquad 0 \le \theta \le \pi$$

$$0 \le \phi \le 2\pi \quad (6-3)$$

If $a = b = r$, then Eq. (6–3) reduces to Eq. (6–2) for a sphere. An ellipsoid of revolution is shown in Fig. 6–6b.

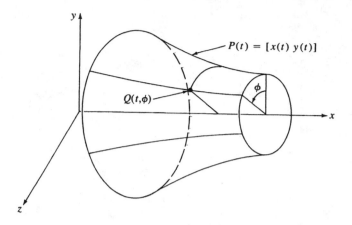

**Figure 6–5**   Biparametric surface of revolution.

If the axis of rotation does not pass through the center of a complete circle or ellipse, then rotation about the axis generates a torus with a circular or elliptical cross section as appropriate. Noting that the parametric equation of a non-origin-centered ellipse in the $xy$ plane is

$$x = h + a \cos \theta \qquad 0 \leq \theta \leq 2\pi$$

$$y = k + b \sin \theta$$

where $(h, k)$ are the $x$ and $y$ coordinates of the center of the ellipse, the parametric equation for any point on the torus is

$$Q(\theta, \phi) = [\, h + a \cos \theta \quad (k + b \sin \theta) \cos \phi \quad (k + b \sin \theta) \sin \phi \,] \qquad (6-4)$$

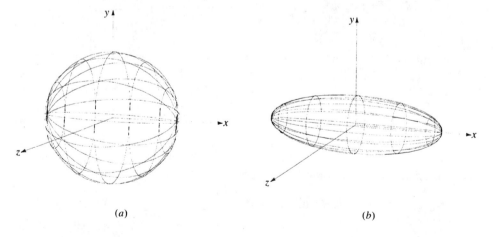

(a)

(b)

**Figure 6–6**   Surfaces of revolution. (a) Sphere; (b) ellipsoid.

where $0 \le \theta \le 2\pi$, $0 \le \phi \le 2\pi$. If $a = b = r$, Eq. (6-4) yields a torus with a circular cross section. If $a \ne b$, then a torus with an elliptical cross section results. Figure 6-7 shows both a circular and an elliptical cross section torus.

A paraboloid of revolution is obtained by rotating the parametric parabola (see Sec. 4-7)

$$x = a\theta^2 \qquad 0 \le \theta \le \theta_{max} \qquad\qquad (4-9)$$
$$y = 2a\theta$$

about the $x$-axis. The parametric surface is given by

$$Q(\theta, \phi) = [\, a\theta^2 \quad 2a\theta \cos\phi \quad 2a\theta \sin\phi \,] \qquad 0 \le \theta \le \theta_{max}$$
$$0 \le \phi \le 2\pi \qquad (6-5)$$

A hyperboloid of revolution is obtained by rotating the parametric hyperbola

$$x = a \sec\theta \qquad 0 \le \theta \le \theta_{max} \qquad\qquad (4-14)$$
$$y = b \tan\theta$$

about the $x$-axis. The parametric surface is given by

$$Q(\theta, \phi) = [\, a\sec\theta \quad b\tan\theta \cos\phi \quad b\tan\theta \sin\phi \,] \qquad 0 \le \theta \le \theta_{max}$$
$$0 \le \phi \le 2\pi \qquad (6-6)$$

Examples are shown in Fig. 6-8.

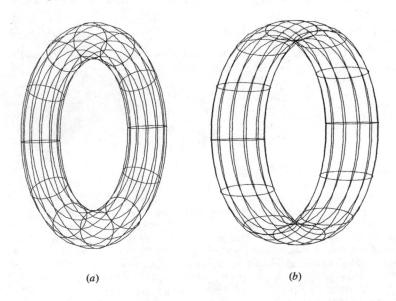

(a)          (b)

**Figure 6-7**  Tori. (a) Circular cross section; (b) elliptical cross section.

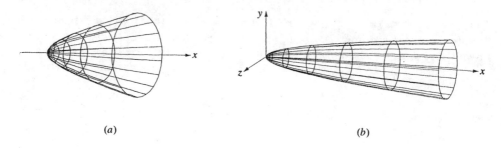

(a)                                                                            (b)

**Figure 6–8**    Surfaces of revolution. (a) Paraboloid; (b) hyperboloid.

Any parametric curve can be used to create a surface of revolution. Obvious possibilities are cubic spline, parabolically blended, Bézier and B-spline curves. Figure 6–9 shows a surface of revolution created using a relatively simple parabolically blended curve. Figure 6–10 shows a handleless mug created as a surface of revolution using a complex open B-spline curve. Notice that the mug has both an inside and an outside. Here rotation is about the $y$-axis.†

Recall that in matrix form a parametric space curve (see Eqs. (5–27), (5–44), (5–67) and (5–94)) is given by

$$P(t) = [\,T\,][\,N\,][\,G\,]$$

where $[\,T\,]$, $[\,N\,]$ and $[\,G\,]$ are parameter, blending function and geometry matrices, respectively. The general form of the matrix equation for a surface of revolution is thus

$$Q(t, \phi) = [\,T\,][\,N\,][\,G\,][\,S\,] \tag{6 – 7}$$

where $[\,S\,]$ represents the contribution due to rotation about an axis by the angle $\phi$. For the specific case of rotation about the $x$-axis

$$[\,S\,] = \begin{bmatrix} 1 & 0 & 0 & 0 \\ 0 & \cos\phi & \sin\phi & 0 \\ 0 & 0 & 0 & 0 \\ 0 & 0 & 0 & 1 \end{bmatrix} \tag{6 – 8}$$

An example illustrates these techniques.

---

† The method used to design the B-spline curve for the mug shown in Fig. 6–10 may be of interest. A sketch of a pottery mug used by the first author was first made on graph paper. Thirty-four points were digitized from the sketch. An initial B-spline polygon ($k = 4, n + 1 = 21$) was derived using the fitting technique described in Sec. 5–11. The defining polygon vertices were then transferred to a real time interactive graphics system for final design (see Ref. 6–7). A B-spline curve created from the final 25 polygon vertices was used to generate the surface of revolution shown. The defining polygon vertices are [ 0   0.684 ], [ 0.302   0.684 ], [ 0.302   0.684 ], [ 1.598  −0.288 ], [ 1.088  0.405 ], [ 0.374  0.773 ], [ 0.848  0.993 ], [ 1.232  1.446 ], [ 1.451  1.875 ], [ 1.502   2.631 ], [ 1.448  3.308 ], [ 1.226  4.076 ], [ 1.397  4.449 ], [ 1.398  4.592 ], [ 1.268  4.572 ], [ 1.241  4.485 ], [ 1.109  4.170 ], [ 1.214  3.669 ], [ 1.313  2.889 ], [ 1.310  2.280 ], [ 1.172  1.575 ], [ 0.629   1.119 ], [ 0.281   0.882 ], [ 0.278   0.891 ], [ 0   0.897 ].

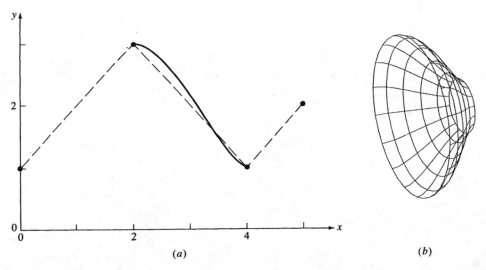

**Figure 6–9**    Parabolically blended surface of revolution. (a) Generating curve; (b) surface.

---

### Example 6–2    Parabolically Blended Surface of Revolution

Consider the parabolically blended curve defined by the points $P_1 [ 0 \quad 1 \quad 0 ]$, $P_2 [ 2 \quad 3 \quad 0 ]$, $P_3 [ 4 \quad 1 \quad 0 ]$, $P_4 [ 5 \quad 2 \quad 0 ]$. Rotate this curve about the $x$-axis through $2\pi$ to obtain a surface of revolution. Calculate the surface point at $t = 0.5$, $\phi = \pi/3$ ($60°$).

Using Eqs. (6–7) and (6–8) the parametric equation of the surface of revolution is

$$Q(t, \phi) = [ T ][ A ][ G ][ S ]$$

where $[ S ]$, $[ T ]$, $[ A ]$ and $[ G ]$ are given by Eqs. (5–44),(5–52) and (5–53), respectively.

Specifically

$$Q(t, \phi) = \left(\frac{1}{2}\right) [\, t^3 \quad t^2 \quad t \quad 1 \,] \begin{bmatrix} -1 & 3 & -3 & 1 \\ 2 & -5 & 4 & -1 \\ -1 & 0 & 1 & 0 \\ 0 & 2 & 0 & 0 \end{bmatrix} \begin{bmatrix} 0 & 1 & 0 & 1 \\ 2 & 3 & 0 & 1 \\ 4 & 1 & 0 & 1 \\ 5 & 2 & 0 & 1 \end{bmatrix} \times$$

$$\begin{bmatrix} 1 & 0 & 0 & 0 \\ 0 & \cos\phi & \sin\phi & 0 \\ 0 & 0 & 0 & 0 \\ 0 & 0 & 0 & 1 \end{bmatrix}$$

$$Q(t, \phi) = \left(\frac{1}{2}\right) [\, t^3 \quad t^2 \quad t \quad 1 \,] \begin{bmatrix} -1 & 7 & 0 & 1 \\ 1 & -11 & 0 & 1 \\ 4 & 0 & 0 & 1 \\ 4 & 6 & 0 & 1 \end{bmatrix} \begin{bmatrix} 1 & 0 & 0 & 0 \\ 0 & \cos\phi & \sin\phi & 0 \\ 0 & 0 & 0 & 0 \\ 0 & 0 & 0 & 1 \end{bmatrix}$$

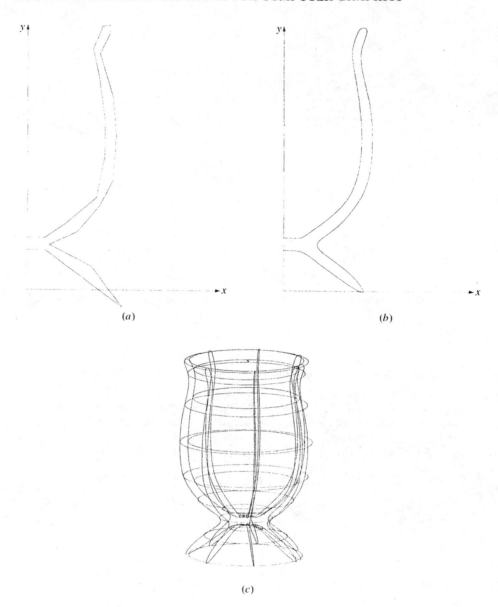

(a)

(b)

(c)

**Figure 6–10** B-spline surface of revolution. (a) Polygon vertices; (b) B-spline curve; (c) surface.

For $t = 0.5$ and $\phi = \pi/3$ (60°)

$$Q(0.5, \pi/3) = \frac{1}{2} \begin{bmatrix} \frac{1}{8} & \frac{1}{4} & \frac{1}{2} & 1 \end{bmatrix} \begin{bmatrix} -1 & 7 & 0 & 1 \\ 1 & -11 & 0 & 1 \\ 4 & 0 & 0 & 1 \\ 4 & 6 & 0 & 1 \end{bmatrix} \begin{bmatrix} 1 & 0 & 0 & 0 \\ 0 & 1/2 & \sqrt{3}/2 & 0 \\ 0 & 0 & 0 & 0 \\ 0 & 0 & 0 & 1 \end{bmatrix}$$

$$= \begin{bmatrix} \dfrac{49}{16} & \dfrac{33}{32} & \dfrac{33\sqrt{3}}{32} & 1 \end{bmatrix} = [\, 3.0625 \quad 1.03125 \quad 1.786181 \quad 1 \,]$$

Complete results are shown in Fig. 6–9. The resulting surface could be the design of a bowl or even a wind tunnel or rocket nozzle.

---

The above results have been obtained by rotating a point, line, polygon or curve about a coordinate axis, specifically the $x$-axis. The more general case of rotation about an arbitrary axis in space is addressed using translations and rotations to position a surface of revolution first generated in a convenient local coordinate system.

Figure 6–11 shows a parametric curve $P(t)$ rotated about an arbitrary axis in space passing through the points $a_0$ and $a_1$ with direction from $a_0$ to $a_1$. After being generated in a convenient coordinate system the following procedure is used to position the surface of revolution:

Translate the point $a_0$ to the origin.

Perform appropriate rotations to make the $a$-axis coincident with the $+z$-axis (see Sec. 5–9).

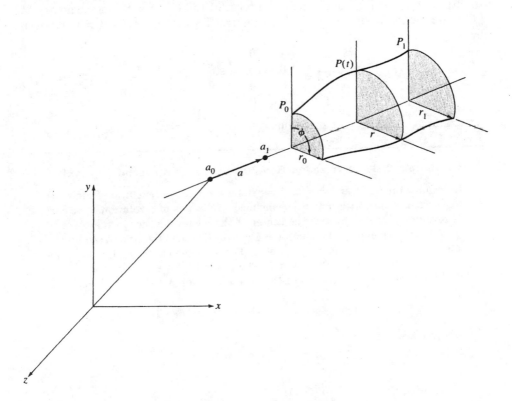

**Figure 6–11**  A surface of revolution about an arbitrary axis.

Rotate about the $y$-axis by $+90°$ to make the $a$-axis coincident with the $x$-axis.[†]

The above three steps are needed only to determine the inverse transformations required to place the surface of revolution correctly in three space. Having generated the surface of revolution by rotation about the $x$-axis, the following three steps correctly place it in three space:

Translate in $x$ to place the center of the surface of revolution at the correct location on the $a$-axis.

Apply the inverse of the combined rotation transformations to the surface of revolution.

Perform the inverse of the translation of the point $a_0$ to the surface of revolution.

A point on the surface of revolution is then given by

$$Q(t, \phi) = [\bar{Q}][Tr][\bar{R}_y]^{-1}[R_y]^{-1}[R_x]^{-1}[Tr]^{-1} \qquad (6-9)$$

where $[Tr]$, $[R_x]$, $[R_y]$ are given by Eqs. (3–22) to (3–24). $[\bar{R}_y]^{-1}$ is given by Eq. (3–8), and $[\bar{Q}]$ is given in the form of Eq. (6–7) with the geometry in $[G]$ represented in homogeneous coordinates. $[S]$ is now a $4 \times 4$ matrix given by

$$[S] = \begin{bmatrix} 1 & 0 & 0 & 0 \\ 0 & \cos\phi & \sin\phi & 0 \\ 0 & 0 & 0 & 0 \\ 0 & 0 & 0 & 1 \end{bmatrix} \qquad (6-10)$$

An example illustrates the procedure.

---

**Example 6–3    Surface of Revolution About an Arbitrary Axis**

Determine the point at $t = \pi/2$, $\phi = \pi/6$ on a surface of revolution formed by rotating an ellipse with major axis inclined to the axis of revolution. The axis of revolution passes through the center of the ellipse and lies in the plane of the ellipse. The angle of inclination is $i = \pi/4$. The semimajor and semiminor axes are $a = 5$, $b = 1$, respectively. The axis passes through the points $a_0 [0 \quad 10 \quad 10]$ and $a_1 [10 \quad 10 \quad 0]$. The center of the ellipse is at $a_1$.

First the direction cosines of the axis of rotation are (see Eq. 3–26)

$$[c_x \quad c_y \quad c_z] = [1/\sqrt{2} \quad 0 \quad -1/\sqrt{2}]$$

and (see Eq. 3–18)

$$d = \sqrt{c_y^2 + c_z^2} = 1/\sqrt{2}$$

Thus, using Eqs. (3–22) to (3–24)

---

[†]This step is necessary *only* to be consistent with previous work. The surface of revolution could as easily be generated about the $z$-axis.

$$[ M_1 ] = [ Tr ][ R_x ][ R_y ]$$

$$= \begin{bmatrix} 1 & 0 & 0 & 0 \\ 0 & 1 & 0 & 0 \\ 0 & 0 & 1 & 0 \\ 0 & -10 & -10 & 1 \end{bmatrix} \begin{bmatrix} 1 & 0 & 0 & 0 \\ 0 & -1 & 0 & 0 \\ 0 & 0 & -1 & 0 \\ 0 & 0 & 0 & 1 \end{bmatrix} \begin{bmatrix} 1/\sqrt{2} & 0 & 1/\sqrt{2} & 0 \\ 0 & 1 & 0 & 0 \\ -1/\sqrt{2} & 0 & 1/\sqrt{2} & 0 \\ 0 & 0 & 0 & 1 \end{bmatrix}$$

$$= \begin{bmatrix} 1/\sqrt{2} & 0 & 1/\sqrt{2} & 0 \\ 0 & -1 & 0 & 0 \\ 1/\sqrt{2} & 0 & -1/\sqrt{2} & 0 \\ -10/\sqrt{2} & 10 & 10/\sqrt{2} & 1 \end{bmatrix}$$

makes the rotation axis coincident with the $z$-axis. Rotating about $y$ by $90°$ yields

$$[ M_2 ] = [ Tr ][ R_x ][ R_y ][ \bar{R}_y ]$$

$$= \begin{bmatrix} 1/\sqrt{2} & 0 & 1/\sqrt{2} & 0 \\ 0 & -1 & 0 & 0 \\ 1/\sqrt{2} & 0 & -1/\sqrt{2} & 0 \\ -10/\sqrt{2} & 10 & 10/\sqrt{2} & 1 \end{bmatrix} \begin{bmatrix} 0 & 0 & -1 & 0 \\ 0 & 1 & 0 & 0 \\ 1 & 0 & 0 & 0 \\ 0 & 0 & 0 & 1 \end{bmatrix}$$

$$= \begin{bmatrix} 1/\sqrt{2} & 0 & -1/\sqrt{2} & 0 \\ 0 & -1 & 0 & 0 \\ -1/\sqrt{2} & 0 & -1/\sqrt{2} & 0 \\ 10/\sqrt{2} & 10 & 10/\sqrt{2} & 1 \end{bmatrix}$$

Using $[ M_2 ]$ and the homogeneous coordinates, the center of the ellipse originally at $a$ is now

$$[ 10 \quad 10 \quad 10 \quad 1 ] \begin{bmatrix} 1/\sqrt{2} & 0 & 1/\sqrt{2} & 0 \\ 0 & -1 & 0 & 0 \\ 1/\sqrt{2} & 0 & -1/\sqrt{2} & 0 \\ -10/\sqrt{2} & 10 & 10/\sqrt{2} & 1 \end{bmatrix} = [ 20/\sqrt{2} \quad 0 \quad 0 \quad 1 ]$$

i.e., at $h = 20/\sqrt{2}$ on the $x$-axis.

Recalling Ex. 4-4 of Sec. 4-6, rotating an origin-centered ellipse about the origin by the angle $i$ yields the parametric equations

$$x = a \cos t \cos i - b \sin t \sin i \qquad 0 \le t \le 2\pi$$

$$y = a \cos t \sin i + b \sin t \cos i$$

which may be written in the form of Eq. (6-7) as

$$[ \cos t \quad \sin t \quad 0 \quad 1 ] \begin{bmatrix} a & 0 & 0 & 0 \\ 0 & b & 0 & 0 \\ 0 & 0 & 0 & 0 \\ 0 & 0 & 0 & 1 \end{bmatrix} \begin{bmatrix} \cos i & \sin i & 0 & 0 \\ -\sin i & \cos i & 0 & 0 \\ 0 & 0 & 1 & 0 \\ 0 & 0 & 0 & 1 \end{bmatrix}$$

The surface of revolution is then

$$[Q] = [T][N][G][S]$$

$$= [\cos t \quad \sin t \quad 0 \quad 1] \begin{bmatrix} a & 0 & 0 & 0 \\ 0 & b & 0 & 0 \\ 0 & 0 & 0 & 0 \\ 0 & 0 & 0 & 1 \end{bmatrix} \begin{bmatrix} \cos i & \sin i & 0 & 0 \\ -\sin i & \cos i & 0 & 0 \\ 0 & 0 & 1 & 0 \\ 0 & 0 & 0 & 1 \end{bmatrix} \times$$

$$\begin{bmatrix} 1 & 0 & 0 & 0 \\ 0 & \cos\phi & \sin\phi & 0 \\ 0 & 0 & 0 & 0 \\ 0 & 0 & 0 & 1 \end{bmatrix}$$

For $a = 5$, $b = 1$, $i = \pi/4$

$$[\bar{Q}] = [\cos t \quad \sin t \quad 0 \quad 1] \begin{bmatrix} 5\sqrt{2}/2 & 5\sqrt{2}/2 & 0 & 0 \\ -\sqrt{2}/2 & \sqrt{2}/2 & 0 & 0 \\ 0 & 0 & 0 & 0 \\ 0 & 0 & 0 & 1 \end{bmatrix} \begin{bmatrix} 1 & 0 & 0 & 0 \\ 0 & \cos\phi & \sin\phi & 0 \\ 0 & 0 & 0 & 0 \\ 0 & 0 & 0 & 1 \end{bmatrix}$$

Translating the origin to $(h, n)$ on the $x$-axis and noting that

$$[M_2]^{-1} = [\bar{R}_y]^{-1}[R_y]^{-1}[R_x]^{-1}[Tr]^{-1}$$

$$= \begin{bmatrix} \sqrt{2}/2 & 0 & -\sqrt{2}/2 & 0 \\ 0 & -1 & 0 & 0 \\ -\sqrt{2}/2 & 0 & -\sqrt{2}/2 & 0 \\ 0 & 10 & 10 & 1 \end{bmatrix}$$

yields
$$[Q] = [T][N][G][S][Tr_x][M_2]^{-1}$$

The point at $Q(t, \phi)$ is

$$Q(t, \phi) = [\cos t \quad \sin t \quad 0 \quad 1] \begin{bmatrix} 5\sqrt{2}/2 & 5\sqrt{2}/2 & 0 & 0 \\ -\sqrt{2}/2 & \sqrt{2}/2 & 0 & 0 \\ 0 & 0 & 0 & 0 \\ 0 & 0 & 0 & 1 \end{bmatrix} \times$$

$$\begin{bmatrix} 1 & 0 & 0 & 0 \\ 0 & \cos\phi & \sin\phi & 0 \\ 0 & 0 & 0 & 0 \\ 0 & 0 & 0 & 1 \end{bmatrix} \begin{bmatrix} 1 & 0 & 0 & 0 \\ 0 & 1 & 0 & 0 \\ 0 & 0 & 1 & 0 \\ 20/\sqrt{2} & 0 & 0 & 1 \end{bmatrix} \times$$

$$\begin{bmatrix} \sqrt{2}/2 & 0 & -\sqrt{2}/2 & 0 \\ 0 & -1 & 0 & 0 \\ -\sqrt{2}/2 & 0 & -\sqrt{2}/2 & 0 \\ 0 & 10 & 10 & 1 \end{bmatrix}$$

or

$$Q(t,\phi) = \left(\frac{1}{2}\right)[\,\cos t \quad \sin t \quad 0 \quad 1\,] \times$$

$$\begin{bmatrix} 5(1-\sin\phi) & -5\sqrt{2}\cos\phi & -5(1+\sin\phi) & 0 \\ -(1+\sin\phi) & -\sqrt{2}\cos\phi & (1-\sin\phi) & 0 \\ 0 & 0 & 0 & 0 \\ 20 & 20 & 0 & 0 \end{bmatrix}$$

For $t = \pi/2,\ \phi = \pi/6$

$$Q(\pi/2,\ \pi/6) = \left(\frac{1}{2}\right)[\,0 \quad 1 \quad 0 \quad 1\,] \begin{bmatrix} 5/2 & -5\sqrt{6}/2 & -15/2 & 0 \\ -3/2 & -\sqrt{6}/2 & 1/2 & 0 \\ 0 & 0 & 0 & 0 \\ 20 & 20 & 0 & 1 \end{bmatrix}$$

$$= [\,37/4 \quad 10 - \sqrt{6}/4 \quad 1/4 \quad 1\,]$$

$$= [\,9.25 \quad 9.388 \quad 0.25 \quad 1\,]$$

The resulting surface is shown in Fig. 6–12. Notice that the surface is both self-intersecting and complex.

---

Formally differentiating Eq. (6–7) yields the parametric derivatives for a surface of revolution. Specifically, the derivative in the axial direction is

$$Q_t(t,\phi) = [\,T'\,][\,N\,][\,G\,][\,S\,] \qquad\qquad (6-11)$$

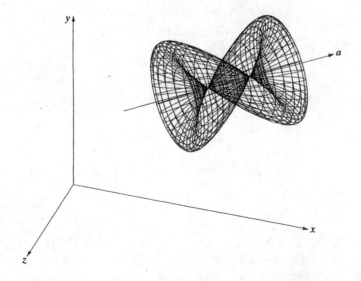

**Figure 6–12** Complex elliptical surface of revolution for Ex. 6–3.

and in the radial direction

$$Q_\phi(t,\phi) = [\,T\,][\,N\,][\,G\,][\,S'\,] \qquad (6-12)$$

where the prime denotes appropriate differentiation.

The surface normal is given by the cross product of the parametric derivatives, i.e.,

$$n = Q_t \times Q_\phi \qquad (6-13)$$

## 6-3    SWEEP SURFACES

A three-dimensional surface is also obtained by traversing an entity, e.g., a line, polygon or curve, along a path in space. The resulting surfaces are called sweep surfaces. Sweep surface generation is frequently used in geometric modeling. The simplest sweep entity is a point. The result of sweeping a point along a path is, of course, not a surface but a space curve. However, it serves to illustrate the fundamental technique.

Consider the position vector $P[\,x \quad y \quad z \quad 1\,]$ swept along the path represented by the sweep transformation $[\,T(s)\,]$. The position vector $Q(s)$ representing the resulting curve is given by

$$Q(s) = P[\,T(s)\,] \qquad s_1 \le s \le s_2 \qquad (6-14)$$

The transformation $[\,T(s)\,]$ determines the shape of the curve. For example, if the path is a straight line of length $n$ parallel to the $z$-axis, then (see Eq. 3–14)

$$[\,T(s)\,] = \begin{bmatrix} 1 & 0 & 0 & 0 \\ 0 & 1 & 0 & 0 \\ 0 & 0 & 1 & 0 \\ 0 & 0 & ns & 1 \end{bmatrix} \qquad 0 \le s \le 1$$

If the path is an origin-centered circle in a $z =$ constant plane, then (see Eq. 3–8)

$$[\,T(s)\,] = \begin{bmatrix} \left(\dfrac{r}{x}\right)\cos\{2\pi(s+s_i)\} & 0 & 0 & 0 \\ 0 & \left(\dfrac{r}{y}\right)\sin\{2\pi(s+s_i)\} & 0 & 0 \\ 0 & 0 & 1 & 0 \\ 0 & 0 & 0 & 1 \end{bmatrix} \qquad 0 \le s \le 1$$

where $s_i = (1/2\pi)\tan^{-1}(y_i/x_i)$ and for $P[\,x \quad y \quad z \quad 1\,]$, $r = \sqrt{x^2+y^2}$. Here, the subscript $i$ is used to indicate the initial or starting point.

Complex paths can be developed by combining simple paths. For example, combining the two previous path transformations yields a single turn of a helical path along the $z$-axis, i.e.,

$$[T(s)] = \begin{bmatrix} \left(\frac{r}{x}\right)\cos\{2\pi(s+s_i)\} & 0 & 0 & 0 \\ 0 & \left(\frac{r}{y}\right)\sin\{2\pi(s+s_i)\} & 0 & 0 \\ 0 & 0 & 1 & 0 \\ 0 & 0 & ns & 1 \end{bmatrix} \quad 0 \le s \le 1$$

The simplest sweep surface is obtained by traversing a line segment along a path. Recalling that the parametric equation of a line segment is

$$P(t) = P_1 + (P_2 - P_1)t \qquad 0 \le t \le 1 \qquad (6-15)$$

The corresponding sweep surface is given by

$$Q(t,s) = P(t)[T(s)] \qquad 0 \le t \le 1, \quad s_1 \le s \le s_2 \qquad (6-16)$$

where again $[T(s)]$ is the sweep transformation. If the sweep transformation contains only translations and/or local or overall scalings, the resulting surface is planar. If the sweep transformation contains rotations, the resulting surface is non-planar. Figure 6–13 shows the helical sweep surface obtained by simultaneously translating along and rotating about the $x$-axis a line originally parallel to the $y$-axis. An example more fully explains the technique.

---

### Example 6–4    Line Sweep Surface

Consider the line segment in the $xy$ plane and parallel to the $y$-axis defined by end points $P_1 [\, 0 \quad 0 \quad 0 \,]$ and $P_2 [\, 0 \quad 3 \quad 0 \,]$. Determine the point at $t = 0.5$, $s = 0.5$ on the sweep surface generated by simultaneously translating the line 10 units along the $x$-axis and rotating it through $2\pi$ about the $x$-axis.

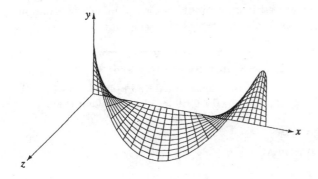

**Figure 6–13**    A helical sweep surface.

Here the sweep transformation matrix is a translation followed by a rotation given by[†]

$$[\,T(s)\,] = \begin{bmatrix} 1 & 0 & 0 & 0 \\ 0 & \cos(2\pi s) & \sin(2\pi s) & 0 \\ 0 & -\sin(2\pi s) & \cos(2\pi s) & 0 \\ ls & 0 & 0 & 1 \end{bmatrix}$$

The parametric equation of the line segment is

$$P(t) = P_1 + (P_2 - P_1)t = [\,0 \quad 0 \quad 0 \quad 1\,] + [\,0-0 \quad 3-0 \quad 0-0 \quad 1-1\,]t$$
$$= [\,0 \quad 3t \quad 0 \quad 1\,]$$

From Eq. (6–15) the sweep surface is given by

$$Q(t, s) = [\,P(t)\,][\,T(s)\,]$$

$$= [\,0 \quad 3t \quad 0 \quad 1\,] \begin{bmatrix} 1 & 0 & 0 & 0 \\ 0 & \cos(2\pi s) & \sin(2\pi s) & 0 \\ 0 & -\sin(2\pi s) & \cos(2\pi s) & 0 \\ ls & 0 & 0 & 1 \end{bmatrix}$$

and

$$Q(0.5, 0.5) = [\,0 \quad 1.5 \quad 0 \quad 1\,] \begin{bmatrix} 1 & 0 & 0 & 0 \\ 0 & -1 & 0 & 0 \\ 0 & 0 & -1 & 0 \\ 5 & 0 & 0 & 1 \end{bmatrix}$$

$$= [\,5 \quad -1.5 \quad 0 \quad 1\,]$$

Complete results are shown in Fig. 6–13.

---

Parametric curves, e.g., cubic splines, parabolically blended, Bézier and B-spline curves, are also used to generate sweep surfaces. The surface equation is identical to Eq. (6–16) where now $P(t)$ represents the parametric curve. Figure 6–14 shows a sweep surface generated from a single cubic spline curve segment swept parallel to the $z$-axis. An example illustrates the technique.

---

### Example 6–5    Cubic Spline Sweep Surface

Sweep the normalized cubic spline curve segment defined by $P_1[\,0 \quad 3 \quad 0 \quad 1\,]$, $P_2[\,3 \quad 0 \quad 0 \quad 1\,]$, $P_1'[\,3 \quad 0 \quad 0 \quad 0\,]$, $P_2'[\,3 \quad 0 \quad 0 \quad 0\,][‡]$ 10 units along the $z$-axis.

The sweep surface is given by

$$Q(t, s) = [\,C(t)\,][\,T(s)\,] \qquad 0 \le t \le 1, \quad 0 \le s \le 1$$

---

[†]The same matrix results from a rotation followed by a translation.
[‡] In homogeneous coordinates a tangent vector has a zero homogeneous coordinate factor.

The normalized cubic spline segment is given by (see Eq. 5–27)

$$[C(t)] = [t^3 \quad t^2 \quad t \quad 1] \begin{bmatrix} 2 & -2 & 1 & 1 \\ -3 & 3 & -2 & 1 \\ 0 & 0 & 1 & 0 \\ 1 & 0 & 0 & 0 \end{bmatrix} \begin{bmatrix} 0 & 3 & 0 & 1 \\ 3 & 0 & 0 & 1 \\ 3 & 0 & 0 & 0 \\ 3 & 0 & 0 & 0 \end{bmatrix}$$

The curve segment is shown in Fig. 6–14a.

The sweep transformation is (see Eq. 3–14)

$$[T(s)] = \begin{bmatrix} 1 & 0 & 0 & 0 \\ 0 & 1 & 0 & 0 \\ 0 & 0 & 1 & 0 \\ 0 & 0 & ns & 1 \end{bmatrix}$$

Hence,

$$Q(t,s) = [t^3 \quad t^2 \quad t \quad 1] \begin{bmatrix} 0 & 6 & 0 & 0 \\ 6 & -9 & 0 & 0 \\ 3 & 0 & 0 & 0 \\ 0 & 3 & 0 & 1 \end{bmatrix} \begin{bmatrix} 1 & 0 & 0 & 0 \\ 0 & 1 & 0 & 0 \\ 0 & 0 & 1 & 0 \\ 0 & 0 & 10s & 1 \end{bmatrix}$$

For $t = 0.5$, $s = 0.5$

$$Q(0.5, 0.5) = [0.125 \quad 0.25 \quad 0.5 \quad 1] \begin{bmatrix} 0 & 6 & 0 & 0 \\ 6 & -9 & 0 & 0 \\ 3 & 0 & 0 & 0 \\ 0 & 3 & 0 & 1 \end{bmatrix} \begin{bmatrix} 1 & 0 & 0 & 0 \\ 0 & 1 & 0 & 0 \\ 0 & 0 & 1 & 0 \\ 0 & 0 & 5 & 1 \end{bmatrix}$$

$$= [3 \quad 1.5 \quad 5 \quad 1]$$

Complete results are shown in Fig. 6–14b.

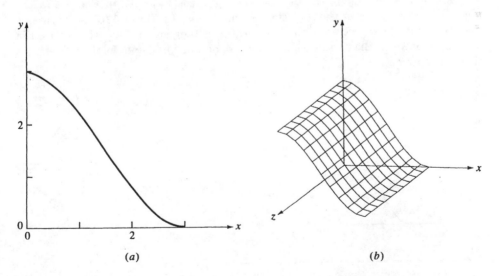

(a)                                    (b)

**Figure 6–14**    A cubic spline based sweep surface. (a) Curve; (b) surface.

Care must be taken to avoid degenerate surfaces or parts of surfaces in generating sweep surfaces from lines and curves. An example is shown in Fig. 6–15. Here an $s$-shaped curve lying in the $xy$ plane is swept parallel to the $x$-axis. Notice that the 'tails' at the left and right sides are degenerate (i.e., lines) of zero area. Such degenerate surface parts can cause difficulty in geometric modeling systems.

In addition to open curves, closed polygons and curves are used to create sweep surfaces. If the end surfaces are included, then the sweep surface encloses a finite volume. Many geometric modeling systems create primitive volumes in this way. A square or rectangle swept along a straight path yields a rectangular parallelepiped. A circle swept along a straight path yields a cylinder. A circle of decreasing radius swept along a straight path yields a cone. Rotation about the sweep axis is also possible. Figure 6–16 shows the sweep surface resulting from a plane square perpendicular to the $x$-axis being swept along and simultaneously rotated through 90° about the $x$-axis.

In sweeping a planar polygon or closed curve along an arbitrary path there are two important considerations. The first is, what point in the polygon continuously lies on the path? In general, any point in a polygon or on a closed curve can continuously lie on the path. For different points, the resulting surfaces are different.

The second is, what is the direction of the normal to the polygon or closed curve as the path is swept out? Here, two approaches are typically taken. The normal to the polygon or closed curve is in the direction of the instantaneous tangent to the path. Alternately, the normal direction is specified independent of the path. This latter alternate is extremely flexible. Two examples are shown in Fig. 6–17. Figure 6–17 shows the sweep surface generated by a square centered on the $x$-axis swept along the path $x = ls$, $y = \cos(\pi s) - 1$. In Fig. 6–17a the normal is maintained in the direction of the $x$-axis. In Fig. 6–17b the normal is maintained in the direction of the instantaneous tangent to the path. Notice the difference between the two sweep surfaces. A detailed example further illustrates this concept.

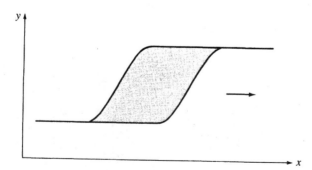

**Figure 6–15**    A sweep surface with degenerate parts.

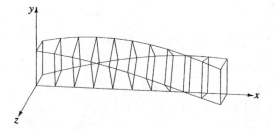

**Figure 6–16**    Sweep surface generated by a square simultaneously sweeping along and rotating about the $x$-axis.

---

### Example 6–6    Complex Sweep Surface

Sweep the planar square defined by vertices $P_1 [\, 0 \quad -1 \quad 1 \,]$, $P_2 [\, 0 \quad -1 \quad -1 \,]$, $P_3 [\, 0 \quad 1 \quad -1 \,]$, $P_4 [\, 0 \quad 1 \quad 1 \,]$ along the path $x = 10s$, $y = \cos(\pi s) - 1$ while maintaining the normal to the polygon in the instantaneous direction of the tangent to the path.

The instantaneous direction of the path tangent is $[\, 10 \quad -\pi \sin(\pi s) \quad 0 \,]$. The rotation angle about the $z$-axis to align the polygon normal with the tangent to the path is thus

$$\psi = \tan^{-1}\left(\frac{-\pi \sin(\pi s)}{10}\right)$$

The sweep transformation is thus

$$[\, T(s) \,] = \begin{bmatrix} \cos\psi & \sin\psi & 0 & 0 \\ -\sin\psi & \cos\psi & 0 & 0 \\ 0 & 0 & 1 & 0 \\ 10s & \cos(\pi s)-1 & 0 & 1 \end{bmatrix}$$

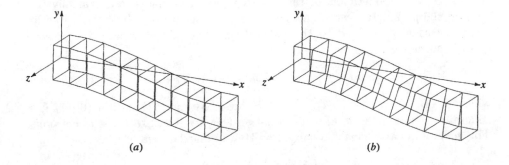

(a)                                    (b)

**Figure 6–17**    A polygon swept along a path. (a) Normal in the $x$ direction; (b) normal in the instantaneous tangent vector direction.

At $s = 0.5$ the rotation angle is

$$\psi = \tan^{-1}\left(\frac{-\pi\sin(\pi/2)}{10}\right) = \tan^{-1}(-\pi/10) = -17.44°$$

The polygonal square at $s = 0.5$ is thus given by

$$Q = \begin{bmatrix} 0 & -1 & 1 & 1 \\ 0 & -1 & -1 & 1 \\ 0 & 1 & -1 & 1 \\ 0 & 1 & 1 & 1 \end{bmatrix} \begin{bmatrix} 0.954 & -0.3 & 0 & 0 \\ 0.3 & 0.954 & 0 & 0 \\ 0 & 0 & 1 & 0 \\ 5 & -1 & 0 & 1 \end{bmatrix}$$

$$= \begin{bmatrix} 4.7 & -1.954 & 1 & 1 \\ 4.7 & -1.954 & -1 & 1 \\ 5.3 & -0.046 & -1 & 1 \\ 5.3 & -0.046 & 1 & 1 \end{bmatrix}$$

Complete results are shown in Fig. 6–17b.

---

Additional information on sweep surfaces is given in Refs. 6–9 and 6–10 and the references therein.

## 6–4  QUADRIC SURFACES

The natural quadric surfaces, the sphere, cone, cylinder, ellipsoid, paraboloid of revolution and the hyperboloid of revolution, are also surfaces of revolution (see Sec. 6–2). These natural quadric surfaces, especially the sphere, cone, and cylinder, play an important part in the manufacture of mechanical parts. The natural quadrics also play an important part in the description of manufactured surfaces. For example, basket- and soccer balls[†] are spherical, funnels are conical, beer cans are cylindrical, and satellite antennas are parabolic. Quadric surfaces also are important in the description of more complex surfaces. For example, the fuselage of the North American P-51 fighter aircraft of WWII vintage was described using conical surface segments (Ref. 6–11). The technique is called conic lofting.

There are two methods for representing quadric surfaces, algebraically (including the parametric representations) and geometrically. Geometric descriptions are usually confined to the natural quadrics. Algebraically the general quadric surface is given by

$$Ax^2 + By^2 + Cz^2 + Dxy + Eyz + Fxz + Gx + Hy + Jz + K = 0 \quad (6-17)$$

where $A$, $B$, $C$, $D$, $E$, $F$, $G$, $H$, $J$, $K$ are constants. Equation (6–17) is a generalization of the general conic equation (see Eq. 4–31) to three dimensions. The general quadric equation can be written in matrix form as

$$[X][S][X]^T = 0 \quad (6-18)$$

---

[†]Soccer is the American name for the game known throughout the rest of the world as football.

where $[X] = [x \quad y \quad z \quad 1]$ and

$$[S] = \begin{bmatrix} A & D/2 & F/2 & G/2 \\ D/2 & B & E/2 & H/2 \\ F/2 & E/2 & C & J/2 \\ G/2 & H/2 & J/2 & K \end{bmatrix} = \left(\tfrac{1}{2}\right) \begin{bmatrix} 2A & D & F & G \\ D & 2B & E & H \\ F & E & 2C & J \\ G & H & J & 2K \end{bmatrix}$$

Similar to the conic sections, the quadric surfaces are either central or non-central. The central quadrics are the ellipsoid and the hyperboloid.[†] The paraboloids are noncentral. If a quadric is central, its center can be translated to the origin. If this is not possible, the quadric is noncentral, i.e., a paraboloid. Translation to the origin eliminates the linear terms in Eq. (6–17).

After translation Eq. (6–18) becomes

$$[X][Tr][S][Tr]^T[X]^T = [X][S'][X]^T = 0 \qquad (6-19)$$

where the translation matrix is

$$[Tr] = \begin{bmatrix} 1 & 0 & 0 & 0 \\ 0 & 1 & 0 & 0 \\ 0 & 0 & 1 & 0 \\ l & m & n & 1 \end{bmatrix}$$

The transformed matrix $[S']$ is

$$[S'] = \left(\tfrac{1}{2}\right) \begin{bmatrix} 2A' & D' & F' & G' \\ D' & 2B' & E' & H' \\ F' & E' & 2C' & J' \\ G' & H' & J' & 2K' \end{bmatrix} \qquad (6-20)$$

with $A' = A$, $B' = B$, $C' = C$, $D' = D$, $\dot{E}' = E$, $F' = F$ and

$$G' = 2Al + Dm + Fn + G$$

$$H' = Dl + 2Bm + En + H$$

$$J' = Fl + Em + 2Cn + J$$

$$2K' = lG' + mH' + nJ' + (Gl + Hm + Jn + 2K)$$

Eliminating the linear terms, i.e., setting $G' = H' = J' = 0$, yields

$$2Al + Dm + Fn + G = 0$$

$$Dl + 2Bm + En + H = 0$$

$$Fl + Em + 2Cn + J = 0$$

---

[†]The sphere is a special case of the ellipsoid. The cylinder is a limiting case of either an ellipsoid or a hyperboloid.

or

$$[\,l \quad m \quad n\,]\begin{bmatrix} 2A & D & F \\ D & 2B & E \\ F & E & 2C \end{bmatrix} = \begin{bmatrix} -G \\ -H \\ -J \end{bmatrix} \qquad (6-21)$$

which may be written as

$$[\,M\,][\,L\,] = [\,G\,]$$

If $[\,L\,]$ is invertible, a solution exists and the quadric is central, i.e., an ellipsoid or a hyperboloid. If $[\,L\,]$ is singular, a solution does not exist and the quadric is a paraboloid. Setting the determinant of $[\,L\,]$ to zero yields the condition for a paraboloid. Thus

$$\det[\,L\,] = \begin{bmatrix} 2A & D & F \\ D & 2B & E \\ F & E & 2C \end{bmatrix} = 0 \qquad (6-22)$$

$A(E^2 - BC) + B(F^2 - AC) + C(D^2 - AB) - (ABC + DEF) = 0$ is the condition for a paraboloid. Further, if $\det[\,L\,] > 0$ a hyperboloid results and if $\det[\,L\,] < 0$ an ellipsoid is obtained.

As with the conic sections (see Sec. 4–10) whether $[\,L\,]$ is invertible or not, the axes of a quadric can be made parallel to the coordinate axes by rotation. Here, three rotations are required, two to make one of the axes of the quadric parallel to a coordinate axis (see Sec. 3–9) and a final rotation about this axis to make the other two axes of the quadric parallel to the other coordinate axes. The solution of the resulting equations for the required rotation angles for a general quadric is nontrivial. It is not given here.

Similarly, if the quadric is noncentral, i.e., a paraboloid, as mentioned previously the linear terms cannot all be eliminated. However, two of the three linear terms can be eliminated. Again, solution of the resulting equations is nontrivial and is not given here.

The result of the above operations is to place the quadric in the standard form. For the central quadric the standard form is with the center at the origin and axis aligned with the coordinate axes. In matrix form the resulting standard form equation is

$$[\,X\,]\begin{bmatrix} \alpha & 0 & 0 & 0 \\ 0 & \beta & 0 & 0 \\ 0 & 0 & \gamma & 0 \\ 0 & 0 & 0 & -\kappa \end{bmatrix}[\,X\,]^T = 0 \qquad (6-23)$$

or

$$\alpha x^2 + \beta y^2 + \gamma z^2 = \kappa \qquad (6-24)$$

If $\alpha \neq \beta \neq \gamma > 0$, $\kappa > 0$ a general ellipsoid results (see Fig. 6–18a). The largest of $\alpha$, $\beta$, $\gamma$ determines the major axis. If two of the three constants are equal, e.g., $\alpha = \beta \neq \gamma > 0$, then an ellipsoid of revolution is obtained. The axis of revolution is associated with the unique constant. If $\alpha = \beta = \gamma > 0$, a sphere of radius $\sqrt{\kappa/\alpha}$ results.

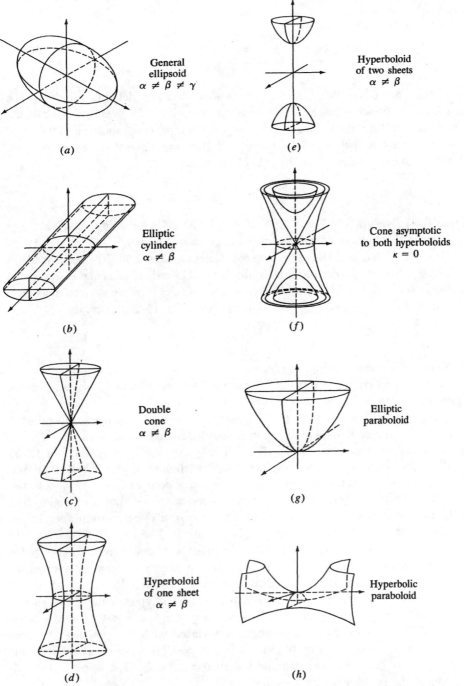

**Figure 6–18**   Quadric surfaces. (a) General ellipsoid $\alpha \neq \beta \neq \gamma$; (b) elliptic cylinder $\alpha \neq \beta$; (c) double cone $\alpha \neq \beta$; (d) hyperboloid of one sheet $\alpha \neq \beta$; (e) hyperboloid of two sheets $\alpha \neq \beta$; (f) cone asymptotic to both hyperboloids $\kappa = 0$; (g) elliptic paraboloid; (h) hyperbolic paraboloid.

Rewriting Eq. (6–24) as

$$\frac{x^2}{a^2} + \frac{y^2}{b^2} + \frac{z^2}{c^2} = 1$$

and letting one of the constants $a$, $b$, $c$ approach infinity yields a cylinder as the limiting case of an ellipsoid. The 'axis' of the ellipsoid, given by the missing coordinate, is 'infinitely' long. If the two remaining constants are equal, e.g., $\alpha = \beta$, a circular cylinder is obtained. If they are unequal, e.g., $\alpha \neq \beta$, an elliptic cylinder results. Here, Eq. (6–24) becomes

$$\alpha x^2 + \beta y^2 = \kappa$$

An example is shown in Fig. 6–18b. If $\kappa = 0$, the cylinder is imaginary because the sum of the squares of two real numbers cannot be zero.

If $\kappa = 0$ with one of the remaining constants negative and the others positive, e.g., $\alpha, \beta > 0$, $\gamma < 0$, a double cone is obtained. The axis of the cone is associated with the coordinate of the negative constant. If $\alpha = \beta$, a right circular cone is obtained. If $\alpha \neq \beta$ an elliptic cone results. Here, Eq. (6–24) becomes

$$\alpha x^2 + \beta y^2 = \gamma z^2$$

An example is shown in Fig. 6–18c.

If $\kappa = 0$ and $\alpha, \beta, \gamma \neq 0$, then the cone is imaginary, because the sum of the squares of three real numbers cannot be zero.

If $\alpha$, $\beta$, $\gamma > 0$ and $\kappa < 0$, an imaginary ellipsoid results because again the sum of the squares of three real numbers cannot be negative.

If one of the constants in Eq. (6–24) is negative, e.g., $\gamma < 0$, and the others positive, the resulting quadric surface is a hyperboloid of one sheet. The axis of the hyperboloid is associated with the negative constant, e.g., if $\gamma < 0$, the hyperboloid's axis is the $z$ coordinate axis. An example is shown in Fig. 6–18d. If the two positive constants are equal, e.g., $\alpha = \beta$, a hyperboloid of revolution results. If not, an elliptic hyperboloid is obtained. The hyperboloid is said to have one sheet because it is possible to connect any point to any other point without leaving the surface. In the limit as the negative constant approaches zero a cylinder, either circular or elliptic, results. A hyperboloid of one sheet is a doubly ruled surface (see Sec. 6–8). In contrast is the hyperboloid of two sheets. Here, two of the constants $\alpha$, $\beta$, $\gamma$ are negative, e.g., $\alpha$, $\beta < 0$, and the other positive. The axis of the hyperboloid is associated with the positive constant. An example is shown in Fig. 6–18e. It is not possible to connect every point to every other point without leaving the surface. For $\alpha$, $\beta < 0$; $\gamma$, $\kappa > 0$, the vertices of the two sheets are at

$$\pm \left(\frac{\alpha \beta \kappa}{\gamma^2}\right)^{1/6}$$

on the $z$ axis.† If the negative constants are equal, a hyperboloid of revolution is obtained. If not, the surface is an elliptic hyperboloid. Note that the number of negative constants equals the number of sheets for the hyperboloid.

If $\kappa = 0$, both hyperboloids degenerate to a cone asymptotic to both of them as shown in Fig. 6–18f.

Now consider the noncentral quadric surfaces, specifically the paraboloids. In standard form, where $z$ is the axis of the paraboloid, these are represented by

$$[X] \begin{bmatrix} \alpha & 0 & 0 & 0 \\ 0 & \beta & 0 & 0 \\ 0 & 0 & 0 & 0 \\ 0 & 0 & \gamma & 0 \end{bmatrix} [X]^T = 0 \tag{6 – 25}$$

or
$$\alpha x^2 + \beta y^2 + \gamma z = 0 \tag{6 – 26}$$

If $\alpha$, $\beta > 0$, an elliptic paraboloid is obtained as shown in Fig. 6–18g. If $\alpha = \beta > 0$, a paraboloid of revolution results. The vertex of the paraboloid is at the origin. For $\gamma < 0$ the surface 'opens' along the positive $z$-axis. Similarly, for $\gamma > 0$ the surface opens along the negative $z$-axis. If $\gamma = 0$, the surface reduces to an ellipse. If either $\alpha$ or $\beta < 0$, then a hyperbolic paraboloid is obtained as shown in Fig. 6–18h. If $\alpha > 0$, $\beta < 0$, the focal axis is the $y$-axis. Similarly, if $\alpha < 0$, $\beta > 0$, the focal axis is the $x$-axis. If $\gamma < 0$, the saddle is upward as shown in Fig. 6–18h. If $\gamma > 0$, the surface is reflected through the $z = 0$ plane and the saddle is downward. If $\gamma = 0$, the surface reduces to a hyperbola. The hyperbolic paraboloid is sometimes called a saddle surface. Note that even if $\alpha = \beta$, the hyperbolic paraboloid is *not* a surface of revolution. However, a hyperbolic paraboloid is a doubly ruled surface (see Sec. 6–8).

Finally, if either $\alpha$ or $\beta = 0$, a parabolic cylinder is obtained. Further information on quadric surfaces and their properties is given in Refs. 6–12 to 6–14.

Although the explicit forms of the quadric surfaces are frequently useful for determining real properties, as with the conic sections the parametric forms yield more pleasing and convincing graphics displays. For quadric surfaces in the standard orientation, parametric representations are given by

Ellipsoid:
$$x = a \, \cos\theta \sin\phi \qquad 0 \le \theta \le 2\pi \tag{6 – 27}$$
$$y = b \, \sin\theta \sin\phi \qquad 0 \le \phi \le 2\pi$$
$$z = c \, \cos\phi$$

Hyperboloid of one sheet:
$$x = a \, \cos\theta \cosh\phi \qquad 0 \le \theta \le 2\pi \tag{6 – 28}$$

---

† $\pm \left( \dfrac{\alpha\beta\kappa}{\gamma^2} \right)^{1/6} = \pm c$ when the equation for an hyperboloid of two sheets is written in the less general notation $\dfrac{z^2}{c^2} - \dfrac{x^2}{a^2} - \dfrac{y^2}{b^2} = 1$.

$$y = b \sin \theta \sinh \phi \qquad -\pi \leq \phi \leq \pi$$
$$z = c \sinh \phi$$

Hyperboloid of two sheets:
$$x = \pm a \cosh \phi \qquad 0 \leq \theta \leq 2\pi$$
$$y = b \sin \theta \sinh \phi \qquad -\pi \leq \phi \leq \pi \tag{6-29}$$
$$z = c \cos \theta \sinh \phi$$

Elliptic paraboloid:
$$x = a \phi \cos \theta \qquad 0 \leq \theta \leq 2\pi$$
$$y = b \phi \sin \theta \qquad 0 \leq \phi \leq \phi_{max} \tag{6-30}$$
$$z = \phi^2$$

Hyperbolic paraboloid:
$$x = a \phi \cosh \theta \qquad -\pi \leq \theta \leq \pi$$
$$y = b \phi \sinh \theta \qquad \phi_{min} \leq \phi \leq \phi_{max} \tag{6-31}$$
$$z = \phi^2$$

Elliptic cone:
$$x = a \phi \cos \theta \qquad 0 \leq \theta \leq 2\pi$$
$$y = b \phi \sin \theta \qquad \phi_{min} \leq \phi \leq \phi_{max} \tag{6-32}$$
$$z = c \phi$$

Elliptic cylinder:
$$x = a \cos \theta \qquad 0 \leq \theta \leq 2\pi$$
$$y = b \sin \theta \qquad \phi_{min} \leq \phi \leq \phi_{max} \tag{6-33}$$
$$z = \phi$$

Parabolic cylinder:
$$x = a \theta^2 \qquad 0 \leq \theta \leq \theta_{max}$$
$$y = 2a \theta \qquad \phi_{min} \leq \phi \leq \phi_{max} \tag{6-34}$$
$$z = \phi$$

Both a parametrically generated ellipsoid and a piece of a hyperbolic paraboloid are shown in Fig. 6–19.

Although it is convenient to use the general second-degree equation (see Eq. 6–17) to represent all the quadric surfaces, and the parametric representations given above are convenient for generating them, for computer modeling the quadrics are most accurately represented geometrically (see Refs. 6–15 and 6–17). Geometrically every quadric surface is represented by a point, two orthogonal (unit) vectors and three scalars. The point, either center or vertex, fixes the location of the surface. The vectors and their cross product determine its axes or orientation. The scalars determine its dimensions or size. For example, a sphere is represented by its center and a radius, a right cylinder by a vector representing its axis, a point on the axis and a radius, an ellipsoid by its center, two vectors representing two of its three orthogonal axes and three scalars representing the lengths along the axes, etc. Table 6–1 lists geometric descriptions of quadric surfaces.

When manipulating geometrically defined quadric surfaces, only the defining points and vectors need be transformed. Scalar quantities remain constant. Thus, they do not accumulate numerical errors due to the finite arithmetic used

## Table 6–1 Geometric Descriptions of Quadric Surfaces

| Surface | Scalars | Point | Vectors |
|---|---|---|---|
| Plane | None | Any on the plane | Unit normal |
| Sphere | Radius | Center | None |
| Right circular cone | Half angle | Center (vertex) | Unit vector parallel to the axis |
| Right circular cylinder | Radius | Any on the axis | Unit vector parallel to the axis |
| Right elliptic cylinder | Lengths of elliptic axes (2) | Any on the axis | Unit vector parallel to the axis |
| Right parabolic cylinder | Focal distance | Vertex | Unit vector parallel to the axis |
| Elliptic cone | Lengths of elliptic axes (2) | Center | Unit vector parallel to the axis |
| Ellipsoid | Length of axes (3) | Center | Two unit vectors parallel to two of the three axes |
| Elliptic paraboloid | Lengths of elliptic axes (2) | Vertex | Unit vector parallel to the axis |
| Hyperbolic paraboloid | Hyperbolic and parabolic foci (3) | Vertex | Unit vector parallel to the axis |
| Hyperboloid of one sheet | Lengths of elliptic axes (2) Hyperbolic focus along the principal axis | Center | Unit vector parallel to the axis |
| Hyperboloid of two sheets | Lengths of axes (2) Location of the vertex along the symmetric axis (1) | Center | Unit vector parallel to the axis |

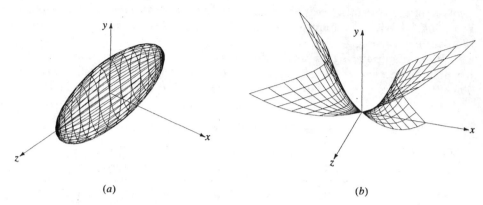

(a)                                                      (b)

**Figure 6–19**    Parametric quadric surfaces. (a) Ellipsoid; (b) hyperbolic paraboloid.

in computers. For example, the geometrically defined radius of a sphere is always $R$. However, the radius of a sphere derived from a transformed algebraic representation (see Eq. 6–17) is $R \pm \epsilon$ where $\epsilon$ is a small numerical error. The numerical stability of the defining scalars is of considerable importance, e.g., in determining the character of the intersection curve of two quadric surfaces or whether two surfaces are identical (see Ref. 6–15).

## 6–5    PIECEWISE SURFACE REPRESENTATION

The previous sections have discussed the generation and characteristics of surfaces for which known analytical descriptions exist. There are, however, many surfaces for which analytical descriptions do not exist. Typical examples are automobile bodies, aircraft fuselages and wings, ship hulls, sculpture, bottles, shoes, etc. These surfaces are represented in a *piecewise* fashion, i.e., similar to a patchwork quilt. A vector valued parametric representation is used because it is axis-independent, avoids infinite slope values with respect to some arbitrary axis system, allows the unambiguous representation of multivalued surfaces or space functions, facilitates the representation of surfaces in homogeneous coordinates and is compatible with the use of the three-dimensional homogeneous coordinate transformations discussed in Chapter 3.

The remainder of this chapter is concerned with a discussion of the techniques and methods of mathematically describing surface patches. The intention is to join individual patches together along their edges to create a complete surface. The discussion closely follows and draws upon that of piecewise curve representation given in Chapter 5. Interestingly enough our discussion begins by considering a portion or patch of an analytical surface, specifically the sphere.

Some properties of curves useful in surface definition are demonstrated by considering a spherical surface. Specific curves on the surface are defined by planes intersecting the sphere. As an example consider the intersection of a unit sphere and the plane defined by the surface equation $z = \cos \phi_1 = a_1 = $ constant shown in Fig. 6-20a. The resulting curve is a parallel of latitude. The equation for the parallel of latitude is obtained by solving the two surface equations simultaneously. The nonparametric equation for a unit sphere is

$$x^2 + y^2 + z^2 = 1.0$$

Thus,

$$x^2 + y^2 = 1 - a_1^2$$

defines the intersection.

In Fig. 6-20b, the plane $\theta = \theta_0 = $ constant is defined by

$$x \sin \theta_0 - y \cos \theta_0 = 0$$

or

$$c_1 x - b_1 y = 0$$

The intersection of this plane and a sphere yields a meridian of longitude. Solving these equations simultaneously yields the resulting curve; i.e.,

$$y^2 \left[ \left( \frac{b_1}{c_1} \right)^2 + 1 \right] + z^2 = 1.0$$

The boundaries of a spherical surface patch on a unit sphere can be formed by four planes, two parallels of latitude and two meridians of longitude, intersecting the sphere, as shown in Fig. 6-21. The vector valued parametric equation for the resulting surface patch $Q(\theta, \phi)$ is

$$Q(\theta, \phi) = [\, \cos \theta \sin \phi \quad \sin \theta \sin \phi \quad \cos \phi \,] \qquad \theta_1 \le \theta \le \theta_2, \qquad \phi_1 \le \phi \le \phi_2$$

$$(6-35)$$

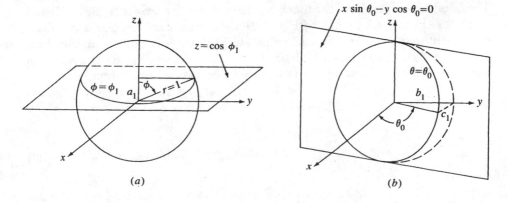

(a)          (b)

**Figure 6-20**   Intersections of a plane and sphere. (a) Parallel of latitude; (b) meridian of longitude.

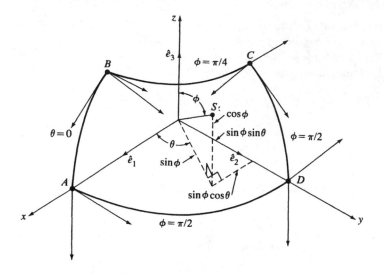

**Figure 6–21**   Spherical surface patch.

The surface patch is the locus of a point in three-dimensional space which moves with two degrees of freedom controlled by the two parameter variables $\theta$ and $\phi$, i.e., it is a biparametric function.

The parametric representation of a unit spherical surface is (see Eq. 6–27 with $a = b = c = 1$)

$$x = \cos\theta\sin\phi$$

$$y = \sin\theta\sin\phi$$

$$z = \cos\phi$$

The patch shown in Fig. 6–21 is defined for $0 \le \theta \le \pi/2$ and $\pi/4 \le \phi \le \pi/2$. The boundaries or edges of the patch are defined by the curves $AB$, $BC$, $CD$ and $DA$. For the spherical patch of Fig. 6–21 these curves are circular arcs. Each curve can be defined by two end points and the tangent vectors at the ends. Consequently the four patch boundary curves are defined by the four position vectors at the corners, and eight tangent vectors, two at each corner.

For the spherical patch of Fig. 6–21 the tangent vectors are given by the parametric derivatives of $Q(\theta, \phi)$, i.e.,

$$Q_\theta(\theta, \phi) = \frac{\partial Q}{\partial \theta}(\theta, \phi) = [\,-\sin\theta\sin\phi \quad \cos\theta\sin\phi \quad 0\,] \qquad (6-36)$$

and
$$Q_\phi(\theta, \phi) = [\,\cos\theta\cos\phi \quad \sin\theta\cos\phi \quad -\sin\phi\,] \qquad (6-37)$$

The tangent vectors at each corner are shown in Fig. 6–21.

The shape of the interior of the surface near each corner is controlled by the twist vector or cross derivative at the corner. For the spherical surface patch given in Fig. 6–21 the cross derivative or twist vector is

$$Q_{\theta,\phi}(\theta, \phi) = \frac{\partial^2 Q}{\partial\theta\partial\phi} = \frac{\partial^2 Q}{\partial\phi\partial\theta} = [\,-\sin\theta\cos\phi \quad \cos\theta\cos\phi \quad 0\,] \qquad (6-38)$$

Evaluation at the corners of the patch yields the twist vectors at the corners. The interior of the patch is given by Eq. (6–35). Equation (6–35) can be considered a spherical *blending* function. Consequently a quadrilateral surface patch can be completely described by

    The 4 position vectors at the corners.

    The 8 tangent vectors, two at each corner.

    The 4 twist vectors at the corners.

and the blending function given by Eq. (6–35).

    The normal to a surface patch at any point is given by the cross product of the parametric derivatives. Specifically for a spherical surface

$$Q_\theta \times Q_\phi = \begin{vmatrix} \mathbf{i} & \mathbf{j} & \mathbf{k} \\ -\sin\theta\sin\phi & \cos\theta\sin\phi & 0 \\ \cos\theta\cos\phi & \sin\theta\cos\phi & -\sin\phi \end{vmatrix}$$

$$= [\,-\cos\theta\sin^2\phi \quad \sin\theta\sin^2\phi \quad -\sin\phi\cos\phi\,] \qquad (6-39)$$

On a surface patch isoparametric lines, i.e., lines of constant parameter values, are orthogonal. Consequently the dot product of the parametric derivatives is zero. For example, for a spherical surface

$$Q_\theta \cdot Q_\phi = [\,-\sin\theta\sin\phi \quad \cos\theta\sin\phi \quad 0\,] \cdot [\,\cos\theta\cos\phi \quad \sin\theta\cos\phi \quad -\sin\phi\,] = 0$$

$$= [\,-\sin\theta\sin\phi \quad \cos\theta\sin\phi \quad 0\,][\,\cos\theta\cos\phi \quad \sin\theta\cos\phi \quad -\sin\phi\,]^T = 0$$

$$= [\,-\cos\theta\sin\theta\cos\phi\sin\phi \quad \cos\theta\sin\theta\cos\phi\sin\phi \quad 0\,] = 0 \qquad (6-40)$$

## 6–6    MAPPING PARAMETRIC SURFACES

The methods of parametric surface description are most conveniently described in terms of the mapping of a two parameter planar surface in $uw$ parametric space into three-dimensional $xyz$ object space. Here the discussion is restricted to mapping the rectangular planar surface in parametric space shown in Fig. 6–22 and given by

$$u = C_1 \qquad C_3 \leq w \leq C_4$$

$$u = C_2 \qquad C_3 \leq w \leq C_4$$

$$w = C_3 \qquad C_1 \leq u \leq C_2$$

$$w = C_4 \qquad C_1 \leq u \leq C_2$$

A surface in object space is represented by the functions that map this parametric surface into $xyz$ object space, i.e.,

$$x = x(u, w)$$

$$y = y(u, w)$$

$$z = z(u, w)$$

A simple two-dimensional example serves to illustrate the technique.

---

**Example 6–7    Two-Dimensional Surface Mapping**

Map the surface described by

$$x = 3u + w \qquad\qquad 0 \le u \le 1$$

$$y = 2u + 3w + uw \qquad 0 \le w \le 1$$

$$z = 0$$

in parametric space into object space. First note that since $z = $ constant $= 0$, the surface in object space is also two-dimensional lying in the $z = 0$ plane.

The boundaries of the surface in object space are defined by mapping the boundaries of the rectangle in parametric space to object space. Thus, for

$$u = 0; \qquad x = w,\ y = 3w \quad \text{and} \quad y = 3x$$

$$u = 1; \qquad x = w + 3,\ y = 2(2w + 1) \quad \text{and} \quad y = 2(2x - 5)$$

$$w = 0; \qquad x = 3u,\ y = 2u \quad \text{and} \quad y = (2/3)x$$

$$w = 1; \qquad x = 3u + 1,\ y = 3u + 3 \quad \text{and} \quad y = x + 2$$

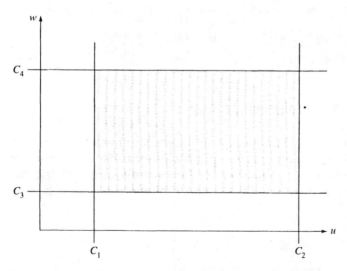

**Figure 6–22**    Rectangular parametric planar surface.

In each case the value of the parameter ($u$ or $w$) was eliminated to obtain $y = y(x)$. The results are shown in Fig. 6–23.

As shown in the example above, holding a single parametric value constant yields a curve on the surface in object space. The curve is called an isoparametric or parametric line. Specifying one parameter as a function of the other in parametric space, i.e., $u = u(w)$, also yields a curve on the surface in object space. For example, the functions

$$u = w \qquad 0 \le w \le 1$$

$$u = 1 - w$$

represent the diagonals of the unit square in parametric space.

Specifying both parametric values yields a point on the surface in object space. Alternately, a point (or points) is specified by the intersection of two curves in parametric space, e.g., $f(u, w) = 0$ and $g(u, w) = 0$. The intersection in parametric space maps or transforms into the intersection in object space.

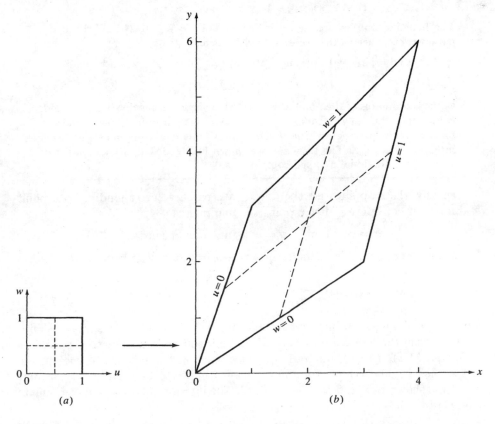

**Figure 6–23**   Two-dimensional surface mapping. (a) Parametric space; (b) object space.

A more complex three-dimensional example further illustrates the mapping concept.

---

**Example 6–8    Three-Dimensional Surface Mapping**

Map the surface described by

$$x(u, w) = (u - w)^2 \qquad 0 \leq u \leq 1$$

$$y(u, w) = u - w^2 \qquad 0 \leq w \leq 1$$

$$z(u, w) = uw$$

in parametric space into object space. Calculate the coordinates of the point at $u = w = 0.5$ on the surface in object space.

First determine the boundary curves

$u = 0; \qquad x = w^2, \; y = -w^2, \; z = 0 \quad$ and $\quad x = -y, \; z = 0$

$u = 1; \qquad x = (1 - w)^2, \; y = 1 - w^2, \; z = w \quad$ and $\quad x = (1 - z)^2, \; y = 1 - z^2$

$w = 0; \qquad x = u^2, \; y = u, \; z = 0 \quad$ and $\quad x = y^2, z = 0$

$w = 1; \qquad x = (u - 1)^2, \; y = u - 1, \; z = u \quad$ and $\quad x = y^2, \; z = 1 + y$

The boundary curves are shown by heavy lines in Fig. 6–24d. Writing the parametric surface as the vector valued function

$$Q(u, w) = [\, x(u, w) \quad y(u, w) \quad z(u, w)\,] = [\,(u - w)^2 \quad u - w^2 \quad uw\,]$$

yields $\qquad\qquad Q(0.5, 0.5) = [\,0 \quad 0.25 \quad 0.25\,]$

as the coordinates of the point at $u = w = 0.5$ shown as the dot in Fig. 6–24d. Notice that each of the components of the surface in object space is also a function of the parameters $u, w$. Each of these individual components is shown in Figs. 6–24a, b, c. The total surface shown in Fig. 6–24d is a composite of each of the individual mapped components.

---

Finally, the mappings for the degenerate patches corresponding to a point and a line are of interest. For a point the mapping is

$$x = \text{constant}, \quad y = \text{constant}, \quad z = \text{constant}$$

For a line the mapping is of the form $x = u, \; y = \text{constant}, \; z = \text{constant}$.

## 6–7    BILINEAR SURFACE

One of the simplest surfaces is the bilinear surface. A bilinear surface is constructed from the four corner points of the unit square in parametric space, i.e., $P(0,0)$, $P(0,1)$, $P(1,1)$ and $P(1,0)$. Any point in the interior of the surface is specified by linearly interpolating between opposite boundaries of the unit square as shown in Fig. 6–25. Any point in the interior of the parametric square is given by

$$Q(u, w) = P(0,0)(1 - u)(1 - w) + P(0,1)(1 - u)w + P(1,0)u(1 - w) + P(1,1)uw$$

$$(6 - 41)$$

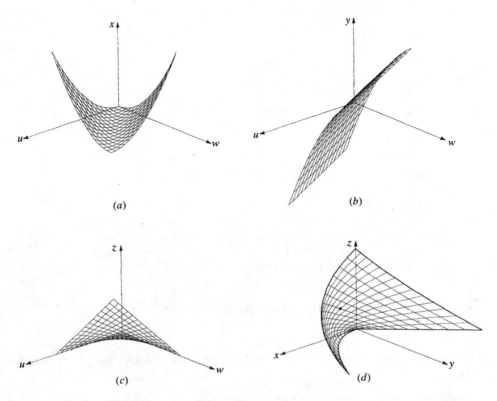

Figure 6–24    Three-dimensional surface mapping. (a) $x$ component; (b) $y$ component; (c) $z$ component; (d) complete.

In matrix form

$$Q(u,w) = [\,1-u \quad u\,] \begin{bmatrix} P(0,0) & P(0,1) \\ P(1,0) & P(1,1) \end{bmatrix} \begin{bmatrix} 1-w \\ w \end{bmatrix} \qquad (6-42)$$

It is necessary that the blended or interpolated surface yield the input data. Here it is easy to verify that corner points are included, i.e., $Q(0,0) = P(0,0)$, etc.

Equation (6–42) is in the form of the general matrix representation of a blended surface, specifically a blending matrix in one of the biparametric variables, a geometry matrix representing the input data and a blending matrix in the other biparametric variable. This form will appear again and again in our study of parametric blended surfaces.

If the position vectors of the four defining points of a bilinear surface are given in three-dimensional object space, the resulting bilinear surface obtained by mapping from parametric space to object space is also three-dimensional. If the four defining points are nonplanar, the bilinear surface is also nonplanar. In fact, it is generally highly curved. An example is shown in Fig. 6–26. The defining points are the ends of the opposite diagonals on opposite faces of a unit

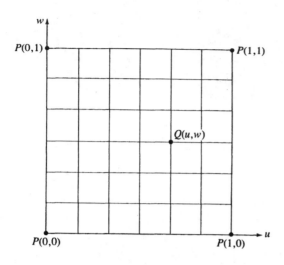

**Figure 6–25**   Bilinear interpolation in parametric space.

cube. The resulting surface is a hyperbolic paraboloid. An example illustrates
this.

---

**Example 6–9    Bilinear Surface.**

Determine the point on the bilinear surface defined by $P(0,0) = [\,0 \quad 0 \quad 1\,]$,
$P(0,1) = [\,1 \quad 1 \quad 1\,]$, $P(1,0) = [\,1 \quad 0 \quad 0\,]$, $P(1,1) = [\,0 \quad 1 \quad 0\,]$, i.e., the
ends of opposite diagonals on opposite faces of a unit cube in object space,
corresponding to $u = w = 0.5$ in parametric space.

Recalling that the surface in object space is a vector valued function

$$Q(u,w) = [\,x(u,w) \quad y(u,w) \quad z(u,w)\,]$$

then from Eq. (6–41) we have

$$Q(0.5, 0.5) = [\,0 \quad 0 \quad 1\,](1 - 0.5)(1 - 0.5) + [\,1 \quad 1 \quad 1\,](1 - 0.5)(0.5)$$

$$+ [\,1 \quad 0 \quad 0\,](0.5)(1 - 0.5) + [\,0 \quad 1 \quad 0\,](0.5)(0.5)$$

$$= 0.25\,[\,0 \quad 0 \quad 1\,] + 0.25\,[\,1 \quad 1 \quad 1\,]$$

$$+ 0.25\,[\,1 \quad 0 \quad 0\,] + 0.25\,[\,0 \quad 1 \quad 0\,]$$

$$= [\,0.5 \quad 0.5 \quad 0.5\,]$$

Complete results are shown in Fig. 6–26b.

---

Notice that every isoparametric line on a bilinear surface is a straight line.
In fact, the surface is doubly ruled (see Sec. 6–8).

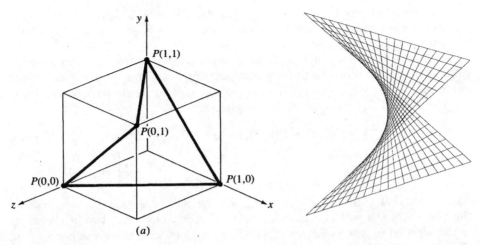

Figure 6-26   Bilinear surface. (a) Defining corner points; (b) surface.

## 6-8   RULED AND DEVELOPABLE SURFACES

Ruled surfaces are frequently used in both the aircraft and the shipbuilding industries. For example, most aircraft wings are cylindrical ruled surfaces. Technically a ruled surface is generated by a straight line moving along a path with one
degree of freedom. Alternately a ruled surface is identified using the following
technique. At any point on the surface, rotate a plane containing the normal
to the surface at that point about the normal (see Fig. 6-27). If in at least one
orientation every point on the edge of the plane contacts the surface, the surface
is ruled in that direction. If the edge of the rotating plane completely touches
the surface in more than one orientation, the surface is multiply ruled at that
point.

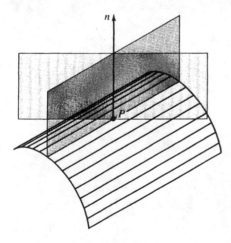

Figure 6-27   Characteristics of a ruled
surface.

The simplest ruled surface is a plane. Of the quadric surfaces, the cones and cylinders are singly ruled; the hyperboloid of one sheet and the hyperbolic paraboloid are doubly ruled.

In the context of a mapping from $u, w$ parametric space to object space, a ruled surface is obtained by linearly interpolating between two known boundary curves associated with the opposite sides of the unit square in parametric space, say $P(u, 0)$ and $P(u, 1)$. The surface is given by

$$Q(u, w) = P(u, 0)(1 - w) + P(u, 1)w \qquad (6 - 43)$$

or $\quad [\, Q \,] = [\, x(u, w) \quad y(u, w) \quad z(u, w) \,] = [\, 1 - w \quad w \,] \begin{bmatrix} P(u, 0) \\ P(u, 1) \end{bmatrix}$

Again note that $Q(0, 0) = P(0, 0)$, etc., i.e., the ends of the specified curves and the corners of the surface, are coincident. Further, note that two of the edges of the blended or interpolated surface are coincident with the given curves, i.e., $Q(u, 0) = P(u, 0)$ and $Q(u, 1) = P(u, 1)$.

Alternately, the curves corresponding to $P(0, w)$ and $P(1, w)$ are assumed known. The ruled surface is then given by

$$Q(u, w) = P(0, w)(1 - u) + P(1, w)u \qquad (6 - 44)$$

or $\quad [\, Q \,] = [\, x(u, w) \quad y(u, w) \quad z(u, w) \,] = [\, 1 - u \quad u \,] \begin{bmatrix} P(0, w) \\ P(1, w) \end{bmatrix}$

Again the corners of the surface are coincident with the ends of the given curve, and the appropriate edges of the blended surface are coincident with the given boundary curves. An example of a ruled surface is shown in Fig. 6–28. Here the edge curves shown offset from the surface are third-order B-spline curves (see Sec. 5–9). An example illustrates the technique.

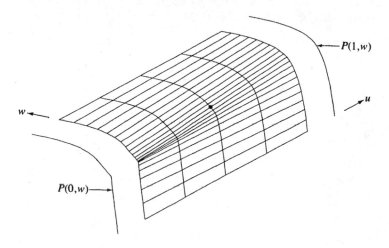

**Figure 6–28**   Example of a ruled surface.

### Example 6–10   Ruled Surface

Consider a ruled surface formed by linearly blending the curves $P(0, w)$ and $P(1, w)$. Determine the point on the surface $Q(u, w)$ at $u = w = 0.5$.

$P(0, w)$ is a third-order ($k = 3$) open B-spline curve with defining polygon vertices given by $B_1 \begin{bmatrix} 0 & 0 & 0 \end{bmatrix}$, $B_2 \begin{bmatrix} 1 & 1 & 0 \end{bmatrix}$, $B_3 \begin{bmatrix} 1 & 1 & 0 \end{bmatrix}$, $B_4 \begin{bmatrix} 2 & 1 & 0 \end{bmatrix}$ and $B_5 \begin{bmatrix} 3 & 0 & 0 \end{bmatrix}$ (see Sec. 5–9). Notice the double vertex $B_2 = B_3$ which yields a cusp in the curve. $P(1, w)$ is also a third-order open B-spline curve. Its defining polygon vertices are $\bar{B}_1 \begin{bmatrix} 0 & 0 & 6 \end{bmatrix}$, $\bar{B}_2 \begin{bmatrix} 1 & 1 & 6 \end{bmatrix}$, $\bar{B}_3 \begin{bmatrix} 2 & 1 & 6 \end{bmatrix}$, $\bar{B}_4 \begin{bmatrix} 3 & 0 & 6 \end{bmatrix}$.

Recalling the previous discussion of B-spline curves yields open uniform knot vectors for $P(0, w)$ and $P(1, w)$, respectively, of

$$[\,X\,] = \begin{bmatrix} 0 & 0 & 0 & 1 & 2 & 3 & 3 & 3 \end{bmatrix}$$

$$[\,Y\,] = \begin{bmatrix} 0 & 0 & 0 & 1 & 2 & 2 & 2 \end{bmatrix}$$

Note that the unnormalized parameter ranges for the two curves are different, $0 \le t \le 3$ for $P(0, w)$ and $0 \le s \le 2$ for $P(1, w)$. The 'normalized' parameter value for the ruled surface $Q$ at $w = 0.5$ corresponds to $t = 1.5$ for $P(0, w)$ and to $s = 1.0$ for $P(1, w)$.

Using Eqs. (5–83) and (5–84) to obtain $P(0, w)$ yields

$$P(0, w) = P(t)$$
$$= B_1 N_{1,3}(t) + B_2 N_{2,3}(t) + B_3 N_{3,3}(t) + B_4 N_{4,3}(t) + B_5 N_{5,3}(t)$$

At $w = 0.5$ or $t = 1.5$

$$P(0, 0.5) = P(1.5) = (0)B_1 + 0.125 B_2 + 0.75 B_3 + 0.125 B_4 + (0)B_5$$
$$= 0.125 \begin{bmatrix} 1 & 1 & 0 \end{bmatrix} + 0.75 \begin{bmatrix} 1 & 1 & 0 \end{bmatrix} + 0.125 \begin{bmatrix} 2 & 1 & 0 \end{bmatrix}$$
$$= \begin{bmatrix} 1.125 & 1 & 0 \end{bmatrix}$$

Similarly,

$$P(1, w) = P(s)$$
$$= \bar{B}_1 \bar{N}_{1,3}(s) + \bar{B}_2 \bar{N}_{2,3}(s) + \bar{B}_3 \bar{N}_{3,3}(s) + \bar{B}_4 \bar{N}_{4,3}(s)$$

At $w = 0.5$ or $s = 1.0$

$$P(1, 0.5) = P(1.0) = (0)\bar{B}_1 + 0.5 \bar{B}_2 + 0.5 \bar{B}_3 + (0)\bar{B}_4$$
$$= 0.5 \begin{bmatrix} 1 & 1 & 6 \end{bmatrix} + 0.5 \begin{bmatrix} 2 & 1 & 6 \end{bmatrix}$$
$$= \begin{bmatrix} 1.5 & 1 & 6 \end{bmatrix}$$

Using Eq. (6–44) to obtain the point on the ruled surface yields

$$Q(u, w) = P(0, w)(1 - u) + P(1, w)u$$

and $\qquad Q(0.5, 0.5) = P(0, 0.5)(1 - 0.5) + P(\dot{1}, 0.5)(0.5)$

$$= 0.5\,[\,1.125 \quad 1 \quad 0\,] + 0.5\,[\,1.5 \quad 1 \quad 6\,]$$

$$= [\,1.3125 \quad 1 \quad 3\,]$$

Complete results are shown in Fig. 6–28. The point on the surface corresponding to $Q(0.5, 0.5)$ is marked with a dot. Notice how the curve containing the cusp, $P(0, w)$, is smoothly blended into the continuous curve $P(1, w)$.

---

Of particular practical interest is whether a ruled surface is developable. Not all ruled surfaces are developable. However, all developable surfaces are ruled surfaces. If a surface is developable, then, by a succession of small rotations of the surface about the generating line, the surface can be unfolded or developed onto a plane without stretching or tearing. Developable surfaces are of considerable importance to sheet-metal- or plate-metal-based industries and to a less extent to fabric-based industries.

It is clear that among the ruled quadric surfaces both the cones and cylinders are developable. However, a few moments' reflection confirms that neither the hyperbola of one sheet (see Fig. 6–18d) nor the hyperbolic paraboloid (see Fig. 6–26), both of which are ruled surfaces, is a developable surface.

To determine if a surface or a portion of a surface is developable, it is necessary to consider the curvature of a parametric surface. At any point $P$ on a surface, the curve of intersection of a plane containing the normal to the surface at $P$ and the surface has a curvature $\kappa$ (see Fig. 6–29). As the plane is rotated about the normal, the curvature changes. Euler, the great Swiss mathematician, showed that unique directions for which the curvature is a minimum and a maximum exists. The curvatures in these directions are called the principal curvatures, $\kappa_{min}$ and $\kappa_{max}$. Further, the principal curvature directions are orthogonal. Two combinations of the principal curvatures are of particular interest, the average and the Gaussian curvatures:

$$H = \frac{\kappa_{min} + \kappa_{max}}{2} \qquad\qquad (6-45)$$

$$K = \kappa_{min}\kappa_{max} \qquad\qquad (6-46)$$

For a developable surface the Gaussian curvature $K$ is everywhere zero, i.e., $K = 0$. Dill (Ref. 6–18) has shown that for biparametric surfaces the average and Gaussian curvatures are given by[†]

$$H = \frac{A|Q_w|^2 - 2BQ_u\cdot Q_w + C|Q_u|^2}{2|Q_u \times Q_w|^3} \qquad\qquad (6-47)$$

---

[†]Here subscript notation is used for partial derivatives, i.e., $Q_u = \partial Q/\partial u$ etc.

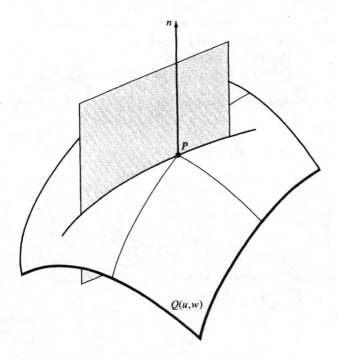

**Figure 6–29**    Curvature of a biparametric surface.

$$K = \frac{AC - B^2}{|Q_u \times Q_w|^4} \qquad (6 - 48)$$

where

$$(A\,B\,C) = [\,Q_u \times Q_w\,]\cdot[\,Q_{uu} \quad Q_{uw} \quad Q_{ww}\,]$$

As shown in Table 6–2 the sign of the Gaussian curvature serves to characterize the local shape of the surface: elliptic, hyperbolic, cylindrical or conical. Since the Gaussian curvature of a developable surface must be zero, the surface must be composed of cylindrical, conical or planar pieces. An example helps to illustrate this discussion.

### Table 6–2 Surface Types

| $\kappa_{min}\kappa_{max}$ | $K$ | Shape |
|---|---|---|
| Same sign | $> 0$ | Elliptic (bump or hollow) |
| Opposite sign | $< 0$ | Hyperbolic (saddle point) |
| One or both zero | $0$ | Cylindrical/conical (ridge, hollow, plane) |

### Example 6–11   Developable Surface

Show that an elliptic cone is a developable surface.

Rewriting Eq. (6–32) for a parametric elliptic cone in terms of $u$ and $w$ yields

$$Q(u, w) = [\, au \cos w \quad bu \sin w \quad cu \,]$$

The partial derivatives are

$$Q_u = [\, a \cos w \quad b \sin w \quad c \,]$$

$$Q_w = [\, -au \sin w \quad bu \cos w \quad 0 \,]$$

$$Q_{uw} = [\, -a \sin w \quad b \cos w \quad 0 \,]$$

$$Q_{uu} = [\, 0 \quad 0 \quad 0 \,]$$

$$Q_{ww} = [\, -au \cos w \quad -bu \sin w \quad 0 \,]$$

$$Q_u \times Q_w = [\, -bcu \cos w \quad -acu \sin w \quad abu \,]$$

$$|Q_u \times Q_w|^2 = (abu)^2 \left\{ \left( \frac{c}{a} \cos w \right)^2 + \left( \frac{c}{b} \sin w \right)^2 + 1 \right\} \neq 0 \qquad u > 0$$

and

$$A = [\, -bcu \cos w \quad -acu \sin w \quad abu \,] \cdot [\, 0 \quad 0 \quad 0 \,] = 0$$

$$B = [\, -bcu \cos w \quad -acu \sin w \quad abu \,] \cdot [\, -a \sin w \quad b \cos w \quad 0 \,]$$

$$= abcu \sin w \cos w - abcu \sin w \cos w = 0$$

$$C = [\, -bcu \cos w \quad -acu \sin w \quad abu \,] \cdot [\, -au \cos w \quad -bu \sin w \quad 0 \,]$$

$$= abcu^2 \cos^2 w + abcu^2 \sin^2 w = abcu^2$$

Hence, using Eqs. (6–48)

$$K = \frac{AC - B^2}{|Q_u \times Q_w|^4} = \frac{(0)(abcu^2) - (0)}{|Q_u \times Q_w|^4} = 0$$

everywhere on the surface, and the surface is developable. Incidentally, note that although for $u = 0$, $|Q_u \times Q_w|^2 = 0$, use of L'Hôpital's rule shows that $K = 0/0 = 0$ at $u = 0$.

## 6–9   LINEAR COONS SURFACE

If the four boundary curves $P(u, 0)$, $P(u, 1)$, $P(0, w)$ and $P(1, w)$ are known, and a bilinear blending function is used for the interior of the surface patch, a linear Coons surface is obtained. At first glance it might be assumed that a simple sum of the singly ruled surfaces (Eqs. (6–43) and (6–44)) in the two directions

$u, w$ would yield the desired result. If this is done, then

$$Q(u, w) = P(u, 0)(1 - w) + P(u, 1)w + P(0, w)(1 - u) + P(1, w)u$$

However, examination of this result at the corners of the surface patch yields, e.g.,

$$Q(0, 0) = P(0, 0) + P(0, 0) = 2P(0, 0)$$

and at the edges, e.g.,

$$Q(0, w) = P(0, 0)(1 - w) + P(0, 1)w + P(0, w)$$

neither of which corresponds to the original data as they should. The problem occurs because the corner points are counted twice, because $P(0, 0)$ is contained in both the $P(u, 0)$ and $P(0, w)$ boundary curves.

The correct result is obtained by subtracting the excess contribution to the surface due to duplication of the corner points. This yields

$$\begin{aligned} Q(u, w) = {} & P(u, 0)(1 - w) + P(u, 1)w + P(0, w)(1 - u) + P(1, w)u \\ & - P(0, 0)(1 - u)(1 - w) - P(0, 1)(1 - u)w \\ & - P(1, 0)u(1 - w) - P(1, 1)uw \end{aligned} \qquad (6 - 49)$$

Here, at the corners,

$$Q(0, 0) = P(0, 0), \text{ etc.}$$

and along the boundaries,

$$Q(0, w) = P(0, w)$$
$$Q(u, 1) = P(u, 1)$$

$$\text{etc.}$$

In matrix form Eq. (6–49) is

$$\begin{aligned} Q(u, w) = {} & [\, 1 - u \quad u \,] \begin{bmatrix} P(0, w) \\ P(1, w) \end{bmatrix} + [\, P(u, 0) \quad P(u, 1) \,] \begin{bmatrix} 1 - w \\ w \end{bmatrix} \\ & - [\, 1 - u \quad u \,] \begin{bmatrix} P(0, 0) & P(0, 1) \\ P(1, 0) & P(1, 1) \end{bmatrix} \begin{bmatrix} 1 - w \\ w \end{bmatrix} \end{aligned}$$

or more compactly as

$$Q(u, w) = [\, 1 - u \quad u \quad 1 \,] \begin{bmatrix} -P(0, 0) & -P(0, 1) & P(0, w) \\ -P(1, 0) & -P(1, 1) & P(1, w) \\ P(u, 0) & P(u, 1) & 0 \end{bmatrix} \begin{bmatrix} 1 - w \\ w \\ 1 \end{bmatrix}$$

$$(6 - 50)$$

The functions $(1 - u)$, $u$, $(1 - w)$, and $w$ are called blending functions because they blend the boundary curves to produce the internal shape of the surface. A linear Coons surface is shown in Fig. 6–30. The linear Coons surface is the simplest of the Coons surfaces. A more general Coons surface is discussed in Sec. 6–10. An example illustrates the method.

**Example 6–12    Linear Coons Surface**

Find the point on a linear Coons surface at $u = w = 0.5$ when the four boundary curves $P(u, 0)$, $P(u, 1)$, $P(0, w)$, $P(1, w)$ are given by open third-order $(k = 3)$ B-spline curves defined by

$P(u, 0)$ :  $B_1 [0 \quad 0 \quad 0]$, $B_2 [1 \quad 1 \quad 0]$, $B_3 [2 \quad 1 \quad 0]$, $B_4 [3 \quad 0 \quad 0]$,
$\qquad\qquad B_5 [3 \quad 0 \quad 3]$

$P(u, 1)$ :  $\bar{B}_1 [0 \quad 0 \quad 3]$, $\bar{B}_2 [1 \quad 1 \quad 3]$, $\bar{B}_3 [2 \quad 1 \quad 3]$, $\bar{B}_4 [2 \quad 1 \quad 3]$

$P(0, w)$ :  $\bar{C}_1 [0 \quad 0 \quad 3]$, $\bar{C}_2 [0 \quad 1 \quad 2]$, $\bar{C}_3 [0 \quad 1 \quad 1]$, $\bar{C}_4 [0 \quad 0 \quad 0]$

$P(1, w)$ :  $C_1 [3 \quad 0 \quad 3]$, $C_2 [3 \quad 1 \quad 2]$, $C_3 [3 \quad 1 \quad 2]$, $C_4 [3 \quad 1 \quad 1]$,
$\qquad\qquad C_5 [3 \quad 0 \quad 0]$

Recalling the previous discussion of B-spline curves (see Sec. 5–9) the knot vector for $P(u, 0)$ and $P(1, w)$ is

$$[X] = [0 \quad 0 \quad 0 \quad 1 \quad 2 \quad 3 \quad 3 \quad 3]$$

Thus, the unnormalized parameter range is $0 \le t \le 3$. For $P(u, 1)$ and $P(0, w)$ the knot vector is

$$[Y] = [0 \quad 0 \quad 0 \quad 1 \quad 2 \quad 2 \quad 2]$$

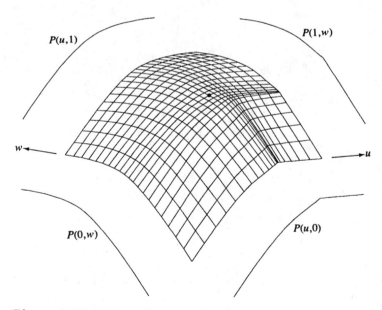

**Figure 6–30**    Linear Coons surface.

with an unnormalized parameter range of $0 \leq s \leq 2$. The corresponding values for the normalized parameter ranges of $0 \leq u, w \leq 1$ are $t = 1.5$ and $s = 1.0$.

Using Eqs. (5–83) and (5–84) yields

$$P(u,0) = P(t) = B_1 N_{1,3}(t) + B_2 N_{2,3}(t) + B_3 N_{3,3}(t) + B_4 N_{4,3}(t) + B_5 N_{5,3}(t)$$

$$P(0.5,0) = P(1.5) = (0)B_1 + 0.125B_2 + 0.75B_3 + 0.125B_4 + (0)B_5$$
$$= 0.125[1 \quad 1 \quad 3] + 0.75[2 \quad 1 \quad 3] + 0.125[2 \quad 1 \quad 3]$$
$$= [1.875 \quad 1 \quad 3]$$

$$P(u,1) = P(s) = \bar{B}_1 \bar{N}_{1,3}(s) + \bar{B}_2 \bar{N}_{2,3}(s) + \bar{B}_3 \bar{N}_{3,3}(s) + \bar{B}_4 \bar{N}_{4,3}(s)$$
$$P(0.5,1) = P(1.0) = (0)\bar{B}_1 + 0.5\bar{B}_2 + 0.5\bar{B}_3 + (0)\bar{B}_4$$
$$= 0.5[1 \quad 1 \quad 0] + 0.5[2 \quad 1 \quad 0]$$
$$= [1.5 \quad 1 \quad 0]$$

$$P(0,w) = P(s) = \bar{C}_1 \bar{N}_{1,3}(s) + \bar{C}_2 \bar{N}_{2,3}(s) + \bar{C}_3 \bar{N}_{3,3}(s) + \bar{C}_4 \bar{N}_{4,3}(s)$$
$$P(0,0.5) = P(1.0) = (0)\bar{C}_1 + 0.5\bar{C}_2 + 0.5\bar{C}_3 + (0)\bar{C}_4$$
$$= 0.5[0 \quad 1 \quad 2] + 0.5[0 \quad 1 \quad 1]$$
$$= [0 \quad 1 \quad 1.5]$$

$$P(1,w) = P(t) = C_1 N_{1,3}(t) + C_2 N_{2,3}(t) + C_3 N_{3,3}(t) + C_4 N_{4,3}(t) + C_5 N_{5,3}(t)$$

$$P(1,0.5) = P(1.5) = (0)C_1 + 0.125C_2 + 0.75C_3 + 0.125C_4 + (0)C_5$$
$$= 0.125[3 \quad 1 \quad 2] + 0.75[3 \quad 1 \quad 2] + 0.125[3 \quad 1 \quad 1]$$
$$= [3 \quad 1 \quad 1.875]$$

Now using Eq. (6–50)

$$Q(u,w) = [1-u \quad u \quad 1] \begin{bmatrix} -P(0,0) & -P(0,1) & P(0,w) \\ -P(1,0) & -P(1,1) & P(1,w) \\ P(u,0) & P(u,1) & 0 \end{bmatrix} \begin{bmatrix} 1-w \\ w \\ 1 \end{bmatrix}$$

$$Q(0.5,0.5) = [0.5 \quad 0.5 \quad 1] \times$$

$$\begin{bmatrix} -[0 \quad 0 \quad 3] & -[0 \quad 0 \quad 0] & [0 \quad 1 \quad 1.5] \\ -[3 \quad 0 \quad 3] & -[3 \quad 0 \quad 0] & [3 \quad 1 \quad 1.875] \\ [1.875 \quad 1 \quad 3] & [1.5 \quad 1 \quad 0] & 0 \end{bmatrix} \begin{bmatrix} 0.5 \\ 0.5 \\ 1 \end{bmatrix}$$

$$= [1.6375 \quad 2.25 \quad 1.6375]$$

Complete results are shown in Fig. 6–30. Notice the flat area. The Gaussian curvature is zero in this area. Consequently, this part of the surface is developable. Elsewhere the Gaussian curvature is positive and the surface is not developable.

## 6–10    COONS BICUBIC SURFACE

Although analytic surfaces, e.g., quadric surfaces, ruled surfaces, and the simple linearly blended surface patches discussed in previous sections, are important for design and manufacturing, they are not sufficiently flexible for many applications. The surface descriptions discussed in this and the remaining sections of the chapter provide the required flexibility by using higher degree polynomials for both the patch boundary curves and the interior blending functions. Surfaces generated by combining patches of this nature are referred to as sculptured surfaces. Of these surface descriptions the Coons bicubic patch is of fundamental importance (see Ref. 6–19).

The Coons bicubic surface patch uses normalized cubic splines (see Sec. 5–4) for all four boundary curves. Cubic blending functions are used to define the interior of the patch. Thus, each boundary curve is of the general form

$$P(t) = B_1 + B_2 t + B_3 t^2 + B_4 t^3 \qquad 0 \le t \le 1 \tag{5-2}$$

For a single normalized cubic spline segment with known tangent and position vectors at the ends, each of the four boundary curves, $P(u,0)$, $P(u,1)$, $P(0,w)$ and $P(1,w)$, is given by (see Eqs. (5-24), (5-26), (5-27))

$$P(t) = [\,T\,][\,N\,][\,G\,]$$

$$= [\,t^3 \quad t^2 \quad t \quad 1\,]
\begin{bmatrix}
2 & -2 & 1 & 1 \\
-3 & 3 & -2 & -1 \\
0 & 0 & 1 & 0 \\
1 & 0 & 0 & 0
\end{bmatrix}
\begin{bmatrix}
P_1 \\
P_2 \\
P'_1 \\
P'_2
\end{bmatrix} \qquad 0 \le t \le 1$$

$$\tag{5-27}$$

where $t$ becomes $u$ or $w$ as appropriate and $P_1$, $P_2$, $P'_1$, $P'_2$ are the position and tangent vectors at the ends of the appropriate boundary curve (see Fig. 6–31). The cubic blending function used for both parametric directions is identical to the one used to blend the interior of a normalized cubic spline curve; i.e.,

$$[\,F\,] = [\,F_1(t) \quad F_2(t) \quad F_3(t) \quad F_4(t)\,] = [\,T\,][\,N\,] \tag{5-26}$$

$$= [\,t^3 \quad t^2 \quad t \quad 1\,]
\begin{bmatrix}
2 & -2 & 1 & 1 \\
-3 & 3 & -2 & -1 \\
0 & 0 & 1 & 0 \\
1 & 0 & 0 & 0
\end{bmatrix}$$

Writing out the blending functions yields

$$F_1(t) = 2t^3 - 3t^2 + 1 \tag{5-25a}$$
$$F_2(t) = -2t^3 + 3t^2 \tag{5-25b}$$
$$F_3(t) = t^3 - 2t^2 + t \tag{5-25c}$$
$$F_4(t) = t^3 - t^2 \tag{5-25d}$$

where $t$ is either $u$ or $w$ as appropriate. These blending functions are shown in Fig. 5–8. The definition for a Coons bicubic patch is then

$$Q(u, w) = [\, F_1(u) \quad F_2(u) \quad F_3(u) \quad F_4(u)\,] \times$$

$$\begin{bmatrix} P(0,0) & P(0,1) & P_w(0,0) & P_w(0,1) \\ P(1,0) & P(1,1) & P_w(1,0) & P_w(1,1) \\ P_u(0,0) & P_u(0,1) & P_{uw}(0,0) & P_{uw}(0,1) \\ P_u(1,0) & P_u(1,1) & P_{uw}(1,0) & P_{uw}(1,1) \end{bmatrix} \begin{bmatrix} F_1(w) \\ F_2(w) \\ F_3(w) \\ F_4(w) \end{bmatrix}$$

$$(6-51)$$

for $0 \le u \le 1$ and $0 \le w \le 1$. Using Eq. (5–26) the definition can be more compactly written as

$$Q(u, w) = [\,U\,][\,N\,][\,P\,][\,N\,]^T[\,W\,] \qquad (6-52)$$

where $[\,U\,] = [\,u^3 \quad u^2 \quad u \quad 1\,]$ and $[\,W\,]^T = [\,w^3 \quad w^2 \quad w \quad 1\,]$.

The $[\,P\,]$ matrix in Eq. (6–51) contains all the geometric information required to generate a single Coons bicubic patch. The $2 \times 2$ submatrices in each corner of $[\,P\,]$ contain

$$[\,P\,] = \begin{bmatrix} \text{corner} & : & w - \text{tangent} \\ \text{position} & : & \text{vectors} \\ \text{vectors} & : & \\ \cdots\cdots & \cdots\cdots & \cdots\cdots \\ u - \text{tangent} & : & \text{twist} \\ \text{vectors} & : & \text{vectors} \end{bmatrix}$$

Thus, a bicubic surface patch is defined by the four position vectors at the corners, eight tangent vectors, two at each corner, the four twist vectors at the corners, and the four cubic blending functions $F_1$, $F_2$, $F_3$ and $F_4$.

An example of a bicubic surface patch is shown in Fig. 6–32. Note that each of the isoparametric lines shown in Fig. 6–32 is a normalized cubic spline curve. Multiple Coons bicubic patches can be joined along their boundaries with $C^1$ continuity to form more complex surfaces that are everywhere $C^1$ continuous. Reference 6–19 discusses the conditions for joining multiple bicubic surface patches in detail.

The parametric derivatives at any point on a bicubic surface are obtained by formally differentiating Eq. (6–52) to yield

$$Q_u(u, w) = [\,U'\,][\,N\,][\,P\,][\,N\,]^T[\,W\,] \qquad (6-53)$$

$$Q_w(u, w) = [\,U\,][\,N\,][\,P\,][\,N\,]^T[\,W'\,] \qquad (6-54)$$

$$Q_{uw}(u, w) = [\,U'\,][\,N\,][\,P\,][\,N\,]^T[\,W'\,] \qquad (6-55)$$

$$Q_{uu}(u, w) = [\,U''\,][\,N\,][\,P\,][\,N\,]^T[\,W\,] \qquad (6-56)$$

$$Q_{ww}(u, w) = [\,U\,][\,N\,][\,P\,][\,N\,]^T[\,W''\,] \qquad (6-57)$$

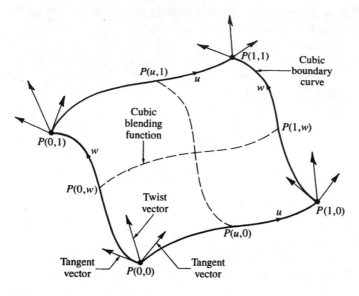

**Figure 6–31**    Geometry for a bicubic Coons surface patch.

where the primes denote differentiation with respect to the appropriate variable
and

$$[\,U'\,] = [\,3u^2 \quad 2u \quad 1 \quad 0\,]$$

$$[\,W'\,]^T = [\,3w^2 \quad 2w \quad 1 \quad 0\,]$$

$$[\,U''\,] = [\,6u \quad 2 \quad 0 \quad 0\,]$$

$$[\,W''\,]^T = [\,6w \quad 2 \quad 0 \quad 0\,]$$

The normal to the surface, which is important in hidden surface, illumination
model (see Ref. 1-1) and numerical control calculations, is given by

$$\mathbf{n} = Q_u \times Q_w$$

A detailed example is illustrative of the calculation procedure for bicubic patches.

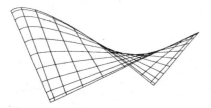

**Figure 6–32**    Coons bicubic surface patch.

**Example 6–13    Coons Bicubic Surface Patch**

Determine the point on a Coons bicubic surface patch corresponding to $u = w = 0.5$. The position vectors for the four corners are $P(0,0) = [\,-100\ \ 0\ \ 100\,]$, $P(0,1) = [\,-100\ \ -100\ \ -100\,]$, $P(1,0) = [\,100\ \ -100\ \ 100\,]$, $P(1,1) = [\,100\ \ 0\ \ -100\,]$. The tangent vectors are $P_u(0,0) = [\,100\ \ 100\ \ 0\,]$, $P_u(0,1) = [\,1\ \ 1\ \ 0\,]$, $P_u(1,0) = [\,1\ \ -1\ \ 0\,]$, $P_u(1,1) = [\,1\ \ -1\ \ 0\,]$, $P_w(0,0) = [\,0\ \ 10\ \ -10\,]$, $P_w(0,1) = [\,0\ \ -1\ \ -1\,]$, $P_w(1,0) = [\,0\ \ 1\ \ -1\,]$, $P_w(1,1) = [\,0\ \ -1\ \ -1\,]$. The twist vectors are $P_{uw}(0,0) = [\,0\ \ 0\ \ 0\,]$, $P_{uw}(0,1) = [\,0.1\ \ 0.1\ \ 0.1\,]$, $P_{uw}(1,0) = [\,0.1\ \ -0.1\ \ -0.1\,]$, $P_{uw}(1,1) = [\,0\ \ 0\ \ 0\,]$. Determine the parametric derivatives $Q_u$, $Q_w$ and the normal vector at $u = w = 0.5$.

Using the matrix formulation given in Eq. (6–51) yields

$$Q(u,w) = [\,U\,][\,N\,] \begin{bmatrix} [\,-100\ \ 0\ \ 100\,] & [\,-100\ \ -100\ \ -100\,] \\ [\,100\ \ -100\ \ 100\,] & [\,100\ \ 0\ \ -100\,] \\ [\,100\ \ 100\ \ 0\,] & [\,1\ \ 1\ \ 0\,] \\ [\,1\ \ -1\ \ 0\,] & [\,1\ \ -1\ \ 0\,] \\[8pt] [\,0\ \ 10\ \ -10\,] & [\,0\ \ -1\ \ -1\,] \\ [\,0\ \ 1\ \ -1\,] & [\,0\ \ -1\ \ -1\,] \\ [\,0\ \ 0\ \ 0\,] & [\,0.1\ \ 0.1\ \ 0.1\,] \\ [\,0.1\ \ -0.1\ \ -0.1\,] & [\,0\ \ 0\ \ 0\,] \end{bmatrix} [\,N\,]^T[\,W\,]^T$$

For $u = 0.5$ the blending functions in $u$ are

$$[\,U\,][\,N\,] = [\,u^3\ \ u^2\ \ u\ \ 1\,] \begin{bmatrix} 2 & -2 & 1 & 1 \\ -3 & 3 & -2 & -1 \\ 0 & 0 & 1 & 0 \\ 1 & 0 & 0 & 0 \end{bmatrix}$$

$$= [\,0.125\ \ 0.25\ \ 0.5\ \ 1\,] \begin{bmatrix} 2 & -2 & 1 & 1 \\ -3 & 3 & -2 & -1 \\ 0 & 0 & 1 & 0 \\ 1 & 0 & 0 & 0 \end{bmatrix}$$

$$= [\,0.5\ \ 0.5\ \ 0.125\ \ -0.125\,]$$

For $w = 0.5$ the blending functions in $w$ are

$$[\,N\,]^T[\,W\,] = \begin{bmatrix} 2 & -3 & 0 & 1 \\ -2 & 3 & 0 & 0 \\ 1 & -2 & 1 & 0 \\ 1 & -1 & 0 & 0 \end{bmatrix} \begin{bmatrix} w^3 \\ w^2 \\ w \\ 1 \end{bmatrix}$$

$$= \begin{bmatrix} 2 & -3 & 0 & 1 \\ -2 & 3 & 0 & 0 \\ 1 & -2 & 1 & 0 \\ 1 & -1 & 0 & 0 \end{bmatrix} \begin{bmatrix} 0.125 \\ 0.25 \\ 0.5 \\ 1 \end{bmatrix}$$

$$= [\,0.5\ \ 0.5\ \ 0.125\ \ -0.125\,]^T$$

Thus the $x$ component of $Q(u, w)$ at $u = w = 0.5$ is

$$Q_x(0.5, 0.5) = [\,0.5 \quad 0.5 \quad 0.125 \quad -0.125\,] \times$$

$$\begin{bmatrix} -100 & -100 & 0 & 0 \\ 100 & 100 & 0 & 0 \\ 100 & 1 & 0 & 0.1 \\ 1 & 1 & 0.1 & 0 \end{bmatrix} \begin{bmatrix} 0.5 \\ 0.5 \\ 0.125 \\ -0.125 \end{bmatrix}$$

$$= [\,12.375 \quad 0 \quad -0.0125 \quad 0.0125\,] \begin{bmatrix} 0.5 \\ 0.5 \\ 0.125 \\ -0.125 \end{bmatrix}$$

$$= 6.18$$

Similarly the $y$ and $z$ components are

$$Q_y(0.5, 0.5) = [\,0.5 \quad 0.5 \quad 0.125 \quad -0.125\,] \times$$

$$\begin{bmatrix} 0 & -100 & 10 & -1 \\ -100 & 0 & 1 & -1 \\ 100 & 1 & 0 & 0.1 \\ -1 & -1 & -0.1 & 0 \end{bmatrix} \begin{bmatrix} 0.5 \\ 0.5 \\ 0.125 \\ -0.125 \end{bmatrix}$$

$$= -42.75$$

$$Q_z(0.5, 0.5) = [\,0.5 \quad 0.5 \quad 0.125 \quad -0.125\,] \times$$

$$\begin{bmatrix} 100 & -100 & -10 & -1 \\ 100 & -100 & -1 & -1 \\ 0 & 0 & 0 & 0.1 \\ 0 & 0 & -0.1 & 0 \end{bmatrix} \begin{bmatrix} 0.5 \\ 0.5 \\ 0.125 \\ -0.125 \end{bmatrix}$$

$$= -0.56$$

Thus, $Q(0.5, 0.5) = [\,6.18 \quad -42.75 \quad -0.56\,]$. Complete results are shown in Fig. 6–32.

Turning now to the derivatives and recalling Eqs. (6–53) to (6–55) and noting that

$$[\,U'\,][\,N\,] = [\,3u^2 \quad 2u \quad 1 \quad 0\,][\,N\,]$$

$$= [\,0.75 \quad 1 \quad 1 \quad 0\,] \begin{bmatrix} 2 & -2 & 1 & 1 \\ -3 & 3 & -2 & -1 \\ 0 & 0 & 1 & 0 \\ 1 & 0 & 0 & 0 \end{bmatrix}$$

$$= [\,-1.5 \quad 1.5 \quad -0.25 \quad -0.25\,]$$

$$[\,N\,]^T[\,W'\,] = [\,N\,]^T[\,3w^2 \quad 2w \quad 1 \quad 0\,]^T$$

$$= \begin{bmatrix} 2 & -3 & 0 & 1 \\ -2 & 3 & 0 & 0 \\ 1 & -2 & 1 & 0 \\ 1 & -1 & 0 & 0 \end{bmatrix} \begin{bmatrix} 0.75 \\ 1 \\ 1 \\ 0 \end{bmatrix}$$

$$= [\,-1.5 \quad 1.5 \quad -0.25 \quad -0.25\,]^T$$

the parametric derivatives at $u = w = 0.5$ are

$$Q_{u_x}(0.5, 0.5) = [\, -1.5 \quad 1.5 \quad -0.25 \quad -0.25\,] \times$$

$$\begin{bmatrix} -100 & -100 & 0 & 0 \\ 100 & 100 & 0 & 0 \\ 100 & 1 & 0 & 0.1 \\ 1 & 1 & 0.1 & 0 \end{bmatrix} \begin{bmatrix} 0.5 \\ 0.5 \\ 0.125 \\ -0.125 \end{bmatrix}$$

$$= [\, 274.75 \quad 299.5 \quad -0.025 \quad -0.025\,] \begin{bmatrix} 0.5 \\ 0.5 \\ 0.125 \\ -0.125 \end{bmatrix}$$

$$= 287.13$$

$Q_{u_y}$ and $Q_{u_z}$ are found in a similar fashion. The result is

$$Q_u(0.5, 0.5) = [\, 287.13 \quad -14.06 \quad 1.69\,]$$

Now

$$Q_{w_x}(0.5, 0.5) = [\, 0.5 \quad 0.5 \quad 0.125 \quad -0.125\,] \times$$

$$\begin{bmatrix} -100 & -100 & 0 & 0 \\ 100 & 100 & 0 & 0 \\ 100 & 1 & 0 & 0.1 \\ 1 & 1 & 0.1 & 0 \end{bmatrix} \begin{bmatrix} -1.5 \\ 1.5 \\ -0.25 \\ -0.25 \end{bmatrix}$$

$$= [\, 12.38 \quad 0 \quad -0.0125 \quad 0.0125\,] \begin{bmatrix} -1.5 \\ 1.5 \\ -0.25 \\ -0.25 \end{bmatrix}$$

$$= -18.56$$

$Q_{w_y}$ and $Q_{w_z}$ are found in a similar fashion to yield

$$Q_w(0.5, 0.5) = [\, -18.56 \quad -19.69 \quad -298.38\,]$$

Finally, the normal vector is

$$\mathbf{n} = Q_u \times Q_w = \begin{vmatrix} \mathbf{i} & \mathbf{j} & \mathbf{k} \\ Q_{u_x} & Q_{u_y} & Q_{u_z} \\ Q_{w_x} & Q_{w_y} & Q_{w_z} \end{vmatrix} = \begin{vmatrix} \mathbf{i} & \mathbf{j} & \mathbf{k} \\ 287.13 & -14.06 & 1.69 \\ -18.56 & -19.69 & -298.38 \end{vmatrix}$$

$$= 4227.5\,\mathbf{i} + 85641.2\,\mathbf{j} - 5915.5\,\mathbf{k}$$

The unit normal is

$$\hat{\mathbf{n}} = [\, 0.049 \quad 0.996 \quad -0.069\,]$$

Note that the twist vectors at the corners have slightly displaced the normal from the $y$ direction.

One of the difficulties in using bicubic surface patches is the disparate magnitudes of position, tangent and twist vectors. All are generally of different orders of magnitude. For example, for a patch 10 units on a side, the tangent vectors might have a magnitude of 10 units, the twist vectors a magnitude of 100 units and the position vectors a magnitude of 1000 units. Further, the effects of changing the magnitude and direction of either tangent and/or twist vectors is not always obvious.

Figure 6–33 shows the effect of varying the magnitude of the tangent vectors at the corners of a bicubic surface patch. The position vectors of the corners of the patch lie in the $y = 0$ plane centered about the origin at $\pm 100x, z$. The tangent vectors lie in planes perpendicular to the plane of the corner position vectors and contain adjacent corners of the patch. The direction of the tangent vectors is such as to make the center of the cubic boundary curve convex upward ('hump up'), e.g., $P_u(0,0) = \begin{bmatrix} 1 & 1 & 0 \end{bmatrix}$, $P_u(1,0) = \begin{bmatrix} 1 & -1 & 0 \end{bmatrix}$, etc. The magnitude of the twist vectors is zero. If the magnitude of the $y$ component of each tangent vector is zero, the patch is flat; if it is nonzero the patch is bowed.

Figure 6–33a shows the resulting bicubic surface patch with unit tangent vector component magnitudes. Although the surface appears flat, it is in fact smoothly rounded. The $y$ component at the surface center, i.e., at $x = z = 0$,

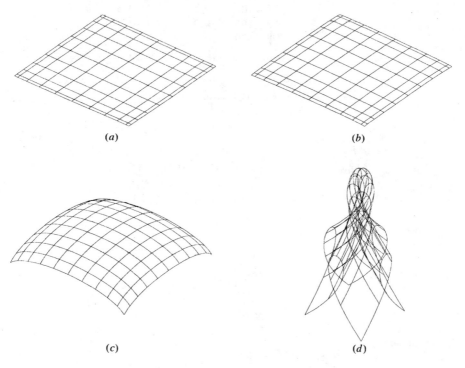

(a)

(b)

(c)

(d)

**Figure 6–33**   Effect of varying tangent vector magnitude on a bicubic surface patch. The tangent vector component magnitudes are (a) 1; (b) 10; (c) 100; (d) 1000.

is 0.5. Figures 6–33b to d show the resulting bicubic surfaces when the tangent vector component magnitudes are increased by 1, 2 and 3 orders of magnitude, respectively, i.e., to 10, 100 and 1000. The center values are now 5, 50 and 500. Note that the center values also increase by an order of magnitude each time the tangent vector magnitude increases.

Figure 6–33d is of particular interest. The surface is self-intersecting. The key to understanding this result is to recall the discussion of cubic spline curves in Sec. 5–3 and in particular Fig. 5–10. Further, recall that each isoparametric line on the surface is a cubic spline curve. Each of the isoparametric lines forms a loop indicating that the tangent vector magnitude at the corner has exceeded the critical value.

The effect of changing the direction of the tangent vector at a corner is shown in Fig. 6–34. Here, the signs of the $y$ components of the tangent vectors at $P(1,0)$ have been changed; the magnitudes are 100. Notice that in Fig. 6–34 the right front corner of the surface is now concave rather than convex as in Fig. 6–33c.

Twist was mentioned previously in Sec. 6–5 in discussing a spherical surface patch. There it was identified as the cross derivative of the surface at the corners. In effect the twist vector at a corner allows modification of the *interior* of a surface *without* modifying the tangent vectors at the corner. Figure 6–35 shows the effect of modifying the twist vector at a single corner, $P(0,0)$, on the surface. For each of the surfaces in Fig. 6–35, $P(0,0)$ is the lowest corner. The surface is the same as that in Fig. 6–33b with the exception of the nonzero twist vector at $P((0,0)$. Figures 6–35a and b, with twist vector component magnitudes of 10 and 100, respectively, show little apparent effect of the nonzero twist vector. In Fig. 6–35c the surface exhibits a definite convex shape due to the nonzero twist vector. Figure 6–35d illustrates the effects of large twist vector magnitudes. However, note that in contrast to Fig. 6–33d the surface does not intersect itself. Further careful examination of Fig. 6–35d shows that the surface is slightly concave at the three corners with zero twist.

A surface with zero twist at a corner is locally 'flat' at that corner. A surface with zero twist at all four corners, as shown in Fig. 6–33, is called a Ferguson or F patch (Ref. 6–20). When joined together to form more complex surfaces, the corner locations of the patches are quite obvious. For this reason they are seldom used in practice.

Although the discussion here is confined to quadrilateral patches, as shown in Fig. 6–36 other patch shapes are important. Triangular patches are discussed

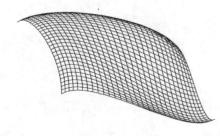

**Figure 6–34**   Effect of changing tangent vector direction on a bicubic surface patch.

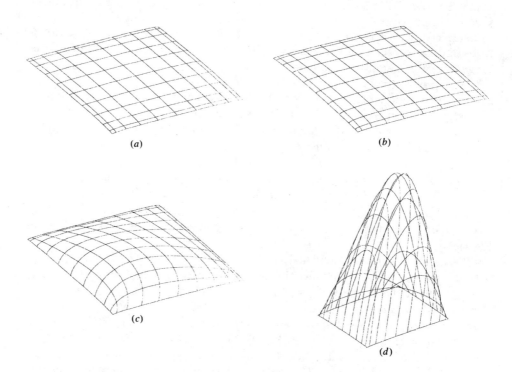

**Figure 6–35** Effect of twist vector on a bicubic surface patch. The magnitude of the twist vector component at $P(0,0)$ is (a) 10; (b) 100; (c) 1000; (d) 10,000.

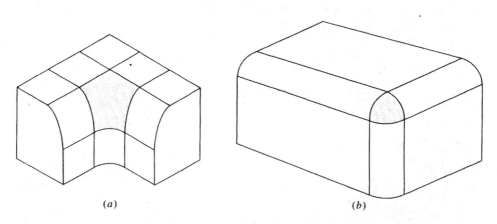

**Figure 6–36** Nonquadrilateral patches. (a) Pentagonal; (b) triangular.

by Barnhill in Refs. 6–21 and 6–22. Pentagonal patches are discussed by Charrot and Gregory in Ref. 6–23.

## 6–11   BÉZIER SURFACES

Coons bicubic surfaces provide a flexible and powerful surface design tool. However, as with cubic spline curves, practical usage suffers from the necessity of specifying precise, nonintuitive mathematical information, e.g., position, tangent and twist vectors. Figures 6–33 to 6–35 amply illustrate some of the difficulties. Most of these difficulties are overcome by the extension of Bézier curves to surfaces.

A Cartesian or tensor product Bézier surface is given by

$$Q(u, w) = \sum_{i=0}^{n} \sum_{j=0}^{m} B_{i,j} J_{n,i}(u) K_{m,j}(w) \qquad (6-58)$$

where $J_{n,i}(u)$ and $K_{m,j}(w)$ are the Bernstein basis functions in the $u$ and $w$ parametric directions (see Eqs. 5–63 and 5–64). Repeating the definition previously given in Sec. 5–8 for convenience yields

$$J_{n,i}(u) = \binom{n}{i} u^i (1-u)^{n-i} \qquad (5-63)$$

$$K_{m,j}(w) = \binom{m}{j} w^j (1-w)^{m-j}$$

with
$$\binom{n}{i} = \frac{n!}{i!(n-i)!} \qquad (5-64)$$

$$\binom{m}{j} = \frac{m!}{j!(m-j)!}$$

The $B_{i,j}$'s are the vertices of a defining polygon net as shown in Fig. 6–37. The indices $n$ and $m$ are one less than the number of polygon vertices in the $u$ and $w$ directions, respectively. For quadrilateral surface patches the defining polygon net must be topologically rectangular, i.e., the net must have the same number of vertices in each 'row'.

Again, as when defining Bézier curves, because the Bernstein basis is used for the surface blending functions, many properties of the surface are known. For example:

The degree of the surface in each parametric direction is one less than the number of defining polygon vertices in that direction.

The continuity of the surface in each parametric direction is two less than

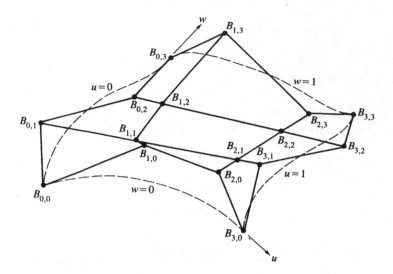

**Figure 6–37**   Bézier surface nomenclature.

the number of defining polygon vertices in that direction.

The surface generally follows the shape of the defining polygon net.

Only the corner points of the defining polygon net and the surface are coincident.

The surface is contained within the convex hull of the defining polygon net.

The surface does not exhibit the variation diminishing property. The variation diminishing property for bivariant surfaces is both undefined and unknown.

The surface is invariant under an affine transformation.

Each of the boundary curves of a Bézier surface is a Bézier curve. Keeping this fact in mind and considering the defining polygon net for a 4 × 4 bicubic Bézier surface shown schematically in Fig. 6–38, it is easy to see that the tangent vectors at the patch corners are controlled both in direction and magnitude by the position of adjacent points along the edges of the net. Specifically, the tangent vectors in the $u$, $w$ directions at $A$ are controlled by the polygon net vertices $B_{0,1}$ and $B_{1,0}$, respectively. Similarly, the polygon net vertices $B_{2,0}$, $B_{3,1}$, $B_{3,2}$, $B_{2,3}$ and $B_{1,3}$, $B_{0,2}$ control the tangent vectors in the $u$, $w$ directions at the corners $B$, $C$, $D$, respectively. The four interior polygon net vertices, $B_{1,1}$, $B_{2,1}$, $B_{2,2}$ and $B_{1,2}$, *influence* the direction and magnitude of the twist vectors at the corners $A$, $B$, $C$, $D$, respectively, of the patch. Consequently, the user can control the shape of the surface patch without an intimate knowledge of tangent or twist vectors.

Figure 6–39 shows several bicubic Bézier surfaces and their defining polygon

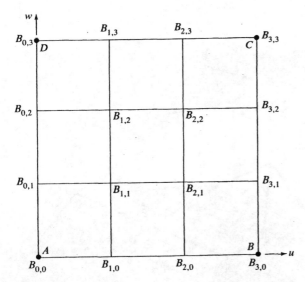

**Figure 6–38**    Schematic of the defining polygon net for a 4 × 4 Bézier surface.

nets. The base polygon net is 4 × 4, centered at the origin with corners at ±15 in $x, z$. The $y$ component of the corner vertices is zero. All other vertices have a $y$ component of five. The base polygon net and the resulting Bézier surface are shown in Fig. 6–39a. In Fig. 6–39 $B_{0,0}$ is the leftmost corner vertex, and $B_{3,3}$ is the rightmost corner vertex. Notice that the center vertices of the base polygon net form a planar cross (shown shaded). Consequently the center of the resulting surface, although not flat, is minimally curved.

Figure 6–39b illustrates the effect of increasing the tangent vector magnitudes at $B_{0,0}$ in both the $u$ and $w$ parametric directions by a factor of 2 by moving $B_{1,0}$ and $B_{0,1}$. The twist has not been changed. Notice the increased curvature of the boundary curves corresponding to $u = 0$ and $w = 0$ and the resulting change in the interior of the surface.

Figure 6–39c shows the effect of reversing the directions of the tangent vectors at $B_{0,3}$ in both the $u$ and $w$ parameter directions by moving $B_{2,3}$ and $B_{3,2}$. Notice the resulting reverse curvature of the boundary curves near $B_{0,3}$ and of the interior of the surface compared with that of the base surface.

Figure 6–39d illustrates the effect of doubling the magnitude of the twist vector at $B_{0,0}$ without changing its direction. Here, only $B_{1,1}$ was moved. The effects are subtle but nonetheless important for design. Careful comparison with the base surface in Fig. 6–39a shows that the parametric lines near $B_{0,0}$ have more curvature. The effect extends nearly to the center of the surface.

In matrix form a Cartesian product Bézier surface is given by

$$Q(u, w) = [\,U\,][\,N\,][\,B\,][\,M\,]^{T}[\,W\,] \qquad (6-59)$$

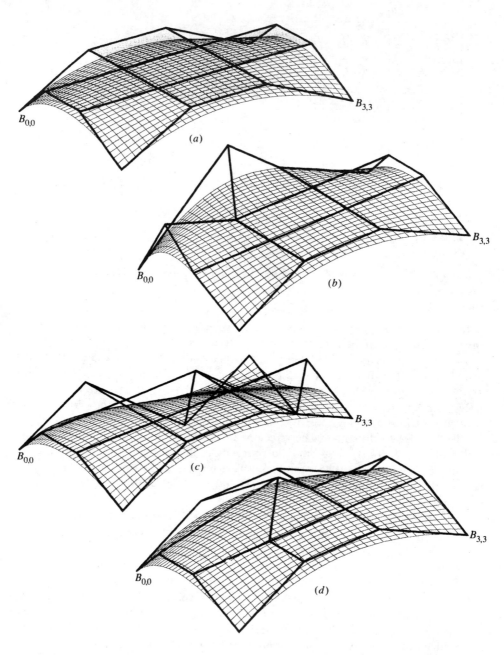

**Figure 6–39**   Bicubic Bézier surfaces. (a) Base surface; (b) effect of a change in both tangent vector magnitudes at $B_{0,0}$; (c) effect of a change in tangent vector direction at $B_{0,3}$; (d) effect of a change in twist vector magnitude at $B_{0,0}$.

where
$$[U] = [u^n \quad u^{n-1} \quad \cdots \quad 1]$$

$$[W] = [w^m \quad w^{m-1} \quad \cdots \quad 1]^T$$

$$[B] = \begin{bmatrix} B_{0,0} & \cdots & B_{0,m} \\ \vdots & \ddots & \vdots \\ B_{n,0} & \cdots & B_{n,m} \end{bmatrix}$$

$[N]$ and $[M]$ are given by Eq. (5–70) or (5–71).

For the specific case of a $4 \times 4$ bicubic Bézier surface Eq. (6–59) reduces to

$$Q(u,w) = [u^3 \quad u^2 \quad u \quad 1] \begin{bmatrix} -1 & 3 & -3 & 1 \\ 3 & -6 & 3 & 0 \\ -3 & 3 & 0 & 0 \\ 1 & 0 & 0 & 0 \end{bmatrix} \times$$

$$\begin{bmatrix} B_{0,0} & B_{0,1} & B_{0,2} & B_{0,3} \\ B_{1,0} & B_{1,1} & B_{1,2} & B_{1,3} \\ B_{2,0} & B_{2,1} & B_{2,2} & B_{2,3} \\ B_{3,0} & B_{3,1} & B_{3,2} & B_{3,3} \end{bmatrix} \begin{bmatrix} -1 & 3 & -3 & 1 \\ 3 & -6 & 3 & 0 \\ -3 & 3 & 0 & 0 \\ 1 & 0 & 0 & 0 \end{bmatrix} \begin{bmatrix} w^3 \\ w^2 \\ w \\ 1 \end{bmatrix}$$

$$(6-60)$$

A Bézier surface need not be square. For a $5 \times 3$ net Eq. (6–59) yields

$$Q(u,w) = [u^4 \quad u^3 \quad u^2 \quad u \quad 1] \begin{bmatrix} 1 & -4 & 6 & -4 & 1 \\ -4 & -12 & -12 & 4 & 0 \\ 6 & -12 & 6 & 0 & 0 \\ -4 & 4 & 0 & 0 & 0 \\ 1 & 0 & 0 & 0 & 0 \end{bmatrix} \times$$

$$\begin{bmatrix} B_{0,0} & B_{0,1} & B_{0,2} \\ B_{1,0} & B_{1,1} & B_{1,2} \\ B_{2,0} & B_{2,1} & B_{2,2} \\ B_{3,0} & B_{3,1} & B_{3,2} \\ B_{4,0} & B_{4,1} & B_{4,2} \end{bmatrix} \begin{bmatrix} 1 & -2 & 1 \\ -2 & 2 & 0 \\ 1 & 0 & 0 \end{bmatrix} \begin{bmatrix} w^2 \\ w \\ 1 \end{bmatrix}$$

$$(6-61)$$

The $5 \times 3$ Bézier surface is composed of quartic polynomial curves in the $u$ parametric direction and quadratic polynomial curves in the $w$ parametric direction. An example of a $5 \times 3$ Bézier surface is shown in Fig. 6–40. Here as shown by Fig. 6–40b changing the central polygon vertex on the defining net side with five defining vertices does not affect the tangent vectors at the corners.

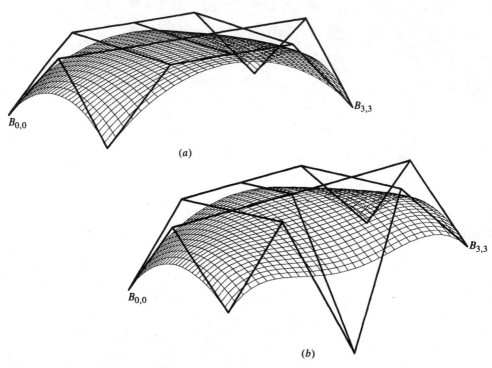

**Figure 6–40** 5 × 3 Bézier surface. (a) Base surface; (b) effect of changing the central polygon vertex on the side with five vertices.

The derivatives of a Bézier surface are obtained by formal differentiation of Eq. (6–58) or (6–59). Specifically using Eq. (6–58) the first and second parametric derivatives are

$$Q_u(u, w) = \sum_{i=0}^{n} \sum_{j=0}^{m} B_{i,j} J'_{n,i}(u) K_{m,j}(w) \qquad (6-62)$$

$$Q_w(u, w) = \sum_{i=0}^{n} \sum_{j=0}^{m} B_{i,j} J_{n,i}(u) K'_{m,j}(w) \qquad (6-63)$$

$$Q_{uw}(u, w) = \sum_{i=0}^{n} \sum_{j=0}^{m} B_{i,j} J'_{n,i}(u) K'_{m,j}(w) \qquad (6-64)$$

$$Q_{uu}(u, w) = \sum_{i=0}^{n} \sum_{j=0}^{m} B_{i,j} J''_{n,i}(u) K_{m,j}(w) \qquad (6-65)$$

$$Q_{ww}(u, w) = \sum_{i=0}^{n} \sum_{j=0}^{m} B_{i,j} J_{n,i}(u) K''_{m,j}(w) \qquad (6-66)$$

where the prime denotes differentiation with respect to the parametric variable. The derivatives of the Bernstein basis functions $J'_{n,i}$, $J''_{n,i}$, $K'_{m,j}$ and $K''_{m,j}$ are given by Eqs. (5-74) and (5-75).

The relationship between a bicubic Bézier and a bicubic Coons surface is easily found. Recalling Eqs. (6-52) and (6-59) and equating them yields

$$Q_{\text{Coons}}(u, w) = Q_{\text{Bézier}}(u, w)$$

$$[U][N_C][P][N_C]^T[W] = [U][N_B][B][N_B]^T[W]$$

where $[N_C]$ is given by Eq. (5-76) and $[N_B]$ by Eq. (5-70). Hence the bicubic Coons surface geometric matrix $[P]$ is given in terms of the Bézier surface polygon net as

$$[P] = [N_C]^{-1}[N_B][B][N_B]^T\left[[N_C]^T\right]^{-1}$$

or

$$
\begin{bmatrix}
P(0,0) & P(0,1) & P_w(0,0) & P_w(0,1) \\
P(1,0) & P(1,1) & P_w(1,0) & P_w(1,1) \\
P_u(0,0) & P_u(0,1) & P_{uw}(0,0) & P_{uw}(0,1) \\
P_u(1,0) & P_u(1,1) & P_{uw}(1,0) & P_{uw}(1,1)
\end{bmatrix}
=
\begin{bmatrix}
B_{0,0} & & B_{0,3} \\
B_{3,0} & & B_{3,3} \\
3(B_{1,0} - B_{0,0}) & & 3(B_{1,3} - B_{0,3}) \\
3(B_{3,0} - B_{2,0}) & & 3(B_{3,3} - B_{2,3})
\end{bmatrix}
$$

$$
\left.
\begin{matrix}
3(B_{0,1} - B_{0,0}) & 3(B_{0,3} - B_{0,2}) \\
3(B_{3,1} - B_{3,0}) & 3(B_{3,3} - B_{3,2}) \\
9(B_{0,0} - B_{1,0} - B_{0,1} + B_{1,1}) & 9(B_{0,2} - B_{1,2} - B_{0,3} + B_{1,3}) \\
9(B_{2,0} - B_{3,0} - B_{2,1} + B_{3,1}) & 9(B_{2,2} - B_{3,2} - B_{2,3} + B_{3,3})
\end{matrix}
\right] \qquad (6-67)
$$

Examining the lower right $2 \times 2$ submatrix in Eq. (6-67) confirms that the center four defining polygon net vertices *influence* the twist at the bicubic Bézier patch corners. However, the twist at a corner is *controlled* by not only the center polygon vertices but also by the adjacent tangent vectors. In fact, the twist at the corner is controlled by the shape of the nonplanar quadrilateral formed by the corner, the two adjacent boundary points and the adjacent center point.

Using Eqs. (6-62) to (6-64) shows that

$$
\begin{bmatrix}
P(0,0) & P(0,1) & P_w(0,0) & P_w(0,1) \\
P(1,0) & P(1,1) & P_w(1,0) & P_w(1,1) \\
P_u(0,0) & P_u(0,1) & P_{uw}(0,0) & P_{uw}(0,1) \\
P_u(1,0) & P_u(1,1) & P_{uw}(1,0) & P_{uw}(1,1)
\end{bmatrix}
=
$$

$$
\begin{bmatrix}
Q(0,0) & Q(0,1) & Q_w(0,0) & Q_w(0,1) \\
Q(1,0) & Q(1,1) & Q_w(1,0) & Q_w(1,1) \\
Q_u(0,0) & Q_u(0,1) & Q_{uw}(0,0) & Q_{uw}(0,1) \\
Q_u(1,0) & Q_u(1,1) & Q_{uw}(1,0) & Q_{uw}(1,1)
\end{bmatrix} \qquad (6-68)
$$

Similarly the inverse relationship between $[P]$ and $[B]$ which gives the Bézier polygon net vertices in terms of the Coons bicubic surface parameters is

$$
\begin{bmatrix}
B_{0,0} & B_{0,1} & B_{0,2} & B_{0,3} \\
B_{1,0} & B_{1,1} & B_{1,2} & B_{1,3} \\
B_{2,0} & B_{2,1} & B_{2,2} & B_{2,3} \\
B_{3,0} & B_{3,1} & B_{3,2} & B_{3,3}
\end{bmatrix} =
$$

$$
\left(\tfrac{1}{3}\right)
\begin{bmatrix}
3P(0,0) & 3P(0,0)+P_w(0,0) \\
3P(0,0)+P_u(0,0) & \tfrac{1}{3}\left\{P_{uw}(0,0)+9P(0,0)-3(P_w(0,0)+P_u(0,0))\right\} \\
3P(1,0)-P_u(1,0) & \tfrac{1}{3}\left\{P_{uw}(1,0)+9P(1,0)+3(P_w(1,0)-P_u(1,0))\right\} \\
3P(1,0) & 3P(1,0)+P_w(1,0)
\end{bmatrix}
$$

$$
\begin{bmatrix}
3P(0,1)-P_w(0,1) & 3P(0,1) \\
\tfrac{1}{3}\left\{P_{uw}(0,1)+9P(0,1)+3(P_u(0,1)-P_w(0,1))\right\} & 3P(0,1)+P_u(0,1) \\
\tfrac{1}{3}\left\{P_{uw}(1,1)+9P(1,1)-3(P_u(1,1)+P_w(1,1))\right\} & 3P(1,1)-P_u(1,1) \\
3P(1,1)-P_w(1,1) & 3P(1,1)
\end{bmatrix}
$$

$$(6-69)$$

An example more fully illustrates the Bézier surface concept.

---

### Example 6–14    Bézier Surface

For the Bézier surface shown in Fig. 6–39a determine the surface point and the first derivatives in both the $u$ and $w$ parametric directions for the parameter values $u = w = 0.5$. Also determine the surface point and the derivatives for the modified surface shown in Fig. 6–39d. Compare the results (also see Prob.6–24). The $4 \times 4$ Bézier polygon vertices are

$$
[B] =
\begin{bmatrix}
[-15\ \ 0\ \ 15] & [-15\ \ 5\ \ 5] & [-15\ \ 5\ \ -5] & [-15\ \ 0\ \ -15] \\
[-5\ \ 5\ \ 15] & [-5\ \ 5\ \ 5] & [-5\ \ 5\ \ -5] & [-5\ \ 5\ \ -15] \\
[5\ \ 5\ \ 15] & [5\ \ 5\ \ 5] & [5\ \ 5\ \ -5] & [5\ \ 5\ \ -15] \\
[15\ \ 0\ \ 15] & [15\ \ 5\ \ 5] & [15\ \ 5\ \ -5] & [15\ \ 0\ \ -15]
\end{bmatrix}
$$

For the modified surface shown in Fig. 6–39d, only the $B_{1,1}[0\ \ \ 10\ \ \ 0]$ vertex changes, i.e., only the twist at the $B_{0,0}$ corner is influenced.

Recall the matrix formulation given in Eqs. (6–59) and (6–60), i.e.,

$$
Q(u,w) = [U][N][B][N]^T[W]
$$

Here

$$[N][B][N]^T = \begin{bmatrix} -1 & 3 & -3 & 1 \\ 3 & -6 & 3 & 0 \\ -3 & 3 & 0 & 0 \\ 1 & 0 & 0 & 0 \end{bmatrix} [B] \begin{bmatrix} -1 & 3 & -3 & 1 \\ 3 & -6 & 3 & 0 \\ -3 & 3 & 0 & 0 \\ 1 & 0 & 0 & 0 \end{bmatrix}$$

$$= \begin{bmatrix} [0 \ 0 \ 0] & [0 \ 0 \ 0] & [0 \ 0 \ 0] & [0 \ 0 \ 0] \\ [0 \ 0 \ 0] & [0 \ -45 \ 0] & [0 \ 45 \ 0] & [0 \ -15 \ 0] \\ [0 \ 0 \ 0] & [0 \ 45 \ 0] & [0 \ -45 \ 0] & [30 \ 15 \ 0] \\ [0 \ 0 \ 0] & [0 \ -15 \ 0] & [0 \ 15 \ -30] & [-15 \ 0 \ 15] \end{bmatrix}$$

The surface point is thus

$$Q(0.5, 0.5) = [0.125 \quad 0.25 \quad 0.5 \quad 1][N][B][N]^T \begin{bmatrix} 0.125 \\ 0.25 \\ 0.5 \\ 1 \end{bmatrix}$$

$$= [0 \quad 4.6875 \quad 0]$$

The derivatives in the parametric directions are

$$Q_u(0.5, 0.5) = [3u^2 \quad 2u \quad 1 \quad 0][N][B][N]^T \begin{bmatrix} w^3 \\ w^2 \\ w \\ 1 \end{bmatrix}$$

$$= [0.75 \quad 1 \quad 1 \quad 0][N][B][N]^T \begin{bmatrix} 0.125 \\ 0.25 \\ 0.5 \\ 1 \end{bmatrix}$$

$$= [30 \quad 0 \quad 0]$$

$$Q_w(0.5, 0.5) = [u^3 \quad u^2 \quad u \quad 1][N][B][N]^T \begin{bmatrix} 3w^2 \\ 2w \\ 1 \\ 0 \end{bmatrix}$$

$$= [0.125 \quad 0.25 \quad 0.5 \quad 1][N][B][N]^T \begin{bmatrix} 0.75 \\ 1 \\ 1 \\ 0 \end{bmatrix}$$

$$= [0 \quad 0 \quad -30]$$

Notice that $Q_u$ and $Q_w$ are orthogonal.

The modified surface of Fig. 6–39d changes only the value $B_{1,1}$ of the standard surface. The new value is $B_{1,1} [\,0 \quad 10 \quad 0\,]$. The new value of

$$[\,N\,][\,B\,][\,N\,]^T =$$

$$
\begin{bmatrix}
[\,45 \quad 45\; -45\,] & [\,-90\; -90 \quad 90\,] & [\,45 \quad 45\; -45\,] & [\,0 \quad 0 \quad 0\,] \\
[\,-90\; -90 \quad 90\,] & [\,180 \quad 135\; -180\,] & [\,-90\; -45 \quad 90\,] & [\,0\; -15 \quad 0\,] \\
[\,45 \quad 45\; -45\,] & [\,-90\; -45 \quad 90\,] & [\,45 \quad 0\; -45\,] & [\,30 \quad 15 \quad 0\,] \\
[\,0 \quad 0 \quad 0\,] & [\,0\; -15 \quad 0\,] & [\,0 \quad 15\; -30\,] & [\,-15 \quad 0 \quad 15\,]
\end{bmatrix}
$$

The new surface point at $u = w = 0.5$ is

$$Q(0.5, 0.5) = [\,0.703 \quad 5.391 \quad -0.703\,]$$

The new parametric derivatives at $u = w = 0.5$ are

$$Q_u(0.5, 0.5) = [\,28.594 \quad -1.406 \quad 1.406\,]$$

$$Q_w(0.5, 0.5) = [\,-1.406 \quad -1.406 \quad -28.594\,]$$

Here, notice that since the defining polygon net is no longer symmetrical about the $y$-axis, the surface is no longer symmetrical about the $y$-axis. Further, notice that although $Q_u$ and $Q_w$ are still orthogonal, both their magnitudes and directions are different. These results show that the twist vector at a single corner has a subtle, but significant, influence on the shape of the entire surface.

---

The above discussion of Bézier surfaces concentrates on the definition and characteristics of a single surface patch. For more complex surfaces multiple Bézier surface patches must be joined together. A complete discussion is beyond the scope of this text. The interested reader is referred to Refs. 6–24 and 6–25. The difficulties of joining Bézier surface patches while maintaining continuity across the edges is illustrated by considering joining two bicubic Bézier surface patches along a single edge as shown in Fig. 6–41.

For positional or $C^0$ continuity along the edge it is necessary for the two boundary curves and hence the two boundary polygons along the edge to be coincident.† To maintain slope or tangent vector or $C^1$ continuity across the patch boundary the surface normal direction along the boundary edge must be the same for both patches. Two conditions may be used to achieve this. The first requires that the four polygon net lines that meet at and cross the boundary edge be colinear as shown by the heavy lines in Fig. 6–41a. The second less restrictive condition requires that only the three polygon net edges meeting at the ends of the boundary curve be coplanar as shown by the heavy lines in Fig. 6–41b.

---

† Recall the discussion in Sec. 5–8 on the continuity of Bézier curve segments.

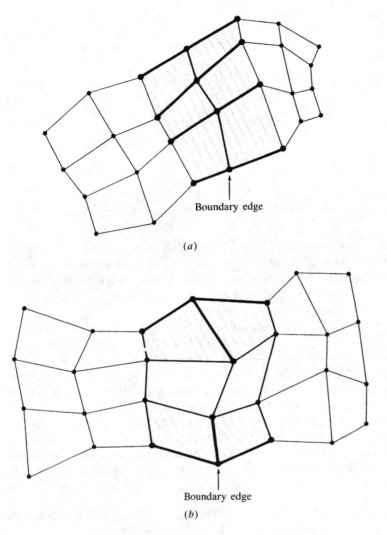

Figure 6–41   Continuity across Bézier surface patches.   (a) Net lines colinear; (b) polygon edges coplanar.

## 6–12   B-SPLINE SURFACES

The natural extension of the Bézier surface is the Cartesian product B-spline surface defined by

$$Q(u, w) = \sum_{i=1}^{n+1} \sum_{j=1}^{m+1} B_{i,j} N_{i,k}(u) M_{j,l}(w) \qquad (6 - 70)$$

where $N_{i,k}(u)$ and $M_{j,l}(w)$ are the B-spline basis functions in the biparametric $u$ and $w$ directions, respectively (see Eq. 5–84). The definition for the basis functions given previously in Sec. 5–9 is repeated here for convenience.

$$N_{i,1}(u) = \begin{cases} 1 & \text{if } x_i \leq u < x_{i+1} \\ 0 & \text{otherwise} \end{cases} \qquad (5-84a)$$

$$N_{i,k}(u) = \frac{(u-x_i)N_{i,k-1}(u)}{x_{i+k-1}-x_i} + \frac{(x_{i+k}-u)N_{i+1,k-1}(u)}{x_{i+k}-x_{i+1}} \qquad (5-84b)$$

and

$$M_{j,1}(w) = \begin{cases} 1 & \text{if } y_j \leq w < y_{j+1} \\ 0 & \text{otherwise} \end{cases} \qquad (5-84a)$$

$$M_{j,l}(w) = \frac{(w-y_j)M_{j,l-1}(w)}{y_{j+l-1}-y_j} + \frac{(y_{j+l}-w)M_{j+1,l-1}(w)}{y_{j+l}-y_{j+1}} \qquad (5-84b)$$

where the $x_i$ and $y_j$ are elements of knot vectors as discussed in Sec. 5–9. Again, the $B_{i,j}$'s are the vertices of a defining polygon net. For quadrilateral surface 'patches' the defining polygon net must be topologically rectangular. The indices $n$ and $m$ are one less than the number of defining polygon vertices in the $u$ and $w$ parametric directions, respectively.

As with B-spline curves the shape and character of a B-spline surface is significantly influenced by the knot vectors $[X]$ and $[Y]$. Open, periodic and nonuniform knot vectors are used. Although it is common to use the same type of knot vector in both parametric directions, it is not required. For example, it is possible to use an open knot vector and its associated B-spline basis functions for one parametric direction and a periodic knot vector and its associated B-spline basis functions for the other. A practical example is a cylindrical surface of varying cross-sectional area.

Because the B-spline basis is used to describe both the boundary curves and to blend the interior of the surface, several properties of the B-spline surface are immediately known:

The maximum order of the surface in each parametric direction is equal to the number of defining polygon vertices in that direction.

The continuity of the surface in each parametric direction is two less than the order in each direction; i.e., $C^{k-2}$ and $C^{l-2}$ in the $u$ and $w$ directions, respectively.

The surface is invariant with respect to an affine transformation; i.e., the surface is transformed by transforming the defining polygon net.

The variation diminishing property for B-spline surfaces is currently not known.

The influence of a single polygon net vertex is limited to $\pm k/2$, $\pm l/2$ spans in each parametric direction.

If the number of defining polygon net vertices is equal to the order in each parametric direction and there are no interior knot values, then the B-spline surface reduces to a Bézier surface (see Fig. 6–39).

If triangulated, the defining polygon net forms a planar approximation to the surface.

The surface lies within the convex hull of the defining polygon net formed by taking the union of all convex hulls of $k, l$ neighboring polygon net vertices.

Recalling the previous discussion of the convex hull properties of B-spline curves (see Sec. 5–9) immediately shows that as a consequence of these strong convex hull properties a B-spline surface can contain imbedded flat regions and lines of sharp discontinuity. This is a particularly desirable characteristic for many design situations. Figures 6–42a to d show a series of open B-spline surfaces and their defining polygon nets that are third-order in each parametric direction. Notice that each of the defining polygon net lines in the $w$ direction is a straight line with four vertices. The resulting surface is ruled in the $w$ direction. The B-spline surface shown in Fig. 6–42a, defined by four polygon net vertices in the $u$ direction, is smoothly curved in that direction.

The B-spline surface shown in Fig. 6–42b is defined by five polygon net vertices in the $u$ direction. The three central vertices are colinear. Notice that the center of the resulting surface is flat. Similarly, five of the seven defining polygon net vertices in the $u$ direction for the surface shown in Fig. 6–42c are colinear. Again, the surface is flat in the central region. The flat area is larger than in Fig. 6–42b.

Figure 6–42d shows that these very strong convex hull properties extend to both parametric directions. Thus, a flat region can be imbedded in the interior of a sculptured surface. The flat region becomes smaller as the order of the surface increases.

Figure 6–43 illustrates the effect of coincident net lines. In Figure 6–43a three coincident net lines are used to generate a hard line or knuckle in the center of a fourth-order B-spline surface. Figure 6–43b shows the result when three coincident net lines are used in *both* parametric directions. Here, the fourth-order B-spline surface contains two ridges that rise to a point in the center of the surface. As with B-spline curves, a hard line or knuckle is formed if $k - 1$ or $l - 1$ net lines are coincident. Further, because a B-spline surface is everywhere $C^{k-2}/C^{l-2}$ continuous, it is continuous at the hard line or knuckle. In addition, this property insures that the transition from curved surface to flat surface is also $C^{k-2}/C^{l-2}$ continuous.

The excellent local control properties of B-spline curves (see Sec. 5–9) carry over to B-spline surfaces. An example is shown in Fig. 6–44. Here, an open bicubic $(k = l = 4)$ B-spline surface is defined by a $9 \times 9$ $(m = n = 8)$ polygon net. The polygon net, shown as the upper surface in Fig. 6–44, is flat except for the center point. The open knot vector in both parametric directions is $[0\ 0\ 0\ 0\ 1\ 2\ 3\ 4\ 5\ 6\ 6\ 6\ 6]$. Thus, there are six parametric spans in each direction, i.e., $0 - 1$, $1 - 2$, $\cdots$, $5 - 6$. Each parametric quadrilateral, e.g., $0 \le u \le 1$, $0 \le w \le 1$, forms a B-spline surface subpatch.† The

---

†Some authors designate each subpatch as a B-spline surface. Here, the surface is considered the entity defined by the complete polygon net taken as an entity.

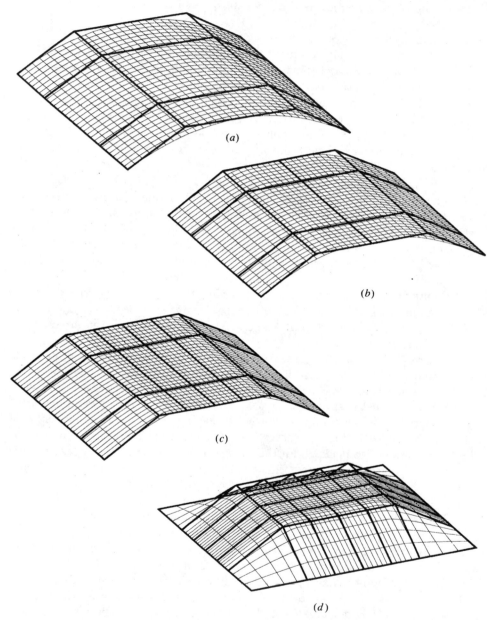

**Figure 6–42** Third-order B-spline surfaces. (a) Smooth ruled surface; (b) small interior flat region caused by three colinear net vertices in $u$; (c) larger interior flat region caused by five colinear net vertices in $u$; (d) flat region imbedded within a sculptured surface.

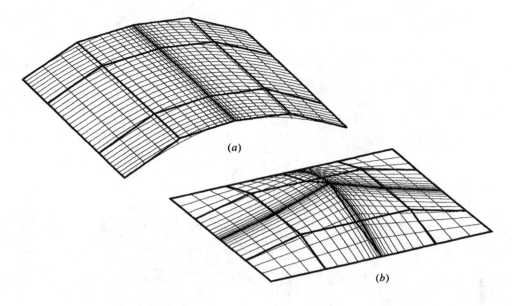

(a)

(b)

**Figure 6–43**    Fourth-order B-spline surfaces with multiple coincident net lines.

middle surface shown in Fig. 6–44 is composed of parametric lines at the ends of each parametric interval, i.e., at $u, w = 0, 1, 2, 3, 4, 5, 6$. Each quadrilateral represents a subpatch. Notice that the influence of the displaced point is confined to $\pm k/2, l/2$ spans or subpatches.

The parametric derivatives of a B-spline surface are obtained by formally

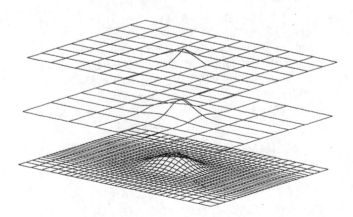

**Figure 6–44**    Local control in B-spline surfaces.

differentiating Eq. (6–70) to yield

$$Q_u(u, w) = \sum_{i=1}^{n+1} \sum_{j=1}^{m+1} B_{i,j} N'_{i,k}(u) M_{j,l}(w) \tag{6 – 71}$$

$$Q_w(u, w) = \sum_{i=1}^{n+1} \sum_{j=1}^{m+1} B_{i,j} N_{i,k}(u) M'_{j,l}(w) \tag{6 – 72}$$

$$Q_{uw}(u, w) = \sum_{i=1}^{n+1} \sum_{j=1}^{m+1} B_{i,j} N'_{i,k}(u) M'_{j,l}(w) \tag{6 – 73}$$

$$Q_{uu}(u, w) = \sum_{i=1}^{n+1} \sum_{j=1}^{m+1} B_{i,j} N''_{i,k}(u) M_{j,l}(w) \tag{6 – 74}$$

$$Q_{ww}(u, w) = \sum_{i=1}^{n+1} \sum_{j=1}^{m+1} B_{i,j} N_{i,k}(u) M''_{j,l}(w) \tag{6 – 75}$$

where the prime denotes differentiation with respect to the appropriate parameter. The derivatives of the B-spline basis functions are given by Eqs. (5–97) to (5–100).

An example illustrates the method for calculating a B-spline surface.

---

### Example 6–15    Calculating an Open B-spline Surface

Consider the B-spline surface defined by the $4 \times 4$ polygon net:

$B_{1,1}\,[\,-15\ \ 0\ \ 15\,]$     $B_{2,1}\,[\,-5\ \ 5\ \ 15\,]$     $B_{3,1}\,[\,5\ \ 5\ \ 15\,]$     $B_{4,1}\,[\,15\ \ 0\ \ 15\,]$
$B_{1,2}\,[\,-15\ \ 5\ \ 5\,]$     $B_{2,2}\,[\,-5\ \ 10\ \ 5\,]$     $B_{3,2}\,[\,5\ \ 10\ \ 5\,]$     $B_{4,2}\,[\,15\ \ 5\ \ 5\,]$
$B_{1,3}\,[\,-15\ \ 5\ \ -5\,]$     $B_{2,3}\,[\,-5\ \ 10\ \ -5\,]$     $B_{3,3}\,[\,5\ \ 10\ \ -5\,]$     $B_{4,3}\,[\,15\ \ 5\ \ -5\,]$
$B_{1,4}\,[\,-15\ \ 0\ \ -15\,]$     $B_{2,4}\,[\,-5\ \ 5\ \ -15\,]$     $B_{3,4}\,[\,5\ \ 5\ \ -15\,]$     $B_{4,4}\,[\,15\ \ 0\ \ -15\,]$

The surface is fourth-order in the $u$ direction ($k = 4$) and third-order in the $w$ direction ($l = 3$). Thus, the surface is composed of two subpatches: one for $0 \le u \le 1, 0 \le w \le 1$ and the other for $0 \le u \le 1, 1 \le w \le 2$. Determine the surface point at the center of the surface, i.e., at $u = 1/2, w = 1$.

Writing out Eq. (6–70) yields

$$Q(u, w) = \sum_{i=1}^{4} \sum_{j=1}^{4} B_{i,j} N_{i,4}(u) M_{j,3}(w)$$

$$= N_{1,4}(B_{1,1}M_{1,3} + B_{1,2}M_{2,3} + B_{1,3}M_{3,3} + B_{1,4}M_{4,3})$$

$$+ N_{2,4}(B_{2,1}M_{1,3} + B_{2,2}M_{2,3} + B_{2,3}M_{3,3} + B_{2,4}M_{4,3})$$

$$+ N_{3,4}(B_{3,1}M_{1,3} + B_{3,2}M_{2,3} + B_{3,3}M_{3,3} + B_{3,4}M_{4,3})$$

$$+ N_{4,4}(B_{4,1}M_{1,3} + B_{4,2}M_{2,3} + B_{4,3}M_{3,3} + B_{4,4}M_{4,3})$$

Here, the knot vector in the $u$ direction is $[X] = [0\ \ 0\ \ 0\ \ 0\ \ 1\ \ 1\ \ 1\ \ 1]$.
Recalling Ex. (5–12) yields the basis functions; i.e.,

$$N_{1,4}\left(\frac{1}{2}\right) = (1-u)^3 = \left(\frac{1}{2}\right)^3 = \frac{1}{8}$$

$$N_{2,4}\left(\frac{1}{2}\right) = 3u(1-u)^2 = (3)\left(\frac{1}{2}\right)\left(\frac{1}{2}\right)^2 = \frac{3}{8}$$

$$N_{3,4}\left(\frac{1}{2}\right) = 3u^2(1-u) = (3)\left(\frac{1}{2}\right)^2\left(\frac{1}{2}\right) = \frac{3}{8}$$

$$N_{4,4}\left(\frac{1}{2}\right) = u^3 = \left(\frac{1}{2}\right)^3 = \frac{1}{8}$$

Similarly, the knot vector in the $w$ direction is $[Y] = [0\ \ 0\ \ 0\ \ 1\ \ 2\ \ 2\ \ 2]$.
Recalling Ex. (5–10) yields the basis functions; i.e.,

$$M_{1,3}(1) = 0$$

$$M_{2,3}(1) = \frac{(2-w)^2}{2} = \frac{(2-1)^2}{2} = \frac{1}{2}$$

$$M_{3,3}(1) = \frac{(2-w)(3w-2)}{2} = \frac{(2-1)(3-2)}{2} = \frac{1}{2}$$

$$M_{4,3}(1) = (w-1)^2 = (1-1) = 0$$

Thus

$$Q(1/2, 1) = \frac{1}{8}\{(0)B_{1,1} + \frac{1}{2}B_{1,2} + \frac{1}{2}B_{1,3} + (0)B_{1,4}\}$$

$$+ \frac{3}{8}\{(0)B_{2,1} + \frac{1}{2}B_{2,2} + \frac{1}{2}B_{2,3} + (0)B_{2,4}\}$$

$$+ \frac{3}{8}\{(0)B_{3,1} + \frac{1}{2}B_{3,2} + \frac{1}{2}B_{3,3} + (0)B_{3,4}\}$$

$$+ \frac{1}{8}\{(0)B_{4,1} + \frac{1}{2}B_{4,2} + \frac{1}{2}B_{4,3} + (0)B_{4,4}\}$$

$$Q(1/2, 1) = \frac{1}{16}(B_{1,2} + B_{1,3}) + \frac{3}{16}(B_{2,2} + B_{2,3})$$

$$+ \frac{3}{16}(B_{3,2} + B_{3,3}) + \frac{1}{16}(B_{4,2} + B_{4,3})$$

$$= \frac{1}{16}\{[-15\ \ 5\ \ 5] + [-15\ \ 5\ \ -5]\}$$

$$+ \frac{3}{16}\{[-5\ \ 10\ \ 5] + [-5\ \ 10\ \ -5]\}$$

$$+ \frac{3}{16}\{[5\ \ 10\ \ 5] + [5\ \ 10\ \ -5]\}$$

$$+ \frac{1}{16}[15\ \ 5\ \ 5] + [15\ \ 5\ \ -5]\}$$

$$= [0\ \ 35/4\ \ 0]$$

Periodic B-spline surfaces are easily generated using periodic knot vectors to obtain periodic basis functions for use in Eq. (6–70). Figure 6–45 shows several examples of periodic B-spline surfaces formed by open defining polygon nets. The defining polygon nets for Figs. 6–45a and b correspond to that of Figs. 6–42a and c and that of Fig. 6–45c to Fig. 6–43b. Notice that in each case, as for periodic B-spline curves, because of the reduced parameter range used for periodic B-spline basis functions, the edge of the surface and the polygon edge do not coincide.

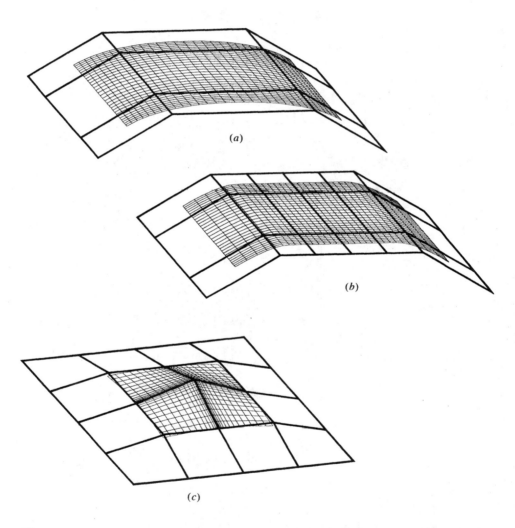

(a)

(b)

(c)

**Figure 6–45**  Periodic B-spline surfaces for open defining polygons. (a) Third-order smooth ruled surface; (b) third-order large interior flat region caused by five colinear net vertices in $u$; (c) point in a fourth-order surface caused by multiple intersecting net lines.

Closed periodic B-spline surfaces exhibit properties analogous to closed periodic B-spline curves. Figure 6–46 shows examples of three third-order surfaces. The defining polygon net for Fig. 6–46a is formed by equally spacing the defining polygon for the closed B-spline curve of Fig. 5–46b along the $z$-axis from $z = -8$ to $z = 8$. The result is a cylindrical surface. Notice that the surface does not touch the planes of the first and last defining polygon. The defining polygon for Fig. 6–46b is obtained by increasing the $x$ and $y$ dimensions of the second and fourth defining polygons of Fig. 6–46a by one. The result is a wavy cylinder. Figure 6–46c shows the local effect of perturbing a single polygon net vertex.

It is possible to combine open and periodic B-spline basis functions in Eq. (6–70). Two examples of the results are shown in Fig. 6–47. Here an open knot vector and basis function are used in one parametric direction and a periodic knot vector and basis function in the other parametric direction. Figure 6–47a shows a combined B-spline surface defined by the open polygon net of Fig. 6–42a. Figure 6–47b shows a combined B-spline surface defined by the closed polygonal net of Fig. 6–46b. Notice that the surface is coincident with the end polygon net lines in the $u$ direction. This characteristic is useful in some design situations.

A matrix formulation for periodic B-spline surfaces is of the form

$$Q_{s,t} = [\, U^* \,][\, N^* \,][\, B_{s,t}^* \,][\, M^* \,]^T [\, W^* \,]^T \qquad (6-76)$$

where $[\, U^* \,]$ and $[\, W^* \,]$ are the reparameterized parametric variables on the intervals $0 \le u^* \le 1$ and $0 \le w^* \le 1$ given in Eq. (5–90). $[\, N^* \,]$ and $[\, M^* \,]$ are given by Eq. (5–91). The matrix $[\, B_{s,t}^* \,]$ represents a $k \times l$ sliding net of defining polygon vertices which define a subpatch on the surface. For periodic B-spline surfaces defined by open polygonal nets

$$[\, B_{s,t}^* \,] = [\, B_{i,j} \,] \qquad (6-77)$$

where
$$1 \le s \le n - k + 2 \quad s \le i \le s + k - 1$$

$$1 \le t \le m - l + 2 \quad t \le j \le t + l - 1 \qquad (6-78)$$

and $B_{i,j}$ represents individual elements of the defining polygon net.

For polygonal nets closed along $u = 0$, i.e., with the first and last net lines in the $u$ direction coincident, the sliding net is given by[†]

$$1 \le s \le n - k + 2$$

$$1 \le t \le m + l$$

$$s \le i \le s + k - 1$$

$$j \in [\{(t - 1) \bmod (m + 1)\} + 1 \; : \; (t + l - 2) \bmod (m + 1) + 1] \qquad (6-79)$$

---

[†] $j \in [a : b]$ means in the set $a \ldots b$. Here the polygon vertex lists must be considered as circular. For example, if $m + 1 = 4$, then $j \in [3 : 2]$ means in the set $3, 4, 1, 2$ in that order.

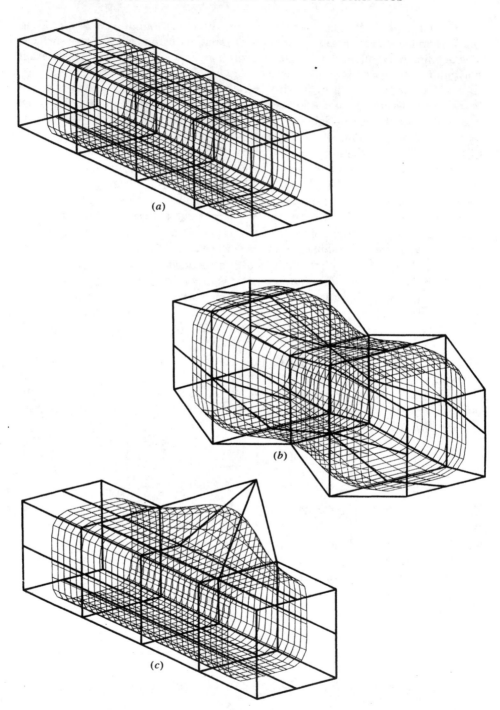

**Figure 6–46**   Closed periodic B-spline surfaces. (a) Straight cylindrical surface; (b) perturbed wavy cylindrical surface; (c) effect of perturbing a single net vertex.

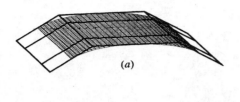

(a)

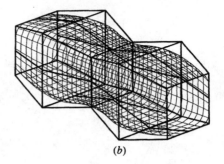

(b)

**Figure 6–47**    Third-order combined B-spline surfaces. (a) Open polygon net; (b) closed polygon net.

Similarly, for polygonal nets closed along $w = 0$ the sliding net is given by

$$1 \leq s \leq n + 1$$

$$1 \leq t \leq m - l + 2$$

$$i \in [\{(s - 1) \bmod (n + 1)\} + 1 \ : \ (s + k - 2) \bmod (n + 1) + 1]$$

$$t \leq j \leq t + l - 1 \tag{6 - 80}$$

Finally, for polygonal nets closed along both $u = 0$ and $w = 0$ the sliding net is given by

$$1 \leq s \leq n - k + 2$$

$$1 \leq t \leq m - l + 2$$

$$i \in [\{(s - 1) \bmod (n + 1)\} + 1 \ : \ (s + k - 2) \bmod (n + 1) + 1]$$

$$j \in [\{(t - 1) \bmod (m + 1)\} + 1 \ : \ (t + l - 2) \bmod (m + 1) + 1] \tag{6 - 81}$$

Here a completely closed surface is formed. An example is shown in Fig. 6–48. The defining polygon net shown in Fig. 6–48a is formed by translating the defining polygon vertices for the periodic B-spline curve of Fig. 5–47 $-2$ units in $x$ and $+4$ units in $y$ and then rotating 360° about the $x$-axis in increments of 45°. The closed periodic bicubic ($k = l = 4$) B-spline surface shown in Fig. 6–48b is toroidal in shape.

The matrix formulation for open B-spline surfaces is of the same form as Eq. (6–76). However, as with the matrix formulation for open B-spline curves, the existence of multiple knot values at the ends of the knot vector makes the result both less compact and less useful than for periodic B-spline surfaces. Consequently, the details are not given here.

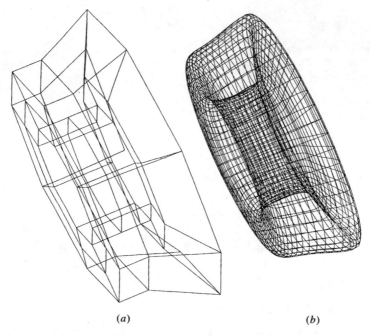

$(a)$                                          $(b)$

**Figure 6–48**   Closed toroidal bicubic ($k = l = 4$) B-spline surface. (a) Defining polygon net; (b) surface.

## 6–13   B-SPLINE SURFACE FITTING

The previous sections discussed the characteristics and generation of B-spline surfaces from a known defining polygon net. The inverse problem is also of interest; i.e., given a known set of data on a surface, determine the defining polygon net for a B-spline surface that best interpolates that data. Since the edges of the surface represented by the data are generally known, only open B-spline surfaces are considered here. Development of an analogous method for closed surfaces using periodic B-spline surfaces is obvious. Here the discussion is confined to topologically rectangular nets; i.e., the data can *conceptually* be arranged to occupy the intersections of a rectangular grid. The problem is shown schematically in Fig. 6–49 where a 4 × 4 defining polygon net for an 8 × 8 data matrix is illustrated. This problem has been studied by Rogers and Satterfield (Ref. 6–5) and by Barsky and Greenberg (Ref. 6–26). Barsky and Greenberg exploited the known characteristics of bicubic B-spline surfaces to obtain additional computational efficiencies. The approach taken here is more straight forward but less computationally efficient (see Sec. 5–11).

Recall Eq. (6–70) and note that here the $Q(u, w)$'s are the known surface data points. The $N_{i,k}(u)$ and $M_{j,l}(w)$ basis functions can be determined for a known order and a known number of defining polygon net vertices in each

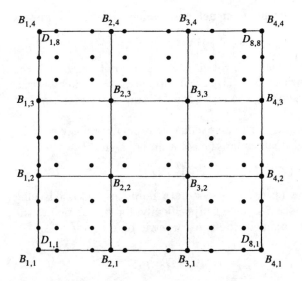

**Figure 6-49**    Determining a B-spline surface from a known data set.

parametric direction provided that the parametric values $u, w$ are known at the surface data points. Hence, for each known surface data point Eq. (6-70) provides a linear equation in the unknown defining polygon net vertices $B_{i,j}$. Writing Eq. (6-70) out for a single surface data point yields

$$D_{1,1}(u_1, w_1) =$$
$$N_{1,k}(u_1)[M_{1,l}(w_1)B_{1,1} + M_{2,l}(w_1)B_{1,2} + \cdots + M_{m+1,l}(w_1)B_{1,m+1}] +$$
$$\vdots$$
$$N_{n+1,k}(u_1)[M_{1,l}(w_1)B_{n+1,1} + M_{2,l}(w_1)B_{n+1,2} + \cdots + M_{m+1,l}(w_1)B_{n+1,m+1}]$$

where for an $r \times s$ topologically rectangular set of data $2 \leq k \leq n+1 \leq r$ and $2 \leq l \leq m+1 \leq s$. Writing an equation of this form for each data point yields a system of simultaneous equations. In matrix form the result is

$$[D] = [C][B] \qquad\qquad (6-82)$$

where $C_{i,j} = N_{i,k}M_{j,l}$. For $r \times s$ topologically rectangular surface point data, $[D]$ is an $r * s \times 3$ matrix containing the three-dimensional coordinates of the surface point data, $[C]$ is an $r * s \times n * m$ matrix of the products of the B-spline basis functions, and $[B]$ is an $n * m \times 3$ matrix of the three-dimensional coordinates of the required polygon net points.

If $[C]$ is square, the defining polygon net is obtained directly by matrix inversion, i.e.,

$$[B] = [C]^{-1}[D] \tag{6-83}$$

In this case the resulting surface passes through each data point. Although the resulting surface will be everywhere $C^{k-2}, C^{l-2}$ continuous, it may not be fair. Experience has shown that, in general, the fewer the defining polygon net points the fairer the surface.

If $[C]$ is not square the problem is overspecified and a solution can only be obtained in some mean sense. In particular the solution is given by

$$[B] = [[C]^T[C]]^{-1}[C]^T[D] \tag{6-84}$$

The $u$ and $w$ parametric values for each surface data point are obtained using a chord length approximation (see Sec. 5–11). Specifically, for $r$ data points the parameter value at the $l$th data point in the $u$ parametric direction is

$$u_1 = 0 \qquad \frac{u_l}{u_{\max}} = \frac{\displaystyle\sum_{g=2}^{l} |D_{g,s} - D_{g-1,s}|}{\displaystyle\sum_{g=2}^{r} |D_{g,s} - D_{g-1,s}|}$$

Similarly, for $s$ data points in the $w$ parametric direction

$$w_1 = 0 \qquad \frac{w_l}{w_{\max}} = \frac{\displaystyle\sum_{g=2}^{l} |D_{r,g} - D_{r,g-1}|}{\displaystyle\sum_{g=2}^{s} |D_{r,g} - D_{r,g-1}|}$$

where $u_{\max}$ and $w_{\max}$ are the maximum values of the appropriate knot vectors. Figure 6–50a shows surface data and the defining polygon net generated using this technique. Figure 6–50b shows the B-spline surface generated from this net.

As previously pointed out for B-spline curve fitting (see Sec. 5–11), neither this technique, nor that of Ref. 6–5, can yield hard points or hard lines (discontinuities in the first or second derivatives) in the resulting surface.

Notice from Fig. 6–50 that the defining polygon net vertices obtained using Eq. (6–84) lie anywhere in the three-dimensional plane. If the surface is to subsequently be modified, this is inconvenient. Rogers and Fog (Ref. 6–27) have developed a technique for iterating on the parametric values $u, w$ that confines the defining polygon net vertices to lie in planes or along lines in three space.

## 6–14   B-SPLINE SURFACE SUBDIVISION

A B-spline surface is subdivided by separately subdividing each defining polygon net line in one or both parametric directions. Any of the B-spline curve subdivision techniques can be used (see Sec. 5–12). The technique is best illustrated by an example.

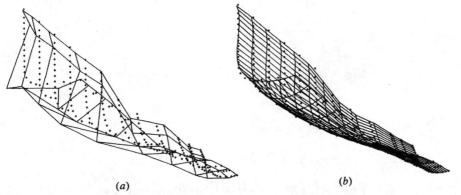

(a)                                                  (b)

**Figure 6–50**    B-spline surface fit. (a) Data points and fit defining polygon net; (b) data points and generated surface.

---

### Example 6–16    Subdivision of an Open B-spline Surface

Consider the open B-spline surface defined by the $4 \times 4$ polygon net:

$B_{1,1}[\,-15\ \ 0\ \ 15\,]$    $B_{2,1}[\,-5\ \ 5\ \ 15\,]$    $B_{3,1}[\,5\ \ 5\ \ 15\,]$    $B_{4,1}[\,15\ \ 0\ \ 15\,]$

$B_{1,2}[\,-15\ \ 5\ \ 5\,]$    $B_{2,2}[\,-5\ \ 10\ \ 5\,]$    $B_{3,2}[\,5\ \ 10\ \ 5\,]$    $B_{4,2}[\,15\ \ 5\ \ 5\,]$

$B_{1,3}[\,-15\ \ 5\ \ -5\,]$    $B_{2,3}[\,-5\ \ 10\ \ -5\,]$    $B_{3,3}[\,5\ \ 10\ \ -5\,]$    $B_{4,3}[\,15\ \ 5\ \ -5\,]$

$B_{1,4}[\,-15\ \ 0\ \ -15\,]$    $B_{2,4}[\,-5\ \ 5\ \ -15\,]$    $B_{3,4}[\,5\ \ 5\ \ -15\,]$    $B_{4,4}[\,15\ \ 0\ \ -15\,]$

The surface is fourth-order in both parametric directions ($k = l = 4$). The surface is composed of a single patch with parameter ranges $0 \le u \le 1$, $0 \le w \le 1$. Subdivide the surface into 4 subpatches. Maintain a uniform open knot vector.

Recalling [ 0  0  0  0  1  1  1  1 ], the knot vector in both parametric directions given in Sec. 5–12 and Ex. 5–18, and reparameterizing it to [ 0  0  0  0  2  2  2  2 ], the surface is subdivided by inserting a knot value of 1 in the interval $0 \to 2$. Thus, the new knot vector is given by [ 0  0  0  0  1  2  2  2  2 ]. Applying Eqs. (5–119) and (5–120) to each of the polygon net lines in both directions yields the defining polygon net for the subdivided surface. For example, consider the subdivision of the net line in the $w$ direction defined by $B_{1,j}$, $1 \le j \le 4$. Here, only

$$\alpha'_{4,1} = \alpha'_{4,2} = \alpha'_{4,3} = \alpha'_{4,4} = \alpha'_{4,5} = 1$$

are nonzero.

Using Eqs. (5–120) then yields

$$\alpha^2_{3,1} = \alpha^2_{3,2} = \alpha^2_{3,3} = \alpha^2_{3,5} = 1; \qquad \alpha^2_{3,4} = \alpha^2_{4,4} = 1/2$$

$$\alpha^3_{2,1} = \alpha^3_{2,2} = \alpha^3_{3,5} = 1; \qquad \alpha^3_{2,3} = \alpha^3_{3,3} = \alpha^3_{3,4} = \alpha^3_{4,4} = 1/2$$

$$\alpha^4_{1,1} = \alpha^4_{3,5} = 1; \qquad \alpha^4_{1,2} = \alpha^4_{2,2} = \alpha^4_{2,3} = \alpha^4_{3,3} = \alpha^4_{3,4} = \alpha^4_{4,4} = 1/2$$

Equation (5–119) then yields the new defining polygon vertices. In particular,

$$C_{1,1} = \alpha_{1,1}^4 B_{1,1} + \alpha_{2,1}^4 B_{1,2} + \alpha_{3,1}^4 B_{1,3} + \alpha_{4,1}^4 B_{1,4}$$

$$= B_{1,1} = [\,-15 \quad 0 \quad 15\,]$$

$$C_{1,2} = \alpha_{1,2}^4 B_{1,1} + \alpha_{2,2}^4 B_{1,2} + \alpha_{3,2}^4 B_{1,3} + \alpha_{4,2}^4 B_{1,4}$$

$$= \frac{1}{2}(B_{1,1} + B_{1,2}) = [\,-15 \quad 2.5 \quad 10\,]$$

$$C_{1,3} = \alpha_{1,3}^4 B_{1,1} + \alpha_{2,3}^4 B_{1,2} + \alpha_{3,3}^4 B_{1,3} + \alpha_{4,3}^4 B_{1,4}$$

$$= \frac{1}{2}(B_{1,2} + B_{1,3}) = [\,-15 \quad 5 \quad 0\,]$$

$$C_{1,4} = \alpha_{1,4}^4 B_{1,1} + \alpha_{2,4}^4 B_{1,2} + \alpha_{3,4}^4 B_{1,3} + \alpha_{4,4}^4 B_{1,4}$$

$$= \frac{1}{2}(B_{1,3} + B_{1,4}) = [\,-15 \quad 2.5 \quad -10\,]$$

$$C_{1,5} = \alpha_{1,5}^4 B_{1,1} + \alpha_{2,5}^4 B_{1,2} + \alpha_{3,5}^4 B_{1,3} + \alpha_{4,5}^4 B_{1,4}$$

$$= B_{1,4} = [\,-15 \quad 0 \quad -15\,]$$

After performing the same operation on each of the net lines in the $w$ direction, the defining $4 \times 5$ polygon net for the surface, which consists of two subpatches in the $w$ direction and one in the $u$ direction, is

$C_{1,1}\,[-15\ 0\ 15]$　　$C_{2,1}\,[-5\ 5\ 15]$　　$C_{3,1}\,[5\ 5\ 15]$　　$C_{4,1}\,[15\ 0\ 15]$
$C_{1,2}\,[-15\ 2.5\ 10]$　$C_{2,2}\,[-5\ 7.5\ 10]$　$C_{3,2}\,[5\ 7.5\ 10]$　$C_{4,2}\,[15\ 2.5\ 10]$
$C_{1,3}\,[-15\ 5\ 0]$　　$C_{2,3}\,[-5\ 10\ 0]$　　$C_{3,3}\,[5\ 10\ 0]$　　$C_{4,3}\,[15\ 5\ 0]$
$C_{1,4}\,[-15\ 2.5\ -10]$ $C_{2,4}\,[-5\ 7.5\ -10]$ $C_{3,4}\,[5\ 7.5\ -10]$ $C_{4,4}\,[15\ 2.5\ -10]$
$C_{1,5}\,[-15\ 0\ -15]$　$C_{2,5}\,[-5\ 5\ -15]$　$C_{3,5}\,[5\ 5\ -15]$　$C_{4,5}\,[15\ 0\ -15]$

The $\alpha_{i,j}^k$'s given above also apply when subdividing the surface in the $u$ direction. The $5 \times 4$ defining polygon net is then

$C_{1,1}\,[-15\ 0\ 15]$　　$C_{2,1}\,[-10\ 2.5\ 15]$
$C_{1,2}\,[-15\ 5\ 5]$　　$C_{2,2}\,[-10\ 7.5\ 5]$
$C_{1,3}\,[-15\ 5\ -5]$　$C_{2,3}\,[-10\ 7.5\ -5]$
$C_{1,4}\,[-15\ 0\ -15]$ $C_{2,4}\,[-10\ 2.5\ -15]$

　　　　　　　　$C_{3,1}\,[0\ 5\ 15]$　　$C_{4,1}\,[10\ 2.5\ 15]$　$C_{5,1}\,[15\ 0\ 15]$
　　　　　　　　$C_{3,2}\,[0\ 10\ 5]$　$C_{4,2}\,[10\ 7.5\ 5]$　$C_{5,2}\,[15\ 5\ 5]$
　　　　　　　　$C_{3,3}\,[0\ 10\ -5]$ $C_{4,3}\,[10\ 7.5\ -5]$ $C_{5,3}\,[15\ 5\ -5]$
　　　　　　　　$C_{3,4}\,[0\ 5\ -15]$ $C_{4,4}\,[10\ 2.5\ -15]$ $C_{5,4}\,[15\ 0\ -15]$

Here, the surface consists of two subpatches in the $u$ direction and one in the $w$ direction.

Subdividing the surface in both the $u$ and $w$ directions yields a $5 \times 5$ defining polygon net given by

$C_{1,1} [-15 \ 0 \ 15]$   $C_{2,1} [-10 \ 2.5 \ 15]$
$C_{1,2} [-15 \ 2.5 \ 10]$   $C_{2,2} [-10 \ 5 \ 10]$
$C_{1,3} [-15 \ 5 \ 0]$   $C_{2,3} [-10 \ 7.5 \ 0]$
$C_{1,4} [-15 \ 2.5 \ -10]$   $C_{2,4} [-10 \ 5 \ -10]$
$C_{1,5} [-15 \ 0 \ -15]$   $C_{2,5} [-10 \ 2.5 \ -15]$

$C_{3,1} [0 \ 5 \ 15]$   $C_{4,1} [10 \ 2.5 \ 15]$   $C_{5,1} [15 \ 0 \ 15]$
$C_{3,2} [0 \ 7.5 \ 10]$   $C_{4,2} [10 \ 5 \ 10]$   $C_{5,2} [15 \ 2.5 \ 10]$
$C_{3,3} [0 \ 10 \ 0]$   $C_{4,3} [10 \ 7.5 \ 0]$   $C_{5,3} [15 \ 5 \ 0]$
$C_{3,4} [0 \ 7.5 \ -10]$   $C_{4,4} [10 \ 5 \ -10]$   $C_{5,4} [15 \ 2.5 \ -10]$
$C_{3,5} [0 \ 5 \ -15]$   $C_{4,5} [10 \ 2.5 \ -15]$   $C_{5,5} [15 \ 0 \ -15]$

Note that this net is derivable from either of the two above using Eqs. (5–119) and (5–120).

The original surface and all three of the subdivided surface nets are shown in Fig. 6–51. Each of the surfaces is identical to the original surface.

---

Clearly, as the surface is further subdivided the defining polygon net converges to the surface.

## 6–15   GAUSSIAN CURVATURE AND SURFACE FAIRNESS

Of fundamental concern in computer aided design is development of appropriate techniques for determining and/or visualizing the fairness or smoothness of surfaces. It is well known that the bicubic surfaces (Coons, Bézier or B-spline) commonly used, although $C^2$ continuous everywhere, can exhibit unfair bumps, flat spots or undulations. Currently the best mathematical techniques for determining surface fairness use Eulerian (orthogonal) nets of minimum and maximum curvature (see Refs. 6–28 and 6–29) and of Gaussian curvature (see Refs. 6–28 to 6–32, and Sec. 6–8).

Recalling the discussion of Sec. 6–8, two combinations of the principal curvatures, called the average and the Gaussian (total) curvatures, characterize the local shape of the surface. The average curvature is

$$\kappa_a = \frac{\kappa_{min} + \kappa_{max}}{2} \qquad (6-45)$$

The Gaussian curvature is

$$\kappa_g = \kappa_{min} \cdot \kappa_{max} \qquad (6-46)$$

where $\kappa_{min}$ and $\kappa_{max}$ are the principal curvatures. The Gaussian curvature at a point on the surface indicates whether the surface is locally elliptic, hyperbolic or parabolic (Gaussian curvature positive, negative or zero).

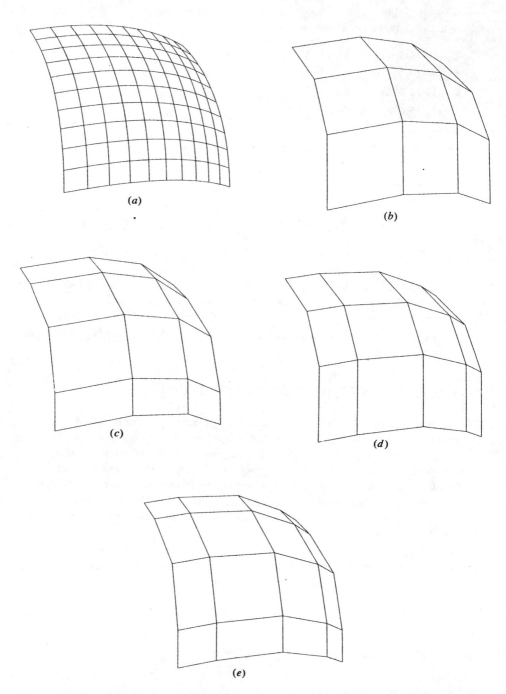

**Figure 6–51**   B-spline surface subdivision. (a) Surface; (b) original defining polygon net; (c) net subdivided in $w$; (d) net subdivided in $u$; (e) net subdivided in both $u$ and $w$.

Here it is interesting to note that if the Gaussian curvature is zero, then the surface is developable; i.e., it can be unfolded onto a plane. A developable surface is singly curved, e.g., a cone or cylinder such as a beverage can. This implies that one of the principal curvatures, $\kappa_{min}$ or $\kappa_{max}$, is zero. Hence, the Gaussian curvature is zero.

The average and Gaussian curvature for a surface can be presented using a number of techniques. If display capabilities are limited to line drawings, then contour plots are most useful (see Refs. 6–28 and 6–29). Dill (Ref. 6–30) and Dill and Rogers (Ref. 6–32) showed that color or gray scale encoded Gaussian curvature raster displays are an effective technique.

Figure 6–52 shows gray scale encoded[†] Gaussian curvature images of several test surfaces along with corresponding defining polygon and wire frame parametric representations of the surfaces. The surfaces are all bicubic ($k = l = 4$) B-spline surfaces. The three surfaces shown in Fig. 6–52 represent increasing degrees of discontinuity in the smoothness or fairness of the surface. Figure 6–52a is completely smooth and fair. In Fig. 6–52b the two pronounced ridges of decreased smoothness are caused by the three coincident polygon net lines at each end. In Fig. 6–52c the extended 'hard' line in the middle of the surface results from the three coincident polygon net lines extending across several interior polygon lines shown in the defining polygon net.

In general, the encoded Gaussian curvature images make the character of the surfaces more obvious. For example, Figs. 6–52a and b show a large negative value at the corners. This negative curvature is a result of constraining the boundaries of the surface to be straight and flat while the interior is full and positively curved. The encoded Gaussian curvature image in Fig. 6–52b emphasizes the flatness of the area between the ridges. Note that since the Gaussian curvature is zero in this region, this portion of the surface is developable. Note also that the defining polygon net in this region is developable. Finally, the band across the middle of the Gaussian encoded image in Fig. 6–52c shows that in this region the surface is a plane folded in the middle. The fact that the fold is a straight line explains the vanishing of the Gaussian curvature along the line.

An example illustrates the technique for calculating the Gaussian curvature.

---

### Example 6–17    Gaussian Curvature

Determine the Gaussian curvature at $u = 1/2$, $w = 1$ for the open B-spline surface previously defined in Ex. 6–15.

First recall the basis functions $N_{i,4}$ and $M_{j,l}$ from Ex. 6–15. From these results the first and second derivatives needed to determine $Q_u$, $Q_w$, $Q_{uw}$,

---

[†]These images are monochrome renderings of color images in Ref. 6–33. In encoding the Gaussian curvature images, curvature values at the four vertices of a dense quadrilateral approximation of the surface were averaged. The average value was assigned to each polygon. The curvature range was divided into a number of equal intervals (except at the ends) corresponding to the available intensity range. A legend giving this range is shown to the right of the image. The aliasing (staircase-like boundaries between different intensities) is due to the limited number of available intensities and *not* to the polygonal approximation.

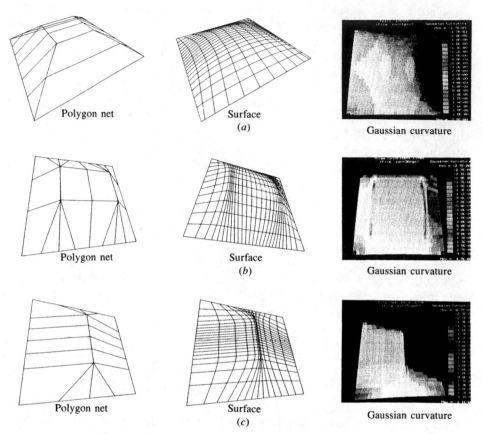

Polygon net       Surface
*(a)*       Gaussian curvature

Polygon net       Surface
*(b)*       Gaussian curvature

Polygon net       Surface
*(c)*       Gaussian curvature

**Figure 6–52**    Gaussian curvature. (a) Smooth surface; (b) short 'hard' line; (c) longer 'hard' line. (Courtesy J. C. Dill and D. F. Rogers.)

$Q_{uu}$ and $Q_{ww}$, and subsequently the Gaussian curvature, can be calculated. Specifically,

$$N_{1,4} = (1 - u)^3 \qquad N'_{1,4} = -3(1 - u)^2 \qquad N_{1,4} = 6(1 - u)$$
$$N_{2,4} = 3u(1 - u)^2 \qquad N'_{2,4} = 3(1 - u)(1 - 3u) \qquad N''_{2,4} = 6(3u - 2)$$
$$N_{3,4} = 3u^2(1 - u) \qquad N'_{3,4} = 3u(2 - 3u) \qquad N''_{3,4} = 6(1 - 3u)$$
$$N_{4,4} = u^3 \qquad N'_{4,4} = 3u^2 \qquad N''_{4,4} = 6u$$

and

$$M_{1,3} = 0 \qquad M'_{1,3} = 0 \qquad M''_{1,3} = 0$$
$$M_{2,3} = \frac{(2 - w)^2}{2} \qquad M'_{2,3} = w - 2 \qquad M''_{2,3} = 1$$
$$M_{3,3} = \frac{(2 - w)(3w - 2)}{2} \qquad M'_{3,3} = 4 - 3w \qquad M''_{3,3} = -3$$
$$M_{4,3} = (w - 1)^2 \qquad M'_{4,3} = 2(w - 1) \qquad M''_{4,3} = 2$$

Evaluating the derivatives at $u = 1/2$, $w = 1$, and substituting into Eqs. (6–71) to (6–75), yields

$$Q(1/2, 1) = [\,0 \quad 35/4 \quad 0\,]$$

$$Q_u(1/2, 1) = [\,30 \quad 0 \quad 0\,]$$

$$Q_w(1/2, 1) = [\,0 \quad 0 \quad 10\,]$$

$$Q_{uw}(1/2, 1) = [\,0 \quad 0 \quad 0\,]$$

$$Q_{uu}(1/2, 1) = [\,0 \quad -30 \quad 0\,]$$

$$Q_{ww}(1/2, 1) = [\,0 \quad -10 \quad 10\,]$$

The components of Eq. (6–48) for the Gaussian curvature are

$$Q_u \times Q_w = [\,30 \quad 0 \quad 0\,] \times [\,0 \quad 0 \quad 10\,] = [\,0 \quad -300 \quad 0\,]$$

$$|Q_u \times Q_w|^4 = (300)^4$$

$$A = [\,Q_u \times Q_w\,] \cdot Q_{uu} = [\,0 \quad -300 \quad 0\,] \cdot [\,0 \quad -30 \quad 0\,] = 9000$$

$$B = [\,Q_u \times Q_w\,] \cdot Q_{uw} = [\,0 \quad -300 \quad 0\,] \cdot [\,0 \quad 0 \quad 0\,] = 0$$

$$C = [\,Q_u \times Q_w\,] \cdot Q_{ww} = [\,0 \quad -300 \quad 0\,] \cdot [\,0 \quad -10 \quad 10\,] = 3000$$

Using Eq. (6–48) the Gaussian curvature is

$$\kappa_g = \frac{AC - B^2}{|Q_u \times Q_w|^4} = \frac{(9000)(3000) - (0)}{(300)^4} = 3.33 \times 10^{-3}$$

Since $\kappa_g > 0$, the surface is locally elliptical.

---

## 6–16    RATIONAL B-SPLINE SURFACES

As with rational curves, rational forms of the quadric surfaces, of Coons bicubic surfaces and of Bézier surfaces are possible. However, both because of space limitations and because they represent a generalization of all these forms, only rational B-spline surfaces are considered.

A Cartesian product rational B-spline surface in four-dimensional homogeneous coordinate space is given by

$$Q(u, w) = \sum_{i=1}^{n+1} \sum_{j=1}^{m+1} B_{i,j}^h N_{i,k}(u) M_{j,l}(w) \qquad (6 - 85)$$

where the $B_{i,j}^h$'s are the 4D homogeneous defining polygon vertices and $N_{i,k}(u)$ and $M_{j,l}(w)$ are the nonrational B-spline basis functions previously given in Eq. (5–84).

Projecting back into three-dimensional space by dividing through by the homogeneous coordinate gives the rational B-spline surface

$$Q(u,w) = \frac{\displaystyle\sum_{i=1}^{n+1}\sum_{j=1}^{m+1} h_{i,j}B_{i,j}N_{i,k}(u)M_{j,l}(w)}{\displaystyle\sum_{i=1}^{n+1}\sum_{j=1}^{m+1} h_{i,j}N_{i,k}(u)M_{j,l}(w)} = \sum_{i=1}^{n+1}\sum_{j=1}^{m+1} B_{i,j}S_{i,j}(u,w) \tag{6-86}$$

where the $B_{i,j}$'s are the 3D defining polygon net points and the $S_{i,j}(u,w)$ are the bivariant rational B-spline surface basis functions

$$S_{i,j}(u,w) = \frac{h_{i,j}N_{i,k}(u)M_{j,l}(w)}{\displaystyle\sum_{i1=1}^{n+1}\sum_{j1=1}^{m+1} h_{i1,j1}N_{i1,k}(u)M_{j1,l}(w)} \tag{6-87}$$

It is convenient to assume $h_{i,j} \geq 0$ for all $i,j$.

Here, it is important to note that $S_{i,j}(u,w)$ is *not* the product of $R_{i,k}(w)$ and $R_{j,l}(w)$ (see Eq. 5–123). However, the $S_{i,j}(u,w)$ have similar shapes and analytic properties to the product function $N_{i,k}(u)M_{j,l}(w)$. Hence, rational B-spline surfaces have similar analytic and geometric properties to their nonrational counterparts. Specifically,

The sum of the rational surface basis functions for any $u,w$ values is

$$\sum_{i=1}^{n+1}\sum_{j=1}^{m+1} S_{i,j}(u,w) \equiv 1 \tag{6-88}$$

Each rational surface basis function is positive or zero for all parameter values $u,w$, i.e., $S_{i,j} \geq 0$.

Except for $k=1$ or $l=1$, each rational surface basis function has precisely one maximum.

The maximum order of a rational B-spline surface in each parametric direction is equal to the number of defining polygon vertices in that direction.

A rational B-spline surface of order $k,l$ (degree $k-1$, $l-1$) is $C^{k-2}$, $C^{l-2}$ continuous everywhere.

A rational B-spline surface is invariant with respect to a *projective* transformation; i.e., any *projective* transformation can be applied to the surface by applying it to the defining polygon net. Note this is a stronger condition than that for a nonrational B-spline surface.

The surface lies within the convex hull of the defining polygon net formed by taking the union of all convex hulls of $k,l$ neighboring polygon net vertices.

The variation diminishing property is not known for rational B-spline sur-

The influence of a single polygon net vertex is limited to $\pm k/2$, $\pm l/2$ spans in each parametric direction.

If triangulated, the defining polygon net forms a planar approximation to the surface.

If the number of defining polygon net vertices is equal to the order in each parametric direction and there are no duplicate interior knot values, the rational B-spline surface is a rational Bézier surface.

From Eqs. (6–86) and (6–87) it is clear that when all $h_{i,j} = 1$, $S_{i,j}(u,w) = N_{i,k}(u)M_{j,l}(w)$. Thus, rational B-spline surface basis functions and surfaces reduce to their nonrational counterparts. Consequently, rational B-spline surfaces represent a proper generalization of nonrational B-spline surfaces and of rational and nonrational Bézier surfaces.

Again, as is the case for rational B-spline curves, algorithms for degree raising, subdivision (see Sec. 6–14) and surface fitting (see Sec. 6–13) of nonrational B-spline surfaces are applicable by simply applying them to the 4D defining polygon net vertices.

Open uniform, periodic uniform and nonuniform knot vectors can be used to generate rational B-spline basis functions and rational B-spline surfaces. Knot vector types can be mixed. For example, an open uniform knot vector can be used in the $u$ parametric direction and a nonuniform knot vector in the $w$ direction. Here we initially concentrate on open uniform knot vectors.

Figure 6–53 shows a bicubic ($k = l = 4$) rational B-spline surface and its defining polygon net for $h_{1,3} = h_{2,3} = 0, 1, 5$. Figure 6–53c, with $h_{1,3} = h_{2,3} = 1$, is identical to the nonrational B-spline surface. The effects of varying the homogeneous coordinate values can be seen by comparing Fig. 6–53c to Figs. 6–53b and d. The effects are analogous to, but not as striking as, those for rational B-spline curves (see Sec. 5–13). Here the effects are reduced by the fact that $S_{i,j}(u,w)$ is a bivariate blending function.

Figures 6–54a and b illustrate the effect obtained by setting all interior $h_{i,j}$'s $= 0$ and 500, respectively; i.e., $h_{2,2} = h_{2,3} = h_{3,2} = h_{3,3} = h_{4,2} = h_{4,3} = 0, 500$. All other $h_{i,j}$'s $= 1$. The defining polygon net is shown in Fig. 6–53a. Setting all the interior $h_{i,j}$'s $= 0$ effectively ignores the interior defining polygon net vertices. Only the edge vertices are interpolated. In contrast, setting all the interior $h_{i,j}$'s $= 500$ reduces the influence of the edge vertices to a minimum. Note that changing the $h_{i,j}$'s affects the parameterization of the surface. This effect is illustrated by the clustering of the parametric lines near the edges of the surface when the interior $h_{i,j}$'s $= 0$ (see Fig. 6–54a) and in the interior of the surface when the interior $h_{i,j}$'s $= 500$ (see Fig. 6–54b).

The effects of multiple vertices or net lines are analogous to those for nonrational B-spline surfaces (see Sec. 6–12) and of rational B-spline curves (see Sec. 5–13). The results of moving a single vertex on the surface are also analogous.

One of the strong attractions of rational B-spline surfaces is their ability to represent quadric surfaces *and* to blend them smoothly into higher degree

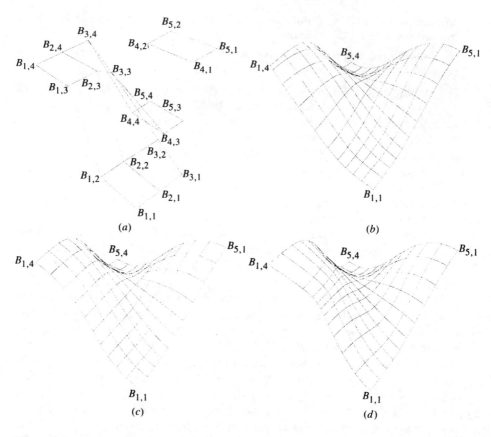

**Figure 6–53**   Rational B-spline surfaces with $n + 1 = 5$, $m + 1 = 4$, $k = l = 4$. (a) Defining polygonal net; (b) $h_{1,3} = h_{2,3} = 0$; (c) $h_{1,3} = h_{2,3} = 1$; (d) $h_{1,3} = h_{2,3} = 5$.

sculptured surfaces. As a simple example of a quadric surface consider a general cylinder formed by sweeping a curve. It is clear that the surface must be second order, i.e., a straight line, in the sweep direction. Consequently, with the surface swept out in the $u$ parametric direction, the surface representation is (see Ref. 6–33)

$$Q(u, w) = \sum_{i=1}^{2} \sum_{j=1}^{m+1} B_{i,j} S_{i,j}(u, w) \qquad (6 - 89)$$

where $S_{i,j}(u, w)$ is of the order of the curve in the $w$ parametric direction and of order 2 in the $u$ parametric direction. Further, the defining polygon net vertices in the $u$ direction are $B_{1,j} = B_j$ and $B_{2,j} = B_j + sD$, where $D$ gives the direction and distance to be swept. $s$ is a parameter in the range $0 \le s \le 1$. The $B_j$'s are the defining polygon vertices for the swept curve. The homogeneous coordinates are maintained constant in the sweep direction; i.e., $h_{1,j} = h_{2,j} = h_j$ where $h_j$ is

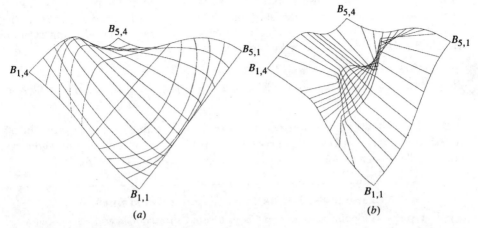

$B_{5,4}$

$B_{5,1}$

$B_{1,4}$

$B_{1,1}$

(a)

$B_{5,4}$

$B_{5,1}$

$B_{1,4}$

$B_{1,1}$

(b)

**Figure 6–54**  Rational B-spline surfaces with $n + 1 = 5$, $m + 1 = 4$, $k = l = 4$. (a) All interior $h_{i,j}$'s $= 0$; (b) all interior $h_{i,j}$'s $= 500$.

the homogeneous coordinate for the swept curve. Figure 6–55 shows an elliptic cylinder generated using the elliptic curve given in Fig. 5–67b. The swept curve is shown offset at each end.

Rational B-spline surfaces are also used to generate ruled surfaces. The elliptic cylinder shown in Fig. 6–55 is of course a ruled surface. The conditions required to generate a more general ruled surface, using rational B-splines, require that both curves be of the same order (degree), have the same knot vector and have the same number of defining polygon vertices. If the curves are not of the same order (degree) the degree of the lower order curve is raised (see Sec. 5–8 and Ex. 6–18). The required knot vector is the union of the knot vectors of the two curves. Any multiplicity of knot values for either curve is included in the

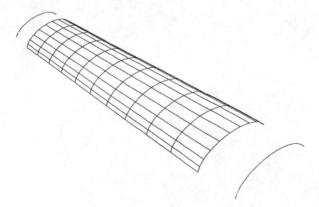

**Figure 6–55**  Rational B-spline elliptic cylinder generated by sweeping the rational elliptic curve of Fig. 5–67b.

final knot vector. Knot insertion (see Sec. 5–12) is used to insure that both knot vectors are identical. Degree raising and knot insertion insure that the number of defining polygon vertices is identical for both curves. The resulting rational B-spline ruled surface is described by Eq. (6–89) with

$$P_1(w) = Q(0, w) = \sum_{j=1}^{m+1} B_{1,j} R_{j,l}(w) \quad \text{and} \quad P_2(w) = \sum_{j=1}^{m+1} B_{2,j} R_{j,l}(w) = Q(1, w)$$

Figure 6–56 shows an example of a ruled surface blending a quarter circle into a fourth order rational B-spline curve. The curves and their defining polygons are shown offset at each end. An example better illustrates the technique.

---

### Example 6–18    Rational B-spline Ruled Surface

Determine the point at $u = w = 0.5$ on a ruled surface formed by blending a $120°$ circular arc represented by a third order rational B-spline curve defined by $B_{1,1}[0 \quad 0 \quad 0]$, $B_{1,2}[1 \quad \sqrt{3} \quad 0]$, $B_{1,3}[2 \quad 0 \quad 0]$ and $[H] = [1 \quad 1/2 \quad 1]$, with a fourth order rational curve defined by $B_{2,1}[0 \quad 0 \quad 10]$, $B_{2,2}[1 \quad 1 \quad 10]$, $B_{3,2}[2 \quad 0 \quad 10]$, $B_{4,2}[3 \quad 1 \quad 10]$ with $[H] = [1 \quad 3/4 \quad 5 \quad 1]$.

First it is necessary to raise the degree of the circular arc. The circular arc is in fact a rational Bézier curve. For the rational case the degree raising technique discussed in Sec. 5–8 is applied to the 4D homogeneous coordinates. The results are:

$$B_1^{h*} = B_1^h$$

$$B_i^{h*} = \alpha_i B_{i-1}^h + (1 - \alpha_i) B_i^h \qquad \alpha_i = \frac{i}{n+1} \qquad i = 2, \cdots, n$$

$$B_{n+1}^{h*} = B_n^h$$

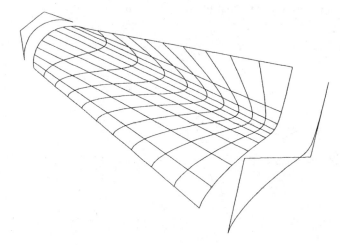

**Figure 6–56**   Rational B-spline ruled surface.

Projecting back into 3D space yields

$$B_1^* = B_1$$

$$B_i^* = \frac{\alpha_i h_{i-1} B_{i-1} + (1 - \alpha_i) h_i B_i}{\alpha_i h_{i-1} + (1 - \alpha_i) h_i} \qquad i = 2, \cdots, n$$

$$h_i^* = \alpha_i h_{i-1} + (1 - \alpha_i) h_i$$

Using these results to raise the degree of the 120° arc yields

$$h_{1,1}^* = h_{1,1} = 1$$

$$B_{1,1}^* = B_{1,1} = [\,0 \quad 0 \quad 0\,]$$

$$h_{1,2}^* = \left(\frac{1}{3}\right)(1) + \left(\frac{2}{3}\right)\left(\frac{1}{2}\right) = \frac{2}{3}$$

$$B_{1,2}^* = \left\{\frac{1}{3}(1)[\,0 \quad 0 \quad 0\,] + \frac{2}{3}\left(\frac{1}{2}\right)[\,1 \quad \sqrt{3} \quad 0\,]\right\} / \left(\frac{2}{3}\right) = \left[\,\frac{1}{2} \quad \frac{\sqrt{3}}{2} \quad 0\,\right]$$

$$h_{1,3}^* = \left(\frac{2}{3}\right)\left(\frac{1}{2}\right) + \left(\frac{1}{3}\right)(1) = \frac{2}{3}$$

$$B_{1,3}^* = \left\{\left(\frac{2}{3}\right)\left(\frac{1}{2}\right)[\,1 \quad \sqrt{3} \quad 0\,] + \frac{1}{3}(1)[\,2 \quad 0 \quad 0\,]\right\} / \left(\frac{2}{3}\right) = \left[\,\frac{3}{2} \quad \frac{\sqrt{3}}{2} \quad 0\,\right]$$

$$h_{1,4}^* = h_{1,3} = 1$$

$$B_{1,4}^* = B_{1,3} = [\,2 \quad 0 \quad 0\,]$$

Each curve now has four defining polygon vertices. The knot vector for each curve is $[\,X\,] = [\,Y\,] = [\,0 \quad 0 \quad 0 \quad 0 \quad 1 \quad 1 \quad 1 \quad 1\,]$. Hence knot insertion is unnecessary.

For $u = w = 0.5$ Eq. (5–84) yields

$$N_{1,2} = 0.5; \qquad N_{2,2} = 0.5$$

$$M_{1,4} = 0.125; \qquad M_{2,4} = 0.375; \qquad M_{3,4} = 0.375; \qquad M_{4,4} = 0.125$$

Eq. (6–87) then yields

$$S_{1,1} = 0.0396; \qquad S_{1,2} = 0.0792 \qquad S_{1,3} = 0.0792 \qquad S_{1,4} = 0.0396$$

$$S_{2,1} = 0.0396; \qquad S_{2,2} = 0.0891 \qquad S_{2,3} = 0.594 \qquad S_{2,4} = 0.0396$$

The surface point is

$$Q(0.5, 0.5) = [\,1.634 \quad 0.266 \quad 7.624\,]$$

Complete results are shown in Fig. 6–56.

Surfaces of revolution can also be represented by rational B-splines. Assuming that

$$P(w) = \sum_{j=1}^{m+1} B_j R_{j,l}(w)$$

with knot vector $[\,Y\,]$ is a rational B-spline curve, and recalling that a full circle is obtained by combining four quarter circles defined by nine polygon vertices (see Sec. 5–13), leads to a rational B-spline surface of revolution defined by (see Ref. 6–33)

$$Q(u,w) = \sum_{i=1}^{9} \sum_{j=1}^{m+1} B_{i,j} S_{i,j}(u,w) \qquad (6-90)$$

where the knot vector $[\,X\,] = [\,0 \ \ 0 \ \ 0 \ \ 1 \ \ 1 \ \ 2 \ \ 2 \ \ 3 \ \ 3 \ \ 4 \ \ 4 \ \ 4\,]$. Assuming that rotation occurs about the $z$-axis and that the curve $P(w)$ is defined in the $xz$ plane, the $B_{i,j}$'s are given by $B_{1,j} = B_j$ for fixed $j$ with $1 \le i \le 9$. The defining polygon vertices form the corners and midpoints of a square lying in a plane perpendicular to the $z$-axis with side dimension twice the radius of the circle of revolution. The homogeneous weighting factors are the product of those for the defining rational B-spline curve and those required to define the circle of revolution. Specifically, for fixed $j$, $h_{1,j} = h_j$, $h_{2,j} = h_j\sqrt{2}/2$, $h_{3,j} = h_j$, $h_{4,j} = h_j\sqrt{2}/2, \cdots, h_{9,j} = h_j$. Figure 6–57 shows the defining polygon net and curve for the rational B-spline curve to be rotated and the circle of revolution. Also shown in Fig. 6–57 is the composite surface defining polygon net and the surface itself.

The common quadric surfaces of revolution, e.g., the torus and the sphere along with their defining polygon nets, are shown in Figs. 6–58 and 6–59. The torus is generated by revolving an offset circle about one of the axes. The sphere is generated by revolving a semicircle composed of two 90° arcs about an axis which is a diameter of the semicircle.

As mentioned above, one of the most powerful characteristics of rational versus nonrational B-spline surfaces is their ability to 'bury' or include quadric surface elements within a general sculptured surface. For example, a cylindrical surface element can be included as a part of a more general surface. Figure 6–60 shows three examples. The central portion of each fourth order surface is a section of a circular cylinder. Figure 6–60a might represent the leading edge of a wing or turbine blade.[†] Figure 6–60b might represent the cylindrical bow (stem) of a ship. Both surfaces are generated by first defining a third order circular arc (see Sec. 5–13), raising the degree of the arc (see Ex. 6–18), making a ruled surface from the arc and including it between the two fourth order side surface elements. Incidentally, both of the surfaces shown in Figs. 6–60a and b are ruled developable surfaces. Figure 6–60c shows the cylindrical element buried in a more general surface.

The derivatives of a rational B-spline surface are obtained by formal differentiation of Eq. (6–86). The results are

$$Q_u = \frac{\bar{N}}{\bar{D}}\left(\frac{\bar{N}_u}{\bar{N}} - \frac{\bar{D}_u}{\bar{D}}\right) \qquad (6-91a)$$

---

[†]NACA airfoil sections use a circular arc to define the leading edge.

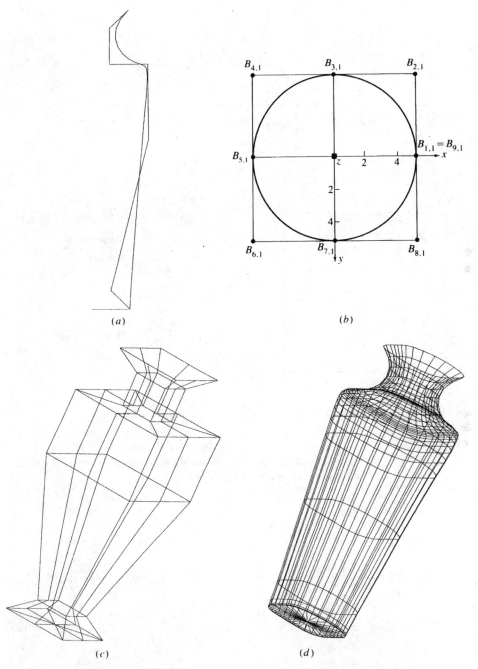

Labels in figure (b):
$B_{4.1}$  $B_{3.1}$  $B_{2.1}$  $B_{5.1}$  $B_{1.1} = B_{9.1}$  $x$  $z$  $B_{6.1}$  $B_{7.1}$  $y$  $B_{8.1}$

(a)

(b)

(c)

(d)

**Figure 6–57**    Rational B-spline surface of revolution.    (a) Generating curve and defining net; (b) circle of revolution; (c) defining surface polygon net; (d) surface of revolution.

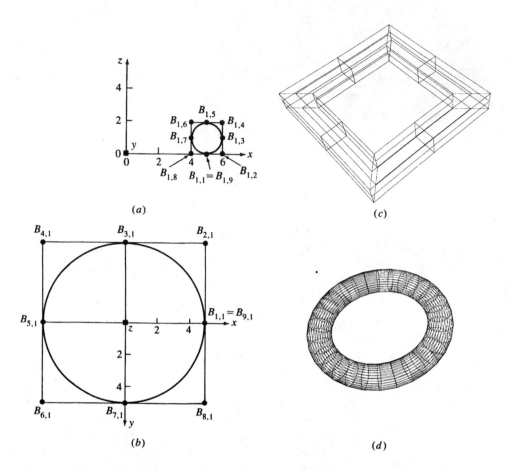

**Figure 6–58**  Torus generated as a rational B-spline surface. (a) Offset circle and defining polygon; (b) circle of revolution and defining polygon; (c) defining polygon net for torus; (d) torus.

$$Q_w = \frac{\bar{N}}{\bar{D}}\left(\frac{\bar{N}_w}{\bar{N}} - \frac{\bar{D}_w}{\bar{D}}\right) \qquad (6-91b)$$

$$Q_{uw} = \frac{\bar{N}}{\bar{D}}\left(\frac{\bar{N}_{uw}}{\bar{N}} - \frac{\bar{N}_u}{\bar{N}}\frac{\bar{D}_w}{\bar{D}} - \frac{\bar{N}_w}{\bar{N}}\frac{\bar{D}_u}{\bar{D}} + 2\frac{\bar{D}_u}{\bar{D}}\frac{\bar{D}_w}{\bar{D}} - \frac{\bar{D}_{uw}}{\bar{D}}\right) \qquad (6-91c)$$

$$Q_{uu} = \frac{\bar{N}}{\bar{D}}\left(\frac{\bar{N}_{uu}}{\bar{N}} - 2\frac{\bar{N}_u}{\bar{N}}\frac{\bar{D}_u}{\bar{D}} + 2\frac{\bar{D}_u^2}{\bar{D}^2} - \frac{\bar{D}_{uu}}{\bar{D}}\right) \qquad (6-91d)$$

$$Q_{ww} = \frac{\bar{N}}{\bar{D}}\left(\frac{\bar{N}_{ww}}{\bar{N}} - 2\frac{\bar{N}_w}{\bar{N}}\frac{\bar{D}_w}{\bar{D}} + 2\frac{\bar{D}_w^2}{\bar{D}^2} - \frac{\bar{D}_{ww}}{\bar{D}}\right) \qquad (6-91e)$$

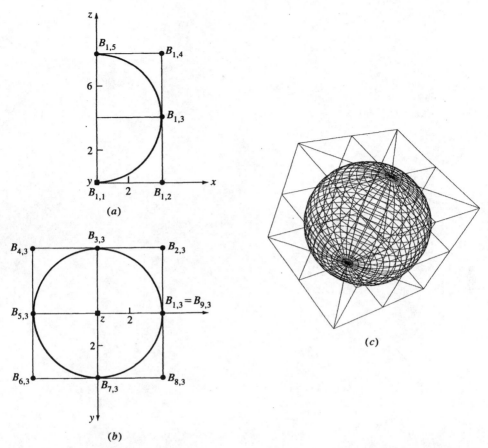

**Figure 6–59**    Sphere generated as a rational B-spline surface.  (a) Offset circle and defining polygon;  (b) circle of revolution and defining polygon;  (c) defining polygon net and sphere.

where $\bar{N}$ and $\bar{D}$ are the numerator and denominator, respectively, of Eq. (6–86) with derivatives

$$\bar{N}_u = \sum_{i=1}^{n+1} \sum_{j=1}^{m+1} h_{i,j} B_{i,j} N'_{i,k}(u) M_{j,l}(w)$$

$$\bar{N}_w = \sum_{i=1}^{n+1} \sum_{j=1}^{m+1} h_{i,j} B_{i,j} N_{i,k}(u) M'_{j,l}(w)$$

$$\bar{N}_{uw} = \sum_{i=1}^{n+1} \sum_{j=1}^{m+1} h_{i,j} B_{i,j} N'_{i,k}(u) M'_{j,l}(w)$$

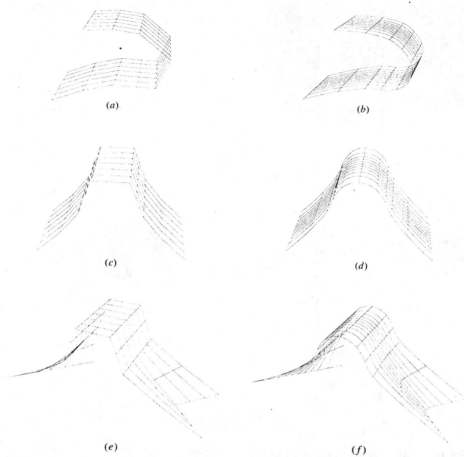

**Figure 6–60**    A quadric surface element within a more general rational B-spline surface. Airfoil leading edge. (a) Polygon net; (b) surface. Ship stern. (c) Polygon net; (d) surface. A cylinder as part of a more general surface. (e) Polygon net; (f) surface.

$$\bar{N}_{uu} = \sum_{i=1}^{n+1} \sum_{j=1}^{m+1} h_{i,j} B_{i,j} N''_{i,k}(u) M_{j,l}(w)$$

$$\bar{N}_{ww} = \sum_{i=1}^{n+1} \sum_{j=1}^{m+1} h_{i,j} B_{i,j} N_{i,k}(u) M''_{j,l}(w)$$

$$\bar{D}_{u} = \sum_{i=1}^{n+1} \sum_{j=1}^{m+1} h_{i,j} N'_{i,k}(u) M_{j,l}(w)$$

$$\bar{D}_w = \sum_{i=1}^{n+1} \sum_{j=1}^{m+1} h_{i,j} N_{i,k}(u) M'_{j,l}(w)$$

$$\bar{D}_{uw} = \sum_{i=1}^{n+1} \sum_{j=1}^{m+1} h_{i,j} N'_{i,k}(u) M'_{j,l}(w)$$

$$\bar{D}_{uu} = \sum_{i=1}^{n+1} \sum_{j=1}^{m+1} h_{i,j} N''_{i,k}(u) M_{j,l}(w)$$

$$\bar{D}_{ww} = \sum_{i=1}^{n+1} \sum_{j=1}^{m+1} h_{i,j} N_{i,k}(u) M''_{j,l}(w)$$

The prime denotes a derivative with respect to the appropriate parametric variable. The $N'_{i,k}(u) M'_{j,l}(w)$, $N''_{i,k}(u)$, $M''_{j,l}(w)$'s are given by Eq. (5–97) to (5–100).

These derivatives are useful in determining the Gaussian curvature (see Sec. 6–15) of the surface, as well as other characteristics.

## 6–17   REFERENCES

6–1 Rogers, D.F., *Procedural Elements for Computer Graphics*, McGraw-Hill, New York, 1985.

6–2 Bézier, P.E., *Emploi des Machines à Commande Numerique*, Masson et Cie, Paris, France, 1970; Bézier, P.E., "Example of an Existing System in the Motor Industry: The Unisurf System," *Proc. Roy. Soc. (London)*, Vol. A321, pp. 207–218, 1971.

6–3 Sabin, M.A., "An Existing System in the Aircraft Industry. The British Aircraft Corporation Numerical Master Geometry System," *Proc. Roy. Soc. (London)*, Vol. A321, pp. 197–205, 1971.

6–4 Peters, G.J., "Interactive Computer Graphics Application of the Bicubic Parametric Surface to Engineering Design Problems," McDonnell Douglas Automation Company, St. Louis, Missouri, presented at SIAM 1973 National Meeting, Hampton, Va., 18–21 June 1973.

6–5 Rogers, D.F., and Satterfield, S.G., "Dynamic B-Spline Surfaces," *Proc. of the Fourth International Conference on Computer Applications in the Automation of Shipyard Operation and Ship Design* (ICCAS 82), 7–10 June 1982, Annapolis, Maryland, pp. 189–196, North Holland, 1982.

6–6 Rogers, D.F., and Satterfield, S.G., "B-Spline Surfaces for Ship Hull Design," *Comp. Graph.*, Vol. 14, pp. 211–217, 1980, (SIGGRAPH 80).

6–7 Rogers, D.F., Rodriguez, F., and Satterfield, S.G., "Computer Aided Ship Design and the Numerically Controlled Production of Towing Tank Models," *Proc. of 16th Des. Auto. Conf.*, San Diego, California, 24–27 June 1979.

6–8 Cohen, E., "Some Mathematical Tools for a Modeler's Workbench," *IEEE Comp. Graph. & Appl.*, Vol. 3, pp. 63–66, October 1983.

6-9 Tan, S.T., Yuen, M.F., and Hui, K.C., "Modeling Solids with Sweep Primitives," *Comp. Mech. Eng.*, Vol. 6, pp. 60–72, 1987.

6-10 Coquillart, S., "A Control-Point-Based Sweeping Technique," *IEEE Comp. Graph. & Appl.*, Vol. 7, pp. 36–45, November 1987.

6-11 Patton, D., Dept. of Mech. and Prod. Engr., Royal Melbourne Inst. of Tech., Melbourne, Australia, private communication, 1988.

6-12 Dresden, A., *Solid Analytic Geometry and Determinants*, Dover Publications, New York, 1964.

6-13 Sommerville, D.M.Y., *Analytical Geometry of Three Dimensions*, Cambridge Univ. Press, 1959.

6-14 Snyder, V., and Sisam, C.H., *Analytic Geometry of Space*, Henry Holt and Co., New York, 1914.

6-15 Goldman, R.N., "Two Approaches to a Computer Model for Quadric Surfaces," *IEEE Comp. Graph. & Appl.*, Vol. 3, pp. 21–24, September 1983.

6-16 Wilson, P.R., "Conic Representation for Shape Description," *IEEE Comp. Graph. & Appl.*, Vol. 7, pp. 23–30, 1987.

6-17 Miller, J.R., "Geometric Approaches to Non-planar Quadric Surfaces Intersection Curves," *ACM Trans. on Graph.*, Vol. 6, pp. 274–307, 1987.

6-18 Dill, J.C., "An Application of Color Graphics to the Display of Surface Curvature," *Comp. Graph.*, Vol. 15, pp. 153–161, 1981, (SIGGRAPH 81).

6-19 Coons, S., "Surfaces for Computer-Aided Design of Space Forms," M. I. T. Proj. MAC, MAC–TR–41, June 1967. (Also as AD 663 504).

6-20 Ferguson, J.C., "Multivariable Curve Interpolation," *J. ACM*, Vol. 2, pp. 221–228, April 1964.

6-21 Barnhill, R.E., "Smooth Interpolation over Triangles," in *Computer Aided Geometric Design*, Barnhill, R.E., and Riesenfeld, R.F. (eds.), Academic Press, New York, pp. 45–70, 1974.

6-22 Barnhill, R.E., "Coons Patches," *Comp. in Ind.*, Vol. 3, pp. 37–43, 1982.

6-23 Charrot, P., and Gregory, J., "A Pentagonal Surface Patch for Computer Aided Geometric Design," *Comp. Aid. Geom. Des.*, Vol. 1, pp. 87–94, 1984.

6-24 Faux, I.D., and Pratt, M.J., *Computational Geometry for Design and Manufacture*, Ellis Horwood (John Wiley & Sons), 1979.

6-25 Bézier, P.E., *The Mathematical Basis of the Unisurf CAD System*, Butterworth, London, 1986.

6-26 Barsky, B.A., and Greenberg, D.P., "Determining a Set of B-spline Control Vertices to Generate an Interpolating Surface," *Comp. Graph. Imag. Proc.*, Vol. 14, pp. 203–226, 1980.

6-27 Rogers, D.F., and Fog, N.G., "Constrained B-spline Curve and Surface Fitting," *CADJ*, Vol. 21, pp. 641–648, 1989.

6-28 Munchmeyer, F.C., Schubert, C., and Nowacki, H., "Interactive Design of Fair Hull Surfaces Using B-splines," *Proc. of the Third International Conference on Computer Applications in the Automation of Shipyard Operation and Ship Design* (ICCAS 79), 18–21 June 1979, University of Strathclyde, Glasgow, Scotland, pp. 67–76, North Holland, 1979.

6–29 Munchmeyer, F.C., "The Gaussian Curvature of Coons Biquintic Patches," *Proc. ASME Century 2 Inter. Comp. Tech. Conf.*, 12–15 August 1980.

6–30 Dill, J.C., "An Application of Color Graphics to the Display of Surface Curvature," *Comp. Graph.*, Vol. 15, pp. 153–161, 1981, (SIGGRAPH 81).

6–31 Forrest, A.R., "On the Rendering of Surfaces," *Comp. Graph.*, Vol. 13, pp. 253–259, 1979, (SIGGRAPH 79).

6–32 Dill, J.C., and Rogers, D.F.,"Color Graphics and Ship Hull Surface Curvature," *Proc. of the Fourth International Conference on Computer Applications in the Automation of Shipyard Operation and Ship Design* (ICCAS 82), pp. 197–205, North Holland, 1982.

6–33 Piegl, L., and Tiller, W., "Curve and Surface Constructions Using Rational B-splines," *Comp. Aid. Des.*, Vol. 19, pp. 485–498, 1987.

## COMPUTER GRAPHICS SOFTWARE

### A–1  INTRODUCTION

In developing the concepts for computer graphics software it is convenient to think in terms of the pipeline shown by the heavy arrows in Fig. 1–63. The pipeline begins with an application program and its associated data base, flows through a computer graphics support package and its associated graphical data base, is processed by appropriate device interface software, to generate a picture on a physical graphics device with which a user may or may not interact. Along the pipeline there are two critical software interfaces: the application programmer's interface and the device interface. Both interfaces are currently the subject of international standards efforts.

The application programmer's interface is usually represented by a subroutine or function package implemented in a higher level programming language, e.g., FORTRAN, C, BASIC or PASCAL. The user interface is usually written using the application programmer's interface subroutines and functions. The application programmer's interface is currently represented by four major standards efforts: the Graphical Kernel System (GKS) (see Refs. A–1 to A–3), GKS–3D (see Ref. A–4), the Programmer's Hierarchical Interactive Graphics System (PHIGS) (see Refs. A–5 and A–6) and PHIGS+ (see Ref. A–7). Many of the routines and functions provided by the application programmer's interface are the main subject of this book and of Ref. A–8. Examples are rotation, translation, perspective projection, clipping, hidden lines and hidden surfaces.

The device interface operates at a much lower level than the application programmer's interface. It is concerned with generating the necessary codes (binary bit patterns) required to drive a specific physical or virtual graphics device. Generally systems programmers or implementors of the application programmer's interface routines and functions are concerned with the device interface. Examples of standard device interfaces are the Computer Graphics Metafile (CGM) (see Refs. A–9 to A–11), the Computer Graphics Interface (CGI) (see Refs. A–10 to A–12) and the Virtual Device Interface (VDI) (see Ref. A–13).

A detailed discussion of the various standards is beyond the scope of this text. Such discussions are provided in the cited references. Here, only brief general descriptions are given.

GKS is a two-dimensional viewing standard; no modeling is included. Only two-dimensional primitives are provided, e.g., polyline, rotation, translation and scaling. Three-dimensional manipulations must be accomplished outside the standard, e.g., a 3D to 2D projection performed (see Chapter 3) and the result displayed using 2D GKS routines. GKS supports a wide variety of graphical input and output devices (see Chapter 1), e.g., monochrome and color CRT displays, printers, plotters, mice, tablets, control dials, function switches, etc. Access to GKS routines is provided in a number of higher-level programming languages, e.g., FORTRAN, PASCAL, ADA and C. GKS is currently both an official International Standards Organization (ISO) and an American National Standards Institute (ANSI) standard (see Ref. A–1).

GKS–3D is an extension of GKS that provides facilities for viewing and defining 3D objects. Again, no modeling functions are provided. Hidden lines and hidden surface capability as well as parallel and perspective projection are included. The GKS–3D standard is still under development (see Ref. A–4).

PHIGS, in contrast to GKS and GKS–3D, was originally designed as both a three-dimensional manipulation and viewing standard *and* as a three-dimensional geometric modeling standard. The emphasis is on support for very highly interactive graphics environments, e.g., CADCAM, molecular modeling, solid modeling and simulation and control. PHIGS allows building, manipulating, modifying and storing three-dimensional geometric models. The PHIGS standard is currently under development (see Ref. A–5).

PHIGS+ extends PHIGS to include lighting, shading and depth cueing as well as curves and surfaces, e.g., rational B-splines (see Sec. 5–13 and 6–16). PHIGS+ is specifically designed to take advantage of the capabilities of highly interactive graphics workstations. For example, rendering effects such as Gouraud and Phong shading are included, as are new geometric attributes such as vertex normals.

The CGI provides the functionality to convert the device independent information generated by the application programmer's standard to the device dependent information required to 'drive' a specific graphics device. The CGI defines a Virtual Device Interface; i.e., an idealized standard graphics device that accepts user input, generates and manipulates graphics information. There is a strong interconnected relationship between GKS and the CGI. The CGM captures and stores graphical information at the CGI level. The result is a formatted file containing 'a picture' that can be stored on a disc or tape and transmitted over telephone lines or computer networks.

Rather than discuss each of the standards in all of their changing details, it is more advantageous to take a fundamental and conceptual view.

## A–2  COMPUTER GRAPHICS PRIMITIVES

In developing any computer graphics software system the physical (or virtual) graphics device is controlled by low-level primitive device dependent commands. A graphics primitive command executes a *single* action. The graphics primitives generally fall into three areas: cursor control, device state control and graphics input. Here cursor and state are used in a very general sense. From these graphics primitives several compound (multiple action) graphics commands called graphics elements are developed in Sec. A–3. The graphics elements are device independent.

There are two graphics primitives associated with cursor control. They are:

Move the cursor — move (x,y).

Turn the cursor on/off — onoff (i).

The functions of these primitives are self-explanatory.

The graphics primitives associated with device state control are many and varied. They are given the generic name Set. Some examples are:

Set alphanumeric mode.

Set graphics mode.

Set absolute coordinate mode.

Set relative coordinate mode.

Set color (r, g, b).

Set clear screen.

etc.

Fundamentally there is only one graphics primitive, Set, with various arguments. Before continuing, a word about the function of each of these various device states helps clarify the intent.

Alphanumeric and graphics modes are generally associated with devices which can interpret a data stream as either alphanumeric (ASCII) characters or graphics commands. Absolute and relative coordinate modes determine whether Cartesian coordinates specified in the graphics primitive, Move, are to be interpreted with respect to an absolute or relative coordinate origin. The Set color command determines the color of the cursor for subsequent commands, e.g., line, point, etc. The Set clear screen command resets the entire display to the default (background) color.

The graphics primitive associated with graphic input is given the generic name, Get.

Get (value).

It is clear from the above that fundamentally there are only four graphics primitives. Generally they may be represented as:

Onoff (control variable).

Move (coordinate,coordinate).

Set (control variable, <argument 1>, <argument 2>, ···).

Get (value).

where < > is used to represent optional arguments.

## A–3    COMPUTER GRAPHICS ELEMENTS

The computer graphics primitives discussed in Sec. A–2 can be combined into computer graphics elements. In general these are compound operations; i.e., they involve more than one of the graphics primitives. Properly implemented, they are device independent.

Again, as with the graphics primitives, the graphics elements divide into three groups: drawing functions, device or picture control functions and interactive input control functions. The drawing functions are derived from the action of a pencil, on or moving over a sheet of paper. A pencil can be *moved* over a sheet of paper without making a mark. While in contact with the paper, movement of the pencil *draws* a line. The pencil can also be moved over the paper to some location, then placed in contact with the paper to make a *point*. It is convenient to be able to specify the movement over the paper or drawing surface of the pencil or cursor in either absolute or relative coordinates. These concepts give rise to six drawing functions or graphics elements:

Move Absolute (x,y).

Move Relative ($\Delta$x,$\Delta$y).

Draw Absolute (x,y).

Draw Relative ($\Delta$x,$\Delta$y).

Point Absolute (x,y).

Point Relative ($\Delta$x,$\Delta$y).

The ability to print character or textual material on the graphics surface is also required, say,

Text (string).

In each case it is convenient to assume that the action initiates from the current location of the cursor. Functionally each of these graphics elements can be described in terms of graphics primitives. For example, the Move Absolute algorithm might be:

Set absolute coordinate mode.

Set graphics mode.

Turn cursor off.

Move the cursor to the specified coordinates.

The Point Absolute algorithm might be:

Set absolute coordinate mode.

Set graphics mode.

Turn cursor off.

Move the cursor to the specified coordinates.

Turn cursor on.

The Draw Absolute algorithm might be:

Set absolute coordinate mode.

Set graphics mode.

Turn cursor on.

Move the cursor to the specified coordinates.

The relative algorithms are identical with the substitution of Set relative coordinate mode.

The device or picture control elements are initializing the device and starting a new frame or picture. For example:

Initialize the Device.

Begin Frame.

could serve these purposes. Functionally, the Initialize the Device command serves to set default conditions. Begin Frame serves to notify a refresh graphics device that the current picture is complete, to set the device to the background color and to begin presenting the next picture, to erase the screen on a storage tube CRT device, to indicate a new plot for pen and ink devices, etc.

The control of graphic input needs to be more sophisticated than the simple Get graphics primitive discussed in Sec. A–2. Some examples of graphic input elements are:

Get Mouse (x,y).

Get Valuator (value).

Get Tablet (x,y).

Get Function Switch (i).

etc.

The graphics primitives can be combined to provide this functionality. Two example algorithms are illustrative. The first is the Get Valuator command. The algorithm might be:

Set absolute coordinate mode.

Set graphics mode.

Get (value).

The Get Mouse command algorithm might be:

Set absolute coordinate mode.

Set graphics mode.

Get (x value).

Get (y value).

In all of the above there has been no discussion of the type of graphics device nor of pixels or scan lines etc. The reader may wonder why Set pixel and Get pixel commands are not explicitly included. However, a moment's thought reveals that in the context of a graphics device a pixel is a point. Consequently, the point commands conceptually suffice for the pixel commands.

The graphics elements are generally the lowest level graphics commands of interest to the application programmer. In many cases the application programmer is unaware of the graphics primitives. They may in fact be unavailable to him. However, they are of interest to the systems programmer. If the total graphics system is broken down into levels or shells, then the graphics elements occupy level 1 or shell 1 and the graphics primitives level 0 or shell 0 (0 because it is hidden from the application programmer).

## A–4   COORDINATE SYSTEMS

In the context of a computer graphics software system there are three coordinate systems of interest — world or user coordinates, a pseudospace with normalized device coordinates and device coordinates. World coordinates are those in which the application is given or specified. They are usually given as floating point numbers. Device coordinates are those understood by the particular graphics device — pixels, addressable points, inches, cm, etc. They may be specified by integer numbers. Normalized device space is a pseudospace used to obtain device independence. Normalized device coordinates are given as floating point numbers in the first quadrant in the range $0 \leq ndcx \leq 1.0$, $0 \leq ndcy \leq 1.0$. Thus, the origin is in the lower left-hand corner.

As shown in Fig. A–1 and discussed in Chapter 1, specification, manipulation and clipping of the data base occurs in world coordinates. The 'window' on the data base thus formed is transformed to normalized device coordinates and then to device coordinates. The window extents are specified in world coordinates. The viewport extents are specified in normalized device coordinates to provide device independence. Both the transformation from world to normalized device coordinates and from normalized device coordinates to device coordinates involve only simple translations and scalings.†

An example serves to illustrate the various coordinate systems and transformations.

---

### Example A–1    Coordinate Transformation

Display an origin-centered square 36 units on a side in the upper left quadrant of a graphics device with $1024 \times 1024$ resolution.

To allow some space around the square, define a window with left, right, bottom, top edges given by $wleft = -20$, $wright = 20$, $wbottom = -20$, $wtop = 20$. It is really the window, not the image, that determines the transformation.

In normalized device coordinates the upper left quadrant is specified by $vleft = 0$, $vright = 0.5$, $vbottom = 0.5$, $vtop = 1.0$.

Transforming from world coordinates to normalized device coordinates requires scaling the window coordinates and then translating the result to the

---

†Perspective transformation is assumed to be accomplished before clipping.

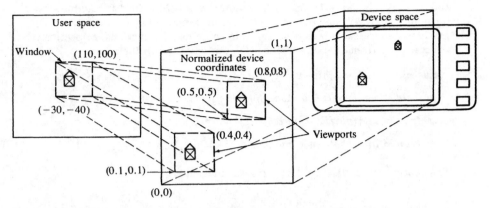

**Figure A-1**    Transformations in the graphics pipeline.

first quadrant. The scale factors are

$$xwscale = \frac{1}{wright - wleft} = \frac{1}{20 - (-20)} = \frac{1}{40}$$

$$ywscale = \frac{1}{wtop - wbottom} = \frac{1}{20 - (-20)} = \frac{1}{40}$$

The translation factors are

$$xwtran = \frac{-wleft}{wright - wleft} = \frac{-(-20)}{20 - (-20)} = \frac{1}{2}$$

$$ywtran = \frac{-wbottom}{wtop - wbottom} = \frac{-(-20)}{20 - (-20)} = \frac{1}{2}$$

The concatenated $3 \times 3$ 2D window to NDC transformation is

$$[\,T_w\,] = [\,S_w\,][\,Tr_w\,] = \begin{bmatrix} xwscale & 0 & 0 \\ 0 & ywscale & 0 \\ xwtran & ywtran & 1 \end{bmatrix}$$

$$= \begin{bmatrix} 1/40 & 0 & 0 \\ 0 & 1/40 & 0 \\ 1/2 & 1/2 & 1 \end{bmatrix}$$

Transforming from normalized device coordinates to device coordinates again involves a scale and a translate. When device coordinates are specified using integer numbers special care is required in determining the scale and translation factors.

Although the resolution of an integer addressable device is $xresolution \times yresolution$ the addressable range of integer numbers is 0 to $xresolution - 1$

and 0 to $yresolution - 1$; e.g., if the resolution is $1024 \times 1024$ the addressable range in both directions is 0 to 1023. Letting $xmaxdev$ and $ymaxdev$ be the maximum addressable integer numbers in the $x$ and $y$ directions, respectively, the scale and translation factors for NDC to device coordinates are

$$xvscale = int\{(vright - vleft)xmaxdev\} = int\{(0.5 - 0)(1023)\} = 511$$

$$yvscale = int\{(vtop - vbottom)ymaxdev\} = int\{(1 - 0.5)(1023)\} = 511$$

$$xvtran = int\{(vleft)(xmaxdev + 1)\} = int\{(0)(1024)\} = 0$$

$$yvtran = int\{(vbottom)(ymaxdev + 1)\} = int\{(0.5)(1024)\} = 512$$

The concatenated NDC to device transformation is

$$[\,T_v\,] = [\,S_v\,][\,Tr_v\,] = \begin{bmatrix} xvscale & 0 & 0 \\ 0 & yvscale & 0 \\ xvtran & yvtran & 1 \end{bmatrix} = \begin{bmatrix} 511 & 0 & 0 \\ 0 & 511 & 0 \\ 0 & 512 & 1 \end{bmatrix}$$

Using these results to transform the corners of the origin-centered square yields

$$\begin{bmatrix} -18 & -18 & 1 \\ 18 & -18 & 1 \\ 18 & 18 & 1 \\ -18 & 18 & 1 \end{bmatrix} \begin{bmatrix} 1/40 & 0 & 0 \\ 0 & 1/40 & 0 \\ 1/2 & 1/2 & 1 \end{bmatrix} = \begin{bmatrix} 1/20 & 1/20 & 1 \\ 19/20 & 1/20 & 1 \\ 19/20 & 19/20 & 1 \\ 1/20 & 19/20 & 1 \end{bmatrix}$$

and

$$\begin{bmatrix} 1/20 & 1/20 & 1 \\ 19/20 & 1/20 & 1 \\ 19/20 & 19/20 & 1 \\ 1/20 & 19/20 & 1 \end{bmatrix} \begin{bmatrix} 511 & 0 & 0 \\ 0 & 511 & 0 \\ 0 & 512 & 1 \end{bmatrix} = \begin{bmatrix} 25.55 & 537.55 & 1 \\ 485.45 & 537.55 & 1 \\ 485.45 & 997.45 & 1 \\ 25.55 & 997.45 & 1 \end{bmatrix}$$

$$= \begin{bmatrix} 25 & 537 \\ 485 & 537 \\ 485 & 997 \\ 25 & 997 \end{bmatrix}$$

Here the integer function has been used to obtain the final integer addressable points.

---

## A–5   A SIMPLE GRAPHICS METAFILE

The concept of storing a picture in a data file has previously been addressed as part of the discussion of graphics standards. The applicable graphics standard is that for the Computer Graphics Metafile (CGM). However, the CGM is somewhat more detailed and complex than required for either personal or student work. A simple alternative, here called the standard display file, is given in Table A–1.[†]

The first line of the standard display file contains an identification string. Each subsequent line of the file begins with an operation code number, followed by the

---

[†]A similar concept has been in use at the authors' home institute for more than a decade.

appropriate information required by that operation. All coordinate values are specified as floating point numbers in normalized device coordinates, i.e., in the range $0 \le x \le 1.0$, $0 \le y \le 1.0$. All items are separated by commas.

A simple standard display file for the square defined in Ex. A–1 is:

The square of Ex. A–1

0, 0.05, 0.05

2, 0.95, 0.05

2, 0.95, 0.95

2, 0.05, 0.95

2, 0.05, 0.05

The format is simple enough that a picture can be generated using a text editor. Normally the file is created by calling a graphics routine that turns command logging on or off. For example,

Set sdf on/off   filename

Programs to display the stored picture on any graphics device are quite simple. The format allows easy extension to include local functionality.

## Table A–1 Standard Display File (.sdf) Codes

| Code | Operation | Parameters[†] |
|------|-----------|------------|
| 0 | Move Absolute | x,y |
| 1 | Point Absolute | x,y |
| 2 | Draw Absolute | x,y |
| 3 | Move Relative | $\Delta x, \Delta y$ |
| 4 | Point Relative | $\Delta x, \Delta y$ |
| 5 | Draw Relative | $\Delta x, \Delta y$ |
| 6 | Text | Text string |
| 7 | Set color | red, green, blue |
| 8 | Set look-up table | red bits, green bits, blue bits |
| 9 | Set pixel | x, y, red, green, blue |
| 10 | New frame | |
| 11 | Pause | |
| 12 | Set resolution | xresolution, yresolution |
| 99 | Print message | Message string |

[†] x,y are floating point numbers in NDC; i.e., in the range $0 \le x, y \le 1.0$. red, green, blue are floating point numbers in the range $0 \le$ red, green, blue $\le 1.0$ with $0 \equiv$ no intensity and $1 \equiv$ full intensity. Red bits, green bits, blue bits are powers of 2 (see Sec. 1–9 for a discussion of look-up tables).

The power of normalized device coordinates and a graphics metafile is illustrated by Fig. A–2. The graphics, including the lettering, were designed and proofed on a storage tube. The resulting picture was stored in a standard display file. The standard display file was transferred to a computer used as a real time controller for a numerically controlled machining center (see Fig. 1–1). A program read in the standard display file and generated the necessary codes to drive the machining center. The result was the engraving shown in Fig. A–2.

## A–6    SIMPLE GRAPHICS INPUT FILE FORMATS

In any computer graphics software system standard input file formats are a necessity. For complex or very large data bases the formalism of data structures and data base management systems is required. However, for relatively small data bases simpler formats based on sequential file access are sufficient. Two are suggested here.

The first input file format, called the 'standard graphics format' (.sgf) and defined in Table A–2, is best suited to plotting and to two- or three-dimensional wire frame displays. The second, defined in Table A–3, is called the 'standard polygon format'. This format is particularly useful for raster displays or as input to hidden line or hidden surface algorithms. Note that when the .spf format is used to generate wire frame drawings each line is drawn twice. In both cases rendering attributes, e.g., line or polygon color, polygon or solid reflection coefficients, etc., are contained in separate companion files.

### Table A–2 Standard Graphics Format (.sgf)

The standard graphics format is a very simple and general-purpose format for describing any two- or three-dimensional data that can be expressed as a list of x,y pairs or x,y,z triplets. Blank lines are allowed in the file. The general form is:

descriptive string          descriptive string

$x_1, y_1$                  $x_1, y_1, z_1$
$x_2, y_2$                  $x_2, y_2, z_2$
.                            .
.
$x_n, y_n$                  $x_n, y_n, z_n$
1e37,1e37                   1e37,1e37,1e37

A group of pairs or triplets is terminated by the delimiter 1e37,1e37 or 1e37, 1e37,1e37.[†] Additional groups may follow. The last line in the file does *not* have to be a delimiter.

Typically, this file format is interpreted to mean that the graphics device moves to the first point of a group and draws to the remaining points forming a connected line until the 1e37 delimiter is found.

[†]The delimiter value is historical.

## Table A–3 Simple Polygon File Format (.spf)

A general description of the polygon file format is first given, followed by a detailed example. The file naturally divides into two parts. The first part is a description of all the position vectors in the scene, the second is a description of the polygon characteristics. Blank lines are allowed in the file. A line-by-line description of the file is

> an identifying string
> number of position vectors, polygons
> x,y,z position vector list
> .
> .
> polygon list
>> Each entry consists of two types of data on a single line: number of points in the polygon, followed by a vertex list with each number corresponding to a row in the position vector list.

A specific example is

> polygon with a hole
> 14,2
> 4,4
> 4,26
> 20,26
> 28,18
> 28,4
> 21,4
> 21,8
> 10,8
> 10,4
> 10,12
> 10,20
> 17,20
> 21,16
> 21,12
> 9,1,2,3,4,5,6,7,8,9
> 5,10,11,12,13,14

This is a single polygon with a hole.
There are 14 position vectors or polygon vertices and two polygons.
The first polygon has 9 vertices.
The second polygon has 5 vertices.
Note that polygons are assumed to be closed; i.e., the first point need not be respecified to close the polygon.

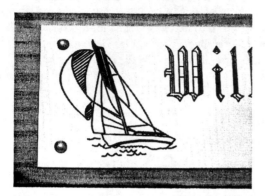

**Figure A–2**   Engraving machined from a standard display file.

Both file formats contain an implied drawing or construction algorithm.[†] The .sgf format drawing is:

> In absolute coordinates move to the first point and then draw to each succeeding point until the delimiter is found.
>
> Repeat until the end of file is found.

The drawing algorithm for the .spf format is given as part of the polygon specification:

> Move in absolute coordinates to the point specified by the first index.
>
> Connect (draw to) the points specified by each succeeding index on the list.
>
> Connect the point specified by the last index to that specified by the first index to close the polygon.

It is generally convenient to be consistent in the direction, either counterclockwise or clockwise, in specifying the polygon vertices.

## A–7   SIMPLE CONNECTIVITY ALGORITHMS

Both the .sgf and .spf file formats specify a simple and limited connectivity or drawing algorithm. Two alternate simple, but separately specified, drawing algorithms are of practical interest. Assuming that the three-dimensional data base of position vectors is represented as a single $n \times 4$ matrix, then a one-dimensional control array, $C(j)$, defining the drawing algorithm is specified as follows:

---

[†] Both the standard graphics format (.sgf) and the standard polygon format (.spf) have been in use at the authors' home institute for more than a decade.

The value of the number, $C(j)$, is used as an index specifying the row in the position vector matrix.

The sign of the number, $C(j)$, is used to specify the drawing operation,

$C(j) < 0$   –   Move Absolute.

$C(j) > 0$   –   Draw Absolute.

Although adequate, the above scheme is somewhat limited. A more flexible and powerful scheme uses a two-dimensional control array, $C(i, j)$. The drawing algorithm is specified as follows:

The value of the number, $C(i, 1)$ is used as an index specifying the row in the position vector matrix.

The value of the number, $C(i, 2)$ defines the drawing operation to be performed (see Table A–1).

$C(i, 2) = 0$   –   Move Absolute.

$C(i, 2) = 1$   –   Move Relative.

$C(i, 2) = 2$   –   Draw Absolute.

$C(i, 2) = 3$   –   Draw Relative.

$C(i, 2) = 4$   –   Point Absolute.

$C(i, 2) = 5$   –   Point Relative.

## A–8   A SIMPLE GRAPHICS PACKAGE

In teaching or in learning a new subject it is generally considered best to start with simple topics and concepts. Providing a minimal set of routines and building upon them using concepts developed in this book and in Ref. A–8 makes pedagogical sense. The Raster Display Graphics Package (RDGP) (see Ref. A–14) is such a minimal set of graphics routines. The routines have been implemented in four languages: ANSI BASIC, FORTRAN 77, C and PASCAL. Specifications for all four languages are given for each of the routines. The specifications are given first for ANSI BASIC, then for FORTRAN 77, C and PASCAL, in that order. Specifications for each routine are separated by horizontal lines. Variable types are indicated for each of the parameters for each routine.

### RDGP – RASTER DISPLAY GRAPHICS PACKAGE[†]

The routines fall naturally into three groups: display state, pixel manipulation and line drawing. The routines are discussed in this order.

---

[†]Copyright ©1985 by David F. Rogers and Stephen D. Rogers.
RDGP routines in TRUE BASIC, FORTRAN 77 and C for IBM PC's and compatibles are available from the first author. Send a self-addressed stamped envelope to Prof. David F. Rogers, 817 Holly Dr. E., Rt.10, Annapolis, MD 21401, USA for details.

| | |
|---|---|
| name: | rdinit (Raster display initialize) |
| purpose: | Initialize the raster display graphics package and the graphics device. |
| declaration: | sub rdinit |
| | subroutine rdinit |
| | rdinit() |
| | procedure rdinit; |
| comments: | rdinit should be called only once at the beginning of the program. |

| | |
|---|---|
| name: | erase (Erase the screen) |
| purpose: | Erase the graphics screen with the specified color. |
| declaration: | sub erase(r,g,b) |
| | subroutine erase(r,g,b)<br>real r,g,b |
| | erase(r,g,b)<br>double r,g,b; |
| | procedure erase(r,g,b : real); |
| comments: | r, g, b are the red, green, and blue components of the color. r, g, b are values in the range 0 to 1. (r,g,b) = (0.,0.,0.) is black and (r,g,b) = (1.,1.,1.) is white. |

| | |
|---|---|
| name: | setrsl (Set resolution) |
| purpose: | Set the pseudoresolution of the display raster. |
| declaration: | sub setrsl(xres,yres) |
| | subroutine setrsl(xres,yres)<br>integer xres,yres |
| | setrsl(xres,yres)<br>int xres,yres; |
| | procedure setrsl(xres,yres : integer); |
| comments: | xres is the pseudoresolution of the display raster in the x or horizontal direction. xres is between 1 and the maximum physical resolution of the display raster in the horizontal direction. |
| | yres is the pseudoresolution of the display raster in the y or vertical direction. yres is between 1 and the maximum physical resolution of the display raster in the vertical direction. |

The pseudoraster is centered in the physical display space.

Pixels are square or as square as it is possible to make them within the limitations of the physical display.

setrsl should be called only once at the beginning of the program.

---

| | |
|---|---|
| name: | setrgb (Set rgb) |
| purpose: | Set the current drawing color. |
| declaration: | sub setrgb(r,g,b) |
| | subroutine setrgb(r,g,b)<br>real r,g,b |
| | setrgb(r,g,b)<br>double r,g,b; |
| | procedure setrgb(r,g,b : real); |
| comments: | r, g, b are the red, green, and blue components of the color. r, g, b are values in the range 0 to 1. (r,g,b) = (0.,0.,0.) is black and (r,g,b) = (1.,1.,1.) is white. |
| | This command is generally used to set the color for the drawing commands ma, pa, da, mr, pr, dr and text given below. Note, however, that calls to setpxl and setscn may change the drawing color. |

---

| | |
|---|---|
| name: | setlut (Set the lookup table) |
| purpose: | Set the color lookup table (LUT). |
| declaration: | sub setlut(table$,rbits,gbits,bbits) |
| | subroutine setlut(table,rbits,gbits,bbits)<br>character table(*)<br>integer rbits,gbits,bbits |
| | setlut(table,rbits,gbits,bbits)<br>char *table;<br>int rbits,gbits,bbits; |
| | rdString = lstring(255);<br>procedure setlut(table : rdString;<br>rbits,gbits,bbits : integer); |
| comments: | Table is a string which indicates the specific lookup table to be set. Possible values are: default (the default lookup table), gray and color. |
| | rbits, gbits and bbits are the number of bit planes assigned to each of the red, green and blue components of the frame buffer. |

The number of pure shades for each color is $2^{bits}$. rbits, gbits, bbits must each individually be less than or equal to the width of the color lookup table (LUT). The sum of rbits, gbits and bbits must be less than the number of physical bit planes $n$ in the frame buffer. The total number of colors displayable at any one time is $2^{(rbits+gbits+bbits)}$ out of a possible palette of $2^{(3*w)}$ where $w \geq n$ is the width of the LUT.

For a gray-level lookup table the gray bits are taken as equal to rbits. The maximum number of gray bits is $w$.

---

| | |
|---|---|
| name: | setdm (Set the display mode) |
| purpose: | Control the display mode. |
| declaration: | sub setdm(str$) |

. subroutine setdm(str)
character str(*)

setdm(str)
char *str;

rdString = lstring(255);
procedure setdm(str : rdString);

| | |
|---|---|
| comments: | The default strings are: monitor (the standard alphanumeric device) and graphics (the standard graphics device). |

---

| | |
|---|---|
| name: | setpxl (Set pixel) |
| purpose: | Set a single pixel on a scanline. |
| declaration: | sub setpxl(x,y,r,g,b) |

subroutine setpxl(x,y,r,g,b)
integer x,y
real r,g,b

setpxl(x,y,r,g,b)
int x,y;
double r,g,b;

procedure setpxl(x,y : integer; r,g,b : real);

| | |
|---|---|
| comments: | x and y are the coordinates of the lower left-hand corner of a pseudopixel as defined by setrsl. The pixel covers an area to the right and above the location x, y. r, g, b are the red, green and blue components of the color for the pixel. r, g, b are values in the range 0 to 1. (r,g,b) = (0.,0.,0.) is black and (r,g,b) = (1.,1.,1.) is white. |

| | |
|---|---|
| name: | setscn (Set scanline) |
| purpose: | Set a group of pixels on a scanline. |
| declaration: | sub setscn(y,ra,ga,ba,xstart,xstop) |

subroutine setscn(y,ra,ga,ba,xstart,xstop)
integer y,xstart,xstop
real ra(*),ga(*),ba(*)

setscn(y,ra,ga,ba,xstart,xstop)
int y,xstart,xstop;
double ra[ ], ga[ ], ba[ ];

rdScanline = array[ 0  $\cdots$  xmax ] of real;
procedure setscn(y : integer; ra,ga,ba : rdScanline; xstart,xstop
    : integer);

| | |
|---|---|
| comments: | y is the pseudoscanline to be set. |

xstart is the starting location of the pixels.
xstop is the location of the last pixel.

ra, ga, ba are arrays containing the red, green and blue values
for the pixels to be set. The elements of ra, ga and ba are in the
range 0 to 1 with (0.,0.,0.) as black and (1.,1.,1.) as white. The
first element in each of the arrays is used for the pixel at xstart.
Succeeding pixels along the scanline use the values in succeeding
elements of the array.

| | |
|---|---|
| name: | getpxl (Get pixel) |
| purpose: | Get a single pixel on a scanline. |
| declaration: | sub getpxl(x,y,r,g,b) |

subroutine getpxl(x,y,r,g,b)
integer x,y
real r,g,b

getpxl(x,y,r,g,b)
int x,y;
double *r,*g,*b;

procedure getpxl(x,y : integer; var r,g,b : real);

| | |
|---|---|
| comments: | x and y are the coordinates of the lower left-hand corner of a |

pseudopixel as defined by setrsl. The pixel covers an area to the
right and above the location x, y.

r, g, b are (in C pointers to) the red, green, and blue components of the color for the pixel. r, g, b are values in the range 0 to 1. (r,g,b) = (0.,0.,0.) is black and (r,g,b) = (1.,1.,1.) is white.

---

| | |
|---|---|
| name: | getscn (Get scanline) |
| purpose: | Get a group of pixels on a scanline. |
| declaration: | sub getscn(y,ra,ga,ba,xstart,xstop) |

subroutine getscn(y,ra,ga,ba,xstart,xstop)
integer y,xstart,xstop
real ra(*),ga(*),ba(*)

getscn(y,ra,ga,ba,xstart,xstop)
int y,xstart,xstop;
double ra[ ],ga[ ],ba[ ];

rdScanline = array[0...xmax] of real;
procedure getscn(y : integer; var ra,ga,ba : rdScanline;
    xstart,xstop : integer);

comments:   y is the pseudo scanline to be read.
xstart is the starting location of the pixels.
xstop is the location of the last pixel.

ra, ga, ba are arrays which receive the red, green, and blue values for the pixels to be read. ra, ga, and ba are in the range 0 to 1 with (ra,ga,ba) = (0.,0.,0.) as black and (1.,1.,1.) as white. The first element in the arrays is the value for the pixel at xstart. Succeeding elements of the array contain the values for succeeding pixels.

---

| | |
|---|---|
| name: | text (Text) |
| purpose: | Display text. |
| declaration: | sub text(str$) |

subroutine text(str)
character str(*)

text(str)
char *str;

rdString = lstring(255);
procedure txt(str : rdString);

comments:   Text is displayed at the last cursor position in the default character size. The cursor position is the lower left corner of the first character cell. The cursor is left at the lower right of the last character cell of the text string.

Note: The text/character string in FORTRAN 77 must end with a $, e.g. HELLO$ is used to display HELLO.

Note: Because text is a reserved word in PASCAL the abbreviation txt is used.

---

| | |
|---|---|
| name: | ma (Move absolute) |
| purpose: | Move the cursor invisibly to the absolute location x, y. |
| declaration: | sub ma(x,y) |
| | subroutine ma(x,y) <br> real x,y |
| | ma(x,y) <br> double x,y; |
| | procedure ma(x,y : real); |
| comments: | x and y are real numbers. x and y are in absolute coordinates for the pseudoraster set in setrsl. 0, 0 is the lower left corner of the pseudoraster. |

---

| | |
|---|---|
| name: | mr (Move relative) |
| purpose: | Move the cursor invisibly by the relative amounts dx, dy. |
| declaration: | sub mr(dx,dy) |
| | subroutine mr(dx,dy) <br> real dx,dy |
| | mr(dx,dy) <br> double dx,dy; |
| | procedure mr(dx,dy : real); |
| comments: | dx and dy are real numbers. Movement is relative to the last location of the cursor in the dimensions of the pseudoraster set in setrsl. |

---

| | |
|---|---|
| name: | da (Draw absolute) |
| purpose: | Draw a thin line in absolute coordinates. |
| declaration: | sub da(x,y) |
| | subroutine da(x,y) <br> real x,y |
| | da(x,y) <br> double x,y; |

procedure da(x,y : real);

comments:

x and y are real numbers given in the dimensions of the pseudo-raster set in setrsl. A thin (1 physical pixel wide) line is drawn from the cursor location to x, y. x, y are given in absolute coordinates with 0, 0 as the lower left corner of the pseudoraster set in setrsl.

The current color is used to draw the line. setrgb is used to set the current color.

---

name: dr (Draw relative)

purpose: Draw a thin line using relative coordinates.

declaration: sub dr(dx,dy)

subroutine dr(dx,dy)
real dx,dy

dr(dx,dy)
double dx,dy;

procedure dr(dx,dy : real);

comments:

dx and dy are real numbers given in the dimensions of the pseu-doraster set in setrsl. A thin (1 physical pixel wide) line is drawn from the last cursor location x0, y0 to x0 + dx, y0 + dy. dx and dy are given in relative coordinates with x0, y0 as the last cursor position.

The current color is used to draw the line. setrgb is used to set the current color.

---

name: pa (Point absolute)

purpose: Display a point in absolute coordinates.

declaration: sub pa(x,y)

subroutine pa(x,y)
real x,y

pa(x,y)
double x,y;

procedure pa(x,y : real);

comments:

x and y are real numbers given in the dimensions of the pseudo-raster set in setrsl. A small dot (1 physical pixel size) is displayed at the location x, y. x, y are given in absolute coordinates with (0,0) as the lower left corner of the pseudoraster set in setrsl.

The current color is used to display the dot. setrgb is used to set the current color.

---

| | |
|---|---|
| name: | pr (Point relative) |
| purpose: | Display a point using relative coordinates. |
| declaration: | sub pr(dx,dy) |

subroutine pr(dx,dy)
real dx,dy

pr(dx,dy)
double dx,dy;

procedure pr(dx,dy : real);

comments: dx and dy are real numbers given in the dimensions of the pseudoraster set in setrsl. A small dot (1 physical pixel size) is displayed at the location x0 + dx, y0 + dy. dx, dy are relative coordinates with respect to the last cursor location x0, y0.

The current color is used to display the dot. setrgb is used to set the current color.

---

# A–9   REFERENCES†

A–1  "Graphical Kernel System (GKS)," ISO 7942, 15 August 1985; also, ANSI X3.124-1985, 24 June 1985.

A–2  Bono, P., and Herman, I. (eds.), *GKS Theory and Practice*, Springer-Verlag, Heidelberg, 1987.

A–3  Enderle, G., Kansy, K., and Pfaff, G., *Computer Graphics Programming, GKS– The Graphics Standard*, Springer-Verlag, Heidelberg, 2nd ed., 1987.

A–4  "Graphical Kernel System for Three Dimensions (GKS-3D)," ISO DIS 8805, July 1987.

A–5  "Programmer's Hierarchical Interactive Graphics System (PHIGS)," ISO DIS 9592, December 1987; also, dpANS X3.144.

A–6  Brown, M., and Heck, M., *Understanding PHIGS*, Megatek Corp., San Diego, 1985.

A–7  Van Dam, A., "PHIGS+, Functional Description Revision 3.0," *Comp. Graph.*, Vol. 22, pp. 125–218, 1988.

A–8  Rogers, D.F., *Procedural Elements for Computer Graphics*, McGraw-Hill, New York, 1985.

A–9  "Computer Graphics Metafile for the Storage and Transfer of Picture Description Information (CGM)," ISO 8632-Parts 1 through 4: 1987; also, ANSI/X3.122-1986.

A–10  Arnold, D.B., and Bono, P.R., *CGM and CGI*, Springer-Verlag, Heidelberg, 1988.

A–11 McKay, L., *CGI/CGM PRIMER*, Nova Graphics International, Austin, TX 1987.

A–12 "Computer Graphics Interfacing Techniques for Dialogues with Graphical Devices (CGI)," ISO DP 9636, 6 December 1986; also, dpANS X3.161.

A–13 International Organization for Standardization: Information Processing Systems — Computer Graphics — Interface Techniques for Dialogues with Graphical Devices. Baseline Document. ISO/TC97 N1511 (1985).

A–14 Rogers, D. F., and Rogers, S. D., "A Raster Display Graphics Package for Education," *IEEE Comp. Graph. & Appl.*, Vol. 6, pp. 51–58, April 1986.

---

†These documents are available from a variety of sources:

The published ANSI standards (viz., GKS and CGM) and the ISO documents (CGI, CGM, GKS, GKS-3D, PHIGS) can be obtained from ANSI, 1430 Broadway, New York, NY 10018. Outside the United States, ISO documents can be obtained from the national standardization organization (e.g., BSI in the UK, AFNOR in France, DIN in Germany and JIS in Japan).

The draft ANSI standards (CGI, GKS–3D and PHIGS) can be obtained from the X3 Secretariat, CBEMA, 311 First Street, Suite 500, Washington, DC 20001.

The IGES and PDES documents can be obtained from the IGES Committee Chairman, Mr. Bradford Smith, National Bureau of Standards, Gaithersburg, MD 20760.

# MATRIX OPERATIONS

A few simple rules from matrix algebra are given here for convenience. A *matrix* is simply a rectangular array of numbers governed by these rules.

## B–1 TERMINOLOGY

The numbers which make up a matrix are called its elements. These elements form rows and columns within a matrix. If the number of rows and columns are equal the matrix is *square*. Consider the $4 \times 4$ square matrix given by

$$\begin{bmatrix} a_{11} & a_{12} & a_{13} & a_{14} \\ a_{21} & a_{22} & a_{23} & a_{24} \\ a_{31} & a_{32} & a_{33} & a_{34} \\ a_{41} & a_{42} & a_{43} & a_{44} \end{bmatrix}$$

The elements of the matrix are referred to by $a_{ij}$. The first subscript refers to the row and the second to the column. Thus, $a_{34}$ is the matrix element in the third row and fourth column. A matrix of $m$ rows and $n$ columns has dimensions $m \times n$. In the square matrix above, $m = n$. The elements $a_{11}$, $a_{22}$, $a_{33}$ and $a_{44}$ of the matrix above, i.e., $a_{ij}$, $i = j$, are called diagonal elements. The sum of the diagonal elements in a square matrix is its trace.

A diagonal matrix is a square matrix in which only the diagonal elements are nonzero, i.e., $a_{ij} = 0$, $i \neq j$. An identity matrix is a diagonal matrix with all ones on the diagonal, i.e., $a_{ij} = 0$, $i \neq j$; $a_{ij} = 1$, $i = j$. An example of a $3 \times 3$ identity matrix is

$$\begin{bmatrix} 1 & 0 & 0 \\ 0 & 1 & 0 \\ 0 & 0 & 1 \end{bmatrix}$$

Every element of a zero or null matrix is zero, i.e., $a_{ij} = 0$. Two matrices are equal only when every element in one is equal to the corresponding element in the other, i.e., $a_{ij} = b_{ij}$.

A symmetrical matrix is a square matrix with $a_{ij} = a_{ji}$. For example,

$$\begin{bmatrix} 2 & 3 & 6 \\ 3 & 17 & 5 \\ 6 & 5 & 12 \end{bmatrix}$$

**503**

A row matrix is a $1 \times n$ matrix. Row matrices are occasionally called row vectors or just vectors. A column matrix is an $n \times 1$ matrix. Column matrices are occasionally called column vectors or just vectors.

A scalar is a $1 \times 1$ matrix.

## B–2   ADDITION AND SUBTRACTION

If two matrices have the same dimension, then addition and subtraction are defined. To add or subtract two matrices, each of the corresponding elements is added or subtracted, i.e., $c_{ij} = a_{ij} + b_{ij}$ or $c_{ij} = a_{ij} - b_{ij}$, respectively. As an example,

$$\begin{bmatrix} 1 & 2 & 3 \\ 4 & 5 & 6 \\ 7 & 8 & 9 \end{bmatrix} + \begin{bmatrix} 1 & 4 & 7 \\ 2 & 5 & 8 \\ 3 & 6 & 9 \end{bmatrix} = \begin{bmatrix} 2 & 6 & 10 \\ 6 & 10 & 14 \\ 10 & 14 & 18 \end{bmatrix}$$

and

$$\begin{bmatrix} 1 & 2 & 3 \\ 4 & 5 & 6 \\ 7 & 8 & 9 \end{bmatrix} - \begin{bmatrix} 1 & 4 & 7 \\ 2 & 5 & 8 \\ 3 & 6 & 9 \end{bmatrix} = \begin{bmatrix} 0 & -2 & -4 \\ 2 & 0 & -2 \\ 4 & 2 & 0 \end{bmatrix}$$

The negative of a matrix means that $b_{ij} = -a_{ij}$.

## B–3   MULTIPLICATION

Matrix multiplication is the most useful operation for computer graphics. Consider a matrix of order $n \times m$ and a second matrix of order $r \times s$. For multiplication of two matrices to be defined, the value of $m$ must equal the value of $r$. That is, the number of columns in the first matrix must equal the number of rows in the second matrix.

The rules for matrix multiplication are best described by the following example. If $[\,A\,]$ is a $4 \times 3$ matrix and $[\,B\,]$ is a $3 \times 3$ square matrix then the matrix product $[\,A\,][\,B\,]$ is defined by

$$\begin{bmatrix} a_{11} & a_{12} & a_{13} \\ a_{21} & a_{22} & a_{23} \\ a_{31} & a_{32} & a_{33} \\ a_{41} & a_{42} & a_{43} \end{bmatrix} \begin{bmatrix} b_{11} & b_{12} & b_{13} \\ b_{21} & b_{22} & b_{23} \\ b_{31} & b_{32} & b_{33} \end{bmatrix}$$

$$= \begin{bmatrix} a_{11}b_{11} + a_{12}b_{21} + a_{13}b_{31} & a_{11}b_{12} + a_{12}b_{22} + a_{13}b_{32} & a_{11}b_{13} + a_{12}b_{23} + a_{13}b_{33} \\ a_{21}b_{11} + a_{22}b_{21} + a_{23}b_{31} & a_{21}b_{12} + a_{22}b_{22} + a_{23}b_{32} & a_{21}b_{13} + a_{22}b_{23} + a_{23}b_{33} \\ a_{31}b_{11} + a_{32}b_{21} + a_{33}b_{31} & a_{31}b_{12} + a_{32}b_{22} + a_{33}b_{32} & a_{31}b_{13} + a_{32}b_{23} + a_{33}b_{33} \\ a_{41}b_{11} + a_{42}b_{21} + a_{43}b_{31} & a_{41}b_{12} + a_{42}b_{22} + a_{43}b_{32} & a_{41}b_{13} + a_{42}b_{23} + a_{43}b_{33} \end{bmatrix}$$

Specifically, each element in successive rows of $[\,A\,]$ is multiplied element-by-element with the elements of successive columns of $[\,B\,]$, and the results are added to yield a single element of the result $[\,C\,]$. Notice that a $4 \times 3$ matrix multiplied by a $3 \times 3$ matrix produces a $4 \times 3$ matrix. In general, an $n \times m$ matrix times an $r \times s$ matrix, where $m = r$, produces an $n \times s$ matrix. As a numerical example, consider

$$\begin{bmatrix} 1 & 3 \\ 4 & 2 \\ 1 & 1 \\ 6 & 4 \\ 3 & 2 \end{bmatrix} \begin{bmatrix} 1 & 2 \\ 3 & 4 \end{bmatrix} = \begin{bmatrix} 1+9 & 2+12 \\ 4+6 & 8+8 \\ 1+3 & 2+4 \\ 6+12 & 12+16 \\ 3+6 & 6+8 \end{bmatrix} = \begin{bmatrix} 10 & 14 \\ 10 & 16 \\ 4 & 6 \\ 18 & 28 \\ 9 & 14 \end{bmatrix}$$

The operation of matrix multiplication is not commutative. That is, in general, $[A][B]$ is not equal to $[B][A]$. Thus, the order (sequence) of multiplication is important. Matrix operations follow the first and second distributive laws; e.g., $A(B + C) = AB + AC$ and $(A + B)C = AC + BC$. Also, the associative law $A(BC) = (AB)C$ applies.

## B-4    DETERMINANT OF A SQUARE MATRIX

The determinant of a square matrix $[A]$ is denoted by $|A|$. The determinant has many useful properties in matrix theory. For our purpose, it is sufficient to illustrate the method for finding the determinant of a $3 \times 3$ square matrix. For the matrix

$$M = \begin{bmatrix} a_{11} & a_{12} & a_{13} \\ a_{21} & a_{22} & a_{23} \\ a_{31} & a_{32} & a_{33} \end{bmatrix}$$

the determinant is

$$\begin{vmatrix} a_{11} & a_{12} & a_{13} \\ a_{21} & a_{22} & a_{23} \\ a_{31} & a_{32} & a_{33} \end{vmatrix} = a_{11} \begin{vmatrix} a_{22} & a_{23} \\ a_{32} & a_{33} \end{vmatrix} - a_{12} \begin{vmatrix} a_{21} & a_{23} \\ a_{31} & a_{33} \end{vmatrix} + a_{13} \begin{vmatrix} a_{21} & a_{22} \\ a_{31} & a_{32} \end{vmatrix}$$

$$= a_{11}(a_{22}a_{33} - a_{23}a_{32}) - a_{12}(a_{21}a_{33} - a_{23}a_{31}) + a_{13}(a_{21}a_{32} - a_{22}a_{31})$$

This gives a single numerical value for the determinant. As an example consider the evaluation of

$$\begin{vmatrix} 3 & 9 & 4 \\ 6 & 1 & 8 \\ 2 & 5 & 3 \end{vmatrix}$$

The result is

$$3(3 - 40) - 9(18 - 16) + 4(30 - 2) = 3(-37) - 9(2) + 4(28) = -17$$

## B-5    TRANSPOSE OF A MATRIX

The transpose of a matrix is the original matrix with the rows and columns interchanged, i.e., $b_{ij} = a_{ji}$. For example,

$$\begin{bmatrix} 1 & 6 & 3 & 7 \\ 2 & 8 & 11 & 4 \\ 6 & 3 & 2 & 1 \end{bmatrix}^{T} = \begin{bmatrix} 1 & 2 & 6 \\ 6 & 8 & 3 \\ 3 & 11 & 2 \\ 7 & 4 & 1 \end{bmatrix}$$

where the superscript $T$ indicates the transpose. Notice that if the original matrix had dimensions $m \times n$ the transposed matrix has dimensions $n \times m$.

## B–6    INVERSE OF A SQUARE MATRIX

In algebra, where single variables are considered, if $ax = y$, then $x = a^{-1}y$, where $a^{-1}$ is simply the reciprocal of $a$, i.e., $a^{-1} = 1/a$. In matrix algebra division is not defined, and the reciprocal of a matrix does not exist. However, if $[A][X] = [Y]$, then $[X] = [A]^{-1}[Y]$, where $[A]^{-1}$ is the inverse of the square matrix $[A]$.

A matrix inverse exists if the matrix is square *and* if the matrix is nonsingular. Thus, not every square matrix has an inverse. However, if the determinant of the square matrix is nonzero and an inverse exists, then that inverse is unique. If the inverse exists then $[A][A]^{-1} = [I]$, where $[I]$ is the identity matrix.

Consider the matrix product of the two $3 \times 3$ matrices

$$\begin{bmatrix} 1 & 2 & 3 \\ 1 & 3 & 3 \\ 1 & 2 & 4 \end{bmatrix} \begin{bmatrix} 6 & -2 & -3 \\ -1 & 1 & 0 \\ -1 & 0 & 1 \end{bmatrix} = \begin{bmatrix} 1 & 0 & 0 \\ 0 & 1 & 0 \\ 0 & 0 & 1 \end{bmatrix}$$

If this product is represented by $[A][B] = [I]$, then $[B] = [A]^{-1}$; i.e., $[B]$ is the inverse of $[A]$.

There are numerous techniques for calculating the inverse of a square matrix. Most computer languages have functions or subroutines which perform the repetitive calculations necessary to evaluate the elements of the inverse of a given matrix. Inclusion of these techniques is beyond the scope of these brief notes.

# PSEUDOCODE

The pseudocode described is intended as an aid in understanding and implementing the algorithms presented in the text. It is not intended as a precise syntactically correct complete language. The elements of the pseudocode are drawn from several common computer programming languages: BASIC, FORTRAN, PASCAL, C, etc. The pseudocode contains structured constructs, specifically **if-then-else** and **while**. The common unconditional **go to** statement is included for convenience. The **for-next** loop statement is taken from BASIC. Subroutine modules are included. Matrix functions are included. Special functions and routines, e.g., **Min, Max, Push, Pop** are individually defined within the algorithms.

The general conventions used in presenting the algorithms are briefly given here. All key words are set in boldface, lower case characters. All statements within the body of an **if-then-else, while,** or **for-next** loop are indented. All comments are set in italics and indented, along with the statements to which they refer. Variable names longer than one character are generally set in lower case. Single character variables may be either lower case or upper case. Functions are set boldface with the first character capitalized. Detailed descriptions of these conventions follow.

## C–1    COMMENTS

Comment statements are set in italic. They are indented, along with the statements to which they refer. Sufficient comments are given at the beginning of an algorithm to briefly describe its purpose and to define the variables used.

## C–2    CONSTANTS

All constants are decimal numbers unless specified otherwise in comments. For example, 9, -3, 6.732, $1. \times 10^{-9}$, 3.

## C–3    VARIABLES

A variable is a name used to store a value. This value may change. The characters of a long variable name characters are set in lower case unless the use of a capitalized character aids in understanding by comparison with the notation used in the body of the text. Single character variables may be either lower case or upper case. Subscripted characters may be used for understanding. Typical examples are flag, $P_2'$, $x$, $y$.

## C–4    ARRAY VARIABLES

An array variable is the name for an indexed collection of values. Naming conventions are the same as those for variables. An entire array is referenced by its variable name alone. Individual elements of the array are referenced by the variable name followed by a subscript in parentheses. Examples are window, window(1, 3).

## C–5    ASSIGNMENT STATEMENT

The equal sign is used to assign the value of the expression on the right-hand side to the variable on the left-hand side.

## C–6    ARITHMETIC EXPRESSIONS

The common arithmetic operators, multiplication, division, addition, subtraction and exponentiation are indicated by $*$, $/$, $+$, $-$, $\wedge$.

## C–7    LOGICAL AND RELATIONAL OPERATORS

The logical operators **and** and **or** are set in boldface lower case, as shown. The relational operators equal, not equal, less than, greater than, less than or equal, greater than or equal are indicated by $=$, $\neq$, $<$, $>$, $\leq$, $\geq$, respectively. These operators are used for testing purposes. The result of the test is either true or false.

## C–8    THE **finish** STATEMENT

The **finish** statement is used to show termination of the algorithm.

## C–9    THE **while** AND **end while** STATEMENTS

The statements within the **while-end while** block are executed repeatedly while some condition is true. The condition is tested at the beginning of the block. When the condition is no longer true, execution continues with the statement following the **end while**. The **end while** statement is used to indicate the end of a block. All statements within a **while-end while** block are indented. The general form is

```
while (condition)
     [statements to be executed]
end while
```

As an example

```
i = 0
while (i < 5)
     x = x + 5
     i = i + 1
end while
finish
```

## C–10    THE if-then STATEMENT

The **if-then** statement is used to select an alternate execution path or to assign an alternate value to a variable depending on whether a condition is true or false.

If the argument of the **then** is a statement number, and if the condition is true, execution continues with that statement. If not, execution continues with the next sequential statement. Statement numbers are labels.

If the argument of the **then** is an assignment statement, and if the condition is true, then the assignment statement is executed. If not, the assignment statement is not executed and execution continues with the next sequential statement. The general forms are

```
if (condition) then (statement number)
if (condition) then (assignment statement)
```

Examples are

```
if (i < 10) then 3
if (i < 10) then x = x + 1
```

## C–11    THE if-then-else AND end if STATEMENTS

The **if-then-else** statement is used to select alternate blocks of statements for execution depending on whether a condition is true or false. The **end if** statement is used to indicate the end of the **if-then-else** block. The **if-then-else** statement does not imply repetition. Only one of the alternate statement blocks is executed. Execution then continues with the next sequential statement after the **end if** statement. All statements within the **if-then-else** block are indented. The general form is

```
if (condition) then
     [statements to be executed if the condition is true]
else
     [ statements to be executed if the condition is false]
end if
```

An example is

```
if (i ≥ 0) then
    x = x + 1
else
    x = x - 1
end if       .
```

If an **if-then-else** statement is written on a single line the **end if** statement is omitted. Note also that if the **else** and the second group of statements is omitted, a block **if-then** statement results.

## C–12   THE for-next STATEMENT

Loop control is achieved with a **for-next** statement as well as the **while** statement. Execution of the statements within the body of the **for-next** loop occurs repeatedly while the index value is within the specified range. All statements within the body of the loop are indented. The general form is

```
for (index variable) = (initial value) to (final value) step (index value increment)
    [ statements to be executed]
next (index variable)
```

If **step** is absent the increment is assumed to be one. Negative **step** values are allowed. The initial, final and increment values may be variables. An example is

```
for x = 1 to n step a
    y = y + x
next x
```

## C–13   THE go to STATEMENT

The **go to** statement causes an unconditional branch to the statement identified by its argument. The general form is

```
go to (statement number)
```

Statement numbers are labels. They are positioned at the extreme left edge of the statement.

## C–14   SUBROUTINE MODULES

A subroutine is a separate program module. It is invoked by means of the **call** statement. The beginning of a subroutine is defined by the **subroutine** statement. Exit from a subroutine module is indicated by the **return** statement. Upon exit from the subroutine module, control returns to the next sequential statement after the **call** statement in the calling program. The **subroutine** statement contains a list of input and a list of output variables. Communication between the calling program and the subroutine module occurs only through these variables. All other variables within a subroutine module are local to the module. The general form of the **call**, **subroutine** and **return** statements is

> **call** name(input variables; output variables)
>
> **subroutine** name(input variables; output variables)
> **return**

The input and output variable lists for the **call** and **subroutine** statements are separated by a ;. The lists must match. Subroutine names are set in boldface lower case. An example of a subroutine module is

> **subroutine check**(x,y; flag)
>     **if** x < y **then**
>         flag = 0
>     **else**
>         flag = 1
>     **end if**
> **return**

## C–15    TRIGONOMETRIC FUNCTIONS

The arguments for the common trigonometric functions, e.g., **Sin**($\theta$), **Cos**($\theta$), **Tan**($\theta$), and their inverses, e.g., **Arcsin**($x$), **Arccos**($x$), **Arctan**($x$), take and return values in degrees if the **option angle degrees** switch is set. The common hyperbolic functions and their inverses, e.g., **Sinh**($\theta$), **Cosh**($\theta$), **tanh**($\theta$), **Arcsinh**($x$), **Arccosh**($x$), **Arctanh**($x$) also take and return values in degrees if the **option angle degrees** switch is set. Otherwise, they take and return values in radians. Trigonometric and hyperbolic functions are set in boldface type with their first letter capitalized.

## C–16    MATRIX FUNCTIONS

The matrix functions are used to perform the typical operations of matrix algebra, e.g., addition, subtraction, multiplication, inversion and transpose. The matrix functions manipulate entire arrays. Each array argument in a matrix function must be of the proper dimensions for the specified operation. The matrix that results from the specified operation is of the proper dimension. For example, the result of postmultiplying a [ 3 × 2 ] matrix by a [ 2 × 3 ] matrix is a [ 3 × 3 ] matrix. Matrix arrays are read and written in row major order. Matrix arrays can be redimensioned during program execution. A matrix array can appear on both sides of an assignment statement. Matrix functions are set in boldface type with their first letter capitalized. The matrix functions are

| | |
|---|---|
| addition | **Mat** A = B + C |
| subtraction | **Mat** A = B − C |
| multiplication | **Mat** A = A∗B |
| inverse | **Mat** A = **Inv**(B) |
| transpose | **Mat** A = **Trn**(B) |

| determinant | Value | $= \textbf{Det}(B)$ |
| identity matrix | **Mat** A | $= \textbf{Idn}$ |
| zero matrix | **Mat** A | $= \textbf{Zer}(n1,n2)$ |
| constant matrix | **Mat** A | $= \textbf{Con}(n1)$ |
| dot product | Value | $= \textbf{Dot}(A,B)$ |

The **Zer** function *redimensions* the matrix array to $[\,n1 \times n2\,]$ and fills it with zeros. The **Con** function fills a previously dimensioned array with the constant value n1.

## C–17  SPECIAL FUNCTIONS

Various special functions are defined within specific algorithms. Again the function names are set in boldface type with the first letter capitalized. An example is

$$\textbf{Max}(x_1, x_2)$$

which returns the larger of the values of $x_1$ and $x_2$.

# B-SPLINE SURFACE FILE FORMAT

With the considerable current interest in B-spline surfaces a number of diverse file formats for the interchange of surface descriptions have developed. Another is proposed in Table D-1. Four-dimensional homogeneous coordinates are used to specify the defining polygon net points. This allows incorporating both the three-dimensional physical polygon net point location *and* the homogeneous coordinate (weighting) factor into a single specification. The proposed format is general enough to handle rational uniform and nonuniform, periodic and open B-spline surfaces. Nonrational B-spline surfaces are specified by setting all the homogeneous coordinate factors (weights) to unity. Rational Bézier surfaces are specified by using uniform open knot vectors of the form [ *k zeros   k ones* ] with appropriate homogeneous coordinate factors. Nonrational Bézier surfaces are specified by using the appropriate knot vectors and setting all the homogeneous coordinate factors (weights) to unity. Multiple surfaces are specified by simply repeating the complete description for each separate surface. Note that this allows specifying different types of B-spline and Bézier surfaces in the same file. The commas must be present as shown. Spaces and blank lines are allowed.

### Table D-1 Formal B-spline Surface File Format Description

| | |
|---|---|
| Surface identification string | for example: hull number (see Fig. 6–50) |
| nonrational, rational | rational or nonrational in $u$, $w$, respectively |
| open, periodic | open, periodic, nonuniform in $u$, $w$, respectively |
| order of basis, order of basis | order in $u$, order in $w$ |
| no. net pts., no. net pts. | no. net pts. in $u$ dir., no. net pts. in $w$ dir. |
| knot vector in $u$ | sequence of numbers 1, 2, 3, ... |
| knot vector in $w$ | sequence of numbers 1, 2, 3, ... |
| 4D net points list | $B(i,j)$ a ((no. net pts. in $u$)×(no. net pts. in $w$),4) array. For $B(i,j)$, j varies fastest with fixed i. Each row contains x,y,z,h components of $B(i,j)$ where $h$ is the homogeneous (weighting) factor for each net point. Note: For nonrational B-splines, all $h = 1$. |

513

## Example File

Example Surface (see Fig. 6–50)
nonrational, nonrational      The surface is nonrational in both directions.
open, open      Open basis functions are used in both directions.
4, 4      Fourth-order in both directions.
8, 8      An $8 \times 8$ defining polygon net is used.
0, 0, 0, 0, 1, 2, 3, 4, 5, 5, 5, 5      Open uniform knot vector for $u$ direction.
0, 0, 0, 0, 1, 2, 3, 4, 5, 5, 5, 5      Open uniform knot vector for $w$ direction.

| | | | | |
|---|---|---|---|---|
| 0 | , 62.7896 | , −14.2345 | , 1 | Net points $B(i,j)$, j varies fastest |
| 0 | , 58.3546 | , −11.7746 | , 1 | with fixed i. |
| 0 | , 50.7321 | , −7.7246 | , 1 | |
| 0 | , 37.2752 | , −0.7445 | , 1 | |
| 0 | , 24.6114 | , 0.2266 | , 1 | |
| 0 | , 12.2841 | , −.7321 | , 1 | |
| 0 | , 0.9638 | , −4.2096 | , 1 | |
| 0 | , −0.02351 | , −0.06207 | , 1 | |
| 13.2994 | , 57.2518 | , 0 | , 1 | |
| 8.6079 | , 50.7918 | , 0 | , 1 | |
| 7.2922 | , 52.4931 | , 0 | , 1 | |
| −0.6518 | , 33.3121 | , 0 | , 1 | |
| 1.5411 | , 14.3331 | , 0 | , 1 | |
| 3.7183 | , 13.4063 | , 0 | , 1 | |
| 7.87419 | , 1.8224 | , 0 | , 1 | |
| 0.9025 | , −0.4589 | , 0 | , 1 | |
| 17.0482 | , 57.6166 | , 13.5 | , 1 | |
| 14.0925 | , 55.5365 | , 13.5 | , 1 | |
| 11.067 | , 48.282 | , 13.5 | , 1 | |
| 3.0433 | , 40.1302 | , 13.5 | , 1 | |
| 0.2289 | , 21.5281 | , 13.5 | , 1 | |
| 3.5539 | , 7.0775 | , 13.5 | , 1 | |
| 3.0443 | , 0.7293 | , 13.5 | , 1 | |
| −0.2092 | , 0.08977 | , 13.5 | , 1 | |
| 29.2903 | , 53.3467 | , 54 | , 1 | |
| 30.7639 | , 54.1187 | , 54 | , 1 | |
| 21.1234 | , 48.1403 | , 54 | , 1 | |
| 12.0645 | , 35.461 | , 54 | , 1 | |
| 9.0546 | , 17.3787 | , 54 | , 1 | |
| 8.6407 | , 6.64932 | , 54 | , 1 | |
| 5.1127 | , −0.7182 | , 54 | , 1 | |
| 0.1572 | , −0.03143 | , 54 | , 1 | |
| 37.8884 | , 50.5464 | , 108 | , 1 | |
| 33.861 | , 47.4467 | , 108 | , 1 | |
| 27.1525 | , 36.9685 | , 108 | , 1 | |
| 23.2976 | , 19.6017 | , 108 | , 1 | |
| 19.832 | , 11.186 | , 108 | , 1 | |
| 12.7107 | , 2.5924 | , 108 | , 1 | |
| 5.5457 | , −0.4150 | , 108 | , 1 | |
| −0.01007 | , −0.04313 | , 108 | , 1 | |
| 41.0213 | , 48.1632 | , 162 | , 1 | |

| | | | |
|---|---|---|---|
| 39.6319 | , 39.2661 | , 162 | , 1 |
| 38.6344 | , 30.4192 | , 162 | , 1 |
| 33.8422 | , 16.8768 | , 162 | , 1 |
| 28.2826 | , 6.96425 | , 162 | , 1 |
| 18.2607 | , −1.0973 | , 162 | , 1 |
| 4.4469 | , 0.2564 | , 162 | , 1 |
| 0.1344 | , 0.01421 | , 162 | , 1 |
| 40.4748 | , 47.8315 | , 216 | , 1 |
| 41.1403 | , 43.5986 | , 216 | , 1 |
| 40.9666 | , 30.6183 | , 216 | , 1 |
| 41.4111 | , 14.9213 | , 216 | , 1 |
| 34.093 | , 0.2635 | , 216 | , 1 |
| 16.9322 | , 0.9311 | , 216 | , 1 |
| 5.55319 | , 0.167384 | , 216 | , 1 |
| 0.06208 | , −0.07885 | , 216 | , 1 |
| 40.536 | , 47.9986 | , 270 | , 1 |
| 40.8065 | , 41.4721 | , 270 | , 1 |
| 39.8169 | , 33.6058 | , 270 | , 1 |
| 41.8009 | , 13.1977 | , 270 | , 1 |
| 37.0837 | , 0.3062 | , 270 | , 1 |
| 13.1546 | , 1.2999 | , 270 | , 1 |
| 7.0730 | , −0.2726 | , 270 | , 1 |
| 0.07475 | , −0.04795 | , 270 | , 1 |

PROBLEMS

Because computer graphics is very much a learn by doing discipline, a number of problems and programming projects are included. Problems generally attempt to confirm or extend a concept presented in the text or to provide computational experience with a technique. They generally are focused on a single aspect of the material. They may or may not require programming.

Programming projects are designed to not only illustrate concepts and techniques presented in the text but also to provide experience in developing a reasonably complex computer graphics program. Properly executed, they result in the development of a toolbox of useful graphics routines. Completed projects frequently result in generally useful programs.

This appendix contains problems. Appendix F contains programming projects. Problems and projects are grouped by chapter.

## CHAPTER 2

**2–1**   Show that a 2D reflection through the $x$-axis, followed by a 2D reflection through the line $y = -x$, is equivalent to a pure rotation about the origin.

**2–2**   For the position vectors $P_1 [\,1 \quad 1\,]$, $P_2 [\,3 \quad 1\,]$, $P_3 [\,4 \quad 2\,]$, $P_4 [\,2 \quad 3\,]$ that define a 2D polygon, develop a single transformation matrix that

Reflects about the line $x = 0$.
Translates by $-1$ in both the x and y directions.
Rotates about the origin by $180°$.

Using this transformation, determine the transformed position vectors. Plot both the original and the transformed polygon on the same graph.

**2–3**   Show that the $2 \times 2$ matrix

$$[\,T\,] = \begin{bmatrix} \dfrac{1 - t^2}{1 + t^2} & \dfrac{2t}{1 + t^2} \\[2ex] \dfrac{-2t}{1 + t^2} & \dfrac{1 - t^2}{1 + t^2} \end{bmatrix}$$

represents a pure rotation.

**517**

**2–4**   A unit square is transformed by a $2 \times 2$ transformation matrix. The resulting position vectors are

$$\begin{bmatrix} 0 & 0 \\ 2 & 3 \\ 8 & 4 \\ 6 & 1 \end{bmatrix}$$

What was the transformation matrix?

**2–5**   Show that for $x = t^2$, $y = t$ the transformation

$$[\, x \quad y \quad 1\,] \begin{bmatrix} 0 & -2 & 2 \\ -2 & 2 & -2 \\ 1 & 0 & 1 \end{bmatrix}$$

yields points that lie on a unit circle.

## CHAPTER 3

**3–1**   Show that to obtain the same transformed effect on an object by preconcatenating matrices requires that they be applied in *reverse* order to that when postconcatenation is used; i.e.,

$$[\,Tr\,][\,Rx\,][\,Ry\,][\,Data\,] = [\,Data\,][\,Ry\,][\,Rx\,][\,Tr\,]$$

where $[\,Data\,]$ is the data matrix for the object.

**3–2**   Derive the concatenated transformation matrix for: translation by $m$, $n$, $l$ in the $x$, $y$, $z$ directions, respectively; rotation about the $y$-axis by the angle $\phi$; rotation about the $x$-axis by the angle $\theta$; followed by a single-point perspective projection onto the $z = 0$ plane from a center of projection on the $z$-axis at $z = k$. Compare the result to Eq. (3–63).

**3–3**   Reverse the order of application of the rotation in Prob. 3–2. Compare the results.

**3–4**   For the cube of Ex. 3–23, determine the position vectors after transformation using the concatenated matrix derived in Prob. 3–2 with $m = l = n = 0$, $\phi = 60°$, $\theta = 30°$ and $k = 2.5$. Compare the results to those of Ex. 3–23 by plotting both results side by side on a single piece of graph paper.

**3–5**   Reverse the order of application of the rotation in Prob. 3–4. Compare the results to those of Prob. 3–4 and of Ex. 3–23 by plotting the three results side by side on a single piece of graph paper.

**3–6**   Develop the $4 \times 4$ transformation matrix for the object defined by the position vectors

$$\begin{bmatrix} 0 & 0 & 2 & 1 \\ 2 & 0 & 2 & 1 \\ 2 & 1 & 2 & 1 \\ 1 & 2 & 2 & 1 \\ 0 & 2 & 2 & 1 \\ 0 & 0 & 0 & 1 \\ 2 & 0 & 0 & 1 \\ 2 & 2 & 0 & 1 \\ 0 & 2 & 0 & 1 \\ 2 & 2 & 1 & 1 \end{bmatrix}$$

with connectivity algorithm (see Sec. A–7)

$$C(j) = -1, 2, 3, 4, 5, 1, -6, 7, 8, 9, 6, -1, 6, -2, 7, -5, 9, -4, 10, 8, -10, 3$$

as viewed from an eye position (center of projection) 50 units to the right, 60 units above and 150 units in front of the object's center. Remember, we see in perspective.

**3–7** Rotate the cube with the corner cut off (see Prob. 3–6) 30° about an axis through the points $P_1 [-3 \quad -3 \quad 2]$ and $P_2 [-3 \quad -2 \quad -2]$. Determine the transformed position vectors. Draw the result using a dimetric projection with a foreshortening factor of 0.625. Assume both dimetric rotation angles are positive.

**3–8** Show that any combination of pure rotations and/or an even number of reflections can be represented by at most 3 rotations about the coordinate axes.

**3–9** Extend the analysis of Sec. 3–20 to the case where the sight vector from the center of projection is *not* perpendicular to the plane of projection.

## CHAPTER 4

**4–1** Derive the relationship between the number of points, the radius and the tolerance when representing a circle by its inscribed polygon. The tolerance is defined as the maximum perpendicular distance from the arc to the chord between two points on the circumference of the circle.

**4–2** A Lamé oval is described by

$$\frac{x^n}{c_1} + \frac{y^n}{c_2} = 1$$

Determine the equation of the oval through the three points $P_1 [0 \quad 6]$, $P_2 [5 \quad 5]$, $P_3 [6 \quad 0]$. Determine the intersection of this oval with the circle of radius 3 centered at $x = 6$, $y = 0$.

**4–3** Calculate an equal number of points on the perimeter of the quarter circle in the first quadrant using a nonparametric explicit (Eq. 4–1), a trigonometric parametric (Eq. 4–2) and the alternate parametric (Eq. 4–3) analysis. Plot and compare the results.

**4–4** Derive Eq. 4-13.

**4–5** Develop and implement an algorithm for the vertex definition of a parametric parabola given by Eq. 4–13.

**4–6** Extend the method of Sec. 4–9 to the case of a circle through a point tangent to a line.

**4–7** Extend the method of Sec. 4–9 to the case of a line through a point tangent to a circle of known radius and location.

**4–8** Extend the method of Sec. 4–9 to the case of a circle of known radius tangent to two circles of known radius and known location. Hints: There are 16 possible solutions. Construct a decision tree of possible solutions depending on the radius of the tangent circle and the distance between the two known circles.

**4–9**   Extend the method of Sec. 4–9 to the case of a circle of known radius simultaneously tangent to a line and a circle of known radius and location. Hints: There are 8 possible solutions. The line may or may not intersect the circle.

**4–10**   Extend the method of Sec. 4–9 to the case of an ellipse of known semimajor and semiminor axes tangent to two intersecting lines. What additional information, if any, is required?

**4–11**   For each of Probs. 4–5 to 4–8, substitute an ellipse of known semimajor and semiminor axes for each of the circles. In each case state what additional information, if any, is required.

**4–12**   What type of conic section is represented by each of the following equations:

$$x^2 + y^2 + 4x - 2y = 10$$
$$x^2 + y^2 + xy - x + y = 3$$
$$x^2 - 4xy + 4y^2 + 3x = 6$$
$$2x^2 - y^2 + 4xy + 2x - 3y = 6$$
$$x^2 - 4xy + 3y^2 + 5y = 7$$
$$x^2 - y^2 = 1$$

**4–13**   Transform each of the equations in Prob. 4–12 into standard form.

**4–14**   Show that Eq. (4–33) is equivalent to

$$A(x + m)^2 + B(y + n)(x + m) + C(y + n)^2 + F(x + m) + G(y + n) + H = 0$$

**4–15**   Show that the following quadratic equation is a parabola and draw the segment between $x = 1$ and $x = 3$ for $y_{min}$:

$$16x^2 - 24xy + 9y^2 - 60x - 80y + 20 = 0$$

**4–16**   The first quadrant of a unit circle is parametrically represented by

$$x = \frac{(1 - \sqrt{2})t^2 + (\sqrt{2} - 2)t + 1}{(2 - \sqrt{2})t^2 + (\sqrt{2} - 2)t + 1}$$

$$y = \frac{(1 - \sqrt{2})t^2 + \sqrt{2}t}{(2 - \sqrt{2})t^2 + (\sqrt{2} - 2)t + 1}$$

Determine the value of $y$ for $x = 0.5$. Hint: use an iterative technique to first find $t$ for $x = 0.5$.

## CHAPTER 5

**5–1**   Generate the parametric curves shown in Fig. 5–3.

**5–2**   Given the four position vectors $P_1 [\,0 \quad 0 \quad 0\,]$, $P_2 [\,1 \quad 1 \quad 1\,]$, $P_3 [\,2 \quad -1 \quad -1\,]$, $P_4 [\,3 \quad 0 \quad 0\,]$, determine the piecewise cubic spline curve through them using the chord length approximation for the $t_k$'s. The tangent vectors at the ends are $P_1' [\,1 \quad 1 \quad 1\,]$ and $P_4' [\,1 \quad 1 \quad 1\,]$. Calculate 7 points on each spline segment. Compare the results for $\tau = 1/3, 2/3$ with those of Ex. 5–2, the 2D analog of this problem.

**5-3**    Using the position vectors of Ex. 5–2, calculate and compare the cubic spline curve shapes for tangent vectors at $P_1$ of $P_1'\,[\ \sqrt{2}\cos\theta\quad \sqrt{2}\sin\theta\ ]$ for $\theta = 0°$, 22.5°, 45°, 67.5°, 90° while keeping $P_2\,[\,1\quad 1\,]$ constant. Compare these results to those obtained by varying both $P_1'\,[\ \sqrt{2}\cos\theta\quad \sqrt{2}\sin\theta\ ]$ and $P_2'\,[\ \sqrt{2}\cos\theta\quad \sqrt{2}\sin\theta\ ]$. Notice that the magnitude of the tangent vectors is constant; only the direction changes.

**5-4**    Using the position vectors of Ex. 5–2, calculate and compare the cubic spline curve shapes for tangent vectors at $P_1$ and $P_2$ of $P_1'\,[\,a\quad a\,]$, $P_2'\,[\,a\quad a\,]$ for $a = 1/4$, 1/2, 1, 2, 4, 8. Notice that the direction of the tangent vectors is constant but the magnitude changes.

**5-5**    Using the position vectors of Ex. 5–2, calculate and compare the cubic spline curve shapes for relaxed end conditions. Compare the results to those of Prob. 5–2 and Ex. 5–2.

**5-6**    Given the five 2D position vectors

$$[\,P\,] = \begin{bmatrix} 0 & 0 \\ 0.5 & 0.6 \\ 1.0 & 1.0 \\ 1.5 & 0.8 \\ 1.0 & 0 \end{bmatrix}$$

along with the two end tangent vectors $P_1' = [\,1\quad 1\,]$ and $P_2' = [\,0\quad -1\,]$, determine $P(0.5)$ for each of the four cubic spline segments using the normalized approximation, i.e., $0 \le t \le 1$

**5-7**    Repeat Prob. 5–2 using the normalized approximation for the $t_k$'s, i.e., $t_k = 1.0$. Compare the results with those of Prob. 5–2 and with Ex. 5–2, the 2D analog of this problem.

**5-8**    Determine the cubic spline curve through the 5 position vectors $P_1\,[\,1\quad \pi/4\quad 0\,]$, $P_2\,[\,1\quad 3\pi/4\quad 1\,]$, $P_3\,[\,1\quad 5\pi/4\quad 2\,]$, $P_4\,[\,1\quad 7\pi/4\quad 3\,]$, $P_5\,[\,1\quad \pi/4\quad 4\,]$, where the position vector components are given in cylindrical coordinates, i.e., $P_i\,[\,r\quad \theta\quad z\,]$. Use relaxed end conditions.

**5-9**    Calculate the parabolically blended curve through the data points given in Prob. 5–2. Use the technique described in Sec. 5–6. Compare the results with those of Prob. 5–2 and Ex. 5–2.

**5-10**    Derive the $[\,A\,]$ matrix (see Eq. 5–60) for a parabolically blended curve using the chord lengths as the maximum parameter value, i.e., assume

$$p(r) = [\,r^2\quad r\quad 1\,][\,B\,] \qquad\qquad 0 \le r \le d_{13}$$
$$q(s) = [\,s^2\quad s\quad 1\,][\,D\,] \qquad\qquad 0 \le s \le d_{24}$$
$$C(t) = [\,t^3\quad t^2\quad t\quad 1\,][\,A\,][\,G\,] \qquad 0 \le t \le d_{23}$$

where $d_{12}$, $d_{23}$, $d_{34}$ are the chord lengths for $P_1 P_2$, $P_2 P_3$, $P_3 P_4$ and $d_{13} = d_{12} + d_{23}$, $d_{24} = d_{23} + d_{34}$. Note that this is still not precisely Overhauser's result.

**5-11**    Derive Overhauser's result using the matrix methods of Sec. 5–7.

**5-12**    Determine the Bézier curve using the position vectors defined in Ex. 5–2 as the defining polygons. Calculate results for parametric values of 0, 1/3, 2/3, 1.

**5–13**   Determine the position vector $P_3$ that gives tangent vector continuity across the joint between the two Bézier curve segments otherwise defined by $P_1[\,0 \quad 0 \quad 0\,]$, $P_2[\,2 \quad 2 \quad -2\,]$, $P_4[\,4 \quad 0 \quad 0\,]$ and $Q_1[\,4 \quad 0 \quad 0\,]$, $Q_2[\,6 \quad -2 \quad 1\,]$, $Q_3[\,8 \quad -3 \quad 2\,]$, $Q_4[\,10 \quad 0 \quad 1\,]$

**5–14**   For the Bézier curve defined by the polygon vertices of Ex. 5–7, determine the defining polygon vertices required to generate the sixth-degree Bézier curve equivalent to the fourth-degree curve of Ex. 5–7. Hint: Raise the degree in successive steps.

**5–15**   Determine the defining polygon vertices that subdivide the Bézier curve defined in Ex. 5–7 into two cubic Bézier curves.

**5–16**   Apply the Bézier curve subdivision technique successively to the Bézier curve and its defining polygon vertices of Ex. 5–7, and show by example that the defining polygon and the curve converge.

**5–17**   Repeat Ex. 5–11 for the knot vector $[\,0 \quad 0 \quad 0 \quad 2 \quad 2 \quad 3 \quad 3 \quad 3\,]$. The results are shown in Fig. 5–38e. Compare these results with those of Ex. 5–11 and Fig. 5–38d.

**5–18**   Determine algebraic relations for the nonuniform basis functions obtained with knot vectors $[\,0 \quad 0 \quad 0 \quad 0.4 \quad 2.6 \quad 3 \quad 3 \quad 3\,]$ and $[\,0 \quad 0 \quad 0 \quad 1.8 \quad 2.2 \quad 3 \quad 3 \quad 3\,]$. The results are shown in Figs. 5–38b and c. Compare the results with each other and with those of Figs. 5–38d and e.

**5–19**   Illustrate the dependencies of the B-spline basis functions for curves of orders 4 and 5 defined by six polygon vertices. Use a technique similar to that in Sec. 5–9.

**5–20**   Determine the fourth-order B-spline curve using the position vectors of Ex. 5–2 as the defining polygons. Compare the results to the Bézier curve calculated in Prob. 5–12.

**5–21**   Determine the third-order B-spline curve using the position vectors defined in Ex. 5–2 as the defining polygons. Use parameter values of 0, 1/2, 1, 3/2, 2.

**5–22**   For the defining polygon given in Ex. 5–13, determine the pseudovertices necessary to make the end points of the periodic B-spline curve coincide with $B_1$ and $B_4$, respectively. Compare the results with those shown in Fig. 5–54.

**5–23**   For the defining polygon given in Ex. 5–13, determine the pseudovertices necessary to make the tangent vectors at the ends of the curve be $[\,-1 \quad 1\,]$ and $[\,1 \quad -1\,]$, respectively. Also calculate the starting and ending points of the curve. Compare the results with those shown in Fig. 5–54.

**5–24**   Using the chord length approximation discussed in Sec. 5–9, determine the fourth-order open B-spline curve for the defining polygon given in Ex. 5–14. Compare the results to those given in Ex. 5–14.

**5–25**   Using the chord length approximation discussed in Sec. 5–9, determine the third-order periodic B-spline curve for the defining polygon given in Ex. 5–14. Compare the results to those given in Ex. 5–14.

**5–26**   Using the chord length approximation discussed in Sec. 5–9, determine the fourth-order periodic B-spline curve for the defining polygon given in Ex. 5–14. Compare the results to those given in Ex. 5–14 and in Prob. 5–24 above.

**5-27** Show that the two B-spline curves defined in Ex. 5–18 by polygon vertices $B_1 [0 \quad 0], B_2 [1 \quad 1], B_3 [2 \quad 1], B_4 [3 \quad 0]$ with alternate knot vectors defined by $[X'] = [0 \quad 0 \quad 0 \quad 1 \quad 2 \quad 2 \quad 2]$ and $[X] = [0 \quad 0 \quad 0 \quad 2 \quad 4 \quad 4 \quad 4]$ are identical. Hint: Calculate a number of points on the first curve $0 \le t' \le 2$ and on the second curve $0 \le t = 2t' \le 4$, and compare the results.

**5-28** Show that the subdivided B-spline curve in Ex. 5–18 is the same as the original curve. Hint: Calculate several points on the two curves, and plot them to the same scale.

**5-29** Show that the subdivided B-spline curve in Ex. 5–19 is the same as the original curve. Hint: Calculate several points on the two curves, and plot them to the same scale.

**5-30** Show that if, after the original curve in Ex. 5–19 is subdivided, the new polygon vertex $C_3$ is moved to coincide with $C_2$, then the resulting curve has a sharp corner at $C_2 = C_3$.

**5-31** To obtain a better understanding of the nature of a vector valued function such as $P(t) = [x(t) \quad y(t)]$, plot graphs of $x(t)$ vs $t$, $y(t)$ vs $t$ and $y(t)$ vs $x(t)$ for the fourth-order ($k = 4$) B-spline curve defined by $B_1 [0 \quad 0], B_2 [2 \quad 2], B_3 [4 \quad 2], B_4 [6 \quad 0]$ with the open knot vector $[0 \quad 0 \quad 0 \quad 0 \quad 1 \quad 1 \quad 1 \quad 1]$. Repeat for the third-order ($k = 3$) B-spline curve with the open knot vector $[0 \quad 0 \quad 0 \quad 1 \quad 2 \quad 2 \quad 2]$.

**5-32** Determine the analytical expressions for the second derivative along a rational B-spline curve. Evaluate the results for $t = 0$ and $t = n + k - 2$.

**5-33** Generate the rational B-spline curves for defining polygon vertices $B_1 [0 \quad 0]$, $B_2 [1 \quad 2], B_3 [2.5 \quad 0], B_4 [2.5 \quad 0], B_5 [2.5 \quad 0], B_6 [4 \quad 2], B_7 [5 \quad 0]$, with $[H] = [1 \quad 1 \quad h_3 \quad h_4 \quad h_5 \quad 1 \quad 1]$ for values of $h_3 = h_4 = h_5 = 0, 0.25, 1, 5$. Compare the results to Fig. 5–66.

**5-34** Do Ex. 5–20 for $k = 4$.

**5-35** Determine the first and second derivatives at $t = 0$ and $t = 3$ for the defining polygon in Ex. 5–20.

**5-36** Determine the first and second derivatives at $t = 0$ and $t = 2$ for $k = 4$ for the defining polygon in Ex. 5–20.

**5-37** Generate a torus as a rational B-spline surface by rotating the circle of radius 1 centered at $x = 5$, $z = 1$ about the z-axis. (See Fig. 6–58.)

**5-38** Generate a sphere of radius 1 as a rational B-spline surface by rotating the semicircle of radius 1 centered at $x = 0$, $z = 1$ about the z-axis. (See Fig. 6–59.)

## CHAPTER 6

**6-1** Generate the surfaces shown in Fig. 6–6.

**6-2** Generate surfaces of revolution for the curves calculated in Probs. 5–6 and 5–9.

**6-3** Generate the mug shown in Fig. 6–10.

**6-4** Add a handle to the mug shown in Fig. 6–10 using a sweep surface.

**6–5**   Generate the sweep surface shown in Fig. 6–16.

**6–6**   Determine the type of quadric surface defined by each of these equations:

$$2x^2 - 2yz + 2zx - 2xy - x - 2y + 3z - 2 = 0$$
$$x^2 + z^2 + 2xy + 2xz - 2yz - 2x + 4y - 4 = 0$$
$$x^2 + 4Y^2 + z^2 - 4yz - 12zx + 24xy + 4x + 16y - 26z - 3 = 0$$
$$4x^2 + y^2 + z^2 - 4xy + 6z + 8 = 0$$
$$4y^2 + 4z^2 + 4xy - 2x - 14y - 22z + 33 = 0$$

**6–7**   Using a parametric representation, generate a hyperbolic paraboloid.

**6–8**   Draw the individual component mapped surfaces, i.e., $Q(u, v, x)$, $Q(u, v, y)$, $Q(u, v, z)$ (see Fig. 6–24), and the complete surface $Q(x, y, z)$, for a point, a line and a plane.

**6–9**   For the ruled surface with edge curves defined by

$$z = 0 \qquad y = 0.25 \cos(2\pi x) \qquad 0 \le x \le 1$$
$$z = 1 \qquad y = 0.25 \sin(2\pi x) \qquad 0 \le x \le 1$$

determine the surface point at $Q(0.5, 0.5)$.

**6–10**   Construct the bilinear surface corresponding to the four points $P(0, 0) = [\,0.25 \quad 0\,]$, $P(1, 0) = [\,0.75 \quad 0\,]$, $P(0, 1) = [\,0.75 \quad 0.9\,]$, $P(0, 0) = [\,0.25 \quad 0.8\,]$.

**6–11**   Construct the bilinear surfaces that correspond to the four points defined by the opposite ends of the diameters of two unit circles lying in parallel planes 1 unit apart as they rotate in opposite directions through 180° at 15° intervals.

**6–12**   Generate the complete ruled surface shown in Fig. 6–28 and discussed in Ex. 6–10. Is the surface developable?

**6–13**   Generate the complete ruled surface shown in Fig. 6–30 and discussed in Ex. 6–12. Show that the corner part of the surface is developable.

**6–14**   Show by example that a planar Coons bicubic surface results when the position, tangent and twist vectors all lie in the same plane.

**6–15**   Find the matrix $[\,P\,]$ that yields a cylindrical Coons bicubic surface patch.

**6–16**   Find the matrix $[\,P\,]$ that yields a general ruled Coons bicubic surface patch.

**6–17**   Determine the surface point at $u = w = 0.5$ for the Coons bicubic surface with the following position: $P(0,0) = [\,-100 \quad 0 \quad 100\,]$, $P(0,1) = [\,100 \quad -100 \quad 100\,]$, $P(1,1) = [\,-100 \quad 0 \quad -100\,]$, $P(1,0) = [\,-100 \quad -100 \quad -100\,]$; u-tangent $P^{1,0}(0,0) = [\,10 \quad 10 \quad 0\,]$, $P^{1,0}(0,1) = [\,-1 \quad -1 \quad 0\,]$, $P^{1,0}(1,1) = [\,-1 \quad 1 \quad 0\,]$, $P^{1,0}(1,0) = [\,1 \quad -1 \quad 0\,]$; w-tangent $P^{0,1}(0,0) = [\,0 \quad -10 \quad -10\,]$, $P^{0,1}(0,1) = [\,0 \quad 1 \quad -1\,]$, $P^{0,1}(1,1) = [\,0 \quad 1 \quad 1\,]$, $P^{0,1}(1,0) = [\,0 \quad 1 \quad 1\,]$; and twist vectors given by $P^{1,1}(0,0) = [\,0 \quad 0 \quad 0\,]$, $P^{1,1}(0,1) = [\,0.1 \quad 0.1 \quad 0.1\,]$, $P^{1,1}(1,1) = [\,0 \quad 0 \quad 0\,]$, $P^{1,1}(1,0) = [\,-0.1 \quad -0.1 \quad -0.1\,]$. Systematically vary the tangent and twist vectors, and compare the results.

**6–18**   Extend the analysis of parabolically blended curves to parabolically blended surfaces (see Ref. 5–10). Hint: Use parabolically blended curves for the four boundary curves and a Coons linear surface style formulation with blending functions given by $F_1(t) = 1 - 3t^2 + 2t^3$, $F_2(t) = 3t^2 - 2t^3$. Note that the resulting surface is controlled by the four corner points and by two additional pseudovertices at each corner that control the tangent vectors at the ends of the boundary curves. What is the continuity of individual patches? What degree of continuity can be maintained across patch boundaries? What is the extent of the influence of moving a single point on a surface built up of multiple patches?

**6–19** Show for a $4 \times 4$ bicubic Bézier surface that for $u = w = 0$

$$Q_{uw}(0,0) = 9 \left[ (B_{1,1} - B_{0,1}) - (B_{1,0} - B_{0,0}) \right]$$

Compare the result to the appropriate term in Eq. (6–60).

**6–20** Determine the $4 \times 4$ defining Bézier polygon net vertices that yield the bicubic Coons surface patch of Ex. 6-13.

**6–21** Generate the Bézier surface of Ex. 6–14 without using matrix methods.

**6–22** Show that neither a hyperbolic paraboloid nor a hyperbola of one sheet is a developable surface.

**6–23** For the surface in Ex. 6–12, show that the Gaussian curvature is zero in the flat area and positive elsewhere.

**6–24** Determine the Gaussian curvature at $u = w = 0.5$ for the surfaces described in Ex. 6–14 and shown in Figs. 6–39a to d. Compare the results.

**6–25** Generate the closed periodic B-spline surfaces shown in Fig. 6–46.

**6–26** Generate the combined open and periodic B-spline surface shown in Fig. 6–47.

**6–27** Generate the closed periodic B-spline torroidal surface shown in Fig. 6–48.

**6–28** Compute the fourth order B-spline surface for the $4 \times 5$ defining polygon net given by

$$B_{1,1} [\, 0 \quad 0 \quad 100 \,] \qquad B_{2,1} [\, 25 \quad 0 \quad 150 \,] \qquad B_{3,1} [\, 50 \quad 0 \quad 100 \,]$$
$$B_{4,1} [\, 75 \quad 0 \quad 50 \,] \qquad B_{5,1} [\, 100 \quad 0 \quad 100 \,]$$

$$B_{1,2} [\, 0 \quad 33 \quad 150 \,] \qquad B_{2,2} [\, 25 \quad 33 \quad 200 \,] \qquad B_{3,2} [\, 50 \quad 33 \quad 100 \,]$$
$$B_{4,2} [\, 75 \quad 33 \quad 50 \,] \qquad B_{5,2} [\, 100 \quad 33 \quad 50 \,]$$

$$B_{1,3} [\, 0 \quad 66 \quad 50 \,] \qquad B_{2,3} [\, 25 \quad 66 \quad 25 \,] \qquad B_{3,3} [\, 50 \quad 66 \quad 100 \,]$$
$$B_{4,3} [\, 75 \quad 66 \quad 150 \,] \qquad B_{5,3} [\, 100 \quad 66 \quad 150 \,]$$

$$B_{1,4} [\, 0 \quad 100 \quad 100 \,] \qquad B_{2,4} [\, 25 \quad 100 \quad 50 \,] \qquad B_{3,4} [\, 50 \quad 100 \quad 100 \,]$$
$$B_{4,4} [\, 75 \quad 100 \quad 150 \,] \qquad B_{5,4} [\, 100 \quad 100 \quad 100 \,]$$

Determine by hand calculation the point in the center of an $11 \times 15$ parametric surface net.

Write a program to compute the two diagonal parametric lines $u = 2w$ and $u = 2(1-w)$. List the points from (0, 0) to (2, 1) for $u = 2w$ and from (0, 1) to (2, 0) for $u = 2(1-w)$. List 11 values for each diagonal.

Compute and display the $11 \times 15$ parametric surface. List 15 $u$ and 11 $w$ values. Use an appropriate viewing transformation. Suggestion: Output the results to a file in either standard graphics format (.sgf) or standard polygon format (.spf) and use the three-dimensional manipulator developed in Proj. 3–1 to display the surface.

# PROGRAMMING PROJECTS

Programming projects are designed to not only illustrate concepts and techniques presented in the text but also to provide experience in developing a reasonably complex computer graphics program. Properly executed, they result in the development of a toolbox of useful graphics routines. Many of the routines and techniques developed for one project are usable in developing subsequent projects. Completed projects frequently result in generally useful programs. The projects are grouped by chapter.

Two of the projects are particularly recommended. The first is the scientific plotting program (Proj. 2–4). Writing a good scientific plotting program is a nontrivial task. However, it is well within the capabilities of either undergraduate or graduate students. It is recommended that for undergraduates it be assigned as one of two term projects (the other being the three-dimensional manipulator (Proj. 3–1)). Graduate students should be allowed approximately three weeks to complete the project.

The second is the three-dimensional manipulator (Proj. 3–1). A three-dimensional manipulator allows the display and manipulation (rotation, translation, scaling, projection, etc.) of three-dimensional objects. A three-dimensional manipulator significantly aids in the visualization of objects. Further, it improves the ability to visualize in three dimensions. Finally, it is useful in developing an understanding of the material on three-dimensional curves and surfaces presented in Chapters 5 and 6. For undergraduates this should be the second of two term projects. Again, for graduate students this is about a three week project.

In designing and developing these programs the concepts of structured programming and in particular modular programming must be emphasized. Each of the projects is easily broken down into a reasonably small set of graphics tool type modules. For example, most of the graphics tools for the three-dimensional manipulator are given as pseudocode in Appendix G. The implementation language is unimportant. All the projects have been implemented, by students, on a variety of machines in a variety of languages.

Good documentation is required. An example of an acceptable documentation header is shown in Table F–1. Copious internal documentation is also required.

### Table F–1 Program Documentation Header

name:

programmer:

date:

history:

purpose:

method:

system:

language:

subroutines called:

input files:

compile command:

link command:

calling arguments:

variable list:

Since a number of projects are intended to be interactive, a word about user interfaces is appropriate. In a nonreal time graphics environment, the alphanumeric keyboard is the most frequently used interactive device. In this environment, a properly designed keyboard interface is easy to learn, fast and efficient.

Unless a numeric value is specifically required, a keyboard interface should accept alphabetic words for inputs. Numbered lists of responses are unacceptable. The fundamental reason is that the user thinks in terms of words and phrases, *not* numbered items on a list. For example, if the desired action is to rotate an object, the user thinks rotate and *not* item 3 on the option list.

Not all individuals are touch typists. Consequently, the number of characters required to initiate a command should be kept to a minimum. However, individuals who are touch typists should not be placed at a disadvantage (annoyed) by the use of odd sequences of characters. One solution is to allow full words as input and then *truncate* those words to the minimum number of characters necessary to uniquely define the command. For example, the command rotate is truncated to the first two characters, i.e., ro. Acceptable truncation that yields unique character sequences is indicated by parentheses, e.g., (ro)tate. Numeric input must be accepted in free format; i.e., decimal points are *not* required for floating point numbers. For example, 30 and 30. are equivalent.

A command menu should be provided. The question of how and when it is provided is important. It should be displayed once upon initial execution of the program and upon request thereafter. It should *not* be redisplayed after each command is accepted. Doing so is both annoying and time consuming. The command menu should occupy a single screen. Appropriate command menus should be provided at all levels within the program that accept commands. In lieu of continuous display of the command menu a single command line is used. The command line consists of a single word or character, e.g., ? or Option? or Command?

There are as many ways of requesting a command or help menu (screen) as there are programmers, e.g., typing h or help or ? or ?? or menu or whatever! Discovering the appropriate command is often rather interesting. A simple solution is to accept any of them or a simple carriage return. Implementation is simple. If, in parsing the command input, a legal input is not found, then the command menu (help screen) appropriate to that level is displayed.

The efficiency of the interface is increased by a concept called 'command stacking'. The concept is best illustrated by an example. For the three-dimensional manipulator project (see Proj. 3–1) the rotate command might require the specification of the axis of rotation ($x$, $y$, $z$, or general) and the rotation angle in degrees. The top level command processor accepts the rotate command and invokes a lower level command processor that asks for and accepts the axis and angle inputs. Command stacking allows the familiar user to type

    ro x 30

where here the command responses are separated by spaces. The top level command processor parses the input string, determines if the first command ro is acceptable and, if acceptable, passes the remaining commands to lower level command processors. Command stacking allows the familiar user to accomplish multiple manipulations with little input and minimal waiting while allowing the occasional user access to the same capabilities. As an example, with command stacking

    sc o 2
    ro x 30
    ro y −45
    dr

scales the object by a factor of 2 using overall scaling, rotates about the $x$-axis by 30°, rotates about the $y$-axis by −45° and draws the result on the $z = 0$ plane using an orthographic projection.

Finally, a user interface must be consistent at all levels. It must also adhere to the 'principle of least astonishment'. The principle of least astonishment, simply stated, is that when a response to a command can be implemented in multiple ways the choice is made on the basis of 'what response will least astonish the user'.

## CHAPTER 2

The first two projects are designed to familiarize students with the local graphics package and to begin the development of a basic toolbox of graphics modules. The third is designed to provide experience with the concepts of window and viewport and to begin the development of manipulative transformations. The fourth is the development of a scientific plotting program.

**2–1**   Design and implement a program to draw the closed polygon with vertices $P_1 [ 0 \quad 0 ]$, $P_2 [ 2 \quad -2 ]$, $P_3 [ 2 \quad 1 ]$, $P_4 [ 0 \quad 3 ]$, $P_5 [ -2 \quad 1 ]$, $P_6 [ -2 \quad -2 ]$ taken in order counterclockwise. Use a window and/or viewport command as appropriate to make the polygon fill the display area. Be careful to maintain the correct geometric relationships; i.e., 1 unit on the $x$-axis is equal to 1 unit on the $y$-axis. Include axes through the origin. Place tick marks on the axes at unit intervals. Label the tick marks.

As part of the program design and implementation include modules to:

Draw axes through the point $x0, y0$ for $x$-min to $x$-max and for $y$-min to $y$-max.

Place left, right or through the axis tick marks on an $x$- or $y$-axis of a specified length passing through a specified location at specified intervals.

Label the tick marks with the appropriate values.

Draw an arbitrary polygon. Hint: See Appendix A–7.

**2–2**    Design and develop a program to generate and display the curves described by the parametric equations:

a. $x = \{2 + 7\cos(\sin(\theta) + \sin(121\theta))\}\cos(\theta)$    $\pi/2500 \leq \theta \leq 2\pi$
   $y = \{2 + 7\cos(\sin(\theta) + \sin(121\theta))\}\sin(\theta)$

b. $x = \{11/10 + \cos(8\theta)^{19}\}\cos(\theta)$    $\pi/2000 \leq \theta \leq 2\pi$
   $y = \{1.1 + \cos(8\theta)^{19}\}\sin(\theta)$

c. $x = \{1 + 2\sin(17\theta/4)\}\cos(\theta)$    $\pi/500 \leq \theta \leq 8\pi$
   $y = \{1 + 2\sin(17\theta/4)\}\sin(\theta)$

d. $x = \{-\theta\sin(\pi\theta)/8\}\cos(\theta)$    $9\pi/1000 \leq \theta \leq 36\pi$
   $y = \{-\theta\sin(\pi\theta)/8\}\sin(\theta)$

e. $x = \{\sin(13\theta/4\}\cos(\theta)$    $\pi/100 \leq \theta \leq 100\pi$
   $y = \{\sin(13\theta/4\}\sin(\theta)$

Use a window and/or viewport command as appropriate to make the figure fill the display area. Be careful to maintain the correct geometric relationships, i.e., 1 unit on the $x$-axis is equal to 1 unit on the $y$-axis. Include axes through the origin. Place tick marks on the axes at unit intervals. Label the tick marks. Allow the user to turn the axes off.

As part of the program design and implementation include modules to:

Draw axes through the point $x0, y0$ for $x$-min to $x$-max and for $y$-min to $y$-max.

Place left, right or through the axis tick marks on an $x$ or $y$ axis of a specified length passing through a specified location at specified intervals.

Label the tick marks with the appropriate values.

Draw the figure. Hint: See Appendix A–7.

**2–3**    Perform the following transformations individually on the pair of lines $P_1 P_2$ and $P_3 P_4$ defined by $P_1 [ -2 \quad -1 ]$, $P_2 [ 1 \quad 2 ]$, $P_3 [ -1 \quad -1 ]$, $P_4 [ -1 \quad 2 ]$

a. Rotate through $-60°$.
b. Reflect about the line $y = x$.
c. Scale by a factor of 2.

Perform the following transformations individually on a second pair of lines $P_5 P_6$ and $P_7 P_8$ defined by $P_5 [ -1 \quad -1 ]$, $P_6 [ 2 \quad 2 ]$, $P_7 [ -3 \quad -1 ]$, $P_8 [ 0 \quad 2 ]$

a. Rotate through $60°$ followed by reflection through the $x$-axis.
b. Reflect through the $x$-axis followed by rotation through $60°$.
c. Apply the transformation $\begin{bmatrix} -1 & 3 \\ 2 & 4 \end{bmatrix}$.

Obtain the indicated results by hand calculation.

Design and develop a program to display the results on a single screen in the format shown in the sketch below. The three left hand boxes in the lower row each contain the first pair of untransformed lines. The three right hand boxes contain the second pair of untransformed lines. The upper row contains the corresponding transformed lines. Each box is to contain an axis with tick marks. Because of space limitations it may be desirable to *not* label the individual tick marks. However, it is necessary to indicate, in some manner, the value of each tick mark in each box. The display is to be labeled as indicated.

Transformed

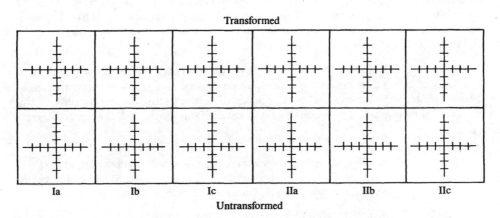

Ia          Ib          Ic          IIa          IIb          IIc

Untransformed

In designing and implementing this program good use is made of the concepts of window and viewport discussed in Sec. 1–4 and Appendix A–4. Except for the window size, the placement of the box on the screen and the application of a transformation, if any, the operations required to generate each of the boxes is identical. Thus, the main program consists of:

```
for i = 1 to 6
        apply transformation, if any
        determine window size
        call window
        for j = 1 to 2
                call viewport(j)
                call box
                call axes
                call tick
                call label
                call drawlines(j)
        next j
    next i
```

As part of the program design and implementation include modules to:

Determine the required window size.

Draw a box around the window.

Draw axes through the point $x0, y0$ from $x$-min to $x$-max and from $y$-min to $y$-max.

Place left, right or through the axis tick marks on an $x$ or $y$ axis of a specified length passing through a specified location at specified intervals.

Label the tick marks with the appropriate values.

Draw the lines.

Also be sure to implement general two-dimensional rotation, reflection and scaling modules (see Appendix G). Use these modules to generate the required transformation matrices within the program. When multiple transformations are required (items a and b for the second pair of lines) concatenate the matrices *before* applying them to the original pair of lines.

**2–4** Design and implement a scientific plotting program that accepts input data in the form of a two-dimensional .sgf file as described in Table A–2 of Appendix A–6. The user interface comments at the beginning of this appendix are appropriate to the design of the program. The required characteristics and options for the program are:

input
: Inputs data from a two-dimensional .sgf file.

plot
: Display the graph according to range, labels, annotation, etc. specifications. Defaults are autoranging, data connected by solid lines, no labels, box with no grid and no annotation. (See below.)

labels
: Label the graph, the $x$-axis and the $y$-axis.

axes
: Both axes linear, one or both axes log. Neat axis ranges are required. Possible axis ranges begin or end at 0, $\pm 1$, $\pm 2$, $\pm 5$. Thus, an axis may have a range of $0 \rightarrow 1$, $0 \rightarrow 2$, $0 \rightarrow 5$, $-1 \rightarrow 1$, $-1 \rightarrow 5$, $-2 \rightarrow 5$, etc. Odd axis ranges, e.g., $0 \rightarrow 1.736$, are not permitted unless specifically requested via the range command. Axis labels are of order of magnitude 1. The magnitude of the labels is indicated by a multiplier located next to the last tick label on the axis. It is of the form $\times 10^2$. Log axes are labeled only at intervals corresponding to 1, 5, and 10.

range
: Change the range of the graph. $x$ and $y$ minimums and maximums are requested.

autorange
: Automatically determine appropriate $x$- and $y$-axis ranges. (See axes.)

style
: Select a line style for a specified curve. A menu of available styles is presented. As a minimum, a dashed line, a solid line, a dot at each point, a star at each point, a plus at each point or an $\times$ at each point is provided. Combinations of a point and line style are allowed.

tick
: Select a style of tick mark. A menu of available styles is presented. As a minimum, ticks on the left or right side of the axis looking from the origin in the positive axis direction, ticks on both sides of the axis, long ticks at major axis divisions and short ticks at minor axis divisions are provided.

| | |
|---|---|
| ylabel | Toggles the $y$-axis label to read from the side or vertically downward. The default is vertically downward. |
| grid | Toggle a grid on/off. |
| square | Provides a square graph that preserves geometric relations, i.e., 1 unit on the $x$-axis equals 1 unit on the $y$-axis. |
| box | Toggles between a box graph with axes and tick marks on all four sides and one with only coordinate axes and tick marks. |
| scale | Change the graph size by specifying $x$ and $y$ scale factors. |
| color | Color each data curve separately by mixing a palette of red, green and blue values. Red, green and blue values are given in the range $0 \leq r, g, b \leq 1$ where 0 is no contribution and 1 is the maximum contribution of that component. |
| annotate | Place appropriate annotation on the graph at arbitrary locations. Both automatic and interactive placement of the annotation is possible. The automatic option prompts for input strings and displays them in the upper left hand corner of the graph. The interactive option allows positioning each entered annotation string by requesting $x$, $y$ coordinates for the lower left corner of the string. A menu of available annotation fonts is presented. (See fonts.) |
| undo | Allows any previous command to be turned off, e.g., labels, annotation, range, etc., specifically including the last command. A menu of undo options is presented. |
| reset | Resets all options to the default values. (See plot.) |
| font | Select alternate font styles. A menu of available fonts is presented. |
| hardcopy | Make a hardcopy of the displayed graph. A menu of available options is presented. Output to an .sdf (see Table A–1 of Appendix A–5) format file is included. |
| save | Save the current graph in a file. |
| restore | Load a previously saved graph from a file. Further modification of the graph is allowed. |
| fit | Generate a curve fit for individual data curves. A menu of available fitting techniques is presented. Among these should be polynomial, power law and exponential least-squares, cubic spline, Bézier and B-spline fitting techniques. |
| quit | Terminate the program and return to the operating system. |

## CHAPTER 3

The single project here is the design and development of a three-dimensional manipulator. The assumption is that objects are displayed using a wire frame style. Input of multiple objects is allowed. Successful implementation requires the development of a suite of modules for three-dimensional rotation, translation, scaling, etc., as well as those for orthographic, oblique and perspective projection, etc.

**3–1**   Design and implement a three-dimensional manipulator program that accepts input data in the form of either an .sgf or .spf file as described in Table A–2 and A–3 of Appendix A–6. The user interface comments at the beginning of this appendix are appropriate to the design of the program. The required characteristics and options for the program are:

| | |
|---|---|
| input | Input object data from a file in either .sgf or .spf format. |
| delete # | Delete the object(s) specified by #. |
| rotation | Rotate the object(s) about the $x$, $y$ or $z$ coordinate axes or about a general rotation axis. The general rotation axis is specified by either a point and three direction cosines or by two points on the axis. The general rotation is built-up from rotations about the coordinate axes. Rotations occur about either the world coordinate axes or about local body axes. |
| translation | Translate the object(s) in the $x$, $y$ or $z$ direction. |
| reflection | Reflect the object(s) through the $x = 0$, $y = 0$ or $z = 0$ planes. |
| scale | Scale the object(s) either locally, i.e., in the individual $x$, $y$ or $z$ directions or overall, i.e., equally in all directions. |
| axis | Two types of three-dimensional axes are required: body and fixed. Either or both are displayable at any one time. Size is variable. Tick marks may optionally be on or off. Body axes are fixed to the centroid of an object or of a group of objects. They move, i.e., rotate, translate, reflect, etc., with the object. The fixed axes are located at the origin of the world coordinate system. They are subject to the scene transformation, e.g., isometric, dimetric, oblique or perspective projection. |
| projection | Projection of the object(s) onto the $z = 0$ plane using an isometric, dimetric, oblique, cabinet, cavalier or single-point perspective projection. Isometric and dimetric transformations provide a choice of positive or negative rotation about both the $x$- and $y$-axes. Dimetric and oblique projections allow for variable foreshortening factors. Oblique, cabinet and cavalier projections allow for variable angle with the horizontal ($\alpha$). Only a single-point perspective projection onto the $z = 0$ plane with variable center of projection on the $z$-axis is implemented. |
| zoom | Zoom in or out on the *entire* scene. Note: this is not the same as scaling the object(s). |
| original | Restore the original object data. |
| draw | Draw the transformed object(s) using an orthographic projection onto the $z = 0$ plane. |
| output | Save the current transformed data points in a file in either .sgf or .spf format, as appropriate. |
| savmat | Save the current transformation matrix in a file. |

| | |
|---|---|
| shade | Create a shaded image.[†] Requires that data be entered in .spf format. |
| hidden | Create a hidden line/surface display.[†] Requires that the data be entered in .spf format. |
| hardcopy | Make a hardcopy of the displayed image. A menu of available output devices is presented. Output to an .sdf format file is required (see Table A–1 of Appendix A–5). |
| center | Display object(s) centered about the geometric center of the data. |
| object # | Turns individual or groups of objects specified by # on/off. |
| 4view | Creates four views of the object(s): front, side and top orthographic projections in the lower left, lower right and upper left quadrants of the screen, plus the current projection in the upper right quadrant. |
| background | Deletes any background items on the display, e.g., menus. |
| quit | Terminate the program and return to the operating system. |

The program is structured such that all transformation matrices are concatenated until either a draw command or one of the projection commands is executed. Upon execution of either the draw or one of the projection commands, the concatenated transformation matrix is applied to the data base and the resulting transformed two-dimensional position vectors are drawn on the output device. The original three-dimensional data base is *not* modified by a draw or projection command.

The main program basically consists of an option loop of the form:

Quit = arbitrary string
**while** Quit <> q **then**
    **print** Option ? to the screen
    **input** Response from the keyboard
    **truncate** Response to first two characters
    **convert** Response to lower case character
    **if** Response = ro **then call** rotation submenu
    **if** Response = re **then call** reflection submenu
    **if** Response = pr **then call** projection submenu

    .
    .
    .

    **print** main help screen
**end while**

A typical submenu program might look like

---

[†] See Rogers, D.F., *Procedural Elements for Computer Graphics*, McGraw-Hill Book Co., New York, 1985, Chapter 4.

Quit = arbitrary string

**while** Quit <> q **then**

    **print** Rotation about what axis?

    **input** Response from the keyboard

    **truncate** Response to first character

    **convert** Response to all lower case characters

    **if** Response = x **then call** x-rotation routine

    **if** Response = y **then call** y-rotation routine

    **if** Response = z **then call** z-rotation routine

    **if** Response = g **then call** general rotation routine

    **print** local help screen

**end while**

With this basic concept it is easy to see that the program has at least three operational levels. The first selects the principle operation, e.g., rotation, the second selects the specific operation, e.g., the axis of rotation, and the third performs the operation.

If required, the scope of the project can be reduced by deleting requirements.

As a specific test example consider the T-block defined by

$$\begin{bmatrix} 0 & 0 & 4 \\ 4 & 0 & 4 \\ 4 & 2 & 4 \\ 3 & 2 & 4 \\ 3 & 4 & 4 \\ 1 & 4 & 4 \\ 1 & 2 & 4 \\ 0 & 2 & 4 \\ 0 & 0 & 0 \\ 4 & 0 & 0 \\ 4 & 2 & 0 \\ 3 & 2 & 0 \\ 3 & 4 & 0 \\ 1 & 4 & 0 \\ 1 & 2 & 0 \\ 0 & 2 & 0 \end{bmatrix} \begin{matrix} A \\ B \\ C \\ D \\ E \\ F \\ G \\ H \\ I \\ J \\ K \\ L \\ M \\ N \\ O \\ P \end{matrix}$$

Develop a single transformation matrix which:

Reduces the size by 1/2.

Rotates about the $x$-axis by 30°.

Rotates about the $y$-axis by −30°.

Translates −2 units in the $y$ direction.

Performs a single-point perspective projection on to $z = 0$ from $z = 10$.

First develop and then apply the concatenated transformation matrix for these operations to the data base by hand calculation. Plot the result on graph paper. Calculate and plot any vanishing points. Use these hand calculations to verify the operation of the three-dimensional manipulator.

## CHAPTER 4

The single project here is based on extensions of the material in Sec. 4–9. Suggested extensions are given in Problems 4–6 to 4–10. Similar constructions are required in computer aided drafting systems and in numerical control applications.

**4–1**   Design and implement a program to interactively define the geometry specified in Sec. 4–9 and/or its extensions given in Problems 4–6 to 4–10. Be careful to maintain the correct geometric relationship when displaying the results; e.g., circles should look like circles, not ellipses. The user interface comments at the beginning of this appendix are appropriate to the design of the program. The required characteristics and options for the program are:

| | |
|---|---|
| line | Define a line by its two end points. |
| circle | Define a circle by its radius and center $(h, k)$. |
| add | Add a circle or line to the geometry. |
| delete | Delete a circle or line from the geometry. |
| move | Move a previously defined circle or line. |
| axes | Turn axes on/off. |
| ticks | Turn axis tick marks on/off. |
| labels | Turn axis tick mark labels on/off. |
| solution | Select the appropriate solution from the possible solutions using concepts such as left, right, near, far, inside and outside as presented in Sec. 4–9. |

As part of the program design and implementation, include modules to:

Draw axes through the point $x0, y0$ for $x$-min to $x$-max and for $y$-min to $y$-max.

Place left, right or through the axis tick marks on an $x$- or $y$-axis of a specified length passing through a specified location at specified intervals.

Label the tick marks with the appropriate values.

Generate and draw a circle or circular arc.

Also be sure to develop the necessary two-dimensional manipulation modules, e.g., rotation, translation, reflection, etc., required to place the geometry in a standard orientation. When multiple transformations are required, concatenate the matrices *before* applying them to the geometry. Develop the necessary modules to support traversing the decision tree required to select the necessary solution, determine if the selected solution is physically possible and perform the necessary calculations required to determine any unknown geometric values.

## CHAPTER 5

The project here is a curve generation and manipulation program. Any of the curves discussed in Chapter 5, e.g., cubic spline, parabolically blended, Bézier or B-spline curves, both nonrational and rational, are used as the basis of the program. Including the ability to generate multiple curve types within the same program makes comparison particularly convenient.

**5–1**   Design and implement a three-dimensional curve generation and manipulation program that accepts input data in the form of a three-dimensional .sgf file as described in Table A–2 of Appendix A–6. The generated three-dimensional curve(s) are plotted using an orthographic projection onto the $z = 0$ plane. The user interface comments at the beginning of this appendix are appropriate to the design of the program. The required characteristics and options for the program are:

| | |
|---|---|
| input | Input data from a file in three-dimensional .sgf format. |
| type | Selects the type of curve to be generated. A menu of available curve types, e.g., cubic spline, parabolically blended, Bézier and B-spline, is presented. For cubic spline curves, both normalized and chordwise approximations with at least clamped and relaxed end conditions are implemented. For parabolically blended curves, variable $\alpha$ and chordwise approximation of $\alpha$ and $\beta$ are implemented. The default value of $\alpha$ is 0.5. For Bézier and B-spline curves, both nonrational and rational variants as well as degree raising and subdivision capabilities are implemented. |
| polygon | Draws straight lines between the input data points. For Bézier and B-spline curves, this shows the defining polygon. |
| label | Display labels next to the individual input data points, e.g., $P_1$, $P_2$, $P_3$, etc. |
| add | Add a data point. Be sure to allow for adding a point *before* the first data point. |
| delete | Delete a data point. |
| move | Move a data point. |
| erase | Toggles whether or not the screen is erased before the current curve is drawn. |
| axes | Toggles the graph axes on/off. The axes include appropriate tick marks and labels. |
| range | Change the range of the graph. $x$ and $y$ minimums and maximums are requested. |
| autorange | Automatically determine appropriate $x$ and $y$ axis ranges. |
| style | Select a line style for a specified curve. A menu of available styles is presented. As a minimum, a dashed line and a solid line are provided. |
| curve # | Turns individual or groups of curves specified by # on/off. |
| remove # | Remove the curve(s) specified by # from the program database. |
| original | Restore the original curve data. |

print        Print the curve constructive data to the screen, e.g., the defining polygon for a Bézier or B-spline curve.

hardcopy     Make a hardcopy of the displayed image. A menu of available output devices is presented. Output to an .sdf format file is required (see Table A–1 of Appendix A–5).

output       Save the generated three-dimensional curve data points in a file in three-dimensional .sgf format for subsequent display and manipulation using the three-dimensional manipulator (see Project 3–1).

quit         Terminate the program and return to the operating system.

If desired, the scope of the project can be reduced by deleting requirements.

Use the calculations of Ex. 5–2 and Problems 5–2, 5–5, 5–7, 5–9, 5–10, 5–12, 5–20 and 5–21 to verify the operation of the three-dimensional curve generator and manipulator program.

**5–2** Add the capability for Bézier and B-spline curve fitting, both nonrational and rational to Project 5–1. Data is input from an .sgf format file.

## CHAPTER 6

The project here is a surface generation and manipulation program. It is very similar to the curve generation and manipulation program for Chapter 5. It has many of the same characteristics of that program. It can also be built on top of the three-dimensional manipulator program of Proj. 3–1. In that case surface generation and manipulation are simply additional functions.

Any of the surfaces discussed in Chapter 6, e.g., bilinear, ruled, linear or bicubic Coons, Bézier or B-spline surfaces, both nonrational and rational, are used as the basis of the program. Including the ability to generate and display multiple surfaces makes investigation of the effects of input data variations particularly convenient.

**6–1** Design and implement a three-dimensional surface generation and manipulation program that accepts input data in the form of a three-dimensional .sgf file, as described in Table A–2 of Appendix A–6 or for Bézier and B-spline surface polygon net point file in the form of a .pnp file, as described in Table D–1 of Appendix D. The generated surfaces are displayed using an appropriate projection onto the $z = 0$ plane, e.g., isometric, dimetric, cabinet or cavalier. Output of results in either .sgf or .spf format allows subsequent use. The user interface comments at the beginning of this appendix are appropriate to the design of the program. The required characteristics and options for the program are:

input        Input data from a file in three-dimensional .sgf or .pnp format.

surface      Generates the surface. For Bézier and B-spline surfaces both nonrational and rational variants as well as degree raising and subdivision capabilities are implemented. (See Probs. 6–17 and 6–28 for suggested test surfaces.)

boundary     Calculate and display the four boundary curves for the surface.

diagonals    Calculate and display the two diagonal curves for the surface.

parametric   Calculate and display an orthogonal net of isoparametric lines on the surface. The number of lines in each parametric direction is requested.

draw   Display the surface using an appropriate projection, e.g., isometric, dimetric, cabinet or cavalier.

polygon   Draws straight lines between the input data points. Implemented for Bézier and B-spline surfaces to show the defining polygon.

axis   Two types of three-dimensional axes are required: body and fixed. Either or both are displayable at any one time. Size is variable. Tick marks may optionally be on or off. Body axes are fixed to the centroid of an object or of a group of objects. They move, i.e., rotate, translate, reflect, etc., with the object. The fixed axes are located at the origin of the world coordinate system. They are subject to the scene transformation, e.g., isometric, dimetric, oblique or perspective projection.

label   Display labels next to the individual input data points, e.g., $P_1$, $P_2$, $P_3$, etc.

modify   Modify the characteristics of the surface. A menu of possible modifications, of which one is to move the position vector, is presented. For a bicubic Coons surface, modification of the tangent and twist vectors is also included.

zoom   Zoom in or out on the *entire* scene. Note: this is not the same as scaling the surface.

erase   Toggles whether or not the screen is erased before the current surface is drawn.

original   Restore the original surface data.

print   Print the surface constructive data to the screen, e.g., the defining polygon net for a Bézier or B-spline surface.

hardcopy   Make a hardcopy of the displayed image. A menu of available output devices is presented. Output to an .sdf format file is required (see Table A–1 of Appendix A–5).

output   Save the generated surface data points in a file in .sgf or .spf format for subsequent display and manipulation using the three-dimensional manipulator (see Project 3–1).

quit   Terminate the program and return to the operating system.

If desired, the scope of the project can be reduced by deleting requirements.

Use the calculations of Exs. 6–9, 6–10, 6–12 to 6–15 and 6–18 and Problems 6–9 to 6–11 to verify the operation of the surface generator and manipulator program.

**6–2**   Add the capability for three-dimensional surface fitting to Project 6–1. Input data in the form of a three-dimensional .sgf file as described in Table A–2 of Appendix A–6.

# ALGORITHMS

Gathered here are a number of useful algorithms. The algorithms are presented using the pseudocode described in Appendix C. The choice of 'language' to use in presenting the algorithms was difficult. Pascal, Fortran, C and ANSI Basic were all strong candidates. Each language has its strengths and weaknesses for computer graphics. Each has its strong supporters and proponents and its equally strong detractors. The final decision was made on pedagogical grounds. Presentation using pseudocode requires that the algorithms be translated into a 'real' programming language. Hopefully, this process increases the understanding of the algorithms and hence of the underlying mathematics.

The pseudocode versions of the algorithms were algorithmically derived from working programs. Hopefully, this process resulted in more accurate algorithms. However, errors may have been introduced in the typesetting process. Consequently, implementers should carefully check the algorithms against the mathematics presented in the text.

The algorithms are designed to be educational, i.e., they are intended to support the mathematical techniques discussed in the text. They are *not* intended to be the *most* efficient implementations possible. Frequently, computational inefficiencies are accepted if the resulting algorithm more closely follows the discussion in the text. Computational inefficiencies are also accepted to reduce memory requirements. Consequently, programs derived from the implemented algorithms are usable with microcomputer operating systems having limited memory access. An example is the B-spline surface algorithm **bsplsurf**. In the pseudocode algorithm given below, the B-spline basis functions for each parameter value are calculated inside the main loop. This reduces memory requirements. However, it is computationally more efficient to calculate all of the basis functions externally to the main loop, form their products and store them in a large array. Appropriate elements of the array are then used within the main loop to calculate position vectors on the surface. A few minutes thought shows that, for reasonably complex surfaces, the array size becomes quite large. However, the algorithm runs several times faster than the pseudocode algorithm presented. When implementing the pseudocode algorithms, it is suggested that the algorithm first be implemented as given.[†] Once the program is proven correct, then both the underlying mathematics *and* the algorithm should be closely examined to determine methods for increasing efficiency.

The algorithms are grouped by chapter and alphabetically within each chapter.

## CHAPTER 2

The algorithms given here perform the basic two dimensional manipulations. In alphabetical order these are: **reflt2d, rot2d, scale2d, tran2d**.

### reflt2d

Subroutine to form and concatenate a 2D reflection matrix with the current transformation matrix (see Eqs. 2–34 to 2–36).

$reflt(,)$ = *reflection matrix*
$rfltcode$ = *reflection code*
    $1$ = *thru x-axis*
    $2$ = *thru y-axis*
$t(,)$    = *current transfomation matrix with which the translation matrix*
      *is to be concatenated*

**subroutine reflt2d**(rfltcode; t(,))

**dimension** reflt(3,3)

**Mat** reflt = **Idn**

**if** rfltcode = 1 **then** reflt(2,2) = −1           *set the appropriate element to* −1
**if** rfltcode = 2 **then** reflt(1,1) = −1

**Mat** t = t*reflt                 *concatenate the matrices*

**return**

### rot2d

Subroutine to form and concatenate a 2D rotation matrix with the current transformation matrix (see Eq. 2–29).

$rot(,)$ = *rotation matrix*
$theta$ = *rotation angle in degrees*
$t(,)$    = *applied matrix with which the rotation matrix*
      *is to be concatenated*

---

[†]For information on implementations in ANSI Basic (True Basic), C and Fortran, send a self-addressed, stamped envelope to: David F. Rogers, 817 Holly Drive E., Rt. 10, Annapolis, MD 21401, USA.

**subroutine rot2d**(theta; t(,))

**option angle degrees**

**dimension** rot(3,3)

**Mat** rot = **Idn**

rot(1,1) = **Cos**(theta)                                     *set up the rotation matrix*
rot(1,2) = **Sin**(theta)
rot(2,2) = rot(1,1)
rot(2,1) = −rot(1,2)

**Mat** t = t∗rot                                            *concatenate the matrices*

**return**

## scale2d

Subroutine to form and concatenate a 2D scaling matrix with the current transformation matrix (see Eqs. 2–37 and 2–58).

$a, d$     =  *x and y stretching factors a,d > 1 stretches; a,d < 1 contracts*
$s$        =  *overall scaling factor s > 1 enlarges, s < 1 reduces*
$Scale(,)$ =  *scaling matrix*
$t(,)$     =  *current transformation matrix with which the translation matrix*
              *is to be concatenated*

**subroutine scale2d**(a,d,s; t(,))

**dimension** scale(3,3)

**Mat** scale = **Idn**

scale(1,1) = a                                              *set up the scaling matrix*
scale(2,2) = d
scale(3,3) = 1/s

**Mat** t = t∗scale                                          *concatenate the matrices*

**return**

## tran2d

Subroutine to form and concatenate a 2D translation matrix with the current transformation matrix (see Eq. 2–50).

$m, n$     =  *translation factors in x and y respectively*
$t(,)$     =  *current transformation matrix with which the translation matrix*
              *is to be concatenated*
$tran(,)$  =  *translation matrix*

**subroutine tran2d**(m,n; t(,))

**dimension** tran(3,3)

**Mat** tran = **Idn**

tran(3,1) = m                                               *set up the translation matrix*
tran(3,2) = n

**Mat** t = t∗tran                                           *concatenate the matrices*

**return**

## CHAPTER 3

The algorithms given here perform the basic three dimensional manipulations. A number of algorithms for projection onto a two-dimensional plane are also given. In alphabetical order these are: **cabinet, cavalier, dimetric, genrot, isometric, oblique, perspective, project, reflt3d, scale3d, tran3d, xrot, yrot, zrot.**

### cabinet

Subroutine to form and concatenate a cabinet projection matrix with the current transformation matrix (see p. 175 and Ex. 3–16).

$alpha$ = *the angle between the horizontal and the projected z-axis*
$t(,)$ = *current transformation matrix with which the cabinet matrix is to be concatenated*

**subroutine cabinet**(alpha; t(,))

**option angle degrees**

*perform the cabinet projection by calling oblique with $f = 0.5$*

**call oblique**(alpha,0.5; t(,))

**return**

### cavalier

Subroutine to form and concatenate a cavalier projection matrix with the current transformation matrix (see p. 175 and Ex. 3–16).

$alpha$ = *the angle between the horizontal and the projected z-axis.*
$t(,)$ = *current transformation matrix with which the cavalier matrix is to be concatenated*

**subroutine cavalier**(alpha; t(,))

**option angle degrees**

*perform the cavalier projection by calling oblique with $f = 1$*

**call oblique**(alpha,1; t(,))

**return**

### dimetric

Subroutine to form and concatenate a dimetric projection matrix with the current transformation matrix (see Eqs. 3–32, 3–39, 3–40 and Ex. 3–14).

$f$ = *foreshortening factor in z direction*
$t(,)$ = *current transformation matrix with which the dimetric matrix is to be concatenated*
$xcode$ = *x rotation code*
$\qquad 0 = negative\ rotation\ angle$
$\qquad 1 = positive\ rotation\ angle$
$ycode$ = *y rotation code*
$\qquad 0 = negative\ rotation\ angle$
$\qquad 1 = positive\ rotation\ angle$

**subroutine dimetric**(ycode,xcode,f; t(,))

**option angle degrees**

*find the rotation angles*

phi = **Arcsin**(f/(**Sqrt**(2−f∗f)))
theta = **Arcsin**(f/**Sqrt**(2))

*set up the rotation directions*

**if** ycode = 0 **then** phi = −phi
**if** xcode = 0 **then** theta = −theta

*perform the dimetric transformation by calling yrot, xrot and project*

**call yrot**(phi; t)
**call xrot**(theta; t)
**call project**(3; t)

**return**

## genrot

Subroutine to form and concatenate a 3D rotation matrix about a general axis in space, not parallel to a coordinate axis, with the current transformation matrix. The technique is to make the rotation axis coincident with the z-axis (see Eqs. 3–21 and 3–23 to 3–26).

a(,)  =  *array containing two points of the rotation axis*
delta =  *rotation angle about the general axis in degrees*
t(,)  =  *current transformation matrix with which the general rotation matrix*
        *is to be concatenated*

**subroutine genrot**(a(,),delta; t(,))

**option angle degrees**

**dimension** rx(4,4),ry(4,4),rdelta(4,4),rxinv(4,4),ryinv(4,4)
**dimension** tran(4,4),traninv(4,4)
**dimension** m(4,4),minv(4,4)
**dimension** temp1(4,4),temp2(4,4)

**Mat** rx = **Idn**
**Mat** ry = **Idn**
**Mat** rdelta = **Idn**
**Mat** tran = **Idn**
**Mat** rxinv = **Idn**
**Mat** ryinv = **Idn**
**Mat** traninv = **Idn**

*calculate the direction cosines*

cx = a(2,1) − a(1,1)
cy = a(2,2) − a(1,2)
cz = a(2,3) − a(1,3)

nfactor = **Sqrt**(cx∗cx + cy∗cy + cz∗cz)

cx = cx/nfactor
cy = cy/nfactor
cz = cz/nfactor

d = **Sqrt**(cy*cy + cz*cz)

*set up the various matrices*

*note that because rx and ry are pure rotations the inverse is the transpose*

tran(4,1) = −a(1,1)

tran(4,2) = −a(1,2)

tran(4,3) = −a(1,3)

traninv(4,1) = a(1,1)

traninv(4,2) = a(1,2)

traninv(4,3) = a(1,3)

rx(2,2) = cz/d

rx(2,3) = cy/d

rx(3,2) = −rx(2,3)

rx(3,3) = rx(2,2)

**Mat** rxinv = **Trn**(rx)

ry(1,1) = d

ry(1,3) = cx

ry(3,1) = −cx

ry(3,3) = d

**Mat** ryinv = **Trn**(ry)

rdelta(1,1) = **Cos**(delta)

rdelta(2,2) = rdelta(1,1)

rdelta(1,2) = **Sin**(delta)

rdelta(2,1) = −rdelta(1,2)

*concatenate the various matrices*

**Mat** temp1 = rx*ry

**Mat** m = tran*temp1

**Mat** temp2 = rxinv*traninv

**Mat** minv = ryinv*temp2

**Mat** temp1 = rdelta*minv

**Mat** temp2 = m*temp1

**Mat** t = t*temp2

**return**

## isometric

Subroutine to form and concatenate an isometric projection matrix with the current transformation matrix (see Eqs. 3–32, 3–41 and Ex. 3–15).

t(,)   =  *current transformation matrix with which the isometric matrix*
           *is to be concatenated*

xcode =  *x rotation code*
           *0 = negative rotation angle*
           *1 = positive rotation angle*

ycode =  *y rotation code*
           *0 = negative rotation angle*
           *1 = positive rotation angle*

**subroutine isometric**(ycode,xcode; t(,))

**option angle degrees**

*set up the rotation directions*

**if** ycode = 0 **then** phi = −45
**if** ycode = 1 **then** phi = 45
**if** xcode = 0 **then** theta = −35.26439
**if** xcode = 1 **then** theta = 35.26439

*perform the isometric transformation by calling yrot, xrot and project*

**call yrot**(phi; t)
**call xrot**(theta; t)
**call project**(3; t)

**return**

## oblique

Subroutine to form and concatenate an oblique projection matrix with the current transformation matrix (see Eq. 3–44).

*alpha =*  *the angle between the horizontal and the projected z-axis*
*f*     =  *foreshortening factor in z direction*
*t(,)*   =  *current transformation matrix with which the oblique matrix*
       *is to be concatenated*

**subroutine oblique**(alpha,f; t(,))

**option angle degrees**

**dimension** oblique(4,4)

**Mat** oblique = **Idn**

oblique(3,3) = 0                               *set up the transformation matrix*
oblique(3,1) = −f***Cos**(alpha)
oblique(3,2) = −f***Sin**(alpha)

**Mat** t = t*oblique                            *concatenate the matrices*

**return**

## perspective

Subroutine to form and concatenate a single point perspective projection on to the z = 0 plane matrix with the current transformation matrix (see Eq. 3–47).

*cp*   =  *center of projection on the z-axis*
*t(,)* =  *current transformation matrix with which the perspective matrix*
       *is to be concatenated*

**subroutine perspective**(cp; t(,))

**option angle degrees**

**dimension** perspective(4,4)

**Mat** perspective = **Idn**

perspective(3,3) = 0         *set up the single point perspective projection matrix*
perspective(3,4) = −1/cp

**Mat** t = t*perspective                    *concatenate the matrices*

**return**

## project

Subroutine to form a simple orthographic projection onto one of the coordinate planes and concatenate it with the current transformation matrix (see Eqs. 3–27 to 3–29).

$proj(,)$ = *projection matrix*
$projcode$ = *projection code*
      *1 = onto x=0 plane*
      *2 = onto y=0 plane*
      *3 = onto z=0 plane*
$t(,)$ = *current transfomation matrix with which the projection matrix is to be concatenated*

**subroutine project**(projcode; t(,))

**dimension** proj(4,4)

**Mat** proj = **Idn**

**if** projcode = 1 **then** proj(1,1) = 0      *set the appropriate matrix element to zero*
**if** projcode = 2 **then** proj(2,2) = 0
**if** projcode = 3 **then** proj(3,3) = 0

**Mat** t = t*proj               *concatenate the matrices*

**return**

## reflt3d

Subroutine to form and concatenate a 3D reflection matrix with the current transformation matrix (see Eqs. 3–11 to 3–13).

$rfltcode$ = *reflection code*
      *1 = thru x=0 plane*
      *2 = thru y=0 plane*
      *3 = thru z=0 plane*
$reflt(,)$ = *reflection matrix*
$t(,)$ = *current transfomation matrix with which the translation matrix is to be concatenated*

**subroutine reflt3d**(rfltcode; t(,))

**dimension** reflt(4,4)

**Mat** reflt = **Idn**

**if** rfltcode = 1 **then** reflt(1,1) = −1      *make the appropriate term*
**if** rfltcode = 2 **then** reflt(2,2) = −1      *in the reflection matrix −1*
**if** rfltcode = 3 **then** reflt(3,3) = −1

**Mat** t = t*reflt            *concatenate the matrices*

**return**

## scale3d

Subroutine to form and concatenate a 3D scaling matrix with the current transformation matrix (see Eqs. 3–3 and 3–4).

$a$ = *x stretching factor a > 1 stretches, a < 1·contracts*

$$
\begin{aligned}
e &= y \text{ stretching factor } e > 1 \text{ stretches, } e < 1 \text{ contracts} \\
j &= z \text{ stretching factor } j > 1 \text{ stretches, } j < 1 \text{ contracts} \\
s &= \text{overall scaling factor } s > 1 \text{ enlarges, } s < 1 \text{ reduces}
\end{aligned}
$$

$scale =$ scaling matrix

$t(,) =$ current transformation matrix with which the scaling matrix
is to be concatenated

**subroutine scale3d(a,e,j,s; t(,))**

**option angle degrees**

**dimension** scale(4,4)

**Mat** scale = **Zer**

scale(1,1) = a                                          *set up the scaling matrix*
scale(2,2) = e
scale(3,3) = j
scale(4,4) = 1/s

**Mat** t = t*scale                                     *concatenate the matrics*

**return**

## tran3d

Subroutine to form and concatenate a 3D translation matrix with the current
transformation matrix (see Eq. 3–14).

$$
\begin{aligned}
l &= x \text{ translation factor} \\
m &= y \text{ translation factor} \\
n &= z \text{ translation factor}
\end{aligned}
$$

$tran(,) =$ translation matrix

$t(,) =$ current transformation matrix with which the translation matrix
is to be concatenated

**subroutine tran3d(l,m,n; t(,))**

**dimension** tran(4,4)

**Mat** tran = **Idn**

tran(4,1) = l                                           *set up the translation matrix*
tran(4,2) = m
tran(4,3) = n

**Mat** t = t*tran                                      *concatenate the matrices*

**return**

## xrot

Subroutine to form and concatenate a 3D rotation matrix about the x-axis with
the current transformation matrix (see Eq. 3–6).

$rot(,) =$ rotation matrix

$theta =$ rotation angle in degrees

$t(,) =$ current transformation matrix with which the x rotation matrix
is to be concatenated

**subroutine xrot(theta; t(,))**

```
option angle degrees
dimension rot(4,4)
Mat rot = Idn
rot(2,2) = Cos(theta)                                set up the rotation matrix
rot(2,3) = Sin(theta)
rot(3,3) = rot(2,2)
rot(3,2) = −rot(2,3)
Mat t = t*rot                                        concatenate the matrices
return
```

### yrot

Subroutine to form and concatenate a 3D rotation matrix about the y-axis with the applied matrix (see Eq. 3–8).

phi    =  rotation angle in degrees
rot(,) =  rotation matrix
t(,)   =  current transformation matrix with which the y rotation matrix
          is to be concatenated

```
subroutine yrot(phi; t(,))
option angle degrees
dimension rot(4,4)
Mat rot = Idn
rot(1,1) = Cos(phi)                                  set up the rotation matrix
rot(3,1) = Sin(phi)
rot(3,3) = rot(1,1)
rot(1,3) = −rot(3,1)
Mat t = t*rot                                        concatenate the matrices
return
```

### zrot

Subroutine to form and concatenate a 3D rotation matrix about the x-axis with the current transformation matrix (see Eq. 3–7).

rot(,) =  rotation matrix
theta  =  rotation angle in degrees
t(,)   =  current transformation matrix with which the x rotation matrix
          is to be concatenated

```
subroutine zrot(theta; t(,))
option angle degrees
dimension rot(4,4)
Mat rot = Idn
rot(1,1) = Cos(theta)                                set up the rotation matrix
rot(1,2) = Sin(theta)
rot(2,2) = rot(1,1)
rot(2,1) = −rot(1,2)
Mat t = t*rot                                        concatenate the matrices
return
```

## CHAPTER 4

The algorithms given here are used to generate points on the perimeter of the conic sections. In alphabetical order these are: **circle, ellipse, hyper1, hyper2, parabola.** Each of these algorithms is easily modified to generate points on only a portion of the conic section.

### circle

Subroutine to generate points on the circumference of a circle (see Eq. 4–5).

$cdtheta$ = $\cos(dtheta)$
$circ(,)$ = *array containing the 2D points*
  $circ(,1)$ = *x coordinate*
  $circ(,2)$ = *y coordinate*
$dtheta$ = *increment in theta*
$h$     = *x coordinate of the center of the circle*
$k$     = *y coordinate of the center of the circle*
$n$     = *number of points on the circle*
$r$     = *radius*
$sdtheta$ = $\sin(dtheta)$
$tcirc(,)$ = *array containing the 2D points*
  $tcirc(,1)$ = *x coordinate*
  $tcirc(,2)$ = *y coordinate*
  $tcirc(,3)$ = *1, the homogenous coordinate*
$t(,)$   = *3 × 3 2D translation matrix*

**subroutine circle(h,k,r,n; circ(,))**

**option angle degrees**

**dimension** t(3,3),tcirc(256,3)

*redimension and fill the transformation and temporary tcirc arrays*

**Mat t = Idn**
**Mat tcirc = Zer(n,3)**
**Mat tcirc = Con(n,3)**

*determine the constants*

dtheta = 360/(n−1)

cdtheta = **Cos**(dtheta)
sdtheta = **Sin**(dtheta)

*determine the initial point*

tcirc(1,1) = r
tcirc (1,2) = 0

*calculate the points on an origin-centered circle*

**for** i = 2 **to** n
    tcirc(i,1) = cdtheta∗tcirc(i−1,1) − sdtheta∗tcirc(i-1,2)
    tcirc(i,2) = sdtheta∗tcirc(i−1,1) + cdtheta∗tcirc(i-1,2)
**next** i

*translate the results to h,k*

```
call tran2d(h,k; t)
Mat tcirc = tcirc*t
```

*assign translated values to the 2D circ array*

```
for i = 1 to n
    circ(i,1) = tcirc(i,1)
    circ(i,2) = tcirc(i,2)
next i

return
```

## ellipse

Subroutine to generate points on the perimeter of a ellipse (see Eq. 4–8).

| | | |
|---|---|---|
| a | = | *length of semi-major axis* ` |
| b | = | *length of semi-minor axis* |
| c1 | = | *constant – (a/b)*cdtheta* |
| c2 | = | *constant – (b/a)*sdtheta* |
| cdtheta | = | *constant – cos(dtheta)* |
| dtheta | = | *increment in the parameter* |
| ellip(,) | = | *array containing the points on the ellipse* |
| | | *ellip( ,1) = x component* |
| | | *ellip( ,2) = y component* |
| h | = | *x coordinate of center of the ellipse* |
| inclin | = | *inclination angle of major axis in degrees* |
| k | = | *y coordinate of center of the ellipse* |
| n | = | *number of points on ellipse* |
| sdtheta | = | *constant – sin(dtheta)* |
| tellip(,) | = | *array containing the 3D homogeneous points* |
| | | *tellip( ,1) = x coordinate* |
| | | *tellip( ,2) = y coordinate* |
| | | *tellip( ,3) = 1, the homogenous coordinate* |
| t(,) | = | *3 × 3 2D transformation matrix* |

**subroutine ellipse(h,k,a,b,inclin,n; ellip(,))**

**option angle degrees**

**dimension** t(3,3),tellip(256,3)

*redimension and fill the transformation and temporary tellip arrays*

**Mat** t = **Idn**
**Mat** tellip = **Zer**(n,3)
**Mat** tellip = **Con**(n,3)

*determine the constants*

dtheta = 360/(n−1)
cdtheta = **Cos**(dtheta)
sdtheta = **Sin**(dtheta)
c1 = (a/b)*sdtheta
c2 = (b/a)*sdtheta

*determine the initial point*

tellip(1,1) = a

tellip(1,2) = 0

*calculate the points on the origin-centered ellipse*

**for** i = 2 **to** n
   tellip(i,1) = tellip(i−1,1)*cdtheta − c1*tellip(i−1,2)
   tellip(i,2) = c2*tellip(i−1,1) + tellip(i−1,2)*cdtheta
**next** i

*rotate by i and translate the results to h,k*

**call rot2d**(inclin; t)
**call tran2d**(h,k; t)

**Mat** tellip = tellip*t

*assign translated values to the 2D circ array*

**for** i = 1 **to** n
   ellip(i,1) = tellip(i,1)
   ellip(i,2) = tellip(i,2)
**next** i

**return**

## hyper1

Subroutine to generate points on a hyperbola (see Eq. 4–15). Only the hyperbola in the first quadrant, opening to the right with the x-axis as the axis of symmetry is generated. The complete hyperbola is externally obtained by reflection, first about the x-axis and then about the y-axis. Arbitrary orientations and center positions are obtained by appropriate rotations and translations.

| | | |
|---|---|---|
| *a* | = | *distance from the center of the hyperbola to the vertex* |
| *b* | = | *determines the slope of the asymptotes* = ± *b/a* |
| *c1* | = | *constant − b*tdtheta* |
| *c2* | = | *constant − b*cdtheta* |
| *cdtheta* | = | *constant − cos(dtheta)* |
| *dtheta* | = | *increment in the parameter* |
| *hyper(,)* | = | *array containing the points on the hyperbola* |
| | | *hyper( ,1) = x component* |
| | | *hyper( ,2) = y component* |
| *n* | = | *number of points on hyperbola* |
| *tdtheta* | = | *constant − tan(dtheta)* |
| *sdtheta* | = | *constant − sin(dtheta)* |

**subroutine hyper1**(a,b,n; hyper(,))

*redimension and fill the hyper array with zeros*

**Mat** hyper = **Zer**(n,2)

*determine the constants*

dtheta = (**Pi**/2)/(n−1)
cdtheta = **Cos**(dtheta)
sdtheta = **Sin**(dtheta)
tdtheta = **Tan**(dtheta)
c1 = b*tdtheta
c2 = b*cdtheta

*determine the initial point*

hyper(1,1) = a
hyper(1,2) = 0

*calculate the points on the origin-centered hyperbola*

**for** i = 2 **to** n
   hyper(i,1) = b*hyper(i−1,1)/(c2−sdtheta*hyper(i−1,2))
   hyper(i,2) = b*(hyper(i−1,2)+c1)/(b−hyper(i−1,2)*tdtheta)
**next** i

**return**

## hyper2

Subroutine to generate points on a hyperbola using hyperbolic functions (see Eq. 4–17). Only the hyperbola in the first quadrant, opening to the right with the x-axis as the axis of symmetry is generated. The complete hyperbola is subsequently obtained by reflection, first about the x-axis and then about the y-axis. Arbitrary orientations and center positions are obtained by appropriate rotations and translations.

| | | |
|---|---|---|
| *a* | = | *distance from the center of the hyperbola to the vertex* |
| *b* | = | *determines the slope of the asymptotes = ±b/a* |
| *c1* | = | *constant − (a/b)*sdtheta* |
| *c2* | = | *constant − (b/a)*sdtheta* |
| *cdtheta* | = | *constant − cosh(dtheta)* |
| *dtheta* | = | *increment in the parameter* |
| *hyper(,)* | = | *array containing the points on the hyperbola* |
| | | *hyper( ,1) = x component* |
| | | *hyper( ,2) = y component* |
| *n* | = | *number of points on hyperbola* |
| *sdtheta* | = | *constant − sinh(dtheta)* |
| *thetamax* | = | *maximum parameter value* |

**subroutine hyper2**(a,b,thetamax,n; hyper(,))

*redimension and fill the hyper array with zeros*

**Mat** hyper = **Zer**(n,2)

*determine the constants*

dtheta = thetamax/(n−1)
cdtheta = **Cosh**(dtheta)
sdtheta = **Sinh**(dtheta)
c1 = (a/b)*sdtheta
c2 = (b/a)*sdtheta

*determine the initial point*

hyper(1,1) = a
hyper(1,2) = 0

*calculate the points on the origin-centered hyperbola*

**for** i = 2 **to** n
   hyper(i,1) = hyper(i−1,1)*cdtheta + c1*hyper(i−1,2)

hyper(i,2) = c2*hyper(i−1,1) + hyper(i−1,2)*cdtheta
**next** i

**return**

## parabola

Subroutine to generate points on a parabola in the first quadrant symmetrical about the x-axis opening to the right (see Eq. 4–12). Appropriate reflection, rotation and translation transformations are subsequently applied to generate the complete parabola and place it in the proper position and orientation.

$a$        =   *distance from focus to vertex of parabola*
$a1$       =   *constant – a\*dtheta\*dtheta*
$b1$       =   *constant – 2\*a\*dtheta*
*dtheta*   =   *increment in the parameter*
$n$        =   *number of points on the parabola*
*para(,)*  =   *array containing the 2D points on the parabola*
                  *para( ,1) = x coordinate*
                  *para( ,2) = y coordinate*
*thetamax* =   *maximum value of the parameter*

**subroutine parabola**(a,thetamax,n; para(,))

*redimension and fill the para array with zeros*

**Mat** para = **Zer**(n,2)

*determine the constants*

dtheta = thetamax/(n−1)
a1 = a*dtheta*dtheta
b1 = 2*a*dtheta

*determine the initial point*

para(1,1) = 0
para(1,2) = 0

*calculate the points on the parabola*

**for** i = 2 **to** n
    para(i,1) = para(i−1,1) + dtheta*para(i−1,2) + a1
    para(i,2) = para(i−1,2) + b1
**next** i

**return**


# CHAPTER 5

The algorithms given here encompass both curve fitting and fairing techniques. Curve fitting algorithms are given for cubic spline, parabolically blended and B-spline curves. Curve fairing algorithms for both Bézier and nonrational and rational B-spline curves are included along with supporting algorithms for the generation of open and periodic uniform and nonuniform knot vectors and B-spline basis functions. In alphabetic order these are: **basis, bezier, bsplfit, bspline, bsplineu, cblend, cspline, dbasis, dbasisu, dbezier, dbspline, dbsplineu, knot, knotc, knotu, matpbspl, nmatrix, parabld, param, rbasis, rbspline, rbsplinu.**

## basis

Subroutine to generate B-spline basis functions for open uniform knot vectors (see Eq. 5–84).

$c$      =   *order of the B-spline basis function*
$d$      =   *first term of the basis function recursion relation*
$e$      =   *second term of the basis function recursion relation*
$npts$   =   *number of defining polygon vertices*
$n(,)$   =   *array containing the basis functions*
           *$n(1,1)$ contains the basis function associated with $B_1$ etc.*
$nplusc$ =   *constant – npts + c – maximum number of knot values*
$t$      =   *parameter value*
$temp()$ =   *temporary array*
$x()$    =   *knot vector*

**subroutine basis**(c,t,npts,x(); n(,))

**dimension** temp(20)                           *allows for 20 polygon vertices*

nplusc = npts+c

*calculate the first order basis functions $N_{i,1}$ (see Eq. 5–84a)*

**for** i = 1 **to** nplusc−1
    **if** t >= x(i) and t < x(i+1) **then**
       temp(i) = 1
    **else**
       temp(i) = 0
    **end if**
**next** i

*calculate the higher order basis functions (see Eq. 5–84b)*

**for** k = 2 **to** c
    **for** i = 1 **to** nplusc−k
       **if** temp(i) $\neq$ 0 **then**           *if basis function is zero skip the calculation*
          d = ((t−x(i))*temp(i))/(x(i+k−1)−x(i))
       **else**
          d = 0
       **end if**
       **if** temp(i+1) $\neq$ 0 **then**         *if basis function is zero skip the calculation*
          e = ((x(i+k)−t)*temp(i+1))/(x(i+k)−x(i+1))
       **else**
          e = 0
       **end if**
       temp(i) = d + e
    **next** i
**next** k

**if** t = x(nplusc) **then** temp(npts) = 1               *pick up last point*

*put in n array*

**for** i = 1 **to** npts

```
    n(1,i) = temp(i)
next i
if t = x(nplusc) then n(1,npts) = 1                    pick up last point
return
```

## bezier

Subroutine to calculate a Bezier curve (see Eq. 5–62).

$b(,)$ = *array containing the defining polygon vertices*
        *$b( ,1)$ contains the x component of the vertex*
        *$b( ,2)$ contains the y component of the vertex*
        *$b( ,3)$ contains the z component of the vertex*
$Basis$ = *function to calculate the Bernstein basis value (see Eq. 5–63)*
$cpts$ = *number of points to be calculated on the curve*
$Factrl$ = *function to calculate the factorial of a number*
$j(,)$ = *Bernstein basis function*
$Ni$ = *factorial function for the Bernstein basis*
$npts$ = *number of defining polygon vertices*
$p(,)$ = *array containing the curve points*
        *$p( ,1)$ contains the x component of the point*
        *$p( ,2)$ contains the y component of the point*
        *$p( ,3)$ contains the z component of the point*
$t$ = *parameter value $0 \leq t \leq 1$*

```
subroutine bezier(npts,b(,),cpts; p(,))
def Ni(n,i) = Factrl(n)/(Factrl(i)*Factrl(n−i))          factorial function
def Basis(n,i,t) = Ni(n,i)*(t^i)*((1−t)^(n−i))       Bernstein basis function

dimension j(1,20)                                allows for 20 polygon vertices
dimension temp(1,3)
icount = 0
Mat j = Zer(1,npts)
for t = 0 to 1 step 1/(cpts−1)
    icount = icount+1
    determine the Bernstein basis function (see Eq. 5–63)
    for i = 1 to npts
        j(1,i) = Basis(npts−1,i−1,t)
    next i
    determine a point on the curve
    Mat temp = j*b
    place in array
    for i = 1 to 3
        p(icount,i) = temp(1,i)
    next i
next t
return
```

## bsplfit

Subroutine to fit a B-spline curve using an open uniform knot vector (see Eq. 5–117).

| | | |
|---|---|---|
| $b(,)$ | = | array containing the defining polygon vertices |
| | | $b(\ ,1)$ contains the x component of the vertex |
| | | $b(\ ,2)$ contains the y component of the vertex |
| | | $b(\ ,3)$ contains the z component of the vertex |
| dpts | = | number of data points |
| $d(,)$ | = | array containing the data points |
| | | $d(\ ,1)$ contains the x component of the data point |
| | | $d(\ ,2)$ contains the y component of the data point |
| | | $d(\ ,3)$ contains the z component of the data point |
| k | = | order of the B-spline basis function |
| n | = | matrix of basis function |
| nbasis | = | array containing the basis functions for a single value of t |
| ninv | = | inverse of $trn(n) \times n$ |
| nplusc | = | number of knot values |
| npts | = | number of defining polygon vertices |
| ntemp | = | temporary matrix to hold $trn(n) \times n$ |
| ntmp | = | temporary matrix to hold inverse of $trn(n) \times n \times d$ |
| ntrn | = | transpose of the n matrix |
| t | = | parameter value $0 \le t \le 1$ |
| tpar() | = | array containing the chordwise approximation to the parameter values |
| x() | = | array containing the knot vector |

**subroutine bsplfit**(dpts,d(,),npts,k; b(,))

**dimension** nbasis(1,20),x(30),n(20,20),temp(1,3)          *allow for 20 data points*
**dimension** tpar(20),ninv(20,20),ntrn(20,20),ntemp(20,20),ntmp(20,3)

*zero and redimension the matrices*

**Mat** nbasis = **Zer**(1,npts)
**Mat** x = **Zer**(npts+k)
**Mat** n = **Zer**(dpts,npts)
**Mat** ntrn = **Zer**(npts,dpts)
**Mat** ntemp = **Zer**(npts,npts)
**Mat** ntmp = **Zer**(npts,2)
**Mat** ninv = **Zer**(npts,npts)
**Mat** tpar = **Zer**(dpts)

**call knot**(npts,k; x())

**call param**(dpts,d; tpar)

nplusc = npts+k

*generate the matrix of basis functions*

**for** i = 1 **to** dpts
   t = tpar(i)*x(nplusc)                    *calculate the parameter value for one row*
   **call basis**(k,t,npts,x; nbasis)          *calculate the basis function for one row*
   **for** j = 1 **to** npts
      n(i,j) = nbasis(1,j)                    *build the matrix row by row*
   **next** j
**next** i

*generate the defining polygon vertices using the least squares technique*

**Mat** ntrn = trn(n)                     *find the transpose of the matrix of basis functions*
**Mat** ntemp = ntrn∗n                                      $trn(n) \times n$
**Mat** ninv = **Inv**(ntemp)                          *inverse of* $trn(n) \times n$
**Mat** ntmp = ntrn∗d                          *inverse of* $trn(n) \times n \times d$
**Mat** b = ninv∗ntmp                      *calculate the defining polygon vertices*

**return**

## bspline

Subroutine to generate a B-spline curve using an open uniform knot vector (see Eq. 5–83).

$b(,)$     =  *array containing the defining polygon vertices*
            $b( ,1)$ *contains the x component of the vertex*
            $b( ,2)$ *contains the y component of the vertex*
            $b( ,3)$ *contains the z component of the vertex*
$k$      =  *order of the B-spline basis function*
*nbasis* =  *array containing the basis functions for a single value of t*
*nplusc* =  *number of knot values*
*npts*    =  *number of defining polygon vertices*
$p(,)$    =  *array containing the curve points*
            $p( ,1)$ *contains the x component of the point*
            $p( ,2)$ *contains the y component of the point*
            $p( ,3)$ *contains the z component of the point*
$p1$      =  *number of points to be calculated on the curve*
$t$       =  *parameter value* $0 \leq t \leq 1$
$x()$     =  *array containing the knot vector*

**subroutine bspline**(npts,k,p1,b(,); p(,))

**dimension** nbasis(1,20),x(30),temp(1,3)          *allows for 20 polygon vertices*
                                              *with basis function of order 5*

nplusc = npts+k

*zero and redimension the knot vector and the basis array*

**Mat** nbasis = **Zer**(1,npts)
**Mat** x = **Zer**(nplusc)

*generate the uniform open knot vector*

**call knot**(npts,k; x)

icount = 0

*calculate the points on the B-spline curve*

**for** t = 0 **to** x(npts+k) **step** x(npts+k)/(p1−1)
    icount = icount+1
    **call basis**(k,t,npts,x; nbasis)     *generate the basis function for this value of t*
    **Mat** temp = nbasis∗b                      *generate the point on the curve*
    p(icount,1) = temp(1,1)     *assign the current value of the point on the curve*
    p(icount,2) = temp(1,2)                      *to the curve array*
    p(icount,3) = temp(1,3)
**next** t

**return**

## bsplineu

Subroutine to generate a B-spline curve using an periodic uniform knot vector (see Eq. 5–83).

$b(,)$   =   *array containing the defining polygon vertices*
               *$b(,1)$ contains the x component of the vertex*
               *$b(,2)$ contains the y component of the vertex*
               *$b(,3)$ contains the z component of the vertex*
$k$      =   *order of the B-spline basis function*
$nbasis$ =   *array containing the basis functions for a single value of t*
$nplusc$ =   *number of knot values*
$npts$  =   *number of defining polygon vertices*
$p(,)$   =   *array containing the curve points*
               *$p(,1)$ contains the x component of the point*
               *$p(,2)\cdot$ contains the y component of the point*
               *$p(,3)$ contains the z component of the point*
$p1$     =   *number of points to be calculated on the curve*
$t$      =   *parameter value $0 \leq t \leq 1$*
$x()$   =   *array containing the knot vector*

**subroutine bsplineu**(npts,k,p1,b(,); p(,))

**dimension** nbasis(1,20),x(30),temp(1,3)         *allows for 20 polygon vertices*
                                               *with basis function of order 5*

*zero and redimension the knot vector and the basis array*

**Mat** nbasis = **Zer**(1,npts)
**Mat** x = **Zer**(npts+k)

nplusc = npts+k

*generate the uniform periodic knot vector*

**call knotu**(npts,k; x)

icount = 0

*calculate the points on the B-spline curve*

**for** t = (k−1) **to** (npts−1+1) **step** ((npts−1+1)−(k−1))/(p1−1)
    icount = icount+1
    **call basis**(k,t,npts,x; nbasis)     *generate the basis function for this value of t*
    **Mat** temp = nbasis∗b              *generate the point on the curve*
    p(icount,1) = temp(1,1)     *assign the current value of the point on the curve*
    p(icount,2) = temp(1,2)                       *to the curve array*
**next** t

**return**

## cblend

Subroutine to calculate the normalized cubic blending functions (see Eq. 5–21).

$f(,)$ =   *$1 \times 4$ array containing the blending functions*
        *$f(1,1)$ contains $F_1$*
        *$f(1,2)$ contains $F_2$*
        *$f(1,3)$ contains $F_3$*
        *$f(1,4)$ contains $F_4$*

$tau$ = $\:$ *normalized parameter value $0 \leq tau \leq 1$*

**subroutine cblend**(tau; f(,))

f(1,1) = 2*(tau)^3 − 3*(tau)^2 + 1

f(1,2) = −2*(tau)^3 + 3*(tau)^2

f(1,3) = tau*((tau)^2 − 2*tau + 1)

f(1,4) = tau*((tau)^2 − tau)

**return**

## cspline

Subroutine to calculate a cubic spline curve (see Eq. 5–1).

| | | |
|---|---|---|
| *bcflag* | = | *boundary condition flag* |
| *bcflag* | = | *1 – clamped end conditions* |
| *bcflag* | = | *2 – relaxed end conditions* |
| *d(,)* | = | *array containing the data points to be fit* |
| | | *d( ,1) contains the x component of the point* |
| | | *d( ,2) contains the y component of the point* |
| | | *d( ,3) contains the z component of the point* |
| *f(,)* | = | *1 × 4 array containing the blending functions* |
| | | *f(1,1) contains $F_1$* |
| | | *f(1,2) contains $F_2$* |
| | | *f(1,3) contains $F_3$* |
| | | *f(1,4) contains $F_4$* |
| *g* | = | *geometry matrix* |
| *icount* | = | *counter for the number of points on the curve* |
| *m(,)* | = | *coefficient matrix [M] (see Eq. 5–15)* |
| *minv(,)* | = | *inverse of the coefficient matrix [M]* |
| *npts* | = | *number of points to be fit* |
| *p(,)* | = | *array containing the curve points* |
| | | *p( ,1) contains the x component of the point* |
| | | *p( ,2) contains the y component of the point* |
| | | *p( ,3) contains the z component of the point* |
| *point(,)* | = | *single point on the curve* |
| | | *point(1,1) contains the x component of the point* |
| | | *point(1,2) contains the y component of the point* |
| | | *point(1,3) contains the z component of the point* |
| *p1* | = | *number of points to be calculated on each curve span* |
| *r(,)* | = | *right hand side matrix [R] (see Eq. 5–15)* |
| *t(,)* | = | *chordwise approximated parameter matrix* |
| *tangent(,)* | = | *tangent vector matrix (see Eq. 5–15)* |
| *tau* | = | *normalized parameter value $0 \leq tau \leq 1$* |

**subroutine cspline**(npts,p1,d(,),bcflag,icount,tangent(,); p(,))

**dimension** t(20),m(20,20),minv(20,20),r(20,3)          *allows for 20 data points*

**dimension** g(4,3),point(1,3),f(1,4)

**Mat** m = **Zer**(npts,npts)

**Mat** minv = **Zer**(npts,npts)

**Mat** r = **Zer**(npts,3)

**Mat** t = **Zer**(npts)

*determine the parameter values using a chord approximation (see Ex. 5-2)*

**for** i = 2 **to** npts
    t(i) = **Sqrt**((d(i,1)−d(i−1,1))^2 + (d(i,2)−d(i−1,2))^2)
**next** i

*set up the coefficient matrix [M] (see Eq. 5-15).*

**for** i = 2 **to** npts−1
    m(i,i−1) = t(i+1)
    m(i,i) = 2*(t(i) + t(i+1))
    m(i,i+1) = t(i)
**next** i

*set up the right hand side matrix [R] (see Eq. 5-15)*

**for** i = 2 **to** npts−1
    coeff = (3/(t(i)*t(i+1)))
    **for** j = 1 **to** 3
        r(i,j) = coeff*((t(i)^2)*(d(i+1,j)−d(i,j)) + (t(i+1)^2)*(d(i,j)−d(i−1,j)))
    **next** j
**next** i

*add the boundary conditions to the matrices (see Table 5-3)*
*bcflag = 1 - clamped end conditions*
*bcflag = 2 - relaxed end conditions*
            *cyclic and anticyclic boundary conditions are left as an exercise.*

**if** bcflag = 1 **then**
    m(1,1) = 1
    m(npts,npts) = 1

    **for** j = 1 **to** 3
        r(1,j) = tangent(1,j)
        r(npts,j) = tangent(npts,j)
    **next** j

**end if**

**if** bcflag = 2 **then**
    m(1,1) = 1
    m(1,2) = 1/2
    m(npts,npts−1) = 2
    m(npts,npts) = 4

    **for** j = 1 **to** 3
        r(1,j) = (3/(2*t(2)))*(d(2,j)−d(1,j))
        r(npts,j) = (6/t(npts))*(d(npts,j)−d(npts−1,j))
    **next** j

**end if**

*invert the coefficient matrix [M] (see Eq. 5-16)*

**Mat** minv = **Inv**(m)

*calculate the internal tangent vectors $[M]^{-1}[R]$*

**Mat** tangent = minv*r

*generate the points on the cubic spline curve (see Eq. 5-22)*

*restrict interval to prevent calculating point at the end of the span twice*
*pick up the last point later*

icount = 0

**for** i = 2 **to** npts

   **for** tau = 0 **to** 1−(1/(p1−1)) **step** 1/(p1 −1)        *p1 > 1 or an error results*

      icount = icount+1

      *set up the blending function matrix (see Eq. 5-21)*

      f(1,1) = 2*(tau^3) − 3*(tau^2) + 1

      f(1,2) = −2*(tau^3) + 3*(tau^2)

      f(1,3) = tau*(tau^2 − 2*tau+1)*t(i)

      f(1,4) = tau*(tau^2 − tau)*t(i)

      *set up the geometry matrix (see Eq. 5-20)*

      **for** j = 1 **to** 3

         g(1,j) = d(i−1,j)

         g(2,j) = d(i,j)

         g(3,j) = tangent(i−1,j)

         g(4,j) = tangent(i,j)

      **next** j

      *calculate a single point on the curve (see Eq. 5-22)*

      **Mat** point = f*g

      *assign to position vector matrix*

      **for** j = 1 **to** 3

         p(icount,j) = point(1,j)

      **next** j

   **next** tau

**next** i

*pick up the last point specially*

icount = icount+1

**for** j = 1 **to** 3

   p(icount,j) = d(npts,j)

**next** j

**return**

## dbasis

Subroutine to generate B-spline basis functions and their derivatives for uniform open knot vectors (see Eqs. 5-84 and 5-97 to 5-100).

| | | |
|---|---|---|
| b1 | = | *first term of the basis function* |
| b2 | = | *second term of the basis function* |
| c | = | *order of the B-spline basis function* |
| d1(,) | = | *array containing the derivative of the basis functions* |
| | | *d1(1,1) contains the derivative of the basis function for $B_1$ etc.* |
| d2(,) | = | *array containing the derivative of the basis functions* |
| | | *d2(1,1) contains the derivative of the basis function for $B_1$ etc.* |
| f1 | = | *first term of the first derivative of the basis function* |

| | | |
|---|---|---|
| *f2* | = | *second term of the first derivative of the basis function* |
| *f3* | = | *third term of the first derivative of the basis function* |
| *f4* | = | *fourth term of the first derivative of the basis function* |
| *npts* | = | *number of defining polygon vertices* |
| *n(,)* | = | *array containing the basis functions* |
| | | *n(1,1) contains the basis function for $B_1$ etc.* |
| *nplusc* = | | *constant – npts + c – maximum knot value* |
| *s1* | = | *first term of the second derivative of the basis function* |
| *s2* | = | *second term of the second derivative of the basis function* |
| *s3* | = | *third term of the second derivative of the basis function* |
| *s4* | = | *fourth term of the second derivative of the basis function* |
| *t* | = | *parameter value* |
| *temp()* = | | *temporary array* |
| *x()* | = | *knot vector* |

**subroutine dbasis**(c,t,npts,x(); n(,),d1(,),d2(,))

**dimension** temp(20),temp1(20),temp2(20)     *up to 20 defining polygon vertices*

nplusc = npts+c

*zero the temporary arrays*

**Mat** temp = **Zer**(npts+c)
**Mat** temp1 = **Zer**(npts+c)
**Mat** temp2 = **Zer**(npts+c)

*calculate the first order basis functions n(i,1) (see Eq. 5–84a)*

**for** i = 1 **to** nplusc−1
   **if** t ≥ x(i) **and** t < x(i+1) **then**
      temp(i) = 1
   **else**
      temp(i) = 0
   **end if**
**next** i

**if** t = x(nplusc) **then** temp(npts) = 1                 *handle the end specially*

*calculate higher order basis functions and their derivatives*
*(see Eqs. 5–84b and 5–97 to 5–100)*

**for** k = 2 **to** c
   **for** i = 1 **to** nplusc−k

     *calculate basis function*

     **if** temp(i) ≠ 0 **then**          *if basis function is zero, skip the calculation*
        b1 = ((t−x(i))*temp(i))/(x(i+k−1)−x(i))
     **else**
        b1 = 0
     **end if**

     **if** temp(i+1) ≠ 0 **then**          *if basis function is zero, skip the calculation*
        b2 = ((x(i+k)−t)*temp(i+1))/(x(i+k)−x(i+1))
     **else**
        b2 = 0
     **end if**

     *calculate first derivative*

```
    if temp(i) ≠ 0 then            if basis function is zero, skip the calculation
        f1 = temp(i)/(x(i+k−1)−x(i))
    else
        f1 = 0
    end if
    if temp(i+1) ≠ 0 then          if basis function is zero, skip the calculation
        f2 = −temp(i+1)/(x(i+k)−x(i+1))
    else
        f2 = 0
    end if
    if temp1(i) ≠ 0 then           if basis function is zero, skip the calculation
        f3 = (t−x(i))*temp1(i)/(x(i+k−1)−x(i))
    else
        f3 = 0
    end if
    if temp1(i+1) ≠ 0 then         if basis function is zero, skip the calculation
        f4 = (x(i+k)−t)*temp1(i+1)/(x(i+k)−x(i+1))
    else
        f4 = 0
    end if
```

*calculate second derivative*

```
    if temp1(i) ≠ 0 then           if basis function is zero, skip the calculation
        s1 = 2*temp1(i)/(x(i+k−1)−x(i))
    else
        s1 = 0
    end if
    if temp1(i+1) ≠ 0 then         if basis function is zero, skip the calculation
        s2 = −2*temp1(i+1)/(x(i+k)−x(i+1))
    else
        s2 = 0
    end if
    if temp2(i) ≠ 0 then           if basis function is zero, skip the calculation
        s3 = (t−x(i))*temp2(i)/(x(i+k−1)−x(i))
    else
        s3 = 0
    end if
    if temp2(i+1) ≠ 0 then         if basis function is zero, skip the calculation
        s4 = (x(i+k)−t)*temp2(i+1)/(x(i+k)−x(i+1))
    else
        s4 = 0
    end if
    temp(i) = b1 + b2
    temp1(i) = f1 + f2 + f3 + f4
    temp2(i) = s1 + s2 + s3 + s4
  next i
next k
```

*put in arrays*

```
for i = 1 to npts
    n(1,i) = temp(i)
```

```
    d1(1,i) = temp1(i)
    d2(1,i) = temp2(i)
next i
return
```

## dbasisu

Subroutine to generate B-spline basis functions and their derivatives for uniform periodic knot vectors (see Eqs. 5–84 and 5–97 to 5–100).

$b1$      = *first term of the basis function*
$b2$      = *second term of the basis function*
$c$       = *order of the B-spline basis function*
$d1(,)$ = *array containing the derivative of the basis functions*
           *$d1(1,1)$ contains the derivative of the basis function for $B_1$ etc.*
$d2(,)$ = *array containing the derivative of the basis functions*
           *$d2(1,1)$ contains the derivative of the basis function for $B_1$ etc.*
$f1$      = *first term of the first derivative of the basis function*
$f2$      = *second term of the first derivative of the basis function*
$f3$      = *third term of the first derivative of the basis function*
$f4$      = *fourth term of the first derivative of the basis function*
$npts$ = *number of defining polygon vertices*
$n(,)$    = *array containing the basis functions*
           *$n(1,1)$ contains the basis function for $B_1$ etc.*
$nplusc$ = *constant – npts + c – maximum knot value*
$s1$      = *first term of the second derivative of the basis function*
$s2$      = *second term of the second derivative of the basis function*
$s3$      = *third term of the second derivative of the basis function*
$s4$      = *fourth term of the second derivative of the basis function*
$t$       = *parameter value*
$temp()$ = *temporary array*
$x()$    = *knot vector*

**subroutine dbasisu**(c,t,npts,x(); n(,),d1(,),d2(,))

**dimension** temp(20),temp1(20),temp2(20)      *up to 20 defining polygon vertices*

nplusc = npts+c

*zero the temporary arrays*

**Mat** temp = **Zer**(nplusc)
**Mat** temp1 = **Zer**(nplusc)
**Mat** temp2 = **Zer**(nplusc)

*calculate the first order basis functions $N_{i,1}$(see Eq. 5–84a)*

```
for i = 1 to nplusc−1
  if t ≥ x(i) and t < x(i+1) then
      temp(i) = 1
  else
      temp(i) = 0
  end if
next i
```

if t = x(npts+1) then                               *handle the end specially by resetting the*
    temp(npts) = 1                                  *first order basis functions.*
    temp(npts+1) = 0
**end if**

*calculate higher order basis functions and their derivatives*
*(see Eqs. 5-84b and 5-97 to 5-100)*

**for** k = 2 **to** c
  **for** i = 1 **to** nplusc−k

   *calculate basis function*

   **if** temp(i) ≠ 0 **then**                      *if basis function is zero, skip the calculation*
        b1 = ((t−x(i))*temp(i))/(x(i+k−1)−x(i))
   **else**
        b1 = 0
   **end if**

   **if** temp(i+1) ≠ 0 **then**                    *if basis function is zero, skip the calculation*
        b2 = ((x(i+k)−t)*temp(i+1))/(x(i+k)−x(i+1))
   **else**
        b2 = 0
   **end if**

   *calculate first derivative*

   **if** temp(i) ≠ 0 **then**                      *if basis function is zero, skip the calculation*
        f1 = temp(i)/(x(i+k−1)−x(i))
   **else**
        f1 = 0
   **end if**
   **if** temp(i+1) ≠ 0 **then**                    *if basis function is zero, skip the calculation*
        f2 = −temp(i+1)/(x(i+k)−x(i+1))
   **else**
        f2 = 0
   **end if**
   **if** temp1(i) ≠ 0 **then**                     *if basis function is zero, skip the calculation*
        f3 = (t−x(i))*temp1(i)/(x(i+k−1)−x(i))
   **else**
        f3 = 0
   **end if**
   **if** temp1(i+1) ≠ 0 **then**                   *if basis function is zero, skip the calculation*
        f4 = (x(i+k)−t)*temp1(i+1)/(x(i+k)−x(i+1))
   **else**
        f4 = 0
   **end if**

   *calculate second derivative*

   **if** temp1(i) ≠ 0 **then**                     *if basis function is zero, skip the calculation*
        s1 = 2*temp1(i)/(x(i+k−1)−x(i))
   **else**
        s1 = 0
   **end if**
   **if** temp1(i+1) ≠ 0 **then**                   *if basis function is zero, skip the calculation*
        s2 = −2*temp1(i+1)/(x(i+k)−x(i+1))

```
        else
            s2 = 0
        end if
        if temp2(i) ≠ 0 then            if basis function is zero, skip the calculation
            s3 = (t−x(i))*temp2(i)/(x(i+k−1)−x(i))
        else
            s3 = 0
        end if
        if temp2(i+1) ≠ 0 then          if basis function is zero, skip the calculation
            s4 = (x(i+k)−t)*temp2(i+1)/(x(i+k)−x(i+1))
        else
            s4 = 0
        end if
        temp(i) = b1 + b2
        temp1(i) = f1 + f2 + f3 + f4
        temp2(i) = s1 + s2 + s3 + s4
    next i
next k

put in arrays

for i = 1 to npts
    n(1,i) = temp(i)
    d1(1,i) = temp1(i)
    d2(1,i) = temp2(i)
next i

return
```

## dbezier

Subroutine to calculate a Bezier curve and its first and second derivatives (see Eqs. 5–62, 5–72 and 5–73)

$b(,)$ = *array containing the defining polygon vertices*
   $b(,1)$ *contains the x component of the vertex*
   $b(,2)$ *contains the y component of the vertex*
   $b(,3)$ *contains the z component of the vertex*
$Basis$ = *function to calculate the Bernstein basis value*
$cpts$ = *number of points to be calculated on the curve*
$d1(,)$ = *array containing the first derivative of the curve*
   $d1(,1)$ *contains the x component of the derivative*
   $d1(,2)$ *contains the y component of the derivative*
   $d1(,3)$ *contains the z component of the derivative*
$d2(,)$ = *array containing the second derivative of the curve*
   $d2(,1)$ *contains the x component of the derivative*
   $d2(,2)$ *contains the y component of the derivative*
   $d2(,3)$ *contains the z component of the derivative*
$Factrl$ = *function to calculate the factorial of a number*
$j(,)$ = *Bernstein basis function*
$j1(,)$ = *first derivative of the Bernstein basis function*
$j2(,)$ = *second derivative of the Bernstein basis function*
$Ni$ = *factorial function for the Bernstein basis*

$npts$  =  *number of defining polygon vertices*
$p(,)$  =  *array containing the curve points*
  *p( ,1) contains the x component of the point*
  *p( ,2) contains the y component of the point*
  *p( ,3) contains the z component of the point*
$t$  =  *parameter value $0 \le t \le 1$*

**subroutine dbezier**(npts,b(,),cpts; p(,),d1(,),d2(,))

**def Ni**(n,i) = **Factrl**(n)/(**Factrl**(i)∗**Factrl**(n−i))    *factorial function*
**def Basis**(n,i,t) = **Ni**(n,i)∗(t^i)∗((1−t)^(n−i))    *Bernstein basis function*

**dimension** j(1,20),j1(1,20),j2(1,20)    *allows for 20 polygon vertices*
**dimension** temp(1,3),temp1(1,3),temp2(1,3)

*zero and redimension matrices*

**Mat** j = **Zer**(1,npts)
**Mat** j1 = **Zer**(1,npts)
**Mat** j2 = **Zer**(1,npts)

**for** t = 0 **to** 1 **step** 1/(cpts−1)

  icount = icount+1
  **if** icount = cpts **then** t = 1    *necessary to handle incremental calculation of t*

  *determine the Bernstein basis function and its first and second derivative*
  *(see Eqs. 5–63, 5–74 and 5–75)*

  **for** i = 1 **to** npts
    j(1,i) = **Basis**(npts−1, i−1,t)
    **if** t ≠ 0 **and** t ≠ 1 **then**    *handle the end points specially*
      j1(1,i) = (((i−1)−(npts−1)∗t)/(t∗(1−t)))∗j(1,i)
      j2(1,i) = ((i−1)−(npts−1)∗t)^2 − (npts−1)∗t∗t − (i−1)∗(1−2∗t)
      j2(1,i) = j(1,i)∗j2(1,i)/(t∗t∗(1−t)∗(1−t))
    **end if**
  **next** i

  *determine a point on the curve*

  **Mat** temp = j∗b

  *determine the curve first and second derivatives (Eqs. 5–62, 5–72 and 5–73)*

  **if** t <> 0 **and** t ≠ 1 **then**    *handle the end points specially*
    **Mat** temp1 = j1∗b
    **Mat** temp2 = j2∗b
  **else**
    **if** t = 0 **then**
      temp1(1,1) = (npts−1)∗(b(2,1)−b(1,1))
      temp1(1,2) = (npts−1)∗(b(2,2)−b(1,2))
    **end if**
    **if** t = 0 **then**
      temp2(1,1) = (npts−1)∗(npts−2)∗(b(1,1)−2∗b(2,1)+b(3,1))
      temp2(1,2) = (npts−1)∗(npts−2)∗(b(1,2)−2∗b(2,2)+b(3,2))
    **end if**
    **if** t = 1 **then**
      temp1(1,1) = (npts−1)∗(b(npts,1)−b(npts−1,1))
      temp1(1,2) = (npts−1)∗(b(npts,2)−b(npts−1,2))

```
        end if
        if t = 1 then
            temp2(1,1) = (b(npts,1)−2*b(npts−1,1)+b(npts−2,1))
            temp2(1,1) = (npts−1)*(npts−2)*temp2(1,1)
            temp2(1,2) = (b(npts,2)−2*b(npts−1,2)+b(npts−2,2))
            temp2(1,2) = (npts−1)*(npts−2)*temp2(1,2)
        end if
    end if

    place in arrays

    for i = 1 to 3
        p(icount,i) = temp(1,i)
        d1(icount,i) = temp1(1,i)
        d2(icount,i) = temp2(1,i)
    next i

next t

return
```

## dbspline

Subroutine to generate a B-spline curve and its derivatives using an open uniform knot vector (see Eqs. 5–83, 5–95 and 5–96).

| | | |
|---|---|---|
| $b(,)$ | = | array containing the defining polygon vertices |
| | | $b(\ ,1)$ contains the $x$ component of the vertex |
| | | $b(\ ,2)$ contains the $y$ component of the vertex |
| | | $b(\ ,3)$ contains the $z$ component of the vertex |
| $d1(,)$ | = | array containing the first derivative of the curve |
| | | $d1(\ ,1)$ contains the $x$ component |
| | | $d1(\ ,2)$ contains the $y$ component |
| | | $d1(\ ,3)$ contains the $z$ component |
| $d2(,)$ | = | array containing the second derivative of the curve |
| | | $d2(\ ,1)$ contains the $x$ component |
| | | $d2(\ ,2)$ contains the $y$ component |
| | | $d3(\ ,3)$ contains the $z$ component |
| $d1nbasis(,)$ | = | first derivative of the basis functions for a single value of $t$ |
| $d2nbasis(,)$ | = | second derivative of the basis functions for a single value of $t$ |
| $k$ | = | order of the B-spline basis function |
| $nbasis$ | = | array containing the basis functions for a single value of $t$ |
| $nplusc$ | = | number of knot values |
| $npts$ | = | number of defining polygon vertices |
| $p(,)$ | = | array containing the curve points |
| | | $p(\ ,1)$ contains the $x$ component of the point |
| | | $p(\ ,2)$ contains the $y$ component of the point |
| | | $p(\ ,3)$ contains the $z$ component of the point |
| $p1$ | = | number of points to be calculated on the curve |
| $t$ | = | parameter value $0 \leq t \leq 1$ |
| $x()$ | = | array containing the knot vector |

subroutine dbspline(npts,k,p1,b(,); p(,),d1(,),d2(,))

*allows for 20 polygon vertices with basis function of order 5*

dimension x(30),nbasis(1,20),d1nbasis(1,20),d2nbasis(1,20)
dimension temp(1,3),temp1(1,3),temp2(1,3)

*zero and redimension the knot vector, basis, curve and derivative arrays*

**Mat** p = **Zer**(p1,3)
**Mat** d1 = **Zer**(p1,3)
**Mat** d2 = **Zer**(p1,3)
**Mat** nbasis = **Zer**(1,npts)
**Mat** d1nbasis = **Zer**(1,npts)
**Mat** d2nbasis = **Zer**(1,npts)
**Mat** x = **Zer**(npts+k)

nplusc = npts+k

*generate the uniform open knot vector*

**call knot**(npts,k; x)

icount = 0

*calculate the points on the B-spline curve and their first and second derivatives*

**for** t = 0 **to** x(nplusc) **step** x(nplusc)/(p1−1)
    icount = icount+1
    **if** icount = p1 **then** t = x(nplusc)  *compensate for incremental calculation of t*

    *generate the basis function and its derivatives for this value of t*
    (*see Eqs. 5-84 and 5-97 to 5-100*)

    **call dbasis**(k,t,npts,x; nbasis,d1nbasis,d2nbasis)
    **Mat** temp = nbasis*b                    *generate the point on the curve*
    **Mat** temp1 = d1nbasis*b          *first derivative at that point on the curve*
    **Mat** temp2 = d2nbasis*b       *second derivative at that point on the curve*

    p(icount,1) = temp(1,1)      *assign the current value of the point on the curve*
    p(icount,2) = temp(1,2)                                  *to the curve array*
    d1(icount,1) = temp1(1,1)    *assign the current value of the derivative at that*
    d1(icount,2) = temp1(1,2)         *point on the curve to the derivative array*
    d2(icount,1) = temp2(1,1)    *assign the current value of the derivative at that*
    d2(icount,2) = temp2(1,2)         *point on the curve to the derivative array*

**next** t

**return**

## dbomplineu

dbsplineu

Subroutine to generate a B-spline curve and its derivatives using an open uniform knot vector (see Eqs. 5-83, 5-95 and 5-96).

$b(,)$   = *array containing the defining polygon vertices*
        *b( ,1) contains the x component of the vertex*
        *b( ,2) contains the y component of the vertex*
        *b( ,3) contains the z component of the vertex*
$d1(,)$ = *array containing the first derivative of the curve*
        *d1( ,1) contains the x component*
        *d1( ,2) contains the y component*
        *d1( ,3) contains the z component*
$d2(,)$ = *array containing the second derivative of the curve*
        *d2( ,1) contains the x component*

$d2(\ ,2)$ *contains the y component*
$d3(\ ,3)$ *contains the z component*
$d1nbasis(,) =$ *first derivative of the basis functions for a single value of t*
$d2nbasis(,) =$ *second derivative of the basis functions for a single value of t*
$k$       *= order of the B-spline basis function*
*nbasis    = array containing the basis functions for a single value of t*
*nplusc    = number of knot values*
*npts      = number of defining polygon vertices*
$p(,)$     *= array containing the curve points*
               $p(\ ,1)$ *contains the x component of the point*
               $p(\ ,2)$ *contains the y component of the point*
               $p(\ ,3)$ *contains the z component of the point*
*p1        = number of points to be calculated on the curve*
$t$        *= parameter value* $0 \le t \le 1$
$x()$      *= array containing the knot vector*

**subroutine dbsplineu(npts,k,p1,b(,); p(,),d1(,),d2(,))**

*allows for 20 polygon vertices with basis function of order 5*

**dimension** x(30),nbasis(1,20),d1nbasis(1,20),d2nbasis(1,20)
**dimension** temp(1,3),temp1(1,3),temp2(1,3)

*zero and redimension the knot vector, basis, curve and derivative arrays*

**Mat** p = **Zer**(p1,3)
**Mat** d1 = **Zer**(p1,3)
**Mat** d2 = **Zer**(p1,3)
**Mat** nbasis = **Zer**(1,npts)
**Mat** d1nbasis = **Zer**(1,npts)
**Mat** d2nbasis = **Zer**(1,npts)
**Mat** x = **Zer**(npts+k)

nplusc = npts+k

*generate the open uniform knot vector*

**call knotu**(npts,k; x)

icount = 0

*calculate the points on the B-spline curve and their first and second derivatives*
*(see Eqs. 5–84, 5–93 and 5–94)*

**for** t = (k−1) **to** npts **step** (npts−(k−1))/(p1−1)
   icount = icount+1
   **if** icount = p1 **then** t = npts       *compensate for incremental calculation of t*
   *generate the basis function and its derivatives for this value of t*
   **call dbasisu**(k,t,npts,x; nbasis,d1nbasis,d2nbasis)
   **Mat** temp = nbasis∗b                    *generate the point on the curve*
   **Mat** temp1 = d1nbasis∗b              *first derivative at that point on the curve*
   **Mat** temp2 = d2nbasis∗b          *second derivative at that point on the curve*
   p(icount,1) = temp(1,1)       *assign the current value of the point on the curve*
   p(icount,2) = temp(1,2)                              *to the curve array*
   d1(icount,1) = temp1(1,1)     *assign the current value of the derivative at that*
   d1(icount,2) = temp1(1,2)          *point on the curve to the derivative array*
   d2(icount,1) = temp2(1,1)     *assign the current value of the derivative at that*

d2(icount,2) = temp2(1,2)                    *point on the curve to the derivative array*

**next** t

**return**

## knot

Subroutine to generate a B-spline open knot vector with multiplicity k at the ends (see p. 311).

$c$         =   *order of the basis function*
$n$         =   *the number of defining polygon vertices*
$nplus2$ =   *index of $x()$ for the first occurrence of the maximum knot vector value*
$nplusc$ =   *maximum value of the knot vector* $- n + c$
$x()$      =   *array containing the knot vector*

**subroutine knot**(n,c; x())

nplusc = n+c
nplus2 = n+2

x(1) = 0
**for** i = 2 **to** nplusc
    **if** i > c **and** i < nplus2 **then**
        x(i) = x(i−1) + 1
    **else**
        x(i) = x(i−1)
    **end if**
**next** i

**return**

## knotc

Subroutine to generate a nonuniform open knot vector proportional to the chord lengths between defining polygon vertices (see Eq. 5–86).

$b(,)$         =   *array containing the defining polygon vertices*
                  *$b( ,1)$ contains the x component of the vertex*
                  *$b( ,2)$ contains the y component of the vertex*
                  *$b( ,3)$ contains the z component of the vertex*
$c$            =   *order of the basis function*
$chord$        =   *chord distance between defining polygon vertices*
$csum$         =   *accumulated sum of the chord distances*
$maxchord$   =   *sum of the chord distances between defining polygon vertices*
$npts$         =   *the number of defining polygon vertices*
$nplusc$       =   *maximum value of the knot vector* $- n + c$
$numerator$ =   *numerator of Eq. (5–86)*
$x()$          =   *array containing the knot vector*
$xchord$       =   *x component of the distance between defining polygon vertices*
$ychord$       =   *y component of the distance between defining polygon vertices*

**subroutine knotc**(npts,c,b(,); x())

**dimension** chord(20)

nplusc = npts+c

```
n = npts−1
```

*zero and redimension the knot vector and chord values*

**Mat** chord=**Zer**(n)

*determine chord distance between defining polygon vertices and their sum*

```
maxchord = 0
for i = 2 to npts
    xchord = b(i,1) − b(i−1,1)
    ychord = b(i,2) − b(i−1,2)
    chord(i−1) = Sqrt(xchord*xchord + ychord*ychord)
    maxchord = maxchord + chord(i−1)
next i
```

*multiplicity of k zeros at the beginning of the open knot vector*

```
for i = 1 to c
    x(i)=0
next i
```

*generate the internal knot values*

```
for i = 1 to n−c+1
    csum = 0
    for j = 1 to i
        csum = csum+chord(j)
    next j
    numerator = (i/(n−c+2))*chord(i+1) + csum
    x(c+i) = (numerator/maxchord)*(n−c+2)
next i
```

*multiplicity of k zeros at the end of the open knot vector*

```
for i = n+2 to nplusc
    x(i) = n−c+2
next i
return
```

## knotu

Subroutine to generate a B-spline periodic uniform knot vector (see p. 307).

c       =  *order of the basis function*
n       =  *the number of defining polygon vertices*
nplusc =  *maximum value of the knot vector - n + c*
$x()$    =  *array containing the knot vector*

**subroutine knotu**(n,c; x())

```
nplusc = n+c
for i = 1 to nplusc
    x(i) = i−1
next i
return
```

## matpbspl

Subroutine to generate a B-spline curve using matrix methods and a periodic uniform knot vector (see Eq. 5–93).

$b(,)$     = *array containing the defining polygon vertices in the sliding window*
          *$b( ,1)$ contains the x component of the vertex in the sliding window*
          *$b( ,2)$ contains the y component of the vertex in the sliding window*
          *$b( ,3)$ contains the z component of the vertex in the sliding window*

$d(,)$     = *array containing the defining polygon vertices*
          *$d( ,1)$ contains the x component of the vertex*
          *$d( ,2)$ contains the y component of the vertex*
          *$d( ,3)$ contains the z component of the vertex*

*fcoeff*   = *coefficient for the integer $N^*$ matrix*
*k*       = *order of the B-spline basis function*
*nbasis*  = *array containing the basis functions for a single value of t*
*nplusc*  = *number of knot values*
*npts*   = *number of defining polygon vertices*
$p(,)$     = *array containing the curve points*
          *$p( ,1)$ contains the x component of the point*
          *$p( ,2)$ contains the y component of the point*
          *$p( ,3)$ contains the z component of the point*

*p1*     = *number of points to be calculated on the span of the curve*
*ptemp(,)* = *temporary matrix containing a single curve point – t∗n∗b*
$t(,)$     = *parameter matrix*
*temp(,)* = *temporary matrix – t∗n*
*u*       = *normalized parameter value $0 \leq u \leq 1$*

**subroutine matpbspl(k,npts,p1,d(,); p(,))**

**dimension** t(1,9),b(9,3),n(9,9),temp(1,9),ptemp(1,3)     *allows for 9th order*

*zero and redimension matrices*

**Mat b = Zer(k,3)**
**Mat n = Zer(k,k)**
**Mat t = Zer(1,k)**
**Mat temp = Zer(1,k)**

*set up the [N] matrix*

**call nmatrix(k; fcoeff,n)**

*set up the sliding polygon vertex matrix and calculate the points*

icount = 0

**for j = 0 to npts**                      *set up sliding polygon vertex matrix*
    **for l = 0 to k−1**
        b(l+1,1)=d(mod(j+l,npts)+1,1)
        b(l+1,2)=d(mod(j+l,npts)+1,2)
        b(l+1,3)=d(mod(j+l,npts)+1,3)
    **next l**
    **for u = 0 to 1 −(1/(p1−1)) step 1/(p1−1)**
        icount = icount+1
        **for i = 1 to k**                   *set up the parameter matrix*
            t(1,i) = u^(k−i)

```
        next i
        Mat t = fcoeff*t                    calculate the points on this segment
        Mat temp = t*n
        Mat ptemp = temp*b
        p(icount,1) = ptemp(1,1)            assign the current value of the point
        p(icount,2) = ptemp(1,2)                on the curve to the curve array
        p(icount,3) = ptemp(1,3)
     next u
  next j
  return
```

## nmatrix

Subroutine to calculate the general B-spline periodic basis matrix (see Eq. 5–91).

$Factrl$ = *function that calculates the factorial of a number*
$fcoeff$ = *coefficient of the integer matrix* $- 1/(k-1)!$
$k$        = *order of the periodic basis function*
$n(,)$   = *integer form of the* $[N^*]$ *matrix*
$Ni(n,i)$ = *function that calculates* $\binom{n}{i}$

**subroutine nmatrix(k; fcoeff,n(,))**

def **Ni(n,i) = Factrl(n)/(Factrl(i)\*Factrl(n−i))**

*zero and redimension the* [N] *matrix*

**Mat n = Zer(k,k)**

fcoeff = 1/**Factrl(k−1)**                    calculate the constant multiplicative factor

*set up the matrix*

```
for i = 0 to k−1
   temp = Ni(k−1,i)
   for j = 0 to k−1
      sum = 0
      for l = j to k−1
         sum1 = (k −(l+1))^i
         sum2 = (−1)^(l−j)
         sum3 = Ni(k,l−j)
         sum = sum + sum1*sum2*sum3
      next l
      n(i+1,j+1) = temp*sum
   next j
next i
return
```

## parabld

Subroutine to perform parabolic blending – alpha $\neq$ beta – using a chord length approximation (see Eq. 5–44 and Ex. 5–6).

The assumption is that this routine is provided with data points four at a time. Points along the interior span on the parabolically blended curve are calculated.

$a(,)$ $\quad=\quad$ *the $4 \times 4$ parabolic blending function matrix*
$alpha$ $\quad=\quad$ *r parameter value at $P_2$*
$beta$ $\quad=\quad$ *s parameter value at $P_3$*
$c(,)$ $\quad=\quad$ *array containing points on the blended curve*
$\qquad\qquad$ *c( ,1) contains the x component of a point on the curve*
$\qquad\qquad$ *c( ,2) contains the y component of a point on the curve*
$\qquad\qquad$ *c( ,3) contains the z component of a point on the curve*
$c12$ $\quad=\quad$ *chord distance between points 1 & 2*
$c23$ $\quad=\quad$ *chord distance between points 2 & 3*
$c34$ $\quad=\quad$ *chord distance between points 3 & 4*
$icount$ $\quad=\quad$ *counter for the number of points on the blended curve*
$inter(,) =$ *intermediate matrix $[A][G]$*
$p(,)$ $\quad=\quad$ *array containing four data points*
$\qquad\qquad$ *p( ,1) contains the x component of the point*
$\qquad\qquad$ *p( ,2) contains the y component of the point*
$\qquad\qquad$ *p( ,3) contains the z component of the point*
$point(,) =$ *single point on the blended curve*
$\qquad\qquad$ *point(1,1) contains the x component of the point*
$\qquad\qquad$ *point(1,2) contains the y component of the point*
$\qquad\qquad$ *point(1,3) contains the z component of the point*
$p1$ $\quad=\quad$ *number of points to be calculated on this span*
$t(,)$ $\quad=\quad$ *cubic parameter matrix*
$t1$ $\quad=\quad$ *parameter value along the blended curve*

**subroutine parabld**$(p(,); c(,),p1,icount)$

**dimension** a(4,4),t(1,4),inter(4,3),point(1,3)

*calculate chord lengths*

c12 = **Sqrt**((p(2,1)−p(1,1))^2 + (p(2,2)−p(1,2))^2)
c23 = **Sqrt**((p(3,1)−p(2,1))^2 + (p(3,2)−p(2,2))^2)
c34 = **Sqrt**((p(4,1)−p(3,1))^2 + (p(4,2)−p(3,2))^2)

*calculate alpha and beta*

alpha = c12/(c23+c12)
beta = c23/(c23+c34)

*calculate [A]*

a(1,1) = −((1−alpha)^2)/alpha
a(2,1) = 2*((1−alpha)^2)/alpha
a(3,1) = a(1,1)
a(4,1) = 0
a(1,2) = ((1−alpha) + alpha*beta)/alpha
a(2,2) = −(2*(1−alpha) + alpha*beta)/alpha
a(3,2) = (1−2*alpha)/alpha
a(4,2) = 1
a(1,3) = (−(1−alpha) − alpha*beta)/(1−beta)
a(2,3) = (2*(1−alpha) − beta*(1−2*alpha))/(1−beta)
a(3,3) = alpha
a(4,3) = 0

$a(1,4) = (beta^2)/(1-beta)$
$a(2,4) = -a(1,4)$
$a(3,4) = 0$
$a(4,4) = 0$

*calculate the matrix* $[A][G]$

**Mat** inter = a*p

*determine the points on the curve segment*

**for** t1 = 0 **to** 1−(1/(p1−1)) **step** 1/(p1−1)

    *set up the* $[T]$ *matrix*

    $t(1,1) = t1^3$

    $t(1,2) = t1^2$

    $t(1,3) = t1$

    $t(1,4) = 1$

    *calculate a point on the blended curve and assign it to* $C(t)$

    **Mat** point = t*inter

    icount = icount+1

    **for** i = 1 **to** 3

        c(icount,i) = point(1,i)

    **next** i

**next** t1

**return**


## param

Subroutine to calculate parameter values based on chord distances.

| | | |
|---|---|---|
| $d(,)$ | = | *array containing the data points* |
| *dpts* | = | *number of data points* |
| *isum* | = | *incremental sum of the chord distances* |
| *sum* | = | *sum of all the chord distances* |
| *tparm()* | = | *array containing the parameter values* |

**subroutine param**(dpts,d(,); tparm())

sum = 0
isum = 0
tparm(1) = 0

*calculate the sum of the chord distances for all the data points*

**for** i = 2 **to** dpts

    sum = sum + **Sqrt**$((d(i,1)-d(i-1,1))^2 + (d(i,2)-d(i-1,2))^2)$

**next** i

*calculate the parameter values*

**for** i = 2 **to** dpts

    isum = isum + **Sqrt**$((d(i,1)-d(i-1,1))^2 + (d(i,2)-d(i-1,2))^2)$

    tparm(i) = isum/sum

**next** i

**return**

## rbasis

Subroutine to generate a rational B-spline basis function for open knot vectors (see Eq. 5–123).

$c$       = *order of the B-spline basis function*
$d$       = *first term of the basis function recursion relation*
$e$       = *second term of the basis function recursion relation*
$h()$    = *array containing the homogeneous coordinate weighting factors*
*npts*   = *number of defining polygon vertices*
*nplusc* = *constant – npts + c – maximum number of knot values*
$r(,)$    = *array containing the basis functions*
           *r(1,1) contains the basis function associated with $B_1$ etc.*
*sum*    = *sum of the products of the nonrational basis functions and the homogeneous coordinate weighting factors*
$t$       = *parameter value*
*temp()* = *temporary array*
$x()$    = *knot vector*

**subroutine rbasis**(c,t,npts,x(),h(); r(,))

**dimension** temp(20)                      *allows for 20 polygon vertices*

nplusc = npts+c

*calculate the first order nonrational basis functions $N_{i,1}$ (see Eq. 5–84a)*

**for** i = 1 **to** nplusc−1
    **if** t $\geq$ x(i) and t $<$ x(i+1) **then**
       temp(i) = 1
    **else**
       temp(i) = 0
    **end if**
**next** i

*calculate the higher order nonrational basis functions (see Eq. 5–84b)*

**for** k = 2 **to** c
    **for** i = 1 **to** nplusc−k
       **if** temp(i) $\neq$ 0 **then**               *if zero skip the calculation*
          d = ((t−x(i))∗temp(i))/(x(i+k−1)−x(i))
       **else**
          d = 0
       **end if**
       **if** temp(i+1) $\neq$ 0 **then**           *if zero skip the calculation*
          e = ((x(i+k)−t)∗temp(i+1))/(x(i+k)−x(i+1))
       **else**
          e = 0
       **end if**
       temp(i) = d + e
    **next** i
**next** k

**if** t = x(nplusc) **then** temp(npts) = 1            *pick up last point*

*calculate sum for denominator of rational basis functions (see Eq. 5–123)*

sum = 0

```
for i = 1 to npts
    sum = sum + temp(i)*h(i)
next i
```

*form rational basis functions and put in r vector (see Eq. 5–123)*

```
for i = 1 to npts
    if sum ≠ 0 then
        r(1,i) = temp(i)*h(i)/sum
    else
        r(1,i) = 0
    end if
next i

return
```

## rbspline

Subroutine to generate a rational B-spline curve using an open uniform knot vector (see Eqs. 5–122 and 5–124).

$b(,)$   = *array containing the defining polygon vertices*
           $b(\,,1)$ *contains the x component of the vertex*
           $b(\,,2)$ *contains the y component of the vertex*
           $b(\,,3)$ *contains the z component of the vertex*
$h()$   = *array containing the homogeneous coordinate weighting factors*
$k$     = *order of the B-spline basis function*
$nbasis$ = *array containing the rational basis functions for a single value of t*
$nplusc$ = *number of knot values*
$npts$   = *number of defining polygon vertices*
$p(,)$   = *array containing the curve points*
           $p(\,,1)$ *contains the x component of the point*
           $p(\,,2)$ *contains the y component of the point*
           $p(\,,3)$ *contains the z component of the point*
$p1$    = *number of points to be calculated on the curve*
$t$     = *parameter value $0 \le t \le 1$*
$x()$   = *array containing the knot vector*

**subroutine rbspline**(npts,k,p1,b(,),h(); p(,))

**dimension** nbasis(1,20),x(30),temp(1,3)     *allows for 20 data points with basis function of order 5*

nplusc = npts+k

*zero and redimension the knot vector and the basis array*

**Mat** nbasis = **Zer**(1,npts)
**Mat** x = **Zer**(nplusc)

*generate the open uniform knot vector*

**call knot**(npts,k; x)

icount = 0

*calculate the points on the rational B-spline curve*

```
for t = 0 to x(npts+k) step x(npts+k)/(p1−1)
    icount = icount+1
```

```
        call rbasis(k,t,npts,x,h; nbasis)      rational basis functions for this value of t
        Mat temp = nbasis*b                           generate the point on the curve
        p(icount,1) = temp(1,1)        assign the current value of the point on the curve
        p(icount,2) = temp(1,2)                                  to the curve array
        p(icount,3) = temp(1,3)

    next t

    return
```

## rbsplinu

Subroutine to generate a rational B-spline curve using a periodic uniform knot vector (see Eqs. 5–123 and 5–124).

$b(,)$   =  *array containing the defining polygon vertices*
            *$b( ,1)$ contains the x component of the vertex*
            *$b( ,2)$ contains the y component of the vertex*
            *$b( ,3)$ contains the z component of the vertex*
$h()$   =  *array containing the homogeneous coordinate weighting factors*
$k$     =  *order of the B-spline basis function*
$nbasis$ =  *array containing the rational basis functions for a single value of t*
$nplusc$ =  *number of knot values*
$npts$  =  *number of defining polygon vertices*
$p(,)$   =  *array containing the curve points*
            *$p( ,1)$ contains the x component of the point*
            *$p( ,2)$ contains the y component of the point*
            *$p( ,3)$ contains the z component of the point*
$p1$    =  *number of points to be calculated on the curve*
$t$     =  *parameter value $0 \leq t \leq 1$*
$x()$   =  *array containing the knot vector*

**subroutine rbsplinu(npts,k,p1,b(,),h(); p(,))**

**dimension** nbasis(1,20),x(30),temp(1,3)     *allows for 20 data points with basis function of order 5*

nplusc = npts+k

*zero and redimension the knot vector and the basis array*

**Mat** nbasis = **Zer**(1,npts)
**Mat** x = **Zer**(nplusc)

*generate the open uniform knot vector*

**call knotu**(npts,k; x)

icount = 0

*calculate the points on the rational B-spline curve*

**for** t = (k−1) **to** (npts−1+1) **step** ((npts−1+1)−(k−1))/(p1−1)
    icount = icount+1
    **call rbasis**(k,t,npts,x,h; nbasis)    *rational basis functions for this value of t*
    **Mat** temp = nbasis*b              *generate the point on the curve*
    p(icount,1) = temp(1,1)    *assign the current value of the point on the curve*
    p(icount,2) = temp(1,2)                 *to the curve array*

```
        p(icount,3) = temp(1,3)
    next t
    return
```

## CHAPTER 6

The algorithms given here generate three dimensional surfaces. Algorithms for bilinear, ruled, Coons linear and bicubic, Bézier and both nonrational and rational B-spline surfaces are included. In alphabetical order the algorithms are: **bilinear, bsplsurf, bspsurfu, coonslin, dbicubic, dbsurf, loftlinu, loftlinw, mbezsurf, rbspsurf, sumrbas.**

### bezsurf

Subroutine to calculate a Bézier surface (see Eq. 6–58).

$b(,)$ = *array containing the polygon vertices*
  $b(,1)$ *contains the x component of the vertex*
  $b(,2)$ *contains the y component of the vertex*
  $b(,3)$ *contains the z component of the vertex*
  *Note:* $B_{i,j} = b(,)$ *has dimensions of* $n*m \times 3$ *with j varying fastest*
Basis = *function to calculate the Bernstein basis value*
Factrl= *function to calculate the factorial of a number*
jin  = *Bernstein basis function in the u direction (see Eq. 5–63)*
kjm  = *Bernstein basis function in the w direction (see Eq. 5–63)*
m    = *one less than the number of polygon vertices in w direction*
n    = *one less than the number of polygon vertices in u direction*
Ni   = *factorial function for the Bernstein basis*
p1   = *number of parametric lines in the u direction*
p2   = *number of parametric lines in the w direction*
$q(,)$ = *position vectors for points on the surface*
  $q(,1)$ *contains the x component of the vector*
  $q(,2)$ *contains the y component of the vector*
  $q(,3)$ *contains the z component of the vector*
  *for a fixed value of u the next m elements contain*
  *the values for the curve* $q(u_i, w)$ *q has dimensions*
  *of* $p1*p2 \times 3$

```
subroutine bezsurf(b(,),n,m,p1,p2; q(,))
def Ni(n,i) = Factrl(n)/(Factrl(i)*Factrl(n−i))
def Basis(n,i,t) = Ni(n,i)*(t^i)*((1−t)^(n−i))
icount = 0
for u = 0 to 1 step 1/(p1−1)              for fixed u calculate various w's
    for w = 0 to 1 step 1/(p2−1)
        icount = icount+1
        for i = 0 to n
        jin = Basis(n,i,u)               Bernstein basis function in the u direction
            for j = 0 to m
                j1 = (m+1)*i + (j+1)
```

```
            kjm = Basis(m,j,w)        Bernstein basis function in the w direction
            for k = 1 to 3
                q(icount,k) = q(icount,k) + b(j1,k)*jin*kjm calculate surface point
            next k
          next j
        next i
      next w
    next u
    return
```

## bicubic

Subroutine to generate a Coons bicubic surface (see Eq. 6–51).

$n(,)$ = $4 \times 4$ blending function matrix (see Eq. 6–31)
$p(,)$ = $4 \times 4$ boundary condition matrix (see Eq. 6–36)
$p1$ = number of points along u-direction
$p2$ = number of points along w-direction
$q(,)$ = matrix containing the position vectors for the
            bicubic surface, has dimensions of $p1*p2 \times 3$
            first column is x component
            second column is y component
            third column is z component
            first p2 elements for $u = 0$
            second p2 elements for $u = 1/(p1-1)$, etc.
$u(,)$ = $1 \times 4$ cubic blending vector (see Eq. 6–37)
$w(,)$ = $4 \times 1$ cubic blending vector (see Eq. 6–37)
$x(,)$ = $4 \times 4$ array containing the x components of the
            p boundary condition matrix (see Eq. 6–36)
$y(,)$ = $4 \times 4$ array containing the y components of the
            p boundary condition matrix (see Eq. 6–36)
$z(,)$ = $4 \times 4$ array containing the z components of the
            p boundary condition matrix (see Eq. 6–36)

**subroutine blcubic**(p1,p2,x(,),y(,),z(,); q(,))

**dimension** p(4,4),n(4,4),ntrn(4,4),u(1,4),w(4,1)
**dimension** temp1(4,4),temp2(4,4),temp3(1,4),temp4(1,1)

*redimension matrices and fill with zeros*

**Mat** p = **Zer**(4,4)
**Mat** n = **Zer**(4,4)
**Mat** u = **Zer**(1,4)
**Mat** w = **Zer**(4,1)
**Mat** q = **Zer**(p1*p2,3)
**Mat** temp1 = **Zer**(4,1)
**Mat** temp2 = **Zer**(4,1)
**Mat** temp3 = **Zer**(4,1)
**Mat** temp4 = **Zer**(1,1)

*set up n-matrix*

n(1,1) = 2
n(1,2) = −2

```
n(1,3) = 1
n(1,4) = 1
n(2,1) = -3
n(2,2) = 3
n(2,3) = -2
n(2,4) = -1
n(3,3) = 1
n(4,1) = 1
```

*calculate transpose of n-matrix*

**Mat** ntrn = trn(n)

**for** k = 1 **to** 3

    icount = 0

    **if** k = 1 **then Mat** p = x
    **if** k = 2 **then Mat** p = y
    **if** k = 3 **then Mat** p = z

    **Mat** temp1 = p*ntrn                 *calculate p*ntrn – constant for all u,w*
    **Mat** temp2 = n*temp1            *calculate n*p*ntrn – constant for all u,w*

    **for** u1 = 0 **to** 1 **step** 1/(p1−1)           *set up u-matrix*
        u(1,1) = u1*u1*u1
        u(1,2) = u1*u1
        u(1,3) = u1
        u(1,4) = 1
        **for** w1 = 0 **to** 1 **step** 1/(p2−1)        *set up w-matrix*

           icount = icount+1

           w(1,1) = w1*w1*w1
           w(2,1) = w1*w1
           w(3,1) = w1
           w(4,1) = 1

           **Mat** temp3 = u*temp2         *calculate u*n*p*ntrn*
           **Mat** temp4 = temp3*w          *calculate q(u,w)*

           q(icount,k) = temp4(1,1)         *store q(u,w)*

      **next** w1
    **next** u1
  **next** k
  **return**

## bilinear

Subroutine to calculate a bilinear surface (see Eq. 6–41).

$n$   =  *number of increments in u*
$m$  =  *number of increments in w*
$p(,)$ =  *contains the coordinates of the corner points*
         *p has dimensions of 4 × 3. The first column contains*
         *x components, the second y components, the third*
         *z components of the corner position vectors.*
$q(,)$ =  *contains the coordinates of the interpolated surface*

> *q has dimensions of m\*n × 3*
> *the first m coordinates correspond to u = 0 = constant*
> *the second m coordinates correspond to u = 1/(n−1) = constant*
> *third m coordinates correspond to u = 2/(n−1) = constant,*
> *etc.*

**subroutine bilinear**(n,m,p(,); q(,))

**Mat** q = **Zer**(n\*m,3)                    *redimension q and fill with zeros*

icount = 0

*calculate the surface*

**for** u = 0 **to** 1 **step** 1/(n−1)              *set up u = constant loop*
  **for** w = 0 **to** 1 **step** 1/(m−1)              *set up w loop*

    icount = icount+1                    *increment point counter*

    q(icount,1) = p(1,1)\*(1−u)\*(1−w) + p(2,1)\*(1−u)\*w + p(3,1)\*u\*(1−w)
    q(icount,1) = q(icount,1) + p(4,1)\*u\*w
    q(icount,2) = p(1,2)\*(1−u)\*(1−w) + p(2,2)\*(1−u)\*w + p(3,2)\*u\*(1−w)
    q(icount,2) = q(icount,2) + p(4,2)\*u\*w
    q(icount,3) = p(1,3)\*(1−u)\*(1−w) + p(2,3)\*(1−u)\*w + p(3,3)\*u\*(1−w)
    q(icount,3) = q(icount,3) + p(4,3)\*u\*w

  **next w**

**next u**

**return**

## bsplsurf

Subroutine to calculate a Cartesian product B-spline surface using open uniform knot vectors (see Eq. 6–58).

b()      = *array containing the polygon net points*
       *b( ,1) contains the x component of the vertex*
       *b( ,2) contains the y component of the vertex*
       *b( ,3) contains the z component of the vertex*
       *Note: $B_{i,j} = b(,)$ has dimensions of n\*m × 3 with j varying fastest*
       *The polygon net is n × m*
k        = *order in the u direction*
l        = *order in the w direction*
mbasis(,) = *nonrational basis functions for one value of w (see Eq. 5-84)*
mpts     = *the number of polygon vertices in w direction*
nbasis(,) = *nonrational basis functions for one value of u (see Eq. 5-84)*
npts     = *the number of polygon vertices in u direction*
p1       = *number of parametric lines in the u direction*
p2       = *number of parametric lines in the w direction*
q()      = *array containing the resulting surface*
       *q( ,1) contains the x component of the vector*
       *q( ,2) contains the y component of the vector*
       *q( ,3) contains the z component of the vector*
       *for a fixed value of u the next m elements contain*
       *the values for the curve $q(u_i, w)$ q has dimensions*
       *of p1\*p2 × 3. The display surface is p1 × p2*

**subroutine bsplsurf**(b(,),k,l,npts,mpts,p1,p2; q(,))

*allows for 20 data points with basis function of order 5*

**dimension** x(30),y(30),nbasis(1,20),mbasis(1,20)

*zero and redimension the arrays*

**Mat** x = **Zer**(npts+k)
**Mat** y = **Zer**(mpts+l)
**Mat** nbasis = **Zer**(1,npts)
**Mat** mbasis = **Zer**(1,mpts)
**Mat** q = **Zer**(p1*p2,3)

*generate the open uniform knot vectors*

**call knot**(npts,k; x())                          *calculate u knot vector*
**call knot**(mpts,l; y())                          *calculate w knot vector*

nplusc = npts+k
mplusc = mpts+l

icount = 0

*calculate the points on the B-spline surface*

**for** u = 0 **to** x(nplusc) **step** x(nplusc)/(p1−1)
    **call basis**(k,u,npts,x; nbasis)             *basis function for this value of u*
    **for** w = 0 **to** y(mplusc) **step** y(mplusc)/(p2−1)
        **call basis**(l,w,mpts,y; mbasis)         *basis function for this value of w*
        icount = icount + 1
        **for** i = 1 **to** npts
            **for** j = 1 **to** mpts
                j1 = mpts*(i−1) + j
                **for** s = 1 **to** 3
                    q(icount,s) = q(icount,s) + b(j1,s)*nbasis(1,i)*mbasis(1,j)
                **next** s
            **next** j
        **next** i
    **next** w
**next** u
**return**

## bspsurfu

Subroutine to calculate a Cartesian product B-spline surface using periodic uniform knot vectors (see Eq. 6–58).

b()        =  *array containing the polygon net points*
              b( ,1) *contains the x component of the vertex*
              b( ,2) *contains the y component of the vertex*
              b( ,3) *contains the z component of the vertex*
              *Note: $B_{i,j} = b(,)$ has dimensions of $n*m \times 3$ with j varying fastest*
              *The polygon net is $n \times m$*
q()        =  *array containing the resulting surface*
              q( ,1) *contains the x component of the vector*

$q(\ ,2)$ *contains the y component of the vector*
$q(\ ,3)$ *contains the z component of the vector*
*for a fixed value of u the next m elements contain*
*the values for the curve $q(u_i, w)$ q has dimensions*
*of p1\*p2 $\times$ 3. The display surface is p1 $\times$ p2*

| | | |
|---|---|---|
| *k* | = | *order in the u direction* |
| *l* | = | *order in the w direction* |
| *mbasis(,)* | = | *nonrational basis functions for one value of w (see Eq. 5-84)* |
| *mpts* | = | *the number of polygon vertices in w direction* |
| *nbasis(,)* | = | *nonrational basis functions for one value of u (see Eq. 5-84)* |
| *npts* | = | *the number of polygon vertices in u direction* |
| *p1* | = | *number of parametric lines in the u direction* |
| *p2* | = | *number of parametric lines in the w direction* |

**subroutine bspsurfu**(b(,),k,l,npts,mpts,p1,p2; q(,))

*allows for 20 data points with basis function of order 5*

**dimension** x(30),y(30),nbasis(1,20),mbasis(1,20)

*zero and redimension the arrays*

**Mat** x = **Zer**(npts+k)
**Mat** y = **Zer**(mpts+l)
**Mat** nbasis = **Zer**(1,npts)
**Mat** mbasis = **Zer**(1,mpts)
**Mat** q = **Zer**(p1\*p2,3)

*generate the periodic uniform knot vectors*

**call knotu**(npts,k; x())                                    *calculate u knot vector*
**call knotu**(mpts,l; y())                                    *calculate w knot vector*

nplusc = npts+k
mplusc = mpts+l
icount = 0

*calculate the points on the B-spline surface*

**for** u = (k−1) **to** (npts−1+1) **step** ((npts−1+1)−(k−1))/(p1−1)
  **call basis**(k,u,npts,x; nbasis)                    *basis function for this value of u*
  **for** w = (l−1) **to** (mpts−1+1) **step** ((mpts−1+1)−(l−1))/(p2−1)
    **call basis**(l,w,mpts,y; mbasis)              *basis function for this value of w*

    icount = icount+1

    **for** i = 1 **to** npts
      **for** j = 1 **to** mpts
        **for** s = 1 **to** 3
        j1 = mpts\*(i−1)+j
        q(icount,s) = q(icount,s) + b(j1,s)\*nbasis(1,i)\*mbasis(1,j)
        **next s**
      **next j**
    **next i**
  **next w**
**next u**
**return**

### coonslin

Subroutine to calculate a linear Coons surface (see Eq. 6–49).

$a(,)$ = array containing the points on the $p(u,0)$ curve
has dimensions of $n \times 3$

$b(,)$ = array containing the points on the $p(u,1)$ curve
has dimensions of $n \times 3$

$c(,)$ = array containing the points on the $p(0,w)$ curve
has dimensions of $m \times 3$

$d(,)$ = array containing the points on the $p(1,w)$ curve
has dimensions of $m \times 3$

$n$ = number of points on the $p(u,0)$ and $p(u,1)$ boundary curves

$m$ = number of points on the $p(0,w)$ and $p(1,w)$ boundary curves

$q(,)$ = array containing the curves which describe the surface
has dimensions of $n*m \times 3$. the format is for a fixed
value of $u$, the next $m$ rows of the $q$ matrix contain
the values for variable $w$

**subroutine coonslin(n,m,a(,),b(,),c(,),d(,); q(,))**

**Mat q = Zer(n*m,3)**                    *redimension q and fill with zeros*

*calculate the surface*

**for** u = 0 **to** 1 **step** 1/(m−1)
  **for** w = 0 **to** 1 **step** 1/(n−1)
    icount = icount+1
    **for** l = 1 **to** 3
      q(icount,l) = a(k,l)*(1−w) + b(k,l)*w + c(j,l)*(1−u) + d(j,l)*u
      q(icount,l) = q(icount,l) − a(1,l)*(1−u)*(1−w) − b(1,l)*(1−u)*w
      q(icount,l) = q(icount,l) − a(n,l)*u*(1−w) − b(n,l)*u*w
    **next** l
  **next** w
**next** u
**return**

### dbicubic

Subroutine to calculate a Coons bicubic surface and its derivatives (see Eq. 6–51
and Eqs. 6–53 to 6–57).

$du(,)$ = $1 \times 4$ derivative blending vector (see Eq. 6–53)

$dw(,)$ = $4 \times 1$ derivative blending vector (see Eq. 6–54)

$n(,)$ = $4 \times 4$ blending function matrix (see Eq. 5–26)

$p(,)$ = $4 \times 4$ boundary condition matrix (see Eq. 6–51)

$p1$ = no of points along u direction

$p2$ = no of points along w direction

$q(,)$ = matrix containing the position vectors for the
bicubic surface, has dimensions of $p1*p2 \times 3$
first column is $x$ component
second column is $y$ component
third column is $z$ component
first $p2$ elements for $u = 0$

second p2 elements for $u = 1/(p1 - 1)$, etc.
all the derivatives are arranged in a similar manner

$qu(,)$ = matrix containing the u derivative vectors for the bicubic surface, has dimensions of $p1*p2 \times 3$

$qw(,)$ = matrix containing the w derivative vectors for the bicubic surface, has dimensions of $p1*p2 \times 3$

$quu(,)$ = matrix containing the uu derivative vectors for the bicubic surface, has dimensions of $p1*p2 \times 3$

$quw(,)$ = matrix containing the uw derivative vectors for the bicubic surface, has dimensions of $p1*p2 \times 3$

$qww(,)$ = matrix containing the ww derivative vectors for the bicubic surface, has dimensions of $p1*p2 \times 3$

$u(,)$ = $1 \times 4$ cubic blending vector (see Eq. 5-26)

$w(,)$ = $4 \times 1$ cubic blending vector (see Eq. 5-26)

$x(,)$ = $4 \times 4$ array containing the x components of the p boundary condition matrix (see Eq. 6-36)

$y(,)$ = $4 \times 4$ array containing the y components of the p boundary condition matrix (see Eq. 6-36)

$z(,)$ = $4 \times 4$ array containing the z components of the p boundary condition matrix (see Eq. 6-36)

**subroutine dbicubic**(p1,p2,x(,),y(,),z(,); q(,),qu(,), qw(,),quu(,),quw(,),qww(,))

**dimension** p(4,4),n(4,4),ntrn(4,4),u(1,4),w(4,1)
**dimension** du(1,4),dw(4,1),duu(1,4),dww(1,4)
**dimension** temp1(4,4),temp2(4,4),temp3(1,4),temp4(4,1)
**dimension** temp5(4,1),temp6(4,1),temp7(4,1)
**dimension** dtemp1(1,1),dtemp2(1,1),dtemp3(1,1),dtemp4(1,1),dtemp5(1,1)

*redimension matrices and fill with zeros*

**Mat** p = **Zer**(4,4)
**Mat** n = **Zer**(4,4)
**Mat** u = **Zer**(1,4)
**Mat** w = **Zer**(4,1)
**Mat** q = **Zer**(p1*p2,3)
**Mat** qu = **Zer**(p1*p2,3)
**Mat** qw = **Zer**(p1*p2,3)
**Mat** quu = **Zer**(p1*p2,3)
**Mat** quw = **Zer**(p1*p2,3)
**Mat** qww = **Zer**(p1*p2,3)
**Mat** temp1 = **Zer**(4,4)
**Mat** temp2 = **Zer**(4,4)
**Mat** temp3 = **Zer**(1,4)
**Mat** temp4 = **Zer**(4,1)
**Mat** temp5 = **Zer**(1,1)
**Mat** dtemp1 = **Zer**(1,1)
**Mat** dtemp2 = **Zer**(1,1)

*set up n matrix*

n(1,1) = 2
n(1,2) = −2
n(1,3) = 1

n(1,4) = 1
n(2,1) = −3
n(2,2) = 3
n(2,3) = −2
n(2,4) = −1
n(3,3) = 1
n(4,1) = 1

*calculate transpose of n matrix*

**Mat** ntrn = **Trn**(n)

**for** k = 1 **to** 3
   icount = 0
   **if** k = 1 **then Mat** p = x
   **if** k = 2 **then Mat** p = y
   **if** k = 3 **then Mat** p = z

| | |
|---|---|
| **Mat** temp1 = p*ntrn | *calculate p*ntrn − constant for all u,w* |
| **Mat** temp2 = n*temp1 | *calculate n*p*ntrn − constant for all u,w* |

   **for** u1 = 0 **to** 1 **step** 1/(p1−1)          *set up u matrix*
      u(1,1) = u1*u1*u1
      u(1,2) = u1*u1
      u(1,3) = u1
      u(1,4) = 1
      du(1,1) = 3*u1*u1          *set up du matrix*
      du(1,2) = 2*u1
      du(1,3) = 1
      du(1,4) = 0
      duu(1,1) = 6*u1          *set up duu matrix*
      duu(1,2) = 2
      duu(1,3) = 0
      duu(1,4) = 0

      **for** w1 = 0 **to** 1 **step** 1/(p2 − 1)       *set up w matrix*
         icount = icount+1

         w(1,1) = w1*w1*w1
         w(2,1) = w1*w1
         w(3,1) = w1
         w(4,1) = 1
         dw(1,1) = 3*w1*w1          *set up dw matrix*
         dw(2,1) = 2*w1
         dw(3,1) = 1
         dw(4,1) = 0
         dw(1,1) = 6*w1          *set up dww matrix*
         dw(2,1) = 2
         dw(3,1) = 0
         dw(4,1) = 0

| | |
|---|---|
| **Mat** temp3 = u*temp2 | *calculate u*n*p*ntrn* |
| **Mat** temp4 = temp2*w | *calculate n*p*ntrn*w* |
| **Mat** temp5 = du*temp2 | *calculate du*n*p*ntrn* |
| **Mat** temp6 = temp2*dw | *calculate n*p*ntrn*dw* |
| **Mat** temp7 = temp3*w | *calculate q(u,w)* |

$$\begin{array}{ll}
\textbf{Mat } \text{dtemp1} = \text{du}*\text{temp4} & \textit{calculate } qu(u,w) \\
\textbf{Mat } \text{dtemp2} = \text{temp3}*\text{dw} & \textit{calculate } qw(u,w) \\
\textbf{Mat } \text{dtemp3} = \text{temp5}*\text{dw} & \textit{calculate } quw(u,w) \\
\textbf{Mat } \text{dtemp4} = \text{duu}*\text{temp4} & \textit{calculate } quu(u,w) \\
\textbf{Mat } \text{dtemp5} = \text{temp3}*\text{dww} & \textit{calculate } qww(u,w) \\
\text{q(icount,k)} = \text{temp7(1,1)} & \textit{store surface point } q \\
\text{qu(icount,k)} = \text{dtemp1(1,1)} & \textit{store surface derivative } qu \\
\text{qw(icount,k)} = \text{dtemp2(1,1)} & \textit{store surface derivative } qw \\
\text{quw(icount,k)} = \text{dtemp3(1,1)} & \textit{store surface derivative } quw \\
\text{quu(icount,k)} = \text{dtemp4(1,1)} & \textit{store surface derivative } quu \\
\text{qww(icount,k)} = \text{dtemp5(1,1)} & \textit{store surface derivative } qww \\
\end{array}$$

> **next** w1
>> **next** u1
**next** k
**return**

## dbsurf

Subroutine to calculate a Cartesian product B-spline surface and its derivatives using open uniform knot vectors (see Eq. 6–58 and Eqs. 6–62 to 6–66).

$b()$ = *array containing the polygon net points*
    *$b(\ ,1)$ contains the $x$ component of the vertex*
    *$b(\ ,2)$ contains the $y$ component of the vertex*
    *$b(\ ,3)$ contains the $z$ component of the vertex*
    *Note: $Bi, j = b(,)$ has dimensions of $n*m \times 3$ $j$ varies fastest*
    *The polygon net is $n \times m$*

$d1mbasis(,)$ = *first derivative of the basis functions for $w$ (see Eq. 5–95)*
$d1nbasis(,)$ = *first derivative of the basis functions for $u$ (see Eq. 5–95)*
$d2mbasis(,)$ = *second derivative of the basis functions for $w$ (see Eq. 5–96)*
$d2nbasis(,)$ = *second derivative of the basis functions for $u$ (see Eq. 5–96)*
$k$ = *order in the $u$ direction*
$l$ = *order in the $w$ direction*
$mbasis(,)$ = *basis functions for $w$ (see Eq. 5–84)*
$mpts$ = *the number of polygon vertices in $w$ direction (see Eq. 5–83)*
$nbasis(,)$ = *basis functions for $u$ (see Eq. 5–84)*
$nptw$ = *the number of polygon vertices in $u$ direction (see Eq. 5–83)*
$p1$ = *number of parametric lines in the $u$ direction*
$p2$ = *number of parametric lines in the $w$ direction*
$q()$ = *resulting surface (see Eq. 6–58)*
    *$q(\ ,1)$ contains the $x$ component of the vector*
    *$q(\ ,2)$ contains the $y$ component of the vector*
    *$q(\ ,3)$ contains the $z$ component of the vector*
    *for a fixed value of $u$ the next $m$ elements contain*
    *the values for the curve $q(u(sub\ i),w)$ $q$ has dimensions*
    *of $p1*p2 \times 3$. The display surface is $p1 \times p2$*

$qu(,)$ = *$u$ derivative vectors for the*
    *B-spline surface, has dimensions of $p1*p2 \times 3$ (see Eq. 6–62)*
$qw(,)$ = *$w$ derivative vectors for the*
    *B-spline surface, has dimensions of $p1*p2 \times 3$ (see Eq. 6–63)*

quu(,)      = *uu derivative vectors for the*
              *B-spline surface, has dimensions of p1∗p2* × *3 (see Eq. 6-64)*
quw(,)      = *uw derivative vectors for the*
              *B-spline surface, has dimensions of p1∗p2* × *3 (see Eq. 6-65)*
qww(,)      = *ww derivative vectors for the*
              *B-spline surface, has dimensions of p1∗p2* × *3 (see Eq. 6-66)*

**subroutine dbsurf**(b(,),k,l,npts,mpts,p1,p2; q(,),qu(,),qw(,),quw(,),quu(,),qww(,))

*allows for 20 data points with basis function of order 5*

**dimension** x(30),y(30)
**dimension** nbasis(1,20),mbasis(1,20)
**dimension** d1nbasis(1,20),d1mbasis(1,20)
**dimension** d2nbasis(1,20),d2mbasis(1,20)

*zero and redimension the arrays*

**Mat** x = **Zer**(npts+k)
**Mat** y = **Zer**(mpts+l)
**Mat** nbasis = **Zer**(1,npts)
**Mat** mbasis = **Zer**(1,mpts)
**Mat** d1nbasis = **Zer**(1,npts)
**Mat** d1mbasis = **Zer**(1,mpts)
**Mat** d2nbasis = **Zer**(1,npts)
**Mat** d2mbasis = **Zer**(1,mpts)
**Mat** q = **Zer**(p1∗p2,3)
**Mat** qu = **Zer**(p1∗p2,3)
**Mat** qw = **Zer**(p1∗p2,3)
**Mat** quw = **Zer**(p1∗p2,3)
**Mat** quu = **Zer**(p1∗p2,3)
**Mat** qww = **Zer**(p1∗p2,3)

*generate the open uniform knot vectors*

**call knot**(npts,k; x())                    *calculate u knot vector*
**call knot**(mpts,l; y())                    *calculate w knot vector*

nplusc = npts+k
mplusc = mpts+l

icount = 0

*calculate the points on the B-spline surface*

**for** u = 0 **to** x(nplusc) **step** x(nplusc)/(p1−1)
   **call dbasis**(k,u,npts,x; nbasis,d1nbasis,d2nbasis)   *basis function & derivatives*
   **for** w = 0 **to** y(mplusc) **step** y(mplusc)/(p2−1)
      **call dbasis** (l,w,mpts,y; mbasis,d1mbasis,d2mbasis)
      icount = icount+1
      **for** i = 1 **to** npts
         **for** j = 1 **to** mpts
            **for** s = 1 **to** 3
            j1 = mpts∗(i−1) + j
            q(icount,s) = q(icount,s) + b(j1,s)∗nbasis(1,i)∗mbasis(1,j)
            qu(icount,s) = qu(icount,s) + b(j1,s)∗d1nbasis(1,i)∗mbasis(1,j)
            qw(icount,s) = qw(icount,s) + b(j1,s)∗nbasis(1,i)∗d1mbasis(1,j)
            quw(icount,s) = quw(icount,s) + b(j1,s)∗d1nbasis(1,i)∗d1mbasis(1,j)

```
            quu(icount,s) = quu(icount,s) + b(j1,s)*d2nbasis(1,i)*mbasis(1,j)
            qww(icount,s) = qww(icount,s) + b(j1,s)*nbasis(1,i)*d2mbasis(1,j)
          next s
        next j
      next i
    next w
  next u

  return
```

## loftlinu

Subroutine to calculate ruled surface in the u direction (see Eq. 6–43).

$a(,)$  =  *array containing the points on the $p(u,0)$ curve*
            *has dimensions of $n \times 3$.*
$b(,)$  =  *array containing the points on the $p(u,1)$ curve*
            *has dimensions of $n \times 3$*
$inum$ =  *number of points on each ruled line*
$n$    =  *number of points on the boundary curves*
$q(,)$  =  *array containing points on the intermediate curves*
            *has dimensions of $n*inum \times 3$*

**subroutine loftlinu**(n,a(,),b(,),inum; q(,))

icount = 0

*calculate the surface*

**for** w = 0 **to** 1 **step** 1/(inum−1)
  **for** l = 1 to n

    icount = icount+1

    **for** k = 1 to 3
        q(icount,k) = a(l,k)*(1−w) + b(l,k)*w   *calculate surface (see Eq. 6–43)*
    **next** k
  **next** l
**next** w

**return**

## loftlinw

Subroutine to calculate ruled surface in the w direction (see Eq. 6–44).

$a(,)$  =  *array containing the points on the $p(0,w)$ curve*
            *has dimensions of $n \times 3$.*
$b(,)$  =  *array containing the points on the $p(1,w)$ curve*
            *has dimensions of $n \times 3$*
$inum$ =  *number of points on the ruled line*
$n$    =  *number of points on the boundary curves*
$p(,)$  =  *array containing points on the ruled lines*
            *has dimensions of $n*inum \times 3$*

**subroutine loftlinw**(n,a(,),b(,),inum; p(,))

*calculate the surface*

```
for u = 0 to 1 step 1/(inum−1)
    for l = 1 to n
        icount = icount+1
        for k = 1 to 3
            p(icount,k) = a(l,k)*(1−u) + b(l,k)*u    calculate surface (see Eq. 6–44)
        next k
    next l
next u
return
```

## mbezsurf

Subroutine to calculate a Bézier surface using matrix methods (see Eq. 6–59).

$b(,)$    = *array containing the polygon vertices*
           *b( ,1) contains the x component of the vertex*
           *b( ,2) contains the y component of the vertex*
           *b( ,3) contains the z component of the vertex*
           *Note: $B_{i,j}$ = b(,) has dimensions of n*m × 3 j varies fastest*
$jin$    = *Bernstein basis function in the u direction (see Eq. 5–63)*
$kjm$   = *Bernstein basis function in the w direction (see Eq. 5–63)*
$m(,)$   = *the [M] matrix (see Eq. 6–59)*
$m1$    = *one less than the number of polygon vertices in w direction*
$n1$     = *one less than the number of polygon vertices in u direction*
$Factrl$ = *function that calculates the factorial of a number*
$n(,)$    = *the [N] matrix (see Eq. 6–59)*
$Ni(n,i)$ = *function that calculates $\binom{n}{i}$ (see Eq. 5–64)*
$p1$     = *number of parametric lines in the u direction*
$p2$     = *number of parametric lines in the w direction*
$q(,)$    = *position vectors for points on the surface*
           *q( ,1) contains the x component of the vector*
           *q( ,2) contains the y component of the vector*
           *q( ,3) contains the z component of the vector*
           *for a fixed value of u the next m elements contain*
           *the values for the curve $q(u_i, w)$ q has dimensions*
           *of p1*p2 × 3*
$u(,)$    = *[U] parameter matrix (see Eq. 6–59)*
$w(,)$   = *[W] parameter matrix (see Eq. 6–59)*

**subroutine mbezsurf**(b(,),n1,m1,p1,p2; q(,))

*allows for a 10 × 10 Bézier net*

**dimension** x(10,10),y(10,10),z(10,10),g(10,10)
**dimension** n(10,10),m(10,10),u(1,10),w(10,1)
**dimension** temp1(10,10),temp2(10,10),temp3(1,10),temp4(1,1)

def **Ni**(n,i) = **Factrl**(n)/(**Factrl**(i)***Factrl**(n−i))

*redimension matrices and fill with zeros*

**Mat** n = **Zer**(n1+1,n1+1)
**Mat** m = **Zer**(m1+1,m1+1)
**Mat** x = **Zer**(n1+1,m1+1)

**Mat** y = **Zer**(n1+1,m1+1)
**Mat** z = **Zer**(n1+1,m1+1)
**Mat** g = **Zer**(n1+1,m1+1)
**Mat** u = **Zer**(1,n1+1)
**Mat** w = **Zer**(m1+1,1)
**Mat** temp1 = **Zer**(n1+1,m1+1)
**Mat** temp2 = **Zer**(n1+1,m1+1)
**Mat** temp3 = **Zer**(1,m1+1)
**Mat** temp4 = **Zer**(1,1)

*set up the x,y,z matrices, i.e., the components of* [B]

**for** i = 1 **to** n1+1
  **for** j = 1 **to** m1+1
    ij = (m1+1)*(i−1) + j
    x(i,j) = b(ij,1)
    y(i,j) = b(ij,2)
    z(i,j) = b(ij,3)
  **next** j
**next** i

*set up the* [N] *and* [M] *matrices*

**for** i = 0 **to** n1
  **for** j = 0 **to** n1
    **if** i+j <= n1 **then**
      n(i+1,j+1) = **Ni**(n1,j)***Ni**(n1−j,n1−i−j)*(−1)^(n1−i−j)
    **else**
      n(i+1,j+1) = 0
    **end if**
  **next** j
**next** i

**for** i = 0 **to** m1
  **for** j = 0 **to** m1
    **if** i+j <= m1 **then**
      m(i+1,j+1) = **Ni**(m1,j)***Ni**(m1−j, m1−i−j)*(−1)^(m1−i−j)
    **else**
      m(i+1,j+1) = 0
    **end if**
  **next** j
**next** i

**Mat** m = **Trn**(m)                    *transpose of* [M] *for later use*

**for** k = 1 **to** 3

  icount = 0                    *reset the surface point counter*

  **if** k = 1 **then Mat** g = x       *assign each component of* [B] *in turn to* [G]
  **if** k = 2 **then Mat** g = y
  **if** k = 3 **then Mat** g = z

  *set up the unchanging* [N][B][M] *matrix for each pass (recall* [M] = [M]$^T$)
  **Mat** temp1 = g*m                    [B][M]$^T$
  **Mat** temp2 = n*temp1                [N][B][M]$^T$
  **for** t = 0 **to** 1 **step** 1/(p1−1)        *set up the u matrix*

```
for i = 0 to n1
    u(1,i+1) = t^(n1−i)
next i
Mat temp3 = u*temp2          [U][N][B][M]^T − constant for this u value
for s = 0 to 1 step 1/(p2−1)              set up the w matrix
    icount = icount+1
    for i = 0 to m1
        w(i+1,1) = s^(m1−i)
    next i
    Mat temp4 = temp3*w              calculate the surface point
    q(icount,k) = temp4(1,1)      assign the point to the q array
next s
next t
next k
return
```

### rbspsurf

Subroutine to calculate a Cartesian product rational B-spline surface using an open uniform knot vector (see Eq. 6–85).

$b()$      = *array containing the polygon net points*
         *$b(\ ,1)$ contains the x component of the vertex*
         *$b(\ ,2)$ contains the y component of the vertex*
         *$b(\ ,3)$ contains the z component of the vertex*
         *$b(\ ,4)$ contains the homogeneous coordinate weighting factor*
         *Note: $B_{i,j} = b(,)$ has dimensions of $n*m \times 4$ with j varying fastest*
         *The polygon net is $n \times m$*
$k$      = *order in the u direction*
$l$      = *order in the w direction*
$mbasis(,)$ = *array containing the nonrational basis functions for w (see Eq. 5–84)*
$mpts$      = *the number of polygon vertices in w direction*
$nbasis(,)$ = *array containing the nonrational basis functions for u (see Eq. 5–84)*
$npts$      = *the number of polygon vertices in u direction*
$p1$      = *number of parametric lines in the u direction*
$p2$      = *number of parametric lines in the w direction*
$q()$      = *array containing the resulting surface*
         *$q(\ ,1)$ contains the x component of the vector*
         *$q(\ ,2)$ contains the y component of the vector*
         *$q(\ ,3)$ contains the z component of the vector*
         *for a fixed value of u the next m elements contain*
         *the values for the curve $q(u_i, w)$ q has dimensions*
         *of $p1*p2 \times 3$. The display surface is $p1 \times p2$*
$sum$      = *summation of the rational surface basis functions*

**subroutine rbspsurf**(b(,),k,l,npts,mpts,p1,p2; q(,))

*allows for 20 data points with basis function of order 5*

**dimension** x(30),y(30),nbasis(1,20),mbasis(1,20)

*zero and redimension the arrays*

**Mat** x = **Zer**(npts+k)
**Mat** y = **Zer**(mpts+l)
**Mat** nbasis = **Zer**(1,npts)
**Mat** mbasis = **Zer**(1,mpts)
**Mat** q = **Zer**(p1*p2,3)

*generate the open uniform knot vectors*

**call knot**(npts,k; x())                                     *calculate u knot vector*
**call knot**(mpts,l; y())                                     *calculate w knot vector*

nplusc = npts+k
mplusc = mpts+l

icount = 0

*calculate the points on the B-spline surface*

**for** u = 0 **to** x(nplusc) **step** x(nplusc)/(p1−1)
  **call basis**(k,u,npts,x; nbasis)                 *nonrational basis function for u*
  **for** w = 0 **to** y(mplusc) **step** y(mplusc)/(p2−1)
    **call basis**(l,w,mpts,y; mbasis)               *nonrational basis function for w*
    **call sumrbas**(b,nbasis,mbasis,npts,mpts; sum)   *sum of basis functions*

    icount = icount+1

    **for** i = 1 **to** npts
      **for** j = 1 **to** mpts
        **for** s = 1 **to** 3
          j1 = mpts*(i−1) + j
          qtemp = b(j1,4)*b(j1,s)*nbasis(1,i)*mbasis(1,j)/sum  *surface point*
          q(icount,s) = q(icount,s) + qtemp              *assign to surface array*
        **next** s
      **next** j
    **next** i
  **next** w
**next** u

**return**

## sumrbas

Subroutine to calculate the sum of the nonrational basis functions (see Eq. 6–87).

b()          =  *array containing the polygon net points*
              *b( ,1) contains the x component of the vertex*
              *b( ,2) contains the y component of the vertex*
              *b( ,3) contains the z component of the vertex*
              *b( ,4) contains the homogeneous coordinate weighting factor*
              *Note: $B_{i,j} = b(,)$ has dimensions of $n*m \times 4$ j varies fastest*
              *The polygon net is $n \times m$*
mbasis(,) =  *the nonrational basis functions for w*
mpts        =  *the number of polygon vertices in w direction*
nbasis(,) =  *the nonrational basis functions for u*
npts        =  *the number of polygon vertices in u direction*
sum         =  *sum of the basis functions*

**subroutine sumrbas**(b(,),nbasis(,),mbasis(,),npts,mpts; sum)

```
sum = 0
for i = 1 to npts
   for j = 1 to mpts
      j1 = mpts*(i−1) + j
      sum = sum + b(j1,4)*nbasis(1,i)*mbasis(1,j)          calculate the sum
   next j
next i
return
```

# INDEX